DATE DUE

DEC 0 6 2010	
NOV 2 8 2011	

The Central Intelligence Agency

The Central Intelligence Agency

A Documentary History

Scott C. Monje

GREENWOOD PRESS
WESTPORT, CONNECTICUT • LONDON

Library of Congress Cataloging-in-Publication Data

Monje, Scott C.
   The Central Intelligence Agency : a documentary history / Scott C. Monje
     p. cm.
   Includes bibliographical references and indexes.
   ISBN 978-0-313-35028-3 (alk. paper)
    1. United States. Central Intelligence Agency—History. 2. United States. Central
Intelligence Agency—History—Sources. I. Title
   JK468.I6 M63 2008
327.1273009—dc22   2008010075

British Library Cataloguing in Publication Data is available.

Library of Congress Catalog Card Number: 2008010075
ISBN: 978-0-313-35028-3

First published in 2008

Greenwood Press, 88 Post Road West, Westport, CT 06881
An imprint of Greenwood Publishing Group, Inc.
www.greenwood.com

Printed in the United States of America

∞

The paper used in this book complies with the
Permanent Paper Standard issued by the National
Information Standards Organization (Z39.48-1984).

10 9 8 7 6 5 4

Contents

Preface

Not so long ago, writing a documentary history of the Central Intelligence Agency would have been a futile endeavor. There were simply not enough documents available to be worth the effort. Histories and analyses—valuable as they are—have been compelled to rely heavily on self-serving leaks, faded memories of participants, or speculation. The situation is still far from ideal, yet the change has been tremendous. Eagerly or reluctantly, the CIA and other agencies have released a flood of information on the history of American intelligence. The end of the Cold War and the active use of the Freedom of Information Act by historians and civil libertarians contributed to this.

Symbolic of the change was the declassification in 2007 of the "Family Jewels" file—the result of an internal CIA effort in 1973 to discover whether it had been violating its own charter—after thirty-four years. Although it may sound oxymoronic, this was surely the most famous set of secret documents in the agency's history. Many gaps remain, of course. More documents remain hidden than have come to light. Many of those that have been revealed, including the "Family Jewels," contain more than a few holes inasmuch as selected words, phrases, and pages have been deleted prior to release. Yet, a process has begun. The time has come to take a first, tentative step at putting some of these documents together in a more or less cohesive narrative.

Any book on such a vast topic, even if it seems to be overly long, necessarily involves choices. In this case, some of those choices have been made for us. The CIA decides which records it will release to the public and which it will not. Clearly, the documentary record is not complete, although it is now probably fuller than that of any intelligence agency in history that was not attached to a defeated and occupied country.

We cannot know all of the ways in which the record is skewed because, well, that would be giving away secrets. We do know, of course, that the CIA will be reluctant to reveal current operations, so releases are biased in favor of the past. (On the other hand, certain political leaders of both parties occasionally reveal selective portions of current secret evidence to bolster their positions. On occa-sion, some in the CIA may do something similar, especially when they decide that the revelations already occurring are not only selective but inaccurate or designed to blame the agency for policy failures.) Obviously, certain weapons systems cannot be discussed. Documents pertaining to the design of nuclear weapons or formulas for nerve gas will not be released, at least not intention-ally, and that is fine. The divulgence of intelligence sources and methods or of the names of certain CIA employees is prohibited by law. In a sense, this is unfortunate—the definition of "methods," in particular, is elastic and can be stretched to cover many things—but we will probably have to live with it.[1] Pre-sumably, a number of things have been kept secret because they are embarrass-ing or politically damaging, even though that is expressly prohibited as a criterion. Many of these are, no doubt, categorized as sources and methods.

We are also aware of another bias. The CIA is more reluctant to open its *operational* records, so the evidentiary base is skewed toward the *analytical.* In other words, the agency is generally more willing to discuss what it thought others were doing in the past than to disclose what it was doing. When it does release operational records, and it does on occasion, they are usually connected to an operation that is already fairly well known. This can be interesting, too, but it is clearly incomplete. It is possible that all the past operations are known and therefore the bias is specious, but this is not very likely.

In this book we shall try to give a sampling of document excerpts from throughout the CIA's history that will be necessarily incomplete even in relation to the documents that are now publicly available. Some periods will be more heavily represented and others less so. We will not cover some of the most fa-mous operations, such as Iran (1953), Guatemala (1954), and the Bay of Pigs (1961), which have been thoroughly handled elsewhere. An unfortunate lacuna will be a lack of space devoted to the Soviet Union, which was the major focus of CIA attention for most of the agency's existence. Perhaps, someday, that can be the subject of another book.

An effort has been made to incorporate both analytical and operational reports as well as critical internal reviews. Several chapters rely heavily on the "Family Jewels" collection, which focuses primarily on activities of the late 1960s and early 1970s that could be considered domestic in nature. On occasion, documents from other agencies, such as the National Security Council, will be offered when they discuss the CIA, include CIA representatives, or contribute to understanding a given situation. Chapters dealing with more recent events, for which fewer internal documents are available, make use of the declassified reports of Congressional oversight committees and official investigative com-missions examining CIA and intelligence-related activities. The chapter dealing with the Iraq War examines both the intelligence and the way it was used by the administration in its argument in support of war. The background for the estimate on Iran's nuclear program released in December 2007 is provided through open testimony on Iran before the Senate Select Committee on Intelli-gence. With luck, this book will contribute to an understanding of the CIA and what it does, and of the dilemmas associated with any secret organization in a free society.

Like all researchers in this field, I owe an enormous debt of gratitude to the National Security Archive at George Washington University, which is responsible for making available most of the formerly classified documents pre-sented here.[2] Other documents are available through two important programs of the Federation of American Scientists (the Intelligence Resource Program and the Project on Government Secrecy),[3] the general news media and various departments and agencies of the U.S. government, including the CIA itself.[4]

I would like to express my gratitude to Dr. Mary Curry of the National Secu-rity Archive and to Margaret M. Wood of the Law Library of Congress for help in finding resources and in explaining things. I extend my appreciation to Sandy Towers of Greenwood Press for her consistent enthusiasm and encour-agement. I especially thank my wife, Audrey, and our daughter, Patricia, for their patience and understanding through the many months as I huddled over the computer and grumbled.

NOTES

1. On the flexibility of the concept of "methods" as a reason for classifying things, and also for the reasons that some publicly known facts may be subject to classification, see Joseph Weisberg, "The CIA's Open Secrets," *New York Times* (27 August 2007). Weis-berg was formerly with the CIA Directorate of Operations.
2. See http://www.gwu.edu/~nsarchiv.
3. See http://www.fas.org.
4. See http://www.cia.gov.

Introduction: A Secret Organization in a Free and Open Society

It was an unusual event for an academic meeting, one marked by a certain degree of irony. On 21 June 2007, Gen. Michael V. Hayden, Director of the Central Intelligence Agency, addressed the annual conference of the Society for Historians of American Foreign Relations (SHAFR). As a professional association, SHAFR had long championed ready access to historical government documents, whereas the CIA was the very embodiment of government secrecy. Yet Hayden—who had earned a master's degree in history at Duquesne University in 1969—noted that he both respected and enjoyed the historian's task. He allowed that the CIA had a social contract with the American people to explain to them, to the best of its ability, the things that it did on their behalf. In doing so, he also boasted of his agency's openness: "No other intelligence agency in the world rivals our record on declassification."[1] Over the years, he noted, the CIA had reviewed and released some 31 million pages of previously classified documents, and it continued to receive 3,000 new requests each year for declassifications under the Freedom of Information Act (FOIA) of 1967.

The very nature of intelligence activities, however, creates problems in this regard. For a democratic society to hold its government accountable, it must know what the government is doing. This should be all the more important with regard to vital issues such as national security, which concerns questions of war and peace, life and death. Yet the very nature of intelligence activity requires that it remain secret. The CIA's charter, the National Security Act of 1947, makes the Director of Central Intelligence responsible for "protecting intelligence sources and methods from unauthorized disclosure." Thus, "a secret organization serving an open and free society," as Hayden put it, faces a perpetual dilemma. It must "wrestle constantly with the twin imperatives of essential openness and essential secrecy."

We must balance our responsibility to the public, and to history, to explain our actions and their impact, with our obligation to protect sources, methods, and ongoing intelligence relationships. These are not simple, cut-and-dried issues. They spark vigorous internal debates that ultimately require informed, yet subjective, judgments. We have those debates and make those judgments knowing that mistakes can jeopardize American security, and, in some cases, place lives at risk. An intelligence organization that fails to protect those who work with it—foreign intel services and individuals—will eventually see sources dry up and cooperation diminish. So, as you can see, this is an existential question for us.

Hayden was correct, of course; the dilemma of a secret organization in an open society is a very real one. Real as the predicament may be, however, it also provides endless opportunities and temptations for abuse. The public must simply accept that the CIA will review the appropriate documents, make the proper determination regarding what can and cannot be revealed, and then follow that determination fully and without distortion. This may be problematic when the information proves embarrassing to the agency, its director, or the president of the United States—even when the law forbids such considerations—or when revelations threaten to complicate diplomatic relations with other countries.

Despite the enormous number of documents released by the CIA in recent years, the agency's history of declassification has been more uneven than Hayden implied. While the agency had just released some 31 million pages, it had reportedly reviewed and declined to release about 70 million others.[2] These presumably included some of the most sensitive and, therefore, most interesting. Moreover, most documents that are released are first "redacted." That is to say, they are edited and left with gaping holes, usually without any indication of what information was removed or why. In some cases, it is clearly the name of an individual or a foreign intelligence service. In others, whole paragraphs or entire pages may simply fail to appear.

Hayden himself personifies the irony here. In his speech to the SHAFR conference, he noted: "Of course, we cannot tell the American people everything we do to protect them without damaging our ability to protect them. When it comes to secret intelligence, public sovereignty and oversight reside in the Congress." The careful reader will note that he never specifically said that the Congress is told either, although he clearly meant to leave his audience with that impression. Sometimes, consulting Congress has meant informing the two ranking members of the intelligence committee of each house and then telling them that the matter is secret; they cannot effectively act upon the information or even discuss it with their colleagues or staffs. That takes much of the meaning out of "consultation."

Before coming to the CIA, Hayden had been the director of the National Security Agency, where he initiated the warrantless wiretapping of communications between the United States and foreign countries following the terrorist attacks of 11 September 2001 ("9/11"). Most members of Congress learned of this program in late 2005, four years after it began. They discovered only in April 2007 that legal questions surrounding an earlier version of the program had nearly provoked the resignation of the attorney general, the deputy attorney general, and the director of the FBI in 2004. The week after Hayden's speech at the SHAFR conference, the Senate Judiciary Committee found it necessary to issue subpoenas to the White House in its years-long effort to learn the details of the program and the reasoning behind it. (The subpoenas were ignored.) Even Congress, the repository of "public sovereignty and oversight," is not guaranteed timely and effective access to information.

The early beginnings of the CIA's declassification program came in the 1970s, when the agency released some of the analytic records of its World War II predecessor, the Office of Strategic Services (OSS). Operational records of the OSS followed in the early 1980s. With this precedent in mind, the agency established its own voluntary Historical Review Program in 1985, as part of a deal with Congress exempting CIA operational records from FOIA requests. The agency's various subdivisions, however, were reluctant to cooperate with the program, and its initial releases consisted not of documents but of previously classified internal histories written by the agency's own staff historians.[3]

The heyday of CIA declassification came in the 1990s, in the immediate aftermath of the Cold War's end. Director of Central Intelligence (later, Secretary of Defense) Robert M. Gates convened the Task Force on Greater CIA Openness, which in December 1991 recommended that the agency declassify and release certain historical documents that had been withheld from the public. Although the CIA's initial reaction was to classify the task force's recommendations as secret, it soon repented, published the recommendation, and began releasing documents. Notable was the publication of *CIA Documents on the Cuban Missile Crisis, 1962*, for a conference commemorating the thirtieth anniversary of that event.[4] The Center for the Study of Intelligence, which had been established in 1974, was expanded at this time.

Then, President Bill Clinton, on 17 April 1995, signed Executive Order 12958, "Classified National Security Information," which called on all government agencies to declassify historical records automatically if they were more than twenty-five years old. This was radical new thinking for the government in general, and especially for the CIA. But, as is so often the case, it came with some substantial qualifications. The main point, paragraph (a) in this instance, was followed by a lengthy list of exceptions in paragraph (b), several of which had direct and significant implications for the CIA. While all of them were understandable, and probably even necessary, they meant that significant gaps in the published record would remain. In part, the executive order reads:

Sec. 3.4. Automatic Declassification.

(a) Subject to paragraph (b), below, within 5 years from the date of this order, all classified information contained in records that (1) are more than 25 years old, and (2) have been determined to have permanent historical value under title 44, United States Code, shall be automatically declassified whether or not the records have been reviewed. Subsequently, all classified information in such records shall be automatically declassified no longer than 25 years from the date of its original classification, except as provided in paragraph (b), below.

(b) An agency head may exempt from automatic declassification under paragraph (a), above, specific information, the release of which should be expected to:

(1) reveal the identity of a confidential human source, or reveal information about the application of an intelligence source or method, or reveal the identity of a human intelligence source when the unauthorized

disclosure of that source would clearly and demonstrably damage the national security interests of the United States;

(2) reveal information that would assist in the development or use of weapons of mass destruction;

(3) reveal information that would impair U.S. cryptologic systems or activities;

(4) reveal information that would impair the application of state of the art technology within a U.S. weapon system;

(5) reveal actual U.S. military war plans that remain in effect;

(6) reveal information that would seriously and demonstrably impair relations between the United States and a foreign government, or seriously and demonstrably undermine ongoing diplomatic activities of the United States;

(7) reveal information that would clearly and demonstrably impair the current ability of United States Government officials to protect the President, Vice President, and other officials for whom protection services, in the interest of national security, are authorized;

(8) reveal information that would seriously and demonstrably impair current national security emergency preparedness; or

(9) violate a statute, treaty, or international agreement.

While some information was excluded from automatic declassification, it was still subject to a process of systematic declassification review to determine whether declassification might be permissible in individual cases. There was also the mandatory review of items specifically requested under FOIA. (Mandatory review, of course, does not mean mandatory declassification and release.) It is noteworthy that the lengthy executive order also specified the following among the limitations on the government's ability to classify information:

Sec. 1.8. Classification Prohibitions and Limitations.

(a) In no case shall information be classified in order to:

(1) conceal violations of law, inefficiency, or administrative error;

(2) prevent embarrassment to a person, organization, or agency;

(3) restrain competition; or

(4) prevent or delay the release of information that does not require protection in the interest of national security.

The initial enthusiasm for declassification at the CIA, such as it existed, faded quickly. Through the early and mid-1990s, successive directors pledged to declassify and release the documentary record of eleven major covert operations in France and Italy (1940s–1950s), North Korea (1950s), Iran (1953), Guatemala (1954), Indonesia (1958), Tibet (1950s–1960s), the Congo (1960s), the Dominican Republic (1960s), Laos (1960s), and Cuba (1960s). Yet only documents related to Guatemala and the Bay of Pigs operation in Cuba were released officially, while Iran documents were leaked unofficially. In mid-1998, it was announced that, while a declassification program would continue, budgetary limitations would not permit the review and declassification of documents for the remaining covert operations.[5]

At the same time, while the Department of State and the Department of Energy were aggressively releasing documents, the CIA and the Department of Defense were openly resisting pressure to broaden their declassification programs.[6] At no time did the agency promise to release information about any operation whose existence was not already known to the public. Indeed, when records were released, they concerned operations (such as Guatemala and the Bay of Pigs) on which wide-reaching details were already available through leaks, Congressional investigations, or previous FOIA releases.[7]

The official mood regarding openness began to shift during the Clinton administration, in 1998–1999, owing to concerns that the Department of Energy had inadvertently released some documents related to the design of nuclear weapons. This concern was then made salient by accusations of possible espionage by Wen Ho Lee, a U.S. government scientist at the Los Alamos National Laboratory who occasionally visited the People's Republic of China.[8] In October 1998, Congress passed the Kyl-Lott Amendment (officially titled "Protection against Inadvertent Release of Restricted Data or Formerly Restricted Data"), permitting the Energy Department to remove sensitive weapons-related material from public repositories. Under this program, 5,508 pages of documents were reclassified and removed from public shelves.[9]

Quite aside from the issue of arms-related information, however, by 1999 the CIA was increasingly less cooperative in turning over papers for publication in the State Department's regular documentary series *Foreign Relations of the United States* (FRUS). That autumn the CIA, the Justice Department, the Defense Department, and the three military services complained that State was releasing material in which they had "equity" (by virtue of the interdepartmental nature of the intelligence process) without their permission. These agencies, although lacking any specific Congressional authorization, then began reviewing released documents and withdrawing them from public shelves.

The process of reclassification apparently accelerated under the administration of President George W. Bush and in the wake of the terrorist attacks of 11 September 2001. In October 2001, the process was formalized in a secret memorandum of understanding (MOU) signed by the National Archives and Records Administration (NARA) and the CIA. The MOU was made public in 2006.

MEMORANDUM OF UNDERSTANDING BETWEEN THE NATIONAL
ARCHIVES AND RECORDS ADMINISTRATION AND THE
CENTRAL INTELLIGENCE AGENCY

The purpose of this Memorandum of Understanding is to establish standard procedures to handle instances where classified or sensitive information containing possible Central Intelligence Agency (CIA) equities may have been inadvertently or improperly released. The goal should be to protect CIA equities while resolving the issue as expeditiously as possible in a way that will not draw unnecessary public attention to the steps taken to correct the problem. It is in the interests of both the CIA and the National Archives and Records Administration (NARA) to avoid the kind of public notice and researcher complaints that may arise from removing from the open shelves for extended periods of time records that had been publicly available.

1. When NARA is notified by CIA or another agency, or otherwise becomes aware that CIA documents containing classified or sensitive information, or other government agency documents containing sensitive or classified CIA equities may have been inadvertently or improperly released in records that were reviewed for declassification by NARA or another agency and made available to the public, NARA will notify CIA immediately and hold those

records off the open shelf for a period of 30 days following CIA receipt of notification to give CIA an opportunity to investigate the extent of the problem.

2. CIA will attempt to resolve the exposure within 30 days after it receives notification from NARA. If CIA informs NARA that it cannot resolve the issue within 30 days, NARA and the CIA will agree upon a date by which the CIA will resolve the exposure.

3. If CIA has not resolved its concerns by the agreed upon date, NARA can require an explanation of the CIA's inability to resolve the issue within the agreed upon time limit. NARA can further require an update on CIA's progress monthly until resolution is reached. If a final determination is not reached within six months, NARA will withdraw the documents in question and return the rest of the files to the open shelves. CIA may review such documents that are returned to the open shelves, for additional withdrawals, on a box-by-box basis.

4. If after examining the records, CIA finds that there has been no improper release of classified or still sensitive information, CIA will promptly inform NARA that the records can be returned to the open shelf.

5. If CIA finds that information containing classified or still sensitive CIA equities has been improperly released, CIA will tab these documents. The tabs will include the justification for continued classification or withholding.

6. NARA will withhold the tabbed documents in accordance with the justification cited on the tab. The place markers inserted for withheld documents will not contain any reference to CIA removal of the documents or any reason for the withholding of the documents. The common generic descriptor "intelligence document" shall also not be used.

7. NARA will not attribute to CIA any part of the review or the withholding of documents from this exposed collection. Researcher requests for withheld documents shall be accepted for processing by NARA and researchers shall not be directed to CIA for response. NARA will contact CIA regarding such requests, and will act as a surrogate for CIA in dealing with requestors of these withheld documents.

8. When examining documents at NARA, whether for declassification purposes or investigation of an inadvertent release, CIA personnel will follow NARA requirements for the handling of archival records and will take care to preserve the integrity of the records.

9. NARA staff will provide training for CIA personnel and contractors in NARA requirements and procedures for the handling and preservation of archival documents.

10. NARA will inform CIA immediately if CIA personnel or contractors are mishandling or rearranging archival records. CIA will take prompt action to correct such problems including, if NARA deems necessary, requiring personnel to take refresher training in handling and preserving archival records.

11. NARA will inform CIA immediately if NARA personnel or contractors have mishandled classified information. NARA will take prompt action to correct such problems including, if CIA deems necessary, requiring personnel or contractors to take refresher training in handling classified information.

This Memorandum of Understanding is subject to amendment by agreement of both parties.

In August 2001, the Bush administration initiated a review of the 1995 executive order mandating automatic declassification, although the newly revised order was not issued until 25 March 2003.[10] A great deal of the document—perhaps a surprising amount, given the administration's reported penchant for secrecy—remained unchanged, including all the prohibitions listed in section 1.8 against classifying embarrassing information. One change was delaying the deadline for clearing the backlog of classified material to the end of 2006. (It already had been delayed from 2000 to 2003 by Executive Order 13142 of 1999.) The release of documents by the tens of millions did, in fact, commence at the end of 2006.[11] Another key difference pertained to the issue of reclassification. The Clinton document said, "Information may not be reclassified after it has been declassified and released to the public under proper authority." The new version said:

> Information may be reclassified after declassification and release to the public under proper authority only in accordance with the following conditions:
>
> (1) the reclassification action is taken under the personal authority of the agency head or deputy agency head, who determines in writing that the reclassification of the information is necessary in the interest of the national security;
> (2) the information may be reasonably recovered; and
> (3) the reclassification action is reported promptly to the Director of the Information Security Oversight Office.

The revised executive order reconfirmed the role of the Interagency Security Classification Appeals Panel (ISCAP) in the declassification process. Nonetheless, it granted the director of central intelligence the authority and responsibility to protect information regarding sources and methods by vetoing ISCAP decisions in those areas. In addition, the revised order gives certain officials the right, in an emergency, to "share" classified information with unauthorized individuals without that information then being considered declassified. According to NARA, this is to permit unhindered cooperation with state and local authorities in the context of homeland security.[12] Interestingly, all the powers of classification and declassification granted to the president in the original order are also explicitly extended to the vice president in the revised order, no doubt reflecting the unusually prominent policy role of Vice President Dick Cheney.

Between 2001 and 2006, the CIA and five other agencies reclassified some 9,500 documents (totaling more than 55,500 pages) that had already been made available to the public. At least eight of the documents had already been published, either in print or on microfiche, as part of the State Department's FRUS series.[13]

The clandestine reclassification project went unnoticed until December 2005, when Matthew Aid, a visiting fellow at the National Security Archive (a nongovernmental research center at George Washington University) found that documents he had already used were no longer available in collections of NARA, the official government archives. Researchers familiar with the documents deemed some of them mundane, while others were conceivably embarrassing to the agency. Still available on the public shelves, however, were various manuals explaining how to engage in sabotage or assemble explosives as well as technical documents regarding chemical and biological weapons.[14] The revelation by Aid prompted a review of the declassification standards by NARA's Interagency Security Oversight Office (ISOO).[15]

THE "FAMILY JEWELS"

With that background, many were surprised by the announcement at the June 2007 SHAFR conference that the CIA was releasing the "Family Jewels" in response to a FOIA request made by the National Security Archive fifteen years earlier. The "Family Jewels" file was easily the most famous and most sought-after collection of secret documents in U.S. intelligence history, even though many of its secrets had long been public knowledge.

The 693-page collection had been assembled in the era of Vietnam and Watergate, and it eventually triggered the era of the Congressional intelligence investigations. The order to collect the documents was given on 9 May 1973 by James R. Schlesinger during the seventeen weeks he served as DCI before being named secretary of defense.[16] It came in response to a newspaper report about the trial of Daniel Ellsberg, which revealed that a former CIA operative, E. Howard Hunt, had burglarized the office of Ellsberg's psychiatrist with CIA equipment on behalf of the Nixon White House.

David Robarge, chief historian at the CIA, believes that William Colby himself contributed to misconceptions about the nature of the documents with exaggerated descriptions in his memoirs.[17] If the gravity of the misdeeds was in fact exaggerated, and people may differ on that, that raises another potential question. Did the exaggeration—in some minds, glorification—of the CIA's past misdeeds contribute to public and official acceptance of later, larger-scale misdeeds as merely more of the same? The test of this, however, has been compromised. The terrorist attacks of 9/11 bequeathed such an atmosphere of menace that the public call has been for even more direct action, for the unleashing of the CIA. Controversies focused not on unauthorized or illegal deeds, but on deeds incompetently or insufficiently done. Indeed, whereas in the 1970s Congress was outraged to discover that the CIA had engaged in assassination plots, after 9/11 Congress derided the agency for not having sought authority to assassinate Usama bin Ladin or, barring that, for not "taking advantage of ambiguities" in the authorization it did receive to do it anyhow. The CIA Office of Inspector General found itself explaining to Congress that "CIA managers refused to take advantage of ambiguities" and that "this position was reasonable and correct."[18]

Now, at least, the public can see firsthand what is in the "Family Jewels," or almost. Like many declassified documents, this collection has been heavily redacted. In this case, the entire first document, approximately two and a half pages, has been redacted. Not even a title appears. Well, not completely blanked out: Each page has been marked "Secret: Eyes Only," and on each page this designation has been crossed out in ink because, after all, the document has been "declassified." Likewise, page 260 of the file consists of a letter to Schlesinger, dated 29 May 1973, from House Armed Services Committee chairman F. Edward Hebert. It reads:

> Dear Mr. Schlesinger:
>
> Attached is correspondence from [—about half a line deleted—] which is forwarded for information and whatever action might be appropriate.
>
> With best regards.
>
> > Sincerely,
> > /signed/
> > F. Edw. Hebert
> > Chairman

What follows, pages 261–265 of the file, is completely blank. Yet this document, too, is presumably listed as having been released in redacted form.

One further question comes to many minds: Why did the CIA choose to release the package at this time, thirty-four years after it was assembled and fifteen years after the National Security Archive submitted its FOIA request? The reason could be related to the fact that the automatic declassification program that President Clinton put in place in 1995 finally came into effect at the end of 2006, although the agency has rejected the declassification of tens of millions of pages of other documents and is, generally speaking, within its legal rights to do so. Some commentators have called the release of the "Family Jewels" a distraction, an effort to draw attention to the controversies of past decades at a time when the CIA and other intelligence agencies are accused of engaging in similar activities again, on a far larger scale. It was noted that the agency had still not released the results of its internal review of intelligence failures related to the terrorist attacks of 2001, which had been completed in 2005, even in an unclassified summary or redacted form. As a result, in the following month, July 2007, Congress mandated the release of a declassified summary of that report, and the CIA complied in August.

THE FUNCTION OF INTELLIGENCE

The purpose of intelligence, simply put, is to provide necessary information to government decision makers. Since much information can be gathered by conventional means, ranging from diplomacy to journalism, the focus of intelligence activities is usually on information related to national security that other governments are trying to conceal. It is then integrated with information from open sources to create a more complete picture of the capabilities and intentions of foreign governments or other entities, such as revolutionary movements or terrorist organizations.

The information passes through a set of steps identified as the intelligence cycle.[19] The normal procession is planning and direction, collection, processing, analysis, and dissemination. Planning and direction take account of policy makers' information requirements, given a particular set of threats, concerns, or objectives. Collection is the gathering of information, whether by means of clandestine agents, electronic eavesdropping, satellite photography, or the careful perusal of public sources. Naturally, different means may be more or less appropriate to a given task. Satellite photos will reveal a great deal about missile silos or large-scale troop movements but very little about the intentions of political leaders or the actions of small groups of terrorists. For the latter, spies and informers inside the target organization ("human intelligence") are more useful. During the Cold War, U.S. intelligence tended to rely most heavily on the technical means, leaving a notable gap in human intelligence capabilities in the post–Cold War environment.

Once gathered, the bits of information must be processed. Film must be developed, intercepted messages must be translated, and codes must be deciphered. Next, the processed information must be analyzed. Expert analysts examine the disparate bits of information, calculate the value and reliability of the sources, try to distinguish the relevant ("signals") from the distractions ("noise"), see how the relevant parts fit together, and attempt to decipher whether there is a hidden message and, if so, what it is.[20] Finally, the result is disseminated to policy makers, who, many analysts insist, too often simply ignore it or "cherry-pick" the parts they like to support their preferred policies.

In addition to revealing "secrets," of course, intelligence agencies are also expected to resolve "mysteries." A secret is information that others are trying to keep from you. The task is to find out what they already know. Mysteries are questions to which there are no real answers: What will a given dictator decide to do when he finally makes up his mind? Will a certain government fall? How will a particular leader react to a range of likely or unlikely events? Will an insurgency grow stronger or weaker with time? No one really knows; no amount of wiretapping or satellite photos will disclose the truth. This task calls for a somewhat different set of analytical talents, using both public and clandestine information and relying heavily on the analysis of trends and the laws of probability.

Error may be introduced at any stage of the intelligence cycle. Even the relatively straightforward opening stage of laying out the goals rarely seems to happen in a clear, concise, and useful manner. The key point to remember is that intelligence always deals with uncertainties. This is more obvious in cases involving mysteries, but it is also true of secrets. Much evidence is ambiguous and subject to multiple interpretations. True signals are often indistinguishable from noise until after the fact. Thus, the preconceived notions or preferences of analysts may easily shape the interpretation that emerges. The way an analyst "connects the dots," to use a phrase much in vogue these days, may in fact tell us more about the analyst than about the dots. Human intelligence is the most valuable resource when analysts are trying to determine the intentions of a foreign leader, but sometimes sources are mistaken, vague, unreliable, self-interested, or downright deceitful; and sometimes they are truthful and accurate but unconvincing. Perhaps the best that can be said of the intelligence task is that trying is likely to produce better results than not trying.

As noted earlier, the main purpose of intelligence agencies is to provide information to decision makers, but that is not all that intelligence agencies do. Although the role was not spelled out in its founding legislation, the CIA, early in its existence, assumed the task of running covert operations, or "special activities." Imbued with a spirit of gung-ho enthusiasm for fighting the Cold War and equipped with a network of clandestine agents stationed around the world, the CIA was the place to go when government leaders decided they needed an option "between doing nothing and sending in the Marines." The agency involved itself in the postwar electoral politics of Italy and France in order to prevent a Communist victory and then went on to organize and support a series of attempted coups, revolutions, civil wars, insurgencies, and counterinsurgencies.[21]

Calculating a realistic balance of successes and failures among covert operations is difficult to do given the veil of secrecy that still obscures so much of the history. It is customary for agency officials to claim that everyone knows about their failures but no one knows about their successes, because these remain secret. It appears that it is, in fact, a history replete with failure, possibly because presidents who do not really understand the nature of covert operations turn to the CIA for a miracle when everything else has failed. Impossible tasks are unlikely to fare well. Even known successes have sometimes proved counterproductive in the long run, including the successful overthrow of the Mossadegh government in Iran in 1953 (contributing to animosity toward the

"American shah" and the Islamic revolution of 1979), the successful overthrow of the Arbenz government in Guatemala in 1954 (which contributed to decades of civil war in that country and stoked anti-Americanism throughout Latin America), or the successful arming of anti-Soviet Islamic militants in Afghanistan in the 1980s (which contributed to the rise of the Taliban and al-Qa'ida). When political leaders initiated covert action, only to see it fail spectacularly, they often avoided responsibility afterward by allowing the CIA to be depicted as a "rogue agency" operating on its own.

THE CENTRAL INTELLIGENCE AGENCY AND THE INTELLIGENCE COMMUNITY

It is worth noting that the CIA is only one piece of the overall United States Intelligence Community (IC). Moreover, it is far from the largest agency in terms of budget or personnel. Most intelligence agencies, and an estimated 80 percent of the overall intelligence budget, are subordinated to the Department of Defense, and of all the departments of the executive branch, that department has generated the most resistance to institutional reform. In all, sixteen agencies are considered members of the IC, the oldest being the Office of Naval Intelligence (ONI, 1882) and the youngest being the Coast Guard Intelligence and Criminal Investigations Program (CGICIP, 2001). The Drug Enforcement Administration (DEA) was separated from the IC in 1981 to avoid risking the improper mixing of intelligence and law enforcement functions, only to be readmitted in 2006 to deal with the growing overlap among drug-trafficking, revolutionary, and terrorist organizations. (See Appendix B for a list of IC members.)

The CIA is perhaps the most comprehensive member of the community, in terms of its range of interests, intelligence collection, and analysis. The CIA and the Defense Intelligence Agency (DIA) are experienced in conducting all-source analysis. On the other hand, the three largest agencies in terms of budget and personnel—the National Security Agency (NSA), the National Reconnaissance Office (NRO), and the National Geospatial-Intelligence Agency (NGA), all part of the Pentagon—are highly specialized. The NSA is concerned with signals intelligence (SIGINT), the exploitation of foreign communications for intelligence and counterintelligence purposes. The NRO deals with satellite reconnaissance. Spy satellites were once considered so controversial that the mere existence of the NRO was officially acknowledged only in 1992, more than thirty years after its establishment in 1961. Also making use of satellites, the NGA concerns itself with imagery and mapping. Beyond the official IC, there are offices that primarily keep track of the community's intelligence products in search of information relevant to their parent organizations' concerns, such as the Office of Intelligence, Security, and Emergency Response within the Department of Transportation.

Prior to 2004, the CIA had an especially central role in the community; the Director of Central Intelligence (DCI) was both the administrative leader of the CIA and the nominal leader of the IC as a whole. In a commonly used corporate analogy, the DCI was both the chief executive officer of the CIA and the chairman of the board of the IC. This meant that he (or, theoretically, she) was expected to coordinate intelligence functions across agencies, but the position was given little real authority outside the CIA itself.

One way in which the DCI could perform an interagency role was through the National Intelligence Council (NIC), an entity formed in 1973 and subordinated directly to the office of the DCI. The NIC brought together representatives of all intelligence agencies to produce consensus-based assessments known as National Intelligence Estimates (NIEs). An unclassified summary of an NIE released in July 2007 gives an idea of how the system is supposed to operate.

> The Estimate, *Terrorist Threats to the US Homeland*, followed the standard process for producing National Intelligence Estimates (NIEs), including a thorough review of sourcing, in-depth Community coordination, the use of alternative analysis, and review by outside experts. Starting in October 2006, the NIC organized a series of roundtables with IC experts to scope out terms of reference (TOR) for the Estimate. Drafters from throughout the Community contributed to the draft. In May, a draft was submitted to the IC officers in advance of a series of coordination meetings that spanned several days. The National Clandestine Service, FBI, and other IC collection officers reviewed the text for the reliability and proper use of sourcing. As part of the normal coordination process, analysts had the opportunity—and were encouraged—to register "dissents" and provide alternative analysis. Reactions by the two outside experts who read the final product were highlighted in the text. The National Intelligence Board, composed of the heads of the 16 IC agencies and chaired by the ODNI, reviewed and approved the Estimate on 21 June. As with other NIEs, it is being distributed to senior Administration officials and Members of Congress.

Just how many NIEs go through so complete a process—and how many of them have eight or nine months available to do so—is difficult to say. The DCI's coordinating function, however, extended little beyond the production of these occasional joint estimates.

After the terrorist attacks of 2001, the Intelligence Community was blamed for not predicting the incident, and a bipartisan board was established to conduct a thorough investigation. Officially called the National Commission on the Terrorist Attacks upon the United States—but almost universally referred to as the 9/11 Commission—it proposed changes in the structure of the IC.[22] Prior to the attacks, the community had failed to put together disparate bits of relevant information that might have become meaningful clues in juxtaposition. Thus, the recommendations focused on the lack of real coordination and intelligence sharing among the various entities of the Intelligence Community, especially the "firewall" between foreign intelligence and domestic law enforcement. Congress, responding with customary hyperbole, passed the Intelligence Reform and Terrorism Prevention Act (IRTPA) of 2004, instituting the largest reorganization of the intelligence community since its creation in 1947. That achievement was all the more notable when one considers that between 1989 and 2001, no fewer than six independent commissions and three government reviews had attempted to address the need for intelligence reform, without results.[23]

The task of increasing coordination and information sharing is a difficult one, given the variety of agency mandates, interests, procedures, competencies, cultures, mythologies, and incompatible computer systems. The key to this reform was the creation of a new focal point, the Director of National Intelligence (DNI).[24] The former Director of Central Intelligence was downgraded to Director of the Central Intelligence Agency (DCIA). The idea was to create a new and stronger "intelligence czar." Although the DNI may have been new, after the customary bureaucratic infighting and legislative wrangling—which uncustomarily pitted a bipartisan group of senators against the more skeptical House Republicans—one could question how much stronger the new position really was.

The DNI replaced the DCI as the president's principal intelligence adviser. The NIC was transferred to the Office of the DNI (ODNI), as was the recently formed analytic, interagency National Counterterrorism Center (NCTC; not to be confused with the CIA's more operationally oriented Counterterrorist Center, CTC, which retained responsibility for disrupting terrorist activities). The DNI now had responsibility for coordinating, guiding, and focusing the community as a whole without the biases that might derive from being attached to one of the community members. The new leader was also granted official budgetary authority over the country's civilian intelligence program, although—at the insistence of House Republicans—he was limited to participating with the secretary of defense in drawing up the budget for military intelligence programs. On paper, the DNI also has authority to shift funds and personnel among agencies.

Nevertheless, the new office lacked the clout of an agency leader; the DNI was, in other words, a bureaucrat without a bureaucracy (despite the fact that the ODNI staff quickly grew to 1,500). Congressional responsibilities for intelligence and intelligence-budget matters remained totally unreformed and highly fragmented, which also complicates life at the ODNI. Despite proposals for an open and unified intelligence budget, the community's budget remained secret and hidden in multiple "black accounts" throughout the government. The peculiar combination of extensive responsibilities with relatively few and vaguely defined powers actually made it difficult to fill the new leadership position; several potential candidates turned down the offer.

Exercising authority over Defense Department agencies proved particularly difficult, especially while they were under the strong-willed leadership of Donald Rumsfeld (2001–2006). The CIA was granted communitywide responsibility for the management of overseas human intelligence (HUMINT), but then the Defense Intelligence Agency created its own Defense HUMINT Management Office in 2005, the year after the reform law was enacted. Despite the coordinating role of ODNI, the DIA took on new intelligence management responsibilities among the military intelligence agencies.[25]

In April 2007, Mike McConnell, already the second person to hold the position of DNI, responded to a question as to whether the Intelligence Community had finally found the proper organizational structure.

> We don't have it right yet. The part of the debate earlier was to create a department of intelligence, and that was not warmly embraced in some circles, I would say. So now, as DNI, I'm responsible for basically two things if you just sort of reduce it to the bottom line: the budget for the 16 components of the community and ensuring that no one breaks the law. Now, 15 of those agencies work for another Cabinet official, so I would submit that's a challenge. If you're going to dictate someone else's budget in another department and worry about compliance with the law and the regulations where you don't have direct line management responsibility, you cannot hire or fire, it puts you in a challenging management condition.[26]

As important as improved coordination and information sharing may be, however, there are limits to what can be accomplished through reorganization.

A more efficient structure will not make up for the lack of a human source inside a targeted government or organization. Furthermore, institutional changes designed to offset one problem may very well exacerbate another. Like the National Security Act of 1947, which created the CIA, the IRTPA focused on a particular array of problems highlighted by a given set of recent events. Whether or not the act adequately resolves those problems, other issues—unhighlighted and therefore unaddressed—may cause different problems in the future. For instance, the emphasis placed on coordination, guidance, and focus would seem to promise a homogenized intelligence product without regard for the different, and even competing, needs of various intelligence users. Focusing on the priorities imposed by political leaders might mean overlooking clues to other, unexpected events, which would seem to be the very definition of intelligence failure. Finally, increased centralization and control raise the prospect of "groupthink," an aspect of group dynamics whereby unorthodox, innovative, and other dissident ideas are suppressed by formal or informal pressures to conform to the group consensus.[27]

In the past, the Intelligence Community has always prided itself on a sloppy and cantankerous process that gave rise to a variety of views, interpretations, and explanations, as well as dissents. As Thomas Fingar, deputy director of national intelligence for analysis, put it: "The basic idea is to avoid a premature rush to an artificial consensus.... The interesting thing is not when analysts agree. It's when they disagree."[28] Political leaders, on the other hand, chafe at the caveats and ambiguities that sometimes seem to predict everything and nothing. They generally prefer a single, consensus-based, "correct" answer—even when no one can possibly know what the "correct" answer is. The debate over which approach is superior will be with us for some time.

THE ORGANIZATION OF THE CENTRAL INTELLIGENCE AGENCY

The CIA is subdivided into four directorates. This basic structure has been fairly stable since it was innovated by DCI Walter Bedell Smith in the early 1950s. It is functional and not inherently complicated, but over the years there have been so many nominal reorganizations and name changes that keeping track of whether one is discussing the same directorate over time or a series of different directorates can be highly taxing.

One formality that we shall forgo in this discussion is the shift to "Directorates." At one time they were called "Deputy Directorates" because they usually were—until the most recent reform, led by the agency's Deputy Directors. Thereafter, the divisions were called "Directorates," although the division heads were still called "Deputy Directors." Here, the term "Directorate" will be used throughout.

The essential but routine administrative issues are handled by the Directorate of Support (DS), which deals with human resources, financial and logistical operations, and other housekeeping matters. Originally, the DS was called the Directorate of Administration, but the name was changed to Directorate of Support in 1955, then to Directorate of Management and Services in 1973, and then back to Directorate of Administration in 1974. DCI George Tenet abolished the Directorate of Administration, although its component parts lived on, and DCI Porter Goss reconstituted it as the Directorate of Support.

The branch that stations officers around the world, collects and disseminates foreign intelligence, and conducts "special activities" (covert operations) is currently called the National Clandestine Service (NCS). It began life as the Directorate of Operations, but by the time its first Deputy Director assumed his post, it had taken on a more euphemistic name, Directorate of Plans. In 1973, its name was changed back to the Directorate of Operations, and it remained such until it was given its current designation in 2005. It is led by the Director of the National Clandestine Service (before 2004, by the Deputy Director for Operations, and so forth). In addition to the CIA's clandestine operations, under the 2004 reform the Director of the NCS has overall management responsibility for human intelligence (HUMINT) operations throughout the intelligence community. This includes the development of common standards for all aspects of clandestine human intelligence operations, "including human-enabled technical operations," and the "integration, coordination, de-confliction, and evaluation of clandestine HUMINT operations."[29] Those readers who wish to be correct should note that full-time CIA employees are not called "agents." American officials in the employ of the National Clandestine Service (or, previously, the Directorate of Operations, etc.) are called "case officers." Individuals, usually foreign nationals, whom the case officers recruit, are called "agents." Individuals who are sources of information are "assets." Case officers are assigned overseas to a "station" or a "base." A base is subordinate to a station, whether or not it is located near one. Thus, a Chief of Station (COS) ranks higher than a Chief of Base (COB).

The Directorate of Intelligence (DI) is the analytical branch, generating comprehensive "all-source" intelligence assessments, combining clandestine and open sources of information. It concerns itself with both functional and regional issues, and its output includes quickly produced responses to recent events, long-term research studies, and projections of future trends. As such, it is the branch of the CIA that interacts most with the intelligence users situated in other parts of the government, and it is expected to learn their specific intelligence requirements so that intelligence products can be kept relevant. It has almost always been called the Directorate of Intelligence, except between 1977 and 1982, when it was the National Foreign Assessment Center. Its leader is the Director of Intelligence, formerly the Deputy Director for Intelligence (or Director of the National Foreign Assessment Center). The key employees of the Directorate of Intelligence are called "analysts."

The final major branch is the Directorate of Science and Technology (DS&T), which was formed as the Directorate of Research in 1962 but took its current name the following year. It supports the National Clandestine Service and the Directorate of Intelligence with scientific, engineering, and technical solutions to intelligence problems, devising ways to gain access to information, support clandestine operations, and so forth. The Director of (formerly, Deputy Director for) Science and Technology is the senior scientific and technical adviser to the DCIA. It also maintains the capacity to gather outside experts in many fields on short notice in case of fast-breaking needs.

As an innovation in response to the changing business environment, DS&T founded In-Q-Tel in 1999. In-Q-Tel is a nonprofit venture-capital firm intended to keep the Intelligence Community in contact with innovators of emerging technologies in the private sector and to give financial support to promising projects. As an independent legal entity, it has a board of directors drawn from among former cabinet secretaries, military and intelligence officials, and figures from business and finance. The DS&T office that deals directly with it is the In-Q-Tel Interface Center.

NOTES

1. All Hayden quotes are from "General Hayden's Remarks at SHAFR Conference" (21 June 2007), https://www.cia.gov/news-information/speeches-testimony/2007/general-hayden-remarks-at-shafr-conference.html.

2. Scott Shane, "Secrets to Be Declassified under New Rule at Age 25," *New York Times* (21 December 2006).

3. J. Kenneth McDonald, "Commentary on 'History Declassified,' " *Diplomatic History* 18:4 (Fall 1994): 627–34. McDonald was, at the time, chief historian of the CIA. Examples of declassified internal histories are Arthur B. Darling, *The Central Intelligence Agency: An Instrument of Government, to 1950* (University Park, PA: Pennsylvania State University Press, 1990); Ludwell Lee Montague, *General Walter Bedell Smith as Director of Central Intelligence, October 1950–February 1953* (University Park, PA: Pennsylvania State University Press, 1992). A rare earlier example was Thomas F. Troy, *Donovan and the CIA: A History of the Establishment of the Central Intelligence Agency* (Frederick, MD: Aletheia Books, 1981). The Darling book had been written in 1953. The Troy book had been published internally in 1975 with two copies printed.

4. McDonald, "Commentary;" Zachary Karabell and Timothy Naftali, "History Declassified: The Perils and Promise of CIA Documents," *Diplomatic History* 18:4 (Fall 1994): 615–26; Mary S. McAuliffe, ed., *CIA Documents on the Cuban Missile Crisis, 1962* (Washington, D.C.: Central Intelligence Agency, 1992).

5. "Editorial: The Price of History," *New York Times* (19 July 1998).

6. Matthew M. Aid, "Declassification in Reverse: The U.S. Intelligence Community's Secret Historical Document Reclassification Program," *The National Security Archive* (21 February 2006), http://www.gwu.edu/~nsarchiv/NSAEBB/NSAEBB179/index.htm.

7. Karabell and Naftali, op. cit.; Anna Kasten Nelson, "History with Holes: The CIA Reveals Its Past," *Diplomatic History* 22:3 (Summer 1998): 503–8.

8. Dan Stober and Ian Hoffman, *A Convenient Spy: Wen Ho Lee and the Politics of Nuclear Espionage* (New York: Simon & Schuster, 2001).

9. Aid, "Declassification in Reverse."

10. Executive Order 13292: "Further Amendment to Executive Order 12958, As Amended, Classified National Security Information." See also "Revisions to Executive Order 12958 on Classified National Security Information," http://www.archives.gov/isoo/speeches-and-articles/article-revised-eo-12958.html. The August 2001 date is from Frank Rich, "When the Vice President Does It, That Means It's Not Illegal," *New York Times* (1 July 2007).

11. Shane, "Secrets to Be Declassified," notes that the archives did not have adequate staff to handle all the records that would be released.

12. "Revisions to Executive Order 12958."

13. Aid, "Declassification in Reverse."

14. Aid, "Declassification in Reverse"; Scott Shane, "U.S. Reclassifies Many Documents in Secret Review," *New York Times* (21 February 2006).

15. "Secret Understanding between National Archives and CIA Exposes Framework for Surreptitious Reclassification Program," *The National Security Archive* (19 April 2006), http://www.gwu.edu/~nsarchiv/news/20060419/index.htm. The ISOO, once part of the Office of Management and Budget, now part of NARA, oversees the handling of classified documents. It gained public attention when the Office of the Vice President refused to cooperate with it (over the course of four years) and then proposed to abolish it (as

part of a new revision of Executive Order 12958) when the ISOO director insisted that the vice president comply with the executive order. See Mark Silva, "Cheney Keeps Classification Activity Secret," *Chicago Tribune* (27 May 2006); Scott Shane, "Agency Is Target in Cheney Fight on Secrecy Data," *New York Times* (22 June 2007); and Rep. Henry A. Waxman's letter to Vice President Dick Cheney (21 June 2007), http://oversight.house.gov/documents/20070621093952.pdf.

16. Brief tenure was common in the Watergate era. At the Department of Defense, Schlesinger was following the four-month term of Elliott Richardson, who then served six months as attorney general before he was dismissed for refusing to fire the special prosecutor investigating Watergate.

17. David Robarge, "Perspective on the Jewels from the C.I.A.'s Chief Historian," available on a *New York Times* blog, "Examining the Archives: The CIA's 'Family Jewels,'" http://washington.blogs.nytimes.com/2007/06/27/perspective-on-the-jewels-from-the-cias-chief-historian/#more-28. The memoir in question is William Colby, *Honorable Men: My Life in the CIA* (New York: Simon & Schuster, 1978).

18. See "OIG Report on CIA Accountability With Respect to the 9/11 Attacks" in the chapter "9/11."

19. Mark M. Lowenthal, *Intelligence: From Secrets to Policy*, 3rd ed. (Washington, D.C.: CQ Press, 2006); Loch K. Johnson, *America's Secret Power: The CIA in a Democratic Society* (New York: Oxford University Press, 1989); and Walter Laqueur, *The Uses and Limits of Intelligence* (New Brunswick, NJ: Transaction Publishers, 1993).

20. For a seminal study of how "noise" can crowd out "signals" (even when the signals appear obvious in retrospect), see Roberta Wohlstetter, *Pearl Harbor: Warning and Decision* (Stanford, CA: Stanford University Press, 1962).

21. See, for example, John Prados, *Safe for Democracy: The Secret Wars of the CIA* (Chicago: Ivan R. Dee, 2006); and Tim Weiner, *Legacy of Ashes: The History of the CIA* (New York: Doubleday, 2007).

22. *The 9/11 Commission Report: Final Report of the National Commission on the Terrorist Attacks upon the United States* (New York: W. W. Norton, 2004). Unusually readable, and covering an unusually salient topic, the report quickly became a bestseller.

23. Helen Fessenden, "The Limits of Intelligence Reform," *Foreign Affairs* 84:6 (November/December 2005).

24. Mike McConnell, "Overhauling Intelligence," *Foreign Affairs* 86:4 (July/August 2007).

25. See "Defense Intelligence Agency," in *An Overview of the United States Intelligence Community* (Washington, D.C.: Office of the Director of National Intelligence, 2007).

26. "Remarks and Q&A by the Director of National Intelligence, Mr. Mike McConnell, 2007 Excellence in Government Conference, Washington, D.C., April 4, 2007," http://www.odni.gov/speeches/20070404_speech.pdf.

27. Irving L. Janis, *Groupthink: Psychological Studies of Political Decisions and Fiascoes*, 2nd ed. (Boston: Houghton Mifflin, 1982). In an effort to counter this risk, the Intelligence Community has experimented with "devil's advocate" and alternative analyses. McConnell, "Overhauling Intelligence."

28. Quoted in the *New York Times* blog The Lede, http://thelede.blogs.nytimes.com/2007/07/17/national-intelligence-estimate-day/#more651.

29. *Overview of the United States Intelligence Community.*

Timeline: Selected Events in the History of the Central Intelligence Agency

11 JULY 1941

President Franklin D. Roosevelt creates the Office of the Coordinator of Information (COI) and appoints attorney William J. "Wild Bill" Donovan to the position. The COI is to collect and analyze information that bears on the national security, issue publications, and facilitate the securing of information.

13 JUNE 1942

President Roosevelt reorganizes the Office of the COI as the Office of Strategic Services (OSS) and places it under the Joint Chiefs of Staff. The OSS is to collect and analyze strategic information and perform "special services" as may be directed by the Joint Chiefs of Staff. Donovan is appointed as Director of Strategic Services.

18 NOVEMBER 1944

Donovan recommends that the president create a permanent civilian intelligence agency after World War II.

1 OCTOBER 1945

With the war over, President Harry S. Truman dissolves the OSS and transfers its assets to the State and War departments.

22 JANUARY 1946

President Truman establishes the National Intelligence Authority (NIA)—consisting of the secretaries of State, War, and the Navy and a presidential representative—to plan, develop, and coordinate intelligence activities. He also establishes the Central Intelligence Group (CIG), with a Director of Central

Intelligence and a staff of officers on loan from the War, Navy, State, and Justice departments. The creation of a permanent intelligence agency is to be part of the planned "unification" of the military, which is still under debate.

26 JULY 1947

Congress approves military unification with the passage of the National Security Act of 1947. The Act establishes the Department of Defense (merging the War and Navy departments), the National Security Council, and a new permanent civilian intelligence body, the Central Intelligence Agency (CIA).

18 SEPTEMBER 1947

The National Security Act comes into effect, and the CIA opens for business. The Director of Central Intelligence becomes the head of the new agency.

22 MARCH 1948

The CIA Office of Special Operations is established to conduct espionage and counterespionage. This office will later be merged into the Directorate of Plans.

SPRING 1948

The CIA pays subsidies to the Christian Democratic Party of Italy to assist it in its electoral campaign against the Communist Party of Italy.

18 JUNE 1948

The National Security Council issues a secret directive, NSC 10/2, that authorizes the CIA to undertake "covert operations" to counter similar activities engaged in by the Soviet Union. These activities are to be conducted in accordance with U.S. foreign policy and military goals.

1 SEPTEMBER 1948

The CIA Office of Policy Coordination is established under Frank Wisner to conduct psychological operations. Its responsibilities will soon expand to include sabotage and economic warfare. This office will later be merged into the Directorate of Plans.

16 NOVEMBER 1948

Wisner arranges to use Marshall Plan money to bolster non-Communist labor unions in Italy and France.

20 JUNE 1949

Congress passes the Central Intelligence Agency Act, formally spelling out the agency's authority, responsibilities, and special privileges, including exemptions from civil service rules and normal budgetary and accounting requirements. The CIA may also conceal information regarding is organization, functions, and personnel.

5 SEPTEMBER 1949

In the CIA's first penetration of the Soviet Union, the agency parachutes members of the Supreme Council for the Liberation of Ukraine into the Carpathian Mountains of western Ukraine. Soviet forces mop up the Ukrainian insurgency by 1953.

OCTOBER 1949

In coordination with British intelligence, the CIA begins infiltrating anti-Communist rebels into Albania. Nearly all are immediately killed or captured. It later emerged that Communist agents had infiltrated the Albanian émigré community and training camps, and the British liaison, Kim Philby, was secretly passing information to the Soviet Union.

1 DECEMBER 1950

An administrative reorganization creates the positions of Deputy Director for Administration and Deputy Director for Operations (changed to Deputy Director for Plans on 4 January 1951).

8 DECEMBER 1951

The CIA initiates a program to monitor all mail passing through New York City to and from the Soviet Union. Beginning in 1955, this mail is opened.

1 JANUARY 1952

An administrative reorganization creates the position of Deputy Director for Intelligence.

13 APRIL 1953

DCI Allen Dulles approves a proposal to develop biological and chemical materials. The program, called MKULTRA, leads to drug experiments on unsuspecting individuals.

19 AUGUST 1953

A coup d'état instigated by the CIA overthrows the government of Prime Minister Muhammad Mossadeq in Iran, leading to the restoration of the Shah.

27 NOVEMBER 1953

Dr. Frank Olson, a civilian scientist in the employ of the U.S. Army, commits suicide. The act is attributed to his role as an unwitting subject in the CIA drug program MKULTRA.

27 JUNE 1954

President Jacobo Arbenz is forced form office in Guatemala, despite the failure of a CIA-instigated coup d'état led by Carlos Castillo Armas. As a result of pressure from the United States, Castillo Armas becomes president on 1 September.

23 NOVEMBER 1954

President Dwight Eisenhower approves a plan to develop the U-2 spy plane, which is to fly at altitudes undetectable by the Soviet Union.

14 JANUARY 1955

Montana Senator Mike Mansfield introduces a resolution to establish a joint Congressional oversight committee to monitor the CIA. The measure fails in the face of opposition from the Senate Armed Services Committee and the Eisenhower administration.

3 FEBRUARY 1955

The Deputy Director for Administration becomes the Deputy Director for Support.

4 JULY 1956

The first U-2 overflight of the Soviet Union is conducted.

SPRING 1957

The CIA begins offering training and support to anti-Chinese guerrillas in Tibet. The agency will later establish a training center for the Tibetan operation in the Rocky Mountains in Colorado. Although not very effective, the operation continues into the early 1970s, when President Richard Nixon ends it as part of the policy of improving relations with China.

22 SEPTEMBER 1957

The National Security Council approves a covert operation to overthrow the government of President Sukarno in Indonesia by supporting rebel forces.

4 OCTOBER 1957

The Soviet Union unexpectedly launches *Sputnik*, the first artificial space satellite. A presidential commission later concludes that the Soviets must be building intercontinental missiles at a rapid pace, giving rise to fears of a "missile gap."

19 APRIL 1958

CIA pilots begin engaging directly in combat operations in Indonesia, bombing and strafing government positions in support of armed dissidents.

19 MAY 1958

DCI Dulles orders the Indonesian operation ended after the U.S. ambassador and the commander of Pacific forces declare it a transparent failure.

DECEMBER 1959

Vang Pao, an ethnic Hmong military leader in Laos, tells the CIA that, if he had the weapons, he could raise an army of 10,000 Hmong to fight the pro-Communist

Pathet Lao movement in the country's escalating civil war. Arms begin arriving in January 1961.

17 MARCH 1960

President Eisenhower approves plans to recruit and train Cuban émigrés for an invasion of Cuba.

1 MAY 1960

A CIA U-2 spy plane flown by Francis Gary Powers is shot down over the Soviet Union. A U.S.-Soviet summit meeting scheduled for 16 May is canceled. U-2 flights over Soviet territory are ended and are to be replaced by surveillance satellites.

AUGUST 1960

The National Security Council authorizes the assassination of Premier Patrice Lumumba of the Congo and Prime Minister Fidel Castro of Cuba.

12 AUGUST 1960

Colonel Oleg Penkovsky of Soviet military intelligence (GRU), a "walk-in" informant, offers the CIA highly useful information about Soviet missile technology and intelligence operations. Penkovsky's activities are discovered by Soviet authorities on 12 October 1962, and he is executed on 16 May 1963.

18 AUGUST 1960

The first CIA surveillance satellite is launched in the CORONA program. It is to photograph the Soviet Union in search of missiles.

17 APRIL 1961

Cuban exiles recruited and trained by the CIA invade Cuba at the Bay of Pigs. They are defeated by the Cuban army within three days.

30 MAY 1961

President Rafael Leónidas Trujillo of the Dominican Republic is assassinated by rebels who had, for a time, been encouraged by the CIA.

20 SEPTEMBER 1961

The CIA begins moving into its new headquarters in Langley, Virginia.

NOVEMBER 1961

President John F. Kennedy initiates Operation Mongoose to destabilize Cuba. Being distrustful of the CIA after the Bay of Pigs failure, he places the project under his brother, Attorney General Robert F. Kennedy.

28 NOVEMBER 1961

The CIA headquarters building in Langley, Virginia, is completed.

15 DECEMBER 1961

Soviet intelligence officer Anatoliy Golitsyn defects and offers sensitive information on Soviet intelligence and counterintelligence matters.

19 FEBRUARY 1962

An administrative reorganization creates the position of Deputy Director for Research.

7 MARCH 1962

Under pressure from Attorney General Kennedy, DCI John A. McCone orders the phones of journalists Robert S. Allen and Paul Scott to be monitored in order to identify who was leaking information to them.

14 OCTOBER 1962

A CIA U-2 reports the installation of Soviet missiles in Cuba. Five days later, President Kennedy announces a quarantine of the island, setting off the Cuban Missile Crisis. In the following days, the world comes close to nuclear war.

5 AUGUST 1963

The Deputy Director for Research becomes the Deputy Director for Science and Technology.

1 NOVEMBER 1963

South Vietnamese army officers overthrow and assassinate Premier Ngo Dinh Diem. The CIA denies responsibility for the coup, but it was aware of the planning and opted not to interfere.

4 FEBRUARY 1964

Yuriy Nosenko, an operative of the KGB, defects to a CIA representative in Geneva, Switzerland, claiming to have information on President Kennedy's assassin, Lee Harvey Oswald. Suspicions regarding his authenticity lead to years of incarceration and interrogation in CIA facilities in the United States. Anatoliy Golitsyn encourages suspicion of him.

1965

The CIA-guided Hmong operation in Laos grows into the largest paramilitary operation in the agency's history. In addition to fighting Pathet Lao and North Vietnamese forces in Laos, much activity is directed against Viet Cong supply routes running through Laos from North Vietnam to South Vietnam. The operation continues until June 1974, when it is ended as a consequence of peace accords.

FEBRUARY 1967

Ramparts magazine reports that the CIA has covertly funded the overseas programs of the National Student Association since 1952, raising questions of academic freedom as well as inappropriate domestic activity by the CIA. The Katzenbach Committee later recommends a ban on any direct or indirect funding of American educational or private voluntary organizations, which the CIA accepts.

15 AUGUST 1967

Prodded by President Lyndon B. Johnson, the CIA launches MHCHAOS to investigate possible foreign connections behind U.S. antiwar and civil rights activists. The program continues until 1973.

SUMMER 1968

The CIA issues "Restless Youth," a study of student dissidents around the world, at the behest of National Security Adviser Walter Rostow. A limited number of copies include a chapter on the American organization Students for a Democratic Society (SDS).

31 MARCH 1970

FBI Director J. Edgar Hoover severs the bureau's liaison with the CIA because of his annoyance at the handling of a missing-person case involving a Czech-born history professor in Colorado.

14 JULY 1970

The Huston Plan, devised by White House aide Tom Charles Huston, authorizes intelligence agencies to use "clearly illegal" investigative techniques in domestic operations. The plan is revoked thirteen days later.

15 SEPTEMBER 1970

President Nixon authorizes the CIA to prevent the inauguration of Salvador Allende as president of Chile. Allende has already won the election.

22 OCTOBER 1970

A botched kidnapping attempt results in the death of General René Schneider, commander of the Chilean army. Chilean politicians rally around Allende.

19 NOVEMBER 1970

FBI Director Hoover announces that the Black Panther Party is supported by international terrorists. The CIA finds no evidence in either FBI or CIA files to support such an assertion but is not in a position to say so publicly.

DECEMBER 1970

President Richard M. Nixon forms the Intelligence Evaluation Committee, an interagency group assigned to investigate the foreign roots of internal dissent. It is led by Assistant Attorney General for Internal Security Robert Mardian. The CIA is represented on the committee, but most members are unaware of the CIA's ongoing MHCHAOS.

7 JULY 1971

Presidential adviser John Ehrlichman telephones Deputy Director of Central Intelligence Robert Cushman and instructs him that White House "security consultant" and former CIA officer E. Howard Hunt will be making requests of the agency. The agency is to cooperate with Hunt without asking questions.

JULY–AUGUST 1971

Hunt requests that the CIA provide him with disguises, alias identification, cameras, and a psychological profile of Daniel Ellsberg, who is suspected of releasing the Pentagon Papers to the press. The CIA complies until the end of the summer, when agency managers deem the requests excessive.

3 SEPTEMBER 1971

Hunt breaks into the office of Dr. Louis Fielding, Daniel Ellsberg's psychiatrist.

17 JUNE 1972

Police arrest five men at the National Democratic Committee headquarters in the Watergate complex in Washington. Among them is James McCord, a former CIA employee, and four Cuban Americans with past ties to the CIA, one of whom is carrying a false passport issued to E. Howard Hunt.

23 JUNE 1972

Presidential Chief of Staff H. R. Haldeman presses DCI Richard Helms and Deputy DCI (DDCI) Vernon Walters to intervene with the FBI to limit part of its investigation related to the Watergate break-in. They are to say that further investigation will interfere with CIA operations in Mexico. (The later discovery of a recording of Nixon instructing Haldeman to do this will result in his resignation as president in 1974.)

27 JUNE 1972

DDCI Walters refuses White House Counsel John Dean's request to have the CIA pay the bail and salaries of the Watergate burglars because it would falsely implicate the agency in the break-in.

6 JULY 1972

DDCI Walters informs acting FBI director L. Patrick Gray that his inquiries indicate there is no CIA operation in Mexico, despite what was said the previous month, and he will no longer claim that there is.

JULY 1972

James McCord sends the first of six letters to Richard Helms and other CIA officials implying that the White House is pressing him to implicate the CIA in the Watergate affair.

20 NOVEMBER 1972

Once reelected, despite the CIA's failure to cooperate on the Watergate affair, Nixon dismisses Richard Helms as Director of Central Intelligence.

2 FEBRUARY 1973

James Schlesinger becomes Director of Central Intelligence. He has instructions from President Nixon to shake up the agency.

1 MARCH 1973

The Deputy Director for Plans becomes the Deputy Director for Operations.

22 MARCH 1973

The Deputy Director for Support becomes the Deputy Director for Management and Services.

9 MAY 1973

After learning from newspaper reports that E. Howard Hunt had burglarized a psychiatrist's office with CIA-supplied equipment, DCI Schlesinger issues a memorandum instructing all CIA employees to inform him of any past activities that might transgress the agency's charter. The responses to his memo are collected in a file dubbed the "Family Jewels."

10 MAY 1973

Schlesinger is nominated to be Secretary of Defense. He steps down as DCI on 2 July.

4 SEPTEMBER 1973

William E. Colby becomes Director of Central Intelligence after a period in which Vernon Walters has served as acting director.

11 SEPTEMBER 1973

General Augusto Pinochet overthrows the government of Chile in a violent coup d'état. President Allende dies in the process, apparently by suicide. Many assume the CIA is responsible.

5 AUGUST 1974

The House Judiciary Committee releases the "smoking gun" tape, revealing President Nixon's instructions to have the CIA intervene in the FBI's investigation of Watergate.

9 AUGUST 1974

Richard Nixon resigns from the presidency to avoid impeachment. Gerald R. Ford becomes president.

19 AUGUST 1974

The Deputy Director for Management and Services becomes the Deputy Director for Administration.

17 DECEMBER 1974

DCI Colby informs James J. Angleton that he is relieving him of responsibilities as Chief of the Counterintelligence Staff. Angleton resigns from the agency effective 31 December.

22 DECEMBER 1974

Seymour Hersh reports in *The New York Times* on a "huge CIA operation" against antiwar forces and other dissidents in the United States.

30 DECEMBER 1974

Congress approves the Hughes-Ryan Act, requiring covert operations to have a written "finding," signed by the president, that the operation is in the interest of national security.

4 JANUARY 1975

President Ford creates the President's Commission on CIA Activities within the United States, led by Vice President Nelson Rockefeller (the Rockefeller Commission), to investigate the allegations of domestic surveillance. Some observers later dismiss it as a whitewash.

27 JANUARY 1975

Abandoning a tradition of benign neglect regarding its oversight of intelligence matters, the Senate establishes the Senate Select Committee to Study Governmental Operations with Respect to Intelligence Activities, led by Senator Frank Church (the Church Committee), to investigate allegations of past illegal activities of the CIA and other agencies. The committee conducts 800 interviews, twenty-one public hearings, and 250 executive hearings. Its findings, completed in May 1976, fill fourteen volumes and are called the most comprehensive public review of intelligence activities in history.

19 FEBRUARY 1975

Following the Senate's lead, the House establishes the House Select Intelligence Committee with a similar mandate. Its initial chairman, Lucien Nedzi, resigned from the committee on June 12, 1975, after other Democrats discovered that he had known of the "Family Jewels" file since 1973 (having been informed by Colby). He was replaced by Otis Pike. The Pike Committee develops a less cooperative relationship with the agency than the Church Committee. DCI Colby describes the committee as "totally biased and a disservice to our nation" and privately calls Pike a "jackass." Its report is not officially released to the public, but it is leaked to *The Village Voice*.

MAY 1975

Several retired CIA officials form the Association of Retired Intelligence Officers (after 1978, the Association of Former Intelligence Officers; after 2006, the Association For Intelligence Officers) with the intention of improving the agency's image through public education.

8 JULY 1975

Nine weeks after the fall of Saigon and in the midst of Congressional investigations of CIA activities, President Ford signs a finding authorizing CIA support to two liberation movements in Angola against a third movement, which has connections to the Soviet Union and Cuba.

20 NOVEMBER 1975

The Church Committee issues its most famous interim report, *Alleged Assassination Plots Involving Foreign Leaders.*

23 DECEMBER 1975

Richard Welch, Chief of Station in Athens, Greece, is assassinated after his identity and address are revealed in anti-CIA publications. As a consequence, a law is passed in 1982 making it a crime to disclose the identity of CIA officers.

19 DECEMBER 1975/27 JANUARY 1976

The Senate and then the House approve the Clark Amendment, requiring the termination of all funding for covert operations in Angola.

30 JANUARY 1976

President Ford dismisses Colby as Director of Central Intelligence, in large part for being too forthcoming to the Church Committee. The new DCI is future president George H. W. Bush.

18 FEBRUARY 1976

President Ford issues Executive Order 11905, "United States Foreign Intelligence Activities," to clarify the authority and responsibilities of the Intelligence Community. It includes the following explicit prohibition: "No employee of the United States Government shall engage in, or conspire to engage in, political assassination."

6 MAY 1976

DCI Bush, under political pressure from conservative Republicans challenging President Ford's renomination, creates a panel of outside experts to reevaluate the CIA's assessment of Soviet strategic capabilities and objectives. Team B lambastes the CIA as naïve and paints a picture of a growing and aggressive Soviet military threat. The Team B assessment lays the foundation for Reagan administration policies in the 1980s. An internal CIA review in 1989, with more evidence available, concludes that the CIA had actually overestimated Soviet capabilities somewhat and that the Team B assessment was wildly exaggerated.

19 MAY 1976

The Senate Select Committee on Intelligence is formed as a permanent oversight committee. Previous oversight responsibilities had been handled by subcommittees of the Armed Forces and Appropriations Committees.

14 JULY 1977

The House Permanent Select Committee on Intelligence is formed. The formation of the House committee was delayed owing to controversies over the leaking of the Pike Committee report.

11 OCTOBER 1977

The Deputy Director for Intelligence becomes the Director of the National Foreign Assessment Center.

25 OCTOBER 1978

The Foreign Intelligence Surveillance Act (FISA) establishes a special court and procedures for authorizing electronic surveillance within the United States for foreign intelligence purposes.

14 OCTOBER 1980

The Intelligence Accountability Act amends the 1974 Hughes-Ryan Act by reducing the number of Congressional committees that must be informed of covert actions from eight to two (the two new intelligence committees).

4 DECEMBER 1981

President Ronald Reagan replaces Ford's Executive Order 11905 with Executive Order 12333, "United States Intelligence Activities." The prohibition against assassination is strengthened by extending it to nonemployees of the government and by dropping the modifier "political." It states: "No person employed by or acting on behalf of the United States Government shall engage in, or conspire to engage in, assassination."

4 JANUARY 1982

The Director of the National Foreign Assessment Center reverts to the previous title, Deputy Director for Intelligence.

16 MARCH 1982

William Buckley, CIA Chief of Station in Beirut, Lebanon, is kidnapped by Islamist militants. He is later tortured and killed.

23 JUNE 1982

President Reagan signs the Intelligence Identities Protection Act as an amendment to the National Security Act of 1947. The new law makes it a crime for someone authorized to know the identity of a covert intelligence officer to divulge that identity to someone not so authorized. In part, this is a delayed response to the assassination of Richard Welch in 1975 and to disclosures made by disgruntled former CIA employees such as Philip Agee.

8 DECEMBER 1982

The first Boland Amendment prohibits the use of government funds for the purpose of overthrowing the Nicaraguan government. The Reagan administration claims the CIA's support of the Contras is intended to disrupt arms traffic from Nicaragua to El Salvador, not to overthrow the Nicaraguan government.

12 OCTOBER 1984

The second Boland Amendment prohibits the Department of Defense, the CIA, or "any other agency or entity involved in intelligence activities" from providing military or paramilitary aid to the Nicaraguan Contras for the period from October 1984 to December 1985.

15 OCTOBER 1984

President Reagan signs the Central Intelligence Agency Information Act, exempting the CIA from some of the search and review requirements of the Freedom of Information Act.

27 MARCH 1985

President Reagan signs National Security Decision Directive (NSDD) 166, "U.S. Policy, Programs, and Strategy in Afghanistan," supporting the goal of military victory for the mostly Islamist mujahedeen. Although the United States has been funneling aid through Pakistan's Inter-Services Intelligence (ISI) since 1979, it now increases assistance. The CIA takes a more direct role in arming, training, and supporting the guerrillas. Some of the Afghan guerrillas—and some of their supporters and allies from other Muslim countries—would later become members of the Taliban and al-Qa'ida.

23 AUGUST 1985

President Reagan approves the sale by Israel of U.S.-made weapons to Iran in the hope of facilitating the release of hostages in Lebanon.

5 DECEMBER 1985

President Reagan authorizes direct sales of weapons to Iran.

1 FEBRUARY 1986

DCI William Casey establishes the Counterterrorist Center. Its first head is Duane Clarridge, who earlier was responsible for paramilitary operations in Nicaragua.

5 OCTOBER 1986

Nicaragua shoots down a CIA-chartered aircraft in the process of supplying Contra guerrilla forces. The sole survivor, Eugene Hasenfus, is captured.

3 NOVEMBER 1986

An Islamist newspaper in Lebanon reports that the Reagan administration sought to trade arms for hostages.

25 NOVEMBER 1986

Attorney General Edwin Meese III confirms that arms were traded to Iran to secure the release of hostages in Lebanon and that part of the proceeds were diverted to supply the Contras in Nicaragua in defiance of the Boland Amendment.

1 DECEMBER 1986

The President's Special Review Board, consisting of John Tower, Edmund Muskie, and Brent Scowcroft (the Tower Commission), is established to investigate the Iran-Contra affair and to recommend modifications in the national security policy process.

19 DECEMBER 1986

Lawrence Walsh is appointed Independent Counsel to investigate any criminal activities by the White House, the CIA, or other federal entities in connection with the Iran-Contra affair. The investigation continues for six and a half years.

7 JANUARY 1987

Congress authorizes a joint House and Senate investigation into the Iran-Contra affair.

9 NOVEMBER 1989

Demonstrators tear down the Berlin Wall, symbolizing the end of the Cold War, as East European Communist regimes collapse.

30 NOVEMBER 1989

President George H. W. Bush signs a bill giving the CIA a "statutory" inspector general to be appointed by the president rather than the Director of Central Intelligence.

MARCH 1991

The CIA's New Headquarters Building, attached to the Original Headquarters Building, is completed and occupied.

25 DECEMBER 1991

Mikhail Gorbachev resigns as president of the Union of Soviet Socialist Republics, symbolizing the collapse of the Soviet regime, which for all intents and purposes has already ceased to exist. With the Cold War over, the CIA's budget and staffing are reduced by more than one-fifth over the next decade.

24 DECEMBER 1992

President George H. W. Bush issues pardons to former Secretary of Defense Caspar Weinberger, former Assistant Secretary of State for Inter-American Affairs Elliott Abrams, former National Security Adviser Robert McFarlane, and former CIA officials Duane Clarridge (Chief, Western Hemisphere Division), Alan Fiers (Chief, Central America Task Force), and Clair George (Deputy Director for Operations), all of whom had been indicted in the course of the Iran-Contra investigation.

21 FEBRUARY 1994

Aldrich Ames's thirty-one-year career in the CIA ends when he is arrested for conspiracy to commit espionage. Over the preceding nine years, he sold thousands of classified documents and the names of ten CIA and FBI assets to Soviet and Russian intelligence officials. Several of the individuals he named were executed. In April, after pleading guilty, Ames is sentenced to life in prison without the possibility of parole.

JANUARY 1996

The CIA establishes "Alec Station" as a unit within the Counterterrorist Center at CIA headquarters. Modeled on an overseas CIA station, it fuses analysis, operations, and other functions. The purpose of this "virtual station" is to track Usama bin Ladin and al-Qa'ida, collect intelligence on them, and run operations against them. Its first chief is Michael Scheuer.

19 MAY 1996

Under pressure from Saudi Arabia, Egypt, and the United States, the government of Sudan deports Usama bin Ladin, who had been operating in the country for five years. He and his al-Qa'ida terrorist organization find refuge with the Taliban regime in Afghanistan.

23 FEBRUARY 1998

Usama bin Ladin and associates issue one of a series of anti-Western declarations. It calls on all Muslims to "kill the Americans and plunder their money wherever and whenever they find it." As reasons, he refers to U.S. occupation of the Arabian Peninsula since 1991, continued aggression against Iraq, and support for Israel.

SEPTEMBER 2000

The CIA begins covert flights over Afghanistan with Predator unmanned aerial vehicles in its effort to locate Usama bin Ladin.

6 AUGUST 2001

The Presidential Daily Briefing provided by the CIA includes an item titled "Bin Ladin Determined to Strike in U.S.," but the brief reveals little that is new, actionable, or directly supportive of the claim made by the title.

11 SEPTEMBER 2001 ("9/11")

Terrorists from al-Qa'ida hijack four civilian airliners and crash two into the Twin Towers of the World Trade Center in New York City and one into the Pentagon outside Washington, D.C. The fourth crashes in a Pennsylvania field after the passengers attempt to retake control from the hijackers. The attack results in the deaths of 2,973 people. President George W. Bush soon declares a Global War on Terrorism.

27 SEPTEMBER 2001

CIA officers and Special Operations Forces infiltrate Afghanistan in preparation for U.S. intervention against the Taliban regime and al-Qa'ida. The Northern Alliance Liaison Team is established to coordinate with local anti-Taliban militias.

7 OCTOBER 2001

The overt phase of the Afghan War begins with U.S. aerial bombardment.

7 DECEMBER 2001

The Taliban abandon Kandahar, the last major Taliban stronghold in Afghanistan. Taliban and al-Qa'ida fighters retreat into the countryside and the border areas of Pakistan. Fighting continues.

23 JULY 2002

The chief of British intelligence, according to a confidential memorandum, tells Prime Minister Tony Blair: "Bush wanted to remove Saddam, through military action, justified by the conjunction of terrorism and WMD. But the intelligence and facts were being fixed around the policy."

1 AUGUST 2002

In the so-called Bybee Memo, the Department of Justice defines torture so narrowly as virtually to eliminate limits on the treatment of suspected terrorists. It further suggests that any restrictions on the president's authority to order interrogation techniques of his choosing might be unconstitutional. The opinion remains secret for the next two years.

26 AUGUST 2002

Vice President Dick Cheney delivers a speech that "goes beyond" the current intelligence regarding Iraq's weapons of mass destruction (WMD), according to DCI George Tenet, but Tenet apparently does not protest.

7 OCTOBER 2002

President Bush delivers a speech in Cincinnati pressing the urgent need to address the threat from Iraq. Owing to CIA intervention, a reference to suspect intelligence regarding Iraqi efforts to buy uranium in Africa is dropped from the speech.

OCTOBER 2002

At the request of Congress and in anticipation of a war against Iraq, the CIA issues a National Intelligence Estimate, "Iraq's Continuing Programs for Weapons of Mass Destruction." Post–invasion evidence will indicate that the programs did not exist.

3 NOVEMBER 2002

Using a Hellfire missile fired from a Predator unmanned aerial vehicle, the CIA kills Abu Ali al-Harithi and five others in Yemen. Al-Harithi was believed to be responsible for the October 2000 terrorist attack in Yemen against the destroyer U.S.S. *Cole*, in which seventeen sailors were killed.

25 NOVEMBER 2002

President Bush establishes the National Commission on Terrorist Attacks upon the United States (the 9/11 Commission) to examine the intelligence monitoring of domestic and international terrorist activities prior to the 9/11 attacks.

28 JANUARY 2003

President Bush's State of the Union address makes a forceful argument for war. The address includes the reference to Iraqi efforts to seek uranium in Africa, which was dropped from the Cincinnati speech in October. He attributes the information to British intelligence.

5 FEBRUARY 2003

Secretary of State Colin Powell uses intelligence to make the case for war against Iraq before the United Nations Security Council. Post-invasion evidence will indicate that many of the facts were wrong.

20 MARCH 2003

President Bush announces that the invasion of Iraq has begun.

6 JULY 2003

Former Ambassador Joseph Wilson writes in *The New York Times* that the CIA, prompted by Vice President Cheney, had sent him to Niger in February 2002 to look for evidence that Iraq had sought uranium. He had found none. Cheney later denies any knowledge of the trip.

29 SEPTEMBER 2003

The Department of Justice launches an investigation of senior administration officials to discover who revealed that Joseph Wilson's wife, Valerie Plame, was a covert CIA officer, in violation of the Intelligence Identities Protection Act of 1982. The investigation discovers that several officials had been describing Wilson's trip to Africa as a junket arranged by his wife, ending her career as an undercover officer. Presumably, the reason was to punish Wilson for going public or to distance Cheney from the trip.

6 FEBRUARY 2004

President Bush creates the Commission on the Intelligence Capabilities of the United States regarding WMD (the Robb-Silberman Commission) to investigate the intelligence used to justify the war with Iraq and to examine intelligence regarding North Korea, Libya, Afghanistan, and Iran.

9 JULY 2004

The Senate Select Committee on Intelligence criticizes the CIA and other agencies in a detailed, 511-page report, *U.S. Intelligence Community's Prewar Intelligence Assessments on Iraq.*

22 JULY 2004

The National Commission on Terrorist Attacks upon the United States (the 9/11 Commission) issues its final report, calling for a reorganization of the intelligence community under a Director of National Intelligence.

29 JULY 2004

The Kerr Group issues *Intelligence and Analysis on Iraq: Issues for the Intelligence Community*, the third of a series of reports intended as an internal review by the CIA of its prewar Iraq assessments so as to draw lessons for the future.

AUGUST 2004

President Bush establishes the National Counterterrorism Center (NCTC), which in 2005 becomes part of the new Office of the Director of National Intelligence. There is some jurisdictional confusion between the NCTC and the more opera-tionally oriented Counterterrorist Center (CTC), which continues as part of the CIA.

30 SEPTEMBER 2004

The Iraq Survey Group issues its final report, *Comprehensive Report of the Special Advisor to the DCI on Iraq's WMD*, confirming that Iraq had had no WMD or pro-grams to develop them prior to the invasion. It insists, however, that Saddam Hussein would have liked to have them. Further addenda are added in March 2005.

17 DECEMBER 2004

President Bush signs the Intelligence Reform and Terrorism Prevention Act, enacting several of the recommendations of the 9/11 Commission, including the establishment of the Office of the Director of National Intelligence.

17 DECEMBER 2004

Congress passes the Intelligence Reform and Terrorism Prevention Act (IRTPA) of 2004. The CIA loses its predominant position in the Intelligence Community as the position of Director of Central Intelligence is replaced by two: the Director of

National Intelligence, with responsibility for communitywide coordination, and the Director of the Central Intelligence Agency.

30 DECEMBER 2004

The Department of Justice repudiates the Bybee Memo of 2002 regarding the permissibility of harsh interrogation techniques.

31 MARCH 2005

The Commission on the Intelligence Capabilities of the United States Regarding Weapons of Mass Destruction (the Robb-Silberman Commission) issues its final report, concluding that assessments of other countries' WMD programs were less flawed than that of Iraq's but that errors were still too common.

22 APRIL 2005

The Director of Central Intelligence is replaced by the Director of National Intelligence and the Director of the Central Intelligence Agency.

JUNE 2005

The CIA Office of Inspector General issues the *OIG Report on CIA Accountability with Respect to the 9/11 Attacks.* A redacted version is released to the public at the insistence of Congress in August 2007.

13 OCTOBER 2005

The Deputy Director for Operations becomes the Director of the National Clandestine Service. The director will "coordinate, de-conflict, and assess" human intelligence operations throughout the Intelligence Community.

21 DECEMBER 2005

The Director of National Intelligence establishes the National Counterproliferation Center to coordinate strategic planning within the Intelligence Community to support efforts to stem the proliferation of weapons of mass destruction and the means to deliver them.

30 DECEMBER 2005

President Bush signs the Detainee Treatment Act prohibiting torture and establishing uniform interrogation techniques. A presidential signing statement accompanying the document, however, raises questions as to whether he intends to apply the new law. In addition, secret Justice Department opinions may have already redefined existing harsh techniques as permissible under the new law.

13 JANUARY 2006

An attempt to kill Ayman al-Zawahiri, the deputy leader of al-Qa'ida, in the village of Damadola, Pakistan, with a Predator unmanned aerial vehicle results in the death of eighteen people, mostly women and children. Zawahiri is not present.

29 JUNE 2006

In *Hamdan* v. *Rumsfeld*, the Supreme Court overrules the administration's position that Common Article 3 of the Geneva Conventions, regarding the humane treatment of prisoners, does not apply to suspected terrorists.

6 SEPTEMBER 2006

President Bush publicly acknowledges the existence of the "black sites," secret CIA detention centers for suspected terrorists at undisclosed locations overseas. He announces the transfer of fourteen detainees from these sites to the Defense Department's detention center at Guantánamo Bay Naval Station, Cuba, but does not specify whether there are more detainees at the secret sites.

26 JUNE 2007

After thirty-four years, the CIA releases a redacted version of the "Family Jewels" file, the most famous set of secret documents in the history of the agency.

20 JULY 2007

President Bush signs an executive order applying Common Article 3 of the Geneva Conventions to the detention and interrogation of suspected terrorists by the CIA, in compliance with a Supreme Court decision of the previous year. Certain behaviors are prohibited, but the order remains vague about what is allowed.

SEPTEMBER 2007

The Senate Select Committee on Intelligence releases a less critical report, *Prewar Intelligence Assessments about Postwar Iraq*, but laments the Intelligence Community's failure to influence post-invasion policy.

11 OCTOBER 2007

News reports indicate that the CIA director has been investigating the agency's Office of Inspector General. Some agency officials reportedly believe OIG investigations have lasted too long and may not have been fair and impartial. Members of Congress voiced concern that the DCIA's investigation of OIG could pose a conflict of interest.

21 OCTOBER 2007

Vice President Cheney speaks of Iranian "efforts to destabilize the Middle East and to gain hegemonic power" and of "the inescapable reality of Iran's nuclear program." If Iran "stays on its present course, the international community is prepared to impose serious consequences."

3 DECEMBER 2007

The Director of National Intelligence releases the "Key Judgments" of the National Intelligence Estimate *Iran: Nuclear Intentions and Capabilities*, which assesses that Iran halted the purely military aspects of its nuclear program in

2003. This sudden turnaround from previous assessments is attributed to new information and the application of analytic lessons from the Iraq War.

7 DECEMBER 2007

The *New York Times* reveals that in 2005 the CIA destroyed hundreds of hours of videotapes made in 2002 of the interrogation of two al-Qa'ida suspects held in secret detention. The tapes may have revealed harsh interrogation techniques.

13 DECEMBER 2007

Memorandum by former 9/11 Commission Staff Director Philip Zelikow details the efforts of the commission to acquire information about the interrogation of al-Qa'ida suspects. The CIA had not disclosed the existence of the videotapes.

2 JANUARY 2008

The Department of Justice launches a criminal investigation into the destruction of the CIA's interrogation videotapes.

31 JANUARY 2008

DCIA Michael Hayden announces the establishment of an ombudsman for employees who believe the have been treated unfairly by the Office of Inspector General. The OIG reportedly agreed to tighten control over its investigative procedures.

_____ *Chapter 1* _____

The Charter

The United States did not have a full-time civilian intelligence agency until World War II. The military services had their own agencies, beginning with the Office of Naval Intelligence in 1882. The FBI became involved in some aspects of intelligence work in Latin America in the 1930s and later sought unsuccessfully to reserve the intelligence function in that part of the world to itself.

The first dedicated civilian intelligence agency was the Office of Strategic Services (OSS), established under President Franklin D. Roosevelt in June 1942. It was led by a New York lawyer named William J. "Wild Bill" Donovan, who had previously been named Coordinator of Information. The makeshift agency had both analytic and operational functions, although it had to put up with competitors, including the FBI in Latin America.

The order establishing the OSS was brief:

**Presidential Military Order Establishing
the Office of Strategic Services (OSS)**

12 June 1942

By virtue of the authority of the vested in me as President of the United States and as Commander in Chief of the Army and Navy of the United States, it is ordered as follows:

1. The Office of the Coordinator of Information, established by order of July 11, 1941, exclusive of the foreign information activities transferred to the Office of War Information by executive order of June 13, 1942, shall hereafter be known as the Office of Strategic Services, and is hereby transferred to the jurisdiction of the United States Joint Chiefs of Staff.
2. The Office of Strategic Services shall perform the following duties:

   a. Collect and analyze such strategic information as may be required by the United States Joint Chiefs of Staff.
   b. Plan and operate such special services as may be directed by the United States Joint Chiefs of Staff.

3. At the head of the Office of Strategic Services shall be a Director of Strategic Services who shall be appointed by the President and who shall perform his duties under the direction and supervision of the United States Joint Chiefs of Staff.
4. William J. Donovan is hereby appointed as Director of Strategic Services.

The order of July 11, 1941, is hereby revoked.

Franklin D. Roosevelt
Commander in Chief

Coming out of the war, Congress and President Harry S. Truman still had the surprise attack on Pearl Harbor very much on their minds, and Truman was already becoming concerned about the intentions of the Soviet Union.[1] Congress concluded that the prevention of future Pearl Harbors required unity of command in the military and better intelligence, and this suited Truman as well. Already in 1944 Donovan was mapping out rough ideas for a permanent, civilian intelligence agency for the postwar period. This came in a memorandum to President Roosevelt dated 18 November 1944:

Pursuant to your note of 31 October 1944, I have given consideration to the organization of an intelligence service for the post-war period.

In the early days of the war when the demands upon intelligence services were mainly in and for military operations, the OSS was placed under the direction of the JCS.

Once our enemies are defeated the demand will be equally pressing for information that will aid us in solving the problems of peace.

This will require two things:

1. That intelligence control authority reporting directly to you, with responsibility to frame intelligence objectives and to collect and coordinate the intelligence material required by the Executive Branch in planning and carrying out national policy and strategy.

I attach in form of a draft directive the means by which I think this could be realized without difficulty or loss of time. You will note that coordination and centralization are placed at the policy level but operational intelligence (that pertaining primarily to Department action) remains within the existing agencies concerned. The creation of a central authority thus would not conflict with or limit necessary intelligence functions within the Army, Navy, Department of State, and other agencies.

In accordance with your wish, this is set up as a permanent long-range plan. But you may want to consider whether this (or part of it) should be done now, by executive or legislative action. There are common sense reasons why you may desire to lay the keel of the ship at once.

2. The immediate revisions and coordination of our present intelligence system would effect substantial economies and aid in the more efficient and speedy termination of the war.

Information important to national defense, being gathered now by certain departments and agencies, is not being used to full advantage in the war. Coordination at the strategy level would prevent waste, and avoid the present confusion that leads to waste and unnecessary duplication.

Though in the midst of war, we are also in a period of transition which, before we are aware, will take us into the tumult of rehabilitation. An adequate and orderly intelligence system will contribute to informed decisions.

We have now in the Government the trained and specialized personnel needed to the task. This talent should not be dispersed.

The notion of a new civilian intelligence agency immediately generated its own opposition. Existing bureaucracies, including the military intelligence agencies, the State Department, and the FBI, resented the potential competitor, especially when people talked of giving it centralizing or coordinating functions above them. Some members of Congress feared the establishment of a "secret police" or objected to suggestions that it should have the power to conduct "subversive operations abroad." On the other hand, looming tensions with the Soviet Union reinforced in the minds of many people the need for a centralized intelligence function.

President Truman abolished the makeshift OSS almost immediately after the war ended, in October 1945, and transferred its functions to the Departments of State and War. It was his intention to create a more formal and centralized intelligence agency, but he expected to accomplish this as part of the larger project of "unifying" the armed forces. As an interim measure, Truman established the Central Intelligence Group (CIG) in January 1946, which was to coordinate existing intelligence operations but not to take their place. Its leader was given the title Director of Central Intelligence. That title thus preceded the creation of the Central Intelligence Agency, with which it would become identified. The CIG was to operate under the authority of the National Intelligence Authority, which consisted of a presidential representative and the secretaries of State, War, and the Navy. This arrangement survived a mere twenty months.

In its place came the CIA. The agency's charter was encompassed within the National Security Act of 1947, which was approved by Congress on 26 July 1947 and went into effect on 18 September of that year. In addition to founding the CIA, the act created the Department of Defense (referred to in the bill as the National Military Establishment) by merging the Department of War and the Department of the Navy. At the same time it separated the air force from the army, making the former a military service in its own right, and it gave each of the armed services its own "department" within the new department. In addition, the act created the National Security Council to advise the president with regard to the integration of domestic, foreign, and military policies relating to national security.

The portion of the National Security Act dealing with the CIA is Title I, Section 102. Here is the charter as passed in 1947. Note that it has been amended many times since then.

Central Intelligence Agency

Sec. 102. (a) There is hereby established under the National Security Council a Central Intelligence Agency with a Director of Central Intelligence, who shall be the head thereof. The Director shall be appointed by the President, by and with the advice and consent of the Senate, from among the commissioned officers of the armed services or from among individuals in civilian life. The Director shall receive compensation at the rate of $14,000 a year.[2]

(b) (1) If a commissioned officer of the armed services is appointed as Director then—

(A) in the performance of his duties as Director, he shall be subject to no supervision, control, restriction, or prohibition (military or otherwise) other than would be operative with respect to him if he were a civilian in no way connected with the Department of the Army, the Department of the Navy, the Department of the Air Force, or the armed services or any component thereof; and

(B) he shall not possess or exercise any supervision, control, powers, or functions (other than such as he possesses, or is authorized or directed to exercise, as Director) with respect to the armed services or any component thereof, the Department of the Army, the Department of the Navy, or the Department of the Air Force, or any branch, bureau, unit or division thereof, or with respect to any of the personnel (military or civilian) of any of the foregoing.

(2) Except as provided in paragraph (1), the appointment to the office of Director of a commissioned officer of the armed services, and his acceptance of and service in such office, shall in no way affect any status, office, rank, or grade he may occupy or hold in the armed services, or any emolument, perquisite, right, privilege, or benefit incident to or arising out of any such status, office, rank, or grade. Any such commissioned officer shall, while serving in the office of Director, receive the military pay and allowances (active or retired, as the case may be) payable to a commissioned officer of his grade and length of service and shall be paid, from any funds available to defray the expenses of the Agency, annual compensation at a rate equal to the amount by which $14,000 exceeds the amount of his annual military pay and allowances.

(c) Notwithstanding the provisions of section 6 of the Act of August 24, 1912 (37 Stat. 555), or the provisions of any other law, the Director of Central Intelligence may, in his discretion, terminate the employment of any officer or employee of the Agency whenever he shall deem such termination necessary or advisable in the interests of the United States, but such termination shall not affect the right of such officer or employee to seek or accept employment in any other department or agency of the Government if declared eligible for such employment by the United States Civil Service Commission.

(d) For the purpose of coordinating the intelligence activities of the several Government departments and agencies in the interest of national security, it shall be the duty of the Agency, under the direction of the National Security Council—

(1) to advise the National Security Council in matters concerning such intelligence activities of the Government departments and agencies as relate to national security;

(2) to make recommendations to the National Security Council for the coordination of such intelligence activities of the departments and agencies of the Government as relate to the national security;

(3) to correlate and evaluate intelligence relating to the national security, and provide for the appropriate dissemination of such intelligence within the Government using where appropriate existing agencies and facilities: *Provided,* That the Agency shall have no police, subpoena, law-enforcement powers, or internal-security functions: *Provided further,* That the departments and other agencies of the Government shall continue to collect, evaluate, correlate, and disseminate departmental intelligence: *And provided further,* That the Director of Central Intelligence shall be responsible for protecting intelligence sources and methods from unauthorized disclosure;

(4) to perform, for the benefit of the existing intelligence agencies, such additional services of common concern as the National Security Council determines can be more efficiently accomplished centrally;

(5) to perform such other functions and duties related to intelligence affecting the national security as the National Security Council may from time to time direct.

(e) To the extent recommended by the National Security Council and approved by the President, such intelligence of the departments and agencies of the Government, except as hereinafter provided, relating to the national security shall be open to the inspection of the Director of Central Intelligence, and such intelligence as relates to the national security and is possessed by such departments and other agencies of the Government, except as hereinafter provided, shall be made available to the Director of Central Intelligence for correlation, evaluation, and dissemination: *Provided, however,* That upon the written request of the Director of Central Intelligence, the Director of the Federal Bureau of Investigation shall make available to the Director of Central Intelligence such information for correlation, evaluation, and dissemination as may be essential to the national security.

(f) Effective when the Director first appointed under subsection (a) has taken office—

(1) the National Intelligence Authority (11 Fed. Reg. 1337, 1339, February 5, 1946) shall cease to exist; and

(2) the personnel, property, and records of the Central Intelligence Group are transferred to the Central Intelligence Agency, and such Group shall cease to exist. Any unexpended balances of appropriations, allocations, or other funds available or authorized to be made available for such Group shall be available and shall be authorized to be made available in like manner for expenditure by the Agency.

Note that some of the political, or "police state," concerns about creating a new secret intelligence agency were addressed by expressly denying it "police, subpoena, law-enforcement powers, or internal-security functions." At the same time, some of the bureaucratic concerns were addressed by allowing the existing agencies to continue their own intelligence operations geared to their own purposes: "the departments and other agencies of the Government shall continue to collect, evaluate, correlate, and disseminate departmental intelligence." Still, the Director of Central Intelligence, in addition to running his own agency, was expected to coordinate a large community of independent and semi-independent agencies that he would never really control. This created a central tension in the office that it would never overcome.

The early years of the CIA were marked by the difficulties of creating, organizing, and giving direction to a new bureaucracy. This had to be done amid a background of constant criticism, some of it rooted in fear or bureaucratic rivalry and some of it evidently inspired by actual bad management at the new agency. The bare bones of the charter were filled out through a series of confidential National Security Council Intelligence Directives (NSCIDs).[3] For example:

National Security Council Intelligence Directive No. 5

Washington, December 12, 1947.

ESPIONAGE AND COUNTERESPIONAGE OPERATIONS

Pursuant to the provisions of Section 102(d) of the National Security Act of 1947, the National Security Council hereby authorizes and directs that:

1. The Director of Central Intelligence shall conduct all organized Federal espionage operations outside the United States and its possessions for the collection of foreign intelligence information required to meet the needs of all Departments and Agencies concerned, in connection with the national security, except for certain agreed activities by other Departments and Agencies.

2. The Director of Central Intelligence shall conduct all organized Federal counter-espionage operations outside the United States and its possessions and in occupied areas, provided that this authority shall not be construed to preclude the counter-intelligence activities of any army, navy or air command or installation and certain agreed activities by Departments and Agencies necessary for the security of such organizations.
3. The Director of Central Intelligence shall be responsible for coordinating covert and overt intelligence collection activities.
4. When casual agents are employed or otherwise utilized by an IAC Department or Agency in other than an overt capacity, the Director of Central Intelligence shall coordinate their activities with the organized covert activities.
5. The Director of Central Intelligence shall disseminate such intelligence information to the various Departments and Agencies which have an authorized interest therein.
6. All other National Security Council Intelligence Directives or implementing supplements shall be construed to apply solely to overt intelligence activities unless otherwise specified.

Or, another example:

National Security Council Intelligence Directive No. 3

Washington, January 13, 1948.[4]

COORDINATION OF INTELLIGENCE PRODUCTION

Pursuant to the provisions of Section 102 of the National Security Act of 1947, and for the purposes enunciated in paragraphs (d) and (e) thereof, the National Security Council hereby authorizes and directs that the following over-all policies and objectives are established for the coordination of the production of intelligence:

1. In order that all facilities of the Government may be utilized to their capacity and the responsibilities of each agency may be clearly defined in accordance with its mission, dominant interest, and capabilities, the whole field of intelligence production is divided into the following categories, and responsibilities are allocated as indicated:

   a. Basic Intelligence

     (1) Basic intelligence is that factual intelligence which results from the collation of encyclopedic information of a more or less permanent or static nature and general interest which, as a result of evaluation and interpretation, is determined to be the best available.
     (2) An outline of all basic intelligence required by the Government shall be prepared by the CIA in collaboration with the appropriate agencies. This outline shall be broken down into chapters, sections, and subsections which shall be allocated as production and maintenance responsibilities to CIA and those agencies of the Government which are best qualified by reason of their intelligence requirements, production capabilities, and dominant interest to assume the production and maintenance responsibility.
     (3) When completed, this outline and tentative allocations of production and maintenance responsibilities shall be submitted for NSC approval and issued as an implementation of this Directive. It is expected that as the result of constant consultation with the agencies by the Director of

Central Intelligence, both the outline and the allocations will be revised from time to time to insure the production of the basic intelligence required by the agencies and the fullest possible use of current agency capabilities. Changes in the outline or allocations shall be effected by agreement between the Director of Central Intelligence and the agencies concerned.

(4) This basic intelligence shall be compiled and continuously maintained in National Intelligence Surveys to cover foreign countries, areas, or broad special subjects as appropriate. The National Intelligence Surveys will be disseminated in such form as shall be determined by the Director of Central Intelligence and the agencies concerned.

(5) The Director of Central Intelligence shall be responsible for coordinating production and maintenance and for accomplishing the editing, publication, and dissemination of these National Intelligence Surveys and shall make such requests on the agencies as are necessary for their proper development and maintenance.

(6) Departments or agencies to be called on for contributions to this undertaking may include agencies other than those represented permanently in the IAC.

b. *Current Intelligence*

(1) Current intelligence is that spot information or intelligence of all types and forms of immediate interest and value to operating or policy staffs, which is used by them usually without the delays incident to complete evaluation or interpretation.

(2) The CIA and the several agencies shall produce and disseminate such current intelligence as may be necessary to meet their own internal requirements or external responsibilities.

(3) Interagency dissemination of current intelligence shall be based on interagency agreement including NSC Intelligence Directive No. 1 and the principle of informing all who need to know.

c. *Staff Intelligence*

(1) Staff intelligence is that intelligence prepared by any department or agency through the correlation and interpretation of all intelligence materials available to it in order to meet its specific requirements and responsibilities.

(2) Each intelligence agency has the ultimate responsibility for the preparation of such staff intelligence as its own department shall require. It is recognized that the staff intelligence of each of the departments must be broader in scope than any allocation of collection responsibility or recognition of dominant interest might indicate. In fact, the full foreign intelligence picture is of interest in varying degrees at different times to each of the departments.

(3) Any intelligence agency, either through the Director of Central Intelligence or directly, may call upon other appropriate agencies for intelligence which does not fall within its own field of dominant interest. Such requests shall be made upon the agencies in accordance with their production capabilities and dominant interest.

(4) As a part of the coordination program, the Director of Central Intelligence will seek the assistance of the IAC intelligence agencies in minimizing the necessity for any agency to develop intelligence in fields outside its dominant interests.

(5) The CIA and the agencies shall, for purposes of coordination, exchange information on projects and plans for the production of staff intelligence.

(6) It shall be normal practice that staff intelligence of one agency is available to the other intelligence agencies permanently represented on the IAC.

d. Departmental Intelligence

(1) Departmental intelligence is that intelligence including basic, current, and staff intelligence needed by a Department or independent Agency of the Federal Government, and the subordinate units thereof, to execute its mission and to discharge its lawful responsibilities.

e. National Intelligence

(1) National intelligence is integrated departmental intelligence that covers the broad aspects of national policy and national security, is of concern to more than one Department or Agency, and transcends the exclusive competence of a single Department or Agency or the Military Establishment.

(2) The Director of Central Intelligence shall produce and disseminate national intelligence.

(3) The Director of Central Intelligence shall plan and develop the production of national intelligence in coordination with the IAC Agencies in order that he may obtain from them within the limits of their capabilities the departmental intelligence which will assist him in the production of national intelligence.

(4) The Director of Central Intelligence shall, by agreement with the pertinent Agency or Agencies, request and receive such special estimates, reports, and periodic briefs or summaries prepared by the individual Departments or Agencies in their fields of dominant interest or in accordance with their production capabilities as may be necessary in the production of intelligence reports or estimates undertaken mutually.

2. The research facilities required by any agency to process its own current and staff intelligence shall be adequate to satisfy its individual needs after taking full cognizance of the facilities of the other agencies. Each agency shall endeavor to maintain adequate research facilities, not only to accomplish the intelligence production tasks allocated to it directly under the foregoing provisions but also to provide such additional intelligence reports or estimates within its field of dominant interest as may be necessary to satisfy the requirements of the other agencies under such allocations.

3. For the purposes of intelligence production, the following division of interests, subject to refinement through a continuous program of coordination by the Director of Central Intelligence, shall serve as a general delineation of dominant interests:

Political, Cultural, Sociological Intelligence	Department of State
Military Intelligence	Department of the Army
Naval Intelligence	Department of the Navy
Air Intelligence	Department of the Air Force
Economic, Scientific, and Technological Intelligence	Each agency in accordance with its respective needs

A key, top-secret directive of the National Security Council, NSC 10/2, came on 18 June 1948. With this order, the Truman administration authorized the CIA to engage in "covert operations." Truman had been impressed by actions the agency had already taken earlier that year to distribute money to pro-Western parties and labor unions in Italy to forestall Communist electoral success there. The initial body for conducting these operations, the Office of Special Projects, did not last very long; within a few years it was merged into the new Directorate of Plans. Also to change were provisions requiring the office's chief to be approved by outside officials, such as the Secretary of State. The basic provisions of the directive, however, remain in effect.

National Security Council Directive on Office of Special Projects NSC 10/2

Washington, June 18, 1948.

1. The National Security Council, taking cognizance of the vicious covert activities of the USSR, its satellite countries and Communist groups to discredit and defeat the aims and activities of the United States and other Western powers, has determined that, in the interests of world peace and U.S. national security, the overt foreign activities of the US Government must be supplemented by covert operations.

2. The Central Intelligence Agency is charged by the National Security Council with conducting espionage and counter-espionage operations abroad. It therefore seems desirable, for operational reasons, not to create a new agency for covert operations, but in time of peace to place the responsibility for them within the structure of the Central Intelligence Agency and correlate them with espionage and counter-espionage operations under the over-all control of the Director of Central Intelligence.

3. Therefore, under the authority of Section 102(d)(5) of the National Security Act of 1947, the National Security Council hereby directs that in time of peace:

   a. A new Office of Special Projects shall be created within the Central Intelligence Agency to plan and conduct covert operations; and in coordination with the Joint Chiefs of Staff to plan and prepare for the conduct of such operations in wartime.

   b. A highly qualified person, nominated by the Secretary of State, acceptable to the Director of Central Intelligence and approved by the National Security Council, shall be appointed as Chief of the Office of Special Projects.

   c. The Chief of the Office of Special Projects shall report directly to the Director of Central Intelligence. For purposes of security and of flexibility of operations, and to the maximum degree consistent with efficiency, the Office of Special Projects shall operate independently of other components of Central Intelligence Agency.

   d. The Director of Central Intelligence shall be responsible for:

      (1) Ensuring, through designated representatives of the Secretary of State and of the Secretary of Defense, that covert operations are planned and conducted in a manner consistent with US foreign and military policies and with overt activities. In disagreements arising between the Director of Central Intelligence and the representative of the Secretary of State or the Secretary of Defense over such plans, the matter shall be referred to the National Security Council for decision.

      (2) Ensuring that plans for wartime covert operations are also drawn up with the assistance of a representative of the Joint Chiefs of Staff and

are accepted by the latter as being consistent with and complementary to approved plans for wartime military operations.

(3) Informing, through appropriate channels, agencies of the US Government, both at home and abroad (including diplomatic and military representatives in each area), of such operations as will affect them.

e. Covert operations pertaining to economic warfare will be conducted by the Office of Special Projects under the guidance of the departments and agencies responsible for the planning of economic warfare.

f. Supplemental funds for the conduct of the proposed operations for fiscal year 1949 shall be immediately requested. Thereafter operational funds for these purposes shall be included in normal Central Intelligence Agency Budget requests.

4. In time of war, or when the President directs, all plans for covert operations shall be coordinated with the Joint Chiefs of Staff. In active theaters of war where American forces are engaged, covert operations will be conducted under the direct command of the American Theater Commander and orders therefore will be transmitted through the Joint Chiefs of Staff unless otherwise directed by the President.

5. As used in this directive, "covert operations" are understood to be all activities (except as noted herein) which are conducted or sponsored by this Government against hostile foreign states or groups or in support of friendly foreign states or groups but which are so planned and executed that any US Government responsibility for them is not evident to unauthorized persons and that if uncovered the US Government can plausibly disclaim any responsibility for them. Specifically, such operations shall include any covert activities related to: propaganda, economic warfare; preventive direct action, including sabotage, anti-sabotage, demolition and evacuation measures; subversion against hostile states, including assistance to underground resistance movements, guerrillas and refugee liberation groups, and support of indigenous anti-communist elements in threatened countries of the free world. Such operations shall not include armed conflict by recognized military forces, espionage, counter-espionage, and cover and deception for military operations.

6. This Directive supersedes the directive contained in NSC 4-A, which is hereby cancelled.[5]

Finally, it appears that for the first two years of its existence, the CIA operated without having been formally granted the normal authority to receive or allocate funds or to engage in some of the other basic functions of any government agency. Congress rectified this situation with the Central Intelligence Agency Act of 1949, providing for procurement authorities, education and training, travel allowances, and other related expenses. In the process, however, Congress invented some special rules for the agency. For example, the CIA was authorized to receive funds that had been legally appropriated to other agencies for other purposes and to use them regardless of legal restrictions that might have been placed on them. Such practices would allow the agency to disguise the true dimensions of its budget. Other provisions also reinforced the agency's secretive nature. Some of the precise wording is as follows:

Sec. 6. In the performance of its functions, the Central Intelligence Agency is authorized to—

(a) Transfer to and receive from other Government agencies such sums as may be approved by the Bureau of the Budget,[6] for the performance of any of the functions or activities under sections 102 and 303[7] of the National Security Act of 1947 (Public Law 253, Eightieth Congress), and any other Government agency is authorized to transfer to or receive from the Agency such sums without regard to any provisions of law limiting or prohibiting transfers between appropriations. Sums transferred to the Agency in accordance with this paragraph may be expended for the purposes and under the authority of this Act without regard to limitations of appropriations from which transferred; [...]

Sec. 7. In the interests of the security of the foreign intelligence activities of the United States and in order further to implement the provision of section 102(d)(3) of the National Security Act of 1947 (Public Law 253, Eightieth Congress, first session) that the Director of Central Intelligence shall be responsible for protecting intelligence sources and methods from unauthorized disclosure, the Agency shall be exempted from the provisions of sections 1 and 2, chapter 795 of the Act of August 28, 1935 (49 Stat. 956. 957; 5 U.S.C. 654), and the provisions of any other law which require the publication or disclosure of the organization, functions, names, official titles, salaries, or numbers of personnel employed by the Agency: *Provided,* That in furtherance of this section, the Director of the Bureau of the Budget shall make no reports to the Congress in connection with the Agency under section 607, title VI, chapter 212 of the Act of June 30, 1945, as amended (5 U.S.C. 947 (b)).

[Sec. 10.] (b) The sums made available to the Agency may be expended without regard to the provisions of law and regulations relating to the expenditure of Government funds; and for objects of a confidential, extraordinary, or emergency nature, such expenditures to be accounted for solely on the certificate of the Director and every such certificate shall be deemed a sufficient voucher for the amount therein certified.

There were numerous reforms of the agency over the succeeding decades. The most significant, however, came as a consequence of the terrorist attacks of 11 September 2001 and the subsequent 9/11 Commission, which saw that tragedy as partially rooted in a lack of adequate coordination and information sharing among intelligence agencies. This was the Intelligence Reform and Terrorism Prevention Act of 2004, which went into effect in 2005. Conceived as an amendment to the National Security Act of 1947, it is many times longer than the original.

The principal change that the act brought about was dividing the post of Director of Central Intelligence. Henceforth, the Director of the Central Intelligence Agency would be responsible only for the operation of that agency. The separate, independent position of Director of National Intelligence (DNI) would be responsible for coordinating the Intelligence Community and advising the president. It took the George W. Bush administration some time to fill the position of DNI. According to some observers, this was because the new office took on all the responsibility for failure without any of the powers to assure success.

The following are some brief excerpts of the act:

Subtitle A—Establishment of the Director of National Intelligence

SEC. 1101. REORGANIZATION AND IMPROVEMENT OF MANAGEMENT OF INTELLIGENCE COMMUNITY

(a) In General.—Title I of the National Security Act of 1947 (0 U.S.C. 402 et seq.) is amended by striking sections 102 through 104 and inserting the following new sections:

"DIRECTOR OF NATIONAL INTELLIGENCE

"SEC. 102. (a) DIRECTOR OF NATIONAL INTELLIGENCE.—(1) There is a Director of National Intelligence who shall be appointed by the President, by and with the advice and consent of the Senate. Any individual nominated for appointment as Director of National Intelligence shall have extensive national security expertise.

"(2) The Director of National Intelligence shall not be located within the Executive Office of the President.

"(b) PRINCIPAL RESPONSIBILITY.—Subject to the authority, direction, and control of the President, the Director of National Intelligence shall—

"(1) serve as head of the intelligence community;
"(2) act as the principal adviser to the President, to the National Security Council, and the Homeland Security Council for intelligence matters related to the national security; and
"(3) consistent with section 1018 of the National Security Intelligence Reform Act of 2004, oversee and direct the implementation of the National Intelligence Program.

"(c) PROHIBITION OF DUAL SERVICE.—The individual serving in the position of Director of National Intelligence shall not, while so serving, also serve as Director of the Central Intelligence Agency or as the head of any other element of the intelligence community.

"RESPONSIBILITIES AND AUTHORITIES OF THE DIRECTOR
OF NATIONAL INTELLIGENCE

"SEC. 102A. (a) PROVISION OF INTELLIGENCE.—(1) The Director of National Intelligence shall be responsible for ensuring that national intelligence is provided—

"(A) to the President;
"(B) to the heads of departments and agencies of the executive branch;
"(C) to the Chairman of the Joint Chiefs of Staff and senior military commanders;
"(D) to the Senate and House of Representatives and the committees thereof; and
"(E) to such other persons as the Director of National Intelligence determines to be appropriate.

"(2) Such national intelligence should be timely, objective, independent of political considerations, and based upon all sources available to the intelligence community and other appropriate entities.

"(b) ACCESS TO INTELLIGENCE.—Unless otherwise directed by the President, the Director of National Intelligence shall have access to all national intelligence and intelligence related to the national security which is collected by any Federal department, agency, or other entity, except as otherwise provided by law or, as appropriate, under guidelines agreed upon by the Attorney General and the Director of National Intelligence.

The Director of National Intelligence is then given some power to set priorities and influence the budgets of the various agencies within the Intelligence Community, to transfer funds between agencies, and to transfer personnel between agencies for up to two years. The director develops the consolidated National Intelligence Program budget, but the Secretary of Defense, who controls the largest number of agencies within the community, is given a privileged position. The secretary "develops" his own budget while the director merely "participates."

"(c)(3)(A) The Director of National Intelligence shall participate in the development by the Secretary of Defense of the annual budgets for the Joint Military Intelligence Program and for Tactical Intelligence and Related Activities.

The act also provides for the redefinition of the CIA under the supervision of the Director of National Intelligence. The functions of the CIA remain essentially the same, but it has taken on an expanded role in the direction and coordination of all human intelligence by all agencies. Congress also put considerable emphasis on improving the agency's human intelligence capabilities.

"CENTRAL INTELLIGENCE AGENCY

"Sec. 104. (a) Central Intelligence Agency.—There is a Central Intelligence Agency.

"(b) Function.—The function of the Central Intelligence Agency is to assist the Director of the Central Intelligence Agency in carrying out the responsibilities specified in section 104A(c).

"DIRECTOR OF THE CENTRAL INTELLIGENCE AGENCY

"Sec. 104A. (a) Director of the Central Intelligence Agency.—There is a Director of the Central Intelligence Agency who shall be appointed by the President, by and with the advice and consent of the Senate.

"(b) Supervision.—The Director of the Central Intelligence Agency shall report to the Director of National Intelligence regarding the activities of the Central Intelligence Agency.

"(c) Duties.—The Director of the Central Intelligence Agency shall—

"(1) serve as the head of the Central Intelligence Agency; and
"(2) carry out the responsibilities specified in subsection (d).

"(d) Responsibilities.—The Director of the Central Intelligence Agency shall—

"(1) collect intelligence through human sources and by other appropriate means, except that the Director of the Central Intelligence Agency shall have no police, subpoena, or law enforcement powers or internal security functions;
"(2) correlate and evaluate intelligence related to the national security and provide appropriate dissemination of such intelligence;
"(3) provide overall direction for and coordination of the collection of national intelligence outside the United States through human sources by elements of the intelligence community authorized to undertake such collection and, in coordination with other departments, agencies, or elements of the United States Government which are authorized to undertake such collection, ensure that the most effective use is made of resources and that appropriate account is taken of the risks to the United States and those involved in such collection; and
"(4) perform such other functions and duties related to intelligence affecting the national security as the President or the Director of National Intelligence may direct.

"(e) Termination of Employment of CIA Employees.—(1) Notwithstanding the provisions of any other law, the Director of the Central Intelligence Agency may, in the discretion of the Director, terminate the employment of any officer or employee of the Central Intelligence Agency whenever the Director deems the termination of employment of such officer or employee necessary or advisable in the interests of the United States.

"(2) Any termination of employment of an officer or employee under paragraph (1) shall not affect the right of the officer or employee to seek or accept employment in any other department, agency, or element of the United States Government if declared eligible for such employment by the Office of Personnel Management.

"(f) Coordination With Foreign Governments.—Under the direction of the Director of National Intelligence and in a manner consistent with section 207 of the Foreign Service Act of 1980 (22U.S.C. 3927), the Director of the Central Intelligence Agency shall coordinate the relationships between elements of the intelligence community and the intelligence or security services of foreign governments or international organizations on all matters involving intelligence related to the national security or involving intelligence acquired through clandestine means."[8]

(b) Sense of Congress.—It is the sense of Congress that—

(1) the human intelligence officers of the intelligence community have performed admirably and honorably in the face of great personal dangers;

(2) during an extended period of unprecedented investment and improvements in technical collection means, the human intelligence capabilities of the United States have not received the necessary and commensurate priorities;

(3) human intelligence is becoming an increasingly important capability to provide information on the asymmetric threats to the national security of the United States;

(4) the continued development and improvement of a robust and empowered and flexible human intelligence work force is critical to identifying, understanding, and countering the plans and intentions of the adversaries of the United States; and

(5) an increased emphasis on, and resources applied to, enhancing the depth and breadth of human intelligence capabilities of the United States intelligence community must be among the top priorities of the Director of National Intelligence.

(c) Transformation of the Central Intelligence Agency.—The Director of the Central Intelligence Agency shall, in accordance with standards developed by the Director in consultation with the Director of National Intelligence—

(1) enhance the analytic, human intelligence, and other capabilities of the Central Intelligence Agency;

(2) develop and maintain an effective language program within the Agency;

(3) emphasize the hiring of personnel of diverse backgrounds for purposes of improving the capabilities of the Agency;

(4) establish and maintain effective relationships between human intelligence and signals intelligence within the Agency at the operational level; and

(5) achieve a more effective balance within the Agency with respect to unilateral operations and liaison operations.

(d) Report.—(1) Not later than 180 days after the date of the enactment of this Act, the Director of the Central Intelligence Agency shall submit to the Director of National Intelligence and the congressional intelligence committees a report setting forth the following:

(A) A strategy for improving the conduct of analysis (including strategic analysis) by the Central Intelligence Agency, and the progress of the Agency in implementing that strategy;

(B) A strategy for improving the human intelligence and other capabilities of the Agency, and the progress of the Agency in implementing that strategy.

(2)(A)The information in the report under paragraph (1) on the strategy referred to in paragraph (1)(B) shall—

i. identify the number and types of personnel required to implement that strategy;

    ii. include a plan for the recruitment, training, equipping, and deployment of such personnel; and

    iii. set forth an estimate of the costs of such activities.

(B) If as of the date of the report under paragraph (1), a proper balance does not exist between unilateral operations and liaison operations, such report shall set forth the steps to be taken to achieve such balance.

In addition, the act created a sort of ombudsman to guard against bias or politicization of intelligence products.

SEC. 1020. SAFEGUARD OF OBJECTIVITY IN INTELLIGENCE ANALYSIS.

(a) IN GENERAL.—Not later than 180 days after the effective date of this Act, the Director of National Intelligence shall identify an individual within the Office of the Director of National Intelligence who shall be available to analysts within the Office of the Director of National Intelligence to counsel, conduct arbitration, offer recommendations, and, as appropriate, initiate inquiries into real or perceived problems of analytic tradecraft or politicization, biased reporting, or lack of objectivity in intelligence analysis.

(b) REPORT.—Not later than 270 days after the effective date of this Act, the Director of National Intelligence shall provide a report to the Select Committee on Intelligence of the Senate and the Permanent Select Committee on Intelligence of the House of Representatives on the implementation of subsection (a).

The act transferred the recently created National Counterterrorism Center (NCTC) from the CIA to the Office of the Director of National Intelligence (ODNI). The CIA retained the separate Counterterrorist Center (CTC). The act also created the National Counter Proliferation Center and provided for the establishment of National Intelligence Centers on specialized topics. Note that some of the CIA's prohibitions on domestic activity have been weakened vis-à-vis the NCTC, but it has no operational responsibilities.

"NATIONAL COUNTERTERRORISM CENTER

"SEC. 119. (a) ESTABLISHMENT OF THE CENTER.—There is within the Office of the Director of National Intelligence a National Counterterrorism Center.

"(b) DIRECTOR OF THE NATIONAL COUNTERTERRORISM CENTER.—(1) There is a Director of the National Counterterrorism Center, who shall be the head of the National Counterterrorism Center, and who shall be appointed by the President, by and with the advice and consent of the Senate.

"(2) The Director of the National Counterterrorism Center may not simultaneously serve in any other capacity in the executive branch.

* * *

"(d) PRIMARY MISSIONS.—The primary missions of the National Counterterrorism Center shall be as follows:

    "(1) To serve as the primary organization in the United States Government for analyzing and integrating all intelligence possessed or acquired by the United States Government pertaining to terrorism and counterterrorism, excepting intelligence pertaining exclusively to domestic terrorists and domestic counterterrorism.

    "(2) To conduct strategic operational planning for counterterrorism activities, integrating all instruments of national power, including diplomatic, financial, military, intelligence, homeland security, and law enforcement activities within and among agencies.

"(3) To assign roles and responsibilities as part of its strategic operational planning duties to lead Departments or agencies, as appropriate, for counterterrorism activities that are consistent with applicable law and that support counterterrorism strategic operational plans, but shall not direct the execution of any resulting operations.

"(4) To ensure that agencies, as appropriate, have access to and receive all-source intelligence support needed to execute their counterterrorism plans or perform independent, alternative analysis.

"(5) To ensure that such agencies have access to and receive intelligence needed to accomplish their assigned activities.

"(6) To serve as the central and shared knowledge bank on known and suspected terrorists and international terror groups, as well as their goals, strategies, capabilities, and networks of contacts and support.

"(e) DOMESTIC COUNTERTERRORISM INTELLIGENCE.—(1) The Center may, consistent with applicable law, the direction of the President, and guidelines referred to in section 102A(b), receive intelligence pertaining exclusively to domestic counterterrorism from any Federal, State, or local government or other source necessary to fulfill its responsibilities and retain and disseminate such intelligence.

"(2) Any agency authorized to conduct counterterrorism activities may request information from the Center to assist it in its responsibilities, consistent with applicable law and the guidelines referred to in section 102A(b).

* * *

"(g) LIMITATION.—The Director of the National Counterterrorism Center may not direct the execution of counterterrorism operations.

* * *

"(i) DIRECTORATE OF INTELLIGENCE.—The Director of the National Counterterrorism Center shall establish and maintain within the National Counterterrorism Center a Directorate of Intelligence which shall have primary responsibility within the United States Government for analysis of terrorism and terrorist organizations (except for purely domestic terrorism and domestic terrorist organizations) from all sources of intelligence, whether collected inside or outside the United States.

"(j) DIRECTORATE OF STRATEGIC OPERATIONAL PLANNING.—(1) The Director of the National Counterterrorism Center shall establish and maintain within the National Counterterrorism Center a Directorate of Strategic Operational Planning which shall provide strategic operational plans for counterterrorism operations conducted by the United States Government.

"(2) Strategic operational planning shall include the mission, objectives to be achieved, tasks to be performed, interagency coordination of operational activities, and the assignment of roles and responsibilities.

"(3) The Director of the National Counterterrorism Center shall monitor the implementation of strategic operational plans, and shall obtain information from each element of the intelligence community, and from each other department, agency, or element of the United States Government relevant to monitoring the progress of such entity in implementing such plans."

* * *

"NATIONAL COUNTER PROLIFERATION CENTER

"Sec. 119A. (a) ESTABLISHMENT.—Not later than 18 months after the date of the enactment of the National Security Intelligence Reform Act of 2004, the President shall establish a National Counter Proliferation Center, taking into account all appropriate government tools to prevent and halt the proliferation of weapons of mass destruction, their delivery systems, and related materials and technologies.

"(b) MISSIONS AND OBJECTIVES.—In establishing the National Counter Proliferation Center, the President shall address the following missions and objectives to prevent and halt the proliferation of weapons of mass destruction, their delivery systems, and related materials and technologies:

"(1) Establishing a primary organization within the United States Government for analyzing and integrating all intelligence possessed or acquired by the United States pertaining to proliferation.

"(2) Ensuring that appropriate agencies have full access to and receive all-source intelligence support needed to execute their counter proliferation plans or activities, and perform independent, alternative analyses.

"(3) Establishing a central repository on known and suspected proliferation activities, including the goals, strategies, capabilities, networks, and any individuals, groups, or entities engaged in proliferation.

"(4) Disseminating proliferation information, including proliferation threats and analyses, to the President, to the appropriate departments and agencies, and to the appropriate committees of Congress.

"(5) Conducting net assessments and warnings about the proliferation of weapons of mass destruction, their delivery systems, and related materials and technologies.

"(6) Coordinating counter proliferation plans and activities of the various departments and agencies of the United States Government to prevent and halt the proliferation of weapons of mass destruction, their delivery systems, and related materials and technologies.

"(7) Conducting strategic operational counter proliferation planning for the United States Government to prevent and halt the proliferation of weapons of mass destruction, their delivery systems, and related materials and technologies.

* * *

"NATIONAL INTELLIGENCE CENTERS

"SEC. 119B. (a) AUTHORITY TO ESTABLISH.—The Director of National Intelligence may establish one or more national intelligence centers to address intelligence priorities, including, but not limited to, regional issues.

In addition, the act created the Joint Intelligence Community Council to bring together the appropriate department heads. Note that the act includes express provisions for members to have their dissenting opinions heard so as to avoid excessive consensus and to prevent the Director from dominating the Council. The Director of the Central Intelligence Agency is not listed as among the members.

"JOINT INTELLIGENCE COMMUNITY COUNCIL

"SEC. 101A. (a) JOINT INTELLIGENCE COMMUNITY COUNCIL.—There is a Joint Intelligence Community Council.

"(b) MEMBERSHIP.—The Joint Intelligence Community Council shall consist of the following:

"(1) The Director of National Intelligence, who shall chair the Council.

"(2) The Secretary of State.

"(3) The Secretary of the Treasury.

"(4) The Secretary of Defense.

"(5) The Attorney General.

"(6) The Secretary of Energy.

"(7) The Secretary of Homeland Security.

"(8) Such other officers of the United States Government as the President may designate from time to time.

"(c) FUNCTIONS.—The Joint Intelligence Community Council shall assist the Director of National Intelligence in developing and implementing a joint, unified national intelligence effort to protect national security by—

"(1) advising the Director on establishing requirements, developing budgets, financial management, and monitoring and evaluating the performance of the intelligence community, and on such other matters as the Director may request; and

"(2) ensuring the timely execution of programs, policies, and directives established or developed by the Director.

"(d) MEETINGS.—The Director of National Intelligence shall convene regular meetings of the Joint Intelligence Community Council.

"(e) ADVICE AND OPINIONS OF MEMBERS OTHER THAN CHAIRMAN.—(1) A member of the Joint Intelligence Community Council (other than the Chairman) may submit to the Chairman advice or an opinion in disagreement with, or advice or an opinion in addition to, the advice presented by the Director of National Intelligence to the President or the National Security Council, in the role of the Chairman as Chairman of the Joint Intelligence Community Council. If a member submits such advice or opinion, the Chairman shall present the advice or opinion of such member at the same time the Chairman presents the advice or opinion of the Chairman to the President or the National Security Council, as the case may be.

"(2) The Chairman shall establish procedures to ensure that the presentation of the advice of the Chairman to the President or the National Security Council is not unduly delayed by reason of the submission of the individual advice or opinion of another member of the Council.

"(f) RECOMMENDATIONS TO CONGRESS.—Any member of the Joint Intelligence Community Council may make such recommendations to Congress relating to the intelligence community as such member considers appropriate."

Congress also instituted a requirement for alternative analysis. This was rooted in the belief that the failure to predict the 9/11 attacks was partially rooted in conventional thinking and excessive consensus.

SEC. 1017. ALTERNATIVE ANALYSIS OF INTELLIGENCE BY THE INTELLIGENCE COMMUNITY

(a) IN GENERAL.—Not later than 180 days after the effective date of this Act, the Director of National Intelligence shall establish a process and assign an individual or entity the responsibility for ensuring that, as appropriate, elements of the intelligence community conduct alternative analysis (commonly referred to as "red-team analysis") of the information and conclusions in intelligence products.

(b) REPORT.—Not later than 270 days after the effective date of this Act, the Director of National Intelligence shall provide a report to the Select Committee on Intelligence of the Senate and the Permanent Select Committee of the House of Representatives on the implementation of subsection (a).

NOTES

1. "Historical Perspective," in Michael Warner, ed., *Central Intelligence: Origin and Evolution* (Washington, D.C.: Central Intelligence Agency, Center for the Study of Intelligence, 2001): 1–18.

2. Specific dollar amounts have been removed by amendment.

3. See, for instance, U.S. Department of State, *Foreign Relations of the United States, 1945–1950: Emergence of the Intelligence Establishment* (Washington, D.C.: U.S. Government Printing Office, 1996): documents 422–435.

4. The fact that NSCID No. 3 is dated later than NSCID No. 5 suggests that this is a revision or replacement for an earlier version.

5. NSC 4-A had authorized the CIA to engage in a secret propaganda program.

6. Now called the Office of Management and Budget (OMB).

7. Section 303 permitted the Director of Central Intelligence and certain other officials to appoint advisory committees and other part-time advisory personnel.

8. A note on the confusing format of the Intelligence Reform and Terrorism Prevention Act (IRTPA): Everything up to this point, a total of about nineteen pages, constitutes Section 1101, paragraph (a), of the IRTPA, which is an insert into the National Security Act of 1947. The insert is identified by quotation marks. The following line begins with (b), since it is technically the second paragraph of the new law. The entire 1947 law was a page and a half. The IRTPA is 236 pages. The excerpts do not all follow the original order.

_____ *Chapter 2* _____

The Korean War

The Korean War offers examples of intelligence assessments being shaped by preconceived notions. Not only did the CIA and other agencies fail to predict the North Korean invasion of South Korean, but they neglected to anticipate Chinese intervention in the war despite Chinese warnings and failed for some time to realize that China had in fact intervened.

The proximity and salience of the World War II experience and the notion that they confronted a Soviet-led global Communist movement influenced the participants' expectations. They expected the next war, if one occurred, to be a confrontation on a global scale similar to the last one. They were not thinking in terms of limited warfare, and this delayed their recognition of what was actually happening. When North Korea invaded South Korea in June 1950, one of the United States' first responses was to deploy troops to Europe in case Korea was a feint intended to distract attention from the main thrust.

After the initial invasion, North Korean troops nearly succeeded in occupying the entire Korean Peninsula in a few weeks. American forces from Japan, operating with United Nations authorization, landed at Inchon in mid-September and quickly turned the situation around. Although UN forces initially said they sought only to expel North Korean forces from the south, they crossed the border at the 38th parallel and continued northward through North Korea toward the Chinese border, which ran along the Yalu River. The government of the Chinese People's Republic—which had been established only one year earlier—began to issue warnings of possible intervention if UN forces did not halt their movement toward the border. How to interpret these warnings became the task of the CIA and the Intelligence Community as a whole.

The Department of State, on 12 September 1950, requested "a coordinated intelligence estimate on Chinese Communist intentions concerning intervention in Korea." Before a national intelligence estimate could be produced, the subject came up in a teleconference on 4 October 1950 between Washington and the Far

East Command (FEC). The record included a lengthy discussion of enemy capabilities. One participant suggested the possibility of Chinese intervention in terminology that would probably not have been used today.

> With the collapse of the North Korean armies, the immediate problem facing the UN forces involves the attitude of the Communist Chinese and the Soviets.... Will they intervene openly? ... It is accepted that Russia would find it both convenient and economical to stay out of the conflict and let the idle millions of Communist China perform task as part of master plan to drain US resources into the geographic ratholes of the Orient.... The interest of all intelligence agencies is focused on the Yalu and the movements of the elusive LIN PIAO [the Chinese military commander in Manchuria, the part of China bordering North Korea].... The buildup of Chinese forces along the border has been reported ... massing of forces at Antung and other Manchurian crossings appears conclusive.... Involves a possible 9/18 divisions organized into 3/6 armies of a total of 38 divisions and 9 armies now carried in all Manchuria.... Formosan sources sometimes colored but only serious channel of information from within China flatly stated release or transfer of 9 divisions to North Korea....
>
> In view of these facts the potential exists for Chinese Communist forces to openly intervene in the Korean war if UN forces cross the 38th parallel.

That assessment, however, did not reflect the consensus of the Intelligence Community. On 12 October 1950, the director of the CIA sent the president a memorandum, noting that the State Department, the army, the navy, and the air force concurred in the estimates. The portions dealing with the possibility of Chinese intervention were succinct, depicting that eventuality as possible but not likely. It made similar conclusions regarding the possibility of direct intervention by the Soviet Union. One can detect the underlying assumption that any new war involving either China or the Soviet Union would necessarily be on a scale comparable to World War II. This assumption apparently colored people's assessments and led them to underestimate the possibility of limited intervention.

A. THREAT OF FULL CHINESE COMMUNIST INTERVENTION IN KOREA

II. CAPABILITIES

2. The Chinese Communist ground forces, currently lacking requisite air and naval support, are capable of intervening effectively, but not necessarily decisively, in the Korean conflict.

IV. PROBABILITY OF CHINESE COMMUNIST ACTION

6. While full-scale Chinese Communist intervention in Korea must be regarded as a continuing possibility, a consideration of all known factors leads to the conclusion that barring a Soviet decision for global war, such action in not probable in 1950. During this period, intervention will probably be confined to continued covert assistance to the North Koreans.

B. THREAT OF SOVIET INTERVENTION IN KOREA

II. CAPABILITIES

2. Soviet armed forces now in the Far East are capable of intervening overwhelmingly in Korea virtually without warning.

IV. PROBABILITIES OF SOVIET ACTION

6. It is believed that the Soviet leaders will not consider that their prospective losses in Korea warrant direct military intervention and a consequent grave risk of war. They will intervene in the Korean hostilities only if they have decided, not on the basis of the Korean situation alone, but on the basis of overall considerations, that it is to their interest to precipitate a global war at this time.

The Soviets did not intervene in Korea, apart from the provision of disguised aircraft and pilots, but the Chinese did intervene and did so en masse. In fact, the operation was already under way as the memorandum was issued. The prevailing assumptions surrounding the issue of Chinese intervention, however, and the piecemeal nature of the early evidence of Chinese involvement delayed the realization that it had already happened. In late October, UN forces captured a small number of Chinese soldiers in various incidents, some of them in North Korean uniforms, but the prisoners' stories of large-scale troop movements were initially dismissed or downplayed. Only on 2 November did the Far East Command determine that Chinese intervention was now a "serious proximate threat."

With the realization that intervention was possible, and even happening, the Intelligence Community began to question the assumption that such a war must be "global." They turned to the task of assessing China's intentions and considering whether the war could be contained.

NIE-2, CHINESE COMMUNIST INTERVENTION IN KOREA,
published November 8, 1950.

THE PROBLEM

1. To estimate the scale and purpose of Chinese Communist intervention in North Korea and Chinese Communist capabilities and intentions.

SUMMARY AND CONCLUSIONS

2. Present Chinese Communist troop strength in North Korea is estimated at 30,000 to 40,000. Chinese Communist ground units are engaging UN forces at various points ranging from 30 to 100 miles south of the Korean-Manchurian border. Recent action has been marked also by the appearance of Soviet-type jet fighters in combat with US aircraft over Korea.

3. Present Chinese Communist troop strength in Manchuria is estimated at 700,000. Of this number, there are at least 200,000 regular field forces. These troops strengths, added to the forces already in Korea, are believed to make the Chinese Communists capable of: (a) halting further UN advance northward, through piecemeal commitment of troops; or (b) forcing UN withdrawal to defensive positions farther south by a powerful assault.

4. The objective of the Chinese Communist intervention appears to be to halt the advance of UN forces in Korea and to keep a Communist regime in being on Korean soil. In accomplishing this purpose, the Chinese Communists would: (a) avert the psychological and political consequences of a disastrous outcome of the Korean venture; (b) keep UN forces away from the actual frontiers of China and the USSR; (c) retain an area in Korea as a base of Communist military and guerrilla operations; (d) prolong indefinitely the containment of UN, especially US, forces in Korea; (e) control the distribution of hydroelectric power generated in North Korea and retain other economic

benefits; and (f) create the possibility of a favorable political solution in Korea, despite the military defeat of the North Koreans.

5. The Chinese Communists thus far retain full freedom of action with respect to Korea. They are free to adjust their action in accordance with the development of the situation. If the Chinese Communists were to succeed in destroying the effective strength of UN forces in northern Korea, they would pursue their advantage as far as possible. If the military situation is stabilized, they may well consider that, with advantageous terrain and the onset of winter, their forces now in Korea are sufficient to accomplish their immediate purposes.

6. A likely and logical development of the present situation is that the opposing sides will build up their combat power in successive increments to checkmate the other until forces of major magnitude are involved. At any point in this development, the danger is present that the situation may get out of control and lead to a general war.

7. The Chinese Communists, in intervening in Korea, have accepted a grave risk of retaliation and general war. They would probably ignore an ultimatum requiring their withdrawal. If Chinese territory were to be attacked, they would probably enter Korea in full force.

8. The fact that both the Chinese Communists and the USSR have accepted an increased risk of general war indicates either that the Kremlin is ready to face a showdown with the West at an early date or that circumstances have forced them to accept that risk.

In late November, the CIA returned to the question of China's intentions. Based on their perceptions of Chinese actions up to that point, the amended national intelligence estimate now saw their objectives as limited, although it did not depict their patience as limitless. Moreover, the risk of global war never receded completely from the scene.

NIE-2/1, CHINESE COMMUNIST INTERVENTION IN KOREA,
published November 24, 1950

THE PROBLEM

1. To re-estimate the scale and purpose of Chinese Communist intervention in North Korea.

CONCLUSIONS

2. The Chinese Communists will simultaneously:

   a. Maintain Chinese-North Korean holding operations in North Korea.
   b. Maintain or increase their military strength in Manchuria.
   c. Seek to obtain UN withdrawal from Korea by intimidation and diplomatic means.

3. In case of failure to obtain UN withdrawal by these means, there will be increasing Chinese intervention in Korea. At a minimum, the Chinese will conduct, on an increasing scale, unacknowledged operations designed to immobilize UN forces in Korea, to subject them to prolonged attrition, and to maintain the semblance of a North Korean state in being. Available evidence is not conclusive as to whether or not the Chinese Communists are as yet committed to a full-scale offensive effort. Eventually they may undertake operations designed to bring about the withdrawal of UN forces from Korea. It is estimated that they do not have the military capability of driving the UN

forces from the peninsula, but that they do have the capability of forcing them to withdraw to defensive positions for prolonged and inconclusive operations, which, the Communists might calculate, would lead to eventual UN withdrawal from Korea.

4. So long as Chinese intervention continues, the USSR will continue and possibly increase its support to the Chinese by furnishing equipment, planes, technical advisers, and conceivably, "volunteers" as necessary to man the more intricate equipment.

5. The risk that a general war will develop already exists. The Soviet rulers may underrate this possibility but they appear to have allowed for it and to feel prepared to cope with it.

The risk of open, direct Soviet intervention no longer appeared to be under consideration. Rather, the CIA assessed the possibility of more limited forms of Soviet participation or support, as in this examination of potential Soviet responses to the bombing of Chinese facilities in Manchuria.

NIE-2/2, SOVIET PARTICIPATION IN THE AIR DEFENSE
OF MANCHURIA, published November 27, 1950.

THE PROBLEM

1. To estimate whether, in the event of UN air attack on targets in Manchuria, the Soviet Air Force would participate in the defense of such targets.

SUMMARY AND CONCLUSIONS

2. In the circumstances envisaged in the problem, the USSR would provide aircraft, anti-aircraft artillery, and trained personnel as necessary for the defense of Manchurian targets. Sufficient resources for rendering such aid are available in the Soviet Far East.

3. Soviet participation in the defense of Manchurian targets could take any of the following forms:

   a. Actual participation without identification.
   b. The open participation of ostensibly volunteer units.
   c. The open participation of Soviet units as a limited commitment under the Sino-Soviet treaty.
   d. The open participation of Soviet units as an aspect of a general war forced on the Soviet Union under the Sino-Soviet treaty.

4. At least initially, the most likely form of Soviet participation in the air defense of Manchurian targets would be the first—i.e., actual participation in action without open identification.

5. The open participation of Soviet units would be unlikely unless general war should develop.

6. A substantial risk that the situation may degenerate into a general war already exists. UN air attack on targets in Manchuria, alone, probably would not cause the Soviet rulers to decide to launch a general war, inasmuch as the Kremlin's basic decision for or against war would be based on global considerations. The events likely to follow such attacks, however, would carry with them a greater probability of a general war developing.

In the end, UN forces did not bomb Manchuria, a decision that produced a major dispute with UN commander Gen. Douglas MacArthur. Nonetheless,

Soviet aircraft did participate "without identification" in the air war over Korea, but the Soviet Union limited its direct involvement in the war to that action. In the meantime, CIA estimates of the number of Chinese troops in Korea continued to increase. Then, on 26 November 1950, a teleconference discussing the possibility of a UN counteroffensive was interrupted by the following flash regarding a portion of the front manned by the army of South Korea, or the Republic of Korea (ROK):

> Enemy of unknown strength is attacking across entire ROK II Corps front. All elements of ROK II Corps last reported withdrawing to south with plans to establish a defense line south of Okchon. . . . An unknown size enemy force last reported to have taken Tokchon.

At that point, both the "accepted" and "tentatively accepted" identification of major units of Chinese Communist forces (CCF) and the estimates of deployed troop strengths skyrocketed in a very compressed time period. According to a series of teleconferences with the Far East Command:

> Following strength figures set for CCF units in Korea:
>   Accepted: 38, 29, 40, 42 Armies—46,700–70,900
>   Tentatively Accepted: 66th Army—12,600–18,900
>   Total CCF Strengths: 59,300–89,000 but if
>   20th and 50th Armies become accepted new
>   total becomes: 84,500–127,000
>   [Telecon 27 November 1950]

> Gave following report of CCF strength:
>   Accepted: 119,777
>   Tentatively Accepted: 157,577
>   NK [North Korean] Strength: 41,165
>   [Telecon 28 November 1950]

> Gave accepted Chinese strength as 190,000 and added that there were indications that CCF were actually drawing on Chinese Communist Units in Manchuria. Pointed out that available potential in Manchuria was 355,000 combat troops and 370,000 line of communication troops.
>   [Telecon 30 November 1950]

With the war fully in progress, the CIA took on an additional task, organizing guerrilla and intelligence operations behind enemy lines. Most of the people inserted behind the lines were Korean nationals. The person responsible for the operation was Hans V. Tofte, a Danish-born veteran of the OSS. Tofte arrived in Tokyo to take charge of covert operations in Korea in July 1950, only one month after the war began. He immediately proceeded to recruit agents, train them, and insert them into enemy-controlled territory. One year later, the CIA created an operational arm for this purpose, euphemistically called the Joint Advisory Commission–Korea (JACK).

The U.S. Army and, for a time, the U.S. Air Force were also conducting operations, primarily involving Korean nationals, behind enemy lines. Although the Air Force allowed the CIA the use of some of its aircraft to insert agents, much of the history of the operation—at least at headquarters level—was a tale of jurisdictional conflict and bitterness. This continued even after the Far East Command attempted to streamline jurisdictional issues by subordinating JACK to its Combined Command for Reconnaissance Activities, Korea (CCRAK).[1]

Operationally, the CIA parachuted thousands of Koreans behind enemy lines, 1,500 just in spring–summer 1952. Their assignment was to conduct guerrilla operations, gather intelligence, and rescue downed American fliers. Glowing reports were issued to headquarters about all they were accomplishing. In September 1952, John Limond Hart arrived to take up his post as the new Chief of Station in Seoul, the third since the start of the war. Hart eventually determined that virtually everyone inserted into North Korea had been captured or killed. Those few who had radioed back were compelled to do so at the behest of their captors and were reporting false information. Virtually every report sent to headquarters from the front for the previous one and a half years had been fabricated, either by the enemy, by corrupt assets in South Korea, or by CIA officials themselves. These conclusions were successfully hushed up for nearly half a century.[2]

Donald Gregg, who as a college graduate ran a CIA training camp for Korean and other infiltrators on the Pacific island of Saipan, later commented on the effort to journalist Tim Weiner:

> We didn't know what we were doing. I asked my superiors what the mission was and they wouldn't tell me. They didn't know what the mission was. It was swashbuckling of the worst kind. We were training Koreans and Chinese and a lot of other strange people, dropping Koreans into North Korea, dropping Chinese into China just north of the Korean border, and we'd drop these people in and we'd never hear from them again.[3]

NOTES

1. Richard L. Kiper, "Unconventional Warfare in Korea: Forgotten Aspect of the 'Forgotten War,'" *Special Warfare* 16:2 (August 2003): 26–37; Michael Haas, *In the Devil's Shadow: UN Special Operations during the Korean War* (Annapolis, MD: Naval Institute Press, 2000).

2. Tim Weiner, *Legacy of Ashes: The History of the CIA* (New York: Doubleday, 2007): 49–62.

3. Ibid., 55.

_____ *Chapter 3* _____

Cuba

On 1 January 1959, Cuban president Fulgencio Batista fled Havana, and a guerrilla leader named Fidel Castro Ruz assumed power on the island. Castro was at the head of a fairly broad coalition opposed to the Batista government, but over next few years he shifted his position to the left, forged an alliance with the Soviet Union, and merged his guerrilla movement with the Cuban Communists to form a new ruling party. The Soviet alliance had clear security implications for the United States because Cuba as a potential Soviet base was far more dangerous than Cuba alone. In addition, the Castro government began to sponsor guerrilla wars in other Latin American countries in an effort to create new allies, especially for a time after the Cuban Missile Crisis, when Cuba became disillusioned with the reliability of Soviet protection. Beyond the security threat, many in the United States seemed to be personally affronted that a country in such geographical proximity and so long under U.S. tutelage should turn its back on the United States and join its enemies. In any event, this animosity would last for decades, well beyond the existence of any real threat.

In the very beginning, however, these trends had not yet fully manifested themselves, although controversies were already brewing over issues such as anti-American statements and the trials of former Batista government officials. The questions at that time were: Who is this Fidel Castro, and what are his intentions? On 24 November 1959, the British ambassador to the United States reported to the Foreign Office on a recent meeting with the Director of Central Intelligence. Britain was considering selling jet fighters to Cuba, and the ambassador was feeling out the potential U.S. reaction to such a deal. DCI Allen Dulles, however, had already made up his mind about Castro. For his own strategic purposes, he actually preferred to see the Cubans form a public link to the Soviet Union, which he assumed would be short-lived and useful in mobilizing opposition to the regime.

Following personal for the Secretary of State from the Ambassador.

Your telegram No. 5034: Cuba.

1. I had to see Allen Dulles this morning on another matter and took the opportunity to discuss Cuba on strictly personal basis.
2. In reply to my question how long he thought Castro was likely to last, Mr. Dulles said that, if he had to guess, he would say something in the range of eight months. He thought that the next three or four months were going to be the testing time and, if Castro survived them successfully, he might even carry on for a number of years. Consequently he would far rather delay an answer to my question.
3. He then volunteered that there was at present in Cuba no opposition to Castro who were capable of action. Abroad there were a number of Batista adherents who were trying to get into touch with the United States Administration, but they were, of course, worthless. The most hopeful prospect might lie amongst the people who had originally been supporters of Castro and had only recently become alienated. He gave as instances [Huber] Matos and the Chief of the Air Staff. If Castro continued on his present course, something might be made of an opposition consisting of such elements outside, and inside, Cuba. But the time for that had not yet come, though for our most confidential information, he was already making some contact with these people for possible future use.
4. From his own point of view, he said that he greatly hoped that we would decide not to go ahead with the Hunter deal. His main reason was that this might lead the Cubans to ask for Soviet or Soviet <u>bloc</u> arms. He had not cleared this with the State Department, but it was, of course, a fact that in the case of Guatemala it had been the shipment of Soviet arms that had brought the opposition elements together and created the occasion for what was done. The same might be true in the case of Cuba, and the presence, for instance, of MIGs would have a tremendous effect, not only in the United States, but with other Latin-American countries, quite apart from Trujillo [the dictator of the Dominican Republic].
5. Summing up, he said that there was, of course, always the chance that Castro would get shot. If this did not happen, it was not impossible that within three or four months civil government just might break down. He himself was skeptical whether things would develop in this way to the point which would lead to Castro's downfall. He had heard that the crop had been quite good this year and in these primitive countries where the sun shone, the demands of the people were far less than in more advanced countries. After, say, four months he would hope to be in a position to give a better estimate of Castro's longer term prospects.
6. Meanwhile, he repeated that if, and only if, he had to give an off-the-cuff estimate today, he would plump for something in the order of eight or nine months. But that would not, (repeat not) be for quotation and on this personal basis he again said he hoped that any refusal by us to supply arms would directly lead to a Soviet <u>bloc</u> offer to supply. Then he might be able to do something; for he was convinced that Castro was not only a bad man but had a streak of lunacy in his make-up which might have incalculable results. In other words, he was more like a Cuban Hitler than a Cuban version of Peron [a past Argentine dictator].
7. I did, in fact, repeat to Mr. Hankey what I said in my telegram No. 2334, namely, that in my view, a decision to go ahead would not do deep or lasting damage here. This particularly if the news of our decision broke through a

balanced statement of our own rather than a Press leak based on a Cuban version. But in the three weeks which have elapsed since my telegram, and during the longer period of your personal exchanges with Mr. Herter [the U.S. secretary of state], the situation in Cuba appears to have deteriorated, and attacks on the United States have sharpened. At any rate, public opinion in the United States has continued to harden under the insults of Castro. So far as we are concerned, there could, therefore, be no doubt that a decision on the lines set down in paragraph 5 of your telegram would come as a great relief to the United States Administration and public.

Britain did not supply the aircraft to Cuba, and an arms shipment from Belgium mysteriously exploded in port. At that point, Castro began expropriating U.S. properties. Early in 1960, before final presidential approval had been granted, CIA Deputy Director for Plans Richard Bissell formed a task force under Jacob D. Esterline to plan for an invasion of Cuba to be carried out by Cuban exiles armed and trained by the CIA. Their hope was that the intervention would trigger a broad-based popular uprising against Castro and his regime. The group included many veterans of the Guatemalan operation of 1954. In March, it met with Joseph Caldwell King, the head of operations for Latin America, who was called "the colonel" (although he does not appear to have ever served in the military). The minutes of the meeting suggest that even at this early stage the CIA was aware of the many obstacles to success.

MEMORANDUM FOR THE RECORD

SUBJECT: First Meeting of Branch 4 Task Force, 9 March 1960

1. Mr. Esterline briefed the group on the current situation in Cuba with the report that an alert has been sounded to initiate Phase One of the unified evacuation plan in Cuba. He added that this group would be working largely together in operational programming and planning.
2. Col. King told the group that the DCI is presenting a special policy paper to the NSC 5412 representatives [a committee of the National Security Council]. He mentioned growing evidence that certain of the "heads" in the CASTRO government have been pushing for an attack on the U.S. Navy installation at Guantanamo Bay and said that an attack on the installation is in fact, possible.
3. Col. King stated that the first problem in this operation is how to reach the mass of Cubans with the truth. To date, he said, we have been denied use of certain American islands that might be useful for either PP [political and psychological] or PM [paramilitary] activities. In addition, a number of the Chiefs of State of friendly smaller countries are, at the moment, unwilling to "stick their necks out further to support and operation directed at the overthrow of the CASTRO regime. They are in fact, worried that their respective countries may soon be the victims of Cuban exploitation. He said that unless Fidel and Raul CASTRO and Che GUEVARA could be eliminated in one package—which is highly unlikely—this operation can be a long, drawn-out affair and the present government will only be overthrown by the use of force.
4. Returning to the basic operational premises, Col. King said that the first problem is to reduce the base of support of the CASTRO Government with the masses (reportedly the regime now enjoys the support of between 60 and 70 percent of the population). An additional problem is that opposition forces have no real leader and are divided into many parts with some of the

more susceptible to merger than others. Three groups appear to be satisfactory for initial exploitation and each of these has been asked to come up with names of potential candidates for paramilitary and allied training. After training, this group could become the instructor cadre to train additional Cuban covert action groups.

5. The DCI, Col. King said, has approved the training of the instructor cadre at a U.S. military installation. The principal installation under consideration at the time is Fort Sherman in the Canal Zone which is under the control of the U.S. Army's Jungle Warfare Training Center. The DCI has also approved the Phase Two training, which is the training of Cuban action groups, in non-U.S. territory. A given area in one of the Caribbean countries has been offered and is under consideration. Col. King expressed the opinion that the minimum time that will be consumed in this training will be between 6 and 7 months. It is hoped that during this period the acceptable opposition groups will have been merged and will have formed a government-in-exile to which all trained elements could be attached.

6. Col. King, addressing himself to the enemy's capabilities and programs, said that CASTRO will unquestionably continue to train and arm various worker and student groups who can be mobilized into militia elements in support of the regular military establishment of Cuba. He added that reports indicate that CASTRO has more arms and ammunition available to him now than BATISTA had at the height of his power and warned that under no circumstances should we underestimate the capabilities of the enemy. He said hat the Cuban operation would be far more difficult and complicated than the previous one conducted by this Division and that before this problem is solved, major operations will be necessary.

7. Capsulizing various intelligence reports, Col. King said the Cubans are now initiating operations with an objective of establishing revolutionary movements in the Caribbean area that are not limited to those countries that are under dictatorships. With Ambassadors acting as chiefs of operations, the Cuban Government apparently hopes to overthrow the existing national governments and establish in their place governments that are far left and that are friendly to, and if possible, controlled by Cuba. Naturally, he added, this is generally in line with the objectives of International Communism which are, and for some time have been, to divide the traditional solidarity of the Latin American countries to the detriment of U.S. national security and foreign policy objectives.

8. In terms of operational problems, Col. King stated that he knew of no Latin American country whose people were less secure operationally than Cubans. On the CI [counterintelligence] side, he said that it is known that CASTRO has more than 122 agents in the Miami area alone.

9. In summarizing the more immediate requirements and possibilities, Mr. Esterline said that the support of all offices represented at the meeting will be required on a continuing basis. He added that support from the Office of Security, logistics and OTR and others would be needed comparatively soon:

    a. Assessment of potential recruits to the instructor cadres.
    b. Establishment of an operational base which will probably be located in the Miami area.
    c. The establishment of a secure base in a foreign country for the training of Cuban action groups.

10. He said that while we are awaiting national policy authorizations, Branch is proceeding with its planning operations and is preparing two projects at this

time, one to cover extensive radio operations which probably will include the establishment of a "gray" radio transmitter and another project for the development of air and maritime capabilities for the in-filtration of men and materiel.

11. He suggested that the group of specialists meet here at eh Branch weekly. The next meeting will be held on Tuesday, 15 March.* Although the overall Cuban project per se does not, as yet, have a cryptonym, Mr. Esterline explained the reasons for the formation of Branch 4 in WE Division and suggested the use of "Branch 4" in communications would be sufficient to identify the subject.

12. He mentioned that the following Branch 4 personnel would be in contact with the participants at the meeting from time to time for planning the operational purposes:

    Mr. [—], DC/WH/4
    Mr. David Phillips, Radio Operations
    Mr. Phillip Toomey, PP
    Mr. [—], Economic Action
    Mr. Adolf Lium
    Mr. E. A. Stanulis, Plans and PM Ops

13. Mr. Esterline indicated that an additional step in obtaining policy or operational support from other elements of the U.S. Government would be taken tomorrow, Thursday, 10 March 1960, when certain WE and PP Staff personnel would confer with Captain Spore, USN, a member of the Staff of the Office of Naval Operations, Department of Defense.

*0900 hours

While the initial meeting of the task force appeared cognizant of some of the problems that would confront the operation, the CIA issued an information report on 6 April 1961, shortly before the invasion, that was starkly at odds with the reality of the Castro government's political strength. The subject of the report was "Signs of Discontent among the Cuban Populace; Activities of the Government to Strengthen the Regime."

1. The great mass of Cuban people believe that the hour of decision is at hand and that the survival of the CASTRO regime is in the balance. They expect an invasion to take place before mid-April 1961 and place great reliance in it.

2. The CASTRO regime is steadily losing popularity, and the lack of enthusiasm of the Cuban people is reflected in Habana, where housewives and servants must stand in line for hours to obtain such necessities as soap and lard. Cuban women have become the leaders of opposition activity and urge their husbands to undertake action to alleviate the present situation. The people have begun to lose their fear of the government, and subtle sabotage is common. People deliberately break beer bottles and glasses, knowing that the government cannot replace them, and no one uses change, so that small commercial transactions have become hopelessly involved. CASTRO has said publicly that people who stand in line to purchase scarce items are counterrevolutionaries because they are trying to show that the government cannot provide. As a result nearly everyone stands in line; lines at grocery stores can be seen extending for four to five blocks. Church attendance is at an all-time high as a demonstration of opposition to the government.

3. Travelers through the interior of Cuba have reported that the disenchantment of the masses has spread through all the provinces. Spokesmen of opposition groups

say that Santiago de Cuba and all of Oriente Province is seething with hate. For oppositionists Santiago is the easiest city in Cuba in which too operate. Workers there readily give all the support they can, including hiding underground leaders in their homes. Very few of the aims of the Cuban revolution have passed on to the Cuban masses. The salary of the cane-cutters has been cut about fifty per cent; fishermen must sell their catch to the National Institute for Agrarian Reform at low prices and are paid in script which they consider valueless. Consequently, it is difficult to buy fish, and the fishermen try every means to sell their products illegally on the free or black market. Many government housing units have been constructed, but few are occupied. The reason in some cases is that poor planning or lack of supplies has led to failure to install plumbing and sewage facilities.

4. The defection of Jose PARDO Llada, CASTRO propagandist and news commentator, has been discussed in all walks of life and is regarded as highly significant. Although everyone is aware that PARDO is a complete opportunist, it is also known that he often has the ability to predict the future and change his political affiliations. The ranks of the oppositionists will increase as more and more Cubans seek a means to join the "winning side."

5. It is impossible to estimate the number of arms that have now passed into private hands. It is easy to obtain a gun in Habana; weapons, usually rifles, are furnished by underground organizations. No one wishes to cache any extensive amount of arms because of the difficulty in hiding them successfully.

6. It is generally believed that the Cuban Army has been successfully penetrated by opposition groups and that it will not fight in the event of a showdown. It is also certain that the police, who despise the militia, will not fight. The morale of the militia is falling. They have shown little wish to fight the opposition forces in the Escambray area of central Cuba, and some have been jailed for refusal to go to combat areas. Both militiamen and women try to find an excuse to wear civilian clothing, possibly because members of the opposition have been killing and wounding militia members in the streets and alleys of Habana and taking away their weapons. The government has had to disarm most of the women's militia because opposition groups were taking their weapons away from them.

7. As a result of the evident lack of support for the regime among the armed forces and the militia, CASTRO appears to have shifted his trust to the Asociacion de Jovenes Rebeldes (AJR, Rebel Youth Association), which is composed of a large number of teen-agers from the lower classes. AJR members, uniformed and armed with Czech machine-guns, are arrogant and mean and are feared by the Cuban populace. They are fiercely loyal to CASTRO because of their new-found notoriety and pay. The AJR is divided into military-type platoons and trained in military tactics. AJR members are used to show the force of the government at rallies and demonstrations and also in attacks upon Catholics. Parents of members resent the formation of the AJR because it has brought about less of parental control and respect.

8. CASTRO's decree of 1961 as the "Year of Education" and his order for closing all schools on 15 April and sending the students to rural areas to teach the farmers has caused much resentment among certain groups. Parents, especially of female students, do not want to send their children to rural areas to risk their health and lose the effects of their parental upbringing. Operators of private schools, whose fixed expenses will continue during the period of suspension of school, fear they will become bankrupt and be forced to ask the government to assume the operation of the school.

9. Habana is filled with Soviet, Satellite, and Communist Chinese nationals, who appear to be living comfortably at government expense, probably part of the barter plan between Cuba and bloc countries. Through an arrangement with the government these nationals do not have to pay for expenses in public places but only sign a bill, which the owner of the establishment must present to the government for

reimbursement. Cuban employees do not like this procedure because it eliminates tipping and the owners of the establishment are uncertain over their reimbursement. Soviet and Satellite officers are assigned to Cuban Government offices. Chinese are more of a mystery to the Cubans, since they are seen in large numbers but their function is not known. It is speculated that they are working largely in the Chinese colony, that they are assigned to government agricultural co-operatives in the interior of the country, or that they are helping the militia in the Escambray as instructors in guerrilla warfare.

10. The military camp at Managua is probably the most important one in the Habana area; it is a central depot for cargos arriving on Soviet ships. The cargos are unloaded by Soviet crews under maximum security on to trucks covered with canvas. The convoy route is guarded by militiamen stationed at 25-yard intervals. On one occasion a canvas covering blew off a truck, and oblong boxes, approximately 25 feet long and two feet square, were observed. The airfield at Campo Libertad had recently become a maximum security area and is protected by fences, searchlights, and constantly manned .50-caliber machine-gun emplacements.

The landing of the Cuban exile force at the Bay of Pigs was a fiasco. Castro was aware that they were coming (although some of the reports he received were exaggerated), as was the *New York Times*. The Cuban army was prepared to meet the forces on the beach. High-ranking CIA officials were aware that they had lost the element of surprise, yet they—especially CIA Deputy Director for Plans Bissell—managed to convince themselves and the president that it did not matter. President John F. Kennedy—who had been inaugurated a few months before the landing and had approved the project, which had been in the planning stages for nearly a year—apparently never fully understood the nature of the operation. He canceled most of the planned air strikes against Cuba, believing that they would surely implicate the United States in what was being presented as an independent operation by Cuban exiles based in Central America. Bissell and other ranking officials insisted that this, too, could be done. Many would blame the president's decision limiting air operations for the ultimate failure at the Bay of Pigs. With some 20,000 Cuban troops massed to resist the invasion by 1,500 exiles, however, it appears that strikes by a few World War II–era aircraft would have had relatively little impact.

For his part, Castro was able to use the invasion to bolster his regime, arguing that it proved the United States was a threat and the Cuban oppositionists were merely the tools of a foreign power. Those exiles who were captured and later released included some who would go on to carry out unauthorized terrorist plots against Cuba for years to come.

There were several after-action reviews of the operation. The CIA's own inspector general, Lyman Kirkpatrick, Jr., issued a devastating critique, the "Inspector General's Survey of the Cuban Operation," in October 1961, which included the following:[1]

C. SUMMARY OF EVALUATION

1. In evaluating the Agency's performance it is essential to avoid grasping immediately, as many persons have done, at the explanation that the President's order canceling the D-Day air strikes was the chief cause of failure.
2. Discussion of that one decision would merely raise this underlying question: If the project had been better conceived, better organized, better staffed and

better managed, would that precise issue ever have had to be presented for Presidential decision at all? And would it have been presented under the same ill-prepared, inadequately briefed circumstances?

3. Furthermore, it is essential to keep in mind the possibility that the invasion was doomed in advance, that an initially successful landing by 1,500 men would eventually have been crushed by Castro's combined military resources strengthened by Soviet Bloc-supplied military materiel.

4. The fundamental cause of the disaster was the Agency's failure to give the project, notwithstanding its importance and its immense potentiality for damage to the United States, the top-flight handling which it required— appropriate organization, staffing throughout by highly qualified personnel, and full-time direction and control of the highest quality.

5. Insufficiencies in these vital areas resulted in pressures and distortions, which in turn produced numerous serious operational mistakes and omissions, and in lack of awareness of developing dangers, in failure to take action to counter them, and in grave mistakes of judgment. There was failure at high levels to concentrate informed, unwavering scrutiny on the project and to apply experienced, unbiased judgment to the menacing situations that developed.

Allen Dulles stepped down as Director of Central Intelligence in September 1961. Richard Bissell, the Deputy Director for Plans, did likewise six months later.

The Bay of Pigs soured Kennedy to the CIA, but it did not put an end to covert operations against Cuba. There was already an anti-Castro underground movement on the island and, in the view of the White House, it needed an American official to direct it. That official had to be someone who had the president's confidence but was outside the CIA, even if the agency was responsible for implementation. The solution was the president's brother, Attorney General Robert F. Kennedy, as noted in this memorandum from Richard Goodwin, a presidential aide.

EYES ONLY FOR THE PRESIDENT

November 1, 1961

MEMORANDUM FOR THE PRESIDENT:

I believe that the concept of a "command operation" for Cuba, as discussed with you by the Attorney General, is the only effective way to handle an all-out attack on the Cuban problem. Since I understand you are favorably disposed toward the idea I will not disclose why the present disorganized and uncoordinated operation cannot do the job effectively.

The beauty of such an operation over the next few months is that we cannot lose. If the best happens we will unseat Castro. If not, then at least we will emerge with a stronger underground, better propaganda and a far clearer idea of the dimensions of the problems which affect us.

The question then is who should head this operation. I know of no one currently in Cuban affairs at the State Department who can do it. Nor is it a very to get the State Department involved in depth in such covert activities. I do not think it should be centered in the CIA. Even if the CIA can find someone of sufficient force and stature, one of the major problems will be to revamp CIA operations and thinking—and this will be very hard to do from the inside.

I believe that the Attorney General would be the most effective commander of such an operation. Either I or someone else should be assigned to him as Deputy for this activity, since he obviously will not be able to devote full time to it. The one danger here is that he might become too closely identified with what might not be a successful operation. Indeed, chances of success are very speculative. There are a few answers to this:

(1) Everyone knowledgeable in these affairs—in and out of government—is aware that the United States is already helping the underground. The precise manner of aid may be unknown but the fact of aid is common knowledge. We will be blamed for not winning Cuba back whether or not we have a "command operation" and whether or not the Attorney General heads it.

(2) His role should be told to only a few people at the very top with most of the contact work in carrying out his decisions being left to his deputy. If that deputy is someone already closely identified with the conduct of Cuban affairs then it would appear as if normal channels are being followed except that decisive attention would be given to the decisions which came through those channels.

This still leaves a substantial danger of identifying the Attorney General as the fellow in charge. This danger must be weighed against the increased effectiveness of an operation under his command.

/initialed/
Richard N. Goodwin

Richard Helms, at the time the CIA's chief of operations (the second-ranking position in the Directorate of Plans), attended a meeting the following January with Attorney General Kennedy and representatives of the Joint Chiefs of Staff (JCS), the Office of the Secretary of Defense (OSD), and other representatives of the CIA. He reported back to John A. McCone, the new Director of Central Intelligence, as follows:

EYES ONLY

19 January 1962

MEMORANDUM FOR: The Director of Central Intelligence

SUBJECT: Meeting with the Attorney General of the United States Concerning Cuba

1. I attended a meeting on Cuba at 11:00 A.M., today chaired by the Attorney General. Others present were:

Brig. General E. S. Lansdale (OSD)
Major James Patchell (OSD)
Brig. General William H. Craig (JCS)
Mr. [—] (CIA)
Mr. George McManus (CIA)
(The Department of State was <u>not</u> represented although invited.)

2. The Attorney General outlined to us "How it all started" findings as they developed, and the general framework within which the United States Government should now attack the Cuban problem. Briefly, these were the main points:

(a) After failure of the invasion, the United States Government became less active on the theory "better to lay low."

(b) Over the months the complexion of the refugee flow changed (i.e., upper classes out first, then middle classes—dropping to lower middle class, etc.) which, he stated, indicated a strong feeling of opposition to Castro within Cuba.

(c)   Progress in Cuba toward a police and Communist state was more rapid during this period than that made by any country in Eastern Europe in an equivalent period of time. Because of the rapidity of advance, immediate action on the part of the United States Government was necessary.

(d)   With these factors in mind, the Attorney General had a discussion at the White House during the autumn of 1961 with the President, the Secretary of Defense, and General Lansdale. The Secretary of Defense assigned General Lansdale to survey the Cuban problem, and he (Lansdale) reported to the President, the Secretary of Defense, and the Attorney General (in late November) concluding:

(1)   Overthrow of the Castro regime was possible
(2)   Sugar crop should be attacked at once
(3)   Action to be taken to keep Castro so busy with internal problems (economic, political, and social) that Castro would have no time for meddling abroad especially in Latin America.

DETAIL: United States Government was precluded from destroying the current sugar crop (1) we were late and overly optimistic and (b) "the assets of the United States Government were not as great as we were led to believe."

(e)   Accordingly, a solution to the Cuban problem today carries "The top priority in the United States Government—all else is secondary—no time, money, effort, or manpower is to be spared. There can be no misunderstanding on the involvement of the agencies concerned nor on their responsibility to carry out this job. The agency heads understand that you are to have full backing on what you need."

(f)   Yesterday (18 January 1962), the President indicated to the Attorney General that "the final chapter on Cuba has not been written"—it's got to be done and will be done.

(g)   Therefore, the Attorney General directed those in attendance at the meeting to address themselves to the "32 tasks" unfailingly (see program review—The Cuba Project dated 18 January 1962). He said, "It is not only General Lansdale's job to put the tasks, but yours to carry out with every resource at your command."

3.   The Attorney General inquired about the progress in establishing a refugee interrogation center at Miami and was informed that this would be in operation by 15 February 1962—the target date. With respect to interrogating the back-log of Cubans in the U.S.A., we agreed that we would attack this problem by getting at the more recent arrivals first. The Attorney General was informed that one could not relate, in time, the establishment of an interrogation facility with the placing of agents in Cuba—in other words, a body of information would have to be developed by intensive interrogation of many sources over a period of time.

4.   It was General Lansdale's view that there were several tasks among the "32" outlined upon which action could be taken without awaiting this detailed intelligence information. He noted, for example, the defection of top Cubans as being within the immediate capabilities of the CIA.

/initialed/
Richard Helms
Chief of Operations, DD/P

The planning for the operation, which acquired the code name Mongoose, proceeded apace. Key participants, including Gen. Lansdale, were increasingly convinced that the conditions in Cuba were ripe for an anti-Castro revolution. Indeed, Lansdale did not think the program, as planned, was ambitious enough to take advantage of the evolving political situation. In its first phase, as outlined by Lansdale in a memorandum to the Special Group (augmented) on 25 July 1962, the operation was limited to political, economic, and covert actions "short of inspiring a revolt in Cuba or developing the need for U.S. armed intervention."

Here, Lansdale reports on a meeting with President Kennedy, which included Gen. Maxwell D. Taylor, head of the Special Group, which held overall responsibility for covert actions, and Gen. Lyman Lemnitzer, the chairman of the Joint Chiefs of Staff. Lansdale's briefing, in fact, reflected very little solid intelligence and a great deal of wishful thinking as he projected his own beliefs onto the people of Cuba. Curiously, McCone, the new Director of Central Intelligence, would allow neither Helms, the Chief of Operations, nor William K. Harvey, the head of the CIA's Cuban task force, to attend the session.

16 March 1962

MEMORANDUM FOR THE RECORD

By: Brig. Gen. Lansdale

Subject: Meeting with President, 16 March 1962

Present: The President, General Taylor, the Attorney General, McGeorge Bundy, Mr. Gilpatric, General Lemnitzer, Mr. McCone, Alexis Johnson, myself. At the White House, 1600 hours, 16 March 1962.

Prior to the President's arrival, the group met in the Oval room. General Taylor handed out his "Guidelines for Operation Mongoose," dated 14 March. I asked McCone about having Helms and Harvey, who were waiting outside, join us. McCone asked if I had any differences of opinion with them. I said that we were in agreement on operational procedures, as far as the guidelines would permit operations. McCone then said Helms and Harvey should stay outside (which he told the President later, also).

McCone then asked me if I were in agreement with the concept contained in the "Guidelines." I commented that they didn't fit the conditions inside Cuba that were becoming more apparent to the operational people, including CIA operators, for whom I had respect; the chance of fracturing the regime and creating a valid revolution is becoming more feasible. I felt that we needed much more freedom to work on the revolutionary possibilities than is possible under the guidelines.

The President then came in.

General Taylor gave a brief report on developments since 30 November, said the Special Group felt that hard intelligence was needed before going ahead, and handed the President a copy of the revised Guidelines. (The President glanced at this momentarily and set it down on the table; Taylor had briefed him on the Guidelines the evening before.) The President then turned to me and asked me what was being done.

I gave him a quick summary of the intelligence-collection plan through July, telling him that this was the Special Group's plan, and describing the work so far of CIA and Defense. I told him that we finally were starting to get a really good team together for the operation, after much effort to get the U.S. pointed in the right direction. I noted that agents were to be trained or experienced in guerrilla warfare, that we needed U.S. military participation for support, including air re-supply and maritime actions. He asked for details. Both General Lemnitzer and I told him about "sheep-dipping" U.S. military personnel, "sanitizing" equipment, and use of U.S. bases. I pointed out that PT boat silhouettes required a Navy base as cover, even if we called it "R&E" [Research and Engineering], that air resupply would be done at night from about 800 feet which entailed some risk which the Air Force was now assessing. He asked about maritime runs of the PT-boats; I explained our problems of "mother" ships, the LSD's and 200-300 man crews, which we are trying to lick.

I remarked that the thesis of creating a revolution inside Cuba looked just as valid as ever, and that CIA professionals were now agreeing more and more that both resistance and the possibility of fracturing the regime point to some real opportunities. I noted that we were checking out a number of leads, including relatives of Fidel Castro, to assess the practical opportunities for splitting away some of the regime. If we could get some of the top Cuban leaders, and some units of the Cuban security forces to take to the hills, we would have conditions that would need quick exploitation—and we would have to be ready for this. I noted that we would have to supply arms and equipment; it is possible that this could be done without U.S. forces, if necessary.

The President asked if U.S. military intervention was an issue that the Special Group was posing to him now. Taylor and the Special Group promptly said, "no."

General Lemnitzer commented that the military had contingency plans for U.S. intervention. Also, it had plans for creating plausible pretexts for the use of force, with the pretexts either attacks on U.S. aircraft or a Cuban action in Latin America that we would retaliate.

The President said bluntly that we were not discussing the use of U.S. military force, that General Lemnitzer might find the U.S. so engaged in Berlin or elsewhere that he couldn't use the contemplated 4 divisions in Cuba. So, we cannot say that we are able now to make a decision on the use of U.S. military force.

The President then commented that he hoped something could be done about the press. That the newspapers would start conjecturing on operations just as they did in April 1961. I said that such conjecture was going on all the time, that any solid-looking reports might well be a real blessing, because as talk increases that the U.S. has the intention, somehow, to help the people of Cuba regain their freedom, that the people inside would get some hope. This spiritual factor, of having hope of something better than what they are now saddled with, is vitally important at this time.

The President then asked about immigration. Wouldn't it be better to shut our doors to the people trying to get out, so that they would be forced to stay and take action against the regime? I pointed out that we still were giving them only two choices: either to escape to the U.S. and freedom, or to stay and be slaves. Once we are willing to go all the way in being sure that they win, then we might consider closing our doors—because we then will be helping them gain their freedom at home. Now, with 2,000 people fleeing every week, we would be foolish to remove this symbol of our sympathy and cut off the source of intelligence information and recruits. We must give the Cubans the chance and the help to free themselves.

The Attorney General then mentioned Mary Hemingway [the widow of writer Ernest Hemingway], commenting on reports that Castro was drinking heavily in disgruntlement over the way things were going, and the opportunities offered by the "shrine" to Hemingway [at the house where he had lived in Cuba]. I commented that this was a conversation that [TV journalist] Ed Murrow had had with Mary Hemingway, that we had similar reports from other sources, and that this was worth assessing firmly and pursuing vigorously. If there are grounds for action, CIA had some invaluable assets that might well be committed for such an effort. McCone asked if his operational people were aware of this; I told him that we had discussed this, that they agreed the subject was worth vigorous development, and that we were in agreement that the matter was so delicate and sensitive that it shouldn't be surfaced to the Special Group until we were ready to go, and then not in detail. I pointed out that this pertained to fractioning the regime. If it happened, it could develop like a brush fire, much as in Hungary, and we must be prepared to help it win our goal of Cuba free of a Communist government.

General Lemnitzer mentioned the beach reconnaissance by the U.S. Navy, which was evaluated by the JCS as having little risk. UDT teams would do this at night, and would not need to surface.

Mr. McCone mentioned that we were including sabotage in early actions. I commented that we had a number of such actions listed, but were only planning on a few most necessary ones. One example was the Soviet patrol craft, for which both Navy and CIA were tasked to plan sabotage. The President asked how this might be done. I replied that fuel, lubricants, crews, and the patrol craft were all potential targets—that, for example, a boat laid-up for repair was a boat that wasn't out on patrol at a critical period.

Mr. [Deputy Secretary of Defense Roswell] Gilpatric mentioned that Mr. [Secretary of Defense Robert] McNamara was intensely interested in creating a Defense pool of resources for cover actions, for Colombia for example, so that we wouldn't be faced with the problem of only having 4 PT boats as we do for Cuba.

The meeting then broke up, with the president saying go ahead on the Guidelines. General Taylor asked for his copies of he Guidelines back. I said I needed a copy, for my guidance and to show the operators such as Harvey and Craig. The President expressed his appreciation for what had been done so far. Gen. Taylor didn't persist in getting his copy back, so I retained it.

By early October, the president ("higher authority") was becoming increasingly frustrated with the lack of results. At the same time, those responsible for the project were becoming frustrated with the conflicting limitations set on the operation by higher authority. DCI McCone, Deputy DCI Marshall Carter, and Deputy Under Secretary of State U. Alexis Johnson spoke openly about the contradictions between the requirement to keep the operation secret and the request to increase its scale. Despite the flurry of activity and the talk of "accomplishing the overall objective," the impression emerges that there was no clear-cut plan or even purpose in sight, especially inasmuch as presumed objectives, such as inciting "an uprising," were expressly prohibited.

MEMORANDUM FOR THE RECORD

SUBJECT: Minutes of Meeting of the Special Group (Augmented) on Operation MONGOOSE, 4 October 1962

PRESENT: The Attorney General; Mr. Johnson; Mr. Gilpatric, General Taylor, General Lansdale; Mr. McCone and General Carter; Mr. Wilson

1. The Attorney General opened the meeting by saying that higher authority is concerned about progress on the MONGOOSE program and feels that more priority should be given to trying to mount sabotage operations. The Attorney General said that he wondered if a new look is not required at this time in view of the meager results, especially in the sabotage field. He urged that "massive activity" be mounted within the entire MONGOOSE framework.

There was a good deal of discussion about this, and General Lansdale said that another attempt will be made against the major target which has been the object of three unsuccessful missions, and that approximately six new ones are in the planning stage.

Mr. Johnson said that "massive activity" would have to appear to come from within. He also said that he hopes soon to be able to present to the Group a plan for giving Cuban exiles more of a free hand, with the full realization that his would give more visibility to their activities. On this latter point, Mr. McCone said that he reserves judgment as to the feasibility and desirability of such a program. (Mr. Johnson agreed that he has reservations as well.)

2. Mr. McCone then said that he gets the impression that high levels of the government want to get on with activity but still wish to retain a low noise level. He does not believe that this will be possible. Any sabotage would be blamed on the United States. In this connection, he cited the enormous number of telephone calls that had been directed to the CIA at the time that the skin divers landed in Eastern Cuba and at the time Cuban exile students shot up the apartment house. He urged that responsible officials be prepared to accept a higher noise level if they want to get on with the operations.

In partial rebuttal, the Attorney General said that the reasons people were so concerned at the times mentioned were: (a) the fact that the skin divers were Americans, and (b) that the student activity was irresponsible and foolish, and if either of these had in fact been engineered by the U.S. it would have been a great mistake. He went on to say responsible people do wish to get on with operations but want to relate the possibility of attributability to the importance of the particular undertaking. He also questioned whether we are going down the right road or whether "more direct action" is not indicated. He urged that alternative and imaginative plans be developed for accomplishing the overall objective.

3. Returning to Mr. Johnson's point about the necessity of massive activity coming from within, Mr. McCone pointed out that internal security [measures] are now so rigid that internal uprisings are sure to be suppressed. It was agreed that the current guidelines do not call for inciting such an uprising.

4. Mr. McCone and General Carter explained the tremendous efforts which are necessary to insure that an operation such as the sabotage one previously authorized cannot be pinned directly on the U.S. After considerable discussion, the Group agreed that it is not necessary to go to such extreme lengths to guarantee non-attributability and that short cuts will be acceptable.

5. Mr. Gilpatric reported that Defense is now working hard on establishing a Cuban brigade. Recruits will be trained for four or five months and will then be on call for any future action.

6. General Taylor reported that the Joint Staff is refining various military contingency plans, based on a variety of possible situations. Such situations include: Soviet action against Berlin; presence of Bloc offensive weapons in Cuba; attack against Guantanamo; a popular uprising; armed Cuban subversion in the Hemisphere; and the establishment of a direct threat to the U.S.

7. The Group then turned to the subject of reconnaissance of Cuba. (Dr. Scoville and Colonel Steakley joined the Group for this part of the discussion.) It was pointed out that the Agency is now restricted to using its high performance vehicle in the southeast quadrant of Cuba, because of the SAM [surface-to-air missile] sites. It was questioned whether this is a reasonable restriction at this time, particularly when the SAMs are almost certainly not operational.

Colonel Steakley and Dr. Scoville described for the Group a spectrum of reconnaissance activities which could be undertaken, ranging from low-level Navy fighters through drones, up to the Agency's capabilities, particularly equipped with new radar countermeasures.

The result of this discussion was that it was agreed that DOD and CIA should get together on recommendations for targets within Cuba that require coverage and on recommendations as to how to achieve this coverage. A meeting was set for next Tuesday, at which time DOD and CIA should be prepared to discuss all possibilities, including requirements, capabilities, vulnerabilities, etc.

8. There was some discussion of the desirability of mining Cuban waters. It was pointed out that non-U.S.-attributable mines, which appear to be home-made, are available and could be laid by small craft operated by Cubans.

9. It was agreed that the Attorney General should act as Chairman of the Special Group (Augmented) at least for the time being.

10. It was agreed that four major points emerged from today's discussion:

   a. We ought to go all out for increased intelligence.
   b. There should be considerably more sabotage.
   c. Restrictions on attributability can be relaxed so that training and other preparations can be subject to some short cuts.
   d. All efforts should be made to develop new and imaginative approaches to the possibility of getting rid of the Castro regime.

At that point, the Cuban Missile Crisis of October 1963 erupted. One of the great landmarks of the Cold War, the Cuban Missile Crisis brought the United States and the Soviet Union so close to the brink of nuclear conflict that it led both sides to stop and reconsider their current policies toward both each other and nuclear weapons. This relatively brief period of accord resulted in the signing of a treaty banning open-air nuclear tests (the first effective arms control agreement of the Cold War era) and the establishment of the "hotline," providing direct communications (initially by teletype) between the White House and the Kremlin.

Although most of the world did not know of it for many years, a new opening in U.S.-Cuban relations also came under consideration. Castro made the first move in that he sent out multiple tentative feelers to the Kennedy administration with suggestions that Kennedy might want to make a "first move." One of these came by way of Lisa Howard, a former television actress who had made a name for herself as a correspondent able to get exclusive interviews with world leaders, starting with Nikita Khrushchev in 1960. She reported the proposal to the CIA upon returning from Havana. In the memo below, Richard Helms, although he could not get her name quite right, notified DCI McCone and other top officials of the initiative. Evidently, the CIA took advantage of the opportunity to ask about various peripheral details, including Castro's physical state, his awareness of Cuban police methods, what would happen if he were assassinated (although that paragraph does not specifically cite Howard), the role of Soviet personnel, and how the Swiss ambassador was doing. (The Swiss embassy was representing U.S. interests in the absence of a U.S. embassy. Its role lasted until 1979, when the State Department opened an "interest section" in Havana.) For his part, in addition to asking about the Kennedys, Castro was interested in the influence of Adlai Stevenson, the two-time Democratic presidential nominee who was serving as ambassador to the United Nations and was open to U.S.-Cuban reconciliation, and James Donovan, a New York attorney who helped negotiate the release of Bay of Pigs prisoners and was also eager to serve as a go-between (a fact probably not known to Howard).

1 May 1963

MEMORANDUM FOR: The Director of Central Intelligence

SUBJECT: Interview of U.S. Newswoman with Fidel Castro Indicating Possible Interest in Rapprochement with the United States

1. On 30 April 1963, Liza [sic] Howard, U.S. newswoman associated with the American Broadcasting Company, returned to Miami from Cuba where she had interviewed a number of high-ranking Cuban officials, including Fidel Castro, Raul Castro, Ernesto "Che" Guevara, Vilma Espin de Castro, Raul Roa, and Rene Vallejo. Her conversations with Fidel Castro totaled about ten hours and included one session on 22 April which lasted from 12:45 A.M. to 5:30 A.M. Following is an account of those conversations and Liza Howard's observations concerning the present Cuban situation.

2. It appears that Fidel Castro is looking for a way to reach a rapprochement with the United States Government, probably because he is aware that Cuba is in a state of economic chaos. The October blockade hurt the Cuban economy. Liza Howard believes that Castro talked about this matter with her because she is known as a progressive and she talked with him in frank, blunt, honest terms; Castro has little opportunity to hear this type of conversation. Castro indicated that if a rapprochement was wanted President John F. Kennedy would have to make the first move. In response to the statement that Castro would probably have to make the first move, Castro asked what the U.S. wanted from him. When a return to the original aims of the revolution was suggested, Fidel said that perhaps he, President Kennedy, and Premier Nikita Khrushchev should discuss this. Liza Howard said that she thought it was a more likely topic for Castro to discuss with President Kennedy. Castro said that he doubted that President Kennedy would talk with him without Khrushchev being present. When Howard pressed Castro for further information on how a rapprochement could be achieved he said that steps were already being taken. Pressed further, he said he considered the U.S. limitation on exile raids to be a proper step toward accommodation. It is Liza Howard's opinion that Castro wants to pursue the discussion of rapprochement with proper progressive spokesmen. Based on her discussions with the following persons Liza Howard feels that Guevara, Raul Castro, and Vilma Espin oppose any idea of rapprochement; Roa and Vallejo favor these discussions.

3. Castro asked Howard, who had previously interviewed Khrushchev, for an appraisal of him. When Howard said that Khrushchev was a shrewd politician who would break and dispose of Castro when the Soviets no longer needed him, Castro made no comment but only nodded his head as if in skeptical agreement. Liza Howard had no insight or advance notice on Castro's travel to Moscow.

4. Castro appears healthy, has no visible nervous twitches or tics, and was calm, rational, humorous, and non-argumentative during all discussions. Vallejo, Castro's personal physician, also acts as secretary, interpreter, and confidant.

5. Castro is in complete control in Cuba. No major decision is made without him. Neither Guevara nor Raul Castro would be able to rule Cuba if Fidel wee assassinated.

6. In discussions with Castro about terror and secret police methods Liza Howard received the impression that he was not completely aware of the extent to which terror has gripped Cuba.

7. Castro refers to Soviet troops in Cuba as "technicals" and indicated that they have a training mission in Cuba. He made the point, however, that if an internal revolt takes place in Cuba Soviet "technicals" would fight with Castro to put down a counterrevolution.

8. Liza Howard said that Emil Stadelhofer, Swiss Ambassador to Cuba, is an overworked, timid man who does not have Castro's ear. She believes that the Swiss need a larger staff in Habana and that Stadelhofer needs recognition for a job well done. Howard also said that in her opinion the Western diplomatic community in Habana has no influence on Castro or his government.

9. While discussing a possible rapprochement Castro asked for full assessments of President and Mrs. Kennedy, and Robert Kennedy, and wanted to know if Adlai Stevenson had power in the U.S. and if his voice was heard in President Kennedy's councils. Castro commented that James Donovan was a good man; it was Liza Howard's impression that Donovan had not talked politics with Castro but that Donovan had a platform from which he could launch political discussions on the philosophy of revolution.

10. Liza Howard said that she was willing to undertake further discussions with Castro concerning a possible rapprochement. Other possible candidates whom she suggested were [Assistant Secretary of State for Inter-American Affairs] Edwin M. Martin, Adlai Stevenson, and [Governor of Puerto Rico] Luis Munoz Marin, She also mentioned Donovan but was not quite certain that he was progressive enough. Liza Howard is willing to arrange a meeting for any U.S. Government spokesman with Castro through Vallejo, who will be the point of contact.

11. Liza Howard definitely wants to impress the U.S. Government with two facts: Castro is ready to discuss rapprochement and she herself is ready to discuss it with him if asked to do so by the U.S. Government.

/signed "W. Lloyd George for"/
Richard Helms
Deputy Director (Plans)

The memo, marked "Secret: No Foreign Dissemination/Controlled Dissemination/No Dissemination Abroad/Background Use Only," was considered significant. In addition to being addressed to the DCI, copies were directed to the Special Assistant to the President for National Security Affairs, the Director of Intelligence and Research at the Department of State, the Director of the Defense Intelligence Agency, the Attorney General, and within the CIA to the Deputy Director of Central Intelligence, the Deputy Director for Intelligence, the Assistant Director for National Estimates, and the Assistant Director for Current Intelligence. Marginal notations indicate that it was read by Special Assistant McGeorge Bundy and the president.

Over the course of the next several months, Howard arranged informal meetings in New York between Castro's confidante René Vallejo and William Attwood, Stevenson's deputy at the United Nations. On Cuba's side, Vallejo was replaced by Carlos Lechuga, Cuba's ambassador to the UN. Evidently, the CIA was kept in the dark about the initiative. The whole program came to an end, however, with Kennedy's assassination on 22 November of that year. Gordon

Chase, a member of the National Security Council staff who had advocated "quietly enticing Castro over to us," highlighted the turmoil into which the assassination had thrown the strategy and the political difficulty that Lyndon Johnson, as a new president, would have in trying to renew it.

November 25, 1963

MEMORANDUM FOR MR. BUNDY

SUBJECT: Cuba—Item of Presidential Interest

1. I assume you will want to brief the President on Bill Attwood's Cuban exercise that is presumably still in train.
2. My own thinking on this one, vis a vis the events of November 22, is still very fluid; but here it is. Basically, the events of November 22 would appear to make accomodation with Castro an even more doubtful issue than it was. While I think that President Kennedy could have accomodated with Castro and gotten away with it with a minimum of domestic heat, I'm not sure about President Johnson. For one thing, a new President who has no background of being successfully nasty to Castro and the Communists (e.g. President Kennedy in October, 1962) would probably run a greater risk of being accused, by the American people, of "going soft." In addition, the fact that Lee Oswald has been heralded as a pro-Castro type may make rapprochement with Cuba more difficult—although it is hard to say how much more difficult.
3. If one concludes hat the prospects for accomodation with Castro are much dimmer than they were before November 22, then Bill Attwood's present effort loses much of its meaning. We would appear to have three alternative courses of action in handling the present status of the Attwood-Lechuga tie-line.

   a. We can tell Attwood that if Lechuga calls, Attwood should tell Lechuga that in view of recent events, he is not now prepared to talk about an agenda with Lechuga.
   b. We can tell Attwood that if Lechuga does <u>not</u> call over the next couple weeks (the Cubans may feel that November 22 has stopped all bets), he should take the initiative and get a message to the Cubans, that despite recent events, we are still prepared to hear what is on Castro's mind.
   c. We can tell Attwood that if Lechuga calls about setting up an appointment between Attwood and Lechuga, that Attwood should schedule such a meeting for a few days later and call us immediately. However, if Lechuga does not call him, Attwood should take no initiative until and if he hears from us.

4. I choose 3 (c) above. While November 22 events probably make accomodation an even tougher issue for President Johnson than it was for President Kennedy, a preliminary Attwood-Lechuga talk still seems worthwhile from our point of view—if the Cubans initiate it. We have little or nothing to lose and there will be some benefits; at a minimum, we should get a valuable reading as to what Castro regards as negotiable (e.g. the Soviet tie-line?) and a hint as to how he views the effect of November 22 on Cuban/U.S. relations. At the same time, if the Cubans, who have the ball, feel that all bets are off, we should take no initiative until we have thought the problem through carefully.

   If we decide that course 3 (c) is the right one, the sooner we call Attwood, the better. In view of his and Stevenson's activist tendencies in this matter, it seems conceivable to me that, not hearing from Lechuga in the near future, they will approach him and assure him that we feel the same way and that we are still prepared to hear what Castro has on his mind.

/initialed/
Gordon Chase

Castro again sent out feelers through Lisa Howard. He even noted that if President Johnson had to make bellicose statements about Cuba to win reelection, he would understand. Stevenson also pressed for renewal of the dialog from his office at the UN. Some contacts were made, but little resulted from them. The following spring, Helms sent Bundy the following memo, apparently to let the White House know that the CIA had found out about the initiative on its own through its spies in Cuba.

4 March 1964

MEMORANDUM FOR: Mr. Bundy
                Special Assistant to the President

SUBJECT: Alleged Contacts between Castro and American Government

1. Against the background of the post-Special Group Meeting that you held late in the afternoon on 5 November 1963, I thought you would be interested in the following report which we have just received:

2. About the middle of February 1964, a high-ranking Cuban official who has close personal connections with top-level Government personalities in Cuba was told by Raul <u>Roa</u> Garcia, the Cuban Minister of Foreign Affairs, that President Kennedy, prior to his assassination, had "established certain contacts" with Cuba. Roa said that emissaries from President Kennedy had been sent to make contact with the Cubans; he mentioned specifically that some contacts had taken place in New York, but did not make it clear whether New York was the only place where there had been such contacts. Roa did not describe or identify the emissaries.

3. According to Roa, Fidel Castro felt that it was possible that President Kennedy would have gone on ultimately to negotiate with Cuba. Roa explained that such negotiations would not have been based on any "love for Cuba", but would have been in the nature of an acceptance of a <u>fait</u> <u>accompli</u> for practical reasons; this would have been to Cuba's advantage, in Roa's opinion.

4. Roa added that "it is believed" that President Johnson is unaware of his predecessor's activities in this matter, and for this reason is not continuing President Kennedy's policy. Castro referred to President Johnson in harsh terms in source's presence.

/initialed/
Richard Helms
Deputy Director for Plans

NOTE

1. For the full report and Bissell's rebuttal, see Peter Kornbluh, ed., *Bay of Pigs Declassified: The Secret CIA Report on the Invasion of Cuba* (New York: The New Press, 1998).

Chapter 4

Political Assassinations and Illicit Drug Tests

In early May 1973, a brief, one-page memo was addressed to William E. Colby regarding what the author considered "potentially embarrassing agency activities." It would stand out like a flame among the often tedious and bureaucratic reports that poured into the "Family Jewels" file. The memo began modestly enough, with the case of Hans V. Tofte, who had been dismissed from the CIA in 1966 for mishandling classified documents. Tofte had rented out a basement apartment in his house without bothering to take secret papers out of it first.[1] From there, the memo proceeded through illicit experiments regarding mind-altering drugs to allegations of plots to assassinate foreign heads of state.

8 May 1973

MEMORANDUM FOR: Executive Secretary, CIA Management Committee

SUBJECT: Potentially Embarrassing Agency Activities

The Office of the Inspector General has records on the following sensitive subjects that either have been or might in the future be the source of embarrassment to the Agency.

The report of the Board of Inquiry in the case of Hans Tofte. The Tofte affair was fully exposed in public, of course, but the report itself is closely held within the Agency. This office was designated as the custodian of the report, and we have the only surviving copy.

An annex to the Inspector General's report of survey of the Technical Services Division done in 1963. The annex deals with experiments in influencing human behavior through the administration of mind or personality altering drugs to unwitting subjects.

An Inspector General report of investigation of allegations that the Agency was instrumental in bringing about the assassination of President [Ngo Dinh] Diem [of South Vietnam]. The allegations were determined to be without foundation.

An Inspector General report of investigation of allegations that the Agency was instrumental in bringing about the assassination of President [Rafael Leónidas] Trujillo [of the Dominican Republic]. The investigation disclosed quite extensive Agency involvement with the plotters.

An Inspector General report of investigation of allegations that the Agency conspired to assassinate Fidel Castro. The story first appeared in Drew Pearson's column and has since appeared in Jack Anderson's column. While the columns contained many factual errors, the allegations are basically true.

[—signature, name, and title deleted—]

CASTRO

The CIA's most elaborate and most notorious effort to eliminate a political leader was the attempt to assassinate Cuba's Fidel Castro.[2] It is noteworthy that despite all the movies and novels about professional CIA assassins, when the decision was made to kill Castro the agency did not seem to believe it had anyone suitable on staff. This led it to contract the job out to the criminal underworld. That decision led several years later to the public exposure of the whole operation, when the agency refused to intervene on the gangster's behalf in an unrelated criminal case.

Initially, the assassination plot was more secret than the plan to organize the Bay of Pigs invasion. Even the personnel at JMWAVE, the CIA's anti-Castro operations base in Florida, were not informed. In 1973, when DCI James Schlesinger ordered CIA employees to report on illegal operations, several sources sent in reports regarding this scheme and the solicitation of gangster Johnny Roselli, who was to arrange it. Among the unexpected twists: the "negotiations" with a mob boss led to a botched attempt to spy on comedian Dan Rowan, who would later find fame on television as one of the hosts of *Rowan & Martin's Laugh-In*. The following memorandum from the CIA's Office of Security is one of the more detailed reports on the operation from the "Family Jewels" file.

SUBJECT: Johnny Roselli

1. In August 1960, [Deputy Director for Plans] Mr. Richard M. Bissell approached Colonel Sheffield Edwards to determine if the Office of Security had assets that may assist in a sensitive mission requiring gangster-type action. The mission target was Fidel Castro.
2. Because of its extreme sensitivity, only a small group was made privy to the project. The DCI [Allen Dulles] was briefed and gave his approval. Colonel J. C. King, Chief, WH [Western Hemisphere] Division, was briefed, but all details were deliberately concealed from any of the JMWAVE officials. Certain TSD [Technical Services Division] and Communications personnel participated in the initial planning stages, but were not witting of the purpose of the mission.
3. Robert A. Maheu, a cleared source of the Office of Security [and a former FBI agent], was contacted, briefed generally on the project, and requested to ascertain if he could develop an entrée into the gangster elements as the first step toward accomplishing the desired goal.
4. Mr. Maheu advised that he had met one Johnny Roselli on several occasions while visiting Las Vegas. He only knew him casually through clients, but was given to understand that he was a high-ranking member of the "syndicate" and controlled all of the ice-making machines on the Strip. Maheu reasoned that, if Roselli was in fact a member of the clan, he undoubtedly had connections leading into the Cuban gambling interests.

5. Maheu was asked to approach Roselli, who knew Maheu as a personal relations executive handling domestic and foreign accounts, and tell him that he had recently been retained by a client who represented several international business firms which were suffering heavy financial losses in Cuba as a result of Castro's action. They were convinced that Castro's removal was the answer to their problem and were willing to pay a price of $150,000 for its successful accomplishment. It was to be made clear to Roselli that the United States Government was not, and should not, become aware of this operation.

6. The pitch was made to Roselli on 14 September 1960 at the Hilton Plaza Hotel, New York City. Mr. James O'Connell, Office of Security, was present during this meeting and was identified to Roselli as an employee of Maheu. O'Connell actively served as Roselli's contact until May 1962 at which time he phased out due to an overseas assignment. His [Roselli's] initial reaction was to avoid getting involved, but through Maheu's persuasion, he agreed to introduce him to a friend, Sam Gold, who knew the "Cuban crowd." Roselli made it clear he did not want any money for his part and believed Sam would feel the same way. Neither of these individuals were ever paid out of Agency funds.

7. During the week of 25 September, Maheu was introduced to Sam who was staying at the Fontainebleau Hotel, Miami Beach. It was several weeks after his meeting with Sam and Joe, who was identified to him as a courier operating between Havana and Miami, that he saw photographs of both of these individuals in the Sunday supplemental "Parade." They were identified as Momo Salvatore Giancana and Santos Trafficant, respectively. Both were on the list of the Attorney General's ten most-wanted men. The former was described as the Chicago chieftain of the Cosa Nostra and successor to Al Capone, and the latter, the Cosa Nostra boss of Cuban operations. Maheu called this office immediately upon ascertaining this information.

8. In discussing the possible methods of accomplishing this mission, Sam suggested that they not resort to firearms but, if he could be furnished some type of potent pill, that could be placed in Castro's food or drink, it would be a much more effective operation. Sam indicated that he had a prospective nominee in the person of Juan Orta, a Cuban official who had been receiving kick-back payments from the gambling interests, who still had access to Castro, and was in a financial bind.

9. TSD was requested to produce six pills of high lethal content.

10. Joe delivered the pills to Orta. After several weeks of reported attempts, Orta apparently got cold feet and asked out of the assignment. He suggested another candidate who made several attempts without success.

11. Joe then indicated that Dr. Anthony Verona, one of the principal officers in the Cuban Exile Junta, had become disaffected with the apparent ineffectual progress of the Junta and was willing to handle the mission through his own resources.

12. He [Verona] asked, as a prerequisite to the deal, that he be given $10,000 for organizational expenses and requested $1,000 worth of communications equipment.

13. Dr. Verona's potential was never fully exploited, as the project was canceled shortly after the Bay of Pigs episode. Verona was advised that the offer was withdrawn, and the pills were retrieved.

14. Of significant interest was an incident which involved a request levied by Sam upon Maheu.

  At the height of the project negotiations, Sam expressed concern about his girlfriend, Phyllis McGuire, who he learned was getting much attention from Dan Rowan while both were booked at a Las Vegas night club. Sam asked Maheu to put a bug in Rowan's room to determine the extent of his intimacy with Miss McGuire. The technician involved in the assignment was discovered in the process, arrested, and taken to the Sheriff's office for questioning. He called Maheu and informed him that he had been detained by the police. This call was made in the presence of the Sheriff's personnel.

Subsequently, the Department of Justice announced its intention to prosecute Maheu along with the technician. On 7 February 1962, the Director of Security briefed the Attorney General, Robert Kennedy, on the circumstances leading up to Maheu's involvement in the wiretap. At our request, prosecution was dropped.

15. In May 1962, Mr. William Harvey took over as Case Officer, and it is not known by this office whether Roselli was used operationally from that point on.

16. It was subsequently learned from the FBI that Roselli had been convicted on six counts involving illegal entry into the United States. Our records do not reflect the date of conviction, but it is believed to have been sometime during November 1967.

17. On 2 December 1968, Roselli, along with four other individuals, was convicted of conspiracy to cheat members of the Friars Club of $400,000 in a rigged gin rummy game.

18. Mr. Harvey reported to the Office of Security of his contacts with Roselli during November and December 1967 and January 1968. It was his belief that Johnny would not seek out the Agency for assistance in the deportation proceedings unless he actually faced deportation. Roselli expressed confidence that he would win an appeal.

19. On 17 November 1970, Maheu called James O'Connell, Roselli's first Case Officer, to advise that Maheu's attorney, Ed Morgan, had received a call from a Thomas Waddin, Roselli's lawyer, who stated that all avenues of appeal had been exhausted, and his client now faces deportation. Waddin indicated that, if someone did not intercede on Roselli's behalf, he would make a complete expose of his activities with the Agency.

20. On 18 November 1970, [DCI] Mr. Helms was briefed on the latest development in this case, and it was decided that the Agency would not in any way assist Roselli. Maheu was so advised of the Agency's position, and he was in complete agreement with out stand. He further advised that he was not concerned should Roselli decide to tell all.

21. Subsequently, Roselli or someone on his behalf furnished Jack Anderson details of the operation. Attached are two Anderson columns dealing with this matter.

22. The last known residence of Roselli was the Federal Penitentiary in Seattle, Washington.

As noted, the report came with two articles from *The Washington Post* by columnist Jack Anderson: "6 Attempts to Kill Castro Laid to CIA" (18 January 1971) and "Castro Stalker Worked for the CIA" (23 February 1971). It was through these articles, along with an earlier one by Drew Pearson, that news of the CIA's assassination activities first leaked to the public.

LUMUMBA

The Lumumba case is highly complex. In August 1960, at the same time the order to kill Castro was issued, a similar order was directed against Patrice Lumumba, the thirty-six-year-old prime minister of the Republic of the Congo, which had just gained its independence from Belgium on 30 June 1960. The highly fractious country was so ill-prepared for independence that it had a total of thirteen college graduates and its army was led almost entirely by Belgian officers. Within days of independence, Lumumba faced a rebellion by Congolese troops against their Belgian officers and a subsequent intervention by the Belgian army. Faced with suspicion from the West, he requested military assistance from the United Nations and made ill-considered suggestions that he might turn to the Soviet Union for further help. The Americans did not know at the time that the Soviets turned him down, if only because they lacked the logistical capability.

The CIA station in Leopoldville (later, Kinshasa), the capital of the Congo, had a total of three case officers, all of them hastily reassigned from elsewhere. Not having any particular knowledge of Africa, they relied on Belgian sources and a few French-speaking Congolese for their information. Like many in the U.S. government, including President Eisenhower, they saw Lumumba as incompetent, uncooperative, and a potential Communist or Communist dupe. The Leopoldville station sent the following cable to CIA headquarters on 18 August 1960.[3]

EMBASSY AND STATION BELIEVE CONGO EXPERIENCING CLASSIC COMMUNIST EFFORT TAKEOVER GOVERNMENT. MANY FORCES AT WORK HERE: SOVIETS ... COMMUNIST PARTY, ETC. ALTHOUGH DIFFICULT DETERMINE MAJOR INFLUENCING FACTORS TO PREDICT OUTCOME STRUGGLE FOR POWER, DECISIVE PERIOD NOT FAR OFF. WHETHER OR NOT LUMUMBA ACTUALLY COMMIE OR JUST PLAYING COMMIE GAME TO ASSIST HIS SOLIDIFYING POWER, ANTI-WEST FORCES RAPIDLY INCREASING POWER CONGO AND THERE MAY BE LITTLE TIME LEFT IN WHICH TAKE ACTION TO AVOID ANOTHER CUBA.

Subsequent cables authorized efforts to replace Lumumba with "pro-Western group." Washington preferred President Joseph Kasavubu, Lumumba's partner-rival in a coalition government, but Kasavubu was not sure he wanted to go as far as the some other Congolese politicians. A cable from the Leopoldville station followed on 24 August.

ANTI-LUMUMBA LEADERS APPROACHED KASAVUBU WITH PLAN ASSASSINATE LUMUMBA ... KASAVUBU REFUSED AGREE SAYING HE RELUCTANT RESORT VIOLENCE AND NO OTHER LEADER SUFFICIENT STATURE REPLACE LUMUMBA.

In Washington, the Special Group, a subcommittee of the National Security Council that dealt with covert operations, met on 25 August 1960 and "agreed that planning for the Congo would not necessarily rule out 'consideration' of any particular kind of activity which might contribute to getting rid of Lumumba." On 26 August, DCI Allen Dulles sent a cable to the Leopoldville station. To underline his seriousness, he issued the cable in his own name, rather than the more common "Director," and referred to "high quarters," indicating the approval of the president.

IN HIGH QUARTERS HERE IT IS THE CLEAR-CUT CONCLUSION THAT IF [LUMUMBA] CONTINUES TO HOLD HIGH OFFICE, THE INEVITABLE RESULT

WILL AT BEST BE CHAOS AND AT WORST PAVE THE WAY TO COMMUNIST TAKEOVER OF THE CONGO WITH DISASTROUS CONSEQUENCES FOR THE PRESTIGE OF THE UN AND FOR THE INTERESTS OF THE FREE WORLD GENERALLY. CONSEQUENTLY WE CONCLUDE THAT HIS REMOVAL MUST BE AN URGENT AND PRIME OBJECTIVE AND THAT UNDER EXISTING CONDITIONS THIS SHOULD BE A HIGH PRIORITY OF OUR COVERT ACTION.

CIA headquarters communicated with Leopoldville Chief of Station Larry Devlin through two channels. In the regular CIA channel, messages were distributed to the ambassador as well as to the CIA Chief of Station. In the PROP channel, messages went only to the Chief of Station. The regular channel carried messages noting that Lumumba was a growing problem and that something would have to be done about him because the ambassador would expect the agency to be talking about him. Messages through the secret PROP channel discussed assassination plans and advised Devlin not to pay attention to instructions related to the matter that appeared only in the regular channel.

At the beginning of September, the CIA had agreed to grant "financial support" to President Kasavubu, and four days later Kasavubu dismissed Lumumba as prime minister, citing the latter's inability to suppress a secession movement in the mineral-rich Katanga province. Lumumba responded by dismissing Kasavubu as president; Parliament nullified both actions. In mid-September, Kasavubu was deposed by Colonel Joseph-Désiré Mobutu, a former noncommissioned officer and former Lumumbist who had been made chief of the general staff. (He would later become President Mobutu Sese Seko). Mobutu declared Kasavubu, Lumumba, and all politicians "neutralized" for a period of time. In October, the CIA decided to give backing to "anti-Lumumba resistance groups" and then, in November, specifically to Mobutu.

The operation regarding Lumumba, however, was to continue. As it turned out, Chief of Station Devlin was opposed to the notion of assassinating the prime minister, both for moral reasons and because he considered it unnecessary. Considering the likely career consequences, however, he did not say so openly. In late September 1960, Dr. Sidney Gottlieb, traveling as Joseph Braun or "Joe from Paris," arrived in Leopoldville to deliver the poison for the job. Devlin regularly reported on the progress of his preparations but frequently stressing the difficulty of gaining access to Lumumba. In effect, it appears Devlin simply dawdled until the poison went bad.

The CIA then proposed sending a contract agent or a senior case officer to assassinate Lumumba. It appeared that the agency was considering making this a full-time position for the contract agent.[4]

CONSIDERING DISPATCHING THIRD COUNTRY NATIONAL OPERATIVE WHO, WHEN HE ARRIVES, SHOULD BE ASSESSED BY YOU OVER PERIOD TO SEE WHETHER HE MIGHT PLAY ACTIVE OR CUTOUT ROLE ON FULL TIME BASIS. IF YOU CONCLUDE HE SUITABLE AND BEARING IN MIND EXTRA HEAVY LOAD THIS PLACES ON YOU, WOULD EXPECT DISPATCH [TEMPORARY DUTY] SENIOR CASE OFFICER RUN THIS OP ... UNDER YOUR DIRECTION.

Devlin responded that, in view of his own multiple responsibilities, sending a senior case officer to handle the job was an excellent idea. He also again noted the difficulties of gaining access.

TARGET HAS NOT LEFT BUILDING IN SEVERAL WEEKS. HOUSE GUARDED DAY AND NIGHT BY CONGOLESE AND UN TROOPS.... CONGOLESE TROOPS ARE THERE TO PREVENT TARGET'S ESCAPE AND TO ARREST HIM IF HE ATTEMPTS. UN TROOPS THERE TO PREVENT STORMING OF PALACE BY CONGOLESE. CONCENTRIC RINGS OF DEFENSE MAKE ESTABLISHMENT OF OBSERVATION POST IMPOSSIBLE. ATTEMPTING GET COVERAGE OF ANY MOVEMENT INTO OR OUT OF HOUSE BY CONGOLESE.... TARGET HAS DISMISSED MOST OF SERVANTS SO ENTRY THIS MEANS SEEMS REMOTE.

The senior case officer also claimed he was opposed to the idea of assassination, but he said he would do what he could to "neutralize" him as a political factor. This involved luring him out of his house arrest and into the hands of the Congolese authorities. He appeared to Devlin to be proceeding with preparations for the assassination despite a lack of enthusiasm. The agency then sent the "third-country national" (code name: QJ/WIN) to carry out the task, although he was not informed of the exact nature of the task until he arrived. By that time, however, developments were about to follow a different trajectory.

On 27 November, Lumumba escaped from the protective cordon placed around his offices. In December, Moïse Tshombe, another former Lumumbist, declared the independence of Katanga with the encouragement of Belgium. Lumumba was captured by Mobutu's forces as he tried to make his way to Katanga, in large part because he kept stopping en route and giving public speeches. He was turned over to the Katangan forces. He was tortured and then executed on 17 January 1961 by Belgian and Katangan soldiers.[5]

The "Family Jewels" file has only one further record regarding Lumumba.

14 February 1972

MEMORANDUM FOR THE RECORD:

In November 1962 Mr. [—] advised [Inspector General] Mr. Lyman Kirkpatrick that he had, at one time, been directed by [Deputy Director for Plans] Mr. Richard Bissell to assume responsibility for a project involving the assassination of Patrice Lumumba, then Premier, Republic of Congo. According to [—], poison was to have been the vehicle as he made reference to having been instructed to see Dr. Sidney Gottlieb in order to procure the appropriate vehicle.

The file contains no explanation of why the Inspector General learned of the operation only two years after the fact, if this is indeed the first he heard of it. Neither does it say why it was formally entered into the record ten years after that, still fifteen months before Schlesinger's call for incriminating documents, or (in its redacted form, at least) who entered it.

After the death of Lumumba, civil war continued in the Congo for the next several years, drawing in the UN forces. This was followed by three decades of corrupt and brutal dictatorship under Mobutu (when the country was called Zaïre) and then another civil war, which drew in the armies of several neighboring countries. In 2006, the Congo held its first free election since 1960. This chain of events was not necessarily the fault of the CIA. Nonetheless, the assassination of Lumumba, which the CIA did seek to bring about, was a rallying cry for decades.

TRUJILLO

The Trujillo case, as noted above, involved "quite extensive Agency involvement with the plotters." By 1960, the dictator Rafael Leónidas Trujillo had been running the Dominican Republic for three decades.[6] His regime was not a threat to the United States, nor was it allied to the enemies of the United States, but Trujillo was considered a brutal and increasingly arbitrary dictator. The Eisenhower and Kennedy administrations feared that the regime's continued existence would eventually lead to a Cuban-style revolution, and both supported the activities of democratic Dominican dissidents who hoped to overthrow the regime.

The Eisenhower administration considered contingency plans regarding the Dominican Republic as early as February 1960. That spring some dissidents made a request for twelve sterile (that is, untraceable) rifles with telescopic sights and 500 rounds of ammunition; they did not get them. In May 1960, the United States withdrew most of its diplomats from the country, including the CIA Chief of Station. This resulted in the anomalous circumstance in which the Consul General, Henry Dearborn, became both acting ambassador and de facto CIA Chief of Station.

Diplomatic efforts were made to convince Trujillo to resign the presidency. The dissidents, however, seemingly convinced Dearborn that Trujillo had some outsized ambitions and capabilities. On 10 October 1960, his report to the State Department included the following:

> One further point which I should probably not even make. From a purely practical standpoint, it will be best for us, for the OAS [Organization of American States], and for the Dominican Republic if the Dominicans put an end to Trujillo before he leaves this island. If he has his millions and is a free agent, he will devote his life from exile to preventing stable government in the D.R., to overturning democratic governments and establishing dictatorships in the Caribbean, and to assassinating his enemies. If I were a Dominican, which thank heaven I am not, I would favor destroying Trujillo as being the first necessary step in the salvation of my country and I would regard this, in fact, as my Christian duty. If you recall Dracula, you will remember it was necessary to drive a stake through his heart to prevent a continuation of his crimes. I believe sudden death would be more humane than the solution of the Nuncio who once told me he thought he should pray that Trujillo would have a long and lingering illness.

Dearborn was immediately instructed to stop using normal State Department communications to convey such messages as they were distributed to nineteen different offices. A week earlier, however, on 3 October, the CIA had already drafted a tentative memo titled "Plans of the Dominican Internal Opposition and Dominican Desk for Overthrow of the Trujillo Government." On 12 January 1961, in the closing days of the Eisenhower administration, the minutes of the Special Group, which approved covert operations, included the following:

> Mr. Merchant explained the feeling of the Department of State that limited supplies of small arms and other material should be made available for dissidents inside the Dominican Republic. Mr. Parrott said that we believe this can be managed securely by CIA, and that the plan would call for final transportation into the country being provided by the dissidents themselves. The Group approved the project.

The Special Group minutes do not specifically refer to assassination, although it is known that at least DCI Allen Dulles was aware of the dissidents' intention to assassinate the Dominican president. In February, Dulles and Deputy Director for Plans Richard Bissell informed the new Kennedy administration's Special Group of their predecessors' decisions, including "a list of significant projects" that the CIA planned to continue. The only indication in the minutes that the Dominican Republic was mentioned came in National Security Adviser McGeorge Bundy's request for a memorandum "on the subject of what plans can be made for a successor government to Trujillo." The word "assassination" does not appear in the minutes, but later memoranda mention the provision of arms. A memorandum from Bissell to Bundy on 17 February 1961 anticipates an imminent clash between Trujillo and the opposition "which will end either with the liquidation of Trujillo or with a complete roll up of the internal opposition." No objections were recorded.

In the early months of 1961, CIA officials discussed various possible assassination methods with Dominican dissidents in New York. In March 1961, three .38-caliber pistols were sent to the CIA station in the Dominican Republic at Dearborn's request and turned over to the dissidents. In April, three .30-caliber carbines already located in the consulate were passed to the dissidents with the approval of the CIA. Dearborn was instructed not to inform the State Department.

In February and again in March, the dissidents requested five M3 .45-caliber, or comparable, machine guns and 1,500 rounds of ammunition. This was actually the first request to be explicitly tied to a Trujillo assassination plan, although they were for the assailants' "personal protection," while a silent weapon would be used for the actual deed. By this time, however, CIA headquarters was having qualms. They responded that the time was not right and suggested that the "mere disposal of Trujillo might create more problems than solutions." Moreover, the dissidents did not have the capacity to receive the arms directly and the CIA did not want to use U.S facilities anymore. Nevertheless, in April Bissell approved a waiver of the rule forbidding the use of the diplomatic pouch to carry firearms.

> A determination has been made that the issuance of this equipment to the action group [that is, the dissidents] is desirable if for no other reason than to assure this important group's continued cooperation with and confidence in this Agency's determination to live up to its earlier commitments to the group. These commitments took the form of advising the group in January 1961 that we would provide limited arms and assistance to them provided they develop the capability to receive it. Operational circumstances have prevented this group from developing the assets capable of receiving the above equipment through normal clandestine channels such as air drops or sea infiltration.

In April 1961, however, came the disastrous Bay of Pigs operation against Cuba. After that, both the State Department and the CIA shifted gears and sought to dissuade the dissidents from any precipitous action, especially one that would result in a power vacuum, in view of the "unsettled conditions in Caribbean area." Dearborn was instructed not to pass the machine guns to the dissidents. They responded that this was their affair and they were not taking instructions from the United States. They continued to press for the machine guns but vowed to continue with what they had if necessary. Dearborn advised headquarters that since the CIA was already implicated it may as well go ahead and give them the guns. There followed a stream of reports from Santo Domingo (in those days called Ciudad Trujillo) predicting Trujillo's imminent assassination. Bissell recommended to Dulles that the machine guns be turned over, again in view of the agency's "considerable investment in this dissident group and its plans."

This sentiment was not universal in the CIA, however. On 3 May 1961, the Deputy Chief of the Western Hemisphere Division of the Directorate of Plans met with Adolph Berle, who was at the time Chairman of the Inter-Agency Task Force on Latin America. The Deputy Chief spoke initially of dissident plans to "overthrow" Trujillo. In a memorandum of conversation, Berle recorded:

> On cross examination it developed that the real plan was to assassinate Trujillo and they wanted guns for that purpose. [The CIA officer] wanted to know what the policy should be.
>
> I told him I could not care less for Trujillo and that this was the general sentiment. But we did not wish to have anything to do with any assassination plots anywhere, any time. [The CIA officer] said he felt the same way.

The Special Group met again on 18 May:

> Cabell [Deputy DCI] noted that the internal dissidents were pressing for the release to them of certain small arms now in U.S. hands in the Dominican Republic. He inquired whether the feeling of the Group remained that these arms should not be passed. The members showed no inclination to take a contrary position at this time.

At the same time, Washington continued to be concerned about the possibility of a Cuban-style revolution in other countries of the region, including the Dominican Republic. Efforts to overthrow the Dominican government were still a possibility—once arrangements for a new government could be made—and contingency plans for military intervention were to be drawn up, but not necessarily for assassination. The following record comes from a meeting of the National Security Council held on 5 May 1961. Note that no assassination plot is likely to be "multilateral."

> Agreed that the Task Force on Cuba would prepare promptly both emergency and long-range plans for anti-communist intervention in the event of crises in Haiti or the Dominican Republic. Noted the President's view that the United States should not initiate the overthrow of Trujillo before we knew what government would succeed him, and that any action against Trujillo should be multilateral.

A memorandum dated 13 May 1961 and addressed to White House staff member Richard Goodwin is the first clear indication that the White House had been made fully aware of the situation. Goodwin circled the paragraph and underlined the word "neutralize."

> CIA has had in the direct custody of its Station in Ciudad Trujillo [Santo Domingo], a very limited supply of weapons and grenades. In response to the urgent requests from the internal opposition leaders for personal defense weapons attendant to their projected efforts to neutralize TRUJILLO, three (3) 38 Cal revolvers and three

(3) carbines with accompanying ammunition have been passed by secure means to the opposition. The recipients have repeatedly requested additional armed support.

A cable sent to Dearborn with the approval of the president on 29 May 1961 tried in essence to have it both ways. The U.S. government was intrigued by the notion of being associated with the removal of a hated dictator but did not want to be tied to an assassination.

[W]e must not run the risk of U.S. association with political assassination, since U.S. as matter of general policy cannot condone assassination. This last principal is overriding and must prevail in doubtful situation. . . . Continue to inform dissident elements of U.S. support for their position. . . . [Regarding the refusal to give them the machine guns,] [t]ell them that this is because of our suspicion that method of transfer may be unsafe. In actual fact, we feel that the transfer of arms would serve very little purpose and expose the United States to great danger of association with assassination attempt.

A CIA officer in the Dominican Republic responded that it was too late to avoid the association.

HQ aware extent to which US government already associated with assassination. If we are to at least cover up tracks, CIA personnel directly involved in assassination preparation must be immediately withdrawn.

On 30 May 1961, Trujillo was assassinated by members of the dissident action group using handguns and shotguns. Within days, Dearborn and all CIA personnel who had had contact with the dissidents were withdrawn from the Dominican Republic. The CIA station was ordered to destroy all records of contact and related matters except contingency plans and the 29 May cable to Dearborn.

TORRIJOS

Not all allegations of CIA plots to assassinate leaders turned out to be true, however, even some that originated with sources who ought to know. In 1973, John W. Dean III suggested a plot within the White House to assassinate Omar Torrijos, the populist military ruler of Panama. Dean was a former White House counsel who had been a key witness in testifying against the Nixon administration in the Congressional investigation of the Watergate affair. The statement created a commotion in Panama, the State Department, the National Security Council, and the CIA. The following confidential telegram (designated No. 112189) arrived on 11 June 1973 at the State Department from the U.S. embassy in Panama. (Recall that E. Howard Hunt, a former CIA official, was a member of the White House "plumbers" who had helped organize the Watergate break-in on behalf of the Committee to Re-elect the President.)

SUBJECT: ALLEGATIONS MADE BY JOHN DEAN TO NEWSWEEK MAGAZINE

THE FOLLOWING IS EXCERPTED FROM A FRONT PAGE ARTICLE ON TODAY'S NEW YORK TIMES WHICH REPORTS ON ALLEGATIONS MADE BY JOHN DEAN TO NEWSWEEK MAGAZINE.

"SOME 'LOW-LEVEL' WHITE HOUSE OFFICIALS CONSIDERED ASSASSINAT-
ING PANAMA'S RULER OMAR TORRIJOS, BECAUSE THEY SUSPECTED THE
INVOLVEMENT OF HIGH PANAMANIAN AUTHORITIES IN HEROIN TRAFFIC
AND BECAUSE THEY FELT THE GOVERNMENT HAD BEEN UNCOOPERATIVE
ABOUT RENEGOTIATING THE PANAMA CANAL TREATY. E. HOWARD HUNT
JR., A LEADER OF THE WATERGATE BURGLARS, HAD A TEAM IN MEXICO
"BEFORE THE MISSION WAS ABORTED." NEWSWEEK SAID." RUSH

This prompted an inquiry from the National Security Council to the Western
Hemisphere (WH) Division of the Central Intelligence Agency's Directorate of
Operations. (At the time, Henry Kissinger was both National Security Adviser
and Secretary of State.)

20 June 1973

MEMORANDUM FOR THE RECORD

SUBJECT: John Dean Allegations to <u>Newsweek</u> Magazine

1. Mr. William Jorden, the Latin American referent on Dr. Kissinger's Staff, called
   today in reference to State cable No. 112189, dated 11 June (attached). He said
   that he had specific reference to paragraph 2 of that cable and would like to
   have "everything and anything we know" on that subject in the Agency.
2. The undersigned indicated to Mr. Jorden that he had checked out the allegation that some low level White House officials had considered assassinating
   Torrijos when the story first appeared in <u>Newsweek</u> and, despite checking
   outside WH Division also, could find no one in the Agency who could recol-
   lect or find anything relating to such a plan on the part of any portion of U.S.
   officialdom. I told him that I felt sure that nothing of this nature had come to
   WH Division's attention because for the period in question I had been Deputy
   Chief of WH Division and had heard nothing about any such plan. Mr. Jorden
   asked if the Agency knew anything about Howard Hunt having had a team
   in Mexico "before the mission was aborted" and I indicated that as far as I
   knew, the Agency had no information on Hunt being in Mexico on such a
   mission. I also indicated, however, they could have been and the Agency
   might well not know it simply because he could have used an alias and he is
   an American citizen, which is outside the Agency's province and really the
   FBI's business. I suggested that it might be best if he checked the FBI on that
   particular angle. Subsequently I checked with Mr. William Broe, the IG [In-
   spector General], and Mr. John Horton, recently returned [—] and both indicated that they had not run across any information concerning this latter
   allegation of Hunt and a team in Mexico on a mission related to Panama.
3. It was apparent that Mr. Jorden was under some pressure to refute to refute
   these allegations and was casting about in all directions to make as certain of
   his ground as he possibly could before he tried to do so.

[—signature and name deleted—]
Deputy Chief
Western Hemisphere Division

DIEM

Allegations of assassination arose with regard to two key controversies involving the war in Vietnam. The first concerned the coup d'état against South

Vietnam's leader, Ngo Dinh Diem, in 1963, during which the premier was assassinated.[7] The second was Operation Phoenix, which has been depicted as an assassination campaign against local civilian organizers of the Viet Cong throughout South Vietnam. The agency has regularly denied responsibility for the coup and assassination of Diem, and it has said that the Phoenix program has been misinterpreted.

In 1963, the U.S. government was concerned that South Vietnamese leader Ngo Dinh Diem was destabilizing his own country and undermining the war effort against the Viet Cong guerrillas, which were supported by the government of North Vietnam. In part, this was a result of growing tensions between the Catholic Diem and Buddhist protesters, some of whom had engaged in self-immolation. American officials were particularly concerned about the growing power of Diem's tyrannical and unpopular brother and sister-in-law, Ngo Dinh Nhu and Madame Nhu.[8]

Although the CIA did not stage a coup against the Diem regime, it was aware that a coup was coming. The South Vietnamese military had previously informed CIA operative Lucien Conein of their intention to overthrow Diem, and Conein reported that to headquarters. President John F. Kennedy received a briefing on this the next day from DCI John McCone.

DCI BRIEFING   9 July 1963

SOUTH VIETNAM

    I. South Vietnam continues restive over the unresolved Buddhist issue and a coup attempt is increasingly likely.

    II. South Vietnam's arm commander, Major General Tran Van Don, told a CIA officer on 8 July that there are plans by the military to overthrow President Diem.

        A. Don did not specify the timing of such action, but hinted that it might be within ten days. He said all but one or two general officers were agreed on the plan.

        B. The military is the key to any successful move to oust the government, and Don is a respected officer. That makes this report the most substantial of a recent series on reported coup plots.

        C. Among such reports are a plot centered around Diem's former security chief, Tran Kim Tuyen, alleged to have set a target date of 10 July and to be cooperating with some military elements.[9]

    III. Some of these reports may represent government efforts to smoke out disaffected elements, but Diem's handling of the Buddhist issue has caused serious stresses within the administration in both civilian and military circles.

        A. General Don claims that the military feels it must act to prevent the Viet Cong from capitalizing on the continuing Buddhist crisis.

    IV. Buddhist leaders are skeptical that Diem will honor the concessions he made to them in the 16 June agreement.

        A. They say they are laying plans for further demonstrations and sacrificial suicides if necessary. Extremist Buddhists appear determined to keep up agitation until the government is brought down.

V. Meanwhile, President Diem, presumably reinforced by the known opposition of his brother Nhu to any appeasement of the Buddhists, is taking the line that the religious issue has been resolved, and that the Buddhists now are merely acting as tools of his foreign and domestic enemies—including the Viet Cong.

    A. Diem recently stated privately that however reasonable the Buddhist religious demands might be, concessions to them would only encourage further demands.

    B. Government actions continue to suggest that Diem is using the 16 June agreement to stall until a propitious time to crack down on the chief Buddhist agitators.

VI. The sudden trial of prisoners accused of involvement in the 1960 coup attempt appears designed in part to warn disaffected elements—and the US—against thinking about coups.

    A. While the US Embassy has found no evidence of deliberate government instigation of the police assault against US reporters, Diem is known to feel that US reporting on the Buddhists and on South Vietnam in general has encouraged anti-regime activity.

VII. There continues to be little sign that the Viet Cong have been able to exploit the Buddhist issue effectively. The crisis has as yet had no appreciable effect on the conduct of the war.

President John F. Kennedy eventually decided not to interfere to prevent the coup. This is reflected in a cable, dated 29 August 1963, from Secretary of State Dean Rusk to the U.S. ambassador in Saigon, Henry Cabot Lodge, and the commander of the American military advisory group, General Paul Harkins.

TOP SECRET EYES ONLY FOR AMBASSADOR LODGE & GENERAL HARKINS

1. Highest level meeting noon today reviewed your [Cable No.] 375 and reaffirmed basic course. Specific decisions follow:

2. In response to your recommendation, General Harkins is hereby authorized to repeat to such [South Vietnamese] Generals as you indicate the messages previously transmitted by CAS officers. He should stress that the USG [United States Government] supports the movement to eliminate the Nhus from the government, but that before arriving at specific understandings with the Generals, General Harkins must know who are involved, resources available to them and overall plan for coup. The USG will support a coup which has good chance of succeeding but plans no direct involvement of U.S. Armed Forces. Harkins should state that he is prepared to establish liaison with the coup planners and to review plans, but will not engage directly in joint coup planning.

3. Question of last approach to Diem remains undecided and separate personal message from Secretary to you develops our concerns and asks your comment.

4. On movement of U.S. forces, we do not expect to make any announcement or leak at present and believe that any later decision to publicize such movements should be closely connected to developing events on your side. We cannot of course prevent unauthorized disclosures or speculation, but we will in any event knock down any reports of evacuation.

5. You are hereby authorized to announce suspension of aid through Diem Government at a time and under conditions of your choice. In deciding upon

use of this authority, you should consider importance of timing and managing announcement so as to minimize appearance of collusion with the Generals, and also to minimize danger of unpredictable and disruptive reaction by existing government. We also assume that you will not in fact use this authority unless you think it essential, and we see it as possible that Harkins' approach and increasing process of cooperation may provide assurance of Generals' desire. Our own view is that it will be best to hold this authority for use in close conjunction with the coup, and not for present encouragement of Generals, but decision is yours.

END

RUSK

NOTE: Passed to the White House, OSD [Office of the Secretary of Defense], CIA with special captions.

Sensing what was afoot, Diem's brother, Ngo Dinh Nhu, planted stories about the CIA in the pro-government press in South Vietnam. These were then picked up by the U.S. press. Nhu revealed the name of the Saigon Chief of Station, John Richardson; claimed that the CIA station was trying to undermine the embassy; and generally blamed CIA activities for the adverse turn in political trends. In response, DCI McCone prepared this (typically huffy) CIA briefing for President Kennedy on the agency's role in South Vietnam.

8 October 1963 DRAFT

At your Wednesday [9 October] press conference you will undoubtedly be questioned about CIA's role in South Viet Nam. This as you know has been the subject of countless erroneous and misleading news articles and editorials, the most violent of which have been introduced into the Congressional Record with equally violent speeches condemning CIA as "irresponsible," and winding up with a demand for a Joint Watchdog Committee.

The principal accusations are:

1. CIA makes policy independent of State Department.
2. CIA's estimates and reports on South Viet Nam have been erroneous and many have been willfully withheld from our Ambassador and from U.S. policy makers.
3. CIA had undertaken activities beyond its area of competence, in secrecy and in contradiction of the desires of the Ambassador.
4. CIA is in violent disagreement with the Embassy, the military and other United States agencies in South Viet Nam.

As you know the facts contradict these and a variety of other equally irresponsible statements made in the press or on the Floor of the Congress, the details of which I will not burden you with.

The facts are:

1. CIA does not make policy nor do we express ourselves on policy except to the extent that I do personally as a member of your Executive Committee.
2. CIA estimates and reports on South Viet Nam have been consistently correct. They have reflected the autocratic character of the Diem regime for the past 9 years. They have reflected the tarnishing of the regime's image in the eyes of the people of South Viet Nam and in world opinion for the past 18 months. They have reported on countless coup d'etat rumors and evaluated them as

improbable of coming off because of a lack of unanimity among the military. They have reported favorable progress in the war, at the same time pointing out trouble spots such as the [Mekong] Delta [region].

In fact CIA's reporting supports the logic of your decisions reached following the McNamara-Taylor mission.[10] I might add that [—] who has been under such criticism recently has in my opinion been consistently right in his observations.

3. CIA has undertaken no activities of any nature which have not been approved by the Ambassador and agreed to by the Country Team. Moreover CIA's activities, together with those of the military, USOM, AID, USIA, etc. are held under review by the Southeast Asian Task Force and the special Interdepartmental Counter Insurgency Group, hence there seems no foundation for the allegations that CIA operates without control.[11]

4. Prior to about the first of September there had been no reports of conflicts between the CIA station in Saigon and the Embassy, the military or other agencies. Quite to the contrary, reports of a proper working relationship have been received by me from the Ambassador, from the innumerable missions which have gone to South Viet Nam, i.e. General Wheeler, Gen. Krulak, Mr. Forrestal, Adm. Felt, and indeed, my own observations on my visit there. Additionally a senior CIA officer and our Saigon Station Chief have attended every one of Secretary McNamara's Honolulu meetings and at those meetings the station's activities have been reviewed and approved subject to modifications agreed to at the meeting.

There is no doubt that the criticism which has found its way into hundreds of news articles and editorials is seriously eroding the spirit of this organization which I have now spent two years trying to rekindle. I suggest in view of this it might be timely for you to put the entire matter in focus at your press conference and, if you do so, I believe the problem will disappear.

Through the summer and autumn of 1963, Kennedy and other members of the administration wavered in regard to the coup, proposing alternatives to force Diem to carry out reforms, for instance, and then returning to the coup idea when efforts failed. Members of the National Security Council once again had second thoughts in late October, after hearing a CIA assessment that the number of troops deemed likely to support the coup and the number of troops deemed loyal to Diem were roughly equal. Representatives of the CIA at the meeting were DCI John McCone; Richard Helms, then the Deputy Director for Plans; and William Colby, then the Chief of the Far East Division.

MEMORANDUM OF CONFERENCE WITH THE PRESIDENT

October 29, 1963, 4:20 PM, Subject: Vietnam

Others present: Vice President, Secretary Rusk, Secretary McNamara, Attorney General, Director McCone, General Taylor, General Krulak, Under Secretary Harriman, Mr. Alexis Johnson, Mr. William Bundy, Mr. Helms, Mr. Mendenhall (State), Mr. Colby (CIA), Mr. Bundy, Mr. Forrestal, Mr. Bromley Smith

Mr. Colby of CIA gave the current status of coup forces. He estimated that the pro-Diem and anti-Diem forces were about even, approximately 9800 on each side, with 18,000 listed as neutral. The briefing was illustrated with a CIA order of battle map.

The President asked what Diem had learned from the attempted coup in 1960. Mr. Colby replied that Diem now had much better communications with military forces deployed outside Saigon. He could thus call into Saigon rapidly loyal forces to oppose rebel forces in the city. The 1960 coup was frustrated when forces outside Saigon remained loyal, moved into Saigon, and defeated the forces which had surrounded the palace.

Mr. McGeorge Bundy suggested that the assessment just given the group be sent to Saigon to see if our officials there agreed with it. He asked whether Ambassador Lodge should return to Washington now and mentioned that some of those present felt he should stay in Saigon.

Secretary Rusk said we must assume that Diem and Nhu have heard rumors about a coup. The question for us is whether we think there is enough prospect of a successful coup to make the decision to keep silent. Should we let the coup generals know that a protracted civil war must not be the result of their efforts to overthrow Diem? Should we tell them we would support them only if the coup is short and bloodless? If fighting between the two sides takes place, each will ask for our help. If we support Diem, then we will disrupt the war effort because we will be acting against those generals who are now fighting the war against the Viet Cong. If we support the rebel generals, then we will have to guarantee that they are successful in overthrowing the Diem government.

Ambassador Lodge was asked by General Don to stick to his departure plan so Lodge should go as he had planned. We now have little information. We need 48, not 4, hours advance notice of any coup. We should put or faith in no one, including General Don. We should caution the generals that they must have the situation in hand before they launch a coup. We should tell them we have no interest whatsoever in a long civil war in South Vietnam.

The President agreed that Ambassador Lodge should leave Saigon for Washington as planned. He thought the rebel generals should talk to General Harkins. He said the odds were against a coup. He suggested that General Harkins be put in charge of our mission in Saigon when Ambassador Lodge leaves. If Ambassador Lodge delays his departure, Diem will know we are aware of coup plans. It would be good to have Ambassador Lodge out of the country when a coup takes place.

Regarding the estimate that the pro- and anti-Diem forces are evenly balanced, the President commented that it always looks this way until the coup actually begins. Then support for the coup is forthcoming, as was apparent, for example, in Korea.

General Taylor cautioned against looking at the Vietnam situation as if it were a football game. He said a few key people are crucial to the success of the coup and are more important than total numbers.

The President asked that we try to find out who these key people are.

Secretary McNamara asked who of our officials in Saigon are in charge of the coup planning. He suggested that the Deputy Chief of Mission, Truehart, the Acting Chief of CIA, [—], and General Harkins form a group which would (a) jointly decide on what our agent Conein would say and do, and (b) hear all of Conein's reports. If any of these three disagree, a report would be sent back to Washington at once. General Harkins may not know what the Embassy and CIA are now doing. Truehart should head the Vietnamese country team until the coup was initiated. At that time, General Harkins would take over with Truehart becoming his political adviser.

Director McCone did not agree that a troika should be set up in Saigon. He said it would be better for the CIA officer to take direction rather than participate in a decision-making group.

The Attorney General, acknowledging that he had not seen all of the reports, said that in his opinion the present situation makes no sense to him on the face of it. The situation in Vietnam is not comparable to that in Iraq or in a South American country where a coup could be brought off promptly. The situation now is no different than that of four months ago when the generals were not able to organize a coup. To support a coup would be putting the future of Vietnam and in fact all of Southeast Asia in the hands of one man not now known to us. Diem will not run from a fight or quit under pressure. A failure of a coup risks so much. The reports we have are very thin and the information about the assets which the rebel generals have at their command is limited. We have a right to know what the rebel generals are planning. We can't go half way. If the coup fails, Diem will throw us out. If we send out the draft cable as it stands, it will appear that we are in favor of a coup and only want more information. "My view is the minority view."

Secretary Rusk replied that if we say we are not for a coup, then the coup-minded military leaders will turn against us and the war effort will drop off rapidly.

General Taylor said he agreed with the Attorney General. When pressed by the President, General Taylor said that even a successful coup would slow down the war effort because the new central government would be inexperienced. In addition, all of the provincial chiefs appointed by Diem would probably be replaced by a new government.

Director McCone said he agreed with General Taylor. The failure of a coup would be a disaster and a successful coup would have a harmful effect on the war effort.

The President asked General Taylor why all the province chiefs would be replaced. He replied that as Diem appointees they would be loyal to Diem, and, therefore, not trusted by the rebel generals who had overthrown Diem.

Secretary Rusk said the important question was whether the rebel generals could achieve quick success. He felt that in the long run, if the Diem government continued, the war effort would go down hill.

Mr. Harriman said it was clear that in Vietnam there was less and less enthusiasm for Diem. We cannot predict that the rebel generals can overthrow the Diem government, but Diem cannot carry the country to victory over the Viet Cong. With the passage of time, our objectives in Vietnam will become more and more difficult to achieve with Diem in control.

The President said it appears that the pro- and anti-Diem military forces are about equal. If this is so, any attempt to engineer a coup is silly. If Lodge agrees with this point of view, then we should instruct him to discourage a coup.

Mr. McGeorge Bundy said the most unfortunate development would be a three-day civil war in Saigon. The time remaining for us to instruct Lodge is very short. If a military plane were sent to pick up Lodge, the Ambassador could stay longer in Vietnam during the uncertain days immediately ahead.

Secretary McNamara thought that we ought to leave it up to Ambassador Lodge when he would leave Saigon for Washington. In commenting on the draft cable, he said he thought Lodge would read it as a change of signals. Lodge now believes that he is not to thwart a coup. The draft instructs him to call in Harkins, which would be difficult to do in view of the fact that Lodge is not now keeping General Harkins informed of developments. The Ambassador should be given an option to delay his return if he wishes.

The President asked what were Lodge's existing instructions. In reply, Secretary Rusk read a paragraph from the October 5 telegram.

The President agreed to ask Lodge what he thought he ought to do about returning to Washington. Mr. McGeorge Bundy said the working group would rewrite the draft cable.

Bromley Smith

It proved too late for second thoughts. The coup was carried out on 1 November 1963, and proved successful. On the day of the coup, the CIA's Lucien Conein was summoned to the Joint General Staff Headquarters of the South Vietnamese military. When he went, he brought with him $42,000 in cash. (By some estimates it was closer to $70,000.) It appears that no record was left concerning exactly how the money was used. Years later, a retired CIA official commented to William Colby:

> [A]s you well know, when Lou Conein received his summons to report to the Joint General Staff Headquarters on 1 November 1963 a large amount of cash went with him. My impression is that the accounting for this and its use has never been very frank or complete.[12]

The Vietnamese generals behind the coup had also suggested to their CIA contact their intention to assassinate Diem in the process of the coup. The U.S. government did not approve of this, but neither did it do anything to prevent it. Conein feared that too much moralizing would simply cut off his access to inside information without preventing the outcome. Nevertheless, a case officer did warn Diem that it was coming. Diem was able to escape during the coup, but he turned himself over to the military high command afterward in return for a promise of safe conduct. He was never seen alive again.

OPERATION PHOENIX

The second matter regarding Vietnam was Operation Phoenix, technically not a CIA operation but a program of the South Vietnamese government. It was also known by its Vietnamese name, Phung Hoang. William Colby, later the Director of Central Intelligence, ran this program from 1968 to 1971, while officially detached from the CIA, and he was the one who revealed its existence to the public during Congressional testimony in 1971. The purpose of the program was to identify members of the Viet Cong and to classify them as local leaders, holders of other responsible positions, or just rank-and-file members. That information was then shared with the South Vietnamese army, police, and government at various levels. The Phoenix program had no armed units of its own.

Collectively, Colby termed the subjects of his program as the Viet Cong Infrastructure (VCI) and estimated their number at 70,000. In this way, he figured, action—whether surveillance, persuasion, detention, or attack—could be aimed at specific enemy targets rather than at random segments of the population as frequently occurred in this war as in others.

Colby later objected to the depiction of Operation Phoenix as an assassination program, although a good many of the Viet Cong leaders identified were in fact killed. He issued the following directive in 1969, after a case officer objected to participating in the program based on rumors he had heard about it.

> The Phoenix program is one of advice, support, and assistance to the GVN [Government of Vietnam] Phung Hoang program, aimed at reducing the influence and effectiveness of the Viet Cong Infrastructure in South Vietnam. The Viet Cong Infrastructure is an inherent part of the war effort being waged against the GVN

by the Viet Cong and their North Vietnamese allies. The unlawful status of members of the Viet Cong Infrastructure (as defined by the Green Book and in GVN official decrees) is well established in GVN law and is in full accord with the laws of land warfare followed by the United States Army.

Operations against the Viet Cong Infrastructure include: the collection of intelligence identifying those members, inducing them to abandon their allegiance to the Viet Cong and rally to the government, capturing or arresting them in order to bring them before Province Security Committees for lawful sentencing, and, as a final resort, the use of military or police force against them if no other way of preventing them from carrying out their unlawful activities is possible. Our training emphasizes the desirability of obtaining these target individuals alive and of using intelligent and lawful methods of interrogation to obtain the truth of what they know about other aspects of the VCI. U.S. personnel are under the same legal and moral constraints with respect to operations of a Phoenix character as they are with respect to regular military operations against enemy units in the field. Thus, they are specifically not authorized to engage in assassinations or other violations of the rules of land warfare, but they are entitled to use such reasonable military force as is necessary to obtain the goals of rallying, capturing or eliminating the VCI in the RVN [Republic of (South) Vietnam].

If U.S. personnel come in contact with activities conducted by Vietnamese which do not meet the standards of land warfare, they are certainly not to participate further in the activity. They are also expected to make their objections to this kind of behavior known to the Vietnamese conducting them, and they are expected to report the circumstances to the next higher U.S. authority for decision as to action to be taken with the GVN.

There are individuals who find normal police or even military operations repugnant to them personally, despite the over-all legality and morality of these activities. Arrangements exist whereby individuals having this feeling about military affairs can, according to law, receive specialized assignments or even exemptions from military service. There is no similar legislation with respect to police-type activities of the U.S. military, but if an individual finds the police-type activities of the Phoenix program repugnant to him, on his application, he can be reassigned from the program without prejudice.

During his Congressional testimony in 1971, Colby noted that of those individuals identified by the Phoenix program, approximately 17,000 had been granted amnesty, 28,000 had been captured, and 20,000 had been killed. He maintained that most of those killed had died as a result of "combat actions," not assassination, but he admitted that he could not swear that assassination never occurred.[13]

Colby remained sensitive on the subject of the Phoenix program, especially regarding accusations that it was an assassination campaign. The issue came up, once again, in "Walter Scott's Personality Parade," a regular column in *Parade* magazine, a California-based weekly newspaper supplement carried by *The Washington Post* among others. Despite the name, "Walter Scott's Personality Parade" was written by Lloyd Shearer, editor at large at *Parade*. It regularly offered answers to readers' queries on a diverse range of topics, with a heavy emphasis on celebrities but also including politics. On 9 January 1972, between items on actor Ernest Borgnine's marital problems and Richard Nixon's private golf course, this exchange appeared:

Q. *Is there any agency of the U.S. government which has been authorized to include political assassination in its practices? M. Wilson, Austin, Tex.*

A. The one U.S. agency which uses political assassination as a weapon is the Central Intelligence Agency. Many of its men in Vietnam have assassinated civilian Communists in an effort to destroy the Viet Cong infrastructure. Operation Phoenix run by the CIA established a new high for U.S. political assassinations in Vietnam, largely in response to enemy terrorist tactics which also include assassination, kidnapping, terrorism of all sorts.

Colby, by this time the Executive Director-Comptroller of the CIA, responded with a letter addressed personally to Shearer, although only after sending it to numerous ranking CIA officials for review. There are several copies of a draft returned to Colby with marginal notations in the "Family Jewels" file.

5317 Briley Place
Washington, D.C. 20016
January 11, 1972

Mr. Lloyd Shearer
Editor at Large
<u>Parade</u> Magazine
733 Third Avenue
New York, New York 10017

Dear Mr. Shearer:

In your issue of January 9th, one of Walter Scott's <u>Personality</u> <u>Parade</u> responses stated that CIA "uses political assassination as a weapon" and that Operation Phoenix "run by the CIA established a new high for U.S. political assassinations in Vietnam." Since I have held responsible positions in CIA for many years and was also (during detached service from CIA) responsible for U.S. support to Operation Phoenix, I believe I am uniquely qualified to testify (as I have in public session under oath to Senate and House Committees) that:

a. CIA does not and has not used political assassination as a weapon.
b. Operation Phoenix was run not by the CIA but by the Government of Vietnam, with support of the CORDS [Civil Operations and Revolutionary Development Support] element of the U.S. Military Assistance Command in coordination with several U.S. agencies including CIA.
c. Operation Phoenix is not and was not a program of assassination. It countered the Viet Cong apparatus attempting to overthrow the Government of Vietnam by targeting its leaders. Wherever possible, these were apprehended or invited to defect, but a substantial number were killed in firefights during military operations or resisting capture. There is a vast difference in kind, not merely in degree, between these combat casualties (even including the few abuses which occurred) and the victims of the Viet Cong's systematic campaign of terrorism to which Mr. Scott quite accurately referred.
   In order to clarify this important question to the millions of concerned Americans who read <u>Parade,</u> I should appreciate your publishing this letter.

Sincerely,

/signed/
W. E. Colby

Shearer responded to Colby's letter with skepticism, a hint of sarcasm, and with a challenge of his own.

February 7, 1972

Mr. W. E. Colby
5317 Briley Pl.
Washington, D.C. 20016

Dear Mr. Colby:

Thank you for your kind and informative letter of January 11 concerning Operation Phoenix.

I don't want to get into a running word-battle with you on the subject of political assassination in Indo-China or the role of the CIA and other of our agencies in Operation Phoenix.

I am just wondering if you would care to say flatly that the CIA has never used political assassination in Indo-China or elsewhere and had never induced, employed, or suggested to others that such tactics or devices be employed.

If you will make that flat statement under oath, I will not only apologize, I will tango with Dick Helms in Garfinkel's largest show window at 14th and F—providing, of course, Mrs. Helms gives her permission.

Again, I thank you for your interest and commend you for the really outstanding service you have rendered the country. You are indeed one of Helms' finest.

Respectfully,

/signed/
LLOYD SHEARER

A flat-out, sworn statement denying that the CIA had ever used assassination was more than Colby had bargained for. To begin with, these were the sorts of issues that were concealed from people who did not have a "need to know," regardless of their security clearance. As executive director, however, he could now check with responsible officials beyond the Far East Division, with which he was personally familiar.[14] The "Family Jewels" file contains his handwritten notes as he gathered information on actual and alleged assassination plots. In each case, he tried to reason how it was either not an operation of the CIA or not *really* an assassination.[15]

Notes:

Diem: CIA had no forewarning of Diem's assassination. CIA attempted to arrange a safe conduct out of Vietnam for Diem and Nhu.

Lumumba: CIA had nothing to do with Lumumba's death. Earlier, however, an action was initiated but abandoned.

Castro: Part of the Bay of Pigs plan involved a commando unit targetted on Castro, the leader of the defending forces. This was part of a large paramilitary operation, not a political assassination. On a separate occasion, an action was <u>initiated</u> but abandoned.

Counter-Terror: In Vietnam in 1964, teams were organized and paid by CIA to conduct operations against the Viet Cong. The teams later became the Provincial Reconnaissance Units (PRU). These were a part of the war effort, not political assassination. When questions arose as to their tactics, CIA tightened its and the GVN [Government of Viet Nam] controls over them.

Laos: In the war in Laos, commando and guerrilla squads played an important role against the North Vietnamese. These were a part of paramilitary and military operations, not political assassination.

<u>Phoenix</u>: This has been described in detail to Congressional committees. It was not a program of assassinations.

If Colby considered using such a point-by-point refutation in a letter to Shearer, he abandoned the idea. The explanation that he finally offered was that none of the actual assassination plots had ever succeeded as planned. He artfully built his statement around this notion. He would use the same sort of construction later in dealing with Congress. (A copy of the final version in the "Family Jewels" file carries the handwritten notation, "NB—Mr. Helms approved the dispatch of this letter—WEC").

5317 Briley Place, N.W.
Washington, D.C. 20016
29 February 1972

Mr. Lloyd Shearer
Editor-at-Large
<u>Parade</u> Magazine
140 N. Hamilton Drive
Beverly Hills, California 90211

Dear Mr. Shearer:

Thank you for your letter of February 7, 1972, and its kind words about me. As you can imagine, your challenge set me to work to meet it. As a result I can say, under oath if need be, that the CIA has never carried out a political assassination, nor has it induced, employed or suggested one which occurred. Whether this fully meets your challenge, I cannot say (it takes two to tango), but it is a long way from the original statement in Mr. Scott's column that CIA "uses political assassination as a weapon." Perhaps I am too sensitive, but I would hope you could set the record straight for your readers.

Sincerely,

/signed/
W. E. Colby

If Colby was proud of his subtlety, it was wasted. Shearer was evidently outraged by the statement. He sent a further response, in which sarcasm completely took charge:

April 30, 1972

Dear General Colby:

(1) Thank you for your article, "Should Lesbians Be Allowed to Play Professional Football?" I found it intriguing, and we plan to run it in a future issue under your by-line, of course.

(2) Thank you for arranging a tango with me and Dick Helms of Her Majesty's Tel Aviv Rifles. Even at Williams, Dick was one of the great tango-artists of our time. Garfinkels, Woodrop-Lathrop, even Hechts—in fact, any place and time of your choosing is O.K. with me.

(3) One sad note! Will you tell Angus[16] we cannot use his new car bumper sticker: <u>LICK DICK in '72</u>, because it is open to misinterpretation. In addition, we try to remain politically neutral.

(4) As to your willingness to say under oath that the CIA has never been part to political assassination, I, of late, have been travelling a good deal. In the course of my travels I happened to encounter Oleg Penkovsky—not your Oleg—but Penkovsky, a bartender in Cleveland, Ohio.[17] Penkovsky told me that you signed a secrecy agreement, Form 270, witnessed by Victor L. Marchetti.[18] Under the terms of this agreement you are pledged to eternal silence concerning CIA activities. Unless you have a special Papal dispensation—the kind given Allen Dulles and Lyman Kirkpatrick, Jr.,[19] it seems to me you are lip-sealed.

Perhaps this does not apply to hearings before the Senate Foreign Relations Committee or the prestigious Council on Foreign Relations. If this is so, please let me know; and we will take it from there.

(5) I will be in Washington shortly staying at the home of [columnist] Jack Anderson out in Silver Spring. Perhaps we can meet there for a small summit. I will have with me several former Green Beret members who want to discuss with you the subject of CIA imposters in South Vietnam, who lied to them and me, too.

Let me hear from you.

All the best,

/signed/
LLOYD SHEARER

There is an official routing slip, dated 4 may 1972, associated with the above letter in the "Family Jewels" file, forwarding it to the Director of Central Intelligence, the Deputy Director of Central Intelligence, and Mr. Thuermer. Across the slip, someone has scrawled, "I suggest we let the whole thing drop."

LATER REFLECTIONS

Apart from Operation Phoenix, the issue of assassination came into the open through the leaks and rumors surrounding the creation of the "Family Jewels" file. Colby discovered that it had gotten out when he was approached by Daniel Schorr, then with CBS News. In 1988, Colby was asked about this by the CIA Oral History Program.[20]

> Yes. Daniel Schorr came to me and he dropped that little bombshell on my desk. President Ford, in a background discussion [about the refusal to release the Family Jewels to the public], had been asked, "Why are you defending this?" And he said, "Well, there are a lot of things in there you can't handle." "Such as?" And he said, "Assassinations." They were all under background rules. The *Times* couldn't use it. But as the newsmakers go, they talked [to other reporters]. So, Schorr had the view that there's a story here if I can just get something to hook it on to.
>
> He came to me and said, "I understand from the president that there's been assassinations going on in this country." I said [to myself], "Oh, shit." I really clammed up at that point because I knew I was in deep trouble. I said, "Well," and I reverted to what I have done frequently [which was to] answer exactly what the man said. I said, "Well, no, not in this country." But, I didn't say anything beyond that.

A staff historian went on to ask Colby if he had been "surprised about the assassination issue" itself. He responded:

No, not terribly. I don't think I was morally shocked at it. If you really think about assassination, that's what I was forced to do, it seems to me it just doesn't add up. You think you can solve something by eliminating a guy—it's playing God. You have no idea who is going to succeed him, you have no idea what the repercussions will be, or, the worst, you getting caught doing it. The repercussions are potentially enormous.

For intelligence operations, it seems to me that you have several simple questions to ask before you start one. One, how important is it? What are the risks? What is the impact if it goes sour? And on the last issue, it seems to me you have to turn it down. Now that is being pragmatic, not moral. I think there are moral considerations, too; but being pragmatic, I just think that assassination doesn't work. Politically, it's dynamite. We may do dumb things, we chased all the Japanese-Americans off the west coast because we were scared. Countries do dumb things when they get scared.

In a separate interview by the Oral History Program, Helms was also asked about assassination. He gave a somewhat less nuanced response.

The Agency never assassinated anybody, ever. I was there from the day the doors opened until I left in '73, and I know the Agency never killed anybody, *anybody*. You can take my word for it. If you can find anything in the record of anybody the Agency killed, bring it in here and show it to me. This whole business about Castro was caused largely by the fact that the task force that was working on Cuba had some ideas floated as to ways to get rid of Castro, to make him sick or to do something about him. I don't want to go into a long disquisition about this assassination business. I've said everything I have to say before the Church Committee and there's absolutely no percentage at this late date in my going over this whole area again because it gets complicated by nuances and who said what and who didn't say what. I just really don't want to go into it any further. I've told you we didn't kill anybody, and it seems to me that's the important thing. We didn't even try to kill anybody.

ILLICIT DRUG TESTS

One of the other notorious aspects of the history of the CIA involved "mind-control" experiments on unwitting subjects as part of a program codenamed MKULTRA. In a particularly infamous episode, in 1953, Dr. Sidney Gottlieb, the head of the Chemical Division of the Technical Services Staff of the Directorate of Plans (and the same one who would later deliver the poison to Leopoldville), arranged for a group of scientists from the Special Operations Division of the U.S. Army's Chemical Corps to be served Cointreau laced with LSD. This was reportedly done without approval, even against orders. One of the scientists, Dr. Frank Olson—who was himself developing biological weapons for potential use by the CIA—reportedly went out of his mind and later threw himself out a hotel window to his death. Gottlieb remained with the CIA for another twenty years, eventually becoming the Director of the Technical Services Division, as it was later called. There appear to be no records of the drug experiments, however. It is believed that Richard Helms had them destroyed when he left the agency early in 1973.[21]

Some sort of drug testing continued. The "Family Jewels" file includes the following cryptic note, apparently from William V. Broe, the Inspector General, to William E. Colby, who was at the time Deputy Director for Operations and Executive Secretary of the CIA Management Committee. The undated note concerns activities of the Office of Research and Development (ORD), a branch of the Directorate of Science and Technology. The "attached summary" mentioned does not appear in the "Family Jewels" file as released.

> MEMORANDUM TO: Executive Secretary
>   CIA Management Committee
>
> SUBJECT: Drug Testing Program
>
>   1. The attached summary from ORD describes research into a behavioral drug. Conversations with [Deputy Director for Science and Technology] Carl Duckett indicate that the reported drug was part of a larger program in which the Agency had relations with commercial drug manufacturers, whereby they passed on drugs rejected because of unfavorable side effects. The drugs were screened with the use of ADP equipment, and those selected for experimentation were tested at [—about three-fourths of a line deleted—] using monkeys and mice. Materials having further interest, as demonstrated by this testing, were then tested at Edgewood, using volunteer members of the Armed Forces.
>   2. The program was terminated last fall. The computer program remains in the machine, its final disposition not yet having been decided.
>   3. Carl Duckett emphasizes that the program was considered as defensive, in the sense that we would be able to recognize certain behavior if similar materials were used against Americans.
>
>   WVB

When Helms was asked about the issue of drug experimentation by the CIA Oral History Program in 1988, his response did not suggest that he was very concerned about it.[22]

> Well, that has been a controversial issue from day one. There was the feeling, from Allen Dulles's time on, that these drugs were available, that the Russians had access to them, maybe they were using them, so we should therefore know what they could do and what they couldn't do, both for protection and in case it was felt at some time that it was desirable to make use of them. So that's where the drug-testing program originated. I know there's been a great hoo-hah and lawsuits and all kinds of jiggery-pokery about whether this was done legally or illegally, morally or immorally, and there's absolutely no percentage in my trying to sort this out and say which was which or which I thought was which. But it was established that that was a legitimate function of the Agency to try and do this, and we went ahead and did it.
>   One of the things that I think a thoughtful person might ask is: why is a country spending so much of its time complaining about a minor operation of this kind which has a useful function to it? Why is it that as a country we always have to wait until disaster strikes and then we want to spend billions of dollars trying to solve the problem? AIDS is a good example; cancer is a good example. We're always late in the game, trying to run to catch up. So I have no apologies for that whole affair, and I think that some of the lawsuits have been absolutely egregious, I mean ridiculous. I can't possibly explain why certain psychiatrists did the things that they did, but at least they were supposed to be reputable people at the time that they were given financing.

When the same issue was put to Colby, he allowed that it could have been handled differently.

I was understanding of the fact that you had a group of people in the Agency who were curious about the properties of some of these drugs and were legitimately fearful that they would be used against us. They had an idea of learning something about the properties. You can understand a scientist wanting to know how things work. Now, there are ways to do legitimate testing. You don't want CIA to be on record as doing it, so you need some kind of a front to do it for you. But, there are rules about testing on human beings. The medical profession has them. I think you assume you would follow those rules. Apparently, they didn't. This gets back to the old mystique idea—intelligence is different, we do things differently—which is nonsense.

You know, that's the thing that really scares you about intelligence agencies— where they go wrong is when they do violate people's rights under the "higher good." The KGB should not be our rationale.

NOTES

1. Of course, the documents were not supposed to have left headquarters in the first place. Tofte later attempted to sue DCI Richard Helms, claiming that the CIA security men who came for the documents seized his personal correspondence as well. This was the same Hans V. Tofte who had been in charge of CIA operations behind enemy lines in the Korean War.

2. See also U.S. Senate, Select Committee to Study Governmental Operations with Respect to Intelligence Activities, *Alleged Assassination Plots Involving Foreign Leaders: An Interim Report of the Select Committee to Study Government Operations with Respect to Intelligence Activities, United States Senate: Together with Additional, Supplemental, and Separate Views* (New York: W. W. Norton, 1976).

3. This and subsequent quotes from cables and official minutes regarding Lumumba are taken from *Alleged Assassination Plots Involving Foreign Leaders*.

4. In 1961, the CIA considered establishing a permanent "executive action capability," which would include assassination in its repertoire. The project's code name was ZR/RIFLE. This "third-country national," known by the code name QJ/WIN, was recruited for ZR/RIFLE, but the agency claims that no assassination was ever carried out. See *Alleged Assassination Plots Involving Foreign Leaders*, 181–190.

5. John Prados, *Safe for Democracy: The Secret Wars of the CIA* (Chicago: Ivan R. Dee, 2006): 273–278; Tim Weiner, *Legacy of Ashes: The History of the CIA* (New York: Doubleday, 2007): 162–163; Larry Devlin, *Chief of Station, Congo: A Memoir of 1960–67* (New York: Public Affairs Books, 2007). A book by investigative reporter Ludo de Witte, *De moord op Lumumba* (1999; also published as *L'Assassinat de Lumumba* [2000] and *The Assassination of Lumumba* [New York: Verso, 2001]) prompted the Belgian Parliament to hold an inquiry on Belgium's role in Lumumba's death. Excerpts of its final report, about 630 pages, can be found in Luc de Vos et al., *Les Secrets de l'affaire Lumumba* (Brussels: Racine, 2005). The full version is Belgique, Chambre des représantants, *Enquête Parlementaire visant à déterminer les circonstances exactes de l'assassinat de Patrice Lumumba et l'implication éventuelle des responsables politiques belges dans celui-ci* (Brussels: The Chamber of Representatives of Belguim, 2001).

6. See *Alleged Assassination Plots Involving Foreign Leaders*, 191–215.

7. On the Diem coup generally, see Howard Jones, *Death of a Generation: How the Assassinations of Diem and JFK Prolonged the Vietnam War* (New York: Oxford University Press, 2003); Seth Jacobs, *Cold War Mandarin: Ngo Dinh Diem and the Origins of America's War in Vietnam, 1950–1963* (Lanham, MD: Rowman & Littlefield Publishers, 2006).

8. In the Vietnamese practice, the family name comes first, followed by a generational name. Thus, Diem's family name was Ngo, and members of his generation were named Dinh. However, perhaps because a small number of family names are extremely prevalent (especially Nguyen), people are identified by given name. Hence, President Diem, Madame Nhu, etc. The name Diem is pronounced "Zyem."

9. This plot was foiled.

10. President Kennedy sent Secretary of Defense Robert McNamara and Chairman of the Joint Chiefs of Staff General Maxwell D. Taylor on a fact-finding mission to South Vietnam in late September to early October 1963, where they could speak to Diem privately and evaluate the political and military situation.

11. USOM stands for the U.S. Operations Mission, an economic development office of AID; AID stands for the Agency for International Development; and USIA stands for the U.S. Information Agency.

12. Memorandum from Walter Elder, dated 1 June 1973. See the following chapter.

13. William Colby and Peter Forbath, *Honorable Men: My Life in the CIA* (New York: Simon & Schuster, 1978): 266–276; Colby's directive on 270–271.

14. See also, Colby and Forbath, *Honorable Men*, 311–312.

15. These are handwritten notes, and in some cases, lines run off the end of the page, but care has been made to make this transcription as accurate as possible.

16. Presumably CIA spokesman Angus Thuermer, who was responsible for dealing with the press.

17. Oleg Penkovsky was a Soviet military intelligence officer who provided a considerable amount of information to the CIA in the early 1960s.

18. A former CIA officer turned public critic, he was sued by the CIA for violating his secrecy agreement.

19. A former Director of Central Intelligence and a former CIA Inspector General.

20. "Oral History: Reflections of DCI Colby and Helms on the CIA's 'Time of Troubles,'" *Studies in Intelligence* 51:3 (2007).

21. Jeffrey T. Richelson, *The Wizards of Langley: Inside the CIA's Directorate of Science and Technology* (Boulder, CO: Westview Press, 2001): 9–11; Weiner, *Legacy of Ashes*, 65–66.

22. "Oral History."

_____ *Chapter 5* _____

At Headquarters in the 1960s:
A Brief Note

Most of the memoranda in the "Family Jewels" file deal with events of the late 1960s and the early 1970s. There is relatively little about earlier periods. Memoranda about efforts to find an assassin to kill Fidel Castro are a notable exception, dealt with in another chapter. A smaller exception is a single memorandum from Walter Elder.

William E. Colby, Deputy Director for Operations and Executive Secretary, CIA Management Committee, turned to Elder in an effort to learn of possibly illicit activities of an earlier period for the "Family Jewels" file. Elder had been Assistant to the Director under Allen W. Dulles, John A. McCone, and William F. Raborn, Jr., in the early 1960s. His response to Colby's query, although heavily redacted, offered insights into a variety of topics, including the tapping of reporters' phones, interagency rivalries, the CIA and labor unions, sloppy bookkeeping, reading other departments' secret memos, and the tendency to avoid learning too many inconvenient facts.

1 June 1973

MEMORANDUM FOR: Mr. William E. Colby

SUBJECT: Special Activities

1. Following our recent conversation, I have searched my memory and Mr. McCone's files for examples of activities which to hostile observers or to someone without complete knowledge and with a special kind of motivation could be interpreted as examples of activities exceeding CIA's charter.

2. First, as we discussed, on 7 March 1962, DCI McCone, under pressure from Attorney General Robert F. Kennedy, agreed to tap the telephones of columnists Robert S. Allen and Paul Scott in an effort to identify their sources for classified information which was appearing in their columns. Because the primary source appeared to be in the Department of Defense, McCone

ordered me personally to brief General Joe Carroll, Director of DIA, orally, which I did. I understand more complete information on this operation is available from the Director of Security. I, personally, managed to avoid gaining any knowledge of what precise actions were taken, what information was gained, what was done with it, and when the operation was terminated.

3. [—paragraph deleted; about 37 lines—]

4. Although certain activities never got beyond the planning stage, there are, I believe, three examples of such planning which could be subject to misinterpretation. One involved chemical warfare operations against [—about four-fifths of a line deleted—]. A second involved a paramilitary strike against [—about two-thirds of a line deleted—]. Outside the United States Government, General Eisenhower was briefed on such planning. A third, which assumes a new significance today, involved a proposal by [James J.] Angleton and [Richard] Helms for a greatly increased intelligence collection effort against foreign installations in this country. This planning also involved a scheme for selected exposure of KGB activities and counteractions against the Soviet intelligence service. The reasons are still unclear to me why the FBI chose to brief the PFIAB [President's Foreign Intelligence Advisory Board] to the effect that CIA was planning to wiretap extensively and indiscriminately in this country, to greatly increase the Agency representation in the Moscow Embassy, and generally to use KGB-type tactics, also extensively and indiscriminately. This led to a heated exchange between DCI McCone and Mr. Belmont of the FBI, one such meeting taking place in the presence of the Attorney General. It is clear that the FBI was opposed to any such proposal then, as now, and the plan never went forward.

5. During the period when Des FitzGerald was in charge of the Cuban Task Force, DCI McCone's office learned, quite by accident, that FitzGerald had secured the cooperation of several prominent US business firms in denying economic items to Cuba. There was no question that the businessmen were glad to cooperate, but knowledge of this operation had to be rather widespread.

6. [—about six and a half lines deleted—] in connection with elections in Chile. On 12 May 1964 at a meeting of the 303 Committee [which approved covert operations], it was decided that the offers of American business could not be accepted, it being neither a secure way nor an honorable way of doing such business. This declaration of policy at this time bears on the recent ITT hearings, but I am not surprised that McCone has forgotten that he helped to set the precedent of refusing to accept such collaboration between the Agency's operations and private business.[1]

7. At the direction of Attorney General Robert Kennedy and with the explicit approval of President Kennedy, McCone injected the Agency, and particularly Cord Meyer [from the Directorate of Plans], into the US labor situation, and particularly to try to ameliorate the quarrel between George Meany [of the AFL-CIO] and Walter Reuther [of the UAW]. Cord Meyer steered a very skillful course in this connection, but the Agency could be vulnerable to charges that we went behind Meany's back, or were somehow consorting with Reuther against Meany's wishes.

8. There are three examples of using Agency funds which I know to be controversial. One was the expenditure of money under Project MOSES in securing the release of Cuban brigade prisoners.[2] Details of this operation are best known to Larry Houston, Mike Miskovsky, George MacManus, and James Smith. Second, as you well know, when Lou Conein received his summons to report to the Joint General Staff Headquarters on 1 November 1963 a large amount of cash went with him. My impression is that the

accounting for this and its use has never been very frank or complete.[3] Third, at one of the early Special Group meetings attended by McCone he took strong exception to proposals to spend Agency funds to improve the economic viability of West Berlin, and for an investment program in Mali. His general position was that such expenditures were not within the Agency's charter, and that he would allow such spending only on the direct personal request of the Secretary of State or the Secretary of Defense, or the White House.

9. I raise these issues of funding because I remember the Agency's being severely criticized by the House Appropriations Subcommittee for having spent $3,000 for stamps in connection with a program to buy tractors to secure the release of prisoners from Cuba.

10. Under the heading of old business, I know that any one who has worked in the Director's office has worried about the fact that conversations within the offices and over the telephones were transcribed. During McCone's tenure, there were microphones in his regular office, his inner office, his dining room, his office in East Building, and his study at his residence on White Haven Street. I do not know who would be willing to raise such an issue, but knowledge of such operations tends to spread, and certainly the Agency is vulnerable on this score.

11. Also under the heading of old business, [—just over three lines deleted—]. Shortly after the Cuban missile crisis, there was a disposition in Washington to reexamine the Bay of Pigs, and the fact that several Alabama National Air Guard officers lost their lives in the Bay of Pigs was surfaced with surprisingly little excitement at the time.

12. During my stint on the 7th floor there was a special arrangement with the Office of Communications whereby the Director's office gained access to non-CIA traffic. This surfaced briefly at one point shortly after Admiral Rayborn [sic; Raborn] became DCI. He had visited the Signal Center and removed a copy of a telegram from the Embassy in the Dominican Republic for Under Secretary George Ball, Eyes Only. He returned to his office and proceeded to discuss this telegram with George Ball who was naturally quite curious as to how Rayborn knew about it, and also as to how Rayborn had it in his possession before Ball did. Ben Read in the Secretary of State's office and I spent several weeks putting this one to rest.

13. Finally, DCI McCone, as you and I well know, operated on a very lofty plane, and I think certain of his activities could be misunderstood. One example was his decision in July of 1964 to have [Greek shipping magnate] Aristotle Onassis and [Greek soprano] Maria Callas flown from Rome to Athens on Air Force KC 135. Their arrival in Athens in this airplane attracted the attention of the local press and in due course Mr. John Hightower, Chief of the Associated Press Bureau for Washington, came to see me to ask about the propriety of this action.

14. [—paragraph deleted; about ten lines—]

15. McCone dealt quite extensively with newsmen in Washington. In fact, they gave him a gift and a luncheon when he left Washington, which is perhaps indicative of the press's relations with him. However, in the case of the Ross and Wise book, <u>The Invisible Government</u>, he did try to bring pressure on the publisher and the authors to change things.[4] They did not change a comma, and I doubt that this old saw will ever sing again.

16. [—paragraph deleted; about four lines—]

17. The above listing is uneven, but I have a sinking feeling that discipline has broken down, and that allegations from any quarter which cast these things

in the wrong light would receive great publicity and attention, and no amount of denial would ever set the record straight. If I may be of any assistance in tracking down further details, I am of course at your disposal, but I would point out that I was very much in the position of the enlisted man who knew that the commissioned officers were aware of these activities and better able to judge their propriety and possible impact or misinterpretation.

[—signature deleted—]
WALTER ELDER

NOTES

1. In 1970, International Telephone & Telegraph offered the CIA funds that were allegedly intended to prevent the Marxist candidate Salvador Allende from being elected president of Chile, where ITT had substantial investments. The CIA declined the offer but did suggest ways in which private corporations acting on their own could "create or accelerate economic instability in Chile." Former DCI McCone was a member of the ITT board of directors at the time and was involved in making the offer. At Senate hearings conducted in 1973, there was conflicting testimony regarding the purpose of the funds, with ITT representatives claiming it was intended for investments to improve America's image. See *Time* (9 April 1973).

2. The reference here is to the return of the captives from the Bay of Pigs invasion.

3. The reference here is to the military coup d'état against the South Vietnamese premier Ngo Dinh Diem. See Chapter 4, "Political Assassinations."

4. David Wise and Thomas B. Ross, *The Invisible Government* (New York: Random House, 1964).

_____ *Chapter 6* _____

Counterintelligence:
The Spies among Us

Every intelligence agency must be concerned with the possibility that enemy intelligence agencies are trying to infiltrate it. Double agents and enemy spies are, of course, never as obvious as they appear in the movies. Infiltrators may or may not raise suspicions about themselves; so may perfectly innocent people. The handling of such matters may overlook horrendous security breaches, may "just save the day," or may ruin lives for no good reason.

For two decades, from 1954 to 1974, the head of counterintelligence within the Directorate of Plans was James J. Angleton. His outlook was shaped by an early experience in his career; in the late 1940s and early 1950s he had regularly shared details about secret operations over liquid lunches with the liaison from British intelligence, Kim Philby. Secret intercepts eventually revealed that Philby was a Soviet spy and was forwarding the information to Moscow, although Angleton was reluctant to believe it for some time. Philby was quietly pushed aside at the time, but he defected later, in 1963, and spent the rest of his life in Moscow. Angleton, according to some, became obsessive about the possibility of double agents within the CIA, although his defenders attributed the obsession to the nature of counterintelligence work.

The year after Philby's defection, a Soviet intelligence agent named Yuriy Nosenko defected to the United States. Among other items of interest, Nosenko reported that he had known Lee Harvey Oswald after the latter's defection to the Soviet Union but that the Soviets had had nothing to do with President Kennedy's assassination. Some of the things that Nosenko reported contradicted reports from another recent KGB defector, Anatoliy Golitsyn.

The subsequent dispute over whether Nosenko was a genuine defector or a KGB-controlled plant supplying misleading information divided the CIA for years. Reexaminations of the case, and further disputes, were conducted periodically into the 1980s. Indeed, it has never been resolved to everyone's satisfaction. Angleton and his Counterintelligence Staff and many in the Soviet Bloc

Division of the Directorate of Plans believed that Nosenko had been sent intentionally by the KGB and that the defection was a cover story. Those who
believed Nosenko was a plant also came to think that the CIA was penetrated
by Soviet spies. A widespread search for double agents ensued within the
agency, which some termed a witch hunt.[1] The following report regarding
Nosenko comes from the "Family Jewels" file.

SUBJECT: Yuriy Ivanovich Nosenko

Yuriy Ivanovich Nosenko, an officer of the KGB, defected to a representative of
this Agency in Geneva, Switzerland, on 4 February 1964. The responsibility for his
exploitation was assigned to the then SR [Soviet] Division of the Clandestine Service
and he was brought to this country on 12 February 1964.[2] After initial interrogation
by representatives of the SR Division, he was moved to a safehouse in Clinton,
Maryland, from 4 April 1964 where he as confined and interrogated until 13 August
1965 when he was moved to a specially constructed "jail" in a remote wooded area
at [—]. The SR Division was convinced that he was a dispatched agent but even after a long period of hostile interrogation was unable to prove their contention and
he was confined at [—] in an effort to convince him to "confess."

This Office together with the Office of General Counsel became increasingly concerned with the illegality of the Agency's position in handling a defector under
these conditions for such a long period of time. Strong representations were made
to the Director (Mr. Helms) by this Office, the Office of General Counsel, and the
Legislative Liaison Counsel, and on 27 October 1967, the responsibility for Nosenko's further handling was transferred to the Office of Security under the direction
of the Deputy Director of Central Intelligence, then Admiral Rufus Taylor.

Nosenko was moved to a comfortable safehouse in the Washington area and
was interviewed under friendly, sympathetic conditions by his Security Case Officer, Mr. Bruce Solie, for more than a year. It soon became apparent that Nosenko
was bona fide and he was moved to more comfortable surroundings with considerable freedom of independent movement and has continued to cooperate fully
with the Federal Bureau of Investigation and this Office since that time. He has
proven to be the most valuable and economical defector this Agency has ever had
and leads that were ignored by the SR Division were explored and have resulted
in the arrest and prosecution [—one and a half lines deleted—]. He currently is living under an alias; secured a divorce from his Russian wife and remarried an
American citizen. He is happy, relaxed, and appreciative of the treatment accorded
him and states "while I regret my three years of incarceration, I have no bitterness
and now understand how it could happen."

William E. Colby commented briefly on the Nosenko case to the CIA Oral
History Program in 1988:[3]

I'm not an expert on the Nosenko case, but I spoke to [former Deputy Director for
Plans (DDP) Thomas] Karamessines about it, and I know that both Karamessines
and Helms signed off on the fact that they accepted Nosenko's story as basically
true. Both of them are good, careful guys and they are not going to sign something
that's false. So, period, that did it. The Golitsyn thing is all over the place. I ran into
the fact that some people were shoved out to outer darkness because they had
somehow been in Berlin at the wrong time or something with no evidence—again,
I am a lawyer—no evidence that they were in any way involved, but you had
careers ruined. I said, "Bullshit, we are not going to do that."

Apart from the Nosenko affair, Colby in his memoirs and various memoranda repeatedly drew attention to Angleton's insistence on continuing a program to intercept and photograph first-class mail to and from the Soviet Union. Codenamed SRPOINTER, this program had begun in the early 1950s and continued until 1973. It was based at John F. Kennedy International Airport.[4] A similar operation in San Francisco, called WESTPOINTER, intercepted mail to and from China. The following redacted memorandum provides some of the operational details of SRPOINTER.

22 May 1973

MEMORANDUM FOR: Director of Central Intelligence

THROUGH: Mr. William E. Colby

Mr. Colby advised me that [—], extension [—], had called the Office of the Director in line with the Director's memorandum to all employees dated 9 May 1973, requesting all employees to report activities which might be construed to be outside the legislative charter of the Agency.

[—] is employed as a GS–5 clerk in the Cable Secretariat. He joined the Agency in September 1967 and worked in the Office of Security for 3–1/2 years before transferring to the Cable Secretariat in 1970.

While in the Office of Security he was assigned to a support desk, SD3. The primary function of this desk was to [—just under one line deleted—]. During his assignment to this desk, [—] supported a project entitled SRPOINTER-HTLINGUAL. [—] described the project as follows. The Office of Security [—] had a unit at JFK International Airport that photographed mail going to Soviet Bloc countries. This work was done by Agency staff employees. The mail was placed in bags by the regular Post Office employees and stacked. After their departure for the night, the Agency employees would open the mail and photograph it. Both incoming and outgoing mail, including postcards, were photographed. A watch list was maintained and priority was given to the names listed, but generally all mail was processed.

The results of the operation were sent to Washington Headquarters where they were handled by [—]. He would receive a teletype advising him of the registry number and the number of items. He would check to see if the number of items received was correct and route the material to the appropriate offices. Generally about 1/4 of the material was separated into bundles bound with rubber bands. This portion was sent to TSD [Technical Services Division] for technical processing. The remaining material was sent to the CI [Counterintelligence] Staff, [—].

About twice a month the CI Staff would add names to or delete names from the list. [—] would send the changes in the list to the field office. The watch list was made up primarily of [—about a half line deleted—] who were in the United States. When [—] left the Office of Security in 1970, the project was still active.

[—] was in no way emotional or belligerent. He presented the facts quickly and clearly and said he had no other information. He stated he would have come forward with the information sooner but he had only recently had time to read the Director's memorandum. The writer thanked him for his interest.

/signed/
William V. Broe
Inspector General

In forwarding the previous memorandum from the Inspector General to the Director of Central Intelligence, Colby added a handwritten note to the cover sheet.

Recommend the IG express your appreciation to [—] & assure we will follow this up (which, of course, we already have done by terminating the activity).

WEC

Schlesinger, or someone on his behalf, responded with an even briefer note.

Done—29 May 73

On top of the Nosenko affair and the mail program, it appears that Angleton was inexplicably allowed to take personal control of all relations with Israeli intelligence. In addition, Colby believed that the Counterintelligence Staff was too concerned with looking for spies within the CIA and not sufficiently interested in infiltrating the KGB. Once Colby became DCI, he began to push Angleton out of the agency. The following comments by Colby are from the CIA's Oral History Program:

I had first known of him [Angleton] when I was in Italy [in the 1950s]. He had superb Italian contacts. He had been there in the latter part of the war and met a lot of people. He is a very opinionated guy, which is all right except the idea was that his reports should go straight to God. I remember really getting upset when I heard that he was back in Washington one time, stood on a street corner and a car drove by with Allen Dulles and [his brother] the secretary of state [John Foster Dulles], picked him up and they had a talk in the car. I said, "My God! Is this a serious intelligence agency?" Having this guy with his strong opinions directly at the policy level without any analysis, any comparison with the other factors going on. It just violates my sense of what intelligence is all about.

I spent some time gradually working him into a more normal pattern so that his reports would go in in an ordinary way and go into the ordinary analytical process. While they were valuable, they weren't just rolled gold. I sort of had that sense that the Angleton approach was to run these highly personalized things. Then, remember, I was appointed for a while to take over the Soviet Division. I began the briefing and it was pretty clear that the Soviet Division in the Agency had been all tied up the last several years in this whole series of Nosenko and Golitsyn and all that crap. Every time they tried to move an inch, the CI people said, "No, it's a fake." I think that's why Helms was going to send me there to try to straighten the goddamn thing out. Let Angleton do his thing, but get something going there that made sense.

Then, of course, I went over to Vietnam, but that [the Nosenko affair] left a bad taste in my mouth. Seemed to me that we were hurting ourselves. I never thought that the object of CIA was to protect itself against the KGB. The object of the CIA is to get into the Kremlin; that's what our function is. Sure, you protect yourself, but you goddamn well better have the offensive mission. So, I had doubts about that.

Then I ran into the goddamn mail thing and Jim's insistence on holding it. Then I ran into the Israeli business when I became DDO—here the Israeli account was over here in a corner someplace and had nothing to do with the rest of the Middle East. The officers in those stations were prohibited from communicating with each other. I said, "This can't be serious! You've got a common problem in the Middle East and you've got two separate teams working on it that never talk to each other!" I mean it's just nutty. I understand some of the reasons for it and all this, but I felt I had to change this.

Then I found that he had a whole lot of people, a very large staff—I've forgotten how big it was—and I was under pressure to cut at that point. I had been trying to find out what the hell these people did. I couldn't find that they were doing anything that I could understand. Seemed to me this was a good place to cut. So then when I was DDO, I broke off the Israeli thing, gave it to the NE [Near East] Division; then I made some cuts. Of course, we cut off the mail opening and so forth. It was obvious that I had no confidence in Jim actually running it. So, I tried to sort of edge Jim toward the door in a nice way, in as nice a way as possible by taking these things away, hoping he would get the point. I had a couple of conversations with him, but I didn't force it. I didn't sort of say, "Out." I should have. I now realize that I should have; it would have been much cleaner and noisier. I should have done it right when I came in, but I was, you know, concerned about him. He had done a lot for his country and I did not want to shame him. I wanted to edge him away. I had two or three conversations over the year with him, long conversations about moving, doing something else—all very subtle. He knew exactly what I was talking about and didn't want any part of it. So, he dug his heels in.

Then, finally, when the Hersh thing[5] blew I figured, "Oh, God, we're going to get blamed for this but I am not going to go into this with Jim on my hands. I've got to be able to handle this without Jim's problems." So, I said, "Jim, go. You are finished. I will give you a job of writing the history of the CI Staff or something so you can be around, keep involved and so forth; but I am going to put in a new chief and a new staff, new systems." And I did it.

After the Nosenko affair, counterintelligence cases were handled more discreetly. Indeed, the Nosenko case led some to deride the whole counterintelligence function. The following incident reported in the "Family Jewels" file reflects both suspicion and considerable indecision. As Colby noted to the deputy attorney general on 31 December 1974, this case also involved breaking into the former employee's place of business and attempting to break into her home in search of evidence.[6] Note also that at one time the CIA had a dozen people spying on its own file clerks in the Records Integration Division, although by 1973 the number had dropped to three.

11 May 1973

MEMORANDUM FOR THE RECORD

SUBJECT: General: Office of Security Survey
[—one line deleted—]

1. At the Director's instruction, and with the concurrence of the then DD/P [Deputy Director for Plans], the Office of Security developed informants in RID [Records Integration Division] to report on the activities of RID employees on whom security questions had arisen. This program, which included upwards of a dozen informants at its peak, has declined to its present level of three, only one of whom is reporting regularly on matters of current interest.

2. The principal object of Security's interest through this informant is a female who was employed in RID for a number of years until she resigned in 1969. Her resignation coincided with the initiation of a security review on her by the Office of Security, but Security does not know whether the employee was aware of this security review at the time of her resignation.

3. Security's interest in this employee was occasioned by reports that she had developed an increasingly intimate acquaintance with a Cuban national. Reporting by one informant, who was also being developed by the Cuban, suggested that the Cuban might have an intelligence interest in the female. The same informant also subsequently reported that the Cuban had numerous other

contacts among clerical and secretarial employees of the Agency. [—one and one-fourth lines deleted—]

4. Subsequent to her departure from the Agency, the ex-RID employee entered into a common-law marital relationship with the Cuban and joined him as partner in a photographic business. In this capacity she solicited business among CIA employees, especially those requiring passport photos. Recently, she and the Cuban sought to employ Security's informant in this business on a part-time basis.

5. Information on the background of the Cuban is fairly extensive, but it is inconclusive. He is known to have been a member of anti-Castro organizations in this country. There are also reports that his mother was imprisoned in Cuba at one time. There are other episodes in his life that suggest intelligence involvement on his part with some hostile service, but this is not yet definitely established.

6. The Office of Security has had at times a second informant in this case. His reporting has tended to confirm reporting by the principal informant.
   [—one paragraph deleted; about 13 lines—]

8. The Office of Security has been running this operation for over two years, in an effort to obtain conclusive proof of its intelligence nature. CI Staff has been kept informed The FBI, which was informed of the case at an early stage, has declined to take responsibility for it, on grounds that it concerns CIA's internal security. As a result, the Office of Security has been inhibited in the actions it can take against the Cuban suspect. On the other hand, Security has not taken any action against Agency employees for fear of compromising the operation.

9. It would appear to me that the Office of Security has dallied with this case long enough. Apparently unable through positive measures to resolve doubts about the case, O/S has followed the course of watchful waiting, hoping the Cuban would take precipitant action himself that would give us the evidence we seek. In the meantime, our knowledge of the relationship between the Cuban and the several other current Agency employees with whom he is known to have contact continues
   [—about seventeen lines deleted—] The possibility that the employee in SB [Soviet Bloc] Division may be passing information on CIA's Soviet operations is too great to warrant further delay in moving against her. [—about ten lines deleted—]

The attitude toward the Counterintelligence Staff changed several times. As noted below, the agency began to realize in the mid-1980s that it was leaking information to the Soviet Union. Nonetheless, it took nine years to discover that there was in fact a double agent in the agency and that it was the person responsible for Soviet (and, later, Russian) counterintelligence, Aldrich Ames.[7]

The following is the unclassified summary the CIA Inspector General's report of investigation, *The Aldrich H. Ames Case: An Assessment of CIA's Role in Identifying Ames as an Intelligence Penetration of the Agency*, dated 21 October 1994.

1. In the spring and summer of 1985, Aldrich H. Ames began his espionage activities on behalf of the Soviet Union. In 1985 and 1986, it became increasingly clear to officials within CIA that the Agency was faced with a major CI problem. A significant number of CIA Soviet sources began to be compromised, recalled to the Soviet Union and, in many cases, executed. A number of these cases were believed to have been exposed by Edward Lee Howard, who fled the United States in September 1985 to avoid prosecution for disclosures he made earlier that year. However, it was evident by fall of 1985 that not all of the compromised sources could be attributed to him.

2. Later in 1985, the first Agency efforts were initiated to ascertain whether the unexplained compromises could be the result of a) faulty practices by the sources or the CIA officers who were assigned to handle them (i.e., whether the cases each

contained seeds of their own destruction), b) a physical or electronic intrusion into the Agency's Moscow Station or Agency communications, or c) a human penetration within the Agency (a mole). Although they were never discounted altogether, the first two theories diminished in favor over the years as possible explanations for the losses. A "molehunt"—an effort to determine whether there was a human penetration, a spy, within CIA's ranks—was pursued more or less continuously and with varying degrees of intensity until Ames was convicted of espionage in 1994, nine years after the compromises began to occur.

3. The 1985–1986 compromises were first discussed in late 1985 with DCI William Casey, who directed that the Deputy Director for Operations (DDO) make every effort to determine the reason for them. In January 1986, SE Division instituted new and extraordinary compartmentation measures to prevent further compromises.[8] In the fall of 1986, a small Special Task Force (STF) of four officers operating under the direction of the Counterintelligence Staff (CI Staff) was directed to begin an effort to determine the cause of the compromises. This effort, which was primarily analytic in nature, paralleled a separate FBI task force to determine whether the FBI had been penetrated. The FBI task force ended, and the CIA STF effort diminished significantly in 1988 as its participants became caught up in the creation of the Counterintelligence Center (CIC). Between 1988 and 1990, the CIA molehunt came to a low ebb as the officers involved concentrated on other CI matters that were believed to have higher priority.

4. In late 1989, after his return from Rome, Ames's lifestyle and spending habits had changed as a result of the large amounts of money he had received from the KGB in return for the information he provided. Ames made no special efforts to conceal his newly acquired wealth and, for example, paid cash for a $540,000 home. This unexplained affluence was brought to the attention of the molehunt team by a CIA employee in late 1989, and a CIC officer began a financial inquiry. The preliminary results of the financial inquiry indicated several large cash transactions but were not considered particularly significant at the time.

5. Nevertheless, information regarding Ames's finances was provided to the Office of Security (OS) by CIC in 1990. A background investigation (BI) was conducted and a polygraph examination was scheduled. The BI was very thorough and produced information that indicated further questions about Ames and his spending habits. However, this information was not made available to the polygraph examiners who tested him, and CIC did not take steps to ensure that the examiners would have full knowledge of all it knew about Ames at the time. In April 1991, OS determined that Ames had successfully completed the reinvestigation polygraph with no indications of deception, just as he had five years previously.

6. In 1991, CIA's molehunt was revitalized and rejuvenated. Two counterintelligence officers were assigned full-time to find the cause of the 1985–86 compromises. The FBI provided two officers to work as part of the molehunt team.

7. During this phase, attention was redirected at Ames and a number of other possible suspects. In March 1992, a decision was made to complete the financial inquiry of Ames that had been initiated in 1989. In August 1992, a correlation was made between bank deposits by Ames that were identified by the financial inquiry and meetings between Ames and a Soviet official that the Agency and FBI had authorized in 1985. The joint CIA/FBI analytic effort fort resulted in a report written in March 1993, which concluded that, among other things, there was a penetration of the CIA. It was expected by CIA and FBI officials that the report, which included lists of CIA employees who had access to the compromised cases, would be reviewed by the FBI in consideration of further investigative steps.

8. The totality of the information available to CIC and the FBI prompted the FBI to launch an intensive CI investigation of Ames. During this phase, the FBI

attempted to gather sufficient information to determine whether Ames was in fact engaged in espionage, and the Agency molehunt team was relegated to a supporting role. Every effort was made to avoid alerting Ames to the FBI CI investigation. According to FBI and Agency officials, it was not until a search of Ames's residential trash in September 1993, which produced a copy of an operational note from Ames to the Russians, that they were certain Ames was a spy. After the FBI had gathered additional information, Ames was arrested on February 21, 1994 and pled guilty to espionage on April 28, 1994.

9. The two CIA officers and the two FBI officers who began working in earnest on the possibility of an Agency penetration in 1991 under the auspices of the Agency's CIC, deserve credit for the ultimate identification of Ames as a hostile intelligence penetration of CIA. Without their efforts, it is possible that Ames might never have been successfully identified and prosecuted. Although proof of his espionage activities was not obtained until after the FBI began its CI investigation of Ames in 1993, the CIA molehunt team played a critical role in providing a context for the opening of an intensive investigation by the FBI. Moreover, although the CIA and the FBI have had disagreements and difficulties with coordination in other cases in the past, there is ample evidence to support the statements by both FBI and CIA senior management that the Ames case was a model of CI cooperation between the two agencies.

10. From its beginnings in 1986, however, the management of CIA's molehunt effort was deficient in several respects. These management deficiencies contributed to the delay in identifying Ames as a possible penetration, even though he was a careless spy who was sloppy and inattentive to measures that would conceal his activities. Despite the persistence of the individuals who played a part in the molehunt, it suffered from insufficient senior management attention, a lack of proper resources, and an array of immediate and extended distractions. The existence and toleration of these deficiencies is difficult to understand in light of the seriousness of the 1985–86 compromises and especially when considered in the context of the series of other CI failures that the Agency suffered in the 1980s and the decade-long history of external attention to the weaknesses in the Agency's CI and security programs. The deficiencies reflect a CIA CI function that has not recovered its legitimacy since the excesses of James Angleton, which resulted in his involuntary retirement from CIA in 1974. Furthermore, to some extent, the ''Angleton Syndrome'' has become a canard that is used to downplay the role of CI in the Agency.

11. Even in this context, it is difficult to understand the repeated failure to focus more attention on Ames earlier when his name continued to come up throughout the investigation. He had access to all the compromised cases; his financial resources improved substantially for unestablished reasons; and his laziness and poor performance were rather widely known. All of these are CI indicators that should have drawn attention to Ames. Combined, they should have made him stand out. Arguably, these indicators played a role in the fact that Ames was often named as a prime suspect by those involved in the molehunt.

12. One result of management inattention was the failure of CIA to bring a full range of potential resources to bear on this counterespionage investigation. There was an over-emphasis on operational analysis and the qualifications thought necessary to engage in such analysis, and a failure to employ fully such investigative techniques as financial analysis, the polygraph, behavioral analysis interviews, and the review of public and governmental records. These problems were exacerbated by the ambiguous division of the counterespionage function between CIC and OS and the continuing subordination by the Directorate of Operations (DO) of CI concerns to foreign intelligence collection interests.

Excessive compartmentation has broadened the gap in communications between CIC and OS, and this problem has not been overcome despite efforts to improve coordination. CIC did not share information fully with OS or properly coordinate the OS investigation process.

13. These defects in the Agency's capability to conduct counterespionage investigations have been accompanied by a degradation of the security function within the Agency due to management policies and resource decisions during the past decade. These management policies emphasize generalization over expertise, quantity over quality, and accommodation rather than professionalism in the security field. This degradation of the security function has manifested itself in the reinvestigation and polygraph programs and appears to have contributed to Ames's ability to complete polygraphs successfully in 1986 and 1991 after he began his espionage activities.

14. Beyond defects in counterespionage investigations and related security programs, the Ames case reflects significant deficiencies in the Agency's personnel management policies. No evidence has been found that any Agency manager knowingly and willfully aided Ames in his espionage activities. However, Ames continued to be selected for positions in SE Division, CIC and the Counternarcotics Center that gave him significant access to highly sensitive information despite strong evidence of performance and suitability problems and, in the last few years of his career, substantial suspicion regarding his trustworthiness. A psychological profile of Ames that was prepared as part of this investigation indicates a troubled employee with a significant potential to engage in harmful activities.

15. Although information regarding Ames's professional and personal failings may not have been available in the aggregate to all of his managers or in any complete and official record, little effort was made by those managers who were aware of Ames's poor performance and behavioral problems to identify the problems officially and deal with them. If Agency management had acted more responsibly and responsively as these problems arose, it is possible that the Ames case could have been avoided in that he might not have been placed in a position where he could give away such sensitive source information.

16. The principal deficiency in the Ames case was the failure to ensure that the Agency employed its best efforts and adequate resources in determining on a timely basis the cause, including the possibility of a human penetration, of the compromises in 1985–86 of essentially its entire cadre of Soviet sources. The individual officers who deserve recognition for their roles in the eventual identification of Ames were forced to overcome what appears to have been significant inattentiveness on the part of senior Agency management. As time wore on and other priorities intervened, the 1985–86 compromises received less and less senior management attention. The compromises were not addressed resolutely until the spring of 1991 when it was decided that a concerted effort was required to resolve them. Even then, it took nearly three years to identify and arrest Ames, not because he was careful and crafty, but because the Agency effort was inadequate.

17. Senior Agency management, including several DDOs, DO Division Chiefs, CIC and DO officials, should be held accountable for permitting an officer with obvious problems such as Ames to continue to be placed in sensitive positions where he was able to engage in activities that have caused great harm to the United States. Senior Agency management, including at least several DCIs, Deputy Directors, DO Division Chiefs, and senior CI and security officials, should also be held accountable for not ensuring that the Agency made a maximum effort to resolve the compromises quickly through the conduct of a focused investigation conducted by adequate numbers of qualified personnel.

NOTES

1. On the Nosenko controversy, see Richards J. Heuer, Jr., "Nosenko: Five Paths to Judgment," in H. Bradford Westerfield, ed., *Inside CIA's Private World: Declassified Articles from the Agency's Internal Journal, 1955–1992* (New Haven, CT: Yale University Press, 1995): 379–414. One of Nosenko's original handlers was the author Tennent H. Bagley, who wrote *Spy Wars: Moles, Mysteries, and Deadly Games* (New Haven, CT: Yale University Press, 2007).

2. In 1966, the Soviet (SR) Division was merged with the East European (EE) Division to form the Soviet Bloc (SB) Division.

3. "Oral History: Reflections of DCI Colby and Helms on the CIA's 'Time of Trouble,'" *Studies in Intelligence* 51:3 (2007).

4. The facility was officially designated New York International Airport on 31 July, 1948, but was widely known as Idlewild Airport after the golf course that had been there. It officially became John F. Kennedy International Airport on 24 December, 1963.

5. See Chapter 12, "The Family Jewels."

6. See Chapter 12, "The Family Jewels."

7. See also "An Assessment of the Aldrich H. Ames Espionage Case and Its Implications for U.S. Intelligence," Report prepared by the Staff of the Select Committee on Intelligence, United States Senate, 103rd Congress, 2nd Session (Washington, D.C.: U.S. Government Printing Office, 1994); Tim Weiner et al., *Betrayal: The Story of Aldrich Ames, an American Spy* (New York: Random House, 1995).

8. The Soviet East European Division, later renamed the Central Eurasia Division, directed operations related to the Soviet Union and its successor states.

Chapter 7

The Search for Foreign Instigators: Operation Chaos and the Intelligence Evaluation Committee

Espionage conducted within the United States or against U.S. citizens was one of the few clear prohibitions placed on the CIA by its charter, the National Security Act of 1947. The clearest violation of that was the MHCHAOS program, also known as Operation Chaos. After reports began leaking to the public in the 1970s, MHCHAOS took on legendary proportions in the press and popular books. As depicted in the "Family Jewels" file, it takes on more modest proportions and a greater foreign focus. Nonetheless, it did create files and a computer database on thousands of U.S. citizens in violation of the CIA's charter. It was not, however, a CIA initiative.

The MHCHAOS program commenced in 1967 in response to President Lyndon B. Johnson's insistence that "foreign communists" lay behind the antiwar movement and other dissident groups operating in the United States at that time. The program was continued into the administration of President Richard M. Nixon, who shared Johnson's views on dissidents. It had been created specifically for that purpose and was run by the Special Operations Group (SOG) under Richard Ober.

Closely related to MHCHAOS in concept was the Intelligence Evaluation Committee. An interdepartmental body established under Nixon in 1970, the Intelligence Evaluation Committee was also assigned to study the foreign roots of internal dissidence, and its existence was also regarded as a secret. Counterintelligence Chief James Angleton noted in a memo to William E. Colby (dated 8 May 1973) that the driving force behind the Intelligence Evaluation Committee was Assistant Attorney General for Internal Security Robert Mardian. At that time, May 1973, Mardian was facing a grand jury.[1]

Ober, the chief of the SOG, also served on the staff of the Intelligence Evaluation Committee and as an alternate member of the committee itself. Within the committee, the CIA was assigned to deal only with the foreign aspects of issues.

It appears that most members of the Intelligence Evaluation Committee may have been unaware of the existence of the separate CIA program.

DCI Richard Helms stated that he repeatedly reported to the president that no evidence of significant foreign links had been found. The president repeatedly told him to try harder. Reports from the Intelligence Evaluation Committee, transcribed below, give an indication of how spare some of the findings were. In the process, however, Ober's group within the CIA studied 7,000 FBI files and generated a computerized database containing more than 300,000 names.[2]

The MHCHAOS program was so secret that few within the CIA knew of its existence. It reported directly to Helms, who relayed its findings to the president. An indication of the secrecy surrounding MHCHAOS comes in the following note from the "Family Jewels" file addressed to William Colby from a friend.

15 May 1973

Dear Bill,

Prior to my assignment in Nha Trang [South Vietnam] I was assigned to the CI [Counterintelligence] Staff for approximately 20 months. While I was with the Staff I was led to believe that one of the "Groups" on the ground floor, [—] was involved in domestic operations. I believe their target(s) were minority group(s). The Chief and Deputy Chief of the Group at that time were Dick Ober and [—] respectively. One of their Case Officers, [—] spent over 50% of his time TDY [on temporary duty] within the United States. It was my understanding they reported only to the White House and to Dick Helms. Other members of the Staff, including myself, had limited access to the [—] area, only when necessary and escorted at all times. Perhaps you were or are now aware of what the operations are. However, I believe I would be remiss in not responding to the book cable (407190). And perhaps their operations might have been outside the legislative charter.

Also, during my tour with the CI Staff I accidentally learned they launched someone into Vietnam while you and [—] were there. I believe this was without the knowledge or approval of Chief, [—] (If I recall, the Case Officer was [—].) I mention the latter only because of the following: When they learned that [—] was being reassigned from Saigon to Chief Operations, FE [Far East], they also learned that I was a friend of [—] and from the same area [—]. As a result they cautioned me not to discuss any of their operations with [—]. This I did not do.

[—paragraph deleted; about six lines—]

Sincerely,
[—name deleted—]

In a heavily redacted memorandum to the Director of Central Intelligence (dated 8 May 1973) in the "Family Jewels" file, the Deputy Director for Intelligence includes this brief comment.

OCI [Office of Current Intelligence], in 1967 and 1968, prepared intelligence memoranda on possible foreign connections with the US anti-war movement and worldwide student dissidence (including the SDS) at the request of the White House.

Another memorandum in the file, from the Office of Current Intelligence to the Deputy Director for Intelligence and dated the previous day, elaborated on the surveillance of the antiwar movement without mentioning the code name.

In response to Johnson's instructions, DCI Richard Helms told the Counterintelligence Division to work with the FBI and "to collect whatever information was available through our own sources." It appears that CI's activities were limited to reporting on contacts with foreign "elements" and governments through its stations in other countries. Note that for a few months the CIA or the National Security Agency (NSA) or both had been intercepting phone calls between the United States and foreign countries as well as phone calls between foreign countries that were routed through the United States.[3]

7 May 1973

MEMORANDUM FOR: Director of Central Intelligence

VIA: Deputy Director for Intelligence

FROM: Director of Current Intelligence

SUBJECT: Activity Related to Domestic Events

1. In late 1967 OCI participated in the preparation of several short intelligence memoranda dealing with the foreign connections of US organizations and activists involved in the anti-war movement. The main purpose of these reports, prepared at the request of the White House, was to determine whether any links existed between international Communist elements or foreign governments and the American peace movement. The conclusion reached was that there was some evidence of ad hoc contacts between anti-war activists at home and abroad but no evidence of direction or formal coordination.

2. In October 1967 President Johnson expressed interest in this subject and ordered a high level interdepartmental survey. In response to his personal request to the DCI, Mr. Helms asked the CI Staff to collect whatever information was available through our own sources and through liaison with the FBI and to pass it to OCI, which was directed to prepare a memorandum from the DCI to the President.

3. A book message requirement was sent to all stations to report whatever information was on hand relevant to this subject. Although agent reports on Communist front operations overseas were of some value, the primary source of information on the activities of US activists—and that was quite limited—was sensitive intercepts by NSA [National Security Agency], which had been similarly tasked by the White House.

4. A draft memorandum was jointly prepared by OCI and CI Staff and forwarded to the DCI. He passed this typescript memo, dated 15 November 1967, to the President personally. The White House copy is now in the files of President Johnson's papers at the library in Austin.

5. Brief follow-up memoranda were prepared and forwarded to the White House on 21 December and 17 January 1968. According to our best recollection, no further finished intelligence reports on international connections of the peace movement were produced.

[—signature and name deleted—]
Director of Current Intelligence

Another memorandum from the "Family Jewels" file gives some of the operational details of MHCHAOS. This memo denies strongly that the program involves domestic espionage.

8 May 73

SUBJECT: The MHCHAOS Program

1. The MHCHAOS program is a worldwide program for clandestine collection abroad of information on foreign efforts to support/encourage/exploit/ manipulate domestic U.S. extremism, especially by Cuba, Communist China, North Vietnam, the Soviet Union, North Korea and the Arab fedayeen.

2. The MHCHAOS program has not and is not conducting efforts domestically for internal domestic collection purposes. Agency efforts are foreign. Foreign-oriented activity in the United States has been of two types:

   a. Selected FBI domestic sources who travel abroad in connection with their extremist activity and/or affiliations to make contact with hostile foreign powers or with foreign extremist groups have been briefed and debriefed by Headquarters officers. The briefing has included appropriate operational guidance, including defensive advice.

   b. Americans with existing extremist credentials have been assessed, recruited, tested and dispatched abroad for PCS assignments as contract agents, primarily sources offered for such use by the FBI. When abroad they collect information responsive to MHCHAOS program requirements. They are thus used primarily for targeting against Cubans, Chinese Communists, the North Vietnamese, etc. as their background and their particular access permits. It should be noted that the [—] aspect of the [—] project of the East Asia Division is similar to the MHCHAOS program.[4]

3. As indicated earlier, MHCHAOS is a foreign program, conducted overseas, except for the limited activity described above. The program is and has been managed so as to achieve the maximum feasible utilization of existing resources of the Operations Directorate. No assets have been recruited and run exclusively for the MHCHAOS program. Instead, emphasis has been placed on the exploitation of new and old Agency assets who have a by-product capability or a concurrent capability for provision of information responsive to the program's requirements. This has involved the provision of custom-tailored collection requirements and operational guidance. This collection program is viewed as an integral part of the recruitment and collection programs of China Operations, Vietnam Operations, Cuban Operations, Soviet Bloc Division operations and Korean Branch operations. Agents who have an American "Movement" background or who have known connections with the American "Movement" are useful as access agents to obtain biographic and personality data, to discern possible vulnerabilities and susceptibilities, and to develop operationally exploitable relationships with recruitment targets of the above programs. These assets are of interest to our targets because of their connections with and /or knowledge of the American "Movement." Over the course of the MHCHAOS program, there have been approximately 20 important areas of operational interest, which at the present time have been reduced to about ten: Paris, Stockholm, Brussels, Dar Es Salaam, Conakry, Algiers, Mexico City, Santiago, Ottawa and Hong Kong.

4. The MHCHAOS program also utilizes audio operations, two of which have been implemented to cover targets of special interest.

   a. [—paragraph deleted; about eight lines—]
   b. [—paragraph deleted; about ten lines—]

5. MHCHAOS reporting from abroad relating to the program originates in two ways: Individuals who are noted in contact with Cubans, the Chinese Communists, etc., and who appear to have extremist connections, interests or background are reported upon. Other individuals are reported upon in response to specific Headquarters requirements received from the FBI because such individuals are of active investigatory security interest to the FBI.

6. All cable and dispatch traffic related to the MHCHAOS program is sent via restricted channels. It is not processed by either the Cable Secretariat or the Information Services Division. The control and retrievability of information obtained, including information received from the FBI, is the responsibility of the Special Operations Group.

7. Information responsive to specific FBI requirements is disseminated to the FBI via special controlled dissemination channels, i.e., by restricted handling of cable traffic or via special pouch and specially numbered blind memoranda.

8. Information of particular significance, when collected, has been disseminated by special memorandum over the signature of the Director of Central Intelligence to the White House (Dr. Kissinger or John Dean), as well as to the Attorney General, the Secretary of State and the Director of the FBI.

The following memorandum introduces the Intelligence Evaluation Committee. Attached to it is the table of contents of one of its studies, *The Unauthorized Disclosure of Classified Information*, suggesting that the publication of the Pentagon Papers caused the committee to broaden its interests somewhat beyond foreign instigators. This memorandum comes from the "List of Delicate Matters" within the "Family Jewels" file.

7 May 1973

SUBJECT: Intelligence Evaluation Committee and Staff

1. Background: Formed December 1970. Membership: Department of Justice (Chairman); FBI (active staff participation agreed to only in May 1971); Department of Defense; Secret Service; National Security Agency; CIA and any necessary representatives of other Departments or Agencies. (Following have participated: Treasury, State.) Staff: IES Executive Director John Dougherty and later Bernard Wells supplied by Department of Justice with title of Special Assistant to the Attorney General in reporting through the Assistant Attorney General for Internal Security Robert Mardian and later William Olsen. IES has received requirements directly from and delivered reports directly to John Dean of the White House.

2. CIA Participation: Contributions on foreign aspects (by memorandum with no agency letterhead or attribution). Contributions occasionally include foreign intelligence provided by FBI and NSA.

3. Special Report: The Unauthorized Disclosure of Classified Information, November 1971. Initiated July 1971 by the White House as a consequence of the President's concern about the release of the Pentagon Papers by Daniel Ellsberg. Both Robert Mardian and G. Gordon Liddy initially involved in tasking the IES to produce this evaluation. Drafting done by IES Staff members from Justice and FBI. Only Agency participation was editorial review.

(Table of contents attached).

TABLE OF CONTENTS

By May 1973, CIA Inspector General William Broe was becoming concerned that the agency faced an unfortunate combination of factors: leaks to the press regarding the Intelligence Evaluation Committee and growing resentment within the CIA regarding MHCHAOS.

30 May 1973

MEMORANDUM FOR: Mr. William E. Colby

SUBJECT: MHCHAOS and [—]

I call to your attention the attached sensitive annexes to our 1972 report of survey of EUR [Europe] Division. You have seen them before, but a fresh look at them might be in order in the light of current developments. [—just over one line deleted—] The recent revelations about the activities of the Intelligence Evaluation Committee are getting close to our MHCHAOS program. We are particularly concerned about MHCHAOS because of the high degree of resentment we found among many Agency employees at their being expected to participate in it.

/signed/
William V. Broe
Inspector General

Attachments [not included]

The "Family Jewels" file offers a number of reports from the International Evaluation Committee submitted by Ober as well as a somewhat expanded version of his earlier background memorandum on the committee. These are preceded by two brief notes, the first addressed to Colby and the second to Inspector General Broe. The name of the originator has been deleted from each.

MEMORANDUM FOR: Mr. Colby

Attached is the material we requested from Dick Ober:

A. Ten Reports, Subj: Foreign Support for Activities Planned to Disrupt or Harass the Republican National Convention
B. Five Reports, Subj: Foreign Support for Activities Planned to Disrupt or Harass the Democratic National Convention
C. Two Memoranda re Agency support to Secret Service for Democratic and Republican Conventions

Ober advises that the only American we report on to the IEC is Rennie Davis.

(14 May 73)

Mr. Broe:

Dick Ober has been advised that this package is being sent to you. Since knowledge of the existence of this Committee has been strictly limited, I've asked that it be delivered to you unopened. Although it has an ER number on it, it has not been sent through that office—I gave them only the day, subject, and originator.

15 May 73

[Note on routing sheet from Ober to Evans, dated 14 May 1973:]

Attached are:

1. Background note on the Committee per your request of this morning.
2. Copies of memoranda concerning Agency support to Secret Service (7 April and 23 June 1972).

EYES ONLY

Not to go through any registries.

14 May 1973

SUBJECT: Intelligence Evaluation Committee and Staff

1. Background: Formed December 1970 to produce fully-evaluated national domestic intelligence studies, including studies on demonstrations, subversion, extremism and terrorism. Membership: Department of Justice (Chairman); Federal Bureau of Investigation; Department of Defense; Secret Service; National Security Agency; Central Intelligence Agency; and as necessary representatives of other Departments or Agencies (following have participated: Treasury and State). Staff: IES, Executive Director John Dougherty and later Bernard Wells supplied by Department of Justice with title of Special Assistant to the Attorney General reporting to the Assistant Attorney General for Internal Security Robert Mardian and later William Olson. IES has received requirements directly from and delivered reports directly to John Dean of the White House. The White House has insisted that the existence of this Committee be kept secret. Awareness of its existence within the Agency has been limited to DCI, DDO (DDP), C/CI and four officers of this office.[5]
2. CIA Participation: Contributions on foreign aspects (by memorandum with no Agency letterhead or attribution). Contributions occasionally include foreign intelligence provided by FBI and NSA. The Chief of the Special Operations Group serves as the Agency representative on the Intelligence Evaluation Committee Staff and as the alternate to the Agency representative on the Committee (who is the Chief, Counterintelligence Staff).
3. Special Report: The Unauthorized Disclosure of Classified Information, November 1971. This study was initiated in July 1971 by the White House as a consequence of the President's concern about the release of the Pentagon Papers by Daniel Ellsberg. Both Robert Mardian and G. Gordon Liddy initially involved in tasking the IES to produce this evaluation. Drafting done by IES Staff members from Justice and FBI. Only Agency participation was editorial review.
4. Republican National Convention (21–24 August 1972): At the request of the White House, a series of estimates was prepared by the IES on "Potential Disruptions at the 1972 Republican National Convention, Miami Beach, Florida." The Agency provided from February through August 1972 periodic contributions for these estimates concerning foreign support for activities planned to disrupt or harass the Republican National Convention (copies attached).

5. Democratic National Convention (10–13 July 1972): At the request of the White House, a series of estimates was prepared by the IES on "Potential Disruptions at the 1972 Democratic National Convention, Miami Beach, Florida." The Agency provided between March and July 1972 contributions on foreign support for activities planned to disrupt or harass the Democratic National Convention (copies attached).

Attachments: a/s

23 FEB 1972

SUBJECT: Foreign Support For Activities Planned to Disrupt or Harass the Republican National Convention

1. There are only limited indications thus far of foreign efforts to inspire, support or take advantage of activities designed too disrupt or harass the National Convention of the Republican Party in San Diego, 21–23 August 1972.

2. Some American participants at the Soviet-controlled World Assembly for Peace and Independence of the Peoples of Indochina, held 11–13 February 1972 in Paris/Versailles, attempted unsuccessfully to include a call for international demonstrations to take place at the time of the Republican National Convention. A representative of the San Diego Convention Coalition (SDCC), one of the domestic action groups targeting the Republican Convention, requested the American Delegations' Steering Committee at the World Assembly to include a specific call for international support of activities against the Republican convention in their proposal to the Action Commission of the World Assembly. This request, however, was dropped as too divisive by the Steering Committee, despite initial indications that the proposal would be taken to the floor of the Assembly.

3. John LENNON,[6] a British subject, has provided financial support to Project "YES," which in turn paid the travel expenses to the World Assembly of a representative of leading antiwar activist Rennie DAVIS. (DAVIS' representative is tentatively planning to assist in preparations for disruptive actions at the San Diego Convention.) Project "YES" is an adjunct to another LENNON-supported project, the Election Year Strategy Information Center (EYSIC), of which Rennie DAVIS is a key leader, which was set up to direct New Left protest activities at the Republican National Convention. In Paris Rennie DAVIS' representative to the World Assembly met at least once with officials of the Provisional Revolutionary Government of South Vietnam; it is not known if the Republican National Convention was discussed.

4. The SDCC is planning for foreign support for its harassment of the Republican convention. A working draft plan of the SDCC includes proposals for (a) the use of a special television network to broadcast video-taped messages from other countries, including coverage of sympathetic demonstrations elsewhere; and (b) broadcasts over public address systems of live telephone calls from the Vietnamese in Paris[7] and from the Communist Chinese and others at the United Nations.[8]

21 MAR 1972

Foreign Support for Activities Planned to Disrupt
or Harass the Republican National Convention

SUMMARY AND CONCLUSION:

Indications remain limited, thus far, of foreign efforts to inspire, support or take advantage of activities designed to disrupt or harass the National Convention of the Republican Party in San Diego, 21–23 August 1972. The concept of coordinated international support for domestic activities in the United States was generally endorsed at the recent World Assembly for Peace and Independence of the Peoples of Indochina; however, the Conference issued no specific call for international support of disruptive actions at the American national political conventions.

BACKGROUND:

At the Soviet-controlled World Assembly for Peace and Independence of the Peoples of Indochina, held in Versailles from 10–13 February 1972, there was no mention of American plans for demonstrations at both the Republican and Democratic National Conventions. The final draft resolution from the Conference's "Action Commission" contains an appendix submitted by American delegates whose goal was to secure global coordination for domestic actions in the United States. It calls for international support to six weeks of domestic antiwar actions and demonstrations, from 1 April to 15 May 1972, and concludes with the statement: "This campaign will lead up to the Democratic Party Convention at Miami on July 9, 1972, and the Republican Party Convention in San Diego on August 21, 1972."

The final "Resolution of the Paris World Assembly for the Peace for the Peace and Independence of the Indochinese People" of 13 February 1972, drafted by the "Political Commission" states:

> "In the United States particularly, the protest against the war is voiced more and more strongly, under various forms, such as draft evasions, desertions, resistance, demonstrations which now affect even the soldiers. The Assembly calls for support to these progressive and antiwar forces in the United States, and asks the governments to grant asylum to deserters and to support their right to repatriation. All together, the peoples of the world will efficiently help to impose on the U.S. Government the restoration of peace, and independence and freedom in Vietnam, Laos, and Cambodia."

DEVELOPMENTS:

The San Diego Convention Coalition (SDCC), one of the domestic action groups targetting on the Republican Convention, is planning, in addition to demonstrations, for a "large exposition in the campsights (sic) called Expose 72, which with movies, exhibits, displays will portray the struggles of people all over the world." Plans for activities at Expose 72 are believed to include (a) the use of a special television network to broadcast video-taped messages from other countries, including coverage of sympathetic demonstrations elsewhere; and (b) broadcasts over public address systems of live telephone calls from the Vietnamese in Paris and from the Communist Chinese and others at the United Nations. In addition, the SDCC has suggested that, in order to "outflank NIXON domestically and internationally," international opposition can be expressed "by obtaining the authority of other countries and liberation movements to carry their flags in SDCC demonstrations."

24 APR 1972

Foreign Support for Activities Planned to Disrupt
or Harass the Republican National Convention

SUMMARY:

There is little new evidence of foreign plans or efforts to inspire, support, or take advantage of actions designed to disrupt or harass the Republican National

Convention in San Diego, 21 to 23 August 1972. The Students for a Democratic Society, in joining the ranks of domestic groups planning actions at the Republican Convention, has adopted a proposal to cooperate with Mexican workers and students in a demonstration in Tijuana, Mexico, during the Convention. The San Diego Convention Coalition (SDCC), another domestic group targetting on the Convention, has received a letter of solidarity from the North Vietnamese. The letter is of interest as an indication of North Vietnamese contact with the SDCC; such contact will be required for the SDCC to implement its earlier-reported plans for broadcasts over public address systems during the Convention of live telephone calls from the Vietnamese in Paris.

DEVELOPMENTS:

At its recent convention in Cambridge, Massachusetts, held 30 March to 2 April 1972, the Students for a Democratic Society (SDS) adopted a proposal to hold demonstrations at the San Diego–Tijuana border during the Republican National Convention. The proposal included a call for SDS to cooperate with Mexican workers and students in an action to occur during a fiesta in Tijuana, where Convention delegates will be entertained.

The North Vietnamese have given their endorsement to the San Diego Convention Coalition (SDCC) in the form of a letter from the Vietnam Committee for Solidarity with the American People (VCSWAP), a quasi-official organ of the North Vietnamese Government. The letter, which has been circulated by the SDCC and is dated 27 January 1972, expresses "great delight" with the formation of the SDCC, and conveys the Committee's "best wishes of militant solidarity and friendship." The VCSWAP requests that the SDCC write often and "send us materials you have."

23 MAY 1972

Foreign Support for Activities Planned to Disrupt
or Harass the Republican National Convention

SUMMARY:

Indications remain limited of foreign plans or attempts to inspire, support, influence, or exploit actions designed to disrupt or harass the Republican National Convention in Miami, Florida, 21–23 August 1972.[9] [—about four lines deleted—] The British-based International Confederation for Disarmament and Peace (ICDP) has distributed a "Spring Offensive Calendar" of activities in the United States against the war based on a submission by the People's Coalition for Peace and Justice (PCPJ). The calendar includes actions planned in connection with the Republican Convention.

DEVELOPMENTS:

[—paragraph deleted; about six lines—]
The International Confederation for Disarmament and Peace, a British-based antiwar organization and one of the more prominent member organizations of the Stockholm Conference,[10] has attached a "Spring Offensive Calendar" to the April–May 1972 issue of its regular international publication <u>Vietnam International</u>. The calendar had been furnished by the People's Coalition for Peace and Justice (PCPJ) and included the following entry:

August 21–23 Republican Convention, San Diego.
        Demonstrations organized by the San
        Diego Convention Coalition, Box 8267,
        San Diego, Ca. 92103.

The ICDP commentary on the PCPJ calendar urges demonstrations in support of some of the dates listed but does not specifically call for actions in connection with the Republican Convention.

14 JUN 1972

Foreign Support for Activities Planned to Disrupt
or Harass the Republican National Convention

SUMMARY:

The only new indication of foreign plans or efforts to inspire, support, influence, or exploit actions designed to disrupt or harass the Republican National Convention in Miami, Florida, 21–23 August 1972, is an expression of interest by a member of the North Vietnamese Delegation to the Paris Peace Talks in the plans of the major antiwar organizations in the United States for demonstrations in connection with the political conventions of both major parties.

DEVELOPMENTS:

In mid-May 1972, a member of the North Vietnamese Delegation to the Paris Peace Talks invited a visitor to contact him again when the visitor returned from an imminent trip to the United States. The North Vietnamese official gave the visitor the New York City addresses of the People's Coalition for Peace and Justice (PCPJ) and the National Peace Action Coalition (NPAC), and asked the visitor to inquire at their offices regarding their plans for demonstrations during the coming summer. The North Vietnamese official stated that he was especially interested in plans for actions in connection with the Democratic and Republican National Conventions.

28 JUN 1972

Foreign Support for Activities Planned to Disrupt
or Harass the Republican National Convention

There are no additional indications of any substantial foreign plans or efforts to inspire, support, or take advantage of activities designed to disrupt or harass the National Convention of the Republican Party in Miami, Florida, 21–24 August 1972.

26 JUL 1972

Foreign Support for Activities Planned to Disrupt
or Harass the Republican National Convention

SUMMARY:

New indications of foreign plans or efforts to inspire, support, influence, or exploit activities designed to disrupt or harass the Republican National Convention in Miami, Florida, 21–24 August 1972, consist of the following: A leader of the People's Coalition for Peace and Justice (PCPJ) has stated that demonstrations will be organized to take place at United States and allied military installations abroad during the period immediately before and during the Republican Convention. The PCPJ leader also stated that representatives of the Stockholm Conference on Vietnam will participate in activities in connection with the Convention. The Anti-War

Union (AWU), a domestic organization which has been active in planning demonstrations in connection with the Republican National Convention, has sent a delegation to Paris, France, to meet with officials of the Democratic Republic of Vietnam (DRV)[11] and with the Provisional Revolutionary Government of South Vietnam (PRG).[12] No information is presently available, however, indicating that actions at the Republican Convention have been discussed at these meetings.

DEVELOPMENTS:

In an early July 1972 meeting with prominent members of foreign antiwar organizations, a representative of the People's Coalition for Peace and Justice (PCPJ), who occupies an important position within that organization, discussed the plans of the PCPJ in connection with the upcoming election campaign in the United States. The PCPJ representative stated that during the period 14–23 August, a "People's Campaign Against Bombing" would be waged in U.S. cities involved in the manufacture and shipping of materials for use in Vietnam, and that similar actions will be organized at United States and allied military installations abroad. The PCPJ representative further stated that "dramatic demonstrations" in protest of the bombing of Vietnam are being organized by the "Republican Party National Convention Coalition" to occur on 21 August 1972. In an apparent reference to the 21 August actions, the PCPJ leader added that representatives of the Stockholm Conference on Vietnam will speak on the subject of the alleged American bombing of dikes in North Vietnam. (Comment: We have no present information concerning plans of Stockholm Conference representatives to travel to the United States during the Republican National Convention; nor do we have any additional information concerning plans of Stockholm Conference representatives to participate in activities connected with the Republican Convention.)

The Anti-War Union (AWU), a domestic group engaged in organizing counteractivities at the Republican National Convention, has sponsored the travel of a delegation of activists to Paris, France, to meet with officials of the Democratic Republic of Vietnam (DRV) and the Provisional Revolutionary Government of South Vietnam (PRG). An advance party has already met with the DRV and PRG representatives to discuss the agenda for meetings with the full AWU delegation. Although no information is presently available indicating that actions at the Republican Convention have been discussed or are scheduled to be discussed at meetings between the AWU delegation and the DRV/PRG officials, it is known that members of the AWU advance party have asked for advice from the PRG officials regarding the stance the AWU should take on certain questions relating to the presidential elections. It is also known that the DRV officials have questioned the AWU advance party about the political mood in the United States. One of the AWU delegation members has stated that upon their return to the United States about 26 July 1972, some of the members will speak at rallies, over the radio, and on television, to "educate the American people about the consequences of voting for Nixon, and the need to end the war and defeat Nixon." The delegation member added that the demonstrations at the Republican Convention will be "unique."

2 AUG 1972

Foreign Support for Activities Planned to Disrupt or Harass the Republican National Convention

SUMMARY:

There are no new indications of specific foreign plans or efforts to inspire, support, influence, or exploit activities designed to disrupt or harass the Republican National Convention in Miami, Florida, 21–24 August 1972. Although meetings have been held recently in Paris, France, between American antiwar activists and representatives of the Democratic Republic of Vietnam (DRV) and the Provisional Revolutionary Government of South Vietnam (PRG), currently available information indicates that the DRV/PRG officials made no efforts to encourage or give guidance to the American participants with respect to the upcoming Republican National Convention. Private discussions, separate from the meetings with the entire American delegation, were conducted by both the DRV and the PRG officials; at present, we have no information regarding the substance of these private exchanges. A second group of activists, considered more important than the first delegation, is scheduled to travel to Paris on or about 1 August 1972 for further consultations with the PRG and DRV representatives.

DEVELOPMENTS:

In recent meetings in Paris, France, with members of an American delegations sponsored by the Anti-War Union (AWU), representatives of the Democratic Republic of Vietnam (DRV) and the Provisional Revolutionary Government of South Vietnam (PRG) were very guarded with respect to discussing activities at the Republican National Convention. Although the Vietnamese repeatedly questioned the Americans concerning the mood of the antiwar movement in the United States, they made no direct reference to the Republican Convention, except for one instance when PRG Deputy Chief Nguyen Van TIEN accused President Nixon of using the private and public sessions of the Paris peace talks as "propaganda for the Republican Convention." TIEN then urged the Americans to promote and propagandize the Seven Point Plan offered by the PRG. The Americans, too, for the most part, refrained from discussing the Convention, other than to estimate that demonstrators will number about 10,000 at the Convention.

Following their meeting on 22 July 1972 with the AWU delegation, the PRG officials held additional talks with sub-groups of the delegation. Additionally, at least one of the American participants was invited by the DRV officials to return for further discussions. At present, there is no information available concerning the substance of these private exchanges.

A second, more important delegation of Americans connected with the Anti-War Union is scheduled to travel to Paris circa 1 August 1972 for further consultation with DRV and PRG representatives. This second group is scheduled to be led by Rennie DAVIS, founder and leader of the AWU. This will be DAVIS' second trip to Paris within recent months for discussions with DRV and PRG representatives. Upon his return from his first trip, DAVIS publicly stated that the AWU would demonstrate at both the Democratic and the Republican Convention, but that the AWU's chief target would be the Republican Convention.

9 AUG 1972

Foreign Support for Activities Planned to Disrupt
or Harass the Republican National Convention

There are no new indications, as of this date, of foreign plans or efforts to inspire, support, or take advantage of activities designed to disrupt or harass the National Convention of the Republican Party in Miami, Florida, 21–24 August 1972.

16 AUG 1972

Foreign Support for Activities Planned to Disrupt
or Harass the Republican National Convention

There are no new indications, as of this date, of foreign plans or efforts to inspire, support, or take advantage of activities designed to disrupt or harass the

National Convention of the Republican Party in Miami, Florida, 21–24 August 1972.

A parallel, albeit shorter, series of reports focused on exactly the same question regarding the Democratic National Convention, which was to be held in Miami as well. The conclusions were also similar.

06 MAR 1972

Foreign Support for Activities Planned to Disrupt
Or Harass the Democratic National Convention

SUMMARY AND CONCLUSION:

There are no direct indications thus far of foreign efforts to inspire, support or take advantage of activities designed to disrupt or harass the National Convention of the Democratic Party in Miami, 10–13 July 1972. The concept of coordinated international support for domestic activities in the United States was generally endorsed at the recent World Assembly for Peace and Independence of the Peoples of Indochina; however, the Conference issued no specific call for international support of disruptive actions at the American national political conventions.

BACKGROUND:

At the Soviet-controlled World Assembly for Peace and Independence of the Peoples' of Indochina, held in Versailles from 10–13 February 1972, there was mention of American plans for demonstrations at both the Republican and Democratic National Conventions. The final draft resolution from the conference's "Action Commission" contains an appendix submitted by the American delegates whose goal was to secure global coordination for domestic actions in the United States. It calls for international support to six weeks of domestic antiwar actions and demonstrations, from 1 April to 15 May 1972, and concludes with the statement: "This campaign will lead up to the Democratic Party Convention at Miami on July 9, 1972, and the Republican Party Convention in San Diego on August 21, 1972."

The final "Resolution of the Paris World Assembly for the Peace and Independence of the Indochinese People" of 13 February 1972, drafted by the "Political Commission" states:

> "In the United States particularly, the protest against the war is voiced more and more strongly, under various forms, such as draft evasions, desertions, resistance, and demonstrations which now affect even the soldiers. The Assembly calls for support to these progressive and antiwar forces in the United States, and asks the governments to grant asylum to deserters and to support their right to repatriation. All together, the peoples of the world will efficiently help to impose on the U.S. Government the restoration of peace, independence and freedom in Vietnam, Laos and Cambodia."

09 MAY 1972

Foreign Support for Activities Planned to Disrupt
or Harass the Democratic National Convention

SUMMARY:

New indications of foreign efforts or plans to inspire, support, influence, or exploit actions designed to disrupt or harass the Democratic National Convention in Miami, 10–13 July 1972, are limited to a reiteration by a member of the Secretariat of the Stockholm Conference on Vietnam of a statement previously issued by the World Assembly for Peace and Independence of the Peoples of Indochina. The Assembly's pronouncement generally endorsed the concept of international support to a campaign of anti-Vietnam War activities in the United States leading up to the Democratic and Republican Conventions, but made no specific call for support of disruptive actions at the conventions themselves.

DEVELOPMENTS:

[—paragraph deleted; about eight lines—]
The World Assembly for Peace and Independence of the Peoples of Indochina, of which the Stockholm Conference was a major organizer, had earlier enunciated a similar statement in an appendix to the final draft resolution of the Assembly's "Action Commission." The appendix called for international support to six weeks of domestic antiwar actions and demonstrations, from 1 April to 15 may 1972, and concluded with the statement: "This campaign will lead up to the Democratic Party Convention at Miami on July 9, 1972, and the Republican Party Convention in San Diego on August 21, 1972."

23 MAY 1972

Foreign Support for Activities Planned to Disrupt
or Harass the Democratic National Convention

SUMMARY:

Indications remain limited of foreign plans or attempts to inspire, support, influence, or exploit actions designed to disrupt or harass the Democratic National Convention in Miami, Florida, 10–13 July 1972. [—about four lines deleted—] The British-based International Confederation for Disarmament and Peace (ICDP) has distributed a "Spring Offensive Calendar" of activities in the United States against the war based on a submission by the Peoples' Coalition for Peace and Justice (PCPJ). The calendar includes actions planned in connection with the Democratic Convention.

DEVELOPMENTS:

[—paragraph deleted; about six lines—]
The International Confederation for Disarmament and Peace, a British-based antiwar organization and one of the more prominent member organizations of the Stockholm Conference, has attached a "Spring Offensive Calendar" to the April–May 1972 issue of its regular international publication Vietnam International. The calendar had been furnished by the People's Coalition for Peace and Justice (PCPJ) and included the following entry:

> July 9–12 Democratic Convention, Miami Beach.
> Demonstrations organized by Florida
> People's Coalition, Box 17521, Tampa,
> Florida 33612.

The ICDP commentary on the PCPJ calendar urges demonstrations in support of some of the dates listed but does not specifically call for actions in connection with the Democratic Convention.

7 JUN 1972

Foreign Support for Activities Planned to Disrupt
or Harass the Democratic National Convention

SUMMARY:

The only new indication of foreign plans or efforts to inspire, support, influence, or exploit actions designed to disrupt or harass the Democratic National Convention in Miami, Florida, 10–13 July 1972, is an expression of interest by a member of the North Vietnamese Delegation to the Paris Peace Talks in the plans of the major antiwar organizations in the United States for demonstrations in connection with the political conventions of both major parties.

DEVELOPMENTS:

In mid-May 1972, a member of the North Vietnamese Delegation to the Paris Peace Talks invited a visitor to contact him again when the visitor returned from an imminent trip to the United States. The North Vietnamese official gave the visitor the New York City addresses of the People's Coalition for Peace and Justice (PCPJ) and the National Peace Action Coalition (NPAC), and asked the visitor to inquire at their offices regarding their plans for demonstrations during the coming summer. The North Vietnamese official stated that he was especially interested in plans for actions in connection with the Democratic and National [sic] Conventions.

21 JUN 1972

Foreign Support for Activities Planned to Disrupt
or Harass the Democratic National Convention

There are no additional indications, as of this date, of foreign plans or efforts to inspire, support, or take advantage of activities designed to disrupt or harass the National Convention of the Democratic Party in Miami, Florida, 10–13 July 1972.

As noted above, these reports were accompanied in the file by two relating to CIA support granted to the Secret Service during the conventions. Also included was the original Secret Service request. The CIA's role, based on the unredacted portions of the memo, was primarily concerned with tracking potential foreign threats, including Cuban intelligence operations, but also with vetting thousands of names of hotel and convention employees. The first memo also acknowledges in passing that the agency had formerly targeted Latin American exile groups in the United States, but that responsibility had passed to the FBI.

23 JUN 1972

MEMORANDUM FOR: Executive Director/Comptroller

VIA: Acting Deputy Director for Plans

SUBJECT: Agency Support to the U.S. Secret Service (USSS) for National Democratic (10–14 July 1972) and National Republican (21–24 August 1972) Conventions

1. This memorandum is for the information of the Executive Director/Comptroller.
2. Authorization for CIA support to the U.S. Secret Service for the Democratic and Republican National Conventions is contained in a memorandum of 7 April 1972 from Chief, CI [Counterintelligence] Staff to the DCI which was concurred in by the ADDP [Acting Deputy Director for Plans] and approved by the DCI on 10 April 1972 (copy attached).

3. On 13 April 1972 the [—] met with the Miami USSS representative and Mr. [—] of USSS headquarters to discuss preliminary planning for [—] support to the USSS prior to and during subject conventions. On 17 April 1972 the [—] and [—] met with Mr. [—] at Headquarters to implement the preliminary planning agreed upon in Miami and to determine the extent of Headquarters support required by the USSS.

4. The basic agreement mutually concurred in by the USSS and Headquarters representatives provided that:

   a. [—] would conduct name traces on all Cubans of interest to USSS.
   b. CIA Headquarters would conduct name traces on all other foreign born persons of interest to the USSS.
   c. CIA would keep the USSS informed of any events in the Caribbean and Latin American areas that would have any bearing on the USSS protective mission during the convention periods. This would include briefings on Cuba and Cuban policies toward the United States and on activities of Cuban intelligence operations which could affect the security of the conventions.
   d. Coverage of Latin American exile groups in the United States would be the responsibility of the FBI since CIA had ceased the extensive coverage formerly targeted against these groups since it was now considered an internal security function.

5. [—paragraph deleted; about thirteen lines—]

6. [—] has arranged the rental of a safehouse about five minutes from convention center which will provide a secure and nearby meeting site for USSS and Agency personnel. This safehouse will be available just prior to and during both conventions. A Headquarters officer will TDY [be sent on temporary duty] to Miami prior to the conventions and remain until the conventions adjourn to assist [—] in providing the support described in paragraph four above.

7. Station WH/Miami is in daily contact with the USSS in Miami, utilizing JMFALCON as a meeting site when necessary. The location of Station WH/Miami (JMCOBRA) has not been revealed to the USSS. (JMCOBRA is located some distance from JMFALCON.) Additionally, the Miami Security Filed Office maintains normal liaison with the local USSS Miami unit.[13]

8. The [—] understands that no personnel will be present at the convention hall, that they will not provide any equipment unique to the Agency, nor will it provide the use of any other facilities other than the safehouse described in paragraph six.

9. A copy of this memorandum is being sent to [—] to insure that the [—] is fully conversant with the guidelines and basic agreements with the Secret Service, and has all of the information agreed upon in Headquarters.

/signed/
Theodore G. Shackley
Chief
Western Hemisphere Division

Attachment

7 APR 1972

MEMORANDUM FOR: Director of Central Intelligence

VIA: Deputy Director for Plans

SUBJECT: CIA Support to the Secret Service
   For the Democratic National
   Convention in Miami, Florida
   July 9–15, 1972

1. This memorandum describes the support which the Secret Service has requested from CIA with regard to the Democratic National Convention. It is recommended that the Agency furnish the support outlined in paragraph 3 of this memorandum and your approval is requested.

2. By memorandum 1-30-610.53 of 30 March (attached as reference), the Secret Service has requested a meeting with appropriate Agency officers to discuss the Agency's support to the Secret Service prior to and during the Democratic National Convention. The Secret Service plans to send an agent to Miami on 11 April to commence preparations for the convention and wishes to have the meeting with Agency Headquarters officers prior to the agent's departure for Miami.

3. While details regarding the type of support which the Secret Service will request of the Agency will not be known until there has been a meeting with the Secret Service on this matter, it is evident from the Secret Service memorandum and from our experience in supporting the Secret Service at the Republican Convention in Miami in 1968 that the Secret Service desires:

   A) Briefings on Cuba and Cuban policy towards the United States. Counterintelligence information on Cuban operations against the United States which could affect the security of the convention.
   B) Briefings on Cuban exile activities in the United States.
   C) Name checks on hotel and convention employees; name checks on those persons in the Miami area whom the Secret Service considers a threat to its protective mission.
   D) A watchlist of persons whom the Agency considers a potential threat to the security of the convention.
   E) Liaison with a designated officer [—several words deleted—] for the purpose of conducting name checks against [—] files and other files available [—several words deleted—].

4. Agency support to the Secret Service for the convention will be centralized at Headquarters and will be controlled by Headquarters. Chief, [—], under the general supervision of the CI Staff, will serve as the coordinator of this support.

[—signature deleted—]
James Angleton
Chief, CI Staff

1 Attachment

THE DEPARTMENT OF THE TREASURY
UNITED STATES SECRET SERVICE
WASHINGTON, D.C. 20226

1-30-610.53
Date: March 30, 1972
BY LIAISON: [—]

TO: Central Intelligence Agency
     ATTN: Mr. [—]

FROM: JAMES J. ROWLEY—DIRECTOR

SUBJECT: Democratic National Convention—Miami, Florida, July 9–15, 1972

In view of our responsibilities regarding the protection of Presidential candidates, we have initiated security preparations for the Democratic National Convention, which will be held in Miami, Florida, between July 9–15, 1972.

We request a meeting as soon as possible between representatives of our Intelligence Division and your agency to discuss intelligence support prior to and during the Democratic National Convention. We are specifically interested in discussing the appropriate channels for routing name checks of hotel and convention employees, as well as other individuals of protective interest to this Service. We anticipate there will be several thousand names to be checked. We would also like to discuss the current Cuban situation, particularly any existing relationships between pro-Cuban groups in the Miami area and mainland Cuba, since we consider these groups to be a potential threat to our protective mission.

NOTES

1. For the Angleton memo, see "The List of Delicate Matters." Mardian was convicted along with John Mitchell, H. R. Haldeman, and John Ehrlichman on charges of conspiracy, obstruction of justice, and perjury in connection with the Watergate cover-up. Mardian's conviction was later overturned because his attorney had been ill. Stanley I. Kutler, *The Wars of Watergate: The Last Crisis of Richard Nixon* (New York: Alfred A. Knopf, 1990): 576.

2. Richard Helms, with William Hood, *A Look over My Shoulder: A Life in the Central Intelligence Agency* (New York: Random House, 2003): 279–282; William Colby, *Honorable Men: My Life in the CIA* (New York: Simon & Schuster, 1978): 313–317.

3. See Chapter 9, "Assistance to Police and Other Agencies."

4. To the left of the last sentence is a handwritten marginal notation: "U.S. citizens recruited to go abroad."

5. DCI stands for the Director of Central Intelligence; DDO (DDP) stands for the Deputy Director for Operations (formerly called Deputy Director for Plans); and C/CI stands for the Chief, Counterintelligence.

6. Formerly of the Beatles.

7. Paris was the site of the long-stalled Vietnam peace negotiations.

8. The People's Republic of China had just assumed, in 1971, the United Nations seat previously held by the Republic of China (Taiwan). The Nixon administration, seeking improved relations with the PRC, acquiesced in this change, which it could have vetoed in the UN Security Council.

9. The venue of Republican National Convention, originally San Diego, was changed to Miami Beach in May, just three month before the event. The principal reason was an accusation by columnist Jack Anderson that ITT had made a $400,000 donation for the San Diego convention in return for a favorable decision by the Department of Justice on an antitrust case. See Vincent S. Ancona, "When the Elephants Marched Out of San Diego: The 1972 Republican Convention Fiasco," *Journal of San Diego History* 38:4 (Fall 1992).

10. The Stockholm Conference on Vietnam was a semipermanent body organized by the World Peace Council. Based in Helsinki, Finland, the World Peace Council had direct ties to the Soviet Union and was widely considered to be controlled by the Communist Party or the KGB.

11. The government of North Vietnam.

12. The revolutionary organization seeking to overthrow the government of South Vietnam with the assistance of North Vietnam. It was widely considered an instrument of the North Vietnamese government and was displaced when the two countries were merged under the North Vietnamese government, one year after the fall of Saigon.

13. The CIA's Western Hemisphere Division (WH) maintained a station in Miami (Station WH/Miami, codenamed JMCOBRA) from which to observe Cuba and maintain contact with Cuban exile groups. JMFALCON is presumably a "base" subordinated to the main "station."

Chapter 8

"CIA's Domestic Activities": The Management Advisory Group

The CIA's legislative charter, the National Security Act of 1947, is vague on many issues but clear about the intention to prohibit the agency from any involvement in law enforcement. This has been interpreted as a prohibition against domestic activities. The agency does not appear to have engaged in widespread domestic espionage, but incidents have occurred, either directly or indirectly (as in training given to metropolitan police forces), especially during the antiwar demonstrations of the Vietnam era.

In the years just before the Daniel Ellsberg and Watergate cases, there were already persistent stories of CIA involvement in domestic affairs, including domestic espionage. These stories appeared in the media and were occasionally denied by the CIA leadership. The agency's leaders, however, do not appear to have fully convinced even their own staff. Evidence of this emerges in a series of memoranda triggered in the spring of 1971 by the CIA Management Advisory Group (MAG), which had been created to improve communications between agency leaders and junior personnel. The MAG was concerned about the rumors, prevalent even within the agency, of domestic spying and feared that the CIA was leaving itself exposed to its political adversaries.

25 March 1971

CENTRAL INTELLIGENCE AGENCY

Management Advisory Group

MEMORANDUM FOR: The Director

THROUGH: The Executive Director

SUBJECT: CIA Domestic Activities

MAG is concerned that CIA avoid involvement in the current expose of the domestic intelligence activities of the Army and other federal agencies. We believe that there are CIA activities similar to those under scrutiny which could cause great embarrassment to the Agency because they appear to exceed the scope of the CIA charter. Except for the Agency's statutory CE/CI [Counterespionage/Counterintelligence] responsibilities, MAG opposes any Agency activity that could be construed as targeted against any person who enjoys the protection of the US Constitution—whether or not he resides in the United States. Except in those cases clearly related to national security, no US citizen should be the object of CIA operations. We realize that on occasion the CIA will develop information about some citizen who is engaged in activities inimical to the interests of the United States. Such information should quickly be turned over to the proper agencies of government for further action, even if it means that sometimes an essentially home-oriented agency may be asked to perform in a limited operational capacity overseas.

If we do not pursue such a course, one day the public and the Congress will come to have grave doubts about our role in government, and may severely restrict our ability to perform those tasks properly assigned to the CIA.

The initial MAG memorandum does not appear to have elicited much of a response. Eight months later, prompted by further public accusations, the group issued a more detailed follow-up memorandum.

Nov 71

MEMORANDUM FOR: The Director

THROUGH: The Executive Director–Comptroller

SUBJECT: CIA's Domestic Activities

REFERENCE: MAG Memorandum, "CIA's Domestic Activities," March 1971

1. MAG is seriously concerned about possible repercussions which may arise as the result of CIA's covert domestic activities. Public revelation that CIA has become involved in collecting information on U.S. citizens would likely redound to the Agency's discredit and jeopardize overall Agency programs.

2. MAG first expressed its concern about CIA's covert domestic activities in a memo for the DCI, transmitted through the Executive Director–Comptroller in the Spring of 1971 (Attachment A). MAG's concern has increased recently because of such articles as Vic Marchetti's UPI interview (Attachment B)[1] and the 10 October New York Times article concerning rupture of FBI-CIA relations (Attachment C). Both hint at extremely sensitive Agency involvement in domestic activities. Additionally, the DCI addresses to the American Society of Newspaper Editors (Attachment D) and to the CIA Annual Awards ceremony (Attachment E) make rather categorical denials of Agency covert targeting on U.S. citizens. Agency employees aware of the various sensitive operations in question know that there is qualifying language explaining CIA involvement. However, MAG believes that in the event of an expose, such esoteric qualifiers will be lost on the American public and that there is probably nothing the Agency could say to alleviate a negative reaction from Congress and the U.S. public. It is MAG's fear that such a negative reaction could seriously damage our Congressional relations, affect our work against priority foreign targets and have significant impact on the viability of CIA.

3. There are indications that the Agency, in responding to CE/CI requirements, is collecting information on selected U.S. citizens both at home and abroad. In operational areas which are highly sensitive and potentially explosive (e.g., domestic radical or racial groups) this Agency must carefully weight the needs and pressures for collecting and maintaining this information against the risk

and impact of revelation should the operation become compromised or public knowledge. We therefore urge that all domestic collection and action programs be severely reviewed so that only those be continued which are of the highest priority and which absolutely cannot be undertaken by domestic agencies. CIA should not take on requirements of this type by default.

4. Not all of the members of MAG are privy to CIA's direct or indirect involvement in domestic activities. Those who are aware probably know only parts of the whole picture. But our increasing concern and our intense interest in maximizing the Agency's ability to do its proper job, impel us to bring our serious apprehensions to your attention.

THE MANAGEMENT ADVISORY GROUP

Attachments B, C, D and E

Attachment B—Vic Marchetti's UPI Interview, from U.S. News and World Report, 11 October 1971:

"Fearing today that the <u>CIA may already have begun 'going against the enemy within'</u> the United States as they may conceive it—that is, <u>dissident student groups</u> and <u>civil-rights organizations</u> ..."

"Because the men of the Agency are superpatriots, he said, it is only natural for them to view violent protest and dissidence as a major threat to the nation.... The inbred CIA reaction, he said, would be to launch a <u>clandestine operation to infiltrate dissident groups</u>.

That, said Marchetti, may already have started to happen.

'I don't have very much to go on,' he said. 'Just bits and pieces that indicate the U.S. Intelligence Community <u>is already targeting on groups in this country that they feel to be subversive</u>.

'I know this was being discussed in the halls of the CIA, and that there were a lot of people who felt this should be done.'"

Attachment C—New York Times, 10 October, "FBI-CIA Relations:"

"Information generally exchanged between the FBI and the CIA might concern such subjects as <u>officers of the Black Panther Party</u> traveling overseas ... and <u>American youngsters cutting sugar cane in Cuba</u>."

Attachment D—DCI Address to the American Society of Newspaper Editors:

"And may I emphasize at this point that the statute specifically forbids the Central Intelligence Agency to have any police, subpoena, or law-enforcement powers, or any <u>domestic security functions</u>. I can assure you that except for the normal responsibilities for protecting the physical security of our own personnel, our facilities, and our classified information, we do not have any such powers and function; we have never sought any; we do not exercise any. In short; we <u>do not target on American citizens</u>."

Attachment E—DCI Address to CIA Annual Awards Ceremony:

"I gave a talk to the American Society of Newspaper Editors last winter, as you know, and I did it for only one purpose. That was to try and put in the record a few of these denials that we've all wanted to see put in the public record for some time. And you can rely on those denials. They're true, and you can use that as any text that you may need to demonstrate that we're not in the drug traffic, and that <u>we're not trying to do espionage on American citizens in the United States</u>."

With the second memorandum, the MAG eventually succeeded in getting a meeting with the Deputy Director for Plans, that is, the head of the Clandestine

Service. He took the opportunity to explain to them why their concerns were not going to be fully addressed. At the same time, he tried to assure them that such activities were limited and usually not really espionage.

21 December 1971

MEMORANDUM FOR: Executive Director–Comptroller

SUBJECT: Meeting with MAG Group

1. I met with the MAG group this morning for little over an hour, and I set forth as candidly as possible those counterintelligence and counterespionage responsibilities of ours overseas which make it mandatory for us occasionally to take an interest in American citizens overseas. I explained the requirements placed on us by the Department of Justice for overseas checks, and also the fact that our normal overseas operations against Soviets and others sometimes produce leads to Americans in conspiratorial contact with our Communist targets.

2. I was asked about our having sent Agency representatives to the Democratic National Convention in Chicago in 1968 and I explained that I never heard of such a thing and did not believe it. I pointed out that, as they knew, the press had reported fully on the Agency participation at the beginning of the sky marshalling program and I assumed they saw nothing wrong with this. They agreed. I also pointed out that, at President Kennedy's funeral, with scores of important foreign personalities here, the Agency lent some assistance to the Secret Service, and here again the group understood that this was a legitimate function.

3. The group made it clear that their concern was over the Agency image if the general public were aware that some of our activities, wherever they took place, were targeted against Blacks. I said that we did not target against Americans of any color in this country, and that the Clandestine Service was colorblind when it came to carrying out its overseas CI responsibilities and it would continue to be so.

4. I agreed that the Director should be asked to speak a little more fully and clearly on whether we "target against American citizens" so that there is no ambiguity.

5. I told the group that we must expect all kinds of irresponsible accusations in the press, such as the one in the January 1972 issue of RAMPARTS magazine in which Bob Kiley and Drex Godfrey, it is suggested, are still in the employ of CIA working on a CIA plan to improve police organizations in this country.[2] I said that this was palpably false as anyone who knows Kiley and Godfrey would understand. The group mentioned Dick Ober's unit and said that there was a lot of scuttlebutt that the purpose of this unit was to keep book on Black Power adherents.[3] I denied this saying that our interest was as I had explained it previously.

6. I do not know whether this is a fair assumption, but Dick Ober's machine program is not handled in the Clandestine Service and it is possible that someone is misreading and misinterpreting the intent of Ober's program from fragmentary bits and pieces that may be discernible from the handling of the machine program. I do not state this as a fact because I have not examined it that closely.

7. I told the group that I had offered to enlighten it candidly on what we do so that they would at least have the facts and I said that I assume you would take it from here.

/signed/
Thomas H. Karamessines
Deputy Director for Plans

The MAG members did not express dissatisfaction with the Karamessines meeting, but neither had they been set at ease. They intended to press the issue further.

23 December 1971

MEMORANDUM FOR: The Executive Director–Comptroller

SUBJECT: CIA's Domestic Activities

REFERENCE: MAG Memoranda on same subject dated March 1971 and November 1971

As requested, MAG met with the DDP on 21 December and discussed with him the referenced memoranda on CIA's covert domestic activities. Our exchange consisted primarily of the DDP responding to the MAG memoranda as they related to activities of the Clandestine Service alone. The DDP made it clear that he spoke only for his Service. Since MAG's initial concern over covert domestic activities extended to, while not being restricted to, the Clandestine Service, it recommends that the referenced memoranda be also brought to the attention of appropriate senior officials in other Agency components.

The Management Advisory Group

The Executive Director–Comptroller is a position roughly equivalent to Chief of Staff. The incumbent at the time was Col. Lawrence K. White (known to his friends as "Red" White), who was just about to retire. (He would be replaced by William E. Colby, just back from Vietnam.) White was clearly annoyed with the group's demands, but he met with them and also looked further into the basis for accusations of CIA activity at the 1968 Democratic National Convention. This he found to be insignificant.

DIARY NOTES

Executive Director–Comptroller/initialed LKW/   4 January 1972

1. I met with the outgoing and incoming MAG Cochairmen. We discussed a number of topics but concentrated particularly on their two most recent memoranda concerning domestic activities. I expressed slight irritation with their second memorandum, which is a shotgun approach to the problem, and asked them to be specific if they have anything in mind. I said I understand they have heard that we sent a surveillance team to the Democratic National Convention. Mr. [—] said that he made this statement because an Office of Security employee reported in his presence that he personally was a member of a team which went to the Convention.[4] (I subsequently raised this with [Director of Security] Howard Osborn, who after investigating reported back that the Secret Service asked us for two technicians during the Democratic National Convention. These technicians were formally detailed to the Secret Service and went to Chicago, where they did RF [Radio Frequency] monitoring under the supervision of the Secret Service. The Secret Service apparently calls RF monitoring "audio surveillance," and it seems that, during the discussion that took place at the Senior Seminar, those who heard this assumed that "surveillance" meant actual surveillance of the candidates, when actually the meeting rooms were being checked to ensure they had not been bugged. I have reported all this to the Director and shall discuss it with MAG when I have dinner with them on 11 January.

Colby, as the new Executive Director–Comptroller, later responded to the issues raised by the MAG with a memorandum to the various division chiefs. The memo reiterated and reemphasized existing policies on a number of issues related to domestic activities, but it also gave examples of justifiable partial exceptions to the general rules. (To be sure, some of the exceptions are a bit vague: "Security investigations are conducted on ... security problems which arise.")[5] As a curious consequence of this, the document, which was purportedly intended to soothe staff concerns, was not to be shared openly with the staff as a whole. Colby limited the distribution of the document to ranking personnel, and it appears that the subject was not to be discussed unless employees raised it first.

21 APR 1972

MEMORANDUM FOR: Deputy Director for Intelligence
Deputy Director for Plans
Deputy Director for Support
Deputy Director for Science and Technology
Heads of Independent Offices

(For Distribution to Office/Division Chief Level Only)

SUBJECT: CIA Activities in the United States

1. From time to time some of our employees express concern over various allegations or rumors of CIA activities in the United States. The attached memorandum is designed to clarify this subject so that supervisors can authoritatively reply to any employees indicating such concern. It is a statement of the facts of the situation. If incidents or activities are reported which appear to conflict with this statement, they should be reported to appropriate senior authority for resolution (or correction if unauthorized activities might have occurred).

2. Because of the possible sensitivity of this description of the Agency's methodology, this memorandum is not being given the usual broad distribution of the "FYI—Allegations and Answers" series. Office and Division Chiefs are urged, however, to use it to inform Branch Chiefs so that its points can be readily available to supervisors to react to expressions of employee concern.

/signed/
W. E. Colby
Executive Director–Comptroller

Attachment

ALLEGATION:

In a variety of ways it has been alleged that CIA is working within the United States, with particular attention to extremist groups.

FACTS:

1. Section 102 of the National Security Act of 1947, subparagraph D3, states, "The Agency shall have no police, subpoena, law-enforcement powers, or internal security functions."

In his speech to the American Society of Newspaper Editors on 14 April 1971, the Director stated:

"I can assure you that except for the normal responsibilities for protecting the physical security of our own personnel, our facilities, and our classified information, we do not have any such powers and functions; we have never sought any; we do not exercise any. In short, we do not target on American citizens."

In the Director's "State of the Agency" speech to employees on 17 September 1971, he said:

"I gave a talk to the American Society of Newspaper Editors last winter, as you know, and I did it for only one purpose. That was to try and put in the record a few of these denials that we've all wanted to see put in the public record for some time. And you can rely on those denials. They're true, and you can use that as any text that you may need to demonstrate that we're not in the drug traffic, and that we're not trying to do espionage on American citizens in the United States, and we're not tapping telephone lines, and that we're not doing a lot of other things that we're accused of doing. One of the things that tends to perpetuate some of these silly ideas are jokes that are made about them, particularly about domestic espionage. Although the jokes have no basis in fact they nevertheless give us a name which we don't deserve. I don't say that that makes all that much difference, but it does make some difference, and this tends to spill over, so I would like to suggest that if you have it in your hearts to do so that you speak up when the occasion arises and try to set the facts straight."

2. From time to time some employees have been concerned that Agency activities might conflict with these statements. They can be assured that Agency activities do not. For clarification, some activities which may have been subject to misunderstanding are listed as follows:

   a. Domestic Contacts. The Domestic Contact Service establishes discreet but overt relationships with American private citizens, commercial, academic and other organizations and resident aliens for the purposes of collecting on a voluntary basis foreign intelligence information or soliciting their cooperation in assisting the Agency to perform its mission overseas. Records of the individuals and organizations cooperating with the Agency are maintained as a necessary practical element of this process.

   b. Security Investigations. Security investigations are conducted on prospective employees, contractors, and consultants, and on security problems which arise. These investigations involve a wide range of investigative procedures, including neighborhood inquiries, checks with other Government agencies, review of credit reports, and interviews with former employers and business associates. This is essential to assure that our personnel possess a high degree of integrity, sense of responsibility, and competence and to protect classified information and sensitive intelligence sources and methods. The resulting files are held separately by the Office of Security and are not merged with other Agency files.

   c. Foreign Resources. On some occasions, foreign citizens of interest to CIA are contacted and recruited in America for work abroad. The purpose of this activity is entirely restricted to the Agency's foreign operations.

   d. Recruitment. CIA recruiters maintain a wide variety of contacts within the United States, assisting individuals interested in employment with CIA to learn more about it and to join its employee force.

   e. Contracting. In the course of CIA business and operations, a number of contracts for procurement, research, or analysis are made with a variety of U.S. companies and individuals. This in no way constitutes operations in the U.S. but rather secures the assistance of these groups in carrying out the CIA mission against foreign targets.

f. Operations. The 1967 Katzenbach Committee report was approved by the Director in March 1967 and is binding on any of our relations with American organizations today. It specifically prohibits covert financial assistance or support, direct or indirect, to any U.S. educational or private voluntary organization. Any relationship or operation the Agency has with an American organization must be and is within these guidelines.[6]

g. Details or Loans. On rare occasions, details of technically qualified CIA personnel, technical advice, or loans of CIA equipment have been made available to other U.S. agencies at their request to assist them to carry out their responsibilities. An example is the skymarshal program, in which some CIA personnel were temporarily detailed to the FAA in order to assist in a rapid initiation of that program. Such personnel and equipment are under the operational control of the receiving agency. Assistance of this nature in no way constitutes an assumption of responsibility or authority by CIA for the program.

h. Counterintelligence and Drugs. To carry out its responsibilities for counterintelligence, CIA is interested in the activities of foreign nations or intelligence services aimed at the U.S. To the extent that these activities lie outside the U.S., including activities aimed at the U.S. utilizing U.S. citizens or others, they fall within CIA's responsibilities. Responsibility for coverage of the activities within the U.S. lies with the FBI, as an internal security function. CIA's responsibility and authority are limited to the foreign intelligence aspect of the problem, and any action of a law enforcement or internal security nature lies with the FBI or local police forces. (CIA's assistance to the U.S. Government program against narcotics and drugs is handled in the same fashion.)

i. Operational Support. To support CIA operations, arrangements are made with various U.S. business or other entities to provide cover or other support for CIA personnel or activities abroad. This can include proprietaries formed or controlled by CIA. While these may exist within the U.S., their purpose is to conduct or support operations abroad.

j. Defectors. As provided by law, CIA occasionally resettles in the U.S. defectors and other foreign individuals of operational interest. This resettlement may involve a new identity, relocation, employment, etc. Although this activity takes place in this country, its purpose is the support of operations abroad.

It appears that the MAG was largely responding to rumors, which evidently ran rampant in the secretive atmosphere of the CIA. What was the basis of these rumors? Among the concerns raised by the MAG was the purported surveillance of domestic radical and Black Power groups within the United States. In fact, a series of memoranda in the "Family Jewels" file dealt with reports written on these or closely related topics. While some of the memoranda are vague as to which agency conducted the actual surveillance, others insist it was the FBI and that the CIA had played no domestic investigative role.

In 1968, the Office of Current Intelligence (OCI), within the Directorate of Intelligence, produced a paper on the topic of student dissidents titled "Restless Youth," which included a section dealing with an American youth organization, Students for a Democratic Society (SDS).[7] According to a memo from the Deputy Director for Intelligence to the Inspector General (dated 22 May 1973), two versions had been produced, one with the chapter on the American organization and one without any reference to it.

The full version of the paper was distributed only to President Lyndon B. Johnson, National Security Adviser Walter Rostow, and Deputy Secretary of Defense Cyrus Vance. The sanitized version had a wider distribution, but it was still limited to only twenty people outside the CIA. After the change of administration in 1969, the sanitized version alone was distributed to Vice President Spiro Agnew and National Security Adviser Henry Kissinger. Attorney General John Mitchell received an even more abbreviated edition. A memo from the Director of Current Intelligence, dated 7 May 1973 and reproduced below, stated that an updated version of the full report went to the White House in February 1969.

The following memorandum, from 1968, reflected the cautious attitude taken toward its distribution. Note that the issue raised was not the need for secrecy for national security's sake, but the "considerable notoriety" that would be raised if the CIA admitted to being interested in the topic. Note, too, that the interest was said to have originated not within the CIA, but was forced upon it by the head of the National Security Council staff.

17 September 1968

MEMORANDUM

SUBJECT: Dissemination of OCI Paper on Student Dissidents

1. <u>Dissemination to the Cabinet and within the Intelligence Community</u>—The paper <u>Restless Youth</u> is sensitive because of the subject matter, because of the likelihood that public exposure of the Agency's interest in the problem of student dissidence would result in considerable notoriety, particularly in the university world, and because pursuant to Mr. Rostow's instructions, the author included in his text a study of student radicals in the United States, thereby exceeding the Agency's charter. We have sanitized the paper for dissemination to members of the President's Cabinet and within the Intelligence Community by eliminating altogether the chapter which discusses Students for a Democratic Society (SDS) and by striking from the Prospects section all mention of SDS.
2. <u>Outside the Community but within the Government</u>—We believe that the basic text should be further edited for the purpose of eliminating even the most casual reference to the domestic scene—lest someone infer from such a chance reference that the original paper had contained a section on American students. The nineteen country chapters which form Part II of <u>Restless Youth</u> can be distributed within the Government, provided that the controls appropriate to their classification are observed. To do the editing and reprinting required would take several days at least.
3. <u>Release to the academic world or to the public</u>—For the reasons set forth above, we believe that release of the basic text would harm the Agency. The country chapters could not be released without first being rewritten to eliminate all classified information. Once this was done, they would duplicate information already available in the open press. There is no lack of overt literature on the subject of student dissent; virtually every publisher includes at least one title on his current listing. Moreover, other agencies of government, such as Health, Education and Welfare, have sponsored research on the subject and are prepared to publish their findings. Consequently, we recommend against public release.

The Director of the Office of Current Intelligence provided a memorandum giving background on the *Restless Youth* study. From this memo it appears that the FBI had done the actual domestic spying on which the analysis was based, although there is also reference to assistance in the report's preparation from the CIA's Counterintelligence (CI) and Covert Action (CA) staffs.

7 May 1973

MEMORANDUM FOR: Director of Central Intelligence

VIA: Deputy Director for Intelligence

FROM: Director of Current Intelligence

SUBJECT: Activity Related to Domestic Events

1. In late spring of 1968 Walt Rostow, then Special Assistant to the President for National Security Affairs, tasked the DCI with undertaking a survey of world-wide student dissidence. Confronted by tumult at campuses like Columbia and mindful of the violence accompanying student outbursts at Berlin's Free University and elsewhere, Rostow sought to learn whether youthful dissidence was interconnected; spawned by the same causes; financed and hence manipulated by forces or influences hostile to the interests of the US and its allies; or likely to come under inimical sway to the detriment of US interests.

2. The paper was prepared by [—] of OCI with the assistance of the CA and CI Staffs. The DDI [Deputy Director for Intelligence], D/OCI [Director of the Office of Current Intelligence], and [—] met with Rostow to elicit the reasons for his or the President's concerns and to agree on the sources to be examined, the research methods to be followed, etc.

3. Written during the summer of 1968, the most sensitive version of <u>Restless Youth</u> comprised two sections. The first was a philosophical treatment of student unrest, its motivation, history, and tactics. This section drew heavily on overt literature and FBI reporting on Students for a Democratic Society and affiliated groups. In a sense, the survey of dissent emerged from a shorter (30 pages) typescript study of SDS and its foreign ties the same author had done for Mr. Rostow at the DCI's request in December 1967. (We no longer have a copy.)

4. Because of the paucity of information on foreign student movements, it was necessary to focus on SDS which then monopolized the field of student action here and abroad. A second section comprised 19 country chapters—ranging from Argentina to Yugoslavia—and stood by itself as a review of foreign student dissidence.

5. Because SDS was a <u>domestic</u> organization, the full paper <u>Restless Youth,</u> including the essay on worldwide dissent went only to nine readers. A copy may be in the Johnson Library.

6. Following the paper's favorable reception by the President and Mr. Rostow, the DCI briefed the NSC [National Security Council] on student dissent. The sensitive version subsequently was updated and sent to the White House in February 1969.

7. The less sensitive text was disseminated in September 1968 and then updated and issued again in March 1969 and August 1970.

[—signature deleted—]
Richard Lehman
Director of Current Intelligence

The daily log kept by Inspector General William V. Broe noted on 30 May 1973 that the Office of Current Intelligence (OCI) analysts had not in fact written the SDS chapter at all:

1100: [—] called WVB, to bring to his attention the fact that Kissinger has asked for some papers he'd received in the summer of 1970; now wants to see them again. One, Restless Youth (June 1970). OCI wrote a whole set of country chapters; and [—] of the CS [Clandestine Service] (since left CIA) wrote a more sensitive piece drawing on US and other countries for examples to make its point. OCI balked— didn't want to do anything on the US side. The whole project eventually was turned over to CA [Covert Activities].

A second memorandum from the Director of the Office of Current Intelligence dealt with two studies about black radicalism in the Caribbean that touched upon domestic topics as well. This one does specify the use of "voluminous" material from the Special Operations Group of the Counterintelligence Staff. There was also reporting on the foreign travels of Stokely Carmichael, an American Black Power activist (although he had been born in Trinidad) who in 1966–1967 had been chairman of the Student Nonviolent Coordinating Committee and in 1968 became a leader of the Black Panther Party.

7 May 1973

MEMORANDUM FOR: Director of Central Intelligence

VIA: Deputy Director for Intelligence

FROM: Director of Current Intelligence

SUBJECT: Activity Related to Domestic Events

1. OCI began following Caribbean black radicalism in earnest in 1968. The emphasis of our analysis was on black nationalism as a political force in the Caribbean and as a threat to the security of the Caribbean states. Two DDI [Directorate of Intelligence] memoranda were produced on the subject: "Black Radicalism in the Caribbean" (6 August 1968), and "Black Radicalism in the Caribbean—Another Look" (12 June 1970). In each a single paragraph was devoted to ties with the US black power movement; the discussion primarily concerned visits of Stokely Carmichael and other overt contacts.

2. In June 1970, Archer Bush of OCI was asked to write a memorandum with special attention to links between black radicalism in the Caribbean and advocates of black power in the US. The record is not clear where this request originated, but it came through channels from the DCI. The paper was to be treated as especially sensitive and was to include material provided by the Special Operations group of the CI Staff. The CI Staff material was voluminous but did not provide meaningful evidence of important links between militant blacks in the US and the Caribbean. This, in fact, was one of the conclusions of the paper. The memorandum was produced in typescript form and given to the DCI.

3. For several months in the first half of 1968 the Caribbean Branch wrote periodic typescript memoranda on Stokely Carmichael's travels abroad during a period when he had dropped out of public view. Our recollection is that the memoranda were for internal CIA use only, although a copy of one was inadvertently sent to the FBI.

[—signature deleted—]
Richard Lehman
Director of Current Intelligence

The Ballou case was another source of the rumors that fed the MAG's concerns regarding domestic activities. In this case, these rumors led to an internal investigation. This peculiar matter became the focus of a series of memoranda in the "Family Jewels" file as senior CIA leadership endeavored to figure out just what it was. Here, an allegation was made of CIA involvement in a police raid that ended in a shooting incident.

25 May 1973

MEMORANDUM FOR: Director of Central Intelligence

THROUGH: Mr. William E. Colby

1. On 17 May the name of [—] was referred to this office as having attempted to contact the Director concerning "activities outside the Agency." I attempted to contact [—] on 21 and 22 May, but he was on leave. On 23 May he stated he wanted to check a portion of his information and asked if he could come to my office on 24 May.

2. [—] came into the Agency as a JOT[8] in October 1957 and is currently a [—] assigned to the Soviet/EE Section. He has a very strong personnel file.

3. [—] advised that in August 1971 he attended the Advanced Intelligence Seminar. On the first evening of the seminar the students had a "getting acquainted" session where each one gave a brief description of his duties. One of the students, [—] of the Office of Security, however, carried on after the session was over and expanded on the briefing he had given. He claimed that CIA was cooperating with the Montgomery County Police [in Maryland], stating that the Office of Security gave electronic and other support to that organization.

4. He further indicated that the Office of Security had been involved in the "Ballou case." [—] described the Ballou case as follows: The residence of Mr. Ballou, an antique gun collector in Silver Spring, Maryland, was raided on 7 June 1971 by the Montgomery County Police and some Federal law enforcement officers. After the officers, dressed in civilian clothes, had forced their way into the house, Ballou picked up an antique pistol. The officers immediately opened fire and wounded Ballou seriously. He spent a long time in the hospital and is partly paralyzed at the present time. His case was given much publicity in the Washington Post at the time. There was additional publicity in the last several months when Ballou instigated a lawsuit against the raiding officers.

5. [—] identified another student, [—], who was assigned to IAS, as a friend of [—]. He stated that [—] also seemed to know the specifics of the Ballou case.

6. I thanked [—] and told him this was just the type of information we wanted to receive so that it can be investigated and appropriate action taken if the information is borne out.

7. This office will follow up on this allegation and advise the Director concerning our finding.

[—signature deleted—]
William V. Broe
Inspector General

F. P. Bishop of the Inspector General's office was assigned to get to the bottom of this question. Armed with a list of the participants in the Advanced Intelligence Seminar, he interviewed the various people mentioned in the original allegation. He began, however, with Director of Security Howard Osborn. (This memo appears to be a rough draft.)

30 May 1973

MEMO OF RECORD:

SUBJECT: Talk with Howard Osborn, Dir. Security Re: [—]
          [—] Report of Statements made by [—]

I talked with Mr. Osborn on 30 May about Mr. [—] statements concerning remarks made by Mr. [—] at the Advanced Intelligence Seminar No. 6 during the period 8–24 Sept. 1971. Mr. Osborn said that the fact that the Office of Security had relations with the local police forces in the Metropolitan Washington Area had been reported to the DCI in the Family Jewels memo dated 16 May 1973, but that he had no knowledge of the Ballou case and had not previously heard of any Agency involvement in or connection with the case.

He suggested that I go ahead and talk to Mr. [—] and get what facts I could from him, but that he also intended to talk to Mr. [—] later himself. He remarked that Mr. [—] was a very good briefer, but inclined to be over-expansive at times and talk too much.

[—signature deleted—]
F. P. Bishop

Bishop interviewed the person who had been so talkative at the Advanced Intelligence Seminar.

31 May 1973

MEMORANDUM FOR THE RECORD

SUBJECT: Interview with [—], Office of Security

1. On 31 May 1973 I questioned [—] about what he had said at the Advanced Intelligence Seminar No. 6 and the extent and nature of the relations he had had with the Montgomery County Police. He said that he and others had been encouraged to discuss their work and the problems related thereto with other Seminar members and told that what they said would be "non-attributable." In this context he had discussed the Office of Security's relations with local Police Forces including the Police Force in Montgomery County. He said he mentioned the "Ballou case" as an example of how the Montgomery County Police had used equipment provided by the Agency in their work, but denied that he had said or implied that the Agency was "involved" in the Ballou case. He said that he had also related to the other Seminar members the fact that the Agency had provided assistance to the Secret Service in connection with the protection of the President and Vice President and that he and others had been detailed to work with the Secret Service on counter-audio activities at the 1968 Democratic National Convention in Chicago and the Republican National Convention in Miami. I asked [—], who was on the Chicago detail, if he was detailed to protect the Vice President. He said that he was detailed to Tom Kelly, Deputy Chief of the Secret Service and worked in effect as a member of the Secret Service under Mr. Kelly.

2. I questioned [—] as to whether his relations with the Montgomery County Police was training oriented, equipment oriented, or if he had engaged in any

operations or activities with the police. He said his relations with the Police had been entirely equipment-oriented and had been limited to the Chief of Police and one or two senior Inspectors. The extent of assistance given consisted of the Agency providing the Police with surplus technical equipment which was of no further use to the Agency, and briefing them as to its use. He said he would not define these briefings as training, but admitted that it might be so construed.

3. [—] said that his only knowledge of the "Ballou case," except what he read in the papers, came from one telephone conversation he had with Inspector [—] of the Montgomery County Police sometime after accounts of the Ballou shooting had appeared in the press. He said the Inspector called to thank him for some amplifying equipment the Agency had given the Police and mentioned that it had probably saved the life of a policeman. He said that the Inspector explained to him that the account of the incident appearing in the press was not the whole story, that with the aid of the equipment the Agency had provided the Police had been able to intercept a telephone call from Ballou to a friend in which Ballou had outlined plans to "kill a cop." The Police had then staged a raid to forestall Ballou's plan and it was during this raid that Ballou was shot. [—] said that he had had no other conversations with the Montgomery County Police on that subject. He said he had mentioned it at the Seminar as an example of the sensitivity involved in the Agency's dealings with domestic Police Forces. He said he recalled that there was quite a bit of discussion and argument by the Seminar members about the propriety of the Agency assisting local police forces and working with the Secret Service in the U.S., but that he did not recall any extensive discussion about the Ballou case and that at no time had he said that the Agency was directly involved. [—] said he remembered that [—] seemed particularly concerned about the Agency's involvement in domestic activities and that sometime later, around January or February 1972, [—] talked to Colonel White [the Executive Director–Comptroller] about his concern and Colonel White in turn talked to the Director of Security. Since that date, he said, he has not had any further direct contact with the Montgomery County Police, based upon orders of the Director of Security.

[—signature deleted—]
F. P. Bishop
Inspector

An interview followed with another participant in the Advanced Intelligence Seminar as a witness to the exchanges that had occurred there. This person, who had been a chairman of the MAG, is one of the deleted names in the closing paragraph of the previous memorandum.

31 May 1973

MEMORANDUM FOR THE RECORD

SUBJECT: Interview with [—], FMSAC

1. [—] said he recalled [—] talking about the Office of Security's liaison with the Police Force in the Metropolitan Area and that the Ballou case was mentioned. He also recalled that [—] had mentioned that the Agency had provided assistance to the Secret Service in connection with surveillance work against radical groups at the 1968 Democratic National Convention in

Chicago. He said that he could not remember exactly what [—] said, but he did recall that there was considerable discussion and debate among the class members about the propriety of the Agency engaging in such activities.

2. Later in January or February 1972, at a time when [—] was Chairman of the Management Advisory Group (MAG), he said he discussed these matters and questioned the extent to which the agency should become involved in domestic intelligence activities, with Colonel White and later with Mr. Colby. The MAG also raised the general problem in a couple of their papers, but without citing specific detailed examples. He said he understood that Colonel White had taken the matter up with the Director of Security and that some changes had been made as a result.

[—signature deleted—]
F. P. Bishop

Bishop interviewed yet another participant in the Advanced Intelligence Seminar, presumably in an effort to corroborate the other stories.

29 May 1973

MEMORANDUM FOR THE RECORD

SUBJECT: Possible Agency Involvement in Outside Activities on Basis of Information Provided by [—]

On 29 May 1973 I talked to Mr. [—] who was a classmate of [—] and [—] at the Advanced Intelligence Seminar No. 6 held on 8–24 September 1971. Mr. [—] said that each student was asked to describe and talk about his work in the Agency and he recalled that Mr. [—] had talked about the Office of Security's liaison with, and assistance given to and received from, the Police Departments in the Washington Metropolitan area. He said he could not recall specifically what was said, but to the best of his memory, Mr. [—] described training given to either the Prince George's or Montgomery County Police concerning surveillance methods and electronic techniques. He said that he did not recall any discussion of the "Ballou case" and that he had no knowledge of that case other than what he had read in the newspapers.

[—signature deleted—]
F. P. Bishop

Bishop returned to the Office of Security on 4 June to compare notes with Osborn. On 6 June, the Inspector General reported back to Schlesinger, by way of Colby, to relate the findings and essentially dismiss the original allegations.

The Office of Technical Services (OTS, formerly the Technical Services Division) provided false identification papers for employees operating under cover. The director of the office evidently believed that some of these had been used within the United States, but in this case very few details survived the CIA censor. Nevertheless, the following memo reveals a bit about the procedures used:

28 May 1973

MEMORANDUM FOR: Deputy Director for Operations

SUBJECT: Documentation Support for Use in the United States

1. As you are aware this office provides document support for a variety of covert activities. [—about four lines deleted—] Specific use is not always

available to this office and should properly come from the requesting office who can provide the details. U.S. alias documentation use in the United States is approved by the Office of Security and normally has the concurrence of Central Cover Staff or FI [Foreign Intelligence] and CI [Counterintelligence] Staffs. Requests received by this office from outside the Clandestine Service are approved by an appropriate office of the DDO.

2. A review of this office's document support files for the period 1 January 1972 to date indicates that the following number of U.S. alias document requests were fulfilled for probable use in the United States. The statistics below are broken down by requester:

[—about three and a half pages deleted—]

[—signature and name deleted—]

Director

Office of Technical Services

On the other hand, the Office of Training (OTR) insisted that none of its disguises or false identity papers were used illicitly, although they may have been used at public locations in the United States. The following memo also makes clear that not everything from OTS was "high-tech:"

18 June 1973

MEMORANDUM FOR: Inspector General

SUBJECT: Use of Disguise and Alias Documentation Within the U.S.

REFERENCE: Memo dtd 30 May 73 to DTR fm [—] Subj:
Issuance of Disguise Materials for Probable Use
Within U.S. or Its Territories

1. The Associate Deputy Director for Operations has asked that we give you a detailed report of the actual use that the Office of Training has made within the U.S. of all disguise materials and alias documentation we have obtained for our staff members and students.

2. <u>Disguise Materials</u>

OTR has obtained from OTS disguise materials—including glasses, wigs, mustaches, and special shoes to increase height—for 12 staff instructors at the Domestic Training Station [DTS]. The purpose of these materials is to increase the difficulty that students in the Basic Operations Course and Advanced Operations Course will have in recognizing instructors during problems and exercises conducted [—] near DTS. Exercises include surveillance, countersurveillance, brush passes, and dead-drop problems in which instructors monitor student activity. These exercises are run under carefully controlled conditions only in areas where adequate liaison exists with local authorities to avoid any flap should difficulty arise during an exercise.

[—paragraph of about four lines deleted—]

[—2" x 2" box, centered in page, deleted—]

The sole use of disguise materials by these instructors has been or will be in support of the training exercise noted above. At no time have the materials been used for other purposes.

3. <u>Alias Documents</u>

U.S. alias documents consisting primarily of business and social cards, but also including drivers' licenses and social security cards, have been used for more than a year by students [—one and a half lines deleted—]. At the conclusion of the course, the alias documents are collected from the students and returned to OTS. Again, these documents are used only under carefully controlled conditions in an environment [—] where adequate liaison with local authorities exists to contain any flap; and the documents are used only for the purposes stated.

4. A thorough canvass of all elements of OTR discloses no other instance in recent years in which we have used disguise materials or alias documentation within the U.S. or obtained such materials for that purpose.

[—signature and name deleted—]
Director of Training

Finally, in a memorandum to the Office of the Deputy Director for Intelligence (O/DDI), the Director of the Central Reference Service (CRS) outlined the CIA Library's quite limited holdings on domestic topics. A slight allowance was made, however, for open-source information on "extremists." The memo also has an intriguing gap related to imagery.

7 May 1973

MEMORANDUM FOR: O/DDI

SUBJECT: Involvement in Domestic Affairs

1. This memorandum responds to the DDI's request for a listing of any questionable involvements in domestic affairs. I do not believe that CRS is doing anything that a reasonable man could construe as improper.

2. CRS does, of course, have several programs to acquire still pictures, movies, videotapes [—approximately 10 lines deleted—].

3. CRS files do not generally bear on U.S. citizens or organizations. The biographic file-building criteria specifically excludes U.S. nationals unless the person has become of such major importance in the political life of a foreign country that the file is essential. (To my knowledge, only 2 persons so qualify. [—one and three-fourths lines deleted—]. Our Cuban files probably include some persons who are now U.S. citizens but we have no way to separate them; we have files on U.S. defectors to Cuba.)

4. The CIA Library has several informal snag files intended to aid the librarians in answering the kinds of questions that they know they will get on a continuing basis. An appointments file is a collection of clippings on appointed federal officials: who holds what job when and what is his background? The extremist files are a collection of folders on a variety of organizations and a few people with intricate organizational links. Any sort of extremism is grist for these particular files. And a few persons, e.g., Rap Brown and Eldridge Cleaver [leaders of the Black Panther Party], have dossiers consisting almost exclusively of clippings from public media. These files are unclassified and consist mostly of clippings from the public press: U.S., foreign, underground, scholarly.

5. I am not aware of any other kind of involvement in domestic activities that is not related to development of techniques or logistics or legitimate training of CRS personnel.

[—signature deleted—]
H. C. Eisenbeiss
Director, Central Reference Service

NOTES

1. Victor Marchetti was a former employee of the CIA; indeed, he had been an assistant to Richard Helms. Disillusioned with the agency, he resigned and became its most public critic. A book by Victor Marchetti and John D. Marks, *The CIA and the Cult of Intelligence* (New York: Knopf, 1974), was published shortly before the Senate hearings on intelligence activities and contributed to an anti-CIA attitude among the public. It caused a sensation, in part, because the CIA took Marchetti to court to compel him to delete passages comprising one-fifth of the book prior to publication. (Marchetti, like all former CIA employees, had signed a severance agreement permitting the CIA to review any publication that might reveal classified material.) The court allowed about half of the deletions to be made and permitted Marchetti and Marks to put the other half back in. Knopf printed the book with blank spaces to indicate the deleted passages and printed the reinstated passages in bold for easy identification.

2. This is presumably the same story printed in the *Quicksilver Times*. See below.

3. Richard Ober was in charge of the Special Operations Group (SOG), which sought evidence of foreign support for U.S. dissident groups, especially the antiwar movement. The "machine program" mentioned in the next paragraph refers to the computerized database that Ober developed. See Chapter 7, "The Search for Foreign Instigators: Operation Chaos and the Intelligence Evaluation Committee."

4. See the memoranda below related to the Ballou case.

5. An earlier draft of the memorandum, which was distributed among the highest-level officers and to the MAG cochairmen for comment in March 1972, was also contained in the "Family Jewels" file. The earlier draft suggested that Colby did intend to distribute it in a future issue of "FYI—Allegations and Answers." It specifically mentioned the "Management Advisory Group, among others," as reporting concern. The draft also cited an article in the *Quicksilver Times* (20 January 1972) under the "Allegation" rubric, noting that the "two gentlemen" mentioned in the article were no longer associated with the agency. (An incomplete clipping from the *Quicksilver Times*, an underground newspaper printed in Washington, D.C., was also included in the file. It alleged that agents from the CIA, FBI, and Treasury had engaged in an "effort to pin the bank bombings on radical groups." The two names mentioned were Robert Kiley, identified in the article as a former special assistant to Helms, and Drexel Godfrey, identified as a former Director of Current Intelligence.) The draft reversed the order of items "a" and "b" and did not include "security problems which arise" among the targets of security investigations. Item "h" did not call special attention to the drug program. The item titled "Operational Support" was originally titled "Cover" and placed last on the list. Several items were reworded, presumably to make them clearer.

6. The Katzenbach Committee issued its recommendation on 29 March 1967, and President Lyndon B. Johnson immediately adopted it as policy. The issue had been prompted by news stories alleging long-term financial subsidies from the CIA to certain student organizations both at home and abroad. The committee consisted of Under Secretary of State Nicholas deBelleville Katzenbach, Secretary of Health, Education, and Welfare John W. Gardner, and Director of Central Intelligence Richard Helms. See the Department of State Web site, http://www.state.gov/r/pa/ho/frus/johnsonlb/xxxiii/32679.htm.

7. For OCI memoranda dealing with the antiwar movement, see Chapter 7, "The Search for Foreign Instigators: Operation Chaos and the Intelligence Evaluation Committee."

8. A JOT is a member of the Junior Office Training program.

Chapter 9

Assistance to Police and Other Agencies

The "Family Jewels" file contains numerous memoranda related to assistance that the CIA rendered to federal agencies that were primarily concerned with domestic matters. These were not necessarily the most controversial of CIA activities. Many of them appear in the "Family Jewels" file primarily because they involved contacts with people who were later connected to Watergate. Sometimes, however, they did cross the line that was intended to separate foreign intelligence activity from domestic law enforcement.

In a memorandum to the Director of Central Intelligence dated 8 May 1973, for example, the Deputy Director for Intelligence lists the few and insubstantial contacts his staff had had with various Watergate figures. He then goes on to note "domestic activities which might appear questionable to outsiders." About six of these have been redacted from the text. Some of the others are fairly benign, such as reviewing NASA satellite photos in search of images too "sensitive" for public release. Other topics, however, do relate to domestic dissidents and police activity.[1] The memo noted, for example:

> DCS [Domestic Contact Service] accepts information on possible foreign involvement in US dissident groups and on the narcotics trade when sources refuse to deal with the FBI and BNDD [Bureau of Narcotics and Dangerous Drugs] directly.

Accompanying this memorandum in the file was another one, dated the previous day, to the Deputy Director for Intelligence (DDI) from the Director of the Domestic Contact Service (DCS), which elaborated on that office's role. For an agency prohibited from operating within U.S. borders, this subdivision would seem to particularly problematic. Although it was restricted to using open sources of information, the DCS operated out of small offices in a number of U.S. cities. In the normal course of its operations, it would contact Americans who had visited "closed societies" and inquire about anything they may have noticed that might be of use to the CIA. It also rendered support to other members of the United States Intelligence Board (USIB, that is, the intelligence community). Despite the DCS's seemingly precarious position with regard to domestic activities, its director in 1973 did not believe it had done anything at all untoward. Nevertheless, about 70 percent of the points he had to make were redacted out of the memo in the "Family Jewels" file.

7 May 1973

MEMORANDUM FOR: Deputy Director for Intelligence
SUBJECT: DCS Domestic Activity
To the best of my knowledge, DCS has not engaged in any activity outside the CIA charter or that could be construed as illegal. Some of the functions that we perform under HR 1–13f(i) of providing operational support within the US to all elements of CIA and to the USIB-member agencies, however, are perhaps borderline or could be construed as illegal if misinterpreted. For example:
[—four paragraphs deleted—]
  5. Collect information on possible foreign involvement or penetration of US dissident groups, but only in a passive manner and only when the source has refused to pass the information directly to the FBI.
  6. Collect information on the narcotics trade, but again only in a passive manner when the source has refused to pass the information directly to BNDD or the FBI.
[—three paragraphs deleted—]
  10. Acquire routing slips recording the fact of overseas telephone calls between persons in the US and persons overseas and telephone calls between two foreign points routed through US switchboards. This activity lasted for approximately six months but has ceased.
[—one paragraph deleted—]

/signed/
JAMES R. MURPHY
Director, Domestic Contact Service

The following memos relate to assistance rendered clandestinely to the Bureau of Narcotics and Dangerous Drugs (BNDD), a relatively short-lived agency that was the successor to the Federal Bureau of Narcotics and was in turn replaced by the Drug Enforcement Agency. Because the activity involved a connection with a predominantly domestic law-enforcement agency, it came within the purview of DCI James Schlesinger's request for information on illegal activities.

7 May 1973

Memorandum to: The Inspector General
Subject: Office of Security Survey—Office of Security Support to BNDD
In December 1970, Robert Ingersoll, head of the Bureau of Narcotics and Dangerous Drugs, asked Mr. Helms if the Agency could give him some assistance in shoring up the internal integrity of the BNDD. According to Mr. Ingersoll, the old Federal Bureau of Narcotics had been heavily infiltrated by dishonest and corrupt elements, who were believed to have ties with the narcotics smuggling industry. Ingersoll wanted us to help him recruit some thoroughly reliable people who could be used, not only as special agents in his various offices around the country, but also to serve as informants on the other BNDD employees in these offices.
[—one page deleted—]

A related question concerned whether, and how much, to continue the BNDD program. The following memo was addressed to William E. Colby in his capacity as the Executive Director of the CIA Management Committee. He held this position at the same time that he was Deputy Director for Operations.

25 May 1973

MEMORANDUM FOR: Executive Secretary, CIA Management Committee
SUBJECT: Project TWO-FOLD

1. This memorandum sets forth a recommendation for your approval in paragraph 5.
2. For the past several years, this office has been supporting the Bureau of Narcotics and Dangerous Drugs (BNDD) by spotting, assessing, and recruiting personnel to form an internal security unit whose primary mission is the detection of corruption within the BNDD. Subsequent to the recruitment and training stage, the individuals selected are turned over to the Chief Inspector of BNDD for operational guidance and handling in their various domestic assignments.
3. Recently, this Agency has extended this activity by supporting BNDD in the covert acquisition of individuals who are hired as Staff Agents utilized under nonofficial cover and directed against the principal international drug traffickers. These individuals are true employees of the BNDD and, although all administrative details relative to their employment are handled within the Agency, they are unaware of any Agency involvement.
4. It is felt at this time that a reaffirmation of our support to BNDD in Project TWO-FOLD is necessary and desirable.
5. Therefore, it is recommended that approval be granted for the continuation of Project TWO-FOLD as originally approved by the Director of Central Intelligence on 12 February 1971.

/signed/
Howard J. Osborn
Director of Security

A notation at the bottom of the above memo recorded the response, which indicated the agency's eagerness at the time to remain strictly within the rules.

Per Mr. Colby's recommendation and DCI concurrence, terminate paragraph 2 activity and continue paragraph 3 only as the activity pertains to foreign intelligence abroad. Copy furnished IG [Inspector General].

At times, of course, the CIA did not have much choice when it came to supporting the budgets of other government agencies.

THE WHITE HOUSE WASHINGTON

February 7, 1972

MEMORANDUM FOR BILL COLBY
SUBJECT: BUDGETARY SUPPORT FOR THE CABINET COMMITTEE ON INTERNATIONAL NARCOTICS CONTROL

The Cabinet Committee on International Narcotics Control was created September 7, 1971, by the President to centralize his attack on the international drug traffic.

The Committee does not have a separate budget.

Salary and administrative support for its small, full-time staff has been provided by the Executive Office of the President. Other expenses are being charged to the constituent agencies and departments.

The Bureau of Customs, BNDD, and AID/Office of Public Safety have provided support to date.[2]

The CIA should be prepared to defray not more than fifteen thousand dollars in overseas travel expenses for Cabinet Committee staff during the remainder of FY-1972.

Walter G. Minnick, the Committee's Staff Coordinator, can be contacted for further details.

Thank you for your assistance.

/signed/
Egil Krogh, Jr.[3]
Executive Director
Cabinet Committee on
International Narcotics Control

For many agencies, cooperation with the CIA meant turning to it as a source of sophisticated espionage gadgets as well as disguises, false identity papers, and so forth. At the time the "Family Jewels" were being assembled, the office responsible for issuing such items was involved in a reorganization. Prior to 4 May 1973, it was the Technical Services Division (TSD), a branch of the Directorate of Plans (Operations). At that time, however, DCI Schlesinger moved it to the Directorate of Science and Technology and renamed it the Office of Technical Services (OTS). In the following memo, written four days later, the head of the office is addressing his new boss, the Deputy Director for Science and Technology, but he is describing the past activities of the TSD. In it, he outlines the nature of his office's cooperation with other agencies, ranging from the Defense Department to the U.S. Postal Service, and some of the procedures involved. Perhaps because his boss is new to this responsibility, he goes into some detail. Note that in addition to a variety of mundane topics, there are also items such as teaching "surreptitious entry" techniques to Washington-area police departments. Also, the sometimes complex authorization requirements (and the nagging for the return of borrowed items) give some idea of life in the intelligence bureaucracy.

8 May 1973

MEMORANDUM FOR: Deputy Director for Science & Technology
SUBJECT: TSD Support to Other Agencies

1. Technical Services Division's charter (CSI 1–9) requires that it provide technical assistance to both CIA operations and other activities as may be directed by the Deputy Director for Operations.
2. Over the years the chief non-CIA recipients of this support have been the Department of Defense, the Federal Bureau of Investigation, Bureau of Narcotics and Dangerous Drugs, Immigration and Naturalization Service, Department of State, United States Postal Service, Secret Service, Agency for International Development, and the White House.
3. While varying widely among the different recipients, these services have included training and materials, and in a few instances participation in the fields of audio and visual surveillance, secret writing and related communications, personal protection, alias documentation and questioned document

examination, disguise, concealment devices, electronic beaconry, illicit narcotics detection, and counter-sabotage/terrorism.

4. In most instances requirements for this support are received by TSD through higher echelons (Officer of the Director or Deputy Director for Operations). Unless the service involved is a trivial or continuing one, the request is referred to the Foreign Intelligence Staff Departmental Coordination Group for coordination and approval at the appropriate Agency levels. Approval within TSD by the Chief of Operations or Development and Engineering and the Chief of TSD or his Deputy also is required.

5. The attachment lists the primary services provided to the organizations named in Paragraph two.

6. Issuance of forged personal identity documentation by TSD is controlled according to two broad criteria: type of requester; and type of documentation requested. A request for denied area documentation from a DDO [Directorate of Operations] Area Division is honored after proper validation. Free world documentation may require some extra coordination however. [—just over five lines deleted—]

7. Unless ordered otherwise by higher Agency authority, no U.S. documentation is issued by TSD Headquarters without prior coordination with the Office of Security and the Central Cove Staff. TSD Regional Bases require at least the validation of U.S. documentation requests by the COS [Chief of Station], or his designated representative, of the requesting Station. Because it could be used [—about three-fourths of a line deleted—], no U.S. Birth Certificate is issued without approval of the DDO [Directorate of Operations] via Central Cover Staff. Backstopped major credit cards are issued by Office of Security, not TSD.

8. Provision of forged documentation to non-DDO requesters, whether they be CIA or other Agency requesters, always requires approval of non-TSD offices. Support to the military for instance would be validated by FI [Foreign Intelligence] Staff/Departmental Coordination Group at Headquarters or by the COS overseas having responsibility for coordination of the operation. BNDD requests are coordinated with DDO/NARCOG [Narcotics Coordination Group]. Requests for documentation of Immigration and Naturalization Service is coordinated via the Alien Affairs Staff.

9. Authentication items are issued on a loan basis and must be returned to TSD or accounted for. After any documentation has been issued, TSD retains photographs and records of such support until the documentation has been returned to TSD. If the material is not returned after a reasonable time, the requester is reminded of the outstanding documentation.

/signed/
Sidney Gottlieb
Chief
Technical Services Division

ATTACHMENT

Department of Defense

Documents, disguise, concealment devices, secret writing, flaps and seals [that is, techniques for opening and resealing envelopes]; counterinsurgency and counter-sabotage courses have been furnished to all intelligence elements of the Department of Defense and certain elements of the Special Forces. All requests are coordinated with the FI Departmental Coordination Group at Headquarters and with the Chief of Stations overseas. In turn these elements furnished TSD with exemplars of foreign identities documents, foreign cachets, foreign intelligence secret writing systems, and foreign intelligence concealment devices. Selected audio requirements have been furnished overseas for CI [Counterintelligence]-type cases.

Federal Bureau of Investigation

At the request of the FBI we cooperate with the Bureau in a few audio surveillance operations against sensitive foreign targets in the United States.

Bureau of Narcotics and Dangerous Drugs

Beacons, cameras, audio and telephone devices for overseas operations, identity documents, car-trailing devices, SRAC [short-range agent communications], flaps and seals and training of selected personnel responsible for use thereof has been furnished this Bureau. All requirements are sent to DDO/NARCOG for coordination with area divisions and for action by TSD if appropriate. Requests overseas are coordinated with the COS or his designee before action by TSD is taken.

Immigration and Naturalization

CI analysis of foreign passports and visas, guidance in developing tamperproof alien registration cards, [—a half line deleted—] have been furnished the Service. Requests are forwarded directly to TSD for coordination within TSD if technical, with the FI Departmental Coordination Group if operational.

Department of State

Technical graphics guidance on developing a new United States Passport, analyses of foreign passports, car-armoring and personnel locators (beacons) for Ambassadors have been supplied the State Department. In addition, analyses and exposure of black letter operations against the United States abroad are made. All graphics requirements are forwarded to TSD for further coordination within the Division. The Department of State furnishes exemplars of foreign passports, foreign visas and in the past passports on a priority basis.

Postal Service

The Office of Chief Postal Inspector has had selected personnel attend basic surveillance photographic courses, has been furnished foreign postal information and has been the recipient of letter bomb analyses, furnished [—] typewriter analyses. Requirements are coordinated with the DDO and DDO/EA. The Post Office has furnished TSD with exemplars of letter bombs and [—just over one line deleted—]. We also have an arrangement with the Post Office to examine and reinsert a low volume of certain foreign mail arriving in the United States.

Secret Service

Gate passes, security passes, passes for Presidential campaign, emblems for Presidential vehicles, and a secure ID photo system have been furnished this Service. Blanket approval for graphics support has been granted to the Deputy Director for Operations. In each case TSD requests approval from the DDO.

U.S. Agency for International Development

We furnish instructors to a USAID-sponsored Technical Investigation Course (Counter Terror) at [—about nine and a half lines deleted—].

White House

Stationary, special memoranda, and molds of the Great Seal have been furnished the Social Secretary. The Deputy Director for Operations is apprised of these requirements.

<u>Police Representing Washington, Arlington, Fairfax and Alexandria</u>

During the period 1968–1969 a series of classes reflecting basic and surveillance photography, basic audio, locks and picks, counter-sabotage and surreptitious entry were given to selected members from the above-mentioned cities. Overall training was approved by the Director of Central Intelligence and in turn validation was required for each course from the Director of Security.

It is worth noting that, apart from the redactions, the preceding memorandum from the "Family Jewels" file had marginal ink marks highlighting certain points. These were references to programs involving the FBI, the U.S. Postal Service (specifically, furnishing foreign postal information and receiving foreign mail), and the entire paragraph concerning local police departments. The document was accompanied by a brief note to Colby from Executive Director Benjamin Evans (the chief of staff). Evans evidently thought the memorandum, although intended for an internal file, deserved to be sanitized. Perhaps it is worth noting that Gottlieb was dismissed within two weeks of writing these memos.[4]

MEMORANDUM FOR: Mr. Colby

Carl Duckett [the Deputy Director for Science and Technology] brought this up and said he is very uncomfortable with what Sid Gottlieb is reporting and thinks the Director would be ill-advised to say he is acquainted with this program. Duckett plans to scrub it down with Gottlieb but obviously cannot do it this afternoon.

Ben Evans
8 May 1973

Gottlieb's original memorandum was also accompanied by another set of memoranda, dated the same day, 8 May 1973. (Evans's note may well have been referring to these also.) The cover sheet notes, "Attached herewith are additional explanations of TSD support to other U.S. Government agencies." These additional files have undergone a more thorough redaction than the original. Note that the second memorandum below highlights that, apart from teaching techniques to local police departments, the CIA could also gain useful technical information from the police.

ATTACHMENT
FEDERAL BUREAU OF INVESTIGATION

TSD has had a close working relationship with the FBI over the past few years. The FBI is the only organization that has been fully briefed on TSD audio techniques and equipment. The following are situations where TSD equipment and guidance were involved in operations:

[—about one and a half pages deleted—]

8 May 1973

MEMORANDUM FOR: Chief, TSD
ATTENTION: Executive Officer
SUBJECT: Contacts with Domestic Police Organizations

1. In December 1968, July 1969 and December 1970, SDB [Special Development Branch] provided basic counter-sabotage familiarization training for selected members of the Washington metropolitan area police departments. The training was given at the Fairfax County pistol and rifle range. Authorization for the training came from DDP [Deputy Director for Plans] and Chief, Office of Security.

2. On occasion during the past few years, under the auspices of the Law Enforcement Assistance Administration [LEAA] of the Department of Justice and with the approval of CI Staff and Office of Security, SDB provided training and familiarization to police officers of several domestic police departments in the uses of the Explosives Residue Detection Technique and Trace Metals Detection Technique. These techniques had been declassified and are currently available to the law enforcement community. The National Bomb Data Center publishes periodic guidance in their uses.

3. In order to augment the SDB mission responsibilities in the field of counter-sabotage and counter-terror, SDB officers have in the past two years visited, under appropriate covers, the explosives disposal units of the New York City police department, Dade County (Miami) Florida Dept. and the Los Angeles Police Dept. Also in March 1973, two SDB officers attended the Explosives and Ordnance Disposal Conference in Sacramento, California, sponsored by LEAA. When the recent letter bomb menace began in September 1972, our liaison with the NYCPD bomb squad paid off in that we had complete information on letter bomb construction in hours, enabling the Agency to make worldwide dissemination within a day.

[—signature and name deleted—]
C/TSD/OPS/SDB

SECRET SERVICE

In addition to printing of various passes and identification emblems, TSD has also supplied the Secret Service with some U.S. alias documentation:
[—about 19 lines deleted—]

Of course, the requests handled by TSD were not always highly controversial or exotic. Sometimes, they did not have much of an effect, either.

25 May 1973

MEMORANDUM FOR THE RECORD
SUBJECT: Loan of Tape Recorder to Passport Office

1. Late in 1971 (December, I believe), the Deputy Director for the Passport Office, Department of State, (Mr. Robert Johnson) informally queried me on whether that office might borrow a small tape recorder for use by the Director of the Passport Office (Miss Frances Knight) to record a meeting she had scheduled with representatives of a foreign government.

2. I conveyed this request to the then Chief, [—about a half line deleted—] and subsequently held several discussions with representatives of our [—] office. It was decided to loan the Passport Office a small commercial recorder (Norelco Cassette Recorder, Model 150), which we had in stock.

3. A representative of our Training Branch [—] and I delivered the recorder to Miss Knight's office and [—] demonstrated the recorder's capabilities and instructed her in its use. She did not seem too pleased at the recording quality; however, the recorder was left with her.

4. On this date (21 May 1973) I asked Mr. Johnson to check on the status of the recorder. He said it was never used in any way. I therefore retrieved it from the Passport Office and delivered it to Training Branch [—].

[—signature and name deleted—]
OTS/[—]

In the following memo, a portion of the CIA's support for domestic police activity has come to the attention of the special Watergate prosecutors, giving rise to the possibility that they could uncover further unspecified programs. Note the reference to "highly sensitive activities which could cause the Agency severe embarrassment," the nature of which evidently could not be divulged even in an internal memorandum.

17 December 1973

MEMORANDUM FOR THE RECORD
SUBJECT: Recent Activities of the Watergate Special Prosecution Staff

1. Early in the evening of 10 December 1973, I received a telephone call from [—three-fourths of a line deleted—] who informed me that he, in turn, had received a call from [—half line deleted—] Intelligence Division, Washington Metropolitan Police Department.
2. It seems that [—] had just spent an hour in conversation at his home with a [—half line deleted—] in the Washington Metropolitan Police Department who had reported to him on his interview that afternoon with a Mr. Martin and a Mr. Horowitz, prosecutors of the Watergate Special Prosecution Staff. [—] had been subpoenaed for his appearance and he indicated to [—] that the two prosecutors were principally concerned with two matters:

   a. What type of training had the Agency given members of the Washington Metropolitan Police Department? How long were the courses? How often were they given?
   b. What support did the Agency provide to the Washington Metropolitan Police Department during demonstrations occurring in the Washington area in late 1969 and early 1970?

3. [—] said that he had been shown a long list of names and asked if any of them had been involved either with the training given the Washington Metropolitan Police Department or the support to the Washington Metropolitan Police Department during the demonstrations. [—] could remember only three names on the list. They were: [—half line deleted—]
4. The three individuals named by [—] did in fact participate in both the training and support during the demonstrations. They are only three among others of my [—one-fourth of a line deleted—] special support group who were involved in these activities. Of extreme sensitivity is the fact that these same individuals were engaged in other highly sensitive activities which could cause the Agency severe embarrassment if they were surfaced today in the current "Watergate climate."
5. I briefed the Director personally on this development and he indicated that if the training and demonstrations surfaced that he would simply acknowledge that this had occurred but as he had assured members of Congress, we would not engage in this type of activity in the future. He agreed with my suggestion that we have the Legislative Counsel brief Congressman [Lucien N.] Nedzi and Senator [John C.] Stennis on this since they have already been briefed on all activities of this nature undertaken by the Agency in the past. I briefed Mr. John Warner, Acting General Counsel, and agreed with him that we would make no effort to brief members of my [—one-fourth of a line deleted—] until and if they are subpoenaed. Mr. Warner or members of his Staff will then caution them to only answer questions asked and not volunteer additional information. I am making a copy of this memorandum

available to [—] of the Inspector General's Staff at the suggestion of the Inspector General, who I also briefed on this development.

/signed/
Howard J. Osborn
Director of Security

Some department heads showed annoyance at having to report on contacts with other agencies, listing every innocuous detail and maintaining that each program was legal or even mandated. Others, however, were already growing intimidated by the growing public attention the agency was receiving. The following memorandum came from the Office of Electronic Intelligence (OEL or ELINT), within the Directorate of Science and Technology. Electronic intelligence deals with aspects of electromagnetic signals other than the actual content of the communications. Note that the Director of OEL, John McMahon, went on to become Deputy Director of Central Intelligence in the 1980s.

OEL-010-73

MEMORANDUM FOR: Deputy Director for Science and Technology
SUBJECT: Policy Regarding Assistance to Agencies Outside the Intelligence Community on Speech Processing Problems

1. Recent public concern over Agency affiliations with law enforcement activities has made me wary of offering speech processing assistance to various other government agencies. My concern here is restricted to government activities outside the Intelligence Community. Because of a scientific community awareness of the expertise of members of OEL in speech processing problems, we are often asked by individuals in government for help on various speech problems. The requests are usually informal on a person-to-person basis. While most of these contacts involve only an exchange of unclassified information, several have involved the use of laboratory resources.
2. Contacts have come from the FBI, Attorney General's office, Bureau of Narcotics and Dangerous Drugs (BNDD), Post Office, and the Treasury Department. Of the above, assistance to BNDD had been specifically sanctioned by Mr. Helms [the former DCI]. In one recent instance where a noisy tape was to be used in a court case, care was taken to insure that the processing of the tape was done entirely by a BNDD employee even though it was done in an Agency laboratory using the Agency's Coherent Spectrum Shaper equipment.
3. Providing services of this kind to other agencies has not as yet imposed a significant workload on us and there is a benefit to us in that such contact enables the staff to test techniques and equipment on a variety of speech problems. Informal interactions at the technical level are fruitful in terms of helping us to accomplish Agency goals. Hence we would be willing to continue to support other departments on an ad hoc basis, but would appreciate your guidance re the wisdom of OEL's involvement in "domestic" activities.

[—signature deleted—]
JOHN N. MCMAHON
Director of ELINT
DD/S&T

The National Photographic Interpretation Center (NPIC; then part of the Directorate of Science and Technology, but now absorbed into the separate

National Geospatial-Intelligence Agency) seemingly took pains to list its every contact with another agency. An episode involving the journalist Jack Anderson was an effort to determine the source of leaked agency documents (the memo does not specify whether it worked), a questionable law-enforcement activity, although some might argue that it contained an internal security element since the object was to find the source of leaks within the CIA. The memo also describes the review of NASA satellite images, presumably either to prevent the release of images of secret installations or to find secret installations of other countries that might have been photographed inadvertently. Some of the programs have clear law-enforcement implications, but several others are concerned with assuring public safety.

8 May 1973

Questionable NPIC Projects

1. Leaks of Jack Anderson

   In January 1972, NPIC performed image enhancement techniques on TV tapes of a Jack Anderson show. The purpose was to try to identify serial numbers of CIA documents in Anderson's possession. The request was levied on NPIC through the Office of Security.

2. The Poppy Project

   NPIC has provided the services of one PI [photographic interpreter] to assist an interagency effort to detect poppy cultivation. In addition the Center has provided the contractual mechanism in support of the Bureau of Narcotics and Dangerous Drugs for a multispectral crop study by a private company.

3. Reviews of NASA Collected Imagery

   NPIC has and continues to conduct reviews of satellite imagery from NASA programs to identify ''sensitive'' frames of photography not releasable to the public and to ascertain the intelligence potential of the imagery. This service has been provided for GEMENI and ERTS photography and preparations are underway for review of SKY LAB [sic] imagery.

4. Peaceful Uses of Satellite Imagery

   NPIC has been requested to provide a number of looks at domestic coverage for special purposes. Examples include:

   Santa Barbara Oil Spill
   Los Angeles Earthquake
   Sierra Snow (flood threat)
   Current Mississippi Floods
   Hurricane Cammile [sic] Damage on the Coast of the Gulf of Mexico
   Civil Disturbance in Detroit
   OEP [Office of Emergency Preparedness] U.S. Data Base

One branch of the CIA that one might not expect to find enmeshed in controversy was the Federal Broadcast Information Service (FBIS). FBIS (often pronounced ''fibbis'') subscribes to foreign news services and records foreign public radio and television broadcasts, translates the contents into English, and distributes the transcripts to government agencies, university libraries, and others. The service claims to have a decision from the CIA's Office of General Counsel stating that this is not a violation of copyright laws. Despite the open, unclassified nature of the transcripts, they have customarily carried the false claim that FBIS is part of the Department of Commerce. FBIS potentially violated the restrictions on CIA activity by cooperating with law-enforcement agencies in need of translation services.

8 May 1973

MEMORANDUM FOR: DDI
SUBJECT: Sensitive Activities

1. FBIS has been engaged in no activities related to the Ellsberg and Watergate cases.
2. FBIS operations occasionally extend to the domestic arena. From time to time, FBIS linguists are made available to DDO [Directorate of Operations] or Office of Communications components for special operations (usually abroad) involving close-support SIGINT [signals intelligence] work or translation of audio take. On one occasion recently DDO, on behalf of the FBI, requested the services of several FBIS linguists skilled in Arabic to work directly for the FBI on a short-term project here in Washington. The arrangements wee made by Mr. Oberg of the DDO CI [Counterintelligence] Staff. He said the project was very highly classified and that FBIS participation was approved by Mr. Colby [then Deputy Director for Operations] and the Director. FBIS participation was approved by the Director of FBIS after a check with the ADDI [Assistant Deputy Director for Intelligence]. Other examples of sensitive linguistic support work are help [sic] in the handling and resettlement of defectors, the recent assignment of and employee to the Bureau of Narcotics and Dangerous Drugs to transcribe recordings in a rare Chinese dialect, and the detailing of another Chinese linguist on two occasions to assist in the U.S. military training of Chinese Nationalist cadets.
[—paragraph about copyright issues, partially deleted—]
4. The routine FBIS monitoring of foreign radio broadcasts often involves statements or speeches made by U.S. citizens using those radio facilities. Examples are statements made or allegedly made by American POWs in Hanoi [North Vietnam], by Jane Fonda in Hanoi and by Ramsey Clark in Vietnam. At the request of FBI and the Department of Justice, and with the approval of the CIA Office of General Counsel, we have on occasion submitted transcripts of such broadcasts to the Department of Justice as part of that Department's consideration of a possible trial. In such cases, we have been required to submit names of FBIS monitors involved, presumably because of the possibility they might be required as witnesses. (In one case in 1971, an FBIS staff employee was directed to appear as an expert witness in the court-martial of a Marine enlisted man charged with aiding the enemy in a broadcast from Hanoi.) FBIS views all this with misgivings. Monitoring such broadcasts is incidental and we rue attribution of their news to FBIS, and we should not be considered policemen maintaining surveillance of traveling Americans.

[—paragraph deleted—]

[—signature deleted—]
E. H. Knoche
Director
Foreign Broadcast Information Service

Sometimes the clandestine nature of the agency itself—even when secrecy probably was not necessary—could make an activity seem suspicious. When a 1970 speech by President Nixon on the subject of Cambodia elicited of flood of correspondence, Nixon decided that he wanted to respond personally to all the "pro" letters. (The State Department was responding to the "cons.") Since the White House budget would not cover the expenses of postage, the printing of response cards, and the addressing of envelopes by machine for tens of thousands of responses, it was decided to charge part of it to the CIA. The CIA, however, while willing to cover the expenses, was not willing to let any (non-CIA) government auditor know how it spent its money. The CIA's budget is, after all, a secret. Therefore, it was decided that the requisite government form that accompanied the check (Form 1080 or Form 1081, depending on the memo) would explain only that the check was "for classified services per our conversation." This explanation surely was destined to raise more eyebrows than the real reason. Pages 75–104 of the "Family Jewels" file are devoted to this issue.

Finally, let us note that assistance was not restricted to agencies of the executive branch. The following notation is from the minutes of the CIA Executive Committee's regular morning meeting of 3 February 1972.

A/DDS [Associate Deputy Director for Support] reported the House Appropriations Committee request for a finance officer to assist them in work on the budget. He added that we have provided such assistance in the past, and the Director interposed no objection.

NOTES

1. For activities related to surveillance of the antiwar movement, see Chapter 7, "The Search for Foreign Instigators: Operation Chaos and the Intelligence Evaluation Committee."

2. AID stands for the Agency for International Development.

3. Krogh also was in charge of the White House Special Investigations Unit, more commonly known as the "plumbers." See Chapter 11, "Watergate."

4. This was the same Sidney Gottlieb who had engaged in illicit drug tests and who had delivered the poison with which Patrice Lumumba was to be assassinated. See Chapter 4, "Political Assassinations and Illicit Drug Tests."

_____ *Chapter 10* _____

Chile

On 4 September 1970, Salvador Allende Gossens won a plurality of 36.3 percent in a three-way presidential election in Chile. Allende, a Socialist, was the candidate of a fractious leftist coalition of parties called Popular Unity (Unidad Popular, UP). Since he did not have a clear majority of the vote, the Chile constitution required that his election be confirmed by Congress. Such an outcome was not uncommon in Chile, which had a well-developed democratic tradition, and it was customary for Congress to unite behind the first-place candidate.[1]

Outwardly, the Nixon administration feigned an air of indifference. National Security Adviser Henry Kissinger sarcastically dismissed Chile's strategic significance, referring to the country as a "dagger pointed at the heart of Antarctica." In reality, the administration, viewing Allende's election through the prism of the Cold War, feared that Chile would become an ally of Cuba in supporting revolution and subversion throughout Latin America. In the end, it appears that Allende never did act to promote revolution abroad. In fact, those favoring, or engaged in, armed revolution tended to be suspicious of Allende and his "peaceful path to socialism" with its necessary faith in the efficacy of elections and "bourgeois institutions."

The White House assigned the CIA to take action to prevent the expected outcome of the Congressional vote. On 16 September 1970, DCI Richard Helms held his first meeting on an operation to be codenamed FUBELT. FUBELT was kept secret even from the National Security Council. In contrast to the government's more "open" policy toward Chile, it came to be known as Track Two.

16 September 1970

MEMORANDUM FOR THE RECORD

SUBJECT: Genesis of Project FUBELT

1. On this date the Director called a meeting in connection with the Chilean situation. Present in addition to the Director were General Cushman, DDCI;

Col. White, ExDir-Compt; Thomas Karamessines, DDP; Cord Meyer, ADDP; William V. Broe, Chief WH Division; [—] Deputy Chief, WH Division, [— about one line deleted—] Chief, Covert Action, WH Division; and [—] Chief, WH/4.[2]

2. The Director told the group that President Nixon had decided that an Allende regime in Chile was not acceptable to the United States. The President asked the Agency to prevent Allende from coming to power or to unseat him. The President authorized ten million dollars for this purpose, if needed. Further, The Agency is to carry out this mission without coordination with the Departments of State or Defense.

3. During the meeting it was decided that Mr. Thomas Karamessines, DDP, would have overall responsibility for this project. He would be assisted by a special task force set up for this purpose in the Western Hemisphere Division. [—just under two lines deleted—]

4. Col. White was asked by the Director to make all necessary support arrangements in connection with the project.

5. The Director said he had been asked by Dr. Henry Kissinger, Assistant to the President for National Security Affairs, to meet with him on Friday, 18 September to give him the Agency's views on how this mission could be accomplished.

/signed/
William V. Broe
Chief
Western Hemisphere Division

The following month, Karamessines met with Kissinger and Alexander Haig, who at the time was Kissinger's deputy, at the White House to review the progress of the operation. The Chilean Congress was expected to confirm Allende's election, and the army commander, Gen. René Schneider, was adhering to the Chilean military's traditional role of supporting constitutional procedures. The vote in Congress was scheduled for 24 October and the inauguration for 3 November 1970. The CIA, nevertheless, had made contact with several disaffected military factions that were willing to consider organizing a coup d'état. Initial contacts with Roberto Viaux, a recently retired general who the previous year had led a brief military rebellion for higher wages, proved disappointing in the agency's view. In the meantime, Ambassador Edward Korry, whose opinionated cables on Allende had become famous within the U.S. government as the "Korrygrams," had been freelancing on his own.

15 October 1970

MEMORANDUM OF CONVERSATION
Dr. Kissinger, Mr. Karamessines, Gen. Haig
at the White House—15 October 1970
[—paragraph deleted; about fourteen lines—]

1. Then Mr. Karamessines provided a run-down on Viaux, the Canales meeting with Tirado, the latter's new position (after Porta was relieved of command "for health reasons") and, in some detail, the general situation in Chile from the coup possibility viewpoint.

2. A certain amount of information was available to us concerning Viaux's alleged support throughout the Chilean military. We had assessed Viaux's claims carefully, basing our analysis on good intelligence from a number of

sources. Our conclusion was clear: Viaux did not have more than one chance in twenty—perhaps less—to launch a successful coup.

3. The unfortunate repercussions, in Chile and internationally, of an unsuccessful coup were discussed. Dr. Kissinger ticked off his list of these negative possibilities. His items were remarkably similar to the ones Mr. Karamessines had prepared.

4. It was decided by those present that the Agency must get a message to Viaux warning him against any precipitate action. In essence, our message was to state, "We have reviewed your plans, and based on your information and ours, we come to the conclusion that your plans for a coup at this time cannot succeed. Failing, they may reduce your capabilities for the future. Preserve your assets. We will stay in touch. The time will come when you with all your other friends can do something. You will continue to have our support."

5. After the decision to defuse the Viaux coup plot, at least temporarily, Dr. Kissinger instructed Mr. Karamessines to preserve Agency assets in Chile, working clandestinely and securely to maintain the capability for Agency operations against Allende in the future.

6. Dr. Kissinger discussed his desire that the world of our encouragement to the Chilean military in recent weeks be kept as secret as possible. Mr. Karamessines stated emphatically that we have been doing everything possible in this connection, including the use of false flag officers, car meetings and every conceivable precaution. But we and others had done a great deal of talking recently with a number of persons. For example, Ambassador Korry's wide-ranging discussions with numerous people urging a coup "cannot be put back into the bottle." [—about two and a half lines deleted—] (Dr. Kissinger requested that copy of the message be sent to him on 16 October.)

7. The meeting concluded on Dr. Kissinger's note that the Agency should continue keeping the pressure on every Allende weak spot in sight—now, after the 24th of October, after 5 November, and into the future until such time as new marching order are given. Mr. Karamessines stated that the Agency would comply.

When instructions were sent to the Santiago Station the next day, it was clear that by putting the Viaux plot on hold, the CIA had not given up on all coup possibilities. Note that in this cable, someone has substituted handwritten descriptive terms for redacted names.

CITE HEADQUARTERS 802

IMMEDIATE SANTIAGO (EYES ONLY [—])

1. [Track Two] POLICY, OBJECTIVES, AND ACTIONS WERE REVIEWED AT HIGH USG [United States Government] LEVEL AFTERNOON 15 OCTOBER. CONCLUSIONS, WHICH ARE TO BE YOUR OPERATIONAL GUIDE, FOLLOW:

2. IT IS FIRM AND CONTINUING POLICY THAT ALLENDE BE OVERTHROWN BY A COUP. IT WOULD BE MUCH PREFERABLE TO HAVE THIS TRANSPIRE PRIOR TO 24 OCTOBER BUT EFFORTS IN THIS REGARD WILL CONTINUE VIGOROUSLY BEYOND THIS DATE. WE ARE TO CONTINUE TO GENERATE MAXIMUM PRESSURE TOWARD THIS END UTILIZING EVERY APPROPRIATE RESOURCE. IT IS IMPERATIVE THAT THESE ACTIONS BE IMPLEMENTED CLANDESTINELY AND SECURELY SO THAT THE USG AND AMERICAN HAND BE WELL

HIDDEN. WHILE THIS IMPOSES ON US A HIGH DEGREE OF SELECTIV-
ITY IN MAKING MILITARY CONTACTS AND DICTATES THAT THESE
CONTACTS BE MADE IN THE MOST SECURE MANNER IT DEFINITELY
DOES NOT PRECLUDE CONTACTS SUCH AS REPORTED IN SANTIAGO
544 [that is, a previous cable from Santiago Station] WHICH WAS A MAS-
TERFUL PIECE OF WORK.

3. AFTER THE MOST CAREFUL CONSIDERATION IT WAS DETERMINED
THAT A VIAUX COUP ATTEMPT CARRIED OUT BY HIM ALONE WITH
THE FORCES NOW AT HIS DISPOSAL WOULD FAIL. THUS, IT WOULD
BE COUNTERPRODUCTIVE TO OUR [track two] OBJECTIVES, IT WAS
DECIDED THAT [CIA] GET A MESSAGE TO VIAUX WARNING HIM
AGAINST PRECIPITATE ACTION. IN ESSENCE OUR MESSAGE IS TO
STATE, "WE HAVE REVIEWED YOUR PLANS, AND BASED ON YOUR
INFORMATION AND OURS, WE COME TO THE CONCLUSION THAT
YOUR PLANS FOR A COUP AT THIS TIME CANNOT SUCCEED. FAIL-
ING, THEY MAY REDUCE YOUR CAPABILITIES FOR THE FUTURE. PRE-
SERVE YOUR ASSETS. WE WILL STAY IN TOUCH. THE TIME WILL
COME WHEN YOU TOGETHER WITH ALL YOUR FRIENDS CAN DO
SOMETHING. YOU WILL CONTINUE TO HAVE OUR SUPPORT." YOU
ARE REQUESTED TO DELIVER THE MESSAGE TO VIAUX ESSENTIALLY
AS NOTED ABOVE. OUR OBJECTIVES ARE AS FOLLOWS: (A) TO ADVISE
HIM OF OUR OPINION AND DISCOURAGE HIM FROM ACTING ALONE;
(B) CONTINUE TO ENCOURAGE HIM TO AMPLIFY PLANNING; (C) EN-
COURAGE HIM TO JOIN FORCES WITH OTHER COUP PLANNERS SO
THAT THEY MAY ACT IN CONCERT EITHER BEFORE OR AFTER 24 OC-
TOBER. (N.B. SIX GAS MASKS AND SIX CS CANNISTERS ARE BEING
CARRIED TO SANTIAGO BY SPECIAL [—] COURIER ETD [that is, esti-
mated time of departure] WASHINGTON 1100 HOURS 16 OCTOBER.)

4. THERE IS GREAT AND CONTINUING INTEREST IN THE ACTIVITIES OF
TIRADO, CANALES, VALENZUELA ET AL AND WE WISH THEM OPTI-
MUM GOOD FORTUNE.

5. THE ABOVE IS YOUR OPERATING GUIDANCE. NO OTHER POLICY
GUIDANCE YOU MAY RECEIVE FROM [state] OR ITS MAXIMUM EXPO-
NENT IN SANTIAGO, ON HIS RETURN, ARE TO SWAY YOU FROM
YOUR COURSE.

6. PLEASE REVIEW ALL YOUR PRESENT AND POSSIBLY NEW ACTIVITIES
TO INCLUDE PROPAGANDA, BLACK OPERATIONS, SURFACING OF
INTELLIGENCE OR DISINFORMATION, PERSONAL CONTACTS, OR
ANYTHING ELSE YOUR IMAGINATION CAN CONJURE WHICH WILL
PERMIT YOU TO CONTINUE TO PRESS FORWARD TOWARD OUR [—]
OBJECTIVES IN A SECURE MANNER.

END OF MESSAGE

With the Viaux path closed off, the CIA's Santiago Station pursued a plot
developed by Gen. Camilo Valenzuela. Valenzuela's plan, like Viaux's, called
for kidnapping Gen. Schneider, who remained opposed to any military intervention in politics. The kidnapping would not only remove Schneider from the
scene, it would be blamed on pro-Allende forces and would then be used as a
pretext for the army to seize power. To carry out the plan, however, Valenzuela
said he needed "sterile" weapons that could not be traced to him or the Chilean
military. CIA headquarters found a request from the military for a secret shipment of arms to be a bit curious. The following three cables, one (Santiago 562)

sent to CIA headquarters from the Santiago Station and two replies (Headquarters 854 and 856), were all sent on 18 October 1970. These cables, too, have descriptive terms to replace redacted names.

CITE SANTIAGO 562

IMMEDIATE HEADQUARTERS
[—]
REFS: A. SANTIAGO 551
      B. SANTIAGO 558

1. [Station Cooptee] MET CLANDESTINELY EVENING 17 OCT WITH [two Chilean Armed Forces Officers] WHO TOLD HIM THEIR PLANS WERE MOVING ALONG BETTER THAN HAD THOUGHT POSSIBLE. THEY ASKED THAT BY EVENING 18 OCT [Cooptee] ARRANGE FURNISH THEM WITH EIGHT TO TEN TEAR GAS GRENADES. WITHIN 48 HOURS THEY NEED THREE 45 CALIBRE MACHINE GUNS ("GREASE GUNS") WITH 500 ROUNDS AMMO EACH. [one officer] COMMENTED HAS THREE MACHINE GUNS HIMSELF BUT CAN BE IDENTIFIED BY SERIAL NUMBERS AS HAVING BEEN ISSUED TO HIM THEREFORE UNABLE TO USE THEM.
2. [Officers] SAID THEY HAVE TO MOVE BECAUSE THEY BELIEVE THEY NOW UNDER SUSPICION AND BEING WATCHED BY ALLENDE SUPPORTERS. [one officer] WAS LATE TO MEETING HAVING TAKEN EVASIVE ACTION TO SHAKE POSSIBLE SURVEILLANCE BY ONE OR TWO TAXIS WITH DUAL ANTENNAS WHICH HE BELIEVED [were] BEING USED BY OPPOSITION AGAINST HIM.
3. [Cooptee] ASKED IF [officers] HAD AIR FORCE CONTACTS. THEY ANSWERED THEY DID NOT BUT WOULD WELCOME ONE. [Cooptee] SEPARATELY HAS SINCE TRIED CONTACT [a Chilean Air Force General] AND WILL KEEP TRYING UNTIL ESTABLISHED. WILL URGE [Air Force General] MEET WITH [other two officers] ASAP. [Cooptee] COMMENTED TO STATION THAT [Air Force General] HAS NOT TRIED CONTACT HIM SINCE REF A TALK.
4. [Cooptee] COMMENT: CANNOT TELL WHO IS LEADER OF THIS MOVEMENT BUT STRONGLY SUSPECTS IT IS ADMIRAL [—]. IT WOULD APPEAR FROM [his contacts'] ACTIONS AND ALLEGED ALLENDE SUSPICIONS ABOUT THEM THAT UNLESS THEY ACT NOW THEY ARE LOST. TRYING GET MORE INFO FROM THEM EVENING 18 OCT ABOUT SUPPORT THEY BELIEVE THEY HAVE.
5. STATION PLANS GIVE SIX TEAR GAS GRENADES (ARRIVING NOON 18 OCT BY SPECIAL COURIER) TO [Cooptee] FOR DELIVERY TO [armed forces officers] INSTEAD OF HAVING [false flag officer] DELIVER THEM TO VIAUX GROUP. OUR REASONING IS THAT [Cooptee] DEALING WITH ACTIVE DUTY OFFICERS. ALSO [false flag officer] LEAVING EVENING 18 OCT AND WILL NOT BE REPLACED BUT [Cooptee] WILL STAY HERE. HENCE IMPORTANT THAT [Cooptee] CREDIBILITY WITH [armed forces officers] BE STRENGTHENED BY PROMPT DELIVERY WHAT THEY REQUESTING. REQUEST HEADQUARTERS AGREEMENT BY 1500 HOURS LOCAL TIME 18 OCT ON DECISION DELIVERY OF TEAR GAS TO [Cooptee] VICE [false flag officer].
6. REQUEST PROMPT SHIPMENT THREE STERILE 45 CALIBRE MACHINE GUNS AND AMMO PER PARA 1 ABOVE, BY SPECIAL COURIER IF NECESSARY. PLEASE CONFIRM BY 2000 HOURS LOCAL TIME 18 OCT THAT

THIS CAN BE DONE SO [Cooptee] MAY INFORM [his contacts] ACCORDINGLY.

CITE HEADQUARTERS 854

IMMEDIATE SANTIAGO (EYES ONLY [—])
[—]
REF: SANTIAGO 562

1. DEPENDING HOW [Cooptee] CONVERSATION GOES EVENING 18 OC-TOBER YOU MAY WISH SUBMIT INTEL REPORT [—] SO WE CAN DECIDE WHETHER SHOULD BE DISSEM[inat]ED.
2. NEW SUBJECT: IF [Cooptee] PLANS LEAD COUP, OR BE ACTIVELY AND PUBLICLY INVOLVED, WE PUZZLED WHY IT SHOULD BOTHER HIM IF MACHINE GUNS CAN BE TRACED TO HIM. CAN WE DEVELOP RA-TIONALE ON WHY GUNS MUST BE STERILE? WILL CONTINUE MAKE EFFORT PROVIDE THEM BUT FIND OUR CREDULITY STRETCHED BY NAVY [officer] LEADING HIS TROOPS WITH STERILE GUNS? WHAT IS SPECIAL PURPOSE FOR THESE GUNS? WE WILL TRY SEND THEM WHETHER YOU CAN PROVIDE EXPLANATION OR NOT.

END OF MESSAGE

CITE HEADQUARTERS 856

IMMEDIATE SANTIAGO (EYES ONLY [—])
[—]
REF: SANTIAGO 562
SUB-MACHINE GUN AND AMMO BEING SENT BY REGULAR [—] COU-RIER LEAVING WASHINGTON 0700 HOURS 19 OCTOBER DUE ARRIVE SAN-TIAGO LATE EVENING 20 OCTOBER OR EARLY MORNING 21 OCTOBER. PREFERRED USE REGULAR [—] COURIER TO AVOID BRINGING UNDUE ATTENTION TO OP.

END OF MESSAGE

The Valenzuela group attempted to kidnap Gen. Schneider but failed because Schneider altered his travel plans. They were preparing a second attempt when, unexpectedly on 22 October, the Viaux group made its own attempt to kidnap Schneider despite having been warned off by the CIA. Schneider was acciden-tally shot in the process and died. Outraged, the Chilean military rallied around Schneider's replacement, Gen. Carlos Prats, and around Allende. On 24 Octo-ber, the Chilean Congress confirmed Allende's election by 153 votes to thirty-five, with seven abstentions.

The Nixon administration endeavored to isolate and undermine the Chilean government over the course of the next three years and provided financial sup-port to opposition groups, but it backed away from further involvement in coup plotting. Meanwhile, Allende's domestic political situation proved fragile. He faced hostility from some portions of the population from the beginning, as he sought to nationalize mines and other large-scale business enterprises. His plan to carry out a peaceful social revolution within the terms of the constitution was constrained by the fact that he was supported by barely more than one-third of the electorate. The more radical elements inside and outside his government took unauthorized actions that went beyond, or even against, his stated policies, such as seizing and occupying medium-sized factories, and then challenged him to stop them, which he was unwilling or unable to do. Such actions alienated middle-class segments of the population that might have been won over to Allende's peaceful revolution. The economy suffered from antigovernment strikes by small businesses and independent truckers. The government's expansive spending policies fueled hyperinflation. The polity became highly polarized and confrontational.

On 11 September 1973, Allende was overthrown in a violent military coup led by Gen. Augusto Pinochet. It appears that the CIA did not organize or encourage the coup, but knew of the planning, and Pinochet was well aware of the U.S. government's hostility toward Allende.

On 18 September 2000, in response to a Congressional mandate (the Hinchey Amendment to the Intelligence Authorization Act for Fiscal Year 2000), the National Intelligence Council issued a report titled "CIA Activities in Chile," or the Hinchey Report, based on a review of CIA records, oral histories, and memoirs. The following excerpt from the Hinchey Report describes the CIA's actions in the period leading up to the 1973 coup:

> The CIA continued to collect intelligence on Chilean military officers actively opposed to the Allende government, but no effort was made to assist them in any way. Some CIA assets and contacts were in direct contact with coup plotters; CIA guidance was that the purpose of these contacts was only to collect intelligence. As coup rumors and planning escalated by the end of 1972, CIA exercised extreme care in all dealings with Chilean military officers and continued to monitor their activities but under no circumstances attempted to influence them. By October 1972 the consensus within the US government was that the military intended to launch a coup at some point, that it did not need US support for a successful coup, and that US intervention or assistance in a coup should be avoided.
>
> On 21 August 1973 the 40 Committee approved a $1 million supplemental budget to increase support for opposition political parties, bringing the total amount of covert funding spent during the Allende period to approximately $6.5 million. In late August the Station requested authorization to provide maximum support for the opposition's efforts to encourage the entrance of the Chilean military into the Allende cabinet. The resignation of Army Commander General Carlos Prats (whose actions were strongly constitutionalist) and his replacement by General Augusto Pinochet (not a coup plotter, but apparently willing to concede to a coup) appeared to further unify the Armed Forces and strengthened the institution as a political pressure group. The UP Government appeared to fear a possible military coup and was unsure how to react to such a development.
>
> The Station realized that the opposition's objectives had evolved to a point inconsistent with current US policy and sought authorization from Washington to support such an aggressive approach. Although the US Ambassador in Chile agreed with the need for Washington to evaluate its current policy, he did not concur in the Station's proposal, fearing that it could lead to a de facto US commitment to a coup. In response, CIA Headquarters reaffirmed to the Station that there was to be no involvement with the military in any covert action initiative; there was no support for instigating a military coup.
>
> On 10 September 1973—the day before the coup that ended the Allende Government—a Chilean military officer reported to a CIA officer that a coup was being planned and asked for US Government assistance. He was told that the US Government would not provide any assistance because this was strictly an internal Chilean matter. The Station officer also told him that his request would be forwarded to Washington. CIA learned of the exact date of the coup shortly before it

took place. During the attack on the Presidential Palace and its immediate aftermath, the Station's activities were limited to providing intelligence and situation reports.

Allende's death occurred after the President refused an offer from the military to take him and his family out of the country. Available evidence indicates that President Allende committed suicide as putchist troops entered his offices. A credible source on Allende's death was Dr. Patricio Guijon, a physician who served on the President's medical staff. Guijon was in the Presidential Palace, *La Moneda*, with Allende during the assault and claimed that he witnessed Allende shoot himself with a rifle. The Chilean National Commission on Truth and Reconciliation in 1991 also concluded that Allende took his own life. There is no information to indicate that the CIA was involved in Allende's death.

Supporters of the coup later published a "white book" to justify Allende's overthrow. The book included documents related to "Plan Z," a supposed program of the Allende government to assassinate prominent military and political figures in order to forestall a coup. Many commentators have alleged that "Plan Z" was a CIA fabrication. While the CIA agrees that it was most likely a fabrication, it denies any involvement in producing it.

In the aftermath of the coup, the CIA cooperated with the new Pinochet government, which developed a reputation for brutality at home and the assassination of opposition members in exile. Contact was maintained with known violators of human rights when they were determined to be useful as sources of intelligence, including information on the behavior of the Pinochet government and on the activities of the remnants of the leftist opposition. (The policy on maintaining contact with known human-rights violators was changed in the mid-1990s.) The Hinchey Report summarizes the situation post-coup Chile this way:

> Given the wide variety and nature of CIA contacts in Chile, the issue of human rights was handled in various ways over the years. Some examples:
>
> - Before the 1973 coup, the issue of human rights was not addressed in liaison contacts and intelligence reporting.
> - One CIA contact was known to be involved in an abortive coup attempt on 29 June 1973, and another was involved in the successful 11 September 1973 coup.
> - In October 1973, the CIA had credible information that a high-level contact was involved in specific human rights abuses; contact was severed.
> - Although the CIA had information indicating that a high-level contact was a hard-liner and therefore more likely to commit abuses, contact with him was allowed to continue in the absence of concrete information about human rights abuses.
> - CIA maintained indirect contact with a source in close contact with human rights violators. There was no evidence that the source engaged in abuses, but he almost certainly knew about the practice. The intelligence value of the contact was sufficiently important that the contact was not dropped.
> - In the case of an individual about whom the CIA had information concerning a corruption issue that may have been related to human rights issues, a decision was made to seek contact given his position and potential intelligence value.
> - In more than one case, in light of the contacts' service affiliation and position, it seemed likely that they were involved in, knew about or covered up human rights abuses. However, because such contacts allowed the CIA to accomplish

its intelligence-reporting mission and maintain a channel through which to voice concerns about human rights abuses, contact was continued.

- In a few cases, although the CIA had knowledge that the contact represented a service with a known history of human rights abuses, contact was continued because refusing such contact would have had a negative impact on the CIA intelligence collection mission.
- In some cases careful checks of contacts' human rights records were not conducted, and a deliberate risk-versus-gain decision was not made. In such cases, if a contact was deemed to have intelligence value, continuing contact was authorized.
- Information concerning human rights abuses of then current and former CIA contacts was disseminated to the intelligence and policy communities.

Chief among those violators was Manuel Contreras Sepúlveda, the head of Chilean intelligence. Contact with him continued because it was determined to be essential to the CIA's intelligence-gathering function. In addition to abuses within Chile, however, Contreras also proved to be involved in a campaign of assassination abroad that reached the streets of Washington, D.C. On this, the Hinchey Report notes, in part:

> In addition to information concerning external threats, CIA sought from Contreras information regarding evidence that emerged in 1975 of a formal Southern Cone cooperative intelligence effort—"Operation Condor"—building on informal cooperation in tracking and, in at least a few cases, killing political opponents. By October 1976 there was sufficient information that the CIA decided to approach Contreras on the matter. Contreras confirmed Condor's existence as an intelligence-sharing network but denied that it had a role in extra-judicial killings.
>
> Former Allende cabinet member and Ambassador to Washington Orlando Letelier and his American assistant, Ronni Moffit, were killed in a carbombing in Washington on 21September 1976. Almost immediately after the assassination, rumors began circulating that the Chilean government was responsible. CIA's first intelligence report containing this allegation was dated 6 October 1976. During October 1976, the Department of Justice and the CIA worked out how the CIA would support the foreign intelligence (FI) aspects of the legal investigation. At that time, Contreras' possible role in the Letelier assassination became an issue.
>
> By the end of 1976, contacts with Contreras were very infrequent. During 1977, CIA met with Contreras about half a dozen times; three of those contacts were to request information on the Letelier assassination. On 3 November 1977, Contreras was transferred to a function unrelated to intelligence so CIA severed all contact with him.
>
> Nonetheless, CIA intelligence reporting continued to follow Contreras' activities closely. After a short struggle to retain power, Contreras resigned from the Army in 1978. In the interim, CIA gathered specific, detailed intelligence reporting concerning Contreras' involvement in ordering the Letelier assassination. While some of this material has been released, some remains classified and another portion has been withheld at the request of the Department of Justice, which continues to pursue the investigation.

NOTES

1. For further information on the CIA and Chile, see Peter Kornbluh, *The Pinochet File: A Declassified Dossier on Atrocity and Accountability* (New York: New Press, 2003);

Jonathan Haslam, *The Nixon Administration and the Death of Allende's Chile: A Case of Assisted Suicide* (New York: Verso Books, 2005); and Kristian Gustafson, *Hostile Intent: U.S. Covert Operations in Chile, 1964–1974* (Washington, D.C.: Potomac Books, 2007).

2. DDCI stands for Deputy Director of Central Intelligence; ExDir-Compt. stands for Executive Director–Comptroller; DDP stands for Deputy Director for Plans; ADDP stands for Associate Deputy Director for Plans; WH stands for Western Hemisphere; and WH/4 stands for Western Hemisphere Task Force 4 (the Cuba Task Force).

Chapter 11

Watergate

At 2:30 A.M. on Saturday, 17 June 1972, five men were caught breaking into the Democratic National Committee (DNC) headquarters in an effort to adjust listening devices that they had planted there earlier. The DNC was located in a Washington, D.C., apartment-and-office complex known as the Watergate, and thus the name Watergate passed into the everyday lexicon of nearly every American and many others around the world.[1] Despite monumental speculation, false leaks to the press from the White House, and some misleading evidence, the CIA's connection to Watergate was not so much the break-in or even its cover-up, but rather a tale of efforts to avoid being swept up in its political aftermath.

Among the five burglars arrested that night was James W. McCord, a former employee of the CIA's Office of Security who was at the time the security coordinator of Richard Nixon's electoral campaign organization, the Committee for the Re-election of the President (also called the Committee to Re-elect the President; officially abbreviated CRP but widely known as CREEP, even among its staff). The others were Cuban Americans who had been involved in past CIA operations and had been told that the break-in would further the cause of Cuban liberation. One of the Cuban Americans had in his possession a passport in the name of Edward V. Hamilton. This was an alias once assigned to E. Howard Hunt, who had retired from the Clandestine Service two years earlier. The actual purpose of the break-in had been political espionage organized by CRP on behalf of the president's campaign, but the apparent links to the CIA were numerous.

Indicted together with the five Watergate burglars (on 15 September 1972) would be G. Gordon Liddy, a CRP counsel and former FBI agent who had organized the break-in, and E. Howard Hunt. Hunt had been in charge of propaganda activities for the Bay of Pigs invasion in 1961 and was once a Chief of Station in South America, where an ambassador described him as "totally self-absorbed, totally amoral, and a danger to himself and anybody around him." [2] After retiring in 1970, he took a position at the White House. Eventually, he became a member of the White House's informal investigations unit, the "plumbers," which was established in 1971 to stop "leaks" to the press of information about the Vietnam War. The Nixon White House, including National Security Adviser Henry Kissinger, had a deep-rooted concern—some would say obsession—with violations of secrecy and leaks to the press, which they frequently blamed on members of Congress. This was despite the fact that they appear to have been responsible for a great many of the leaks themselves. For example, the minutes of DCI Richard Helms's morning staff meeting for 18 January 1973 included the following item:

> [John] Maury noted that in response to Tom Korologis' (Special Assistant to the President for Legislative Affairs (Senate)) request for materials on instances where classified information had been leaked to the press, he assembled a paper on this topic and provided it with a note that an examination of most leaks reveals that the White House and Executive Branch are the guilty parties.

In any event, Hunt had been responsible for recruiting most of the others involved in the burglary. The FBI investigation continued after the indictments, and it was joined by a Congressional investigation early the following year. The ultimate result came on 9 August 1974, when Richard Nixon became the first U.S. president in history to resign from office in disgrace. In the interim, however, the CIA was in turmoil.

On the day of the break-in, the CIA's Director of Security Howard Osborn informed DCI Richard Helms of the arrest and of the McCord connection. At the time, Osborn was still uncertain of the Cubans' connection to the agency, although he knew they were "Miami," not "Havana." He assured Helms that it had not been a CIA operation.

Starting the following Monday, the break-in was a topic of the director's regular morning staff meetings. Following the agency's natural impulse, CIA representatives were not to be forthcoming with information for outsiders, which probably added to the public atmosphere of suspicion. In the beginning, however, Helms and other members of the Executive Committee seemed to believe that the episode would not have too strong an impact on the CIA. According to the morning meeting minutes, from the "Family Jewels" file:

> 19 June 1972
>
> The Director noted the 17 June arrest of James W. McCord and four others who were apprehended at the Democratic National Committee headquarters at the Watergate. With the Director of Security present to provide biographic details, the Director made it perfectly clear that responses to any inquiry with respect to McCord or Howard Hunt, who may be implicated, are to be limited to a statement that they are former employees who retired in August and April 1970 respectively. The Director asked that this guidance be disseminated via staff meetings. The Director asked that any inquiry from other elements of the government be referred to the Director of Security who is to be the focal point. Inquiries from the press are to be referred to Mr. [John] Unumb who may say that McCord worked in the Office of Security. The Director noted that we have no responsibility with respect to an investigation except to be responsive to the FBI's request for name traces. It

was noted that Howard Hunt may have done some work since retirement in connection with the preparation of supporting material for some awards. The Executive Director was asked to review this topic and report to the Director.

20 June 1972

In response to the Director's request, the Director of Security highlighted developments over the past twenty-four hours with respect to the McCord/Hunt, et al., situation. He noted that the late edition of the New York Times carries a different story by Tad Szulc than that which appeared in the edition received here. The Director of Security anticipates inquiries on [Cuban American burglar] Bernard L. Barker's situation, and it was noted that Mr. Barker was hired by the Agency in 1960 and terminated in 1966. The Director complimented Unumb on his handling of inquiries and asked that future inquiries be met with a response confined to the fact that, now that we have acknowledged that both McCord and Hunt are former Agency employees, we know nothing more about the case and the caller should be referred to the FBI as appropriate.

21 June 1972

In view of the coverage in today's New York Times and Washington Post, [John M.] Maury recommended that Chairman [Lucien N.] Nedzi [of the House Subcommittee on Intelligence Operations] be briefed on the McCord affair and that this briefing include all our information about the others involved. The Director asked Maury to touch base with the Director of Security and prepare a briefing paper on this topic for his review. Citing the number of distorted rumors about this matter, the Executive Director said that during the course of the day he hopes to provide a suggested Headquarters Bulletin for all employees for the Director's review.

Unumb noted a number of inquiries from the press with respect to the Cuban-Americans involved in the bugging attempt at the Democratic National Committee headquarters and their alleged involvement in the Bay of Pigs, etc. The Director asked that such inquiries be met with an explanation that we are not prepared to be helpful on this matter.

22 June 1972

Unumb observed that inquiries on the McCord/Hunt situation seem to be slackening off.

23 June 1972

The Director called D/OCI's [the Director of the Office of Current Intelligence] attention to coverage of the McCord affair in the Metro Section of today's Washington Post and asked that future issues of the "CIA Operations Center Morning Newspaper Highlights" include press items on this topic.

Maury noted that he briefed Chairman Nedzi on the McCord/Hunt situation and on a security case.

On that day, the "McCord affair" was to take a more serious turn for Helms and his associates. Nixon instructed his chief of staff, H. R. Haldeman, to call in Helms and Deputy Director of Central Intelligence Lt. Gen. Vernon Walters (a recent presidential appointee who Nixon thought would be a "good friend" at the CIA) and instruct them to intervene with FBI Acting Director L. Patrick Gray to forestall the investigation into the Watergate break-in.

The following excerpts are from the "smoking gun" tape, recorded by the president with a concealed tape recorder in the Oval Office. Its eventual release, in 1974, prompted the House Judiciary Committee to vote for Nixon's impeachment on the charge of obstruction of justice. He resigned from the presidency before the full House had an opportunity to vote.[3] The scene is in the White House on the morning of 23 June 1972.

HALDEMAN:

Okay—that's fine. Now, on the investigation, you know, the Democratic break-in thing, we're back to the—in the, the problem area because the FBI is not under control, because Gray doesn't exactly know how to control them, and they have, their investigation is now leading into some productive areas, because they've been able to trace the money, not through the money itself, but through the bank, you know, sources—the banker himself. [...] That the way to handle this is for us to have Walters call in Pat Gray and just say, "Stay the hell out of this ... this is ah, business here we don't want you to go any further on it." That's not an unusual development ...

PRESIDENT:

Um huh.

HALDEMAN:

... and, uh, that would take care of it.

PRESIDENT:

What about Pat Gray, ah, you mean he doesn't want to?

HALDEMAN:

Pat does want to. He doesn't know how to, and he doesn't have, he doesn't have any basis for doing it. Given this, he will then have the basis. He'll call Mark Felt in, and the two of them ... and Mark Felt wants to cooperate because ...[4]

PRESIDENT:

Yeah.

HALDEMAN:

He's ambitious ...

PRESIDENT:

Yeah.

HALDEMAN:

Ah, he'll call him in and say, "We've got the signal from across the river [that is, from the CIA] to, to put the hold on this." And that will fit rather well because the FBI agents who are working the case, at this point, feel that's what it is. This is the CIA.

[After discussing whether the burglars' funds could be traced to CRP, they conclude that stopping the investigation is safer than relying on ever larger numbers of people to lie for them.]

HALDEMAN:

Well, if they will. But then we're relying on more and more people all the time. That's the problem. And ah, they'll stop if we could, if we take this other step.

PRESIDENT:

All right. Fine.

HALDEMAN:

And, and they seem to feel the thing to do is get them to stop?

PRESIDENT:

Right, fine.

HALDEMAN:

They say the only way to do that is from White House instructions. And it's got to be to Helms and ah, what's his name . . . ? Walters.

PRESIDENT:

Walters.

HALDEMAN:

And the proposal would be that Ehrlichman (coughs) and I call them in.

PRESIDENT:

All right, fine.

HALDEMAN:

And say, ah . . .

PRESIDENT:

How do you call him in, I mean you just, well, we protected Helms from one hell of lot of things.

HALDEMAN:

That's what Ehrlichman says.

[At this point Nixon tries to construct an argument, or to convince himself, that they are doing the CIA a favor. The Cuban American connection would bring up the Bay of Pigs scandal, although the basic facts were already public knowledge.]

PRESIDENT:

Of course, this is a, this is a hunt, you will—that will uncover a lot of things. You open that scab there's a hell of a lot of things and that we just feel that it would be very detrimental to have this thing go any further. This involves these Cubans, Hunt, and a lot of hanky-panky that we [in the White House] have nothing to do with ourselves.

[Nixon and Haldeman discussed the Watergate role of CRP head John Mitchell and that of G. Gordon Liddy. (Nixon considered Liddy "a little nuts." "I mean he just isn't well screwed on is he? Isn't that the problem?") They then concluded that an FBI interrogation of presidential aide Charles Colson had created an opportunity by turning suspicion away from the White House.]

HALDEMAN:

An interrogation, which he did, and that, the FBI guys working the case had concluded that there were one or two possibilities, one, that this was the White House, they don't think there is anything at the Election Committee, they think it was either a White House operation and they had some obscure reasons for it, nonpolitical . . .

PRESIDENT:

Uh huh.

HALDEMAN:

Or it was a . . .

PRESIDENT:

Cuban thing—

HALDEMAN:

Cubans and the CIA. And after their interrogation of, of . . .

PRESIDENT:

Colson.

HALDEMAN:

Colson, yesterday, they concluded it was not the White House, but are now convinced it is a CIA thing, so the CIA turn off would . . .

PRESIDENT:

Well, not sure of their analysis, I'm not going to get that involved. I'm (unintelligible).

HALDEMAN:

No, sir. We don't want you to.

PRESIDENT:

You call them in.

PRESIDENT:

Good. Good deal! Play it tough. That's the way they play it and that's the way we're going to play it.

HALDEMAN:

O.K. We'll do it.

[Later in the conversation, Nixon returned to the theme, concerned that Helms and Walters not suspect why they are doing this.]

PRESIDENT:

When you get in these people when you . . . get these people in, say: "Look, the problem is that this will open the whole, the whole Bay of Pigs thing, and the President just feels that," ah, without going into the details . . . don't, don't lie to them to the extent to say there is no involvement, but just say this is a sort of comedy of errors, bizarre, without getting into it, "the President believes that it is going to open the whole Bay of Pigs thing up again. And, ah, because these people are plugging for, for keeps and that they should call the FBI in and say that we wish for the country, don't go any further into this case," period!

[In another meeting with Haldeman that afternoon, in the midst of an unrelated conversation, Nixon returned to the theme that ending the investigation was for the good of the CIA but was also concerned that Helms not become suspicious.]

PRESIDENT:

[. . .] Just say that I have to look at the primaries (unintelligiblc) recover (unintelligible) I just don't (unintelligible) very bad, to have this fellow Hunt, ah, you know, ah, it's, he, he knows too damn much and he was involved, we happen to know that. And that it gets out that the whole, this is all involved in the Cuban thing, that it's a fiasco, and it's going to make the FB, ah CIA look bad, it's going to make Hunt look bad, and it's likely to blow the whole, uh, Bay of Pigs thing which we think would be very unfortunate for the CIA and for the country at this time, and for American foreign policy, and he just better tough it and lay it on them. Isn't that what you . . .

HALDEMAN:

Yeah, that's, that's the basis we'll do it on and just leave it at that.

PRESIDENT:

I don't want them to get any ideas we're doing it because our concern is political.

HALDEMAN:

Right.

PRESIDENT:

And at the same time, I wouldn't tell them it is not political.

HALDEMAN:

Right.

PRESIDENT:

I would just say "Look, it's because of the Hunt involvement," [. . .]

Haldeman and Ehrlichman met with Helms and Walters that same afternoon and followed the scenario as laid out with the president. Rather than being convinced by the Bay of Pigs argument, Helms and Walters found it baffling.[5] They came away with the conviction, however, that this was an order from the White House and not a search for the truth. Although they complied initially, they soon reversed course. They came to suspect that the CIA (and perhaps themselves personally) was being framed to appear as the guilty party behind the Watergate break-in.[6]

Later, in Congressional testimony, Walters described the encounter with Haldeman and Ehrlichman and several follow-up meetings with White House Counsel John Dean and Acting FBI Director L. Patrick Gray. The testimony was reprinted in the CIA *Employee Bulletin* of 21 May 1973 and a copy was included in the "Family Jewels" file.

DDCI STATEMENT ABOUT THE WATERGATE CASE

The following statement was made by Lieutenant General Vernon A. Walters during a recent appearance before a Congressional Committee.

On 23 June 1972 I was ordered by a phone message from my office to be at the White House at about 1300 [1:00 P.M.] with Director Helms. I had lunch with Mr. Helms and we went to Mr. Ehrlichman's office at the White House. Present were Mr. Ehrlichman, Mr. Haldeman, Mr. Helms and myself. As I recall it, Mr. Haldeman said that the Watergate incident was causing trouble and was being exploited by the opposition. It had been decided at the White House that I would go to Acting FBI Director Gray and tell him that now that the five suspects were arrested, further enquiries into the Mexican aspects of this matter might jeopardize some of the CIA's covert activities in that area.[7] An appointment was made for me to see Mr. Gray at 1430 [2:30 P.M.] that same day. I went over and told him that I had been directed by top White House officials to tell him that further investigation into the Mexican aspects of the Watergate episode might jeopardize some of the Agency's covert actions in that area. He said that he understood the agreement between the FBI and the Agency regarding their sources but that this was a complicated case. He would not violate the agreement with CIA regarding sources. On my return to the Agency I checked to see whether there was any danger in the Agency's covert sources if the Mexican part of the investigation continued and ascertained that on one believed that this was the case. No one had any knowledge of the plan to bug the Democratic National Committee.

On June 26 the Counsel to the President John Dean called me and asked me to come and see him about the matter I had discussed with Haldeman and Ehrlichman. He said I could check with Ehrlichman and I did. He said I could talk to Dean so I went to Dean's office at 1145 [11:45 A.M.] on June 26.

I informed Dean that I had checked carefully to see whether there was any jeopardy to the Agency's sources by a further investigation of the Mexican sources of this matter and found there was none. Dean then asked whether the CIA might have taken part in the Watergate episode without my knowing it. I said that this was not possible. I knew the Agency had no part in the operation against the Democratic National Committee. I therefore could not say that further investigation would jeopardize Agency sources. I felt that someone had bungled badly and that the responsible parties should be fired. He asked whether there was not some way in which the Agency might have been involved. I said that I had checked with Director Helms and was convinced it was not. Any attempt to stifle this investigation would destroy the effectiveness of the Agency and the FBI and would be a grave disservice to the President. I would have no part in it and was quite prepared to resign on the issue. He asked whether I had any ideas on what might be done and I replied that those responsible should be fired. He seemed disappointed and I left.

The following day I saw Dean again in his office at his request. He again reviewed the Watergate Case saying that some witnesses were getting scared and were "wobbling." I said that no matter how scared they got, they could not involve the CIA because it was not involved in the bugging of the Watergate. He then asked if the CIA could not furnish bail and pay the suspects' salaries while they were in jail, using covert action funds for this purpose.

I replied that this was out of the question. It would implicate the Agency in something in which it was not implicated. Any such action by the Agency would imply an order from the highest level and I would not be a party to any such action. It would be a grave disservice to the President and the country and would destroy the CIA's credibility with the Congress and the people. I would resign rather than do this and, if ordered to do it, I would ask to see the President to explain the reasons for my refusal. Furthermore, when the Agency expended funds in the U.S., we had to report this to the Oversight Committees of the Agency in Congress. He was much taken aback by this and agreed that risks of implicating the CIA and FBI in this matter would be enormous. I said that what was now a painful wound could become a mortal one. What was now a "conventional explosion could be turned into a multi-megaton explosion." I again advised him to fire the responsible parties.

Again Dean sent for me on the 28th of June and I saw him at his office at 1130 that day. He enquired whether I had learned anything more about CIA involvement. I replied that there was no involvement of the Agency in the bugging of the Watergate. He then asked whether I had any ideas and I said that I had none which could be helpful. Perhaps the Cubans who were anti-Castro might have had a hand in it but the CIA did not.

On July 5 I received a call from Acting Director of the FBI Gray saying that he could not stop further investigation of the Mexican aspects of this matter unless he had a formal letter from the Director of CIA or me asking him to do this. I said I would come to his office and I saw him at 1000 the following morning.

I told him that I could not tell him that further investigation would jeopardize the Agency's covert sources. I had checked on this and it was not so. I had ascertained that General Cushman had initially authorized the issuance of some equipment to Howard Hunt without knowing its purpose other than that it was, as I understood it, to shut off "leaks." This was long before the Watergate bugging. Since then I had carefully checked and there was no other involvement of any sort by the CIA in the operation against the Watergate. I said that attempts to cover this up or to implicate the CIA or FBI would be detrimental to their integrity and a disservice to the President and the country. I would have no part in this and was quite prepared to resign on this issue. He said that he shared my views regarding the importance of the integrity of our agencies and he too was prepared to resign on this issue. I gave Gray a list of the equipment the Agency had given Hunt and the account of our dealings with the former CIA employees up to the termination of their employment with the Agency long before the Watergate episode.

I saw Gray again on the 12th of July and gave him one additional memorandum regarding the contact furnished Hunt. We reviewed the matter reiterating the position we had taken previously. I said that I had told Dean that the best solution would be to fire those responsible. Gray said he had made the same recommendation. Once again we agreed that anything that might damage the integrity of the FBI and CIA would be a grave disservice to the President and the Government.

In February 1973 shortly after Dr. Schlesinger became Director I told him of my conversations with Haldeman, Ehrlichman, and Dean. In February Dean called Dr. Schlesinger to see if the Agency could get back from the FBI the material it had sent to the Justice Department concerning our contact with Hunt. Dr. Schlesinger and I agreed that this could not be done. I attempted to contact Dean but he was in Florida. On his return I saw Dean in his office on February 21 and told him that we could not ask the FBI for our material back. That would only serve to implicate the CIA and I could not and would not do it. I had seen Acting FBI Director Gray that morning and told him of Dean's request and our refusal. He agreed saying that he could not do such a thing.

Since that date I have had no further contact with Dean. The above represents my recollection of what occurred and the dates are checked in my appointment book.[8]

Nixon won reelection in November despite the CIA's refusal to cooperate. Three weeks after that, he dismissed Helms (effective February 1973) and replaced him with James Schlesinger, who at the time was the chairman of the Atomic Energy Commission. In 1971, as deputy director of the Office of Management and Budget, Schlesinger had authored *A Review of the Intelligence Community* (the Schlesinger Report), in which he argued that the Intelligence Community had grown too large and expensive and was mismanaged. (One of his recommendations was to establish the post of Director of National Intelligence, a proposal that was adopted thirty-three years later.) Now he was given instructions to shake up the CIA, and he dismissed some 1,400 officials during his brief, seventeen-week tenure.

In the meantime, between July 1972 and January 1973, James McCord had sent six letters to Helms and other agency officials, five anonymous and one signed "Jim." In these letters, which have been described as "confused" and "disjointed," he implied that he was under pressure from the White House to pin the blame for the break-in on the CIA. The first letter, in fact, had initially been dismissed as "crank mail." In a five-page affidavit signed on 23 May 1973,

Director of Security Osborn stated that Helms and the CIA General Counsel had determined that the agency was under no obligation to inform the FBI or the Justice Department of the letters. Helms, with the General Counsel's consent, instructed Osborn "to retain them in a secure file and take no action with regard to them." Schlesinger and Colby learned of the McCord letters only after Schlesinger's 9 May 1973 request to agency employees for information regarding potentially illicit activities.[9] (See Introduction.)

Following up Schlesinger's general request to agency employees for information regarding potentially illicit activities, Colby, who at the time was both Deputy Director for Operations and Executive Secretary of the CIA Management Committee, sent out a specific order regarding information related to the Watergate matter.

23 May 1973

MEMORANDUM FOR: All Employees

SUBJECT: Agency Involvement in the Watergate Case

1. The leadership of the Agency continues to make a determined effort to investigate all aspects of Agency involvement with the "Watergate" case or any of those persons connected with it. The results of these investigations have been given to the appropriate legislative, executive, and judicial elements of the Government investigating these matters. Each employee has been asked and is directed to report to the Director any knowledge he or she has of the Watergate affair and related matters, any persons connected with it, or any other illegal activity in which they believe the Agency was involved in any way.

2. In consonance with the foregoing, anyone who has had any connection or contact with individuals on the attached list, or anyone in their offices or anyone purporting to act for them or acting pursuant to their authority, should report these contacts fully. Activities of these and other individuals include not only the Watergate affair, but any investigative work on the Pentagon Papers/Ellsberg case and any contacts relating to the Executive Branch and White House efforts to locate and stem leaks of classified information to the press starting as early as July 1970.

3. Any work done by anyone in the Agency on any of these subjects, or any knowledge related thereto, should be reported to the IG [Inspector General] through the appropriate Deputy Director, or directly and personally to the Director.

4. It is imperative that every piece of information bearing on these matters be reported immediately for evaluation by the senior management of the Agency. The public interest requires that all information be produced and reported to our oversight committees (on a classified basis if necessary) so that the Agency's actual role will be clarified with respect to various charges and speculation.

/signed/
W. E. Colby
Executive Secretary
CIA Management Committee

Attachment

APPROVED
/signed/
James R. Schlesinger
Director

H. R. Haldeman
John D. Ehrlichman
John Dean
Egil Krogh
David Young
E. Howard Hunt
G. Gordon Liddy
James W. McCord
Charles W. Colson
John J. Caulfield
Eugenio Rolando <u>Martinez</u> Careaga
Juan Rigoberto <u>Ruiz</u> Villegas
Bernard L. Barker
Virgilio Gonzales
Frank Anthony Sturgis

The CIA reviewed its files and found that Hunt and McCord cropped up in some unexpected places, especially after 7 July 1971, when presidential aide John Ehrlichman called to tell the CIA to provide Hunt with any equipment and other assistance he requested. Questions as to the purpose of the equipment were not asked. Evidently, Hunt and McCord saw former CIA employees as the sort of people they needed. They made use of the External Employment Assistance Branch (EEAB), an office that helps employees leaving the agency find outside jobs. For example, a four-page memo on various topics from the Director of Personnel, included in the ''Family Jewels'' file, contains the following paragraphs:

8. <u>Hunt Requests a Lockpicker</u>: This is a record of External Employment Assistance Branch's action on a request from Howard Hunt for a lockpicker who might be retiring or resigning from the Agency.

    Sometime in the spring of 1972, Frank O'Malley of EEAB received a call from Howard Hunt who asked Frank if he had a retiree or resignee who was accomplished at picking locks. Mr. O'Malley sent him a resume on Thomas Amato who retired 31 July 1971. Mr. O'Malley did not document his EEAB record to show the date of this exchange, but [—] (who also works in EEAB) opines that it occurred sometime between March and May 1972.

    All of the above information was reported to the Office of Security on 4 October 1972 following the FBI's contact with the Agency regarding Howard Hunt.

9. <u>Resume Sent to McCord</u>: [—], a contract employee who retired in September 1971, was a client of the External Employment Assistance Branch in his search for a job after retirement. One of the leads given to [—] was James McCord's security business. EEAB sent a resume to McCord, but [—] was not hired.

    In mid-summer 1972, [—] telephoned EEAB from Chicago. (He had a job there with Halifax Security Co., a lead provided by EEAB, but until this telephone call he had not notified EEAB that he had the job and had moved from the D.C. area.) He said he had been visited by a Special Agent of the FBI who told [—] that his resume had been found among McCord's papers. The Agent wanted to know if [—] had any connection with McCord. [—] explained how the resume got to McCord. After the Agent left him, [—] telephoned EEAB. [—] of OP [Office of Personnel] and [—] of OS [Office of Security] were notified immediately.

The same day he requested information on illicit activities, DCI Schlesinger had to testify before the Senate Appropriations Subcommittee on Intelligence Operations regarding the CIA's connections with Hunt, all of which, of course, preceded his tenure at the agency.

DCI STATEMENT BEFORE
SENATE APPROPRIATIONS SUBCOMMITTEE
ON INTELLIGENCE OPERATIONS

9 MAY 1973

OPENING STATEMENT

Mr. Chairman, I am here to discuss the questions that have arisen over CIA's real and alleged role in the events that occurred in 1971 and 1972. I have opened a detailed investigation into the precise nature of that role. I can report to you on what Agency records, now being intensively reviewed, reveal at this juncture. However I do not yet know that I have all the facts in the matter. Nonetheless, I am pleased to present to you such facts as are now available, and I will certainly provide you with any further details as they come to my attention.

Let me start with the Agency's relationship with Mr. Howard Hunt, whose testimony has recently been made public. Mr. Hunt was a staff employee of the Agency from 8 November 1949 to 30 April 1970. At that time he retired from the Agency. He performed one editorial job of writing up a recommendation for an award for one of our officers in November 1970. He was not paid for these services, although the Agency placed the sums of $200.00 and $50.00 in two charitable organizations for the service performed.

In early July 1971, General [Robert] Cushman, then the Deputy Director of Central Intelligence, received a telephone call from the White House. He was informed that Mr. Hunt had become a consultant on security affairs for the White House, and a request was made that Mr. Hunt receive assistance from the Agency. The minutes of the Agency Morning Meeting of 8 July 1971 indicate that the DDCI (General Cushman) reported a call by John Ehrlichman stating that Howard Hunt had been appointed a White House security consultant.

On 22 July 1971, Mr. Hunt visited General Cushman at the CIA building. According to the records, Mr. Hunt stated that he was being charged with a highly sensitive mission by the White House to visit and elicit information from an individual whose ideology he was not entirely sure of, and for that purpose he said he was asked to come to the Agency to see if he could get two things: identification documents in alias and some degree of physical disguise, for a one-time operation. He stressed that he wanted the matter to be held as closely as possible and that he would like to meet the Agency people in an Agency safehouse. Agency records indicate that, in the course of the conversation, Mr. Hunt referred to Mr. Ehrlichman by name and General Cushman acknowledged an earlier call from Mr. Ehrlichman to him. The Committee may desire to query General Cushman whose knowledge would not come from such secondary sources.

General Cushman directed the appropriate technical service of the Agency to be of assistance to Mr. Hunt, based on the above request. On 23 July 1971, Mr. Hunt was given alias documents, including a Social Security card, driver's license, and several association membership cards, in the name of "Edward Joseph Warren" similar to material he had been furnished for operational use while he had been an Agency employee, under the name of "Edward V. Hamilton." The same day Mr. Hunt was also given disguise materials (a wig, glasses, and a speech alteration device).

By calling an unlisted telephone number given him, Mr. Hunt arranged several additional meetings with Agency technical officers, the dates of which cannot be provided with precision. In these, he requested and was provided a commercial tape recorder (in a typewriter case) and a commercial Tessina camera disguised in a tobacco pouch. He also brought in a then-unidentified associate (later identified from press photos as Mr. G. Gordon Liddy) and secured for him a disguise (wig and glasses) and alias documents in the name of "George F. Leonard."

The Agency technical officers met these requests despite the absence of the procedural steps and approvals normally required by Agency regulations. However, they became increasingly concerned at the escalation of Mr. Hunt's requests for assistance. These finally included a request from Mr. Hunt to be met on the morning of 27 August 1971, upon his return from California, to have a film developed and returned to him. This was done the same day. He also asked for a New York mail address and telephone-answering service for operational use.

The technical officers raised their concerns with senior officers, who noted the possibility that these activities could involve the Agency in operations outside its proper functions. As a result, again according to Agency records, General Cushman telephoned Mr. Ehrlichman at the White House on 27 August 1971 and explained that further such assistance could not be given. Mr. Ehrlichman agreed. The request for mail address and telephone answering service was not honored. On 31 August 1971, Mr. Hunt contacted the technical officers again, requesting a credit card, but this was refused. Mr. Hunt had also made a request on 18 August 1971 for the assignment of a secretary he had known during his Agency career. This was also refused. The earlier-furnished alias documents and other material were not recovered, however, except for the Tessina camera which was returned on 27 August as unsuitable. Since the end of August 1971, the Technical Services Division has had no further association with Mr. Hunt. As a point of reference, I would note that the break-in of the office of Mr. Ellsberg's psychiatrist took place on or about 3 September 1971.

The Agency outlined the above events to Mr. Patrick Gray, Acting Director of the FBI, in letters dated 5 and 7 July 1972, and a meeting on 28 July 1972. A series of questions were asked the Agency on 11 October 1972 by Mr. Earl Silbert, Principal Assistant United States Attorney for the District of Columbia. On 24 October 1972, Attorney General Kleindienst and Assistant Attorney General Petersen reviewed the 5 and 7 July transmittals together with additional, more detailed but undated materials that had been provided to Acting FBI Director Gray on 18 October 1972. The Agency is aware that this material was reviewed on 27 November 1972 by Mr. Silbert, who asked additional questions on that date as well as on 29 November 1972. Written responses to the foregoing questions were provided on 13 December 1972. An additional submission was made to the Assistant Attorney General Petersen on 21 December 1972. This material was discussed at a meeting held with Assistant Attorney General Petersen and Mr. Silbert on 22 December 1972. All of the foregoing materials can be made available to the Committee if it so desires.

As a separate matter, which was not known by those who prepared the material for the Department of Justice in the fall of last year, the Office of Medical Services of the Agency prepared and forwarded to the White House two indirect personality assessments of Mr. Daniel Ellsberg. The Agency has had a program of producing, on a selective basis, such assessments or studies on foreign leaders for many years. In July 1971, Mr. Helms, then Director, instructed Agency officers to work with Mr. David Young of the White House Staff relative to security leaks in the Intelligence Community.

Mr. Young requested a study on Mr. Ellsberg in the latter part of July 1971, which Agency activity was apparently approved by Mr. Helms. At that time, Mr. Young supplied raw material consisting principally of newspaper and magazine articles together with some State Department and Justice Department papers. The first assessment delivered to the White House dated 9 August 1971, was judged insufficient. As a result, there were several meetings between Dr. Malloy, Mr. Hunt, and Mr. Liddy, in which classified information of the Justice and State Departments was introduced. One such meeting occurred on 12 August 1971. Additional material was transmitted by Mr. Hunt on 12 October, and another meeting was held on 27 October. These meetings led to a second version of the assessment, dated 9 November 1971. This document was delivered to the Executive Office by Dr. Malloy on 12 November 1971. Agency records indicate that Mr. Helms had previously communicated with Mr. Young indicating that he had read both reports.

In another contact "about October 1971," an Agency officer arranged to provide Mr. Hunt certain unclassified materials from CIA files relative to a 1954 French case of leakage of Government documents. These were delivered to his office at the White House.

In closing, I would like to stress several conclusion of my investigation so far:

a. CIA had no awareness of the details of Mr. Hunt's activities. The Agency's impression was that Mr. Hunt was engaged in an activity related to identifying and closing off the security leaks that were so much a preoccupation of the Government at the time.

b. The Agency was insufficiently cautious in the initiation of its assistance to Mr. Hunt. Later, when the nature of Mr. Hunt's requests for assistance began to indicate a possible active involvement by the Agency in activities beyond its charter, the Agency terminated the relationship and refused further assistance.

c. The preparation of a profile on an American citizen under these circumstances lies beyond the normal activity of the Agency. It shall not be repeated—and I have so instructed the staff. This shall not be made a part of the regulations governing such activities.

d. As Director, I have called for a review of all Agency activities and the termination of any which might be considered outside its legitimate charter. In addition to requesting this review from my subordinates, I have directed each employee and invited each ex-employee to submit to me any cases which they may question. I am determined that the Agency will not engage in activities outside of its charter but will concentrate its energies on its important intelligence mission.

Not everyone at CIA headquarters was impressed with the Director's testimony. A draft circulated for commentary drew the following assessment from the Office of National Estimates in the Director of Intelligence, which is contained in the "Family Jewels" file.

8 May 1973

MEMORANDUM FOR: Mr. W. E. Colby
Executive Secretary, CIA Management Committee

FROM: Director, National Estimates

SUBJECT: Comments on Proposed DCI Statement (Hunt Case)

Since you are aware that I have no facts bearing on the case, I take it that you asked for comment from the following point of view: will the proposed statement be well received by the committee?

The main questions in the committee's mind will be: Did CIA cooperate wittingly in activities which were both illegal and outside its charter? Or did it only respond supinely to higher authority even though it had some reason for suspecting illegal conduct?

Tactically, I think there would be advantage in coming to grips frankly with these questions in the statement itself. The text in its present form could be taken as a minimum factual response which doesn't quite get at the heart of the matter. I think it preferable, in the interest of the Agency's reputation on the Hill, to proceed to candor directly rather than to be drawn to it by subsequent questioning.

Key follow-up questions which can be anticipated would include the following:

Why is there no record of the initial Ehrlichman-Cushman contact?

If Cushman recorded the conversation with Hunt, was he not already suspicious of the latter's purpose and why didn't he ask? At a minimum, could he not have inquired whether "the individual whose ideology we aren't entirely sure of" was an American citizen?

When Cushman told Ehrlichman on 27 August 1971 that CIA was suspending support to Hunt, was it only on the ground that the latter had become "too demanding"?

Why was the personality study on Ellsberg provided when it was obvious hat this action transgressed the Agency's charter?

Obviously most questions that will be raised can only be answered by Helms and Cushman personally. Nevertheless, I think the DCI would be well advised to provide a candid evaluation of these proceedings in his intial statement. To do so voluntarily would make more persuasive the assurances the Committee will want that nothing of the sort will be done under his direction of the Agency.

/initialed/
John Huizenga

In the meantime, CIA employees who had any hint of a connection with the Watergate burglars could expect repeated visits from the FBI. Such was the case of Charles W. Kane and his unnamed friend in Florida.

MEMORANDUM FOR: Deputy Director for Management and Services

SUBJECT: Contacts with Individuals Named in the Watergate Matter

1. I am addressing this to you instead of to the Director of Central Intelligence since I doubt that the information contained herein is of such significance to warrant his interest and because it has been on record with the Agency since July 1972. However, if you feel that the information is of such interest that it should be forwarded to the Director I shall put it in the proper format to do so.

2. My only contact with anyone named in connection with the Watergate and related matters was through [—], a former employee now retired and living in Winterhaven, Florida. In December 1971, [—] called me from Florida and advised that he wanted to get in touch with Howard Hunt. He said that he did not have Hunt's home phone number and that it was probably unlisted but that since Hunt was a former employee, could I contact Hunt and ask him to give [—] a call. I had only met Hunt once about 10 years before but I agreed to relay the message. I called Howard Hunt at his home and told him that [—] did not have his home phone and requested he call [—]. Mr. Hunt thanked me for relaying the message and said that he would call [—]. This seemed of little consequence to me in December 1971 but in July 1972 [—] of the Office of Security contacted me in regard to the FBI investigation of the Watergate situation. At that time I informed [—] of the telephone call from

[—] in December 1971. Attached is a copy of a Memorandum for the Record prepared by [—] as a result of our conversation.

3. In the summer of 1972 I took my family to Disney World in Florida and took the occasion to drop in to see [—]. [—] told me in a private conversation that he had been interviewed three or four times by the FCI in connection with the Watergate affair and he related to me his contact with Howard Hunt. On 19 July 1972 after my return from Florida I reported this conversation to the Director of Security and made it a Memorandum for the Record. This memorandum was sent to Mr. Colby and a copy of the memorandum is attached.

4. Other than knowing Mr. McCord through his employment with the Agency and meeting Mr. Hunt once in about 1959, I do not know nor have I had any contact with any individuals named or knowledge of related matters now receiving attention in the press.

/signed/
Charles W. Kane
Special Assistant to the Deputy Director
for Management and Services

19 July 1972

MEMORANDUM FOR THE RECORD

SUBJECT: Conversation with [—]

1. While on leave visiting Disney World in Florida, I dropped in to see [—], who lives in Winterhaven, Florida. [—] retired from the Agency about five years ago on disability due to a serious heart condition. He was with the Office of Security for about 20 years prior to his retirement.

2. During a private conversation, [—] told me that he had been interviewed three or four times by the FBI in connection with the McCord-Hunt affair. I asked him why he had been interviewed, and he told me that in late 1971 he had been contacted by Howard Hunt who suggested that he consider an assignment as Security Officer for the Republican Party. [—] visited Washington in January 1972 to discuss the proposed position with Howard Hunt who apparently was acting on behalf of the Republican Party. [—] furnished a resume to Hunt and discussed the position with him. Ultimately, he decided not to accept the position because he felt that his heart condition would not allow him to become involved in such activity.

3. According to [—], during the meeting with Mr. Hunt they discussed some of the requirements of the job. At that time they discussed a need for both a positive and a counteraudio [that is, eavesdropping and jamming] program and a need for a good security program both before and during the National Convention. [—] indicated that he sincerely believed that the Republican Party did need a security officer and a good security programmer but felt that he could not afford to accept the job even though it was a very lucrative offer. Apparently, money was not a problem.

4. When [—] declined, he indicated that Mr. Hunt asked for any other recommendations he might have. According to [—], he told Mr. Hunt that most of the people he knew were still in the Agency, but he did furnish the name of [—], who might be possibly ready to retire from the Agency.

5. [—] informed me that he assumed that the Bureau obtained his name due to the resume he furnished Mr. Hunt. He said that the Bureau had talked to him on three or four occasions and that he had written up about a 40 page

statement concerning his dealings with Mr. Hunt. When asked about Mr. McCord, [—] said that he really did not know McCord that well and declined any knowledge of Mr. McCord's technical capability.

6. [—] indicated that he had not been in touch with Mr. Hunt since the early part of 1972 and knew nothing of the Watergate operation. He stated that he had gained the impression from the Bureau interview that the technical devices were being removed at the time of arrest and were not being installed as originally reported.

7. All of the above information was volunteered by [—] and I really did not get involved in any discussion on the matter other than to comment that I hated to see the Agency's name connected with such an incident in any way. The above conversation took place during a 10 or 15 minute period and no other discussion relating to this incident was held. It is being reported for the record and for information of the Director of Security.

/signed/
Charles W. Kane

17 July 1972

MEMORANDUM FOR THE RECORD

SUBJECT: Charles W. Kane
   [—]

1. Last week Special Agent Arnold Parham of the FBI contacted the Acting DD/OS [Deputy Director, Office of Security]. He asked whether the Subjects worked for the Central Intelligence Agency. Previously, requests of this nature were followed up by the FBI with an interview of the subjects.

2. I briefed Mr. Colby who is the Agency's focal point on the "Watergate" case and the Acting DD/S of the FBI inquiry. Mr. Colby suggested that we determine the extent of involvement and indicated that we advise the Bureau of their employment.

3. When Agent Parham was again contacted and advised of the Subjects' employment with the Agency, he indicated that the Bureau does not wish to interview them.

4. The office of the DD/PS will interview [—] in the same fashion as [—] was previously interviewed. [Marginal note: "Already did. See file 7/21."]

5. I called Mr. Kane both at his office and his residence and learned that he is in Florida and will return to duty on 17 July. I called Mr. Kane this morning to advise him of the inquiry.

6. Mr. Kane stated that he had no firm conclusion as to how the Bureau obtained his name. He stated that he has seen Mr. Hunt on only one occasion in 1959. At that time Hunt was the Chief of Station, [—]. The meeting was occasioned by the fact that Mr. Kane [—about one line deleted—] Mr. Kane state further that around Christmas time of 1971 he received a call from [—] who wanted to get in touch with Mr. Hunt. [—] asked Mr. Kane how he could get in touch with him. Mr. Kane obtained Mr. Hunt's telephone number through telephone information channels whereupon he passed the number on to [—].

7. Mr. Kane stated that he has information that [—] has talked to the FBI on several occasions in connection with the current investigation and that he surmises that the Bureau may have obtained his name from him.

[—]
Deputy Director of Security

In some cases, CIA officials feared that the most routine contacts would be picked up and blown out of proportion by a hostile press. This was the case with John Mitchell's briefer from the Office of Current Intelligence. Mitchell, Nixon's campaign manager in the election of 1968, served as attorney general during Nixon's first term and then resigned to become chairman of CRP for the 1972 election. He was deeply involved in the decisions to carry out and cover up the Watergate break-in and, consequently, is believed to be the first cabinet member to do jail time.

7 May 1973

MEMORANDUM FOR: Director of Central Intelligence
VIA: Deputy Director for Intelligence

FROM: Director of Current Intelligence

SUBJECT: Activity Related to Domestic Events

1. OCI provided current intelligence briefings to John Mitchell as Attorney General. With the approval of the DCI, this practice began in the pre-inaugural period in New York and continued until Mr. Mitchell's resignation as Attorney General. The OCI officer assigned to this duty had a daily appointment with Mr. Mitchell in his office at Justice.

2. The briefings provided were strictly on foreign intelligence, and were a legitimate service for CIA to provide to an official advisor to the President who sat on, among other bodies, the 40 Committee [which approved and oversaw covert operations]. It must be presumed, however, that our man's daily visits were known and speculated on elsewhere in Justice. The problem comes in the potential press treatment: "CIA Officer in Continuous Contact with Mitchell."

The Director of the Central Reference Service (CRS) drew attention to an even more innocuous connection with David R. Young, Jr.: Young, a former member of Kissinger's National Security Council staff, had, along with Egil Krogh, Jr., been put in charge of the White House "special investigations unit."

7 May 1973

MEMORANDUM FOR: Deputy Director for Intelligence

SUBJECT: Contacts with David Young

1. In the summer of 1972, I had frequent contacts with David Young. He was in this building under my control once. These contacts related solely to Executive Order 11652 and the NSC [National Security Council] directive concerned therewith. Young was apparently at the time in the process of drafting the NSC directive. The visit to the building under my control was for a briefing on CRS processes for storage and retrieval of documents and is apparently reflected in the paragraph of the directive concerned with the Data Index. I visited him in his White House office at least twice in the company of an inter-Agency group concerned with the Data Index.

2. In August of 1972, [—] also visited Mr. Young's office in the company of an inter-Agency group to discuss CIA compliance with the data index instructions. To the best of my knowledge no one in CRS had any contact with Mr. Young in his role as a "plumber."

[—signature deleted—]
H. C. Eisenbeiss
Director, Central Reference Service

NOTES

1. For a detailed history of the Watergate episode, see Stanley I. Kutler, *The Wars of Watergate: The Last Crisis of Richard Nixon* (New York: Alfred A. Knopf, 1990); and Stanley I. Kutler, *Abuse of Power: The New Nixon Tapes* (New York: Free Press, 1997). A briefer account is Keith W. Olson, *Watergate: The Presidential Scandal that Shook America* (Lawrence, KS: University Press of Kansas, 2003).

2. Quote cited in Tim Weiner, *Legacy of Ashes: The History of the CIA* (New York: Doubleday, 2007): 318.

3. Audio recordings and transcripts are available at the Richard Nixon Presidential Library Web site, http://www.nixonlibrary.gov.

4. W. Mark Felt was the Deputy Director of the FBI. More than thirty years later it was revealed that Felt was "Deep Throat," the inside source who was leaking information about the Watergate cover-up to the *Washington Post*. See Bob Woodward, *The Secret Man: The Story of Watergate's Deep Throat* (New York: Simon & Schuster, 2005); Mark Felt and John O'Connor, *A G-Man's Life: The FBI, Being "Deep Throat," and the Struggle for Honor in Washington* (New York: PublicAffairs Books, 2006).

5. Richard Helms, with William Hood, *A Look over My Shoulder: A Life in the Central Intelligence Agency* (New York: Random House, 2003): 9–10.

6. See Vernon A. Walters, *Silent Missions* (Garden City, NY: Doubleday, 1978): 587–604; Helms, *A Look over My Shoulder*, 3–13; and Weiner, 318–322.

7. The real point was to prevent the FBI from discovering that the money used to pay the burglars came from illegal presidential campaign contributions "laundered" through Mexico.

8. The reprint of Walters's testimony in the "Family Jewels" file is illegible in parts, but the testimony can also be found in Special Subcommittee on Intelligence, House Committee on Armed Services, *Inquiry into the Alleged Involvement of the Central Intelligence Agency in the Watergate and Ellsberg Matters* (Washington, D.C.: U.S. Government Printing Office, 1975): 45–47. The testimony was given on 16 May 1973. Original "memoranda for record" on which the testimony was based can be found on pages 107–114.

9. McCord's letters do not appear in the "Family Jewels" file, although a copy of a UPI news report about the letters is followed by four blank pages. See also William Colby and Peter Forbath, *Honorable Men: My Life in the CIA* (New York: Simon & Schuster, 1978): 339–340.

_____ *Chapter 12* _____

The "Family Jewels"

As noted in the Introduction, the creation of the "Family Jewels" file would prove to be a landmark in the history of the CIA. Coming in the midst of the Watergate scandal, word of the file's existence opened a period of turmoil that could have ended in the agency's dissolution.

The order to collect the documents was given on 9 May 1973 by James R. Schlesinger, during the seventeen weeks he served as DCI before being named Secretary of Defense.[1] It came in response to a newspaper report about the trial of Daniel Ellsberg, which revealed that a former CIA officer, E. Howard Hunt, had burglarized the office of Ellsberg's psychiatrist with CIA equipment on behalf of the Nixon White House.

The Nixon administration had become highly concerned—obsessed, some would say—about leaks to the press regarding the conduct of the Vietnam War, even though administration officials were actually responsible for many of the leaks themselves. A particular focus of their concern was the unauthorized release to the *New York Times* of the Pentagon Papers, a classified multivolume study done in 1968 on how the United States had become involved in the war. (The study had been commissioned because, by 1968, even the Department of Defense had lost track of how it had happened.) In 1971, the White House organized an unofficial investigative unit, which came to be known as the "plumbers," to stop these leaks. Hunt was a key member of this group. It transpired that Daniel Ellsberg had been responsible for the Pentagon Papers affair, but the burglary of his psychiatrist's office was to find compromising material to use against Ellsberg, not to compile evidence of his guilt.

Hunt's name was already known to the public by May 1973 because, in the interim, he and James W. McCord, another former CIA employee, had been indicted for their roles in the break-in at the Democratic National Committee headquarters in the Watergate. If nothing else, the CIA's charter forbade it to conduct operations within the United States, and Hunt's illegal activities threatened to compromise it. Schlesinger—irate at not having been informed of the Hunt connection in the Ellsberg case and his use of CIA equipment— ordered all present and former officials to report to him immediately on any current or past matters that might fall outside of the agency's legal authority.[2]

9 May 1973

MEMORANDUM FOR ALL CIA EMPLOYEES

1. Recent press reports outline in detail certain alleged CIA activities with respect to Mr. Howard Hunt and other parties. The presently known facts behind these stories are those stated in the attached draft of a statement I will be making to the Senate Committee on Appropriations on 9 May.[3] As can be seen, the Agency provided limited assistance in response to a request by senior officials. The Agency has cooperated with and made available to the appropriate law-enforcement bodies information about these activities and will continue to do so.

2. All CIA employees should understand my attitude on this type of issue. I shall do everything in my power to confine CIA activities to those which fall within a strict interpretation of its legislative charter. I take this position because I am determined that the law shall be respected and because this is the best way to foster the legitimate and necessary contributions we in CIA can make to the national security of the United States.

3. I am taking several actions to implement this objective:

   I have ordered all senior operating officials of this Agency to report to me immediately on any activities now going on, or that have gone on in the past, which might be construed to be outside the legislative charter of this Agency.

   I hereby direct every person presently employed by CIA to report to me on any such activities of which he has knowledge. I invite all ex-employees to do the same. Anyone who has such information should call my secretary (extension 6363) and say that he wishes to talk to me about "activities outside CIA's charter."

4. To ensure that Agency activities are proper in the future, I hereby promulgate the following standing order for all CIA employees:

   Any CIA employee who believes that he has received instructions which in any way appear inconsistent with the CIA legislative charter shall inform the Director of Central Intelligence immediately.

/signed/
James R. Schlesinger
Director

The result was a compilation of years of CIA misdeeds. Schlesinger gave Deputy Director for Operations William E. Colby the added title of Executive Secretary, CIA Management Committee, and placed him in charge of the issue. Within weeks, Colby succeeded Schlesinger as Director of Central Intelligence. Colby personally referred to the file as the "our skeletons in the closet," but it soon became known within the agency as the "Family Jewels." This was an allusion to an earlier secret document of that name, a loose-leaf binder in which Allen Dulles listed sensitive sources and German contacts at his OSS station in Switzerland during World War II.[4] In both cases, the "Family Jewels" were to be kept under the strictest confidentiality.

What was actually in the file? It proved not to be representative of overall CIA activities. In fact, it was not even representative of the agency's disreputable activities. The CIA's legislative charter, the National Security Act of 1947, was vague in many respects, but it had specifically prohibited the agency from operating within the United States or investigating U.S. citizens. Therefore, those topics—including some items that were fairly innocuous and others that were not—dominated the material that agency employees forwarded to Schlesinger's office. There is very little about foreign operations. Still, there is at least passing reference to activities of note, including plots to assassinate foreign leaders (none of which seem to have succeeded), drug experiments on unwitting subjects, and, of course, equipment lent to the White House "plumbers" who burglarized the Democratic Party campaign headquarters at the Watergate. Some of the documents simply report that a given department did nothing, in its view, that was outside the charter. Even those items that are not scandalous can be informative, however, as they show various departments within the agency trying to educate a new DCI as to what it is that they do (at least at this specific point in history).

Although the documents in the "Family Jewels" file did not leak to the press, stories and rumors about them eventually did and this produced a scandal. The investigative journalist Seymour Hersh, then with the *New York Times*, picked up "bits and pieces" of information on the subject. On an earlier occasion, Hersh had discovered information on the *Glomar Explorer*, a ship the CIA used to attempt to raise a sunken Soviet submarine, without the Soviets knowing, to see what secrets the agency could learn. At that time, Colby intervened personally with Hersh and convinced him not to publish the story. Now, Colby tried that approach again. The CIA Oral History Program asked him about it in 1988.[5]

Did you ever wonder where he got the bits and pieces?

I long ago gave up trying to figure out where journalists get their information. I mean, they develop lots and lots of sources. Very rarely do they have a source who gives them the whole thing. They are very clever about the way they call somebody to get the remotest kind of a hint that there might be something; then they ask this one, they ask that one, and they ask the other. You know, inside of a few hours on the telephone, they have most of the story in this town.

Did you feel that Hersh had very much information regarding abuses when he met with you in December of '74?

Oh, yes. He had them all in exaggerated terms when he walked in, yes. He said, "you guys have been in wiretaps, you have been in mail openings, you have been in surveillances, you have been breaking into people's houses." He had it all.

Did he mention assassination, by chance?

No. He didn't have assassinations—domestic [operations], you see, that was the thrust of it. He said this thing is bigger than My Lai—he's the guy that broke My Lai.[6] "This is a much bigger story"—that was his phrase. I said, "Sy, you've got it all wrong. What you have gone into is a few little things here and there over the 25 years that we did that were a little bit over the line. They were few and far between. There were no massive, no big [domestic] intelligence operations." And I frankly feel that that was the eventual story even though you had a lot of hullabaloo—when you read the Rockefeller Report, and the Church Report on the domestic side, you really have kind of odds and ends here and there.

So I told him, "Come on in, I'll talk to you. You got it all wrong." I was hoping to bring him down. He was going to write something, I knew it. I was hoping to bring him down a bit and didn't. He took it as a confirmation, you see. That's the other thing that is frequently said, if I had said nothing, he wouldn't have had a confirmation. But since I said, "There are some little things that happened," that was confirmation. He took it as confirmation. even though I was saying it didn't happen.

On 22 December 1974, the *New York Times* carried Hersh's banner headline across its front page: "Huge C.I.A. Operation Reported in U.S. against Antiwar Forces, Other Dissidents in Nixon Years." The "Family Jewels," which began as a damage-control exercise, had become an enormous liability. Inasmuch as Nixon had resigned from the presidency in August 1974, DCI Colby soon found himself having to explain the file to the new administration of President Gerald R. Ford. On the last day of 1974, Colby and the CIA General Counsel met with Deputy Attorney General Laurence H. Silberman (identified in the record as LHS) and Associate Deputy Attorney General James A. Wilderotter (JAW) and presented them with an effective summary of the file's highlights. Several of these points will be discussed in more detail in later chapters.

TO: MEMORANDUM FOR THE FILE   DATE: January 3, 1975

FROM: James A. Wilderotter
          Associate Deputy Attorney General

SUBJECT: CIA Matters

CIA Director William Colby and CIA General Counsel John Warner met with LHS and JAW Tuesday, December 31 to discuss certain matters, including items apparently reported to the President by Colby in connection with the recent New York Times articles. Colby did not show us his report to the President, but paraphrased that portion of its contents which, in Colby and Warner's judgment, presented legal questions.

Colby began the meeting by describing the management style of former CIA Director Richard Helms. According to Colby, Helms utilized a very "compartmentalized" organizational structure, with each head of a constituent unit within the organization reporting directly to Helms. Colby described it as like "spokes from a hub," with Helms as the "hub" and the various compartmentalized units constituting the "spokes." It was possible to be in one "spoke" and have no knowledge of what the other "spokes" were doing.

Colby indicated that the various Watergate revelations touched the CIA in several ways, including: (a) Howard Hunt; (b) the matter of "psychological profiles;" and (c) the McCord letters to the CIA. Colby indicated that former CIA Director James Schlesinger sent a memorandum on May 9, 1973 to all CIA employees, directing them to report on all activities undertaken that may have fallen outside the CIA's charter. When the reports came in, Colby—by then the CIA Director—sent out "corrective" memoranda. According to Colby, the reports submitted in response to Schlesinger's May 9, 1973 memorandum constitute the "skeletons in the closet," and form the basis of Colby's recent report to the President. Colby and Warner are trying to track down more details about the various "skeletons."

The "skeletons" related to us by Colby are as follows:

(1) In 1964, a Russian defector was brought to the United States; apparently, CIA thought he was a "fake." The defector, a Russian citizen, was immediately confined in a house in Maryland, and later in a CIA facility in

Virginia, for about two years. Apparently, he was interrogated during the two-year physical confinement. This defector in now settled in the United States, is married, and still works voluntarily with the CIA. According to Colby, former CIA Director McCone approve this confinement. Colby stated that occasionally, the CIA confines defecting individuals, but only <u>outside</u> the United States. Defectors are interrogated in the United States only voluntarily; according to Colby, "they can walk away any time." Colby speculated that the confinement of the Russian defector from 1964 to 1966 might be regarded as a violation of the kidnapping laws.

(2) In 1963, the CIA wiretapped two columnists—Robert Allen and Paul Scott—following a column in a newspaper in which they disclosed certain national security information. CIA records indicate that the wiretapping was approved by McCone after "discussions" with then Attorney General Robert Kennedy and then Secretary of Defense Robert McNamara. The wiretaps, which continued from March 12 to June 15, 1963, were described as "very productive"—among those overheard calling Allen and Scott were twelve Senators, six Congressmen and so forth. Apparently, the tap did not disclose the source of the security information published in the Allen-Scott column.

(3) From February 15 to April 12, 1972, "personal surveillances" were conducted by CIA on Jack Anderson and members of his staff (Les Whitten, Britt Hume, and Mr. Spear). The physical surveillances consisted only of watching the targets, and involved no breaking, entry, or wiretapping. Apparently, the physical surveillance occurred after Jack Anderson's series of "tilt toward Pakistan" stories.[7] The physical surveillances were authorized by Helms and conducted by the CIA's Office of Security. (The Office of Security was headed by Howard Osborn from 1967 to 1973.)

(4) Between October, 1971 and January, 1972, the CIA conducted a physical surveillance of Mike Getler, a *Washington Post* reporter. Again, there is no indication of wiretaps, a break-in, or entry. Like the Anderson surveillances, the Getler physical surveillance was apparently authorized by Helms and run by the CIA's Office of Security.

(5) In 1971, the CIA had reason to suspect a [former] female CIA employee, who was then living with a foreign (Cuban) national. The former CIA employee and the Cuban national apparently maintained a joint residence and a joint place of business. CIA agents broke into the business premises and unsuccessfully attempted to break into the residence to search for any documents the former employee may have taken with her. The agents found nothing. The break-in apparently occurred in Fairfax, Virginia, and was conducted by the Office of Security.

(6) In July 1970, CIA agents broke into and entered an office occupied by a former defector who was still "on contract" to the CIA, looking for CIA documents he may have had. The operation was conducted by the Office of Security, and occurred in Silver Spring, Maryland.

(7) CIA agents apparently "talked their way into" the apartment of one Toftey [sic; Hans Tofte]—at that time a CIA employee—to recover CIA documents he had converted. The documents were recovered, and Toftey was promptly fired. Toftey apparently sued Helms, alleging that, in addition to the CIA documents, the CIA agents had also taken some of his, Toftey's, personal correspondence. The suit was dismissed.

(8) Between 1953 and 1973, the CIA's Counterintelligence Staff screened—and in some cases opened—mail to and from the Soviet Union going through Kennedy Airport Mail Depot. This operation was terminated in 1973 by

Colby. While it was in existence, it was "cleared by" at least three Post-masters General and CIA records indicate that Helms discussed it with then Attorney General John Mitchell.

(9) From 1969 to October 1972, the Far East Division of the CIA reviewed, in San Francisco, mail going to and from the People's Republic of China in an operation similar to the Soviet one at Kennedy Airport. Apparently the CIA sought in this operation "tips" with respect to possible sources, contacts, etc.; the CIA was apparently also interested in mail handling procedures within the PRC.

(10) Between 1963 and 1973, the CIA funded research in some institutions, apparently including academic institutions, on the general subject of behavioral modification. According to Colby, these activities included the participation—on an "unwitting basis"—of some U.S. citizens, who were not told of the true nature of the testing. The example given by Colby was that of a pole put in the middle of a sidewalk, with people's observations recorded as to which side of the pole they would walk. Apparently, some of the other testing also included reactions to certain drugs, although it is not known whether any "unwitting" individuals were used with respect to that type of experiment. In response to a question from LHS, Colby and Warner indicated they would provide more information on these activities, but that their own knowledge of them was very limited at this point.

(11) The CIA apparently "plotted" the assassination of some foreign leaders, including Castro, Lumumba, and Tujillo. The CIA had no role whatsoever in Lumumba's murder on January 17, 1961. With respect to Trujillo's assassination on May 30, 1961, the CIA had "no active part;" but had a "faint connection" with the groups that in fact did it. In connection with these matters, Warner referred to 18 U.S.C. 960, concerning "expeditions against a friendly nation."

(12) Between 1967 and 1971, the CIA covertly monitored dissident groups in the Washington, D.C., area (and possibly elsewhere) who were considered to pose a threat to CIA installations. The monitoring apparently consisted of physical surveillance only; no wiretaps were involved. Some results might have been distributed to the FBI.

(13) Between May and September 1971, the CIA conducted a physical surveillance of a Latin American female (and others, including U.S. citizens), apparently in the Detroit area, who had advised the CIA of a plot to assassinate Helms and then Vice President Agnew. It is possible that a "mail cover" was also utilized. It is likely that the Secret Service was advised of the assassination threat with respect to the Vice President.

(14) In 1972, the CIA conducted a physical surveillance of Victor Marchetti—who wrote a book about the CIA—to determine his contacts with CIA employees.[8]

Except as noted, Colby and Warner did not indicate whether any of the above items had been approved by any individuals outside the CIA.

* * *

Colby then discussed a program conducted by the CIA beginning in 1967 and aimed at identifying possible foreign links to American dissidents. This program was handled in the CIA by James Angleton and Richard Ober. Around July 1967, Helms sent a cable from CIA Headquarters referring to CIA's "participation in an inter-agency group" with respect to these matters. Apparently, the cable also refers to "overseas coverage of subversive students and related activities."

Apparently, a November, 1967, document in the CIA's possession refers to a CIA survey of anti-war activities, including the U.S. peace movement and foreign groups.

In September, 1969, according to CIA documents, Helms reviewed the CIA's efforts against "the international activities of radicals and black militants."

Apparently, under this program, the CIA alerted people abroad to try to identify the foreign contacts of American dissidents. According to Colby, many requests in this area were originated by the FBI. Colby also indicated that the CIA had apparently placed some agents in the peace movement in the United States, with the purported purpose of establishing credentials to travel abroad. A "by-product" of these agents-in-place was information on the domestic activities of various peace organizations. Apparently, these CIA agents undertook no disruptive activities.

Apparently, the CIA's files under this program contain the names of some 9,900 plus Americans. In response to a question from LHS referring to the New York Times stories about the "files on 10,000 Americans," Colby indicates that the CIA's "9,900 names" is not the same as the IDIS master subject index described in the December 30, 1974, memorandum from LHS to Philip Areeda, Counsel to the President.

According to Colby, approximately two-thirds of the names in the CIA's "9,900 plus" list were the results of either FBI requests or reports from the CIA's foreign offices. The other one-third consists of FBI reports on Americans in the peace movement, but no other information. Colby indicated he does not know why the CIA had these latter reports since no foreign travel was involved, etc. He speculated that they were kept as a result of the tendency of bureaucrats to retain paper whether they needed it or acted on it or not.

According to Colby, the "Huston Plan" and the subsequent establishment of the Intelligence Evaluation Committee "gave stimulus" to this entire effort by the CIA. Colby, after reviewing this program, considers it "worthless" from an intelligence standpoint. Among other things, the Soviets apparently thought U.S. dissidents were too unruly to be trusted with any sensitive operations.

* * *

Colby also reported on three other items:

(1) At the CIA's request, the Sheriff of San Mateo, California, polygraphed certain applicants for employment in an experiment to test the effectiveness of the polygraph.

(2) Colby and Warner indicated that the CIA utilizes certain systems to create alias documents, such as birth certificates. Other documents—such as credit cards—are used for what Warner described as "flash" purposes; that is, they are not utilized in themselves, but are used only to corroborate the operative identifying document (such as a birth certificate). For example, a false credit card or similar materials described by Warner as "pocket litter" will not be used to actually charge credit purchases but rather only to corroborate a driver's license or birth certificate. When documents of a Federal Agency are involved—such as a Social Security Card—the CIA does not manufacture or otherwise create the documents except with the knowledge of that Federal Agency. Warner indicated, however, that it may be a violation of some State Laws to "manufacture" or otherwise forge state agency documents. Colby and Warner indicated that this was an on-going operation.

(3) Colby indicated that the CIA occasionally tests experimental electronic equipment on American telephone circuits. The CIA apparently has established guidelines for these tests, which provide among other things that no records may be kept, no tapes and so forth.

From the Department of Justice, Colby returned to the White House to discuss the report that he had delivered to the president earlier. Political consequences were already threatening, and Congress was preparing to launch investigations. Note that at this time there were still no Congressional committees devoted wholly to intelligence matters. (In this document, the words in square brackets were printed that way in the original.)

MEMORANDUM OF CONVERSATION

PARTICIPANTS: President Ford
William E. Colby, Director, Central Intelligence Agency
Philip W. Buchen, Counsel to the President
John O. Marsh, Jr., Counsellor to the President
Lt. General Brent Scowcroft, Deputy Assistant to the President
for National Security Affairs

DATE AND TIME: Friday, January 3, 1975
5:30 P.M.

PLACE: The Oval Office
The White House

SUBJECT: Allegations of CIA Domestic Activities

President: I asked Phil and Jack to analyze the [Colby] report for me, but first, why don't you tell me where we are.

Colby: We have a couple of problems—one within the agency and one with Congress. Already the two Armed Services committees, the two Appropriations committees, and Muskie[9] want me to testify.

I think we have a 25-year-old institution which has done some things it shouldn't have. On the dissidents, the major effort was to check if there were any foreign connections. But we held it so close there was unease within the Agency—was it really done for the foreign connections or was it anti-dissident? We infiltrated some people so they could go overseas. That was okay, but in the course of training within the groups they wrote on the dissidents. We passed the information to the FBI and they passed information to us. But what would happen is we would file reports the FBI gave us. That, together with our reports from overseas, amounts to about 10,000. So we can't deny that, but I will have to try to clarify it.

President: When were the names gathered?

Colby: Beginning in '67. It was formally terminated in March '74.

President: When was the Schlesinger directive?

Colby: In May 1973. Schlesinger was concerned when things popped up—the psychological profiles, and letters from McCord about CIA and Watergate. So, to find everything, he put out this directive. My report has some of it; I will cover the others now. I briefed Nedzi in July 1973; I gave Stennis a general briefing and Symington a detailed one.[10] [He showed the President a loose-leaf book.]

President: What did the three say?

Colby: I said "Here it is; we are not going to do it again." I then gave specific instructions to the Department. In March 1974, we stopped the program and I put it together with the dissident program and treated them as one. He mentions mail opening. We did have a New York and Los Angeles program in the '50s of opening first-class airmail from the USSR. For example, we have four to Jane Fonda. That is illegal, and we stopped it in 1973. In San Francisco we had one with respect to China, to find out who the contacts were. Some letters were opened. We did break in to some premises to see whether there were classified documents.

President: Were these former employees, or people on the payroll?

Colby: Former employees.

President: Had they been fired?

Colby: One had just left—he wasn't fired.

President: Who would approve such operations?

Colby: I would think only the Director, but possibly at these times the Director of the Office of Security.

The third area is the fact that we surveilled some people to find out why they had classified information. Some of the names are pretty hot. [He mentioned a couple of reporters.] In 1971, we surveilled Mike Getler. He had run a story which was an obvious intelligence leak.

President: Who would have approved that?

Colby: I'm pretty sure it was Helms,[11] but whether it was directed from higher up I don't know.

In 1972, at the time of the India-Pakistan war, we put a tap on Jack Anderson and three of his associates.

President: Who ordered it?

Colby: Helms. Whether on his own or not, I don't know. This was not illegal, but (perhaps) outside our jurisdiction. We also followed some of our employees or former employees. Unfortunately, one was Marchetti. Again, it was not illegal, but it's a highly emotional area.

President: Was this outside the Agency's charter?

Colby: Helms says this is a gray area. We have the responsibility to protect our sources and information.

President: What would you have done?

Colby: I said at my confirmation that I have the duty but not the authority. I would go to the FBI or somewhere like that.

We have also run some wiretaps. Most of them on our employees, but not all. Edgar Snow, for example.[12] Generally, from 1965, they were approved by the Attorney General. One other was a defector, but most of them were employees. I doubt that before 1963 we had attorney general approval.

These were from 1951 through 1965. The last tap recorded was in 1971.

None of these have anything to do with the Hersh story, but he lists all these activities as being part of the anti-dissident effort.

Marsh: But Hersh will say that out of the dissident program came the IEC[13] and this is where the Getler and Anderson taps are very worrisome. He will say we turned to the IEC for operations when we couldn't get action from regular agencies.

Buchen: The directive was 9 May; the report was May 21. Isn't that a bit short?

Colby: Most of these skeletons were around, but just in memory rather than on paper. It didn't take much to get them on paper.

President: Who would have known of the dissident group?

Colby: The Director, Karamessines, the Deputy Director, Ober—30 to 40 people were in the group.

President: Who assigned Ober over here?[14]

Colby: When we terminated the program, I nominated him.

[General Scowcroft described how the NSC got him and what his normal NSC duties were.]

Colby: That's about it. We did collect the names of some Congressmen—who weren't in Congress when we got the names. [He gave the President a paper on this.] An "X" by the names means we ran a clearance for the purposes of collaboration with them; "Y" means the name came up in connection with a foreign country.

[The President leaves.]

Buchen: The last directives are undated. Why?

Colby: They were all issued at the same time.

Marsh: They will try to get this all linked with Watergate. Do you think there is a connection?

Colby: Watergate is a code word. Only that concern about dissidents and leaks may have hyped by political concerns.

[Buchen and Marsh asked a series of questions. The President then returned.]

President: Is counterintelligence work suffering because of a lack of coordination with the FBI?

Colby: No. We are cooperating well. I think NSCID 9 will formally regularize the arrangement we've had with the FBI since 1966.[15]

Colby: We obviously have a problem since we lost four of our top people.

President: Tell me about them.

Colby: It has to be a highly compartmented activity.

Angleton is an unusual type and totally dedicated to his mission. He is very intense. I thought of asking him to retire when I took over. I didn't because of the human factors. He also handled the Israeli account. On Friday before the Hersh article appeared, I told him he could move or retire.

Of the other three, one had already decided to retire. His deputy we told that he wouldn't be the chief and he retired. The third was younger, but he thought apparently he might get the job and he retired when he didn't.

Helms helped Hunt get a job with Mullens when he retired.[16]

President: We plan to do three things: One, early next week, all the Intelligence chiefs will come in and I will say, "You know what the law is and I expect you to obey." Two, I'm going to appoint a Blue Ribbon Committee to look into all of this.[17] Three, I am going to suggest to the Hill that a joint committee is the best way for them to go to investigate.

We don't want to destroy but to preserve the CIA. But we want to make sure that illegal operations and those outside the charter don't happen.

Colby: We have run operations to assassinate foreign leaders. We have never succeeded. [He cited Castro, Trujillo, General Sneider of Chile, et al.][18]

There's another skeleton: A defector we suspected of being a double agent we kept confined for three years.

There is one other very messy problem. After the ITT-Chile Congressional investigation, there was an allegation that our testimony was not all kosher. I don't think there was any criminal action, but there was some skating on thin ice. There is an old rule that to protect sources and information you could stretch things.

But the White House hasn't been told about my book of skeletons.

The next day, President Ford met with Henry Kissinger, who at the time was both Secretary of State and National Security Adviser (technically, Assistant to the President for National Security Affairs). Rather than being concerned about criminal activities by the CIA, Kissinger appeared to be more upset about the political implications of the revelations, including the implications for the CIA itself. Beyond that, he viewed the agency's revelations concerning Chile, which had not been part of the leak, as a sign of a conspiracy against him personally. He favored getting rid of Colby, after a decent interval, for his role in the revelations. The two of them considered possible replacements, including Ronald Reagan, former Secretary of State Dean Rusk, and David Packard, the cofounder of the Hewlett-Packard Company who had served as Deputy Secretary of Defense (1969–1971) during Nixon's first term. (The eventual choice, replacing Colby in 1976, would be George H. W. Bush.)

MEMORANDUM OF CONVERSATION

PARTICIPANTS: President Gerald R. Ford
        Dr. Henry A. Kissinger, Secretary of State
        And Assistant to the President
        for National Security Affairs
        Lt. General Brent Scowcroft, Deputy Assistant
        to the President for National Security Affairs

DATE AND TIME: Saturday, January 4, 1975
         9:40–12:20 P.M.

PLACE: The Oval Office
     The White House

Kissinger: What is happening is worse than in the days of McCarthy. You will end up with a CIA that does only reporting, and not operations. He [Colby] has turned over to the FBI the whole of his operation. He has offered to resign and I refused. It is not my prerogative, but I said not until you are proved guilty of criminal conduct.

The President: I agree.

Kissinger: Helms said all these stories are jus the tip of the iceberg. If they come out, blood will flow. For example, Robert Kennedy personally managed the operation on the assassination of Castro.
 [He described some of the other stories.]
 I told him Buchen would warn him and he won't say anything incriminating.

The President: I know Dick Helms and think very highly of him.

Kissinger: The Chilean thing—that is not in any report. That is sort of blackmail on me.

The President: What can we do? We can get Griswold, Lemnitzer, Friendly, Reagan, Jack Connor, Shannon, Dillon.

Kissinger: You might think of Rusk. This will get very rough and you need people around who know the Presidency, and the national interest. What Colby has done is a disgrace.

The President: Should we suspend him?

Kissinger: No, but after the investigation is over you could move him and put in someone of towering integrity.
  When the FBI has a hunting license into the CIA, this could end up worse for the country than Watergate.

The President: Would Rusk have known any of this stuff?

Kissinger: Why don't you ask him?
  [Discussed the Moorer spying incident and what he did to protect the institution of the JCS.][19]
  [Rumsfeld[20] enters to talk about Rusk.]

Kissinger: [Discusses some of the legislative restrictions.]

The President: [Talks to Rusk.]
  [Tries to call Dave Packard.]
  [Buchen and Marsh come in.]
  [The Blue Ribbon announcement is reviewed.]

In an effort to prevent a Congressional investigation, Ford ordered a Blue Ribbon commission, led by Vice President Nelson Rockefeller, to investigate allegations of domestic spying. Nevertheless, two Congressional investigations, one led by Senator Frank Church and the other by Representative Otis Pike, ensued in 1975–1976.[21] Henry Kissinger chaired a meeting in February 1975 to devise a strategy for dealing with Congressional investigations. Again, whereas Colby was concerned about the CIA's illegal activities, Kissinger appeared to be primarily concerned with the political consequences of the revelations. These included the possibility of constraints on future covert operations and the threat of looking like a "cream puff" if the world discovered how few covert operations there actually were. His continuing concern with leaks also showed. Note that the list of participants included James Schlesinger, whose memorandum started this particular turmoil, but the transcript indicates him making only a single comment.

MEMORANDUM OF CONVERSATION

PARTICIPANTS: Dr. Henry A. Kissinger, Secretary of State and Assistant to the
                        President for National Security Affairs
                Dr. James R. Schlesinger, Secretary of Defense William Colby,
                        Director, Central Intelligence Agency
                Philip Areeda, Deputy Counsel to the President
                Mr. Laurence Silberman, Deputy Attorney General
                Martin R. Hoffman, General Counsel, Department of Defense
                Lt. General Brent Scowcroft, Deputy Assistant to the President
                        for National Security Affairs
DATE AND TIME: Thursday, February 20, 1975
                10:36–11:33 A.M.

PLACE: Secretary Kissinger's Office
                The White House

SUBJECT: Investigations of Allegations of CIA Domestic Activities

<u>Secretary Kissinger</u>: Shouldn't we discuss what we are trying to achieve in these investigations and what we are trying to prevent?

The fact of these investigations could be as damaging to the Intelligence Community as McCarthy was to the Foreign Service. The nature of covert operations will have a curious aspect to the average mind and out of perspective it could look inexplicable. The result could be the drying up of the imaginations of the people on which we depend. If people think they will be indicted ten years later for what they do. That is my overwhelming concern.

NSA [National Security Agency], I don't know what the abuses are.

<u>Secretary Schlesinger</u>: Legally NSA is spotless.

<u>Secretary Kissinger</u>: If they are only looking at illegal activities.

<u>Mr. Silberman</u>: There aren't enough illegal activities for them to chew on.

<u>Director Colby</u>: The issue will be, do we do these things?

<u>Mr. Areeda</u>: Church says he's going back to look into the legal, moral, and political cost-effectiveness aspects of it.

<u>Secretary Kissinger</u>: Then we are in trouble. The committees and staff don't inspire confidence. Harrington and Miller are professional leakers. Miller is also violently anti-Vietnam and he believes the way to get the government is to leak it to death.

<u>Director Colby</u>: My idea to control this is to get secrecy agreements. That keeps them from publishing.

<u>Secretary Kissinger</u>: In their own names. You can't keep them from Sy Hersh.

<u>Director Colby</u>: Our testimony will have numbers in place of names. We will divide them into three categories in increasing order of sensitivity.

<u>Secretary Kissinger</u>: Who gets the lists?

<u>Director Colby</u>: The chairmen. It is under their control. If he insists on a name in category 3, we then move carefully—we either tell him, refuse on my initiative, or buck it to the White House.

<u>Secretary Kissinger</u>: You can initially take a position on professional judgment, but then we must go to the President. Bill should invoke himself first so as not to invoke the President initially in each case. We must say this involves the profoundest national security. Of course, we want to cooperate, but these are basic issues of national survival.

<u>Mr. Areeda</u>: Should the President meet with [Sen. John] Tower and Church to make these points?

<u>Secretary Kissinger</u>: In all the world, the things which hurt us the most are the CIA business and Turkey aid.[22] The British can't understand us. [Foreign Secretary James] Callaghan says insiders there are routinely tapped. Our statements ought to indicate the gravity with which we view the situation.

Why can't Bill testify?

<u>Director Colby</u>: Names, countries of operations.

<u>Secretary Kissinger</u>: You can't even do it by country X. And Church wants to prove you shouldn't do it at all.

<u>Director Colby</u>: I would do it in executive session. If it leaks then we have a good case.

Mr. Silberman: I agree. Our position on executive privilege would be better if we had a leak first.

Secretary Kissinger: What if Miller waited until after the investigation to go to Hersh?

Mr. Silberman: It won't hold that long. We first give them less sensitive information, so if it leaks we aren't hurt so much.

Secretary Kissinger: Suppose you say on covert operations that we support the moderate political parties? On a global basis that is okay, but how does that serve Church's purpose? He will then just prove not only is it immoral but useless. We have to demonstrate to foreign countries we aren't too dangerous to cooperate with because of leaks.

Mr. Areeda: Is there any mileage in having the leaders of the select committee have a meeting with the President?

Mr. Silberman: It's premature. They could only discuss generalities because we couldn't know the line yet. We should keep the President out of it until we get a crunch.

Secretary Kissinger: I agree.

Mr. Silberman: The FBI may be the sexiest part of this. Hoover did things which won't stand scrutiny, especially under Johnson. We will put these out in generic terms as quickly as possible. The Bureau would like it to dribble out. This will divert attention and show relative cooperation with the committee. This relates only to illegal activities.
   [Kissinger relates story about Hoover and the female spy.]

Secretary Kissinger: We have to be clear on what we want them to stay out of.

Director Colby: I will refuse to give them the files on people—on privacy grounds.

Mr. Areeda: That is a good case for a confrontation.

Mr. Hoffman: But don't we have to preserve their ability to keep security?

Secretary Kissinger: Harrington is a leaker—any House member has access to the material we turn over.
   We can't fight on details—only categories. We have to know the rules about the NSA, covert operations and any other areas.

Mr. Areeda: There is a constitutional problem on covert operations. We can't take the posture that we can engage in operations that were kept from the committees which Congress has designated as responsible for oversight.

Secretary Kissinger: First, we must define the issues. Then we could go to court ...

Mr. Silberman: I doubt it would go to court—it would take two years.

Secretary Kissinger: Then we could go to the public that they are undermining the country.

Director Colby: But we are doing so little in covert activities it is not too damaging.

Secretary Kissinger: The disclosing them will show us to the world as a cream puff.
   There are dozens of places where we are letting the situation go by default.
   Let's establish categories of especially sensitive activities. Then whoever testifies will follow these guidelines.

Director Colby: The dangerous thing on NSA is whether they can pick up conversations between Americans.

Secretary Kissinger: My worry is not that they will find illegalities in NSA, but that in the process of finding out about illegalities they will unravel NSA activities. In the process of giving us a clean bill of health he could destroy us.

Do we have a case on executive privilege?

Mr. Silberman: In the case of U.S. v. Nixon, there is something there, but you can't analyze it on a strictly legal basis.

Secretary Kissinger: I think this group should establish categories of what we say, methods for protecting what we need to keep. Then we can set down with the President to understand what the issue is.

Then we would avoid the danger that to get through each week we would jeopardize the next week's hearings.

Colby's approach was to be cooperative toward the investigative committees in the hope that he could elicit a more favorable attitude on their part. He explained his attitude in 1988 to the CIA's Oral History Program.[23]

Sure, there is a basic difference of opinion about my role here. Various of them said that I should have stonewalled the whole thing because intelligence is too important, resigned and all the rest of it. I didn't think that would do any good at all. In the context of the politics of the time, we had just had Watergate, you really weren't going to get away with stonewalling them. It just wasn't going to work. On the other hand, if you could go to a committee which starts out with a prosecuting mission and give them the whole view of American intelligence, which is a very good story, then these become rather small against that larger picture. And in order to do that, you've got to tell them quite a lot, but you don't tell them names. And that was a basic point that we came to with the committees as soon as the chairmen were appointed.

As soon as they were named, I went down and talked to them. I said, "Look, you are going to investigate us; I understand that. Not much I can do about it; you are going do it. I'd like to give you a full picture so that you'll see whatever may have happened in proper proportion and context. Now, I'm not going to argue with you about your constitutional right to know everything in the Agency because we'll never end that argument. You'll take the right that you have constitutional authority to learn everything. I'm just going to convince you that there are some things that you don't want to know; you don't need to know, and consequently, that you should not know. Particularly, you don't need to know the names of people who work for us around the world—foreigners, Americans, all the rest. To convince you that you don't need to know them, I'll tell you something: I don't know them. I've made a deliberate point of not learning names of agents. Why? Because I had no reason to, I didn't have to know them to do my job. I have to know that there is an agent there, about their reliability; but I don't have to know the name. You don't need to know their names. Now, let's make a deal. We'll be responsive to your questions as much as we can, but I'm going to ask you to let me leave the names off." [. . .]

You didn't think the Agency would be dismembered, dissolved?

There were days. But if you asked, thoughtfully, I would have to say that I didn't believe they could possibly do it. I mean, that they would be so stupid. And particularly after I told them what the Agency really was all about. I took the right guys down to brief them every now and again. I happened to have as my personal assistant a fellow who had been in Stanleyville and told about being there—the Simbas coming in the house. Everything was so still when he was telling us there. They got the message that there are some very special people [in the agency]. It was deliberate. I was trying to get it out that these are serious things, serious people.

Some suggest that your cooperation during the investigations saved the Agency from serious harm; do you agree with them?

I still think I took the right choice. Now, I don't know whether that saved the Agency a lot of trouble as a result. I can hardly say it came out scot-free. It created an awful lot of trouble abroad—people saying how can we deal with you, you guys put all your stuff in the newspapers all the time. This was a real problem. So, I wouldn't say it saved it from any problems. It did get hurt. No question about it. It would have gotten hurt more if I had taken the totally negative [approach]. Then I think the thing would have just sort of disintegrated, all sorts of chaotic hullabaloos, then the names would have come out.

Far from everyone at the CIA agreed with Colby's cooperative approach toward testifying. Retired DCI Helms, perhaps, was chief among the dissenters, apart from the fact that Colby tried to have him charged with perjury for his lack of candor in the investigations. This excerpt is from Helms's contribution to the Oral History Program.

What are your impressions of Mr. Colby's cooperation with the Church and Pike Committees?

Well, I have been very careful in the years since to say nothing publicly about Colby. But I think Colby did this just wrong, and I believe that to this day. My feeling about Bill Colby is that he should have gone to the president and said, "I don't think we ought to do this, sending these documents about secret operations and so forth up on Capitol Hill. Will you support me?" And then if they insist on it, you'll have to go to the Supreme Court, and I think that's what should have happened.

Instead of that, Colby went the last mile in cooperating with the Church and Pike Committees. He felt he was constitutionally obligated to do this, and in his book he says this, I believe. I don't know what gave him the idea that he was a constitutional lawyer but, anyway, this is what he did. A lot of people on the inside know my feelings, which, I say, I avoided saying publicly because I think it's unseemly for prior directors to be squabbling with each other in public about who did what to whom.

A lot of people think that I'm mad at Colby because he sent those papers down to the Justice Department to try and get me convicted of perjury. I'm not mad at him about that. I'm mad at him about the way he handled the Congress and about sending all these papers down there. And "being mad at" is a colloquialism. I think he was wrong. As far as that perjury thing is concerned, if his lawyers and the people he appointed felt this way, fine, send the papers down to the Justice Department. I don't think he used very good judgment because I think that in doing something like that about his predecessor he opens himself up to getting the same thing done to him.

But leaving that personal element out of it, it tends to set up a precedent. I mean, he who lives in glass houses shouldn't be throwing stones. But that was a pain in the neck for me, and it was very difficult for me to handle, and it certainly didn't do my reputation any good. But he felt he had to do it.

After the hearings, new laws and executive orders put limits on CIA activities. Congress for the first time established specific committees for intelligence oversight—the Senate Select Committee on Intelligence and the House

Permanent Select Committee for Intelligence—although other committees continued to control intelligence appropriations. Congress also established special courts equipped to authorize warrants when circumstances required domestic investigations in matters related to national security or intelligence; many refer to these as "FISA courts" after the law that created them, the Foreign Intelligence Surveillance Act of 1977.[24] For a time, it appeared that every president felt obliged to issue an executive order setting out the ground rules for intelligence activities: President Gerald Ford issued Executive Order 11905 in 1976; President Jimmy Carter replaced E.O. 11905 with E.O. 12036 in 1978; and President Ronald Reagan replaced that with E.O. 12333 on 4 December 1981, which, in part, remains in effect. The basic provisions of each were quite similar, especially in some of the fundamental prohibitions. For example, from E.O. 12333:[25]

> 2.10 *Human Experimentation.* No agency within the Intelligence Community shall sponsor, contract for or conduct research on human subjects except in accordance with guidelines issued by the Department of Health and Human Services. The subject's informed consent shall be documented as required by those guidelines.
>
> 2.11 *Prohibition on Assassination.* No person employed by or acting on behalf of the United States Government shall engage in, or conspire to engage in, assassination.
>
> 2.12 *Indirect Participation.* No agency of the Intelligence Community shall participate in or request any person to undertake activities forbidden by this Order.

NOTES

1. Brief tenure was common in the Watergate era. At the Department of Defense, Schlesinger was following the four-month term of Elliott Richardson, who then served six months as attorney general before he was dismissed for refusing to fire the special prosecutor investigating Watergate.

2. In his memoir, William Colby, with Peter Forbath, *Honorable Men: My Life in the CIA* (New York: Simon & Schuster, 1978): 339, Colby cites the Hunt revelation as the trigger for the "Family Jewels." In an oral history done ten years later, "Oral History: Reflections of DCI Colby and Helms on the CIA's 'Time of Trouble,'" *Studies in Intelligence* 51:3 (2007), he says it was the discovery that James McCord had written letters to the CIA months before accusing the White House of trying to make him blame the agency for the Watergate break-in.

3. The statement is reproduced in the chapter on Watergate.

4. Richard Helms, with William Hood, *A Look over My Shoulder: My Life in the Central Intelligence Agency* (New York: Random House, 2003): 427.

5. "Oral History."

6. Up to 500 residents of the village of My Lai 4, in South Vietnam, had been killed by U.S. troops on 16 March 1968.

7. The reference is to U.S. policy favorable to Pakistan during the India-Pakistan War of 1971.

8. Victor Marchetti, a former CIA official and public critic of the agency, coauthor of *The CIA and the Cult of Intelligence* (New York: Alfred A. Knopf, 1974).

9. Senator Edmund Muskie, Democrat of Maine.

10. Representative Lucien Nedzi, Democrat of Michigan, chairman of the House Subcommittee on Intelligence Operations; Senator John C. Stennis, Democrat of Mississippi, chairman of the Senate Armed Services Committee (in the hospital at the time); and Senator Stuart Symington, Democrat of Missouri, a ranking member of the Senate Armed Services Committee.

11. Richard Helms, Director of Central Intelligence, 1966–1973.

12. Edgar Snow, journalist and China specialist, author of *Red Star over China* (1937 and other editions); considered sympathetic to the Communist Chinese government.

13. IEC stands for Intelligence Evaluation Committee.

14. Richard Ober, former chief of the dissident project, known as MHCHAOS, had been reassigned to the National Security Council.

15. NSCID 9 stands for National Security Council Intelligence Directive No. 9.

16. After retiring from the CIA and before organizing the Watergate break-in, E. Howard Hunt worked at the Robert R. Mullen Company, a public relations firm in Washington, D.C.

17. The Rockefeller Commission.

18. Fidel Castro of Cuba; Rafael Leónidas Trujillo of the Dominican Republic, assassinated in 1961; and General René Schneider, commander of the Chilean army, who was killed during a botched kidnapping attempt that was intended to provoke a coup in 1970. See Chapter 10, "Chile."

19. In December 1971, the FBI tapped the phone of National Security Council staffer Yeoman Charles Radford, suspecting him of stealing documents and giving them to columnist Jack Anderson, but discovered that he was stealing documents and giving them to Admiral Thomas Moorer, Chairman of the Joint Chiefs of Staff (1970–1974). Presumably, this was a result of the secrecy of the Nixon-Kissinger team in preparing major foreign policy initiatives. Moorer denied any knowledge of it, claiming that Radford had fabricated the story. The incident received relatively little public attention. Stanley I. Kutler, *The Wars of Watergate: The Last Crisis of Richard Nixon* (New York: Alfred A. Knopf, 1990): 116–119.

20. Donald Rumsfeld was President Ford's Chief of Staff at this time. Later that year, Rumsfeld would begin his first tour as Secretary of Defense, the youngest in U.S. history. He would again become Secretary of Defense, the oldest in history, under President George W. Bush. He was replaced as White House Chief of Staff by his assistant, Dick Cheney, who would later be a member of the House of Representatives, Secretary of Defense under George H. W. Bush, and Vice President under George W. Bush.

21. See, for example, *Final Report of the Select Committee to Study Governmental Operations with Respect to Intelligence Activities, United States Senate: Together with Additional, Supplemental, and Separate Views*, Report No. 94-755, 6 vols. (Washington, D.C.: U.S. Government Printing Office, 1976); Loch K. Johnson, *A Season of Inquiry: The Senate Intelligence Investigation* (Lexington, KY: University Press of Kentucky, 1985); and Kathryn Olmsted, *Challenging the Secret Government: The Post-Watergate Investigations of the CIA and FBI* (Chapel Hill, NC: University of North Carolina, 1996).

22. The previous year, Turkey had intervened militarily in Cyprus. Even though the crisis had been initiated by Greece, this made dealings with Turkey politically controversial.

23. "Oral History."

24. The Foreign Intelligence Surveillance Act was amended in August 2007 in such a hasty manner that participants in the process argued afterward over exactly how much they had changed it. Realizing that it was acting hastily, however, Congress had set the amendment to expire at the end of six months so it could reconsider the issue.

25. One difference was that the Carter order strengthened the DCI's influence over the budgets of other agencies, but the Reagan order diluted it again. "Historical Perspective," in Michael Warner, ed., *Central Intelligence: Origin and Evolution* (Washington, D.C.: Central Intelligence Agency, Center for the Study of Intelligence, 2001): 10.

Chapter 13

The List of Delicate Matters

One subset of documents within the "Family Jewels" file is distinguished by having its own table of contents. Oddly, the table of contents sits by itself as page 455 of the file, whereas the documents it describes commence on page 481. Many of these records are redacted. One, from the Central Cover Staff (CCS), is so heavily redacted that the table of contents is actually more revealing than the document itself.

For our purposes, we shall call this subfile the "List of Delicate Matters," following the subject line of a memo from the Foreign Intelligence Staff. This subfile brings together reports on various "activities with possible flap potential" and organizes them by division. Most of the documents are dated 7 May 1973 and therefore precede by two days DCI James Schlesinger's general call that solicited most of the "Family Jewels" documents. (See "Introduction.") These evidently came in response to a specific request to division heads earlier that day from William Colby, then Deputy Director for Operations. The material was apparently intended to prepare Schlesinger for his Congressional testimony on 9 May 1973. (See Chapter 11, "Watergate.")

TABLE OF CONTENTS

	Vesco Case
	Intelligence Evaluation Committee and Staff
	MHCHAOS
CI/Police Group	International Police Academy
Foreign Resources	Locations, Recruitments, Use Alias Documents
Division	

The subfile begins with a brief report from the East Asia Division, describing a program that allowed the division to acclimate its assets to a leftist milieu in the United States before deploying them abroad. This was to give them credentials and credibility when they sought to infiltrate foreign organizations by posing as dissidents. The report also comments on the risks of exposure inherent in the program. Note that this operation dealt with "assets," not "case officers." Thus, the people involved were cooperating with the CIA but were not full-time employees.

SUBJECT: [—]
   Project [—] is a Headquarters-initiated program which has as its fundamental objective the long-term manipulations of selected agent assets operating against EA Division difficult targets in the leftist and communist milieu in various parts of the world. Although targeted overseas, these agents are often exposed to and directed against American radical, leftist, and communist targets to gain a practical knowledge of the leftwing, radical, communist world. There is a possibility that an asset might become suspect and be accused of being an employee of the Agency or the Bureau; or it might happen some asset would, for some reason, become disenchanted with his role and expose his Agency relationship and his activities, with resultant embarrassment. To minimize potential problems, therefore, each case is cleared with the FBI and through CI/SO [Counterintelligence/Special Operations] the Bureau is kept informed on a regular basis.

The set of documents submitted by the CCS, according to the table of contents, contains statistics regarding false identities ("alias documentation") and other support to allow the officers of the Clandestine Service to operate under cover. This section runs from pages 484 to 517, but it is so heavily redacted that it is not worth transcribing. (Note that some pages are revised resubmissions of other pages in the same grouping.) Most of the perhaps two dozen or so lines of text that survived the censors consists of subject heads, such as "Alias U.S. Birth Certificates," or uninformative introductory material ("The following specific information regarding domestic cover support provided by Central Cover Staff is submitted in response to your request.").

   The European Division offered the Vesco case. Vesco is a name that crops up at several points in the "Family Jewels" file, often with someone asking why his name is in the files. As a U.S. citizen, he should not have been the subject of any CIA investigation. Robert L. Vesco, the "fugitive financier," fled the United States in 1973 after being accused of stealing $224 million from four mutual funds managed by his Geneva-based Investors Overseas Service, Ltd. (IOS). At the time it was said to be one of the largest securities frauds ever perpetrated. In addition, in 1972, while the Securities and Exchange Commission was investigating those allegations, Vesco made an illegal contribution in the amount of $200,000, evidently in cash, to the Nixon reelection campaign. The intermediary for this transaction was Vesco's administrative assistant Donald Nixon, Jr., a nephew of the president. The president's brother Edward had also had ties to the company. Refusing to return to the United States, Vesco settled first in Costa Rica, then in the Bahamas, and finally in Cuba. He was convicted in Havana in 1996 of attempting to defraud the Cuban Health Ministry and sentenced to thirteen years in prison.[1]

7 May 1973

MEMORANDUM FOR: Deputy Director for Operations

SUBJECT: Research Project on Robert L. Vesco

1. In mid-October 1972 [—] of the Office of Economic Research [OER] asked [—just over one line deleted—] to participate in a meeting with a number of OER officers. During the meeting, [—] explained that the Director of Central Intelligence had levied a crash project on Dr. Edward Proctor, the Deputy Director for Intelligence, to produce a paper on international financier Robert L. Vesco. Since the Director had specifically requested contributions from the field, [—] asked our Division to help in procuring them.

2. We thereupon cabled various questions suggested by OER to [—about a half line deleted—] and asked for replies by 19 October. Relevant answers were turned over to OER in memorandum form. In the case of a brief reference in one of the field messages to an earlier high-level American intercession on behalf of Mr. Vesco, we asked Mr. Helms through his secretary whether this was relevant information. The response, again received through the secretary, was that it was not relevant.

3. Soon after our memoranda had been submitted, [—] advised [—] that the Director wanted everyone to forget the Vesco project. This was communicated to all DDP Headquarters personnel who had had a hand in the project or had been made aware of it.

4. We never had any indication as to the reason for or the purpose of the project.

5. We understand that OER has recently written a memorandum on this matter for the DCI.

[—signature deleted—]
Archibald B. Roosevelt
Chief, European Division

The Soviet Bloc Division laid out its cooperation with U.S. law-enforcement agencies. Those that were not redacted, at least, did not involve an operational role in the United States. It also listed the forced detention of a Soviet KGB defector, Yuriy Nosenko. (See Chapter 6, "Counterintelligence: The Spies among Us.")

7 May 1973

MEMORANDUM FOR: Deputy Director for Operations

SUBJECT: Items for Possible Use in Briefing the DCI

1. This Memorandum is submitted in order to identify to you for possible briefing of the Director activities which in certain contexts could be construed as delicate or inappropriate.

2. At the request of the Director of Security, from approximately mid-October 1972 to mid-January 1973 safesite [—] was made available to the U.S.

Marshal's Service for use as a secure residence by an Assistant U.S. Attorney who reportedly was under threat of assassination by organized criminal elements.

3. [—paragraph deleted; about six lines deleted—]
4. [—paragraph deleted; about seven lines deleted—]
5. Since late 1972 CIA has taken part in seven FBI training courses at Quantico, Virginia, in response to requests from the FBI. We have shared with them through lectures and discussions lessons we have learned which are relevant to their counterespionage responsibilities.
6. As a means of sharing more fully our operational experience we have invited three FBI officers to be students in our [—] Course from 14 to 25 may 1973.
7. The Soviet defector Yuriy NOSENKO was confined at a CIA facility from April 1964 to September 1967 while efforts were being made to establish whether he was a bona fide defector. Although his present attitude toward the agency is quite satisfactory, the possibility exists that the press could cause undesirable publicity if it were to uncover the story.[2]

[—signature deleted—]
David H. Blee
Chief
Soviet Bloc Division

The Narcotics Coordination Group (NARCOG) in the Directorate of Operations also reported cooperative activities with law-enforcement agencies. In this case, the first page was blank and others were heavily redacted.

7 May 1973

MEMORANDUM FOR: Deputy Director for Operations

SUBJECT: CIA Narcotics Activities Having Domestic Implications

1. This memorandum is in response to your request for a review of activities and relationships that might have domestic implications.
2. We occasionally report on the activities of American citizens involved in narcotics trafficking abroad. This information is normally disseminated to U.S. law-enforcement agencies and other recipients of our reports. We also occasionally request U.S. law-enforcement agencies for name traces on U.S. citizens who are known or suspected to be involved in narcotics trafficking abroad.
   [—equivalent of about fifteen lines deleted—]
5. We have occasionally received requests for alias documentation for U.S. narcotics law-enforcement officials working abroad on foreign narcotics investigations. The present method of handling such requests is for us to request the approval of the Deputy Director for Operations prior to asking the Technical Services Division to comply. We insist on knowing the true identity of the persons to use such documentation and limit them to staff officers of the U.S. law-enforcement agencies. We also require that we know the purpose and intended use of the documents. Finally, we require receipts from the headquarters of the agency involved and the individual, and also require these documents to be returned to us for destruction after they have fulfilled their use. We have turned down requests from BNDD [Bureau of Narcotics and Dangerous Drugs] for alias documentation for domestic use. There are some indications in the files that there have been requests from BNDD for domestic documentation in connection with their domestic investigations.

These predate NARCOG, and we are unable to determine how these requests were handled.

6. We periodically receive requests for technical assistance in the form of photographic and audio devices or guidance for use of such items by U.S. law-enforcement agencies in connection with their foreign investigations of illicit narcotics activities. We require these agencies to adhere to the same procedures we require in our own operations. From time-to-time we have honored these requests and have provided sterile equipment when the requests have been properly presented and approved. Our records show evidence that several such requests were made prior to the existence of NARCOG in connection with narcotics law-enforcement investigations in the United States. We are unable to determine whether the requests were fulfilled.

[—signature and name deleted—]
Chief, DDO/NARCOG

The entity mysteriously designated Division D contributed several documents to the subfile. The first four pages are completely blank except for their address (the Inspector General) and the date (29 May 1973). The next document, however, proves very timely in the political environment of the early 2000s, when it has again become an issue. It concerns the interception of communications between the United States and foreign countries. Notable is the General Counsel's determination that the CIA, at least, should terminate such activity despite finding a potential loophole in the United States Code as it existed at that time.

7 May 1973

MEMORANDUM FOR: Deputy Director for Operations

FROM: Chief, Division D

SUBJECT: Potentially Embarrassing Activities Conducted by Division D

REFERENCE: Your staff meeting, 7 May 1973

1. There is one instance of an activity by Division D, with which you are already familiar, which the Agency General Counsel has ruled to be barred to this Agency by statute: the collection [—about one-third of a line deleted—] of international commercial radio telephone conversations between Latin American cities and New York, aimed at the interception of drug-related communications. The background on this is briefly as follows:

   [—about five lines deleted—] Therefore, on 29 September 1972, NSA [the National Security Agency] asked if Division D would take over the coverage, and on 12 October 1972 we agreed to do so. On 14 October, a team of intercept operators from the [—about two-thirds of a line deleted—] began the coverage experimentally. On 15 [or 13?] January 1973, NSA wrote to say that the test results were good, and that it was hoped this coverage would continue.

   Because a question had arisen within Division D as to the legality of this activity, a query was addressed to the General Counsel on this score (Attachment A hereto). With the receipt of his reply (Attachment B), the intercept was immediately terminated. There has been a subsequent series of exchanges between Division D and the General Counsel as to the legality of radio intercepts made <u>outside</u> the U.S., but with one terminal being in the U.S., and the General Counsel has ruled that such intercept is also in violation of CIA's statutory responsibilities.

2. We are carrying out at present one intercept activity which falls within this technical limitation—i.e., of having one terminal in the U.S. [—four to five lines deleted—] Since the [—] link being monitored carries a large number of totally unrelated conversations, the operators do intercept other traffic, frequently involving U.S. citizens—for example, BNDD staffers talking to their agents. I have described this situation to the General Counsel, and his informal judgment was that, as long as the primary purpose of the coverage is a foreign target, this is acceptable. He suggests, however, that it might be desirable to inform the Attorney General of the occasional incidental intercept of the conversations of U.S. citizens, and thus legalize this activity. We will pursue this with Mr. Houston [the General Counsel].

[—paragraph deleted; about six lines—]

3. An incident which was entirely innocent but is certainly subject to misinterpretation has to do with an equipment test run by CIA [—] technicians in Miami in August 1971. At that time we were working jointly to develop short-range agent DF equipment to use against a Soviet agent in South Vietnam. [—about two-thirds of a line deleted—] and a field test was agreed upon. The Miami area was chosen, and a team consisting of Division D, Commo, [—] personnel went to Miami during the second week of August. Contact was made with a Detective Sergeant [—] of the Miami Beach Police Department, and tests were made from four different hotels, one a block away from the Miami Beach Auditorium and Convention Hall. A desk clerk in this hotel volunteered the comment that the team was part of the official security checking process of all hotels prior to the convention. (The Secret Service had already been checking for possible sniper sites.) As the team's report notes, "The cover use of the hotel is a natural."

4. Another subject worthy of mention is the following:

In February 1972, [—just under one line deleted—] contacts in U.S. telecommunications companies [—just over one line deleted—] for copies of the telephone call slips pertaining to U.S.-China calls. These were then obtained regularly by Domestic Contact Service in New York, pouched to DCS/Washington, and turned over to Division D for passage to FE/China Operations. The DDP was appraised of this activity by Division D in March 1972, and on 28 April 1972 Division D told DCS to forward the call slips to CI Staff, Mr. Richard Ober. Soon thereafter, the source of these slips dried up, and they have ceased to come to Mr. Ober. In an advisory opinion, the Office of General Counsel stated its belief that the collection of these slips did not violate the Communications Act, inasmuch as they are a part of a normal record-keeping function of the telephone company, which does not in any way involve eavesdropping.[3]

[—paragraph deleted—]

[—name, signature, title deleted—]

Atts:

A. DivD to OGC 26 Jan 73

B. OGC to DivD 29 Jan 73

26 January 1973

MEMORANDUM FOR: General Counsel

SUBJECT: Intercept of Communications in the U.S.

1. CIA is intercepting at our communications site [—] high frequency, international radio telephone calls originating [—] in New York and being broadcast to South America or being directed to New York from South America. Some

calls are relay calls through New York but not originating or terminating there. The calls involve both U.S. citizens and foreign nationals.

2. [—about one line deleted—] the intercept team screens the telephone calls for drug-related matters. NSA receives the traffic from CIA in the form of magnetic tape. [—about two and a half lines deleted—]

3. I would appreciate your very early views as to where this intercept activity falls with respect to U.S. law. Even if it is legal or we can secure the necessary authorization, it seems to me there is extra flap potential associated with reports going into the BNDD mechanism, particularly since they may well become the basis for executive action.

[—signature and name deleted—]
Acting Chief, [—office deleted—]

29 January 1973

MEMORANDUM FOR: Acting Chief, Division D

SUBJECT: Intercept of Communications in the U.S.

REFERENCE: 26 Jan 73 Memo for GC fr AC/Division D, Same Subject

1. In referent you request our views as to the legal aspects of a radio telephone intercept activity carried on at our communications site [—].

2. The basic law is contained in section 605 of the Communications Act of 1934, 47 U.S.C. 605, which prohibits interception of any radio communication without the authorization of the sender and also prohibits divulging the substance thereof to any person. Chapter 119 of Title 18, U.S.C., makes the interception of any wire or oral communication a crime punishable by $10,000 or five years' imprisonment, or both. There are two exceptions to these prohibitions:

   a. The first provides for application through the Department of Justice to a Federal court for a court order authorizing such interception for specific purposes in connection with law-enforcement duties. Since this agency is prohibited by statute from any police or law-enforcement activities, obviously we cannot operate under this exception.

   b. The other exception is contained in section 2511 of Title 18, U.S.C., at subsection (3). This provides that the prohibition cited above on interception shall not limit the constitutional power of the President to take such measures as he deems necessary to protect against attack, to obtain foreign intelligence information deemed essential to the security of the United States or to protect such information, and to protect the United States against overthrow by force or other unlawful means or against any other clear and present danger to the structure or existence of the Government.

3. The type of information you describe in your memorandum does not appear to fall within any of these categories and since its ultimate destination is BNDD, it appears to be collection for law-enforcement purposes, which as noted above is barred to this Agency by statute.

4. For your information, in most cases where there is a criminal prosecution for violation of the narcotics laws, the Department of Justice queries us as to whether we have engaged in any interception in connection with the defendants. If a case should involve the interception being made [—several words deleted—] it would be deemed to be unauthorized and in all probability the prosecution would have to be dropped by the Government. It is our view, therefore, that such interception should be carried on by the appropriate

law-enforcement agencies in accordance with the authority of chapter 119 of Title 18, U.S.C.

/signed/
LAWRENCE R. HOUSTON
General Counsel

The Foreign Intelligence Staff also contributed a brief note on the Vesco case. The official mentioned, David Young, a former National Security Council staffer, was one of the leaders of the White House "plumbers." (See Chapter 11, "Watergate.")

7 May 1973

MEMORANDUM FOR: Deputy Director for Operations

SUBJECT: Item for the List of Delicate Matters

The Securities and Exchange Commission has asked CIA to provide information on any foreign connections with organized crime in the United States. The record indicates that Mr. David Young, of the White House staff, asked Mr. Colby to set up a contact for Mr. T. C. Barreaux, of SEC. Mr. Barreaux discussed the matter with Mr. Paul V. Walsh of DDI [the Directorate of Intelligence], and on 4 April 1973, Mr. Barreaux and Mr. Timmeny came to a meeting at CIA with Mr. Lawrence Houston (General Counsel) [—several words deleted—] (Chief, FI Staff, DDO).

Since that meeting, we have received no specific requirements from Mr. Barreaux, but have provided him with one piece of information involving a banking transaction of a [—] associate of Robert Vesco.

[—signature and name deleted—]
Chief
Foreign Intelligence Staff

Following the Foreign Intelligence Staff, the Counterintelligence (CI) Staff offered a brief note on funds lent to the FBI and then its own lengthier report on Robert L. Vesco. Here emerge the reasons for the agency's—or more properly, the White House's—interest in Vesco and his company, IOS.

7 May 1973

SUBJECT: Request for Information on Sensitive Activities

You will recall that in Fiscal Years 1971 and 1972, I believe, Agency funds were made available to the FBI. These funds may still be possibly held in a special account for that use. This is one of the areas where TSD [Technical Services Division] has been much involved. Chuck Briggs would have the details as this was handled through the Executive Director's office and of course [Counterintelligence Chief James] Angleton would have additional information.

/signed/
Edward L. Sherman
Chief
Missions and Programs Staff

8 May 1973

MEMORANDUM FOR: Deputy Director for Operations

SUBJECT: Areas of Possible Embarrassment to the Agency

1. Some time in the spring or early summer of 1971, [White House Counsel] Mr. John Dean levied the requirement on the Agency for information relating to

the Investors Overseas Service (IOS). The original request was non-specific but it gradually emerged that Dean was concerned with the possible adverse publicity that might develop regarding the President's nephew, who was employed by IOS.

2. There were multiple channels from the White House to the Agency on this subject:

   a. Presumably Haldeman and/or Ehrlichman to Director Helms.
   b. Someone (unnamed) in the White House to the DDCI [Deputy Director of Central Intelligence], General [Robert] Cushman (see attached telephone conversation). Note that Ehrlichman is mentioned, and
   c. John Dean to the CI Staff. These various channels were sorted out in time and six reports were passed by the CI Staff to Mr. Fred Fielding for Mr. John Dean.

3. The telephone call of General Cushman's is of interest since it gives the flavor of White House concern. It took several days to uncover the fact that the White House interest centered on the involvement of the President's nephew with IOS and possible adverse publicity. The reports submitted to Dean's office were routine in nature and were coordinated with the DCI. After a few months, interest in this subject died down and we did not pursue it further.

4. Please return the attachments when they have served your purpose.

5. I also include a short note on the Intelligence Evaluation Committee and Staff prepared by Richard Ober. The original meetings were held in the office of John Dean at the White House and the principal sparkplug for this group activity was the then-Assistant Attorney General for Internal Security, Robert Mardian and then later his assistant, William Olsen. It is noted that Mr. Mardian is now appearing before the Grand Jury and it is always possible that he might draw in the Agency.[4]

6. Before appointing Ober to the IES Staff as the Agency representative, I had attended various inter-agency meetings presided over by Mardian. I expressed the view to Director Helms that Mardian would require very careful handling due to his inexperience. Furthermore, Mardian was deeply involved in the split between [FBI Assistant Director] Bill Sullivan and [FBI Director] Mr. [J. Edgar] Hoover. On a confidential basis one or two senior FBI officials stated that Sullivan was secretly passing files to Mardian without Mr. Hoover's permission. This was one of the important reasons why Sullivan was dismissed from the Bureau.

[—signature deleted—]
James Angleton
Chief, Counter Intelligence Staff

Attachments (5)

Among the attachments included with the Angleton memorandum were several newspaper clippings regarding Investors Overseas Service and the connections between it and the president's nephew Donald and brother Edward. Also included was the following transcript between Deputy Director of Central Intelligence Robert Cushman and "someone" in the White House (Richard Nixon?):

Telephone conversation of General Cushman and someone in White House, 23/7/71

Bob, how are you?

———————————

DDCI: Just fine; I just talked to Jack Sherwood and he suggested I give you a buzz.

———————————

I deeply appreciate it. I asked Jack to call you. I spoke to Rose[5] yesterday, and told her, "I had a little project here for John Ehrlichman and I need very discreet assistance from the Company, and I should like to touch base with Bob. I met him at Jack Sherwood's."

———————————

DDCI: That's right.

———————————

That's right and beyond that I would like to just establish a relationship because from time to time we have a few needs in your area. Let me tell you what we need to know here. Your Agency would be the only one to help. I have checked with the Bureau, Bob, and they have nothing on this fellow. Just a mere name check but it apparently has some significance, of course. Ray Finkelstein; born in Belgium about 1940; moved to Brazil about age 12 with his family. This might be helpful. He now is working with one Gilbert Straub, apparently Straub is hooked up with that Kornfeld[6] outfit: IOS. We have a need to know what Finkelstein is all about.

———————————

DDCI: We will do our best, of course; we have some counterintelligence files which sometimes turn up people, but ordinarily, of course, we don't surveil any Americans but this fellow might have come to our notice.

———————————

He may not be an American, just a European Jew; that is the problem, the Bureau has come up with zero.

———————————

DDCI: Do you know where he is physically located?

———————————

He may be in Geneva; Straub is apparently in Geneva.

———————————

DDCI: Well, let me get on this and I will get back to you.

The memoranda submitted by Angleton regarding the Intelligence Evaluation Committee and MHCHAOS can be found in a separate chapter. (See Chapter 7, "The Search for Foreign Instigators: Operation Chaos and the Intelligence Evaluation Committee.")

In addition to the submission by the Counterintelligence Staff, there is a separate submission from the Counterintelligence Staff, Police Group. The packet begins with a description of the group, although significant portions failed to survive the censors.

[No date]

MEMORANDUM FOR: Deputy Director for Operations

SUBJECT: Counterintelligence Staff, Police Group Activities

1. Counterintelligence Staff, Police Group (CI/PG) is responsible for Staff coordination within the Office of the Deputy Director for Operations for activities and programs involving assistance to foreign police/security forces for the purpose of exploiting such activities and programs for intelligence purposes.

2. CI/PG maintains liaison with the Office of Public Safety, Agency for International Development (OPS/AID) and its training facility, the International Police Academy (IPA). CI/PG also administers and supervises Project [—one line deleted—] In addition, CI/PG coordinates a joint [—two-thirds of a line deleted—] Central Intelligence Agency [—] Technical Investigations Course. CI/PG provides guidance and counsel to the Area Divisions in matters pertaining to police/security functions and activities. Specific details of these functions are as follows:

LIAISON WITH OPS/AID

CI/PG liaison with OPS/AID and IPA is conducted on a daily basis and consists principally of:

A. exchange of information on IPA participants, some of whom later attend [—] courses [—one line deleted—],
B. arranging for inclusion of Agency sponsored participants in IPA/OPS/AID training programs,
C. arranging for IPA/OPS/AID briefings and tours for foreign police/security representatives sponsored by CIA Area Divisions,
D. [—paragraph deleted; about three lines—]
E. providing general information pertaining to police/security organizations, activities, equipment, and personalities requested by Agency operating components,
F. coordinating the Agency's participation in the Technical Investigations Course designed to familiarize the trainees with the technique required to properly investigate terrorist activities wherein explosives have been utilized,
G. [—paragraph deleted; about five lines—]
H. [—paragraph deleted; about two lines—]

PROJECT [—one line deleted—]
[—about four lines deleted—] It is engaged principally in training foreign police/security personnel under [—about half a line deleted—] and selling police/security equipment to foreign police/security personnel and organizations. [—] also provides special training programs and briefings to foreign police/security personnel of interest to Agency operating divisions. [—one and one-quarter lines deleted—] Recently [—] has acquired the capability of providing training to foreign police/security personnel in VIP protective security for Chiefs of State.

[—footnote deleted; about three lines—]

COMMENT
[—] does not maintain direct contact or liaison with any law-enforcement organization, local or federal, at home or abroad. When the need arises, such contact is sometimes made on our behalf by [—just over one line deleted—] has such contacts at home and abroad because of the nature of its activities (training of foreign police/security personnel at home and abroad), and its Public Safety programs around the world. [—] has such contacts at home— local and federal level—because its personnel are personally acquainted with law-enforcement officers throughout the United States. Members of the [— about half a line deleted—] have appeared as guest lecturers at such federal institutions as the U.S. Park Police, IPA, the U.S. Secret Service, and the U.S. Treasury Enforcement Division.
3. In addition to the liaison mentioned in the previous paragraph, the Agency maintains liaison in varying degrees with foreign police/security organizations

through its field stations. The existence and extent thereof, however, is a decision to be made by the Area Division, and is not the responsibility of [—].

4. [—about one and two-thirds lines deleted—] with Dan Mitrione, who was murdered by the Tupamaros. Dan Mitrione, an experienced and respected law-enforcement officer, was a bona fide OPS/AID officer assigned to the AID mission in Uruguay, and was never a CIA employee or agent.[7]

[—signature deleted—]
James Angleton
Chief, Counter Intelligence Staff

In the following memorandum, we discover that the Counterintelligence Staff, Police Group teaches its foreign police and security trainees how to deal with terrorist, bomb, and sabotage incidents by teaching them terrorist, bomb, and sabotage techniques, using both manufactured and improvised devices.

07 MAR 1973

MEMORANDUM FOR: Deputy Director for Operations

SUBJECT: Joint CIA/USAID Terrorist (Technical)
Investigations Course #7 (English language)
CI Staff's Project [—]

1. This effort is a joint CIA/USAID training program for foreign police/security personnel. The initial phase of the training will be conducted at the International Police Academy (IPA), Washington, D.C. during the period 2–27 April 1973. The following subject matter is covered in this phase of the training: investigative techniques, collection and preservation of evidence, records, files, and reporting, gathering of information on terrorist groups and their activities, a student seminar devoted to discussions on terrorist and other hostile activities currently existing in their respective countries, etc. This phase of the training is concluded by a two-day orientation by the Bomb Squad of the Dade County Police Department in Florida.

2. The second phase of this training will be conducted by Agency [—about one and one-third lines deleted—] during 30 April–25 May 1973. The [—] technicians utilize [—about a half line deleted—] cover. The objective of this phase of the training is to develop individual student technical capability to realistically conduct investigations into known or suspected incidents of sabotage/terrorist bombings by:

    a. Providing trainees with basic knowledge in the uses of commercial and military demolitions and incendiaries as they may be applied in terrorism and industrial sabotage operations.

    b. Introducing the trainees to commercially available materials and home laboratory techniques likely to be used in the manufacture of explosives and incendiaries by terrorists and saboteurs.

    c. Familiarizing the trainees with the concept of target analysis and operational planning that a saboteur or terrorist must employ.

    d. Introducing the trainees to booby-trapping devices and techniques giving practical experience with both manufactured and improvised devices through actual fabrication. Emphasize the necessity of alertness for detecting and countering booby traps placed by saboteurs or terrorists.

    e. Conducting several field exercises to give each trainee the opportunity for detecting and neutralizing various explosives and incendiary devices

likely to be used by terrorists or saboteurs, including letter bombs, pack-
ages, attache cases, etc.

f. Conducting several investigative field exercises of explosive incidents to
alert the trainee to the need for and manner in which to collect, identify,
and preserve legally admissable evidence for prosecutive action.

3. The program provides the trainees with ample opportunity to develop basic
familiarity and use proficiently through handling, preparing and applying the
various explosive charges, incendiary agents, terrorist devices and sabotage
techniques. USAID, International Police Academy (IPA) has received reports
from former foreign police/security personnel who participated in the program indicating that they were called upon to utilize the skills they acquired
through this training in the handling of explosive devices in their respective
country. Attached is a letter from a participant in TIC #6 [—] stating that he
deactivated a letter-bomb device that was sent to the [—] Embassy in [—].

4. Subject course will have 26 participants from ten (10) foreign countries. Nine (9)
are financed by AID, eight (8) by CIA and nine (9) by their own governments.
[—paragraph deleted; about four lines—]

5. Separate end of course reports will be prepared by USAID and CIA, TSD personnel. [—two or three lines deleted—]

[—signature deleted—]
James Angleton
Chief, Counterintelligence Staff

Attached to the memorandum above is a list of comments on facts and statistics related to the program at the International Police Academy. Some of it survived redaction.

FACTS AND STATISTICS

AID/OPS TRAINING
    AID/OPS, International Police Academy sponsors some seven hundred (700)
foreign police officers for training in the United States each year. These officers are
selected from underdeveloped countries. [—just over two lines deleted—]

[—] TRAINING
    [—about one and a third lines deleted—] trains some 350–400 of these officers in
specialized areas of law enforcement. [—about four lines deleted—]
    During FY 1973 [—] supported two of our field stations by providing training in
VIP protective security for [—about a half line deleted—] personnel.

AID/OPS–CIA TRAINING
    During FY 1973 two joint USAID/OPS/CIA Technical Investigations training
programs were conducted for [—] foreign police/security personnel representing
[—] countries. The purpose of the training is to develop individual student technical capability to realistically conduct investigations into known or suspected incidents of sabotage/terrorist bombing or other activities.

Also accompanying the above memorandum was an excerpt from an article
with "comments on AID," which the sender believed "Mr. Colby might find of
interest." The article was "Strategic Leverage from Aid and Trade," written by
the new Director of Central Intelligence, James Schlesinger, ten years earlier. In
the article, Schlesinger argued that trade and aid decisions should be based neither on humanitarian and idealistic grounds nor on ideological considerations,

as in automatically severing ties to dictatorial or leftist regimes. Rather, trade and aid relationships should be nurtured for the long-term political influence and leverage that can be derived from them. By maintaining trade over the longer term, we make countries, especially developing countries, vulnerable to the threat of curtailing Western markets at a later time. Foreign aid programs should not be manipulated to elicit direct support for specific foreign policy goals or to "export the trappings of American democracy," but used to encourage economic development and stability, thereby strengthening the legitimacy of the existing social order. Goals such as responsive government and an equitable distribution of income conflict with the primary goals of growth and stability.

A brief passage highlighted by the sender reads as follows:

> The statement of objectives by AID is a very ambitious one. The purposes of the assistance program include stimulation of self-help, encouragement of progressive forces, and achievement of governments based on consent, which recognize the dignity and worth of individuals who are expected to participate in determining the nation's goals.[8]

The final submissions in the List of Delicate Matters came from the Foreign Resources Division, which was clearly a focus of concern for Colby. Until the previous year, the Foreign Resources Division had been known as the Domestic Operations Division. Operating inside the United States, its function was to identify and recruit visiting foreigners who would be willing to serve as agents of the CIA when they returned abroad. The fact that it operated within the United States, however, made it particularly sensitive and evidently brought it under close scrutiny. These documents, however, are heavily redacted.

7 May 1973

MEMORANDUM FOR: Deputy Director for Operations

SUBJECT: Foreign Resources Division Operational Activities with Possible
          Flap Potential

1. At the risk of stating the obvious, almost all of the operational activities carried on by FR Division [—several words deleted—] run the risk that unauthorized disclosure could create embarrassment to the Agency. We have accepted this as a condition precedent and have proceeded with our operational activities in the most professional manner possible under the circumstances. There are certain rather unusual activities in which FR Division has participated and/or is participating that contain somewhat greater possibility for embarrassment if discovered. I have listed these below, not necessarily in order of embarrassment potential:

   a. [—several words deleted—] provides a fairly considerable amount of support to Dr. Kissinger in his contacts with the Chinese. This support was authorized by [Deputy Director for Plans] Mr. Karamessines and Mr. Helms. Thus far there has been no problem other than the inordinate amount of time spent by [—several words deleted—] personnel, not to mention the fairly sizeable amount of money that has been expended in support of these efforts.

   b. [—paragraph deleted; about eight lines—]

[—signature, name, and title deleted—]

Whatever it was that the previous memo said, apparently it was not specific enough. In any event, Colby did not find it satisfactory. He returned it to the Foreign Resources Division with four handwritten questions across its cover sheet, the last of which has been mostly deleted. This elicited a follow-up memo the next day.

8 May 1973

MEMORANDUM FOR: Deputy Director for Operations

SUBJECT: Foreign Resources Division Operational Activities with Possible Flap Potential

REFERENCE: FR Memorandum, [—] dated 7 May 1973, same subject

1. The answers to your questions are as follows:

   a. Question: Do we recruit Americans?
      Answer: Yes, we recruit Americans to be used as [—] support assets and access agents. These Americans are used for spotting and assessment purposes only and do not perform any recruitments.

   b. Question: Do we use alias documents on Americans in the course of operations?
      Answer: Yes, we do use alias documents when recruiting American support assets. The great majority of these recruitments are done in alias. <u>All</u> recruitments of foreign targets are done in alias.

   c. Question: What disciplinary controls do we have over alias documents?
      Answer: We maintain a current list in FR Division Headquarters of the alias documents issued to each Base. More importantly, each Base Chief is responsible for supervising and maintaining control over the alias documents used by the case officers on his Base.

   d. Question: [—just over one line deleted—] Any clearances or prohibitions?
      Answer: [—paragraph deleted; about sixteen lines—]

2. If you have further questions, please let me know.

[—signature and name deleted—]
Acting Chief
Foreign Resources Division

The Acting Chief of the Foreign Resources Division provided either an annex or a further memo. The degree of redaction makes it difficult to determine which it is. The first page is simply missing. On the second page, a single paragraph survives:

c. Alias Documentation: Clearly, FR Division does the great majority of its operational work by having it case officers utilize alias documents. All recruitments are done in alias. Thus, the alias documentation is a prerequisite for effective operations [—several words deleted—] Furthermore, our case officers have utilized fully backstopped alias credit cards for renting automobiles, motel rooms, hotel rooms for operational meetings, etc. These credit cards are backstopped by accounts in alias which are promptly paid at the appropriate time. I see no problem in the continued use of alias documentation and moreover, I feel it is absolutely essential to continue using alias documentation wherever and whenever possible.

The third page offers the following:

2. Summarizing the above, I believe that all of the activities outlined are clearly within the acceptable risk frame. [—just over one line deleted—] the other activities, although clearly involving some degree of risk are necessary and valuable and in my opinion should be continued.

[—signature and name deleted—]
Acting Chief
Foreign Resources Division

Following this is an outline for a briefing, also from the Foreign Resources Division. It covers such topics as organization and functions, location of field units, covers, targets, budgets, and statistics (for recruitments, general support assets, and positive intelligence reporting). The briefing itself was presumably once contained in the sixteen pages that follow. Of the sixteen-page briefing, all that survived the censors was this:

FOREIGN RESOURCES DIVISION

    1. 1. Statement of Organization and Functions

NOTES

1. *New York Times* (2, 4, 27 August 1996); *Time* (11 December 1972); and Arthur Herzog, *Vesco: From Wall Street to Castro's Cuba* (Garden City, NY: Doubleday, 1987).
2. On Nosenko, see Chapter 6, "Counterintelligence: The Spies among Us."
3. The distinction being made here is that these were records of calls made (By whom? When? To whom? For how long?) rather than transcripts of conversations. In this the program resembles the National Security Agency's unacknowledged "data mining" program of the early twenty-first century, but differs from actual wiretaps.
4. For this document, see Chapter 7, "The Search for Foreign Instigators: Operation Chaos and the Intelligence Evaluation Committee."
5. Presumably Rose Mary Woods, who had been Richard Nixon's personal secretary since 1951.
6. Bernard Cornfeld was Vesco's predecessor at IOS.
7. The death of Dan Mitrione in 1970 inspired a number of works, including the film *État de Siège* (*State of Siege*) by Constantin Costa-Gavras. In the film, Mitrione (given a different name) is depicted as someone who trains torturers. When the leader of the Tupamaro guerrillas saw the film, after a long prison sentence, he said it in no way reflected their understanding of Mitrione or his role in Uruguay.
8. James R. Schlesinger, "Strategic Leverage from Aid and Trade," in David M. Abshire and Richard V. Allen, eds., *National Security: Political, Military, and Economic Strategies in the Decade Ahead* (New York: Praeger, 1963). The excerpt includes pages 687–688, 696–698. The quote is from page 697.

Chapter 14

Nicaragua, with a Side Trip to Iran

The Iran-Contra affair was the signature political scandal of the Reagan era. It was a complex matter that involved the CIA—at times centrally and at other times more peripherally—but was eventually focused on the National Security Council (NSC). The main elements of the affair were the clandestine solicitation of funds for a (widely publicized but nominally covert) war in Central America after Congress had ordered its funding terminated; the secret sale of arms to the Islamic Republic of Iran, even as the administration denounced it as a supporter of international terrorism; the connection of those arms sales to negotiations for the release of hostages; and the diversion of some of the Iranian arms revenues to finance the Central American war. When the affair came to light, the administration sought to place the preponderance of the blame on Lt. Col. Oliver L. North, the Deputy Director of Political-Military Affairs on the National Security Council staff, who was, to be sure, deeply involved in carrying out these policies.

Note that in the minds of the participants at the time, the "Iran" and the "Contra" parts of the affair were two completely separate operations. What eventually brought them together in the mind of the public was that: (1) both operations were conducted in such secrecy that the oversight committees of the Congress and even prominent people within the administration, much less the public, were not informed; (2) as part of the endeavor to conceal the programs from the rest of the government, the NSC staff (generally the same few staff members) was made responsible for both programs, even though it normally had no operational responsibilities whatsoever; and most directly, (3) funds illicitly gained from the sale of arms to Iran (funds that the NSC could not even admit to having) were used to finance the Contras.

NICARAGUA

In July 1979, the Sandinista National Liberation Front (Frente Sandinista de Liberación Nacional, FSLN) overthrew the Nicaraguan government of President

Anastasio Somoza Debayle after a long guerrilla campaign. Somoza Debayle had been the third member of the Somoza family to run Nicaragua (either officially or from behind the scenes) since his father, Anastasio Somoza García, forced the resignation of another president in 1936. As leader of the Nicaraguan army, the Guardia Nacional, in 1934 Somoza García also had ordered the assassination of César Augusto Sandino, who had conducted a guerrilla war against U.S. troops in Nicaragua (1927–1933) and for whom the Sandinista front was later named. The Somoza family used its control of the government to accumulate vast holdings of land and commercial enterprises, making itself the center of economic as well as political power in the country.[1]

Upon the fall of the Somoza regime, a politically diverse junta was installed, but it did not have final say on decisions, and its more moderate members eventually left. The true center of power was the nine-member Joint National Directorate (Dirección Nacional Conjunta, DNC) of the FSLN, on which the three Sandinista factions had equal representation. Both the junta and the DNC were chaired by Daniel Ortega Saavedra, the Sandinista faction leader who had devised the successful "final offensive" that had overthrown Somoza. The FSLN also established party-run mass organizations for workers, peasants, and women. In neighborhoods throughout the country, it organized Sandinista Defense Committees (Comités de Defensa Sandinista, CDS), which were modeled on Cuba's Committees for the Defense of the Revolution and enabled the Sandinistas to disseminate government views, organize rationing, and keep an eye on dissidents.

At least initially, the new government enjoyed the support of broad and diverse segments of the population that had opposed the Somoza dictatorship. The new regime confiscated the land holdings of the Somoza family and their associates, about 2,000 farms comprising at least 20 percent of the country's cultivable land, and converted them into state enterprises. Other large-scale agribusinesses remained in private hands. Also nationalized were the financial institutions, all of which were in bankruptcy. This was sufficient to give the government considerable influence over the economy. Nicaragua maintained a mixed economy, although some Sandinista leaders spoke of further extending the state sector in the future, which proved counterproductive in terms of its relations with the private sector.

The government became more institutionalized in 1984, when elections were held for the presidency and the National Assembly under a new constitution. By then, however, the country was well into a guerrilla war with a U.S.-backed foe. Although some opposition candidates participated and won seats in the National Assembly, the most prominent figures boycotted the election. International observers declared the elections free and fair, but the opposition decried a climate of intimidation. Daniel Ortega was elected president.

Although divided into factions with different ideological and operational shadings, the Sandinistas were generally Marxists. They had long-established contacts with Fidel Castro's government in Cuba, and the Cubans evidently advocated on their behalf in Moscow with some success.

The Sandinistas' ideology, ties to countries of the Soviet bloc, and support for revolutionaries abroad made them an immediate concern to the U.S. government, although the United States had withdrawn its support from the increasingly unpopular Somoza regime in its final months. The administration of

President Jimmy Carter sought a *modus vivendi* with Nicaragua as an incentive to encourage political diversity and Sandinista self-restraint. Concern grew into hostility with the January 1981 inauguration of President Ronald Reagan, a conservative Republican with a tendency to view the world in terms of Soviet expansionism. A few brief entries from Reagan's diaries sum up his attitude toward Nicaragua and the situation in Central America:

> We have definite evidence Nicaragua transferring hundreds of tons of arms from Cuba to El Salvador. . . . An NSC meeting that has left me with the most profound decision I've ever had to make. Central America is really the world's next hotspot. Nicaragua is an armed camp supplied by Cuba and threatening a communist takeover of all of Central America. . . . It's possible the Soviets will ship "Mig" fighter planes into Nicaragua. George S[hultz] Monday will let [Soviet Foreign Minister Andrei] Gromyko know we'll take very seriously any overt moves by them or their stooge Cuba toward any part of Latin Am. We have contingency plans leading all the way up to troop involvement if Cuba should send troops to stir the pot in Central Am.[2]

In addition to their links to the established Soviet bloc, the Sandinistas also had ties to the Farabundo Martí National Liberation Front (FMLN), which was in the early stages of a revolutionary guerrilla war in nearby El Salvador. The FMLN had previously provided the Sandinistas with financial assistance, raised principally through the kidnapping of Salvadoran notables, and now called upon the Sandinistas to reciprocate. The Sandinistas were reluctant to provide more than token assistance at first. They were concerned about the potential reaction from the United States, especially as long as the Carter administration was offering the possibility of a *modus vivendi*. At the same time, at least some of the Sandinista leaders believed that the revolution could survive only if it triumphed on a regional scale—not in a small, weak, and isolated state surrounded by reactionary governments backed by the United States and "world imperialism." In part, revolutionary activity in other countries was expected to create allies or at least distract the revolution's enemies from Nicaragua, and in this sense it became a strategic necessity. Ironically, this parallels one of the CIA's arguments for "taking the war to Nicaragua," to distract Nicaragua and make it harder to export the revolution abroad.[3] Thus, even before there were facts on the ground, the Sandinistas assumed the United States would seek to crush them just as the Reagan administration assumed the Sandinistas would seek to foment revolution. Events did not really prove either of them wrong.

The FMLN planned to launch a "final offensive" before the inauguration of the new president in January 1981, although the decision may well have been made before the election. The CIA reported a heightened flow of arms from Nicaragua to El Salvador in November and December 1980. At this point, the Carter administration authorized the CIA to provide funding to Nicaraguan opposition groups, including non-Sandinista parties, church groups, farmers' cooperatives, and labor unions. It did not, however, initiate any paramilitary operations.

The guerrilla offensive in El Salvador failed; the Sandinistas felt betrayed (having exposed themselves to U.S. hostility on the basis of exaggerated FMLN claims regarding the imminence of success); and the incoming Reagan administration had the evidence it needed for a hostile stance toward Nicaragua. The flow of arms to El Salvador fell off dramatically for a time in early 1981, but the pattern of hostility was already established and the incentives for further self-restraint vanished.[4]

Many career officers at the CIA were skeptical of the Reagan administration's approach to Central America. In their view, they had just been burned by politics in the 1970s. They were especially wary of conducting covert operations without informing Congress, which they would eventually be asked to do. In such situations, the CIA was generally expected to take the blame when things went bad. By the summer of 1983, Deputy Director of Central Intelligence John McMahon was proposing that the Nicaraguan project be made overt and transferred to the Department of Defense.[5]

Reagan chose William J. Casey to be Director of Central Intelligence. A veteran of the Office of Strategic Services in World War II, Casey had been away from intelligence work for some thirty-five years. Nevertheless, he had long wanted to be Director of Central Intelligence and had sought the position in the Nixon administration, but was named Chairman of the Securities and Exchange Commission instead. Among Directors of Central Intelligence, Casey stood out for his uncooperative attitude toward Congress. Within the CIA, it was said that he would not inform a Congressman if the latter's coat had caught fire. As DCI, Casey took a special interest in the administration's Central American policy, which he viewed as countering Soviet expansionism. According to Robert Gates, who was then a rising star in the agency:

> His greatest concern was with Soviet subversion and aggression in the Third World generally, ... But no individual covert action aroused his passion or significantly occupied his thoughts or even his time, save one. For reasons I never fully comprehended, Bill Casey became obsessed with Central America.[6]

Sensing the agency's skepticism toward the Central American policy that was emerging, Casey established a special task force, with its own analysts, within the Directorate of Operations to isolate the program from the rest of the agency as much as possible. To head the Latin American Division in the Directorate of Operations he chose Duane "Dewey" Clarridge, who knew next to nothing about the region. Clarridge devoted his time to Central America, leaving the rest of Latin America to his deputy, who was a regional specialist.[7] Casey would deal directly with Clarridge, bypassing the normal chain of command, and the two would initiate actions that went beyond written authorizations (such as arming Edén Pastora's forces in Costa Rica, south of Nicaragua, purportedly to stop the flow of arms going north from Nicaragua). Bobby Inman, a respected intelligence professional, resigned as Deputy Director of Central Intelligence because of Casey's handling of Central America.[8] Inman's successor, John McMahon, later complained about Clarridge's tendency to act without informing anyone. On 17 January 1983, for instance, he issued a memo of complaint to Deputy Director for Operations John Stein.

> The DCI and I were distressed to learn that Dewey Clarridge was in Panama talking about the Panamanians developing a 250 man paramilitary force without the DCI or I knowing about it.... I want to be aware of all major activities within Nicaragua by forces under our sponsorship and give prior approval before any conversation with foreign nationals on any proposed covert action.[9]

In March 1981, Reagan authorized further nonlethal covert operations against Nicaragua plus the interdiction of arms from Nicaragua to El Salvador. Secretary of State Alexander Haig disdained covert action and proposed a military buildup against Cuba as a way to dissuade revolutionary activity in Central America. Casey, however, saw covert action as politically more feasible, and he won the day.[10] In the summer of 1981, Casey asked Clarridge for options regarding Nicaragua. In his memoirs, Clarridge recalled his response:[11]

My plan was simple:

1. Take the war to Nicaragua.
2. Start killing Cubans.

The first point, taking the war to Nicaragua, Clarridge argued, was necessary to distract the Sandinistas from El Salvador. The second point was to raise the cost to Cuba of involvement in Central America, although he insisted he never intended to go out of his way to find Cubans to kill. On 1 December 1981, President Reagan signed a one-paragraph "finding," authorizing the CIA to initiate a paramilitary operation against Nicaragua.

<u>Finding Pursuant to Section 662 of
The Foreign Assistance Act of 1961
As Amended, Concerning Operations
Undertaken by the Central Intelligence
Agency in Foreign Countries, Other than
Those Intended Solely for the Purpose
of Intelligence Collection</u>

I hereby find that the following operation in a foreign country (including all support necessary to such operation) is important to the national security of the United States, and direct the Director of Central Intelligence, or his designee, to report this Finding to the intelligence committees of the Congress pursuant to Section 501 of the National Security Act of 1947, as amended, and to provide such briefings as necessary.

SCOPE	**PURPOSE**
<u>Central America</u>	Support and conduct [—]
	Paramilitary operations against [—about one line deleted—]
	Nicaragua [—about two lines deleted—]
The White House	/signed Ronald Reagan/
Washington, D.C.	
December 1, 1981	

This was followed on 4 January 1982 by National Security Decision Directive Number 17, putting the policy into a somewhat broader, regional context. This document has been declassified in part.

<u>NATIONAL SECURITY DECISION DIRECTIVE ON
CUBA AND CENTRAL AMERICA</u>

U.S. policy toward the Americas is characterized by strong support for those nations which embrace the principles of democracy and freedom for their people in a stable and peaceful environment. U.S. policy is therefore to assist in defeating the insurgency in El Salvador, and to oppose actions by Cuba, Nicaragua, or others to introduce into Central America heavy weapons, troops from outside the region, trained subversives, or arms and military supplies for insurgents. To adequately support U.S. policy, the following decisions have been made by the President based on discussion at the November 16, 1981 meeting of the National Security Council:

1. Create a public information task force to inform the public and Congress of the critical situation in the area.
2. Economic support for a number of Central American and Caribbean countries (estimate $250 to $300 million FY 1982 supplemental).
3. Agreement to use most of the $50 million Section 506 authority to increase military assistance to El Salvador and Honduras. Reprogram additional funds as necessary.
4. Provide military training for indigenous units and leaders in and out of country.
5. [—paragraph deleted—]
6. Maintain trade and credit to Nicaragua as long as the government permits the private sector to operate effectively.
7. [—paragraph deleted—]
8. Encourage cooperative efforts to defeat externally supported insurgency by pursuing a multilateral step-by-step approach.
9. Support democratic forces in Nicaragua.
10. [—paragraph deleted—]
11. [—paragraph deleted—]

/signed Ronald Reagan/

The CIA took over tutelage of a fledgling anti-Sandinista guerrilla movement based (at this time) on personnel from Somoza's Guardia Nacional and located in neighboring Honduras. Argentina actually had begun the process and Argentines continued to provide training, allowing the CIA to maintain a lower profile. Officially, the anti-Sandinistas called themselves the Nicaraguan Democratic Force (Fuerza Democrática Nicaragüense, FDN), but to the Sandinistas they were the Counterrevolutionaries (Contrarrevolucionarios). From this, the force became widely known on both sides as the Contras.

Why were the Argentines involved? Apart from the Argentine junta's messianic anticommunism, the commanders of Somoza's Guardia Nacional and Honduran police commander Gustavo Álvarez were all graduates of an Argentine military staff college. In addition, Nicaragua had given refuge to Argentine guerrillas. The CIA inherited the entire operation after the fall of the military junta in Buenos Aires 1983, following Argentina's unsuccessful war with Britain over the Falkland Islands.

The U.S. Congress was divided from 1981 through 1986, with Republicans taking control of the Senate as part of the "Reagan landslide" in the 1980 elections but the Democrats retaining the House of Representatives. Many in Congress, but especially liberal Democrats, considered the administration's notion of a worldwide Soviet threat to be exaggerated and its view that Central American revolutions were primarily rooted in foreign subversion to be off the mark. Rather, they saw the Central American rebellions as a reaction to the repressive policies and structures of their own governments and to past U.S. military interventions and support for dictatorial regimes. The Soviets and especially the

Cubans took advantage of opportunities as they arose and often at the invitation of disgruntled locals. In this view, supporting armed elements of the former Somoza regime (the so-called Somocistas)[12] against an indigenous revolutionary regime was exactly the wrong thing to do. Democrats saw it as an illegitimate and ultimately counterproductive attempt to overthrow a sovereign government. Moreover, Congressional resistance was stiffened by the legacy of Vietnam and concern that the United States could be drawn into direct involvement in another prolonged civil conflict. The hasty evacuation of the U.S. embassy in Saigon had occurred just six years earlier, in 1975, and the memories were quite fresh. (To be sure, some in the administration saw the undermining of the timidity left by the Vietnam legacy as a potential side benefit of their policy.) At the same time, members of Congress—fraught as usual with internal divisions and doubts— were reluctant to cut off the operation completely, lest they be proved wrong and blamed for failure. In any event, DCI Casey made sure that no one in Congress, or in the White House for that matter, learned of the skepticism of the CIA's own analysts regarding the likelihood of a victory by the unpopular Somocistas.[13]

The covert war against Nicaragua was destined to become one of the most public secrets in history. By March 1982, major newspapers and magazines were running stories exposing it before it was fully in operation. In Congress, opposition mounted to both the paramilitary campaign against Nicaragua and to military support for the armed forces of El Salvador. Edward Boland, the Democratic Chairman of the House Permanent Select Committee on Intelligence—himself under attack from his colleagues as a tacit accomplice in the operation—attached an amendment to a supplementary appropriations bill prohibiting the use of government funds for the purpose of overthrowing the government of Nicaragua or provoking a war between Nicaragua and Honduras.

> None of the funds provided in this act may be used by the Central Intelligence Agency or the Department of Defense to furnish military equipment, military training or advice, or other support for military activities, to any group or individual, not part of the country's armed forces, for the purpose of overthrowing the government of Nicaragua or provoking a military exchange between Nicaragua and Honduras.

The Boland Amendment, soon to become known as the First Boland Amendment, passed in the House in October 1982 by a vote of 411 to 0. The lopsided majority was possible, however, because the precise wording of the amendment made it virtually meaningless. The administration merely had to assert a different purpose for what it was doing. Indeed, it already claimed that its intention was merely to disrupt the flow of arms from Nicaragua to rebels in El Salvador.

In response to the Congressional opposition, the administration sponsored a new civilian directorate for the Contra forces and initiated a public relations campaign depicting them as fighting for freedom and democracy. Reagan issued a new finding in 1983 that continued the operation much as before but defined its aims as the interdiction of arms supplies to Salvadoran rebels and the application of pressure to force negotiations for a democratic regime in Nicaragua and for a peaceful settlement in Central America. The authorization was kept broad and vague. To accompany the finding, a supporting "scope note" was issued at the same time.

<u>Finding Pursuant to Section 662 of
The Foreign Assistance Act of 1961
As Amended, Concerning Operations
Undertaken by the Central Intelligence
Agency in Foreign Countries, Other than
Those Intended Solely for the Purpose
of Intelligence Collection</u>

I hereby find that the following activities are important to the national security of the United States, and direct the Director of Central Intelligence, or his designee, to report this Finding to the Intelligence Committees of the Congress pursuant to Section 501 of the National Security Act of 1947, as amended, and to provide such briefings as necessary.

<u>SCOPE</u>   <u>PURPOSE</u>

NICARAGUA   [—] in cooperation with other governments, provide support, equipment, and training assistance to Nicaraguan paramilitary resistance groups as a means to induce the Sandinistas and Cubans and their allies to cease their support for insurgencies in the region; to hamper Cuban/Nicaraguan arms trafficking; to divert Nicaragua's resources and energies from support to Central American guerrilla movements; and to bring the Sandinistas into meaningful negotiations and constructive, verifiable agreement with their neighbors on peace in the region.

[—] in cooperation with other governments, provide support to opposition leaders and organizations [—] Provide training, support and guidance to Nicaraguan resistance leaders [—].

Seek support of and work with other foreign governments and organizations as appropriate to carry out this program and encourage regional cooperation and coordination in pursuit of program objectives. CIA may support [—] in order to hamper arms trafficking through Nicaragua, support indigenous resistance efforts, and pressure the Sandinistas.

U.S. support to paramilitary activities in Nicaragua will be terminated at such time as it is verified that: (a) the Soviets, Cubans, and Sandinistas have ceased providing through Nicaragua arms, training, command and control facilities, and other logistical support to military or paramilitary operations in or against any other country in Central America, and (b) the Government of Nicaragua is demonstrating a commitment to provide amnesty and nondiscriminatory participation in the Nicaraguan political process by all Nicaraguans.

The Director of Central Intelligence is directed to ensure that this program is continuously reviewed to assure that its objectives are being met and its restrictions adhered to.

/signed Ronald Reagan/

The White House
Washington, D.C.

Date: September 19, 1983

SCOPE OF CIA ACTIVITIES
UNDER THE NICARAGUA FINDING

The Finding replaces the 1 December 1981 Finding which authorized certain covert action programs in Nicaragua and Central America. This program remains a critical element of U.S. policy in the region which recognizes that Nicaragua's Sandinista regime, with Soviet and Cuban active support, is implementing a strategy of full support for insurgent elements whose aim is the overthrow of democratic governments in the region. The political and paramilitary pressures created by this program are linked and are essential (1) to enable friendly Central American nations to strengthen democratic political institutions and achieve economic and social development, free from Soviet, Cuban, and Sandinista interference and (2) to induce a negotiated political resolution of international tensions in Central America.

This Finding authorizes the provision of material support and guidance to Nicaraguan resistance groups; its goal is to induce the Sandinista government to enter into meaningful negotiations with its neighboring nations; and to induce the Sandinistas and the Cubans and their allies to cease their provision of arms, training, command and control facilities and sanctuary to regional insurgencies. This support is to be provided [—] in cooperation with others, as appropriate. The provision of political support and funding to opposition leaders and organizations [—]—in order to maintain their viability—is also authorized.

POLITICAL ACTION: Financial and material support will be provided to Nicaraguan opposition leaders and organizations to enable them to deal with the Sandinistas from a position of political strength and to continue to exert political pressure on the Sandinistas to return to the original promises of the revolution— free elections, political pluralism, basic human rights, and a free press.

PARAMILITARY ACTION: Arms and other support will be provided to Nicaraguan paramilitary forces operating inside Nicaragua for the purpose of pressuring the Sandinista government and its Cuban supporters to cease their support for regional insurgencies. [—] instructors will train these forces to attack targets in Nicaragua in order to deny facilities, interrupt support networks, and to raise the price the Cubans and Nicaraguans and their allies must pay for continued support of insurgent groups elsewhere in Central America. [—about one and one-third lines deleted—]

U.S. support for paramilitary forces inside Nicaragua will be terminated when it is verified that: (a) the Soviets, Cubans, and Sandinistas have ceased providing arms, training, command and control facilities, and logistical support for military or paramilitary operations in or against any country in Central America, and (b) Nicaragua has committed itself to providing amnesty and non-discriminatory participation in the Nicaraguan political process by all Nicaraguans.

PROPAGANDA AND CIVIC ACTION: Guidance and media assistance will be provided to Nicaraguan opposition elements and paramilitary forces [—just under one line deleted—] Propaganda will be used to promote pluralism, human rights, freedom of the press, free elections, and democratic processes inside Nicaragua and throughout the region. Paramilitary units will be trained in field medicine, basic agriculture, and political/psychological action in order to assist local populations and to gain and maintain popular support.

FUNDING REQUIRED: $19,000,000 is included in the Fiscal Year 1984 CIA budget for this program. Additional funding requirements, to be determined by developments in the area, could be as much as $14,000,000. Any such additional funding will have to come from the Agency's Reserve for Contingencies or other authorized sources.

RISKS: This proposal carries with it the risks that the Cubans may increase their military presence in Nicaragua to defend their installations and to control rising internal opposition to the Sandinistas, and that the Nicaraguans may increase their covert activities or take direct military action against Honduras. The USSR is not likely to take an active direct military role in Central America.

The Sandinista regime may heighten repression in Nicaragua but this would only continue the course of action in which the Sandinistas have been engaged since 1979 to eliminate democratic pluralism.

The Nicaragua project continued to grow in size. In large part it was fed by disillusionment with the Sandinista government, especially among peasants in northern Nicaragua who crossed the border to join the FDN Contra army. (Guardia Nacional veterans, however, still dominated the command echelon of the FDN.) The Indian and Creole populations along the Atlantic coast had their own grievances against the government's centralizing tendencies and needed little prompting to rebel. In addition, Edén Pastora Gómez ("Comandante Cero"), a former Sandinista field commander, switched sides in April 1982. He founded the Democratic Revolutionary Alliance (Alianza Revolucionaria Democrática, ARDE) and established a smaller anti-Sandinista southern front based in Costa Rica.

With the growing size of the Contra army, members of Congress openly questioned the Regan administration's sincerity in foreswearing the goal of overthrowing the government. That skepticism was bolstered by statements from DCI Casey, who swore that the CIA did not intend to overthrow the Sandinistas . . . even if the Contras did.

By 1984, the CIA was concerned that opposition in Congress could result in the cutoff of all funding for Contra operations. This prospect encouraged the managers of the war to try to bring matters to a head while they still had the resources. In the early months of 1984, the CIA sought to increase economic pressure on the Nicaraguan regime by secretly mining the country's harbors. This was done not directly through the Contras but through separate contractors designated "unilaterally controlled Latino assets" (UCLAs). The mines were neither large nor sophisticated (in keeping with their supposed rebel origins), but it was assumed that even the rumor of mining would inhibit shipping.

In the following memorandum, two members of the NSC staff report on this aspect of the Contra war to Robert C. McFarlane, the third of Reagan's six National Security Advisers. They also outline a plan, mostly redacted, for destroying a tanker in a Nicaraguan port.

NATIONAL SECURITY COUNCIL

TOP SECRET   March 2, 1984

ACTION

MEMORANDUM FOR ROBERT C. MCFARLANE

FROM: OLIVER L. NORTH
　　　　CONSTANTINE MENGES

SUBJECT: Special Activities in Nicaragua

On the night of February 29, [—] emplaced four magnetic mines in the harbor at Corinto, Nicaragua. No attempt was made by the Sandinistas to engage the [—] during the mission. In accord with prior arrangements, ARDE's "Barracuda Commandos" took credit for the operation. ARDE also declared that the entire

Nicaraguan littoral is now a "war zone" and that all shipping within the Nicaraguan claimed 12nm territorial sea is subject to attack. [—about four lines deleted—] Our intention is to severely disrupt the flow of shipping essential to Nicaraguan trade during the peak export period. [—about three lines deleted—] In this case, our objective is to further impair the already critical fuel capacity in Nicaragua. This will substantially reduce EPS mobility and hamper their ability to support the ERP/FMLN guerrillas in El Salvador.[14]

[—about seven lines deleted—] While we could probably find a way to overtly stop the tanker from loading/departing, it is our judgment that destroying the vessel and its cargo will be far more effective in accomplishing our overall goal of applying stringent economic pressure. It is entirely likely that once a ship has been sunk no insurers will cover ships calling in Nicaraguan ports. This will effectively limit their seaborne trade to that which can be carried on Cuban, Soviet bloc, or their own bottoms. The following plan has been developed:

- No legal or financial action will be taken to deter [—about one line deleted—]
- [—four bullet points deleted; about twenty lines—]

Given past performances by Sandinista military seamen under fire (surrender or jumping overboard), there is little reason to expect that the Nicaraguan civilian crews of a gasoline laden will attempt to "run for it." It is anticipated that the operation ban be safely executed without injury or loss of life. No American citizens will be directly involved in the operational event.

RECOMMENDATION

That you approve this operation and brief the President using the points above.
    Approve _____   Disapprove _____

McFarlane wrote his initials in the "Approve" space, but the proposal to destroy the tanker (which is believed to have been Mexican)[15] was never carried out. By the end of March, word of the mining was in the press.[16] The Senate Select Committee on Intelligence, not having been fully briefed on the mining operation, was caught off guard. Daniel Patrick Moynihan, the ranking Democrat, submitted his resignation from the committee, withdrawing it only after Casey issued a personnel apology and promised to draw up improved notification procedures. Barry Goldwater, the Republican who chaired the committee and was normally supportive of the administration, sent the following angry letter to Casey.[17]

April 9, 1984

Hon. William J. Casey
Director of Central Intelligence
Central Intelligence Agency
Washington, D.C.

Dear Bill:

All this past weekend, I've been trying to figure out how I can most easily tell you my feelings about the discovery of the President having approved mining some of the harbors of Central America.

It gets down to one, little, simple phrase: I am pissed off!

I understand you had briefed the House on this matter. I've heard that. Now, during the important debate we had all last week and the week before, on whether we would increase funds for the Nicaragua program, we were doing all right, until a Member of the Committee charged that the President had approved the mining. I strongly denied that because I had never heard of it. I found out the next day that the CIA had, with the written approval of the President, engaged in such mining, and the approval came in February!

Bill, this is no way to run a railroad and I find myself in a hell of a quandary. I am forced to apologize to the Members of the Intelligence Committee because I did not know the facts on this. At the same time, my counterpart in the House did know.

The President has asked us to back his foreign policy. Bill, how can we back his foreign policy when we don't know what the hell he is doing? Lebanon, yes, we all knew that he sent troops over there. But mine the harbors in Nicaragua? This is an act violating international law. It is an act of war. For the life of me, I don't see how we are going to explain it.

My simple guess is that the House is going to defeat this supplemental and we will not be in any position to put up much of an argument after we were not given the information we were entitled to receive; particularly, if my memory serves me correctly, when you briefed us on Central America just a couple of weeks ago. And the order was signed before that.

I don't like this. I don't like it one bit from the President or from you. I don't think we need a lot of lengthy explanations. The deed has been done and, in the future, if anything like this happens, I'm going to raise one hell of a lot of fuss about it in public.

Sincerely,

Barry Goldwater
Chairman

As Senator Goldwater noted, Congressional support for continued funding of the Contra war fell precipitously. The CIA also faced condemnation from the public and criticism from major allies. Clarridge was reassigned out of the Latin American Division (and made Chief of the European Division). Clair George replaced John Stein as Deputy Director for Operations. The Contras faced the prospect of having to curtail operations in Nicaragua and return to their bases in Honduras. Thus, the administration began considering ways to fund the operation without going through Congress, a constitutionally questionable proposition.

Casey and McFarlane apparently were the first to act in anticipation of the funds being terminated. Unbeknownst to Congress, or to most members of the administration, they were already considering raising money from the governments of *other* countries. (Note that some of the words in the following memo are obscured by the large, black letters "CIA" stamped across the page, although some can be easily guessed.)

27 March 1984

MEMORANDUM FOR: The Honorable Robert C. McFarlane
                              Assistant to the President for National Security Affairs

SUBJECT: Supplemental Assistance to Nicaragua Program

   1. In view of possible difficulties in obtaining supplemental appropriations to
      carry out the Nicaraguan covert action project through the remainder of this

year, I am in full agreement that you should explore funding alternatives with the Israelis and perhaps others. I believe your thought of putting one of your staff in touch with the appropriate Israeli official should promptly be pursued. You will recall that the Nicaraguan project runs out of funds in mid-May. Although additional moneys are indeed required to continue the project in the [current] fiscal year, equipment and materiel made available from other sources [might] in part substitute for some funding. We are therefore currently exploring two such alternatives. Please note, however, that we are unlikely to [receive] materiel assistance from these sources by mid-May.

2. The first of these alternatives [is] acquiring from the Israelis additional ordnance captured by them [from the] PLO. A joint CIA/DoD survey team will make a second trip to Israel [—word obscured—] April to inspect captured PLO ordnance. The first trip in 1983 resulted [in] the acquisition of some $10 million worth [—a half line deleted—] machine guns and ammunition. The purpose of the upcoming survey is to determine current Israeli inventories and to negotiate thereafter to receive appropriate weapons free or at a low cost. Of course the cost of packing and delivery will have to be factored in.

3. The second alternative we are exploring is the procurement of assistance from [—another country—] [—A senior military official of that country—] has indicated that he may be able to make some equipment and training available to the [Contras?] through the Hondurans.

4. Finally, after examining legalities, you might consider urging an appropriate private US citizen to establish a foundation that could be the recipient of nongovernmental funds which could be disbursed to ARDE and the FDN.

/initialed/
William J. Casey

SECRET

The United States did not have a large number of troops stationed in Central America, but it did move troops in and out of Honduras for military exercises as a way to show support for Honduras and to exert pressure on Nicaragua. At the same time, there had been some limited direct negotiations between the United States and Nicaragua, and the foreign ministers of Mexico, Venezuela, Colombia, and Panama had initiated negotiations in the hope of finding a comprehensive, regional settlement before the various Central American conflicts combined into a full-blown regional war. This latter effort was called the Contadora process after the Panamanian island where the initiative was launched in January 1983. (The sponsoring countries were called the Contadora Group or the Core Four.)

On 25 June 1984, a key meeting of an NSC subcommittee was held to survey the situation and consider ways to move forward. Most of the participants of this meeting were unaware of the proposal to fund the Contras with donations from other countries, much less that funds and equipment from Israel and Saudi Arabia were already arriving. The meeting otherwise highlighted the divisions within the administration over what exactly it was that they had already authorized (including the possibility of third-party support for the Contras) as well as differences over how they should approach negotiations with Nicaragua. Each paragraph of the minutes, including Reagan's closing joke, was designated at the time as secret (S) except for the subject line and the time of adjournment, which were unclassified (U).

NATIONAL SECURITY COUNCIL
WASHINGTON, D.C. 20504

SECRET

NATIONAL SECURITY PLANNING GROUP MEETING
June 25, 1984; 2:00–3:00 P.M.; Situation Room

SUBJECT: Central America (U)

PARTICIPANTS:

The President
The Vice President

The Vice President's Office:
Admiral Daniel J. Murphy

State:
Secretary George P. Shultz
Mr. Michael Armacost
Mr. Langhorne Motley

Defense:
Secretary Caspar W. Weinberger
Dr. Fred Ikle

OMB:
Dr. Alton Keel

CIA:
Mr. William J. Casey
Mr. Duane Clarridge

USUN:
Ambassador Jeane J. Kirkpatrick

JCS:
General John W. Vessey, Jr.
Admiral Arthur S. Moreau

White House:
Mr. Edwin Meese, III
Mr. Robert C. McFarlane
Admiral John M. Poindexter

NSC:
Dr. Constantine Menges

Minutes

Mr. McFarlane: The purpose of this meeting is to focus on the political, economic, and military situation in Central America; to offer a status report, and to discuss next steps needed to keep our friends together while continuing to make progress toward our overall political goals. There is good news and bad news from Central America, as is always the case. The good news includes the fact that Congress will provide $62M in additional military assistance for El Salvador—$30M of which has already been spent. At the same time, we continue to need the additional $116M in aid for El Salvador which we have requested in the FY 84 supplemental, and we need to continue pressing for that. (S)

The bad news includes the fact that there seems to be no prospect that the Democratic leadership will provide for any vote on the Nicaraguan program. During the last vote in the House of Representatives, we lost by 64 votes, and that means that we need to change 32 votes in order to continue funding the anti-Sandinista program. On June 1, Secretary of State Shultz and Mr. Ortega of the Nicaraguan Directorate met in Nicaragua. The key question we need to consider now is what we believe about the prospects for further talks with Nicaragua; do we believe that Nicaragua wants to come to a reasonable agreement? Based on the answer to that question—how do we keep the friendly Central American governments together and focused on a multilateral, comprehensive, and verifiable treaty: What can we do to reinforce the confidence of the Central American and regional countries in the US in the light of questions about continuing congressional support for the anti-Sandinista program? For example, is there a need for any additional military exercises to disrupt or deter the communist guerrilla offensive which we expect will be coming in El Salvador in late summer or autumn? (S)

What can we do to increase public understanding of the situation in Central America and of our Central American policy not only here in the United States but also in Western Europe and Latin America and among other western countries? (U)

We will begin with Secretary Shultz addressing the diplomatic situation followed by Bill Casey reporting on the freedom fighters in Nicaragua, and Cap Weinberger and General Vessey commenting on the military situation. (S)

Secretary Shultz: Mr. President, we would not have gotten the deployment of Pershing missiles in Europe if people had not seen that we had credible, vigorous negotiation going on.[18] Similarly, you have moved to get yourself in a position with the USSR where we have made credible proposals and they have walked out. This is useful because it shows who is at fault for the lack of progress. (S)

Similarly, in Central America, our basic thrust has to be to generate positive elements of the political and economic situation, and to provide security help so that our efforts to disrupt the Nicaraguan export of subversion are as strong as we can get. An essential ingredient in that strategy is that we can say, if Nicaragua is halfway reasonable, there could be a regional negotiated solution—one which we support as much as we can. It is essential to have something like that going on or else our support on the Hill goes down. So it is not a question of making a prediction about the outcome of negotiations, rather it is important that we don't get sucked into something bad as it is essential to our strategy to key everything we do to support for the Contadora regional processes as I shall call it. (S)

So on our efforts to engage Nicaragua, there is one piece of very bad news. We don't have the votes in the House of Representatives to obtain additional funds for the anti-Sandinistas. The Congress will now be out for three weeks, and, therefore, anything credible going on the negotiating track can only help us. There is a sense of unease in Honduras about what is taking place for a great many reasons. The situation in El Salvador is a great big plus, assuming we get additional US military assistance; and taking what we got after the nun's case was solved,[19] we have a good crack at the omnibus supplemental; and if not, we can use 21(d) again. Nicaragua is in trouble though not badly so, especially if the anti-Sandinista funds run out. There is some shift in attitude of the Mexicans. For example, [Foreign Minister Bernardo] Sepulveda went to El Salvador, and there is some Mexican impatience with Nicaragua about their posture on the negotiations. This morning I spent some time with the US Ambassador to Honduras. There are things we can do to ease the concern of the Government of Honduras. They are very concerned about the US bilateral conversations with Nicaragua, but these concerns can be assuaged. Their main problems are internal—economic, and the military change. President [Roberto] Suazo is upset. The most serious problem is what Honduras can do with the Nicaraguan freedom fighters who return. President Suazo is also bothered by the sharp decline in the US military presence. (S)

In the meantime, we have a negotiation going on both in the Contadora process and in this little effort with Nicaragua. Our approach is: (1) to consult closely with our friends; (2) keep our friends posted so they see we are trying to help. By and large, they see this as helpful, as contributing to the Contadora process, and us as supporting them.

Today is the first US-Nicaragua meeting since June 1. We said we would not meet with the Mexicans present. Nicaragua said we have to keep the Mexicans informed. The United States said, O.K., we will inform all our friends in he Contadora countries. The first meeting was at 10:00 A.M. Mexican time or noon our time. Ambassador Schlaudeman was instructed, in the first session, only to talk about modalities and procedure—not to table anything. But to continue these negotiations, we must have content. We thing the best way for this to go on is to have a home-to-home approach (meaning alternating between the US and Nicaragua). We cannot say much about frequency. Nicaragua has lived up to its agreement about this negotiation. There was no press notification before this meeting. (S)

Our negotiating strategy is to table an Aide Memoire saying here is our approach, which we have written out and which is what we told the Core Four we would do so they would not be surprised. We have not given the Core Four the Aide Memoire, which changed recently, as a result of lengthly [sic] discussion which Fred Ikle and Admiral Moreau. We have to follow the Aide Memoire with an approach to negotiations which I discussed with almost everyone before June 1, except for Jeane Kirkpatrick, who was out of the country. Instead of a vertical approach to the negotiations taking some of the four topics on one at a time, we suggest taking some of each of the four in a horizontal approach. Ambassador Schlaudeman had a tableau of these four steps with blanks where any numbers are involved. From the standpoint of negotiations, we need to get the word to go ahead, or we need to decide on some other approach. Then, we will subvert the whole thing and it will have to abort. I have to get word to Shlaudeman. (S)

Mr. McFarlane: Now we'll receive an overview of the anti-Sandinista program from Bill Casey. (S)

Mr. Casey: The FDN in the North remains strong. ARDE in the South is on the run under pressure. In the North, we see continued support for the FDN. For example, 117 persons walked out of Nicaragua and Honduras to join up just last week, and in the central part of Nicaragua, 900 people are waiting for weapons in order to join up with the FDN. At the moment CIA has $250,000 left; about half of this is being kept in order to hold [—] US personnel in Honduras and Costa Rica until the end of September, 1984 so that we can help immediately in the event that a continuing resolution makes more money available. Our warehouses have arms and ammunition which can hold till August. Many of the anti-Sandinistas will stay in place within the country in order to feed themselves, and they would need about $3 million to get by for the next three months. We estimate that about half will retreat into Honduras and Costa Rica in some disarray, and we have to provide humanitarian assistance to help these individuals and those they bring out with them when they come into Honduras and Costa Rica. (S)

The legal position is that CIA is authorized to cooperate and seek support from third countries. In fact, the finding encourages third country participation and support in this entire effort, and we are considering Salvador, Guatemala, Honduras and [a South American country.] If we notify the oversight committees, we can provide direct assistance to help the FDN get the money they need from third countries. There will be some criticism, but senior members of the oversight committees recognize that we need to do this. We need a decision to authorize our permitting the FDN to obtain third country support. Meanwhile, the FDN, Misura,[20] and ARDE are acting on their own to try to get financial support from third party sources. There is a psychological gap coming up, and we should provide Honduras and Costa Rica with some type of humanitarian relief so they can assist the anti-Sandinistas. The anti-Sandinistas have something stashed away but they will be needing help. (S)

I shall offer a few words now on the Cuban-Nicaraguan military buildup. We see Cuban preparations for another military offensive in El Salvador, while at the same time the Cubans are building up their own military forces in Nicaragua. We now estimate, [—about two lines deleted—] there are actually 7–8 thousand Cuban troops [—about a half line deleted—] in Nicaragua. Castro is telling people such as the Nicaraguan leader Ortega that our willingness to negotiate is intended to permit the United States to buy time until we take military action against Nicaragua. (S)

Cuba and Nicaragua are moving more quickly to complete the construction of the new 3100 meter airport in Punta Huetea. [—about two and a half lines deleted—] could support Nicaraguan and Soviet cargo jets. Two other runways at two other airports are nearing the point where they could take jet fighter planes and also Soviet cargo planes. Further, we see that 45 Nicaraguan pilots trained in the Soviet bloc have returned to Nicaragua. (S)

Secretary Weinberger: The Department of Defense objected strongly to the content of the State Department negotiating proposals with respect to the numerical restrictions that would have been placed on US forces in Central America. The content of that first step negotiating proposal and the Aide Memoire is not a negotiating position that the United States should be presenting. We don't want to appear in old paternalistic North American fashion to be taking over the negotiations. We don't think it seemly to dignify Nicaragua by having the home-to-home meeting approach in which US and Nicaraguan negotiating teams alternate meetings from one capital to the other. Rather, what we should be doing is helping the Central American countries take the lead in the Contadora process in order to get a good Contadora treaty. This is the third choice between no negotiations and the separate bilateral negotiations proposed by State. We favor the third choice of helping the Contadora countries, who are our friends, obtain a comprehensive and verifiable Contadora treaty. (S)

On military issues we have reduced our troop levels, trying to keep to about 700. But let me emphasize, this is a self-imposed limit, and we can increase that number now. If we went along with the first step of the State negotiating proposal to Nicaragua as originally planned, we would have given up all of our flexibility. We would have given up the ability of the Defense Department to increase its physical presence in Central America above a certain low limit that was specified. On the anti-Sandinista issue, I think we need to take the offensive against the Democrats in Congress. We need to hold them accountable for not providing the resources needed to defend democracy. We need to hold the Democrats accountable. We should ask the Democrats whether they want a second Cuba. They see Ortega going after the visit of Secretary Shultz to Havana and then to Moscow. Do the American people want this? We should emphasize this to the Democrats in Congress rather than taking the bilateral negotiating tack where we would be giving Nicaragua economic aid, helping them economically. Whatever else, we need to assure that we can keep a US troop presence in Honduras of whatever size is needed to help defend our friends. (S)

General Vessey: I'm going to go over some of the material that Bill Casey covered in a general overview. In Nicaragua, we see an economy in bad shape. We see the government losing popular support, and we see the airfields being readied for jet fighters. (Admiral Moreau, would you please bring the photos to the President.)

The Contras have achieved considerable success in Nicaragua in disrupting Nicaraguan military operations and preparations. In Honduras, the economy is in difficult condition, but the civilian government is functioning well, although there is a great concern in Honduras about the Contras returning into Honduras. The regional training center has been functioning well, and we have trained about 3,000 Salvadoran troops this year. (S)

Looking in overview at what we are doing to provide support, I want to mention the following things we are doing now: two spring deployment exercises are finished and no additional exercises are scheduled between now and December. The naval presence will remain continuous at about the current level. Congress approved the construction of two temporary military bases; and we are doing a number of things in the area of intelligence collection, such as the following: [—about nine lines deleted—]

The current policy we are following is producing results. We need to help Honduras. They have economic and military problems and they probably need an emergency package of assistance. In El Salvador we need the additional $116 million in military assistance and we need to continue reassuring our friends in Central America through firm commitments. Our policy is working now but if we don't watch it, we'll snatch defeat from the jaws of victory. (S)

President Reagan: It all hangs on support for the anti-Sandinistas. How can we get that support in the Congress? We have to be more active. With respect to your differences on negotiating, our participation is important from that standpoint, to get support from Congress. (S)

Secretary Weinberger: If the core four Central American countries agree on our negotiating proposal, that's fine; but they have not even seen the original Aide Memoire that was to be given to the Nicaraguans today, nor have they seen the new one that was just completed this past Saturday afternoon. Besides, we can't end up with a negotiation that gets us into a separate bilateral deal with Nicaragua. (S)

Secretary Shultz: I think Cap's characterization of what we are trying to do is inaccurate and unfair. As of late Saturday afternoon, the Aide Memoire was okay with the Joint Chiefs of Staff and the Office of the Secretary of Defense. (S)

Secretary Weinberger: None of our friends in Central America have seen the new Aide Memoire that, as you point out, was revised Saturday and finished late Saturday afternoon. (S)

President Reagan: If we are just talking about negotiations with Nicaragua, that is so far-fetched to imagine that a communist government like that would make any reasonable deal with us, but if it is to get Congress to support the anti-Sandinistas, then that can be helpful. (S)

Amb. Kirkpatrick: Mr. President, at the United Nations we negotiate on everything with all the countries in the world, and I believe in diplomacy and negotiations. But it is very important to avoid getting into the situation of assuming responsibility for something that cannot be achieved. As you know, we often find it useful to support other countries which are trying to achieve political settlements when we, ourselves, remain in the background. For example, in Afghanistan, in the Persian Gulf where we are helping those countries trying to settle the war without ourselves moving into the forefront, and, in Lebanon, where we found that we were not able to bring about a negotiated solution and where we are now working in the background to facilitate a solution by working with our friends and through our friends. In my judgment, the analogy of Central America is much closer to the Persian Gulf situation than it is to the issue of the deployment of Pershing missiles in Europe. Let us remember that the Contadora process began in early 1983 as an initiative of the Latin American countries, and that when you sent me to the region in February 1983, they told me that they wanted to try to negotiate a political settlement among themselves. The reason the United States got out of the process directly was because the other countries wanted us out. They wanted to establish their own negotiating process, and they have made some progress. Venezuela, Colombia, and Panama have become more responsible as a result of trying to achieve a negotiated settlement. They are now much less critical of us than they were. Now they realize how difficult Nicaragua is, and now they have come to the hard part of the negotiation. (S)

As we now undertake separate bilateral negotiations with Nicaragua, rather than continuing to support the 21 Contadora objectives, these Latin American countries may well take this as an excuse to stand aside. They will get off the hook, and they will put us on the spot. If we give Mexico any special role, it will further undermine the Contadora process, and in fact, the Contadora process would then probably fall apart because any US preference shown toward Mexico, which has been supporting the Nicaraguans and communist guerrillas, will undermine pressure for a genuine negotiated solution. We would then be under lots of pressure from Congress, if the United States were negotiating bilaterally with Nicaragua, to make additional concessions. These bilateral negotiations with Nicaragua will scare our friends in the region and they will neither help us in the region nor in the US Congress. In fact, the coincidence of our undertaking this bilateral negotiating effort at the same time as the Congress fails to support funding for the Contras is enough to totally unravel our entire position in the region. (S)

If we don't find the money to support the Contras, it will be perceived in the region and the world as our having abandoned them, and this will lead to an increase in refugees in the region and it will permit Nicaragua to infiltrate thousands of Nicaraguan trained forces into El Salvador. And this will be an infiltration we could not stop. The Democrats don't want to vote because they don't want to accept the responsibility for their votes against this program. I believe we need to make their responsibility in the Congress clear to the US public. We must require the Democrats to stand up and be counted. If you showed your commitment and the Administration's commitment with more activity, it would be a positive factor in Congress. If we can't get the money for the anti-Sandinistas, then we should make the maximum effort to find the money elsewhere; even if we couldn't find money elsewhere immediately, we should consider using the anti-Sandinistas elsewhere for the time being, for example, in El Salvador to help defend against the coming guerrilla offensive. (S)

Secretary Shultz: Several points: (1) everyone agrees with the Contra program but there is no way to get a vote this week. If we leave it attached to the bill, we will lose the money we need for El Salvador. (2) We have had a vote on the anti-Sandinista program and the Democrats voted it down. It already is on the record and the Democrats are on the record. (3) I would like to get money for the Contras also, but another lawyer, Jim Baker,[21] said that if we go out and try to get money from third countries, it is an impeachable offense. (S)

Mr. Casey: I am entitled to complete the record. Jim Baker said that if we tried to get money from third countries without notifying the oversight committees, it could be a problem and he was informed that the finding does provide for the participation and cooperation of third countries. Once he learned that the funding [sic; finding] does encourage cooperation from third countries, Jim Baker immediately dropped his view that this could be an "impeachable offense," and you heard him say that, George. (S)

Secretary Shultz: Jim Baker's argument is that the US Government may raise and spend funds only through an appropriation of the Congress. (S)

Secretary Weinberger: I am another lawyer who isn't practicing law, but Jim Baker should realize that the United States would not be spending the money for the anti-Sandinista program; it is merely helping the anti-Sandinistas obtain the money from other sources. Therefore, the United States is not, as a government, spending money obtained from other sources. (S)

Secretary Shultz: I think we need to get an opinion from the Attorney General on whether we can help the Contras obtain money from third sources. It would be the prudent thing to do. On the negotiations, all the other countries support this. The question is, can the US conduct the negotiations so that it is perceived as supporting the Contadora process? If people here are so reluctant, then we can go back and try to abort this whole thing. I am very conscious of all the negative points that have been raised. I give the chances of a positive negotiation outcome with Nicaragua as two-in-ten, but if it doesn't succeed, it needs to be clear where the responsibility is, and that we have tried to help our Contadora friends obtain a positive outcome. (S)

Mr. McFarlane: Mr. President, perhaps I might define the issues as they stand now: (1) a negotiating process in order to get a good Contadora treaty is worthwhile; (2) Marxist-Leninist regimes historically do not negotiate in order to make reasonable concessions, as we saw over many years in North Korea and Vietnam. For them, negotiations are tactical exercises to split up their opponents and to obtain their goals. (3) How can there be a multilateral effort rather than one with Nicaragua in which the US is in the lead? On the military front, we had 2,200 troops and now we have about 700 there. (S)

Secretary Weinberger: We brought the numbers down to 700 on our own in order to deal with the critical perception that we were in some way militarizing the situation down there. We can always move to increase the exercises, and we can move exercises in and out so that we support our friends without creating the appearance that we are increasing the number of troops. (S)

President Reagan: Even the appearance of movement of US troops into Honduras for exercises, the movement of small units, would likely help the morale of Honduras. (S)

General Vessey: Yes, and US troop movements helped El Salvador very much during the communist offensive against the elections this year. The guerrillas in El Salvador had to turn and face the direction of US troop movements because they were afraid that our forces might have attacked or might have backed up a Honduran attack against them. So we played a positive role in blunting the Salvadoran guerrilla actions. (S)

President Reagan: I think there is merit to continuing the current negotiating session with the Nicaraguans, which has already begun because the press is eager to paint us as having failed again, and we don't want to let Nicaragua get off the hook. However, we should see these talks as only an adjunct to the Contadora. What we are doing with the Nicaraguans is that our special ambassador is there to help the Contadora process along. (S)

Secretary Shultz: Our Aide Memoire place heavy emphasis on the Contadora process. We have no intention of getting a separate bilateral agreement or treaty. If there is any glory to be obtained, then we are hoping to have the Contadora countries get this if they can get a good treaty. I am of the same mind as you, Mr. President, that we must get the funds for the Contras. (S)

President Reagan: The Contra funding is like the MX spending.[22] It is what will keep the pressure on Nicaragua, and the only way we are going to get a good Contadora treaty is if we keep the pressure on. (S)

Amb. Kirkpatrick: Mr. President I am no expert on legislative relations, but in the last week I have spoken with many congressmen, and, from what I have heard, they feel that the Administration has not attached the same priority to getting funds for the Contras as we have for the MX program and NATO issues. We have not made the impression that if the Congress cuts off the Contra funding this is of major importance to the Administration. On the question of who negotiates with whom we should remember that the Mexicans have always wanted the US and Cuba in the negotiation process. If we would go along with this path of bilateral negotiations with Nicaragua as the Mexicans want, we will sooner (and I mean before November) face the issue of the Cubans being included. I can tell you, Mr. President, that Venezuela, Colombia, and other countries in the region do not want Cuba involved directly and they do not want the United States involved in direct talks. They have approached the United Nations Secretary General in order to invite him to help the Contadora process along. But if we start direct bilateral negotiations with Nicaragua, then Colombia, Panama, and maybe even Venezuela will blame us for their failure. The Foreign Ministers in those countries, in my judgment, lack experience, and they definitely do not want us involved right now. (S)

Secretary Shultz: Mexico, Panama, Colombia, and Venezuela say they are delighted with our initiative. Concerning our efforts in Congress to obtain the anti-Sandinista funding, Senator Kasten and others say we have really worked on this issue. In the House of Representatives General Vessey and I went up to the Congress and offered to brief the full House of Representatives on Central America—about 150 Members came. We had a good discussion. I have also spent an hour-and-a-quarter on with [House Speaker] Tip O'Neill on this issue—this may be the first time he has listened to anyone from the Administration talk to him about this. (S)

Mr. Casey: It is essential that we tell he Congress what will happen if they fail to provide the funding for the anti-Sandinistas. At the same time, we can go ahead in trying to help obtain funding for the anti-Sandinistas from other sources; the finding does say explicitly "the United States should cooperate with other governments and seek support of other governments." The limitation we have in the Congress is the cap on US spending: we want to get that lifted. We have met no resistance from senior members of the intelligence committees to the idea of getting help with third country funding. (S)

Mr. Meese: As another non-practicing lawyer I want to emphasize that it's important to tell the Department of Justice that we want them to find the proper and legal basis which will permit the United States to assist in obtaining third party resources for the anti-Sandinistas. You have to give lawyers guidance when asking them a question. (S)

Secretary Weinberger: I agree that we should be giving greater emphasis to obtaining funding for the anti-Sandinistas. We should make it a major issue with the Congress, Mr. President. I also agree that we should facilitate third party support for the anti-Sandinista groups. Third, I want to emphasize my concerns about the US trying to conduct separate bilateral negotiations with Nicaragua in order to get a regional settlement. We should be supporting the Contadora countries in order to help them get a good treaty; we should not be taking the lead in doing this ourselves. And, I believe we would have much better success with Congress if we are seen as helping others to obtain a good Contadora treaty and that there would be negative effects if Mexico and Cuba are seen as coming into the whole negotiating process. Honduras is not eager to have the United States undertake separate bilateral negotiations with Nicaragua. In fact, they are very alarmed about this and that is why they are starting to pull away from security cooperation with us. (S)

Mr. McFarlane: With regard to diplomacy, Secretary Shultz should recommend specific measures so that the negotiating process will, in fact, be perceived as supportive of these friendly Central American countries in order to obtain a good Contadora treaty. The Secretary of Defense can propose such additional activities as may help our friends meet the coming guerrilla offensive in El Salvador and improve the morale of our friends in the region; Jim Baker and Ed Meese might examine the best way of getting additional money to expand our public affairs efforts and to have a greater impact in the Congress and to obtain an opinion from the Attorney General. (S)

Mr. Casey: We need the legal opinion which makes clear that the US has the authority to facilitate third country funding for the anti-Sandinistas; and at the same time, we need to find a way to provide humanitarian assistance to any anti-Sandinista and their families who might be going into Costa Rica or Honduras to escape the Nicaraguan military actions against them. We need this humanitarian assistance to be available right away. (S)

President Reagan: There are persons now meeting with the Nicaraguans; and without aborting anything, we do want to keep getting a good Contadora treaty as the focus of our negotiating process. On the anti-Sandinistas, I am behind an all-out push in Congress. We must obtain funds to help these freedom fighters. On the Contadora negotiations, there is a risk right now that our separate talks with the Nicaraguans might be misunderstood, and we need to make sure that does not happen and that our friends know they can rely on us. (S)

Secretary Weinberger: We don't need to shut off or abort any negotiations. As I have said, there is a third way between no negotiations and a separate US/Nicaragua bilateral deal. That third way, Mr. President, is that we continue actively to support our Central American friends in order to get a good Contadora treaty that provides a real solution. (S)

Secretary Shultz: Right now Shlaudeman is instructed to talk only about the US Aide Memoire, and we can keep to the Contadora process as the basis of our talks with the Nicaraguans, but then the US negotiating initiative with Nicaragua is no more. (S)

President Reagan: I don't think we should quit on it. (S)

Secretary Weinberger: We don't need to quit—just use the US talks with Nicaragua in order to support our Central American friends and get a good Contadora treaty. (S)

President Reagan: I just think, now, to back away from talks will also look like a defeat, but I can't imagine that Nicaragua will offer anything reasonable in a bilateral treaty. (S)

Mr. McFarlane: The four friendly Central American countries developed a treaty proposal in late April. Secretary Shultz and the four Contadora countries have the text of a draft Contadora treaty that needs a lot of work to become reasonable. One possible agenda item for the US-Nicaragua talks is that the US could talk about the draft Contadora treaty and use the late April document of the Central American four countries to provide criteria for how this treaty needs to be improved. Then, the US can go back to these four Central American countries with Nicaraguan comments on the draft treaty and suggestions for improving it. (S)

Mr. Meese: Is there any chance to pass the funds for the anti-Sandinistas before the Congress goes on recess? (S)

Mr. Casey: We estimate that of about 8,000 FDN fighters, 4,000 might decide to get out of Nicaragua once their ammunition runs out in August; and each of these may have about four family members with him. Therefore, these 16,000 possible new refugees need to have humanitarian assistance available by August. (S)

Vice President Bush: How can anyone object to the US encouraging third parties to provide help to the anti-Sandinistas under the finding? The only problem that might come up is if the United States were to promise to give these third parties something in return so that some people could interpret this as some kind of an exchange. (S)

Mr. Casey: Jim Baker changed his mind as soon as he saw the finding and saw the language. (S)

Mr. McFarlane: I propose that there be no authority for anyone to seek third party support for the anti-Sandinistas until we have the information we need, and I certainly hope none of this discussion will be made public in any way. (S)

President Reagan: If such a story gets out, we'll all be hanging by our thumbs in front of the White House until we find out who did it. (S)
  The meeting adjourned at 3:50 P.M. (U)

The next day, Casey and the CIA General Counsel went to Attorney General William French Smith to get an opinion on third-party funding. "Smith expressed the view that discussions with third countries for such assistance would be permissible as long as it was made clear that the countries must spend their own funds and would not be reimbursed by the United States."[23]

In autumn 1984, another scandal broke out when the press came across *Psychological Operations in Guerrilla Warfare*, a CIA manual written for the Contras that included advice on subjects such as how to target local officials so as to maximize the political and propaganda effects.[24] Several investigations were launched. The White House renewed its commitment not to permit assassination. The CIA concluded that it had been written and distributed by a contract agent without official authorization or review, and that the press exaggerated the nature of the manual. In any event, the agency suffered from the episode.

Not only did Congress refuse to appropriate further funds for the Contras in the wake of the mining scandal, in October 1984 it passed the second Boland Amendment. This one did away with the ambiguous language of the first. Indeed, it appeared to make every effort to close off any possible loophole.

SEC. 8066. (a) During the fiscal year 1985, no funds available to the Central Intelligence Agency, the Department of Defense, or any other agency or entity of the United States involved in intelligence activities may be obligated or expended for the purpose or which would have the effect of supporting, directly or indirectly, military or paramilitary operations in Nicaragua by any nation, group, organization, movement, or individual.

Of course, there are always loopholes. In this case, the line that stood out was "involved in intelligence activities." In late 1984, responsibility for the Contra operation was transferred from the CIA to the staff of the NSC, which normally had no operational responsibilities whatsoever, let alone involvement in intelligence activities. The focal point on the staff would be Lt. Col. Oliver L. North. As for funding, the administration set out on a three-track course: (1) to pursue funding from other countries, (2) to encourage donations by private citizens, and (3) to lobby Congress to renew direct aid.

In the meantime, Deputy Director for Intelligence Gates decided to "talk absolutely straight about Nicaragua," laying out his view of the situation for Casey. Gates was disturbed by what he saw as a disconnect between the administration's apocalyptic rhetoric regarding a threat in Central America and its failure to promote an open and consistent policy. To be sure, his vision of what needed to be done ("ridding the Continent of this regime") was a far cry from that which prevailed in Congress. Striking are the assertions that Nicaragua was armed "far beyond its defensive needs" (which did not seem to take into account that it was under attack by the United States, even if only indirectly) and that the United States had been trying to reach "some sort of an accommodation," which the Nicaraguans were not reciprocating. Note that, in his memoir, Gates says that he knew little about the private funding of the Contras and nothing about the NSC's operational role until he became Deputy Director of Central Intelligence in April 1986.[25]

14 December 1984

MEMORANDUM FOR: Director of Central Intelligence
FROM: Deputy Director for Intelligence
SUBJECT: Nicaragua

    1. It is time to talk absolutely straight about Nicaragua. To recap where we are:

- Based on all the assessments we have done, the Contras, even with American support, cannot overthrow the Sandinista regime. Whatever small chance they had to do that has been further diminished by the new weaponry being provided by the Soviets and Cubans.
- The Soviets and Cubans are turning Nicaragua into an armed camp with military forces far beyond its defensive needs and in a position to intimidate and coerce its neighbors.
- The Nicaraguan regime is steadily moving toward consolidation of a Marxist-Leninist government and the establishment of a permanent and well-armed ally of the Soviet Union and Cuba on the mainland of the Western Hemisphere. Its avowed aim is to spread further revolution in the Americas.
- The FDN has been denied American assistance. Without further assistance by February, all the information we have suggests the Contras are going to begin heading into Honduras. The Hondurans will then be faced with some 12,500 armed fighters (whom the Honduras see as closely aligned with Alvarez, thereby potentially unsettling Honduras itself).[26]
- Flight of the Contras into Honduras will be followed not only by their families but presumably by a second wave of refugees and others who, seeing abandonment of American efforts to force the Sandinistas to alter their regime, will see the handwriting on the wall, determine that their personal futures are in peril and leave the country. It is altogether conceivable that we could be looking at an initial refugee wave from Nicaragua over the first year of 150,000 to 200,000 people (the families of the Contras alone could account for 50,000).
- Failure of the United States to provide further assistance to the resistance and collapse of the Contra movement would force Honduras to accommodate to the Nicaraguan regime. One result of this would be the

complete reopening of the channels of arms support to the Salvadoran insurgency, thereby reversing the progress made in recent months.

   ○ These unsettled political and military circumstances in Central America
would undoubtedly result in renewed capital flight from Honduras and
Guatemala and result in both new hardship and political instability
throughout the region.

2. These are strong assertions but our research as well as the reports of our
people on the spot (for example our COS [Chief of Station] in Honduras)
make it possible to substantiate each of the above points.

3. What is happening in Central America in many ways vividly calls to mind
the old saw that those who forget the past are condemned to repeat it.

   ○ In 1958–60 we thought that we could reach some sort of an accommodation with Castro that would encourage him to build a pluralistic government in Cuba. We have been trying to do the same thing with the
Nicaraguans, with the same success.

   ○ In Vietnam, our strategy consisted of a series of measures applied very
gradually and over a long period of time. With each step of new US
involvement the gradual approach enabled the enemy to adjust to each
new turn of the screw so that by the end of the war, even in the face of
the most severe bombing, the Vietnamese had developed enormous tolerance. Half measures, half-heartedly applied, will have the same result in
Nicaragua.

   ○ In 1975, The United States President announced that American assistance
to UNITA in Angola was in the national interest of the United States and
strongly urged the Congress to support military assistance to that group.
The Congress turned it down, thereby not only proving that the United
States would not involve itself in any significant way in the Third World to
combat Soviet subversion and activity but, moreover, that the Congress
could effectively block any moves the President did wish to make. The
Boland Amendment and the cutoff of aid to the Contras is having the same
effect again, showing the Soviets and our Third World friends how little
has changed in nine years, even with a President like Ronald Reagan.

   ○ In a variety of places, including Vietnam, negotiations in effect became a
cover for the consolidation and further expansion of Communist control.
While they might observe whatever agreements were reached for the first
weeks or as long as American attention (particularly media attention)
was focused on the situation, they knew they could outlast our attention
span. Usually within a relatively short period of time they were openly
violating whatever agreements had been achieved.

4. The truth of the matter is that our policy has been to muddle along in Nicaragua with an essentially half-hearted policy substantially because there is no
agreement within the Administration or with the Congress on our real
objectives. We started out justifying the program on the basis of curtailing
the flow of weapons to El Salvador. Laudable though that objective might
have been, it was attacking a symptom of a larger problem in Central America and not the problem itself.

5. It seems to me that the only way that we can prevent disaster in Central
America is to acknowledge openly what some have argued privately: that
the existence of a Marxist-Leninist regime in Nicaragua closely allied with
the Soviet Union and Cuba is unacceptable to the United States and that the
United States will do everything in its power short of invasion to put that
regime out. Hopes of causing the regime to reform itself for a more

pluralistic government are essentially silly and hopeless. Moreover, few believe that all those weapons and the more to come are only for defense purposes. Only when we acknowledge what the objective is in Central America, can we begin to have any kind of rational discussion on how to achieve it. As long as one maintains the fig leaf of curtailing the flow of arms to El Salvador, all other efforts an easily be politically dismissed.

6. Once you accept that ridding the Continent of this regime is important to our national interest and must be our primary objective, the issue then becomes a stark one. You either acknowledge that you are willing to take all necessary measures (short of military invasion) to bring down that regime or you admit that you do not have the will to do anything about the problem and you make the best deal you can. Casting aside all fictions, it is the latter course we are on. Even new funding for the Contras, particularly in light of the new Soviet weaponry, is an inadequate answer to this problem. The Contras will be able to sustain an insurgency for a time but the cost and the pain will become very high and the resistance eventually will wither. Any negotiated agreement simply will offer a cover for the consolidation of the regime and two or three years from now we will be in considerably worse shape than we are now.

What to Do

7. The alternative to our present policy—which I predict ultimately and inevitably is leading to the consolidation of the Nicaraguan regime and our facing a second Cuba in Central America—is overtly to try to bring down the regime. This involves a mustering of political force and will, first of all within the Administration, and second with the Congress, that we have not seen on any foreign policy issue (apart from our defense rearmament) in many years. It seems to me that this effort would draw upon the following measures:

   o Withdrawal of diplomatic recognition of the regime in Managua and the recognition of a government in exile.
   o Overt provision to the government in exile of military assistance, funds, propaganda support and so forth including major efforts to gain additional support in international community, including real pressure.
   o Economic sanctions against Nicaragua, perhaps even including a quarantine. These sanctions would affect both exports and imports and would be combined with internal measures by the resistance to maximize the economic dislocation to the regime.
   o Politically most difficult of all, the use of air strikes to destroy a considerable portion of Nicaragua's military buildup (focusing particularly on the tanks and helicopters). This would be accompanied by an announcement that the United States did not intend to invade Nicaragua but that no more arms deliveries of such weapons would be permitted.

8. These are hard measures. They probably are politically unacceptable. But it is time to stop fooling ourselves about what is going to happen in Central America. Putting our heads in the sand will not prevent the events that I outlined at the beginning of this note. Can the United States stand a second Cuba in the Western Hemisphere? One need only look at the difficulty that Cuba has caused this country over the past 25 years to answer that question.

9. The fact is that the Western Hemisphere is the sphere of influence of the United States. If we have decided totally to abandon the Monroe Doctrine, if in the 1980s taking strong actions to protect our interests despite the hail of criticism is too difficult, then we ought to save political capital in Washington, acknowledge our helplessness, and stop wasting everybody's time.

10. Without a comprehensive campaign openly aimed at bringing down the regime, at best we somewhat delay the inevitable. Without US funding for the Contras, the resistance essentially will collapse over the next year or two. While seeking funding from other countries to the Contras could help for a time, it is essential to recognize that almost as important as the money is the fact of the United States support both from an economic and political standpoint. Somehow, knowing that Taiwan, South Korea, and Singapore are behind you does not carry the same weight. Economic sanctions surely would have a significant impact in the initial months, but unless accompanied by a broad range of other actions this impact will diminish over time and we will find ourselves with a Nicaragua even more closely attached to the Soviet Union and Cuba than we have now.

11. All this may be politically out of the question. Probably. But all the cards ought to be on the table and people should understand the consequences of what we do and do not do in Nicaragua. Half measures will not even produce half successes. The course we have been on (even before the funding cut-off—as the last two years suggest—will result in further strengthening of the regime and a Communist Nicaragua which, allied with its Soviet and Cuban friends, will serve as the engine for the destabilization of Central America. Even a well funded Contra movement cannot prevent this; indeed, relying on and supporting the Contras as our only action may actually hasten the ultimate, unfortunate outcome.

/initialed/
Robert M. Gates

Gates was right about one thing. His proposals were politically out of the question at the time, even within the administration. (Nonetheless, he would be justly hailed as a moderate in the George W. Bush administration in 2006.) Gates complained that neither the administration nor Congress was willing to elaborate clear goals or take an unambiguous stand, either granting full public support for the Contras or cutting them off completely and ending the situation.[27] In the meantime, however, the administration was quietly seeking foreign sources of funding to continue a low-scale Contra war in defiance of Congress. A 107-paragraph summary provided by the government in 1989 as evidence in the case of *United States of America* v. *Oliver L. North* provides some details on those efforts. Here are a few excerpts from that document:

You are instructed that the United States has admitted for purposes of this trial the following facts to be true:

1. In 1983, DCI Casey asked Secretary of Defense Weinberger if the Department of Defense (DoD) could obtain infantry weapons that Israel had confiscated from PLO [Palestine Liberation Organization] forces. Following discussions between Major General Meron of Israel and Retired Major General Richard Secord of the United States government ("USG"), Israel secretly provided several hundred tons of weapons to the DoD on a grant basis in May 1983. This was known as Operation TIPPED KETTLE. In February 1984, the CIA asked DoD if it could obtain additional PLO weapons from Israel at little or no cost for CIA operation use. After negotiations between March 1984 and July 1984, Israel secretly provided the additional weapons to DoD in Operation TIPPED KETTLE II. The DoD then transferred the weapons to the CIA. Although the CIA advised Congress that the weapons would be used for

various purposes, in fact many of them were provided to the Nicaraguan Resistance as appropriated funds ran out. (The effort to funnel materiel to the Contras at a time when there were limits on the amount of funds the USG could spend to support the Resistance also found expression in 1984 in Project ELEPHANT HERD, under which the CIA was to stockpile weapons and materiel provided by DoD at the lowest possible cost under the Economy Act.) DoD assured Israel that, in exchange for the weapons, the U.S. Government would be as flexible as possible in its approach to Israeli military and economic needs, and that it would find a way to compensate Israel for its assistance within the restraints of the law and U.S. policy.

2. In late March 1984, National Security Advisor Robert C. McFarlane suggested that he pursue funding alternatives for the Resistance for use after Congressional funding ran out. McFarlane proposed putting a member of the NSC staff in touch with an Israeli official to pursue funding alternatives with the Israelis. In an "Eyes Only" Secret memo, DCI Casey informed McFarlane that the CIA was exploring two alternative means of acquiring equipment and materiel from Israel for use by the Resistance after the funding ran out. First, the CIA was considering the acquisition from Israel of ordnance captured from the PLO. Casey advised McFarlane that in 1983 the USG had acquired some $10 million worth of weapons and ammunition in this manner from the Israelis (in Operation TIPPED KETTLE). Second, the CIA was considering procuring additional assistance from another country. Casey informed McFarlane that a foreign government official had indicated that he might be able to make some equipment and training available to the Resistance through Honduras. [...]

4. In early 1984, in a discussion with the Ambassador from Saudi Arabia, McFarlane encouraged that country to support the Resistance. A short time later, the Ambassador informed McFarlane that his government would contribute $1 million per month. The money became available during the early summer of 1984. [...]

6. In late summer and early fall 1984, CIA stations reported to CIA Headquarters concerning apparent offers by the People's Republic of China ("PRC") to provide assistance to the Resistance.

7. At a meeting in mid-July 1984 between DCI Casey, Deputy DCI John McMahon, and Deputy Secretary of State Dam, Casey indicated that those present ought to get moving on non-USG funding for the Resistance since Attorney General [William French] Smith had recently concluded that raising the funds in this manner would not be an impeachable offense, as had been suggested at the NSPG meeting on June 25, 1984. [...]

11. General John Vessey, Chairman of the Joint Chiefs of Staff ("CJCS"), followed up on LtCol North's approach to the PRC military officer. The PRC agreed to provide anti-aircraft missiles to the Resistance, and Retired General Richard Secord consummated the transaction and arranged shipment through Guatemala. The CIA reported the details of this transaction to McFarlane. [...]

16. In early 1985, President Reagan urged the Head of State of Saudi Arabia to continue its support for the Resistance. Saudi Arabia subsequently made a contribution of more than $25 million.

17. In early February 1985, LtCol North advised McFarlane that, as a consequence of Singlaub's[28] recent trip, both the Taiwanese and the South Koreans had indicated to U.S. officials that they would help the Resistance. Claire George, CIA Deputy Director of Operations ("DDO"), withheld dissemination of the offers and contacted LtCol North privately to ensure that they would not become common knowledge. LtCol North sought and

received McFarlane's permission to have Singlaub approach officials of the Embassies of Taiwan and South Korea to urge them to proceed with their offers, Singlaub would then put [Resistance leader Adolfo] Calero in direct contact with the officials.

As secret, foreign sources of funding were being sought, Oliver North was arranging for the collection of donations from private citizens, while concealing the administration's orchestration of the effort. These would help cover costs for nonmilitary supplies, such as food, while third-country donations covered expenses for arms. It also would serve as part of a public explanation of how the Contras were still getting funds when Congress had cut them off.

NATIONAL SECURITY COUNCIL
March 16, 1985

TOP SECRET   SENSITIVE

ACTION

MEMORANDUM FOR ROBERT C. MCFARLANE
FROM: OLIVER L. NORTH
SUBJECT: Fallback Plan for the Nicaraguan Resistance

The plan attached at Tab I has been developed pursuant to our discussion on Friday regarding fallback options. It is premised on the assumption of a major Congressional budget battle and an assessment that th Congress will not rescind the restrictions in Section 8066 of the FY-85 C.R. (Tab A).[29] Should you determine in your meeting with Senators [David] Durenburger and [Richard] Lugar (Tuesday, March 19, 0730) that the Congress will not endorse a resumption of USG [United States Government] support to the resistance, the plan at Tab I provides a workable alternative.

Secrecy for the plan is paramount. We could not implement such an option if it became know in advance and it also mandates that present donors continue their relationship with the resistance beyond the current funding figure. The plan would require the President to make a major public pronouncement which, in turn, must be supported by other Administration officials, resistance leaders, and regional Heads of State once it has been announced.

RECOMMENDATION

That, if Durenburger and Lugar indicate an unwillingness to support resumption of USG aid to the resistance, you discuss the attached plan with Secretary Shultz following your meeting.

Approve _____   Disapprove _____

Attachments

TOP SECRET   SENSITIVE

FALLBACK OPTION PLAN FOR THE NICARAGUAN RESISTANCE

Assumptions. The Congress is unwilling to support release of $14 M in USG funds for the purpose of supporting, directly or indirectly, military or paramilitary operations in Nicaragua. The FY-86 budget is seriously jeopardized by Congressional action and will require a major effort on the part of the President immediately after the MX vote through mid-July. There will be insufficient time or assets available to organize the kind of Administration-wide effort required to achieve an affirmative vote in both houses on the Nicaraguan resistance program.

Section 8066 of the law (Tab A) expires on October 1, 1985. There are currently $28M requested in the FY-86 intelligence budget for the purpose of supporting paramilitary operations by the Nicaraguan resistance. The current funding relationship which exists between the resistance and its donors is sufficient to purchase arms and munitions between now and October–if additional monies are provided for non-military supplies (e.g., food, clothing, medical items, etc.) The current donors will have to be convinced of the need to continue their funding for munitions after October 1, 1985. A commitment for another $25–30M from the donors will be necessary for munitions in 1986 in anticipation that the $28M requested in the intelligence budget is not approved.

Concept. In lieu of forwarding the report to the Congress required by Section 8066 of PL 98-473, the President would announce on or about April 2 that the American people should contribute funds ("... send your check to the Nicaraguan Freedom Fighters, Box 1776, Gettysburg, PA ...") to support liberty and democracy in the Americas. He would note that the monies raised would be used to support the humanitarian needs of those struggling for freedom against Communist tyranny in Central America. By necessity, the Speech must be dramatic and a surprise. It cannot be leaked in advance.

Prior to the speech, the following steps must be taken:

o [Adolfo] Calero, [Arturo] Cruz, and [Alfonso] Robelo (the principle leadership of the Nicaraguan armed and unarmed resistance) must be covertly advised of this plan and must assure of their support.
o The Nicaraguan Freedom Fund, Inc., a 501(c)3 tax exempt corporation, must be established and obtain a Post Office Box 1776 in Gettysburg, Pennsylvania, Valley Forge, or Yorktown. (This process is already underway.)
o Presidents Suazo, Monge, and Duarte[30] (and the appropriate leadership of each of those countries) must be apprised of this plan 1–2 days in advance of the announcement. They must be prepared to fully support the President's proclamation.
o The current donors must be apprised of the plan and agree to provide additional $25–30M to the resistance for the purchase of arms and munitions.
o Public groups and political action committees already mobilized for the Congressional campaign to relieve the 8066 constraints will have to be mobilized for the new approach (advertising, posters, mailings, phone calls, etc.) several hours before the President speaks.
o Assuming a Presidential speech on or about April 2 at 8:00 P.M., a briefing for senior Administration officials should be held at 7:00 P.M. that day in Room 450 OEOB [Old Executive Office Building] to ensure that public commentary after the speech by these officials is supportive of this proclamation.

Additional Requirements.

o Informal contact several months ago with a lawyer sympathetic to our cause indicated that such a procedure would be within the limits of the law. [White House Counsel] Fred Fielding should be asked to do conduct [sic] a very private evaluation of the President's role in making such a request.
o The name of one of several existing non-profit foundations, we have established in the course of the last year, will be changed to Nicaraguan Freedom Fund, Inc. Several reliable American citizens must be contacted to serve as its corporate leadership on its board of directors along with Cruz, Calero, and Robelo.
o Calero, Cruz, and Robelo will support support [sic] such an option if properly approached. They should then be photographed with the President on

the day of the announcement and prepared to appear on U.S. and other media supporting the President's program.

o You will have to make a quick (one day) trip to the region, preferably the day before announcement in order to brief Heads of State and regional leaders. For obvious reasons, this must be a very secret trip.

o The President's speech must be prepared in total secrecy much the same as Ben Elliott worked on the Grenada announcements.[31]

TOP SECRET SENSITIVE

Marginal notes on the document suggest that McFarlane considered a presidential speech unlikely and the additional $25 to $30 million dollars from existing donors to be doubtful. In November 1986, as the Iran-Contra affair was becoming public, North replaced this memorandum in the files with a fake. The fake memo, a brief note also titled "Fallback Plan for the Nicaraguan Resistance," suggested that McFarlane tell Senators Durenburger and Lugar that if they were not going to fund the Contras, then they should come up with a fallback plan.

In addition to third-country support and private donations, the administration pursued a third track. That consisted of efforts to convince Congress to renew funding so that the CIA could again take control of the Contra operation. Apart from private lobbying, this included an extensive and coordinated public relations campaign. The focal points of that campaign were Walter Raymond, Jr., and Otto J. Reich. Raymond of the CIA was assigned by Casey to chair the Central American Public Diplomacy Task Force as part of the National Security Council staff (the CIA being legally prohibited from engaging in domestic operation or seeking to influence public opinion or the media). Reich was the Coordinator of Public Diplomacy for Latin America and the Caribbean at the State Department (an office designated S/LPD). The following memorandum from Reich to Raymond highlights how the campaign sought to mimic the Pentagon's psychological operations (PSYOP). Although the office is in the State Department and PSYOP normally targets foreign audiences, Reich makes clear that he has "the public and Congress" in his sights.

United States Department of State
Coordinator of Public Diplomacy for
Latin America and the Caribbean
Washington, D.C. 20520
January 2, 1986

TO: NSC - Mr. Walt Raymond
FROM: S/LPD - Otto J. Reich
SUBJECT: Denial of Detail of Personnel by DoD

With Col. David Brown's letter of December 17, 1985 (Tab 1), the Department of Defense has turned down our request for a detail of two officers and two non-commissioned officers to S/LPD on a non-reimbursable basis.

This denial of desperately needed resources appears to conflict with the President's expressed desire for an effective public diplomacy effort, as expressed in the attached NSC memoranda (Tabs 3 and 4). According to Col. Brown's letter to me, the prime basis for the denial of resources was "not uniquely military or of primary benefit to the Department of Defense." The skills requested in S/LPD's letter of September 18, 1985 (Tab 2)—intelligence analysis and production of persuasive communications—are combined only in military Psychological Operations personnel.

Prior to S/LPD's request, five TDY [temporary duty] personnel from the 4th Psychological Operations Group served in S/LPD from June 4 to November 4, 1985. The two officers and three non-commissioned officers did the initial setup of information handling and analyzing systems to be operated by the permanent detailees. These systems, when fully operational, will provide information analysis capability fundamental to the production of effective persuasive public diplomacy documents. Analysis of Soviet, Cuban and Nicaraguan propaganda campaigns and their effect on democratic response to specific Central American issues, the synthesis of all-source intelligence, and the ability to convert abstract analysis into effective U.S. policy responses are skills normally combined in those who have worked in strategic PSYOP. We realize that the cadre of U.S. officers and NCO's possessing these skills is limited and in great demand; however, the overall national interest would be well served if some of these assets are placed in S/LPD to work on a problem of vital national importance—Central American public diplomacy. S/LPD currently coordinates government-wide efforts to ensure that the public and Congress understand U.S. policy in Central America.

The five military personnel who were temporarily detailed to S/LPD were highly effective in support of our mission. They developed systems for continued analysis of Soviet, Cuban and Nicaraguan propaganda and political warfare actions by military analysts. The product of such analysis will permit an effective U.S. reaction to these initiatives at a strategic level. S/LPD's mission will suffer unless personnel are obtained to operate the analytical systems these personnel set up. By placing personnel in these positions, DoD has an opportunity to shape U.S. public diplomacy initiatives on Central America. I urge that DoD reconsider its turndown of support to S/LPD. As outlined by the President, the mission of S/LPD requires support from outside agencies to succeed.

Attachments:

Tab 1 - December 17, 1985, letter from Col. David Brown.
Tab 2 - September 18, 1985, letter to Col. Brown.
Tab 3 - NSC memorandum dated July 1, 1983.
Tab 4 - NSC memorandum dated August 1, 1984.

A memorandum from the S/LPD's Johnathan Miller to Patrick Buchanan at the White House gives an idea of some of the office's activities.

United States Department of State
Washington, D.C. 20320
March 13, 1985

CONFIDENTIAL, EYES ONLY

TO: Mr. Pat Buchanan
           Assistant to the President
           Director of Communications
           The White House

FROM: S/LPD - Johnathan S. Miller
SUBJECT: ''White Propaganda'' Operation
    Five illustrative examples of the Reich ''White Propaganda'' operation:

    ○ Attached is a copy of an op-ed piece that ran two days ago in <u>The Wall Street Journal</u>. Professor Guilmartin has been a consultant to our office and collaborated with our staff in the writing of this piece. It is devastating in its analysis of the Nicaraguan arms build-up. Officially, this office had no role in its preparation.

o In case you missed last night's NBC News with Tom Brokaw, you might ask WHCA to call up the Fred Francis story on the "Contras." This piece was prepared by Francis after he consulted two of our contractors who recently had made a clandestine trip to the freedom fighter camp along the Nicaragua/Honduras border (the purpose of this trip was to serve as a pre-advance for many selected journalists to visit the area and get a true flavor of what the freedom fighters are doing; i.e., not baby killing). Although I wasn't wild about the tag line, it was a positive piece.

o Two op-ed pieces, one for The Washington Post and one for The New York Times, are being prepared for the signatures of opposition leaders Alphonso Rubello [Alfonso Robelo], Adolpho Callero [Adolfo Calero] and Arturo Cruz. These two op-ed pieces are being prepared by one of our consultants and will serve as a reply to the outrageous op-ed piece by Daniel Ortega in today's New York Times.

o Through a cut-out, we are having the opposition leader Alphonso Rubello visit the following news organizations while he is in Washington this week: Hearst Newspapers, Newsweek Magazine, Scripps Howard Newspapers, The Washington Post (Editorial Board), and USA Today. In addition, the CNN "Freeman Report," the "McNeil-Lehrer Report," and the "Today Show" and CBS Morning News have been contacted about the availability of Mr. Rubello.

o Attached is a copy of a cable that we received today from Managua. The cable states that Congressman Lagomarsino took up Daniel Ortega's offer to visit any place in Nicaragua. You may remember that Ortega received a good deal of publicity on his "peace" proposal when he stated that he welcomed visits by members of Congress, stating that they would be free to go anywhere they wished. As the cable notes, the Congressman's request to visit an airfield was denied. Do not be surprised if this cable somehow hits the evening news.

I will not attempt in the future to keep you posted on all activities since we have too many balls in the air at any one time and since the work of our operation is ensured by keeping a low profile. I merely want to give you a flavor of some of the activities that hit our office on any one day and ask that, as you formulate ideas and plans of attack, you give us a heads-up since our office has been crafted to handle the concerns that you have in getting the President's program for the freedom fighters enacted.

Attachments:

1. Op-ed piece by Professor Guilmartin.
2. 85 Managua 1523.

The project to convince Congress to renew aid finally showed results, as representatives and senators wavered over the possibility of ill effects following from their past actions. In the summer of 1985, Congress approved $27 million in humanitarian assistance—food, clothing, medicine, and shelter—to sustain the Contra forces. The funds were not to be used for military purposes, and the CIA and the Department of Defense were expressly prohibited from operating the program. Thus, the Nicaraguan Humanitarian Assistance Office (NHAO) was established in the State Department under the leadership of Robert Duemling, a career diplomat.

The fact that the program was to be fully overt created some diplomatic difficulties inasmuch as Honduras continued to deny that there was any Contra presence on its soil. The new nonlethal supply operations had to be run out of Ilopango Airbase in El Salvador, which made it difficult for NHAO to keep track of actual deliveries in the field. The office also had considerable problems verifying invoices and payments.

With the State Department now handling nonlethal aid, North's operation could concentrate all of its resources on military equipment. Moreover, it could take advantage of the logistical support made available for NHAO. To do that, however, it needed to get someone (Robert Owen) on the inside. This was arranged through the Restricted Inter-Agency Group (RIG), which was chaired by Assistant Secretary of State for Inter-American Affairs Elliott Abrams and included North and Alan D. Fiers, the Chief of the CIA's Central American Task Force. They were all knowledgeable of the clandestine funding operations, which Duemling was not. Duemling's reference to having "the confidence of the persons represented at this meeting" suggests that he suspected they were keeping things from him through their own direct contacts with the Contras. Note that after June 1985, the Contras were nominally led by a collective civilian leadership known as the United Nicaraguan Opposition (UNO), which included Adolfo Calero, Alfonso Robelo, and Arturo Cruz (referred to in this memo as Triple-A).

SECRET

Highlights of RIG Meeting of Oct. 17, 1985

Participants:
    ARA - Abrams, Michel, Walker, Melton
    NSC - North, Burghardt
    CIA - [—]
    NHAO - Duemling, Arcos

N.B. - This meeting was called on urgent basis to discuss fallout from the episode involving NBC-TV crew riding UNO aircraft to Tegucigalpa, and renewed complaints from UNO that aid was not moving fast enough. Also, Triple-A were in town and had met with NHAO the previous day (10/16) for two hours.

Status report
    Duemling opened the meeting with brief status report on recent grants, L/Coms and disbursements. He noted the extreme difficulty of dealing with haphazard and incomplete UNO documents/proposals, citing requests for construction of a hospital and dispensaries without any supporting documentation. He also noted the ineffectiveness of UNO's designees [—a half line deleted—] who have no authority and apparently little understanding of the substance of UNO requests.

Buttressing UNO
    With some asperity, North lamented the NBC-TV crew episode and repeated his concern that funds are not flowing fast enough. He asserted that an expediter (Rob Owen) is needed, contending that the NBC-TV episode would not have occurred if Owen had been employed and on the scene.
    Abrams supported the concept of an expediter. Duemling outlined his reservations about introducing a middleman in the NHAO-UNO relationship and about Owen in particular.
    [—] pointed out from long experience that UNO will never be able to provide tidy or efficient paper work.

After considerable discussion, the meeting agreed that Rob Owen would be employed under the following conditions:

1. He will work for UNO, not NHAO.
2. He will serve as an expediter. Whenever NHAO is dissatisfied with an UNO presentation, it will buck it back to UNO for upgrading by Owen.
3. If Owen fails to perform, or becomes a liability, NHAO's commitment to him will be terminated. (Abrams and North agreed that Owen will be expendable if he becomes a political or diplomatic liability. Duemling pointed out Owen's association with Singlaub and North, and fact that Amb [—] had specifically rejected the idea of an American legman running around [—] on behalf of UNO and NHAO. Abrams said that we could defend his employment to Congress by noting that UNO had specifically asked for him, as he had already demonstrated effectiveness in working on UNO's behalf. If later experience proves otherwise, we will simply say that our experiment did not work and we therefore terminated it.)
4. Owen will be offered a much more restricted mandate than had been requested in the UNO letter. For example, he will not be granted authority to contract for additional assistance; his personal compensation will be at a much lower rate; precise limits will be placed on allowable expenditures for travel, etc.

UNO End-runs

Duemling expressed exasperation with UNO's practice of demanding action with scant consideration for constraints imposed on NHAO, and then complaining to their friends if they are not immediately gratified. Duemling stated that he could put up with the shortcomings of UNO and its members, but he would quit if he did not have the confidence of the persons represented at this meeting. (This announcement appeared to have a sobering effect, and served notice that constant complaining and end-running by UNO would not be tolerated.)

Duemling also pointed out that, in the interest of expediting aid, he had approved several invoices that were impossible to verify. He had done this in response to repeated complaints from Calero that UNO's credit had dried up and people were starving. But his action constituted an act of faith pure and simple, and was without even the minimum documentary evidence to confirm delivery.

Discussion of this problem led to agreement that NHAO will provide CIA with a list of disbursements (on a continuing basis) and CIA will instruct its personnel in the field to attempt to verify deliveries. [—] pointed out that their efforts will not cover 100$ of NHAO's disbursements but they will make a best effort. These reports from the field will be provided to NHAO for use in reporting to Congress on verification measures. Abrams emphasized the importance of verification, stating that it cannot be sacrificed.

RWDuemling 10/18/85
/handwritten: Cleared by Arcos/

IRAN

Seemingly unrelated events in a distant part of the world would eventually become entangled with the story of the Contra war. The Shah of Iran had left his country for the last time in January 1979. Many political activists in Iran had identified the Shah with the CIA since 1953. At that time, the CIA organized a coup that returned the Shah to the throne after he had been deposed by Prime Minister Mohammed Mossadeq.[32] Subsequently, anti-Shah and anti-American sentiments were closely entangled.

The revolution of 1979 brought to power the Ayatollah Ruhollah Khomeini at the head of a broad and diverse coalition. As factions contended over the future course of the revolution and the new Islamic Republic, a militant Islamist student group altered the playing field with a *fait accompli*. Prompted by the entry of the Shah into the United States for medical treatment and by reports that the prime minister of the provisional government had met with U.S. National Security Adviser Zbigniew K. Brzezinski in Algiers, the students seized the U.S. embassy in Tehran on 4 November 1979, taking the employees hostage. Fifty-two of these hostages remained in captivity within the building until January 1981. The act foreclosed any prospect of reconciliation between Iran and the United States and helped bring about the collapse of the moderate provisional government. Still, internal politics remained tumultuous for some time.

Unrelated to this, Israel invaded Lebanon in 1982 in an effort to break the Palestine Liberation Organization (PLO), which had been an active participant in the Lebanese civil war as well as a threat to Israel next door. With the PLO leadership trapped in Beirut, the United States, France, and Italy landed a joint peacekeeping force to permit the removal of the PLO from Lebanon to Tunisia, far from Israeli or Lebanese territory. After the evacuation of the PLO and then of the allied peacekeeping force, Israel permitted Lebanese Christian militiamen to perpetrate a massacre in Palestinian refugee camps around Beirut. With the intention of forestalling a new crisis and imposing order, the U.S., French, and Italian troops—still just off the coast—returned to take up positions around the city. Although well meaning, the new intervention had no plan and or explicit goals. With Lebanon still in a state of civil war, there were many elements that identified the imposition of order with a reimposition of the "old order" that they had been fighting. They therefore began launching attacks against the peacekeepers. Prominent among these elements were Shia (Shiite) Muslims, a large but traditionally disenfranchised population in Lebanon that had recently found a new ally in the Islamic Republic of Iran. In 1984, militant Shia began taking Americans hostage, including William Buckley, the CIA Chief of Station in Beirut.[33]

The United States organized an international arms embargo against Iran in 1983, and the State Department formally listed it as a sponsor of terrorism in January 1984. A number of officials were concerned, however, that the Iran policy might be counterproductive. Isolated internationally and at war with Saddam Hussein's Iraq since 1980, Iran might turn to the Soviet Union for help even if they were not natural allies in terms of ideology. In June 1985, National Security Adviser Robert C. McFarlane proposed an opening to Iran. Part of the proposal was a plan to help Iran bypass the arms embargo the United States had just organized. Defense Secretary Weinberger's response to the proposal was, "This is almost too absurd to comment on." State Secretary Shultz also rejected it immediately. Only DCI Casey seemed enthusiastic about the proposal, which his people had helped write.

In July 1985, the situation was altered by a message that came via Israel. The Iranians had expressed an interest in buying American-made arms from Israel for their war with Iraq. In return, they were willing to secure the release of American hostages held by Shia militants in Lebanon. McFarlane pressed the issue as an opportunity both to gain the release of the hostages and to open a dialog with moderates within the Iranian regime. This time, Secretary Shultz, who was en route to Australia and responded by cable, was not so categorical if still cautious.

SUBJECT: REPLY TO BACKCHANNEL NO. 3 FROM BUD [MCFARLANE]

1. TOP SECRET-ENTIRE TEXT
2. PLEASE HAVE FOLLOWING MESSAGES TYPED ON PLAIN BOND AND HAND-CARRIED E.O. TO BUD. ENVELOPE MUST BE GIVEN DIRECTLY TO HIM AND OPENED BY HIM AND NO ONE ELSE.
3. DEAR BUD.
    THANK YOU FOR YOUR MESSAGE ON THE ISRAEL-IRAN CONTACT. I AGREE WITH YOU THAT WE SHOULD MAKE A TENTATIVE SHOW OF INTEREST WITHOUT COMMITMENT. I DO NOT THINK WE COULD JUSTIFY TURNING OUR BACKS ON THE PROSPECT OF GAINING THE RELEASE OF THE OTHER SEVEN HOSTAGES AND PERHAPS DEVELOPING AN ABILITY TO RENEW TIES WITH IRAN UNDER A MORE SENSIBLE REGIME—ESPECIALLY WHEN PRESENTED TO US THROUGH THE PRIME MINISTER OF ISRAEL.
4. THAT BEING SAID, I FURTHER AGREE WITH YOU THAT THIS SITUATION IS LOADED WITH IMPONDERABLES THAT CALL FOR GREAT CAUTION ON OUR PART. I THINK YOU HAVE COVERED THEM ALL IN YOUR MESSAGE. I WOULD ONLY UNDERSCORE A COUPLE OF THEM. THE FRAUD THAT SEEMS TO ACCOMPANY SO MANY DEALS INVOLVING ARMS AND IRAN AND THE COMPLICATIONS THAT ARISE FROM OUR "BLESSING" AND ISRAEL-IRAN RELATIONSHIP WHERE ISRAEL'S INTERESTS AND OURS ARE NOT NECESSARILY THE SAME.
5. I SUGGEST—ANY YOUR MESSAGE INDICATES YOU LEAN THIS WAY TOO—THAT WE GIVE THE EMISSARY A POSITIVE BUT PASSIVE REPLY. THAT IS TELL HIM THAT HE MAY CONVEY TO HIS IRANIAN CONTACTS THAT THE U.S. HAS BEEN INFORMED OF THE IRANIAN PROPOSAL AND IS RECEPTIVE TO THE IDEA OF A PRIVATE DIALOGUE INVOLVING A SUSTAINED DISCUSSION OF U.S.-IRANIAN RELATIONS. IN OTHER WORDS, WE ARE WILLING TO LISTEN AND SERIOUSLY CONSIDER ANY STATEMENT ON THIS TOPIC THEY MAY WISH TO INITIATE.
6. GIVEN THE NATURE OF THIS MATTER, I AM INCLINED TO THINK IT SHOULD BE MANAGED BY YOU PERSONALLY. ITS SENSITIVITY REQUIRES HIGH-LEVEL MANAGEMENT, BUT THAT IN TURN RAISES THE LIKELIHOOD OF DISCLOSURE. BUT THIS IS SOMETHING THAT WE CAN GO OVER MORE CAREFULLY AFTER I GET BACK. I DO THINK IT IMPORTANT THAT YOU MAKE CLEAR TO THE EMISSARY THAT YOU AND I ARE IN CLOSE CONTACT AND FULL AGREEMENT EVERY STEP OF THE WAY. THIS IS ALL THE MORE IMPORTANT IN VIEW OF THE PRESENT LACK OF UNITY AND FULL COORDINATION ON THE ISRAELI SIDE.
7. THANK YOU AGAIN FOR YOUR MESSAGE. I CAN ONLY REITERATE HOW MUCH I VALUE OUR CLOSE CONSULTATION AND FRIENDSHIP.

GEORGE SHULTZ

There was a long-standing policy against negotiating with terrorists, inasmuch as it would encourage them to take more hostages to get what they want. Nonetheless, Reagan approved a plan to allow Israel to deliver TOW antitank missiles in exchange for four of the seven hostages held at that time. The first TOW missile delivery, however, resulted in the release of no hostages and the second in the release of one. A delivery of HAWK antiaircraft missiles followed that.

The HAWK delivery was a fiasco. Richard Secord, one of the private intermediaries, nearly compromised the mission by trying to bribe an official in Portugal and then allowing the lease on a rented aircraft to lapse. Duane Clarridge, now the Chief of the European Division in the CIA Directorate of Operations, had to intercede with various State Department officials in Portugal to keep Secord out of trouble and call on a CIA proprietary airline to transport the missiles. The missiles then proved not to be the variety of HAWK the Iranians had expected, leading them to reject the delivery. No hostages were released.

The presidential approvals for these operations were all verbal, leaving no written record. Upon learning of Clarridge's role in the HAWK missile delivery, after the fact, Deputy Director of Central Intelligence John McMahon insisted that a presidential finding be drawn up, even if it had to be written and signed retroactively.[34] This fact made the CIA nervous because it was involved in the operation and, if caught, was operating without written authorization.

Note that the finding attributes the efforts to seek the release of hostages to "private parties." These include Michael Ledeen, two Israelis, and Manucher Ghorbanifar who were functioning as intermediaries. Ledeen was a part-time consultant to the National Security Council. Ghorbanifar was an expatriate Iranian arms dealer with a shady past. He reportedly had ties to numerous intelligence agencies, including Iran's (both before and after the revolution) and Israel's. He had offered to sell information to the United States on previous occasions. Just one year earlier, in 1984, the CIA had issued a "burn notice," warning other agencies in the U.S. intelligence community that it considered him to be a fabricator and a nuisance.

> Finding Pursuant to Section 662 of the Foreign
> Assistance Act of 1961, As Amended, Concerning
> Operations Undertaken by the Central Intelligence
> Agency in Foreign Countries, Other Than Those
> Intended Solely for the Purpose of Intelligence
> Collection

I have been briefed on the efforts being made by private parties to obtain the release of Americans held hostage in the Middle East, and hereby find that the following operations in foreign countries (including all support necessary to such operations) are important to the national security of the United States. Because of the extreme sensitivity of these operations, in the exercise of the President's constitutional authorities, I direct the Director of Central Intelligence not to brief the Congress of the United States, as provided for in Section 501 of the National Security Act of 947, as amended, until such time as I may direct otherwise.

SCOPE	DESCRIPTION
Hostage rescue— Middle East	The provision of assistance by the Central Intelligence Agency to private parties in their attempt to obtain the release of Americans held hostage in the Middle East. Such assistance is to include the provision of transportation, communications, and other necessary support. As part of these efforts certain foreign material and munitions may be provided to the Government of Iran which is taking steps to facilitate the release of the American hostages.
	All prior actions taken by U.S. Government officials in furtherance of this effort are hereby ratified.
The White House Washington, D.C.	

In reaction to the turmoil, the administration was determined to take direct control of the Iranian supply mission. This called for yet another finding by President Reagan. On 17 January 1986, John M. Poindexter, Reagan's fourth National Security Adviser, sent him a memorandum and a finding to be signed. This time the reasoning put more emphasis on the geopolitical implications of strengthening moderate tendencies within the Iranian government, downplaying the notion that the administration was bargaining for the release of hostages.

Do not assume, however—as many have—that the quest for an improved geostrategic relationship was a false cover for an endeavor actually intended just to free the hostages. Reagan himself was deeply concerned about the fate of the hostages. Secretary Shultz, on the other hand, was intrigued by the idea of improving relations with Iran but opposed to trading arms for hostages. DCI Casey was nearly alone among top officials in backing the president's position on hostages. Robert Gates later suggested that Casey's interest in the Iran initiative was rooted in three factors: a concern that the Soviet Union might take advantage of Iranian instability to expand its influence in the Middle East; the nagging of Reagan's near-daily plea, "We just have to get those people out"; and a political notion that this would put him on the president's side of an issue that George Shultz was opposing (and if it failed, the NSC would take the heat). Gates also pointed out that, according to CIA analysts, there were moderates in the Iranian political spectrum when it came to domestic issues, such as economic policy, but there were no moderates on the question of relations with the United States. Those who favored the policy, however, chose to ignore this.[35]

THE WHITE HOUSE
WASHINGTON
January 17, 1986

ACTION
MEMORANDUM FOR THE PRESIDENT
FROM: JOHN M. POINDEXTER
SUBJECT: Covert Action Finding Regarding Iran

Prime Minister [Shimon] Peres of Israel secretly dispatched his special advisor on terrorism with instructions to propose a plan by which Israel, with limited assistance from the U.S., can create conditions to help bring about a more moderate government in Iran. The Israelis are very concerned that Iran's deteriorating position in the war with Iraq, the potential for further radicalization in Iran, and the possibility of enhanced Soviet influence in the Gulf all pose significant threats to the security of Israel. They believe it is essential that they act to at least preserve a balance of power in the region.

The Israeli plan is premised on the assumption that moderate elements in Iran can come to power if these factions demonstrate their credibility in defending Iran against Iraq and in deterring Soviet intervention. To achieve the strategic goal of a more moderate Iranian government, the Israelis are prepared to unilaterally commence selling military materiel to Western-oriented Iranian factions. It is their belief that by so doing they can achieve a heretofore unobtainable penetration of the Iranian governing hierarchy. The Israelis are convinced that the Iranians are so desperate for military materiel, expertise and intelligence that the provision of these resources will result in favorable long-term changes in personnel and attitudes within the Iranian government. Further, once the exchange relationship has commenced, a dependency would be established on those who are providing the requisite resources, thus allowing the provider(s) to coercively influence near-term events. Such an outcome is consistent with our policy objectives and would present significant advantages for U.S. national interests. As described by the Prime Minister's emissary, the only requirement the Israelis have is an assurance that they will be allowed to purchase U.S. replenishments for the stocks that they sell to Iran. We have researched the legal problems of Israel's selling U.S. manufactured arms to Iran. Because of the requirement in U.S. law for recipients of U.S. arms to notify the U.S. government of transfers to third countries, I do not recommend that you agree with the specific details of the Israeli plan. However, there is another possibility. Some time ago Attorney General William French Smith determined that under an appropriate finding you could authorize the CIA to sell arms to countries outside of the provisions of the laws and reporting requirements for foreign military sales. The objectives of the Israeli plan could be met if the CIA, using an authorized agent as necessary, purchased arms from the Department of Defense under the Economy Act and then transferred them to Iran directly after receiving appropriate payment from Iran.

The Covert Action Finding attached at Tab A provides the latitude for the transactions indicated above to proceed. The Iranians have indicated an immediate requirement for 4,000 basic TOW weapons for use in the launchers they already hold.

The Israelis are also sensitive to a strong U.S. desire to free our Beirut hostages and have insisted that the Iranians demonstrate both influence and good intent by an early release of the five Americans. Both sides have agreed that the hostages will be immediately released upon commencement of this action. Prime Minister Peres had his emissary pointedly note that they well understand our position on not making concessions to terrorists, and organizations are significantly easier to influence through governments than they are by direct approach. In that we have been unable to exercise any suasion over Hizballah[36] during the course of nearly two years of kidnappings, this approach through the government of Iran may well be our <u>only</u> way to achieve the release of the Americans held in Beirut. It must again be noted that since this dialogue with the Iranians began in September, Reverend Weir has been released and there have been no Shia terrorist attacks against American or Israeli persons, property, or interests.

Therefore it is proposed that Israel make the necessary arrangements for the sale of 4,000 TOW weapons to Iran. Sufficient funds to cover the sale would be transferred to an agent of the CIA. The CIA would then purchase the weapons from the Department of Defense and deliver the weapons to Iran through the agent. If all of the hostages are not released after the first shipment of 1,000 weapons, further transfers would cease.

On the other hand, since hostage release is in some respect a byproduct of a larger effort to develop ties to potentially moderate forces in Iran, you may wish to redirect such transfers to other groups within the government at a later time.

The Israelis have asked for our urgent response to this proposal so that they can plan accordingly. They note that conditions inside both Iran and Lebanon are highly volatile. The Israelis are cognizant that this entire operation will be terminated if the Iranians abandon their goal of moderating their government or allow further acts of terrorism. You have discussed the general outlines of the Israeli plan with Secretaries Shultz and Weinberger, Attorney General Meese[37] and Director Casey. The Secretaries do not recommend you proceed with this plan. Attorney General Meese and Director Casey believe the short-term and long-term objectives of the plan warrant the policy risks involved and recommend you approve the attached Finding. Because of the extreme sensitivity of this project, it is recommended that you exercise your statutory prerogative to withhold notification of the Finding to the Congressional oversight committees until such time that you deem it to be appropriate.

Recommendation

<u>OK</u> <u>NO</u>

___ ___ That you sign the attached Finding.

Prepared by:
Oliver L. North

Attachment
    Tab A-Covert Action Finding

<u>Finding Pursuant to Section 662 of</u>
<u>The Foreign Assistance Act of 1961</u>
<u>As Amended, Concerning Operations</u>
<u>Undertaken by the Central Intelligence</u>
<u>Agency in Foreign Countries, Other Than</u>
<u>Those Intended Solely for the Purpose</u>
<u>of Intelligence Collection</u>

I hereby find that the following operation in a foreign country (including all support necessary to such operation) is important to the national security of the United States, and due to its extreme sensitivity and security risks, I determine it is essential to limit prior notice, and direct the Director of Central Intelligence to refrain from reporting this Finding to the Congress as provided in Section 501 of the National Security Act of 1947, as amended, until I otherwise direct.

<u>SCOPE</u>   <u>DESCRIPTION</u>

Iran   Assist selected friendly foreign liaison services, third countries and third parties which have established relationships with Iranian elements, groups, and individuals sympathetic to U.S. Government interests and which do not conduct or support terrorist actions directed against U.S. persons, property or interests, for the purpose of: (1) establishing a more moderate government in Iran, (2) obtaining from them significant intelligence not otherwise obtainable, to determine the current Iranian Government's intentions with respect to its neighbors and with respect to terrorist acts, and (3) furthering the release of the American hostages held in Beirut and preventing additional terrorist acts by these groups. Provide funds, intelligence, counter-intelligence, training, guidance and communications and other necessary assistance to these elements, groups, individuals, liaison services and third countries in support of these activities.

The USG will act to facilitate efforts by third parties and third countries to establish contact with moderate elements within and outside the Government of Iran by providing these elements with arms, equipment and related material in order to enhance the credibility of these elements in their effort to achieve a more pro-U.S. government in Iran by demonstrating their ability to obtain requisite resources to defend their country against Iraq and intervention by the Soviet Union. This support will be discontinued if the U.S. Government learns that these elements have abandoned their goals of moderating their government and appropriated the materiel for purposes other than that provided by this Finding.

/signed Ronald Reagan/

The White House
Washington, D.C.
Date January 17, 1986

The finding was signed by the president as indicated. Curiously, the "OK" space of the attached cover memo was initialed "RR per JP," indicating that National Security Adviser Poindexter initialed it on Reagan's behalf. A hand-written note at the end of the memo stated, "President was briefed verbally from this paper. VP, Don Regan, and Don Fortier were present. JP."[38]

On or about 4 April 1986, Oliver North wrote a memorandum to President Reagan titled "Release of American Hostages in Beirut." The memo outlines some of the practical complications involved in the negotiations with the Iranians and also with the intermediaries. It also gives some idea of the monies being siphoned off by various intermediaries at different points in the process. Most significantly, however, it designates that part of the monies raised by selling arms to Iran would be diverted to support the Contra war in Nicaragua. A "smoking gun" of sorts, the recommendation came to be known as the "Diversion Memo."

TOP SECRET   SENSITIVE

RELEASE OF AMERICAN HOSTAGES IN BEIRUT

Background. In June 1985, private American and Israeli citizens commenced an operation to effect the release of the American hostages in Beirut in exchange for providing certain factions in Iran with U.S.-origin Israeli military materiel. By September, U.S. and Israeli Government officials became involved in this endeavor in order to ensure that the USG would:

- ○ not object to the Israeli transfer of embargoed materiel to Iran;
- ○ sell replacement items to Israel as replenishment for like items sold to Iran by Israel.

On September 15, the Israeli Government, with the endorsement of the USG, transferred 508 basic TOW missiles to Iran. Forty-eight hours later, Reverend Benjamin Weir was released in Beirut.[39]

Subsequent efforts by both governments to continue this process have met with frustration due to the need to communicate our intentions through an Iranian expatriate arms dealer [Manucher Ghorbanifar] in Europe. In January 1986, under the provisions of a new Covert Action Finding, the USG demanded a meeting with responsible Iranian government officials.

On February 20, a U.S. Government official met with [—just over one line deleted—] the first direct U.S.-Iranian contact in over five years. At this meeting, the U.S. side made an effort to refocus Iranian attention on the threat posed by the Soviet Union and the need to establish a longer term relationship between our two countries based on more than arms transactions. It was emphasized that the hostage issue was a "hurdle" which must be crossed before this improved relationship could prosper. During the meeting, it also became apparent that our conditions/demands had not been accurately transmitted to the Iranian Government by the intermediary and it was agreed that:

- ○ The USG would establish its good faith and bona fides by immediately providing 1,000 TOW missiles for sale to Iran. This transaction was covertly completed on February 21, using a private U.S. firm and the Israelis as intermediaries.
- ○ A subsequent meeting would be held in Iran with senior U.S. and Iranian officials during which the U.S. hostages would be released.
- ○ Immediately after the hostages were safely in our hands, the U.S. would sell an additional 3,000 TOW missiles to Iran using the same procedures employed during the September 1985 transfer.

In early March, the Iranian expatriate intermediary demanded that Iranian conditions for release of the hostages now included the prior sale of 200 PHOE-NIX missiles and an unspecified number of HARPOON missiles, in addition to the 3,000 TOWs which would be delivered after the hostages were released. A subsequent meeting was held with the intermediary in Paris on March 8, wherein it was explained that the requirement for prior deliveries violated the understanding reached in Frankfurt on February 20, and were therefore unacceptable. It was further noted that the Iranian aircraft and ship launchers for these missiles were in such disrepair that the missiles could not be launched even if provided.

From March 9 until March 30, there was no further effort undertaken on our behalf to contact the Iranian Government or the intermediary. On March 26, [—] made an unsolicited call to the phone-drop in Maryland which we had established for this purpose. [—] asked why we had not been in contact and urged that we proceed expeditiously since the situation in Beirut was deteriorating rapidly. He was informed by our Farsi-speaking interpreter that the conditions requiring additional materiel beyond the 3,000 TOWs were unacceptable and that we could in no case provide anything else prior to release of our hostages. [—] observed that we were correct in our assessment of their inability to use PHOENIX and HARPOON missiles and that the most urgent requirement that Iran had was to place their current HAWK missile inventory in working condition. In a subsequent phone call, we agreed to discuss this matter with him and he indicated that he would prepare an inventory of parts required to make their HAWK systems operational. This parts list was received on March 28, and verified by CIA.

Current Situation. On April 3, Ari Gorbanifahr [sic], the Iranian intermediary, arrived in Washington, D.C., with instructions from [—] to consummate final arrangements for the return of the hostages. Gorbanifahr was reportedly enfranchised to negotiate the types, quantities, and delivery procedures for materiel the U.S. would sell to Iran through Israel. The meeting lasted nearly all night on April 3–4, and involved numerous calls to Tehran. [—about four lines deleted—]A Farsi-speaking CIA officer in attendance was able to verify the substance of his calls to Tehran during the meeting. Subject to Presidential approval, it was agreed to proceed as follows:

- o By Monday, April 7, the Iranian Government will transfer $17 million to an Israeli account in Switzerland. The Israelis will, in turn, transfer to a private U.S. corporation account in Switzerland the sum of $15 million.
- o On Tuesday, April 8 (or as soon as the transactions are verified), the private U.S. corporation will transfer $3.651 million to a CIA account in Switzerland. CIA will then transfer this sum to a covert Department of the Army account in the U.S.
- o On Wednesday, April 9, the CIA will commence procuring $3.651 million worth of HAWK missile parts (240 separate line items) and transferring these parts to [—just under one line deleted—] This process is estimated to take seven working days.
- o On Friday, April 18, a private U.S. aircraft (707B) will pick up the HAWK missile parts at [—] and fly them to a covert Israeli airfield for prepositioning (this field was used for the earlier delivery of the 1,000 TOWs). At this field, the parts will be transferred to an Israeli Defense Forces' (IDF) aircraft with false markings. A SATCOM [satellite communications] capability will be positioned at this location
- o On Saturday, April 19, McFarlane, North, Teicher, Cave,[40] [—] and a SATCOM communicator will board a CIA aircraft in Frankfurt, Germany, en route to Tehran. [—just over one line deleted—]

o On Sunday, April 20, the following series of events will occur:

  o U.S. party arrives Tehran (A-hour)—met by Rafsanjani,[41] as head of the Iranian delegation.
  o At A+7 hours, the U.S. hostages will be released in Beirut.
  o At A+15 hours, the IDF aircraft with the HAWK missile parts aboard will land at Bandar Abbas, Iran.

<u>Discussion</u>. The following points are relevant to this transaction, the discussions in Iran, and the establishment of a broader relationship between the United States and Iran:

  o The Iranians have been told that our presence in Iran is a "holy commitment" on the part of the USG that we are sincere and can be trusted. There is great distrust of the U.S. among the various Iranian parties involved. Without our presence on the ground in Iran, they will not believe hat we will fulfill our end of the bargain after the hostages are released.
  o [—just over two lines deleted—] Gorbanifahr specifically mentioned that [Libyan leader Muammar al-] Qhadhaffi's efforts to "buy" the hostages could succeed in the near future. Further, the Iranians are well aware that the situation in Beirut is deteriorating rapidly and that the ability of the IRGC [Islamic Revolutionary Guard Corps] to effect the release of the hostages will become increasingly more difficult over time.
  o We have convinced the Iranians of a significant near term and long-range threat from the Soviet Union. We have real and deceptive intelligence to demonstrate this threat during the visit. They have expressed considerable interest in this matter as part of the longer-term relationship.
  o [—paragraph deleted; about four lines—]
  o The Iranians have been told that their provision of assistance to Nicaragua is unacceptable to us and they have agreed to discuss this matter in Tehran.
  o We have further indicated to the Iranians that we wish to discuss steps leading to a cessation of hostilities between Iran and Iraq. [—about four lines deleted—]
  o The Iranians are well aware that their most immediate needs are for technical assistance in maintaining their air force and navy. We should expect that they will raise this issue during the discussion in Tehran. Further conversation with Gorbanifahr on April 4 indicates that they will want to raise the matter of the original 3,000 TOWs as a significant deterrent to a potential Soviet move against Iran. They have also suggested that, if agreement is reached to provide the TOWs [—about four lines deleted—]
  o The Iranians have been told and agreed that they will receive neither blame nor credit for the seizure of the hostages. [—about two-thirds of a line deleted—]
  o The residual funds from this transaction are allocated as follows:

    o $2 million will be used to purchase replacement TOWs for the original 508 sold by Israel to Iran for the release of Benjamin Weir. This is the only way that we have found to meet our commitment to replenish these stocks.
    o $12 million will be used to purchase critically needed supplies for the Nicaraguan Democratic Resistance Forces. This materiel is essential to cover shortages in resistance inventories resulting from their current offensives and Sandinista counter-attacks and to "bridge" the period between now and when Congressionally-approved lethal assistance (beyond the $25 million in "defensive" arms) can be delivered.

The ultimate objective in the trip to Tehran is to commence the process of improving U.S.-Iranian relations. Both sides are aware that the Iran-Iraq War is a major factor that must be discussed. We should not, however, view this meeting as a session which will result in immediate Iranian agreement to proceed to a settlement with Iraq. Rather, this meeting, the first high-level U.S.-Iranian contact in five years, should be seen as a chance to move in this direction. These discussions, as well as follow-on talks, should be governed by the Terms of Reference (TOR) (Tab A) with the recognition that this is, hopefully, the first of many meetings and that the hostage issue, once behind us, improves the opportunities for this relationship.

Finally, we should recognize that the Iranians will undoubtedly want to discuss additional arms and commercial transactions as "quids" for accommodating [—about a half line deleted—] Nicaragua, and Iraq. Our emphasis on the Soviet military and subversive threat, a useful mechanism in bringing them to agreement on the hostage issue, has also served to increase their desire for means to protect themselves against/deter the Soviets.

RECOMMENDATION

That the President approve the structure depicted above under "Current Situation" and the Terms of Reference at Tab A.

Approve _____ Disapprove _____

Attachment
  Tab A - U.S.-Iranian Terms of Reference

THE END OF THE AFFAIR

In the summer of 1986, Congress reversed itself and approved $100 million in aid for the Contras to be distributed by the CIA. The program was to take effect at the beginning of the new fiscal year, on 1 October 1986. As a consequence, North sought to *sell* the assets he had accumulated through his operation, Project Democracy (PRODEM), to the agency. On the other hand, the CIA was no doubt concerned about how it would explain where the equipment came from. The following is a PROFS note (an early form of e-mail) from North to National Security Adviser John M. Poindexter. Note that North makes no mention of the money already available from the Iran arms sale diversion. It has been speculated that North was building resources for future unauthorized operations.

From: NSOLN—CPUA   Date and time 07/24/86 15:55:57
To: NSJMP—CPUA

*** Reply to note of 07/15/85 14:07
NOTE FROM OLIVER NORTH
Subject: PRIVATE BLANK CHECK

We are rapidly approaching the point where the PROJECT DEMOCRACY assets in CentAm need to be turned over to the CIA for use in the new program. The total value of the assets (six aircraft, warehouses, vehicles, supplies, munitions, communications equipment, and a 6520' runway on property owned by a PRODEM proprietary) is over $4.5M.

All the assets—and the personnel—are owned/paid by overseas companies with no U.S. connection. All of the equipment is in first-rate condition and is already in place. It wd be ludicrous for this to simply disappear just because CIA does not want to be "tainted" with picking up the assets and then have them spend $8–10M of the $100M to replace it—weeks or months later. Yet, that seems to be the direction they are heading, apparently based on NSC guidance.

If you have already given Casey instructions to this effect, I would very much like to talk to you about it in hopes that we can reclama [sic] the issue. All seriously believe that immediately after the Senate vote the DRF [Democratic Resistance Forces] will be subjected to a major Sandinista effort to break them before the U.S. aid can become effective. PRODEM currently has the only assets available to support the DRF and the CIA's most ambitious estimate is 30 days after a bill is signed before their own assets will be available. This will be a disaster for the DRF if they have to wait that long. Given our lack of movement on other funding options, and Elliott/Allen's plea for PRODEM to get food to the resistance ASAP, PRODEM will have to borrow at least $2M to pay for the food. That's O.K., and Dick [Secord] is willing to do so tomorrow—but only if there is reasonable assurance that the lenders can be repaid. The only way that the $2M in food money can be repaid is if CIA purchases the $4.5M+ worth of PRODEM equipment for about $2.25M when the law passes. You should be aware that CIA has already approached PRODEM's chief pilot to ask him where they (CIA) can purchase more of the C-135 A/C [aircraft]. The chief pilot told them where they can get them commercially from the USAF as excess—the same way PRODEM bought them under proprietary arrangements. It is just unbelievable. If you wish I can send you a copy of the PROJECT DEMOCRACY status report which includes a breakdown of assets. It is useful, nonattributable reading. Warm regards. North.

The CIA, however, sought to distance itself from North's illicit operations, specifically the donations from private parties. The Boland Amendment had expressly forbidden the CIA from arming the Contras. Casey had strongly favored raising money from foreign governments, but, according to Gates, he made a distinction between this and soliciting private funds, despite the fact that he had himself suggested establishing a private foundation in his memo of 27 March 1984. Gates, recently named Deputy Director of Central Intelligence, made a note of the following exculpatory statement solicited from North.

EYES ONLY
10 October 1986

MEMORANDUM FOR THE RECORD
SUBJECT: Lunch with Ollie North

1. The DCI and I had lunch with Ollie North on 9 October to receive a debriefing on his meetings in Frankfurt. During the course of the lunch, North confirmed to the DCI and to me that, based on his knowledge of the private funding efforts for the Contras, CIA is completely clean on the question of any contact with those organizing the funding and the operation. He affirmed that a clear separation had been maintained between the private efforts and all CIA assets and individuals, including proprietaries. (TS)
2. During the course of the meeting, I urged the DCI to insist on getting a copy of the Iran Finding from John Poindexter. (S)

/initialed/
Robert M. Gates
Deputy Director of Central Intelligence

The timing of this lunch and statement may have been influenced, as suggested by Gates, by the fact that the National Intelligence Officer for Terrorism had told Casey on 7 October that he suspected monies from the Iranian arms sales were being diverted to fund the Contras.[42] However, it may also have been influenced by the fact that on 5 October, one of the contract aircraft resupplying the Contras out of El Salvador's Ilopango Airbase went missing, as recorded in the following CIA cable.

SUBJECT: DISAPPEARANCE OF SOUTHERN FRONT SUPPLY AIRCRAFT

1. C/MILGROUP TOLD [—] ON MORNING OF 6 OCT THAT PRIVATE BENEFACTOR C-123 ENGAGED IN DROPPING SUPPLIES TO SOUTHERN FRONT DID NOT RETURN TO ILOPANGO FROM SCHEDULED DAYLIGHT MISSION ON 5 OCT. AIRCRAFT LEFT ILOPANGO AT 0930 LOCAL, WAS TO FLY DOWN PACIFIC COAST OF NICARAGUA, TURN WEST OVER CABO SANTA ELENA IN COSTA RICA, AND THEN EVENTUALLY TURN NORTH, ENTER NICARAGUA AND MAKE DROP. AIRCRAFT WAS NEVER HEARD FROM AGAIN AFTER LEAVING ILOPANGO AND RECIPIENTS ON GROUND IN NICARAGUA NEVER SAW OR HEARD IT. AIRCRAFT CREW CONSISTS OF THREE U.S. CITIZENS AND ONE NICARAGUAN.

2. ACCORDING TO C/MILGROUP THERE IS A REMOTE POSSIBILITY THAT AIRCRAFT IS DOWN AT MURCIELAGO OR ONE OF THE OTHER SMALL AIRFIELDS IN CABO SANTA ELENA AREA BECAUSE OF MECHANICAL PROBLEMS AND THAT IT HAS BEEN SO FAR UNABLE TO COMMUNICATE ITS LOCATION. OTHER POSSIBILITIES ARE THAT IS CRASHED, EITHER AT SEA OR IN COSTA RICA OR NICARAGUA. EXACT INFO ON AIRCRAFT CARGO IS NOT AVAILABLE HERE. HOWEVER, C/MILGROUP INDICATES THERE IS A GOOD POSSIBILITY THAT WEAPONS AND/OR AMMO WERE ABOARD.

3. ABOVE IS BASICALLY FOR INFO OF ADDEES [that is, addressees], PARTICULARLY IN LIGHT OF POSSIBLE POLITICAL PROBLEMS WHICH MIGHT RESULT IN REGION IF AIRCRAFT DID INDEED GO DOWN IN NICARAGUA OR COSTA RICA. WOULD ALSO APPRECIATE, HOWEVER, ANY OTHER INFO ON THIS INCIDENT WHICH ADDEES MIGHT BE ABLE TO PROVIDE, PARTICULARLY FROM SAN JOSE END.

4. NO FILE. DECL OADR DRV [—] ALL SECRET.

END OF MESSAGE   SECRET

The missing plane was the beginning of the end for the entire operation. The aircraft had been shot down over Nicaragua by a shoulder-fired missile. Soon, the sole surviving crewmember, Eugene Hasenfus, appeared on Nicaraguan television. The story of the clandestine resupply of the Contras was out. Then on 3 November 1986, a Lebanese magazine broke the story of Robert McFarlane's trip to Iran, confirmed the next day by Ali Akbar Hashemi Rafsanjani. Hezbollah announced that it had recently released a hostage because of American "overtures." Soon word of the diversion of funds was public as well. North was dismissed and Poindexter was "allowed to resign" as the administration sought to avoid a political crisis and distance itself from the notions that it had conducted an illegal war, negotiated with terrorists, and sold missiles to a country it was trying to isolate as a supporter of international terrorism.

The results of the Iranian arms-for-hostages initiative had been mixed, at best. Not only did some deliveries fail to result in the release of hostages, but more hostages were taken. William Buckley, the CIA Chief of Station in Beirut, and some of the others were killed. The release of the last surviving hostage came only in December 1991 and had less to do with American policy then with changing political circumstances in Lebanon and the Middle East.

In Nicaragua, the collapse of the clandestine program actually contributed to a regional settlement. The renewed CIA funding was allowed to flow from October 1986 through September 1987 but, in the wake of the Iran-Contra revelations, Congress refused to approve another yearlong extension. There were monthly extensions through February 1988, and then the money ended forever. Without any future prospects, the Contras agreed to a settlement with the Sandinistas, which was mediated by other Central American leaders (in particular, Costa Rican President Óscar Arias, who won the 1987 Nobel Peace Prize for his efforts). The treaty called for cease-fires, amnesties, and free elections in countries throughout the region. People in the CIA and elsewhere in the Reagan administration dismissed the promises of the Sandinistas out of hand and viewed the treaty as the final defeat of the Contra war.[43]

The Sandinistas, however, were in equally dire straits, which explains their willingness to negotiate even after the Contras had lost their support. After years of guerrilla warfare and U.S.-enforced sanctions, the Nicaraguan economy was in ruins and half of the national budget was dedicated to fighting Contras. The Soviet Union, now led by Mikhail Gorbachev, was uninterested sustaining another destitute Third World ally and was increasing unable to do so. Ortega actually moved the Nicaraguan election up to February 1990 from the promised date of 1991. The election was free and fair. The Sandinistas lost, and Nicaragua's revolutionary experiment was at an end.[44]

NOTES

1. For general background on Nicaragua, the Contra war, and the Iran-Contra affair, see Tim Merrill, ed., *Nicaragua: A Country Study*, 3rd ed. (Washington, D.C.: U.S. Government Printing Office, 1994); Thomas W. Walker, *Nicaragua: Living in the Shadow of the Eagle*, 4th ed. (Boulder, CO: Westview Press, 2003); Dennis Gilbert, *Sandinistas: The Party and the Revolution* (New York: Blackwell, 1988); Robert Kagan, *A Twilight Struggle: American Power and Nicaragua, 1977–1990* (New York: Free Press, 1996); Helen Chapin Metz, ed., *Iran: A Country Study* (Washington, D.C.: U.S. Government Printing Office, 1989); Theodore Draper, *A Very Thin Line: The Iran-Contra Affairs* (New York: Wang and Hill, 1991); Lawrence E. Walsh, *Final Report of the Independent Counsel for Iran/Contra Matters*, 3 vols. (Washington, D.C.: U.S. Government Printing Office, 1993); Lawrence E. Walsh, *Firewall: The Iran-Contra Conspiracy and Cover-Up* (New York: W. W. Norton, 1997). For further documentation, see Peter Kornbluh and Malcolm Byrne, eds., *The Iran-Contra Scandal: The Declassified History* (New York: New Press, 1993).

2. Ronald Reagan, *The Reagan Diaries*, ed. By Douglas Brinkley (New York: HarperCollins, 2007): entries for 31 January 1981 (p. 2), 16 October 1981 (p. 44), 24 September 1982 (p. 102).

3. Kagan, *A Twilight Struggle*, 161.

4. Kagan, *A Twilight Struggle*, 159–164; Gilbert, *Sandinistas*, 163–164; William M. LeoGrande, "The United States and Nicaragua," in Thomas W. Walker, ed., *Nicaragua: The First Five Years* (New York: Praeger, 1985): 427–430.

5. Robert M. Gates, *From the Shadows: The Ultimate Insider's Story of Five Presidents and How They Won the Cold War* (New York: Simon & Schuster, 1997): 304.

6. Gates, *From the Shadows*, 242. Gates became Deputy Director for Intelligence early in 1982, at the age of thirty-eight, and Deputy Director of Central Intelligence in 1986. He was nominated by President Reagan to be Director of Central Intelligence in 1987, after Casey's death, but failed to win confirmation in the Senate at that time because of suspicions about his role regarding Nicaragua. He became Director of Central Intelligence under President George H. W. Bush and Secretary of Defense in the last years of the administration of President George W. Bush.

7. Duane R. Clarridge, with Digby Diehl, *A Spy for All Seasons: My Life in the CIA* (New York: Scribner, 1997): 193.

8. Gates, *From the Shadows*, 246, 293–294; Clarridge, *A Spy for All Seasons*, 203.

9. Cited in Gates, *From the Shadows*, 294. Gates doubts that Stein knew any more than McMahon. Whether Casey really did not know may be another question.

10. Gates, *From the Shadows*, 242–243; Clarridge, *A Spy for All Seasons*, 194. See also Alexander M. Haig, Jr., *Caveat: Realism, Reagan, and Foreign Policy* (New York: Macmillan, 1984).

11. Clarridge, *A Spy for All Seasons*, 197.

12. In Spanish orthography, "c" alternates with "z," with "c" used before "i" and "e" and "z" used before all other letters. Hence, Somoza becomes Somocista. In Castillian Spanish, both letters are pronounced "th," but in Latin America they are pronounced the same as "s." For the "k" sound, "c" alternates with "qu." Hence, a follower of Franco is a Franquista.

13. Tim Weiner, *Legacy of Ashes*, 380.

14. EPS stands for Ejército Popular Sandinista (Sandinista People's Army, the army of Nicaragua); ERP stands for Ejército Revolucionario del Pueblo (People's Revolutionary Army), a member of the rebel FMLN alliance in El Salvador.

15. Kornbluh and Byrne, *Iran-Contra Scandal*, 3.

16. Stephen Kinzer, "Nicaraguan Port Thought to Be Mined," *New York Times* (16 March 1984); Philip Taubman, "Americans on Ship Said to Supervise Nicaragua Mining," *New York Times* (8 April 1984).

17. *Congressional Record—Senate* (5 November 1991): S15923.

18. The Pershing missiles were intermediate-range ballistic missiles deployed by the United States in certain NATO countries in 1982 despite widespread popular resistance by Europeans who believed their presence would disrupt relations with the Soviet Union.

19. In 1980, three American nuns and one lay missionary were abducted, raped, and murdered by Salvadoran troops. According to a 1993 State Department report, "This particular act of barbarism did more to inflame the debate over El Salvador in the United States than any other single incident."

20. Misura was an armed Indian group from the Atlantic coast allied with the FDN.

21. James Baker was White House Chief of Staff at this time, during Reagan's first term. He served as Secretary of the Treasury in Reagan's second term and as Secretary of State under President George H. W. Bush.

22. MX was a new intercontinental ballistic missile under development by the Reagan administration while arms control negotiations continued with the Soviet Union.

23. Walsh, *Final Report of the Independent Counsel*, vol. 1, 202.

24. The manual was later published in the United States as *Psychological Operations in Guerrilla Warfare* (New York: Vintage, 1985).

25. Gates, *From the Shadows*, 294–295, 391.

26. General Gustavo Álvarez Martínez, formally the police commander, had become commander in chief of the Honduran armed forces. He was reportedly connected to death squads and privately praised the "Argentine method" of dealing with subversives. His fellow officers accused him of abusing his authority and forced him into exile in March 1984.

27. Gates, *From the Shadows*, 391–395.

28. John K. Singlaub, a retired major general and former commander of U.S. forces in South Korea, was the chairman of the World Anti-Communist League and its affiliate, the United States Council for World Freedom. In addition to actively soliciting funds for the Contra forces, he claimed that monies being raised by the NSC staff from foreign governments were actually donations from private citizens to his organization.

29. Reference is to the second Boland Amendment.

30. Roberto Suazo, Luis Alberto Monge, and José Napoleón Duarte were the presidents of Honduras, Costa Rica, and El Salvador, respectively.

31. Grenada is a small island nation in the eastern Caribbean. In 1982, President Reagan ordered U.S. troops to invade the island and overthrow its leftist government, prompted by a coup d'état by one Grenadan government faction against another.

32. Gasiorowski, Mark J., and Malcolm Byrne, eds., *Mohammad Mossadeq and the 1953 Coup in Iran* (Syracuse, NY: Syracuse University Press, 2004); Kermit Roosevelt, *Countercoup: The Struggle for the Control of Iran* (New York: McGraw-Hill, 1979).

33. Not to be confused with William F. Buckley, Jr., founder of the *National Review*, who also worked for the CIA at one time.

34. Gates, *From the Shadows*, 396.

35. Ibid., 397–398.

36. Hizballah ("Party of God"), also spelled Hezbollah, is a pro-Iranian Shia party in Lebanon.

37. Former White House aide Edwin Meese III had replaced William French Smith as Attorney General.

38. The vice president was George H. W. Bush. Donald Regan, the treasury secretary during Reagan's first term, was now the White House Chief of Staff. Donald Fortier (the least legible name) was a member of the National Security Council staff.

39. This was actually the second arms delivery. The first had been on 20 August and had resulted in the release of no hostages. The Iranians claimed that the missiles had ended up with the wrong faction in Iran.

40. George W. Cave was a retired Iran expert from the CIA who was brought back for the arms-sale operation. Howard J. Teicher was a member of the National Security Council staff specializing in political-military affairs.

41. Ali Akbar Hashemi Rafsanjani, speaker of the Iranian Parliament and later president.

42. Gates, *From the Shadows*, 313, 403.

43. Ibid., 434–436.

44. Ortega was elected president again, in another fair election, in November 2006.

Chapter 15

9/11

The inability to predict the terrorist attacks on the World Trade Center and the Pentagon on 11 September 2001 ("9/11") was a failure of tactical intelligence within a relatively successful program of strategic intelligence. Speaking strategically, the CIA was aware that there was a terrorist group called al-Qa'ida (also, al-Qaeda, al-Qida, etc.) based in Afghanistan, knew in general what its intentions were, and understood that it posed a threat to U.S. interests and possibly to the American homeland. Agents dedicated to the task were following it and doing what they could to stop it. Tactically, however, the agency had no information on the specific operation that ended on 9/11, and therein, of course, lies the tragedy.

Intelligence failures of this sort are not unusual; it is similar to the Pearl Harbor case, except that the United States was more aware that an attack (of some sort, somewhere) was imminent in December 1941. Foreseeing the specific actions of a group that is determined to hide them and is making use of innovative techniques is, unfortunately, more a matter of luck than skill. Attracting the notice of government leaders when the particular threat is far from the center of political attention is also difficult.

A designated set of intelligence officers had been tracking the activities of al-Qa'ida for years before the attacks of 9/11. The organization's founder and leader, Usama bin Ladin (Osama bin Laden), had been involved in financing the resistance war against the leftist regime in Afghanistan and the Soviet army supporting it (1979–1989). At the time, that made him a de facto ally of the CIA, which was also providing support to the anti-Soviet resistance. Bin Ladin came to the agency's attention as a financial backer of anti-American terrorism by 1993. In an unusual move, the CIA established a special unit devoted just to him. It was modeled on an overseas station and given the code name Alec Station, although it was also called the Bin Ladin Issue Station and UBL Station (for Usama bin Ladin).[1]

A National Intelligence Estimate, *The Foreign Terrorist Threat in the United States*, issued in 1995, highlighted the possibility of "large-scale terrorist attacks" along the lines of the earlier attack against the World Trade Center, in 1993, in which six people died. It noted the Islamist networks originating in the Afghan war as the source of the threat.[2] The agency also warned that "aerial terrorism seems likely at some point—filling an airplane with explosives and dive-bombing a target."[3] The CIA and FBI briefed the aviation industry on this possibility but were unable to convince them that the threat was serious enough to invest in security measures.[4] This warning, however, was merely hypothetical. It was not linked to any evidence, was not necessarily tied to al-Qa'ida, gave no indication of time or place, and was indistinguishable from numerous similar warnings of possibilities that did not come to pass. It was certainly not a warning of the specific events that would occur on 9/11.

The CIA released the following description of Bin Ladin to the media in 1996. At that time he was based in Sudan, which was ruled by the National Islamic Front (NIF).

Usama Bin Ladin: Islamic Extremist Financier

Usama bin Muhammad bin Awad Bin Ladin is one of the most significant financial sponsors of Islamic extremist activities in the world today. One of some 20 sons of wealthy Saudi construction magnate Muhammad Bin Ladin—founder of the Kingdom's Bin Ladin Group business empire—Usama joined the Afghan resistance movement following the 26 December 1979 Soviet invasion of Afghanistan. "I was enraged and went there at once," he claimed in a 1993 interview, "I arrived within days, before the end of 1979."

Bin Ladin gained prominence during the Afghan war for his role in financing the recruitment, transportation, and training of Arab nationals who volunteered to fight alongside the Afghan mujahedin. By 1985, Bin Ladin had drawn on his family's wealth, plus donations received from sympathetic merchant families in the Gulf region, to organize the Islamic Salvation Foundation, or al-Qaida, for this purpose.

- A network of al-Qaida recruitment centers and guesthouses in Egypt, Saudi Arabia, and Pakistan has enlisted and sheltered thousands of Arab recruits. This network remains active.
- Working in conjunction with extremist groups like the Egyptian al-Gama'at al-Islamiyyah, also known as the Islamic Group, al-Qaida organized and funded camps in Afghanistan and Pakistan that provided new recruits paramilitary training in preparation for the fighting in Afghanistan.
- Under al-Qaida auspices, Bin Ladin imported bulldozers and other heavy equipment to cut roads, tunnels, hospitals, and storage depots through Afghanistan's mountainous terrain to move and shelter fighters and supplies.

After the Soviets withdrew from Afghanistan in 1989, Bin Ladin returned to work in the family's Jeddah-based construction business. However, he continued to support militant Islamic groups that had begun targeting moderate Islamic governments in the region. Saudi officials held Bin Ladin's passport during 1989–1991 in a bid to prevent him from solidifying contacts with extremists whom he had befriended during the Afghan war.

Bin Ladin relocated to Sudan in 1991, where he was welcomed by National Islamic Front (NIF) leader Hasan al-Turabi. In a 1994 interview, Bin Ladin claimed to have surveyed business and agricultural investment opportunities in Sudan as early as 1983. He embarked on several business ventures in Sudan in 1990, which began to thrive following his move to Khartoum. Bin Ladin also formed symbiotic business relationships with wealthy NIF members by undertaking civil infrastructure development projects on the regime's behalf.

- Bin Ladin's company Al-Hijrah for Construction and Development, Ltd., built the tahaddi (challenge) road linking Khartoum with Port Sudan, as well as a modern international airport near Port Sudan.
- Bin Ladin's import-export firm Wadi al-Aqiq Company, Ltd., in conjunction with his Taba Investment Company, Ltd., acquired a near monopoly over Sudan's major agricultural exports of gum, corn, sunflower, and sesame products in cooperation with prominent NIF members. At the same time, Bin Ladin's Al-Themar al-Mubarakh Agriculture Company, Ltd., grew to encompass large tracts of land near Khartoum and in eastern Sudan.
- Bin Ladin and wealthy NIF members capitalized Al-Shamal Islamic Bank in Khartoum. Bin Ladin invested $50 million in the bank.

Bin Ladin's work force grew to include militant Afghan war veterans seeking to avoid a return to their own countries, where many stood accused of subversive and terrorist activities. In May 1993, for example, Bin Ladin financed the travel of 300 to 480 Afghan war veterans to Sudan after Islamabad launched a crackdown against extremists lingering in Pakistan. In addition to safehaven in Sudan, Bin Ladin has provided financial support to militants actively opposed to moderate Islamic governments and the West:

- Islamic extremists who perpetrated the December 1992 attempted bombings against some 100 U.S. servicemen in Aden [Yemen]—billeted there to support U.N. relief operations in Somalia—claimed that Bin Ladin financed their group.
- A joint Egyptian-Saudi investigation revealed in May 1993 that Bin Ladin business interests helped funnel money to Egyptian extremists, who used the cash to buy unspecified equipment, printing presses, and weapons.
- By January 1994, Bin Ladin had begun financing at least three terrorist training camps in northern Sudan—camp residents included Egyptian, Algerian, Tunisian, and Palestinian extremists—in cooperation with the NIF. Bin Ladin's Al-Hijrah for Construction and Development works directly with Sudanese military officials to transport and provision terrorists training in such camps.
- Pakistani investigators have said that Ramzi Ahmed Yousef, the alleged mastermind of the February 1993 World Trade Center bombing, resided at the Bin Ladin-funded Bayt Ashuhada (house of martyrs) guesthouse in Peshawar during most of the three years before his apprehension in February 1995.
- A leading member of the Egyptian extremist group al-Jihad claimed in a July 1995 interview that Bin Ladin helped fund the group and was at times witting of specific terrorist operations mounted by the group against Egyptian interests.
- Bin Ladin remains the key financier behind the "Kumar" camp in Afghanistan, which provides terrorist training to al-Jihad and al-Gama'at al-Islamiyyah members, according to suspect terrorists captured recently by Egyptian authorities.

Bin Ladin's support for extremist causes continues despite criticisms from regional governments and his family. Algeria, Egypt, and Yemen have accused Bin Ladin of financing militant Islamic groups on their soil (Yemen reportedly sought INTERPOL's assistance to apprehend Bin Ladin during 1994). In February 1994, Riyadh revoked Bin Ladin's Saudi citizenship for behavior that "contradicts the Kingdom's interests and risks harming its relations with fraternal countries."

The move prompted Bin Ladin to form the Advisory and Reformation Committee, a London-based dissident organization that by July 1995 had issued over 350 pamphlets critical of the Saudi Government. Bin Ladin has not responded to condemnation leveled against him in March 1994 by his eldest brother, Bakr Bin Ladin, who expressed through the Saudi media his family's "regret, denunciation, and condemnation" of Bin Ladin's extremist activities.

In December 2000, at the end of the Clinton administration, the National Security Council produced a document, "Strategy for Eliminating the Threat from the Jihadist Networks of al Qida: Status and Prospects," to bring the incoming administration up to date regarding policy toward the al-Qa'ida network. The document included the following multifaceted summary of CIA and other activities carried out up to that point.

4. Implementing the Strategy: The Record to Date

To implement this strategy, the US has used diplomacy, intelligence collection, covert action, law enforcement, foreign assistance, force protection and diplomatic security in a coordinated campaign against al Qida:

- Intelligence Collection: Beginning in 1996, the al Qida network was singled out for special treatment within the US counter-terrorism community. A "Virtual Station" was created by CIA, an organization modeled on a CIA overseas station dedicated to collection and operations against al Qida. NSA [National Security Agency] and CIA made collection against the al Qida network a major requirement, with higher priority given only to support of on-going US military operations.
- Sanctuary Sudan Eliminated: The US placed significant diplomatic pressure on Sudan, resulting in a decision by the Sudanese government to request bin Ladin to abandon Khartoum and move his headquarters to the camps in Afghanistan. US diplomacy with Saudi Arabia resulted in the Kingdom depriving bin Ladin of his citizenship and taking steps to deny him access to financial assets held in his name.
- Diplomacy with Pakistan and the Taliban: Repeated diplomatic efforts with Pakistan gained some limited law enforcement and intelligence cooperation against al Qida. The Pakistani government requested that the Taliban cease to provide sanctuary to al Qida, but the Pakistanis did not condition their support of the Taliban on compliance. Similarly, frequent direct diplomatic contact with the Taliban by the US has failed to gain any cooperation on ending the al Qida presence in Afghanistan. Beginning in late 1998, the US has repeatedly told the Taliban leadership that their complicity in harboring al Qida makes them equally culpable for al Qida operations against us. While some in the Taliban leadership appear willing to cooperate with the US, the ruler (Mullah Omar) has prohibited any action against al Qida.
- Saudi Support Gained: By 1997, CIA was identifying al Qida cells in several nations and working with local security services to disrupt them. Also that year, the Saudis disrupted a plot by the al Qida cell in the Kingdom [Operational detail, removed at the request of the CIA]. Subsequently, the Saudis began taking the al Qida threat seriously and pressured the Taliban to check bin Ladin's activities. Saudi Arabia then joined in demanding bin Ladin's arrest by the Taliban and, when Saudi efforts failed, they severed diplomatic ties and terminated direct assistance to the Taliban.
- UN Security Council Sanctions: By 1999, the Saudis and others joined us in sponsoring limited UN sanctions on Afghanistan because of its harboring of

bin Ladin. The US seized over $250,000,000 in Taliban funds. At the end of 2000, the United States and Russia co-sponsored a further round of UN sanctions that included a one sided arms embargo (only on the Taliban, not on the Northern Alliance) and expanded UN demands to include closure of the terrorist infrastructure in Afghanistan. The resolution passed 13-0-2, China and Malaysia abstaining.

- Renditions and Disruptions: With two, nearly simultaneous, suicide truck-bomb attacks, al Qida destroyed the US embassies in Kenya and Tanzania in 1998. The US stepped up the al Qida cell disruption effort. In addition to disrupting cells, the US found and brought to the US for trial al Qida operatives in Jordan, Egypt, Pakistan, Malaysia, South Africa, Kenya, Tanzania, Germany, and the United Kingdom. Other al Qida operatives not indicted in the US were brought to [countries] where they were wanted by authorities.

- Building Partner Capability: Through the CIA's Counter-terrorism Center (CTC) and State's Anti-Terrorism Assistance Program (ATA) the US has enhanced the capabilities of several nations to collect intelligence on al Qida and to disrupt their operations. [Operations detail, removed at the request of the CIA.] Counter-terrorism training and equipment have been provided to several nations' security forces. As a result of these partnerships, simultaneous disruptions of over twenty al Qida cells were conducted in December, 1999 to prevent possible Millennium celebration period attacks. The FBI has also greatly strengthened counter-terrorism cooperation with foreign counterparts, including stationing of FBI personnel overseas and training partner organizations at home and abroad.

- Inside Afghanistan: CIA developed sources inside Afghanistan who were able to report on the activities and locations of al Qida commanders. One group was developed as a covert action team designed to forcibly apprehend al Qida commanders and hand them off to US arrest teams. An Intelligence Finding authorized the use of lethal force as part of operations against the al Qida commanders. Several efforts to apprehend or attack the al Qida leadership using Afghan personnel were unsuccessful. [A foreign] government unit was trained and equipped for a similar mission, but has not yet been employed in an operation.

  The Afghan Northern Alliance is engaged in civil war with the Taliban. al Qida has been a major source of the Taliban's success, providing the best fighting unit (the 55th Brigade) and literally buying the support of provincial leaders. The Pakistani Army has also provided the Taliban with advisors, intelligence, training, equipment, and placed personnel in Taliban units. The US has provided very limited intelligence and non-lethal equipment to the Northern Alliance, in exchange for intelligence on al Qida. The Northern Alliance has not yet been able to mount an apprehension operation against al Qida commanders.

- Military Operations: In August, 1998 the US struck al Qida facilities in Afghanistan and an al Qida chemical plant in Sudan.[5] Subsequent to those attacks, follow-on attacks were considered and military assets deployed on three occasions when the al Qida commanders were located in Afghanistan by Humint [that is, human, as opposed to technical, intelligence] sources. The Humint sources were not sufficiently reliable and a lack of second source corroboration prevented US military action. Thus in September 2000, the CIA began covert flights into Afghanistan using the Predator UAV [unmanned aerial vehicle] operating out of Uzbekistan. On three occasions, the UAV provided [—] video coverage of what appeared to be gatherings involving the senior al Qida leadership. The UAV operations were suspended [—] but plans are now being developed to allow operations to recommence in late March. The Spring flights may be able to incorporate a new capability: Hellfire anti-tank missiles mounted aboard the Predators. This new capability would permit a "see it/shoot it" option [Operational detail, removed at the request of the CIA].

- <u>Better Self-Defense</u>: Defense, State, and CIA have all taken steps to enhance our capability to defend US installations abroad against al Qida attacks. Physical security measures have been greatly enhanced at likely target facilities. Additional security personnel have been deployed, including covert counter-surveillance units. Intelligence reports indicate that al Qida considered attacks on several facilities, but decided that the enhanced defensive measures would prevent those attacks from succeeding. Ambassadors have been encouraged to take steps, including temporary closing of embassies and consulates, based upon intelligence without waiting for Washington approval. Embassy Dushanbe [in Tajikistan] and Embassy Khartoum [in Sudan] have been closed for security reasons. Embassy Doha [in Qatar] was relocated on an emergency basis. New, more secure embassies are under construction or planned at several locations as part of a multi-year plan, but further funding is needed.

- <u>Financing</u>: Al Qida and several of its affiliates are legally designated Foreign Terrorist Organizations under US law, making it a felony to transfer money to them through US institutions or to raise money for them (or their front organizations) in the US. Moreover, the US can take banking sanctions against foreign banking institutions which facilitate terrorist finances. [CIA has] been able to collect numerous reports about alleged al Qida investments, companies, and transactions. Treasury has had pledges of cooperation from several nations, including Saudi Arabia, the UAE, and Kuwait. Based on the absence of actionable intelligence, however, Treasury has not been able to make specific requests to these countries. State has taken action against several Islamic NGOs which appear to be fronts for al Qida, [—].

Richard A. Clarke, the National Security Council staff member responsible for terrorist-related matters, wrote a memorandum on 25 January 2001 to Condoleezza Rice, the National Security Adviser in the new administration, urging that a "principals" meeting—that is, a meeting of cabinet-level officials—be held quickly to decide what further action should be taken regarding al-Qa'ida. Note that al-Qa'ida had recently, in October 2000, attacked the destroyer USS *Cole* in Yemen using a bomb on a small boat. The attack killed seventeen sailors.

This document featured prominently in the hearings held by the National Commission on the Terrorist Attacks upon the United States (the 9/11 Commission)[6] in 2004. The December 2000 policy review, above, was appended to it and was declassified together with it in 2004.

MEMORANDUM FOR CONDOLEEZZA RICE

FROM: RICHARD A. CLARKE

SUBJECT: Presidential Policy Initiative/Review—the *Al-Qida* Network

Condi[7] asked today that we propose major Presidential policy reviews or initiatives. We <u>*urgently*</u> need such a Principals level review on the *al Qida* network.

<u>Just some Terrorist Group?</u>

As we noted in our briefings for you, *al Qida* is not some narrow, little terrorist issue that need to be included in broader regional policy. Rather, several of our regional policies need to address centrally the transnational challenge to the US and our interests posed by the *al Qida* network. By proceeding with separate policy reviews on Central Asia, the GCC [the Gulf Cooperation Council], North Africa, etc. we would deal inadequately with the need for a comprehensive multi-regional policy on *al Qida*.

al Qida is the active, organized, major force that is using a distorted version of Islam as its vehicle to achieve two goals:

— to drive the US out of the Muslim world, forcing the withdrawal of our military and economic presence in countries from Morocco to Indonesia;
— to replace moderate, modern, Western regime in Muslim countries with theocracies along the lines of the Taliban.

al Qida affects generally our policies on Pakistan, Afghanistan, Central Asia, North Africa, and the GCC. Leaders in Jordan and Saudi Arabia see *al Qida* as a direct threat to them. The strength of the network of organizations limits the scope of support friendly Arab regimes can give to a range of US [—] policies, including Iraq policy and the Peace Process [between Israel and the Palestinians]. We would make a major error if we underestimated the challenge *al Qida* poses, or over estimated the stability of the moderate, friendly regimes *al Qida* threatens.

Pending Time Sensitive Decisions

At the close of the Clinton Administration, two decisions about *al Qida* were deferred to the Bush Administration.

— <u>First, should we provide the Afghan Northern Alliance enough assistance to maintain it as a viable opposition force to the Taliban/al Qida?</u> If we do not, I believe that the Northern Alliance may be effectively taken out of action this Spring when fighting resumes after the winter thaw. The al Qida 55th Brigade, which has been the key fighting force for the Taliban, would then be freed to send its personnel elsewhere, where they would likely threaten US interests. For any assistance to get there in time to effect the Spring fighting, a decision is needed now.
— <u>Second, should we increase assistance to Uzbekistan to allow them to deal with the al Qida/IMU [the Islamic Movement of Uzbekistan] threat?</u> [Operational detail, removed at the request of the CIA.]

Three other issues awaiting addressal now are:

— First, what the new Administration says to the Taliban and Pakistan about the importance we attach to ending the al Qida sanctuary in Afghanistan. We are separately proposing early, strong messages to both.
— Second, do we propose significant program growth in the FY02 [Fiscal Year 2002] budget for anti-al Qida operations by CIA and counter-terrorism training and assistance by State and CIA?
— Third, when and how does the Administration choose to respond to the attack on the USS Cole. That decision is obviously complex. We can make some decisions, such as those above, now without yet coming to grips with the harder decision about the Cole. On the Cole, we should take advantage of the policy that we "will respond at a time, place, and manner of our own choosing" and not be forced into knee-jerk responses.

Attached is the year-end 2000 strategy on al Qida developed by the last Administration to give to you. Also attached is the 1998 strategy. [The latter has not been declassified.] Neither was a "covert action only" approach. Both incorporated diplomatic, economic, military, public diplomacy and intelligence tools. Using the

2000 paper as background, we could prepare a decision paper/guide for a PC [Principals' Committee] review.

I recommend that you have a Principals discussion of *al Qida* soon and address the following issues:

1. <u>Threat Magnitude</u>: Do the Principals agree that the *al Qida* network poses a first order threat to US interests in a number or regions, or is this analysis a "chicken little" over reaching and can we proceed without major new initiatives and by handling this issue in a more routine manner?
2. <u>Strategy</u>: If it is a first order issue, how should the existing strategy be modified or strengthened?

Two elements of the existing strategy that have not been made to work effectively are a) going after *al Qida's* money and b) public information to counter *al Qida* propaganda.

3. <u>FY02 Budget</u>: Should we continue the funding increases into FY02 for State and CIA programs designed to implement the *al Qida* strategy?
4. <u>Immediate [—] Decisions</u>: Should we initiate [—] funding to the Northern Alliance and to the Uzbeks?

Please let us know if you would like such a decision/discussion paper or any modifications to the background paper.

Despite Clarke's insistence on the topic's urgency, the Bush administration assigned it to a deputies' level review, rather than a principals' level review, which in Clarke's view caused needless delay. Other administration officials apparently believed that he was exaggerating the threat. A lack of concrete evidence of an imminent attack and a history of false alarms may have made his warnings easier to ignore. A principals' level meeting was not held until 4 September 2001, exactly one week before 9/11. The National Intelligence Council initiated the drafting of a National Intelligence Estimate on the terrorist threat to the United States in early 2001, the first such assessment in four years; it was in the editing stage when the terrorists struck.

Through the spring and summer of 2001, a stream of intelligence reports referred to the possibility of a terrorist attack by al-Qa'ida against the United States or U.S. interests. Yet the CIA had no information of a specific nature. Most of the evidence was fragmentary and uncorroborated, not the "actionable intelligence" that forces decision makers to focus, and most administration officials paid little attention. On 6 August 2001, the CIA responded to an earlier query from the president regarding the possibility of a terrorist attack against the United States itself. The response came in a section of that day's Presidential Daily Brief. Unfortunately, despite the eye-catching title, the agency still had little actionable intelligence to bring to bear. The report offers no clear warning of the attack that came only five weeks later. Much of the material summarizes information from earlier years. Ironically, the briefing opens with a reference to the smaller-scale bombing attack directed against the World Trade Center in 1993.

Bin Ladin Determined to Strike in US

Clandestine, foreign government, and media reports indicate Bin Ladin since 1997 has wanted to conduct terrorist attack in the US. Bin Ladin implied in US television interviews in 1997 and 1998 that his followers would follow the example of World Trade Center bomber Ramzi Yousef and "bring the fighting to America."

> After US missile strikes on his base in Afghanistan in 1998, Bin Ladin told followers he wanted to retaliate in Washington, according to a [—] service.
>
> An Egyptian Islamic Jihad (EIJ) operative told an [—] service at the same time that Bin Ladin was planning to exploit the operative's access to the US to mount a terrorist strike.

> *The millennium plotting in Canada in 1999 may have been part of Bin Ladin's first serious attempt to implement a terrorist strike in the US.* Convicted plotter Ahmed Ressam has told the FBI that he conceived the idea to attack Los Angeles International Airport himself, but that Bin Ladin lieutenant Abu Zubaydah encouraged him and helped facilitate the operation. Ressam also said that in 1998 Abu Zubaydah was planning his own US attack.

> Ressam says Bin Ladin was aware of the Los Angeles operation.

> *Although Bin Ladin has not succeeded, his attacks against the US Embassies in Kenya and Tanzania in 1998 demonstrate that he prepares operations years in advance and is not deterred by setbacks.* Bin Ladin associates surveilled our Embassies in Nairobi and Dar es Salaam as early as 1993, and some members of the Nairobi cell planning the bombings were arrested and deported in 1997.
>
> *Al-Qa'ida members—including some who are US citizens—have resided in or traveled to the US for years, and the group apparently maintains a support structure that could aid attacks.* Two Al-Qa'ida members found guilty in the conspiracy to bomb our Embassies in East Africa were US citizens, and a senior EIJ member lived in California in the mid-1990s.

> A clandestine source said that a Bin Ladin cell in New York was recruiting Muslim American youth for attacks.

> *We have not been able to corroborate some of the more sensational threat reporting, such as that from a [—] service in 1998 saying that Bin Ladin wanted to hijack a US aircraft to gain the release of "Blind Shaykh" 'Umar 'Abd al-Rahman and other US-held extremists.*

> Nevertheless, FBI information since that time indicates patterns of suspicious activity in this country consistent with preparations for hijackings or other types of attacks, including recent surveillance of federal buildings in New York.
>
> The FBI is conducting approximately 70 full field investigations throughout the US that it considers Bin Ladin-related. CIA and the FBI are investigating a call to our Embassy in the UAE [United Arab Emirates] in May saying that a group of Bin Ladin supporters was in the US planning attacks with explosives.

Intelligence authorities eventually determined that the "patterns of suspicious activity" and the embassy call in the United Arab Emirates were unrelated to the 9/11 attacks. In response to questions from the 9/11 Commission as to why no action had been taken in response to the rising threat, Condoleezza Rice repeatedly pointed out that the briefing had only mentioned the possibility of hijackings, not a plan to crash planes into buildings, although one might expect the prospect of hijackings to warrant some concern as well. The ongoing FBI investigations were also taken as evidence that the situation was under control. Although the FBI itself was concerned that the convictions, in New York in May 2001, of those involved in the embassy bombings in Africa could result in a terrorist attack in the United States, the briefing did not lead to any additional measures.

After the 9/11 attacks, a number of investigations examined the events to determine what might be learned for the future, the most famous being that of the 9/11 Commission. The CIA did its own internal investigation. The study was conducted by the Office of Inspector General (OIG), and a report of several hundred pages was completed in June 2005. The CIA, however, refused to release it to the public, although some of its key findings became known. Among these were the conclusions that the Inspector General, John Helgerson, had found "no single point of failure" and that no "silver bullet" existed that could have predicted or prevented the attacks. Although more concerned with correcting systemic problems in the way the CIA was operating, Helgerson allowed that there were certain leading officials that might be disciplined for shortcomings. In October 2005, CIA Director Porter J. Goss explicitly rejected the recommendation that an Accountability Board be established to take disciplinary action against ranking agency officials. The agency, in general, rejected the assumption that if a catastrophe occurred then someone must have been criminally negligent. Goss suggested that punishing people would inhibit officers from "taking risks" in the future.

Several members of Congress were disturbed by both the agency's reluctance to share its findings and, in their view, its refusal to hold its officials accountable for a major intelligence failure. In August 2007, Congress mandated the release of a declassified summary of the report. In compliance with that law, the CIA published a lightly redacted nineteen-page executive summary a few weeks later. At the same time, the new Director of the Central Intelligence Agency, Michael Hayden, issued a personal statement making clear his belief that the decision to release it was a mistake, likely to reignite past arguments, distract personnel, and undermine morale at a time when the agency should be looking ahead.

Statement to Employees by Director of the Central Intelligence Agency,
General Michael V. Hayden on the Release of the 9/11
IG Report Executive Summary

August 21, 2007

Earlier this month, Congress passed a bill implementing some of the recommendations of the 9/11 Commission. The legislation, lengthy and complex, includes a provision dealing with the report that CIA's Office of Inspector General prepared on the performance of our agency prior to September 11th. The act gave me 30 days to make available to the public a version of the report's executive summary, declassified to the maximum extent possible. Today, well within deadline, I am releasing that material.

While meeting the dictates of the law, I want to make it clear that this declassification was neither my choice nor my preference. Two Directors of National Intelligence have supported the agency's position against release.

The long, grueling fight against terrorism, which depends in very real part on the quality of our intelligence, demands that we keep our focus on the present and the future. We must draw lessons from our past—and we have—without becoming captive to it. I thought the release of this report would distract officers serving their country on the frontlines of a global conflict. It will, at a minimum, consume time and attention revisiting ground that is already well plowed. I also remain deeply concerned about the chilling effect that may follow publication of the previously classified work, findings, and recommendations of the Office of Inspector General. The important work of that unit depends on candor and confidentiality.

In keeping with the letter and spirit of the law, CIA has in its declassification process removed relatively little from the report's executive summary. We focused chiefly on the protection of essential sources and methods. I also thought it unnecessary and unwise to permit identification of officers below the level of Center Chief, even if only by title, and those passages have been deleted, as well.

There is some background that I believe you need to know. In 2002, the Joint Inquiry Committee of Congress instructed our Office of Inspector General to determine if any agency officers should be rewarded for outstanding service in the run-up to 9/11 or held accountable for the unsatisfactory discharge of their duties. In June 2005, the Inspector General presented my predecessor, Porter Goss, with a final report answering that specific mandate. The summary, like the complete report, is a very human document. In it, one group of agency officers—dedicated to their task—looks back to examine and judge the actions of another group of agency officers—dedicated to their task, the task of understanding and combating al-Qai'da.

You should also know that there are very different perspectives on this report. It was important for us to conduct our own review—that is something on which most, if not all of us, can agree. But our colleagues referred to in the document, and others who have read it, took strong exception to its focus, methodology, and conclusions. In October 2005, Director Goss declined to accept its primary recommendation—the creation of an Accountability Board to consider disciplinary action against a handful of individuals at different levels of command. I have re-read the report, carefully evaluated what it says, and have found no reason to revisit his decision.

Director Goss noted at the time that the officers cited include some of our finest. With inadequate resources, they and those they led worked flat out against a tough, secretive foe. As the executive summary points out, there was never a question of misconduct. While they, and our government as a whole, were unable despite their best efforts to shield our nation from attack, their skill, wisdom, energy, and leadership were key elements in the agency's victories over al-Qai'da before and after 9/11. They have made powerful contributions to our national security. They have prevented other acts of terrorism, and they have saved innocent lives, in our country and overseas.

This is *not* about avoiding responsibility. In fact, the opposite is true. CIA has for years spoken publicly, openly, and explicitly about shortcomings in its counter-terror programs before 9/11. Those shortcomings have been the subject of hearings, studies, panels, press reports, books, and critiques of all kinds, some fair, some not. As you will see, the Inspector General found no "silver bullet" that would have prevented the terror attacks of September 11th. There was, in the words of the summary, "no single point of failure."

Nor did CIA wait for this formal review to begin identifying and correcting the systemic flaws discussed in the report. This is an organization that is self-aware, self-critical, and, to a great degree, self-improving. The Inspector General's report, like others before it, found areas in which CIA could do better, and, in the intervening years, we have worked hard to do just that.

Counter-terrorism is an exceptionally difficult challenge. The risks, and the stakes, are extremely high. The enemy is adaptive, resilient, and determined to strike us again here at home. There are limits to what intelligence can accomplish, and there can be no guarantee of perfect security. But the talented, motivated officers who work against this threat day and night give our nation a strong advantage. Together, we recognize that the finest tribute we can pay to the victims of terrorism is a redoubled effort to rip that scourge out by the roots. We can, and should, be proud of the many great things CIA has done, and will do, to defend the United States in a very dangerous world.

Mike Hayden

If the current Director of the CIA was upset, then George J. Tenet, who had been the Director of Central Intelligence in 2001, was livid. The report held him ultimately responsible for the agency's failure to develop a strategic plan for fighting al-Qa'ida prior to 9/11. Even though he had recognized the need for such a plan and even ordered one drawn up, the Inspector General maintained that he did not follow through. The report criticized other officials far more often, especially the chiefs of the Counterterrorist Center, but Tenet seemed to view himself as the scapegoat. He issued a statement of his own, defending his own efforts and drawing attention to a previous assessment by the OIG, made just before the attacks, as well as to various positive statements in the new one.

Statement by George J. Tenet

August 21, 2007

In August of 2001, the Office of the Inspector General produced an insightful and valuable review of CIA's counterterrorism efforts. Unfortunately, it is not the one released today.

Just weeks before 9/11, the Office of the IG reported that "The DCI Counterterrorist Center (CTC) is a well-managed component that successfully carries out the Agency's responsibilities to collect and analyze intelligence on international terrorism and to undermine the capabilities of terrorist groups." The report went on to say: "CTC fulfills interagency responsibility for the DCI by coordinating national intelligence, providing warning and promoting effective use of Intelligence Community resources on terrorism issues." The report noted that, "CTC's resources have steadily increased over the last five years with personnel growing by 74 percent during that period and the budget more than doubling. The Center's comparatively favorable resource situation allows it not only to expand its own programs but also to support operations against terrorists and liaison relationships that DO (Directorate of Operations) area divisions otherwise could not fund."

The August 2001 report stated that, "relationships with the FBI have been vastly improved" and further informed us "CTC's relationship with NSA [National Security Agency] has improved dramatically since the last inspection."

The IG recommended no actions to me to improve our operations against terrorism. It did correctly note that the people of CTC were extraordinarily hard working and were facing a monumental task combating the tide of terrorism. The August 2001 report is sharply at odds with what is being released today.

After 9/11, with the clarity of hindsight, the IG, while acknowledging that "the DCI was actively and forcefully engaged in the counterterrorism efforts of the CIA ... [and] was personally engaged in sounding the alarm about the threat to many different audiences," nevertheless criticized me for not having a strategic plan to fight terrorism and inadequately marshaling resources for such an effort. In these later judgments, the IG is flat wrong.

There was in fact a robust plan, marked by extraordinary effort and dedication to fighting terrorism, dating back to long before 9/11. Without such an effort, we would not have been able to give the President a plan on September 15, 2001 that led to the routing of the Taliban, chasing al Qa'ida from its Afghan sanctuary and combating terrorists across 92 countries. The IG report rightly praises the "most effective interagency effort against UBL [Usama Bin Laden]" as the work of the Assistant DCI for Collection from the early months of 1998 to 9/11. But it fails to note that this effort was at my direction and was regularly monitored by me. This plan was based on actions that were taken over a sustained period using the assets of the Intelligence Community to collect intelligence against al Qa'ida, to develop relationships with key foreign intelligence services, to develop networks of assets inside the Afghan sanctuary, and to develop innovative technologies to deal with an illusive target. All of this was done pursuant to my direction, as quoted in the IG report, that there be "no resources or people spared in this effort, either inside the CIA or the Community."

The latest IG report is equally wrong regarding resources. Although resources available for everything else at CIA went down or stayed flat, counterterrorism resources were going up. The IG report fails to understand where we were starting from or the geopolitical context that the Intelligence Community faced. We had to try to rebuild a seriously under-funded Intelligence Community across the board. During the 1990s, as a Community, we had lost 25 percent of our people and tens of billions of dollars in investment compared to the 1990 baseline. The rebuilding of the entire Community was essential to bolstering our counterterrorism efforts and enabling us to address all the intelligence priorities established by the President. For me, however there was no priority higher than fighting terrorism. The IG fails to understand how intensely I pushed the counterterrorism issue because he failed to interview either me or policymakers from either the Clinton or Bush Administrations on this matter. Had he done so he might have learned that I was relentless in seeking additional funding for the Intelligence Community in general and counterterrorism in particular. I wrote the Administration in 1998 and 1999 imploring for more money to rebuild U.S. intelligence. When only a small portion of what I requested was made available, I went outside established channels to work with then-Speaker Gingrich to obtain a $1.2 billion budgetary supplemental for the Intelligence Community.

The IG's report released today also vastly under appreciates the challenges faced and heroic performance of the hard working men and women of the CIA in general and CTC in specific. As the 9/11 Commission report says: "Before 9/11, no agency did more to attack al Qa'ida than the CIA." The hard work, skill and selfless dedication of Agency officers saved countless lives and enhanced the security of our country. No IG report will ever change that reality.

I do not want my comments to be misconstrued as saying that CIA's performance prior to 9/11 was beyond reproach. We did not obtain the tactical information which may have allowed us to thwart the 9/11 attacks. As I said to the 9/11 Commission: "No matter how hard we worked—of how desperately we tried—it was not enough. The victims and the families of 9/11 deserved better."

But just as we owed it to the country to do better—the CIA IG owed it to the nation and the men and women of the Intelligence Community to do a better job in reviewing the circumstances that led to the tragedy of September 11th.

With that, here is the declassified executive summary of the report as issued by the CIA Office of Inspector General on 21 August 2007. Note that in this document each paragraph and each heading was classified separately. In some cases, the text of a section has been released but the heading has not. These headings may have been the code names of specific operations. In the text below, the original classification is indicated as (U) Unclassified; (C) Confidential; (C//NF) Confidential, No Foreign Dissemination; (S) Secret; (S//NF) Secret, No Foreign Dissemination. In each case, in the original, the designations other than (U) have been crossed off in ink because the document as a whole has been declassified. It is noteworthy that the degree of classification of each paragraph does not necessarily correlate with the degree of redaction to the text.

OIG Report on CIA Accountability with Respect to the 9/11 Attacks

(U) EXECUTIVE SUMMARY

(U) The Senate Select Committee on Intelligence and the House Permanent Select Committee on Intelligence requested that the CIA's Office of Inspector General (OIG) review the findings of their Joint Inquiry (JI) Report and undertake whatever additional investigations were necessary to determine whether any Agency employees were deserving of awards for outstanding service provided before the attacks of September 11, 2001 (9/11), or should be held accountable for failure to perform their responsibilities in a satisfactory manner.

(U) The Accountability Review Team assembled by the Inspector General (IG) focused exclusively on the issues identified by the JI. The IG was not asked by the Congress to conduct a comprehensive review of the capabilities and functioning of the Agency's many components involved with counterterrorism programs, and the Team did not do so. As a result, this account does not document the many successes of the Agency and its officers at all levels (including many whose actions are discussed in this report) in the war on terrorism, both before and after 9/11.

(U) Similarly, because this report was designed to address accountability issues, it does not include recommendations relating to the systemic problems that were identified. Such systemic recommendations as were appropriate to draw from the review of the events of the pre-9/11 period have been forwarded separately to senior Agency managers. In its regular program of audits, investigations, and inspections, the OIG continues to review the counterterrorism programs and operations of the Agency, identifying processes that work well and those that might be improved.

(U) After conducting its review, the Inspector General Team reports that, while its findings differ from those of the JI on a number of matters, it reaches the same overall conclusions on most of the important issues. Concerning certain issues, the Team concluded that the Agency and its officers did not discharge their responsibilities in a satisfactory manner. As a result, the Inspector General recommends that the Director, Central Intelligence Agency establish an Accountability Board made up of individuals who are not employees of the Agency to review the performance of some individuals and assess their potential accountability.

(U) In its deliberations, the Team used a "reasonable person" approach and relied on Agency regulations—which are subjective—concerning standards of accountability. A discussion of those regulations is included in the Foreword. While the Team found that many officers performed their responsibilities in an exemplary fashion, it did not recommend individuals for additional recognition because these officers already have been rewarded.

(U) The Team found no instance in which an employee violated the law, and none of the errors discussed herein involves misconduct. Rather, the review focuses on areas where individuals did not perform their duties in a satisfactory manner; that is, they did not—act "in accordance with a reasonable level of professionalism, skill, and diligence," as required by Agency regulation. On occasion, the

Team has found that a specific officer was responsible for a particular action or lack of action, but has not recommended that an Accountability Board review the officer's performance. Such a conclusion reflects the Team's view that extenuating circumstances mitigate the case.

(U) The findings of greatest concern are those that identify systemic problems where the Agency's programs or processes did not work as they should have, and concerning which a number of persons were involved or aware, or should have been. Where the Team found systemic failures, it has recommended that an Accountability Board assess the performance and accountability of those managers who, by virtue of their position and authorities, might reasonably have been expected to oversee and correct the process. In general, the fact that failures were systemic should not absolve responsible officials from accountability.

(U) The Review Team found that Agency officers from the top down worked hard against the al-Qa'ida and Usama Bin Ladin (UBL) targets. They did not always work effectively and cooperatively, however. The Team found neither a "single point of failure" nor a "silver bullet" that would have enabled the Intelligence Community (IC) to predict or prevent the 9/11 attacks. The team did find, however, failures to implement and manage important processes, to follow through with operations, and to properly share and analyze critical data. If IC officers had been able to view and analyze the full range of information available before 11 September 2001, they could have developed a more informed context in which to assess the threat reporting of the spring and summer that year.

(U) This review focuses only on those findings of the Joint Inquiry that relate to the Central Intelligence Agency. The Team cooperated with the Department of Justice Inspector General and the Kean Commission[8] as they pursued their separate inquiries. For this report, the Team interviewed officers from other agencies who had been detailed to the CIA in the period before 9/11, but did not undertake to interview systematically other officers outside CIA and the IC Management Staff. This report reaches no conclusions about the performance of other agencies or their personnel.

(U) Senior Leadership and Management of the Counterterrorism Effort

(U) The JI concluded that, before 9/11, neither the US Government nor the IC had a comprehensive strategy for combating al-Qa'ida. It charged that the Director of Central Intelligence (DCI) was either unwilling or unable to marshal the full range of IC resources necessary to combat the growing threat to the United States. The OIG Team also found that the IC did not have a documented, comprehensive approach to al-Qa'ida and that the DCI did not use all of his authority in leading the IC's strategic effort against UBL.

(C) The Team found that the DCI was actively and forcefully engaged in the counterterrorism efforts of the CIA. Beginning in 1999, he received regular updates, often daily, on efforts to track and disrupt UBL. He was personally engaged in sounding the alarm about the threat to many different audiences in the policy community, military, Congress, and public, and he worked directly and personally with foreign counterparts to encourage their cooperation.

(S//NF) In December 1998, the DCI signed a memorandum in which he declared: "We are at war." In addition to directives related to collection programs and other matters, this memorandum stated that the Deputy Director for Central Intelligence (DDCI) would chair an interagency group to formulate an integrated, interagency plan to counter the terrorist challenge posed by Usama Bin Ladin. The DCI wrote that he wanted "... no resources or people spared in this effort, either inside CIA or the Community."

(S//NF) The Team found that neither the DCI nor the DDCI followed up these warnings and admonitions by creating a documented, comprehensive plan to guide the counterterrorism effort at the Intelligence Community level. The DDCI chaired at least one meeting in response to the DCI directive, but the forum soon devolved into one of tactical and operational, rather than strategic, discussions. These subsequent meetings were chaired by the Executive Director of the CIA and included few if any officers from other IC agencies. While CIA and other agencies had individual plans and important initiatives underway, senior officers in the Agency and Community told the Team that no comprehensive strategic plan for the IC to counter UBL was created in response to the DCI's memorandum, or at any time prior to 9/11.

(S//NF) The DCI Counterterrorist Center (CTC) was not used effectively as a strategic coordinator of the IC's counterterrorism efforts. CTC's stated mission includes the production of all-source intelligence and the coordination of the IC's counterterrorism efforts. Before 9/11, however, the Center's focus was primarily operational and tactical. While focusing on operations is critically important and does not necessarily mean that other elements of mission will be ignored, the Team found that this nearly exclusive focus—which resulted in many operational successes—had a negative impact on CTC's effectiveness as a coordinator of IC counterterrorism strategy. The Team found that the most effective interagency effort against UBL was that of the Assistant DCI for Collection, who, from the early months of 1998 to 9/11, worked with representatives of several intelligence agencies to stimulate collection.

(S//NF) In the years leading up to 9/11, the DCI worked hard and with some success, at the most senior levels of government, to secure additional budgetary resources to rebuild the CIA and the IC. At the same time, the Team found that he did not use his senior position and unique authorities to work with the National Security Council to elevate the relative standing of counterterrorism in the formal ranking of intelligence priorities, or to alter the deployment of human and financial resources across agencies in a coordinated approach to the terrorism target. While the nature of the IC makes the mission of managing it problematic and difficult, the DCI at the time has some authority to move manpower and funds among agencies. The Team found that, in the five years prior to 9/11, the DCI on six occasions used these authorities to move almost [—] in funds from other agencies to the CIA for a number of important purposes [—four-fifths of a line deleted—]. One of these transfers helped fund a Middle East program that was terrorism-related, but none supported programs designed to counter UBL or al-Qa'ida. Nor were DCI authorities used to transfer any personnel into these programs in the five years prior to 9/11.

(C//NF) The Team notes that the former DCI recognized the need for an integrated, interagency plan, and believes that such a plan was needed to mobilize all of the operational, analytic, and resource capabilities of the IC to enable the several agencies of the Community to work cooperatively and with maximum effectiveness against al-Qa'ida. At the same time, the Team concludes that the former DCI, by virtue of his position, bears ultimate responsibility for the fact that no such plan was ever created, despite his specific direction that this should be done.

(S//NF) The JI report discussed a persistent strain in relations between CIA and the National Security Agency (NSA) that impeded collaboration between the two agencies in dealing with the terrorist challenge from al-Qa'ida. The Team, likewise, found that significant differences existed between CIA and NSA over their respective authorities. The Team did not document in detail or take a position on the merits of this disagreement, but notes that the differences remained unresolved well into 2001 in spite of the fact that considerable management attention was devoted to the issue, including at the level of the Agency's Deputy Executive Director. Senior officers of the CIA and the IC Management Staff stated that these interagency differences had a negative impact on the IC's ability to perform its mission and that only the DCI's vigorous personal involvement could have led to a timely resolution of the matter.

(C) The Team recommends that an Accountability Board review the performance of the former DCI for failing to act personally to resolve the differences between CIA and NSA in an effective and timely manner.

(U) See the Team's discussions of Systemic Findings 2 (The DCI's Role); 4 (Application of Technology); and 7 (Computer Exploitation) for discussion of these issues.

(U) Management of CIA's Resources for Counterterrorism

(C) Funding for the Agency's counterterrorism programs increased significantly from Fiscal Year (FY) 1998 to FY 2001 as a result of supplemental appropriations. These funds were appropriated, in part, because of efforts of the CIA's Director and senior leaders to convince the Administration and Congress that the Agency was short of resources for counterterrorism and other key programs. The Team preparing this report did not attempt to reach a conclusion regarding the proper level of funding for counterterrorism programs.

(S) The Team did find, however, that during the same period they were appealing the shortage of resources, senior officials were not effectively managing the Agency's counterterrorism funds. In particular, Agency managers moved funds from the base budgets of the Counterterrorist Center and other counterterrorism programs to meet other corporate and Directorate of Operations (DO) needs. The Team found that from FY 1997 to FY 2001 (as of 9/11), [—] was redistributed from counterterrorism programs to other Agency priorities. Some of these funds were used to strengthen the infrastructure of the DO and, thus, indirectly supported counterterrorism efforts; other funds were used to cover nonspecific corporate "taxes" and for a variety of purposes that, based on the Agency's budgetary definitions, were unrelated to terrorism. Conversely, no resources were reprogrammed from other Agency programs to counterterrorism, even after the DCI's statement in December 1998 that he wanted no resources spared in the effort. The Team found that the Agency made little use of the Reserve for Contingencies to support its counterterrorism effort. Finally, CTC managers did not spend all of the funds in their base budget, even after it had been reduced by diversions of funds to other programs.

(C) The Team recommends that an Accountability Board review the performance of the Executive Director, the Deputy Director for Operations, and the Chief of CTC during the years prior to 9/11 regarding their management of the Agency's counterterrorism financial resources, including specifically their redirection of funds from counterterrorism programs to other priorities.

(C) Concerning human resources, the Team found that the unit within CTC responsible for Usama Bin Ladin, UBL Station, by the accounts of all who worked there, had an excessive workload. Most of its officers did not have the operational experience, expertise, and training necessary to accomplish their mission in an effective manner. Taken together, these weaknesses contributed to performance lapses related to the handling of materials concerning individuals who were to become the 9/11 hijackers. The Team recommends that an Accountability Board review the performance of the Chiefs of CTC during the period 1997–2001 regarding the manner in which they staffed the UBL component.

(C) The Team found that certain units within CTC did not work effectively together to understand the structure and operations of al-Qa'ida. This situation had a particularly negative impact on performance with respect to Khalid Shaykh Muhammad (KSM), the mastermind of the 9/11 attacks. The Team, like the Joint Inquiry, found that CTC's assigning principal responsibility for KSM to the Renditions Branch had the consequence that the resources of the Sunni Extremist Group, UBL Station, and CTC analysts were not effectively brought to bear on the problem. CTC considered KSM to be a high-priority target for apprehension and rendition, but did not recognize the significance of reporting from credible sources in 2000 and 2001 that portrayed him as a senior al-Qa'ida lieutenant and thus missed important indicators of terrorist planning. This intelligence reporting was not voluminous and its significance is obviously easier to determine in hindsight, but it was noteworthy even in the pre-9/11 period because it included the allegation that KSM was sending terrorists to the United States to engage in activities on behalf of Bin Ladin.

(C) The evidence indicates that the management approach employed in CTC had the effect of actively reinforcing the separation of responsibilities among the key CTC units working on KSM. The Team recommends that an Accountability Board review the performance of the [—several words deleted—] and [—several words deleted—] for failure to provide proper oversight and guidance to their officers; to coordinate effectively with other units; and to allocate the workload to ensure that KSM was being covered appropriately. The Team also recommends that an Accountability Board review the performance of the Chief of CTC for failure to ensure that CTC units worked in a coordinated, effective manner against KSM. Finally, the Team recommends that an Accountability Board review the performance of the [—several words deleted—] for failure to produce any [—] coverage of Khalid Shaykh Muhammad from 1997 to 2001.[9]

(U) See the Team's discussions of Systemic Finding 3 (Counterterrorism Resources) and Factual Finding 5i (Khalid Shaykh Muhammad) for further information on these issues.

(U) Information Sharing

(C) The Team's findings related to the issue of information sharing are in general accord with the JI's overall assessment of CIA's performance. Like the JI, the Team found problems in the functioning of two separate but related processes in the specific case of the Malaysia operation of early 2000: entering the names of suspected al-Qa'ida terrorists on the "watchlist" of the Department of State and providing information to the Federal Bureau of Investigation (FBI) in proper channels. The Team also found that CTC did not forward relevant information to [—about one and a half lines deleted—] In regard to broader issues of information sharing, the Team found basic problems with processes designed to facilitate such sharing. In particular, CTC managers did not clarify the roles and responsibilities of officers detailed to CTC by other agencies.

(S//NF) The Malaysia Operation. Agency officers did not, on a timely basis, recommend to the Department of State the watchlisting of two suspected al-Qa'ida terrorists, Nawaf al-Hazmi and Khalid al-Mihdhar. These individuals, who later were among the hijackers of 9/11, were known by the Agency in early 2000 to have traveled to Kuala Lumpur, Malaysia, to participate in a meeting of suspected terrorists. From Kuala Lumpur, they traveled to Bangkok. In January 2000, CTC officers received information that one of these suspected terrorists had a US visa; in March 2000, these officers had information that the other had flown from Bangkok to Los Angeles.

(S//NF) In the period January through March 2000, some 50 to 60 individuals read one or more of six Agency cables containing travel information related to these terrorists. These cables originated in four field locations and Headquarters. They were read by overseas officers and Headquarters personnel, operations officers and analysts, managers and junior employees, and CIA staff personnel as well as officers in rotation from NSA and FBI. Over an 18-month period, some of these officers had opportunities to review the information on multiple occasions, when they might have recognized its significance and shared it appropriately with other components and agencies. Ultimately, the two terrorists were watchlisted in late August 2001 as a result of questions raised in May 2001 by a CIA officer on assignment at the FBI.

(S) In 1998, CTC assumed responsibility for communicating watchlisting guidance in the Agency. As recently as December 1999, less than a month before the events of early January 2000, CTC had sent to all field offices of the CIA a cable reminding them of their obligation to watchlist suspected terrorists and the procedures for doing so. Field components and Headquarters units had obligations related to watchlisting, but they varied widely in their performance. That so many individuals failed to act in this case reflects a systemic breakdown—a breakdown caused by excessive workload, ambiguities about responsibilities, and mismanagement of the program. Basically, there was no coherent, functioning watchlisting program.

(S) The Review Team recommends that an Accountability Board review the performance of the two Chiefs of CTC in the years between 1998 and 2001 concerning their leadership and management oversight of the watchlisting program.

(S//NF) Agency officers also failed to pass the travel information about the two terrorists to the FBI in the prescribed channels. The Team found that an FBI officer assigned to CTC on 5 January 2000 drafted a message about the terrorists' travel that was to be sent from CIA to FBI in the proper channels. Apparently because it was in the wrong format or needed editing, the message was never sent. On the same day, another CTC officer sent a cable to several Agency addresses reporting that the information and al-Mihdhar's travel documents had been passed to the FBI. The officer who drafted this cable does not recall how this information was passed. The Team has not been able to confirm that the information was passed, or that it was not passed. Whatever the case, the Team found no indication that anyone in CTC checked to ensure FBI receipt of the information, which, a few UBL Station officers said, should have been routine practice.

(S) Separately, in March 2000, two CIA field locations sent to a number of addresses cables reporting that al-Hazmi and another al-Qa'ida associate had traveled to the United States. They were clearly identified in the cable as "UBL associates." The Team has found no evidence, and heard no claim from any party, that this information was shared in any manner with the FBI or that anyone in UBL Station took other appropriate operational action at that time.

(C) In the months following the Malaysia operation, the CIA missed several additional opportunities to nominate al-Hazmi and al-Mihdhar for watchlisting; to inform the FBI about their intended or actual travel to the United States; and to take appropriate operational action. These included a few occasions identified by the Joint Inquiry as well as several others.

(C) The consequences of the failures to share information and perform proper operational followthrough on these terrorists were potentially significant. Earlier watchlisting of al-Mihdhar could have prevented his re-entry into the United States in July 2001. Informing the FBI and good operational follow through by CIA and FBI might have resulted in surveillance of both al-Mihdhar and al-Hazmi. Surveillance, in turn, would have had the potential to yield information on flight training, financing, and links to others who were complicit in the 9/11 attacks.

(S) The Team recommends that an Accountability Board review the performance of [—about two and a half lines deleted—] for failing to ensure that someone in the Station informed the FBI and took appropriate operational action regarding al-Hazmi in March 2000. In addition, the Team recommends that the Accountability Board assess the performance of the latter three managers for failing to ensure prompt action relevant to al-Hazmi and al-Mihdhar during several later opportunities between March 2000 and August 2001.

(U) **Broader Information Sharing Issues.** The Joint Inquiry charged that CIA's information-sharing problems derived from differences among agencies with respect to missions, legal authorities, and cultures. It argued that CIA efforts to protect sources and methods fostered a reluctance to share information and limited disclosures to criminal investigators. The report also alleged that most Agency officers did not focus sufficiently on the domestic terrorism front, viewing this as an FBI mission. The 9/11 Review Team's findings are similar in many respects, but the Team believes the systemic failures in this case do not lie in reluctance to share. Rather, the basic problems were poor implementation, guidance, and oversight of processes established to foster the exchange of information, including the detailee program.

(C) CTC and UBL Station had on their rosters detailees from many different agencies, including the FBI, NSA, Federal Aviation Administration, and State Department. The manner in which these detailees were managed left many of them unclear about the nature of their responsibilities. Many CIA managers and officers believed the detailees were responsible for conveying information to their home agencies, while most of the detailees maintained that they were working as CTC officers and had neither the time nor the responsibility to serve as links to their home agencies. The Team found, at a minimum, that there were fundamental ambiguities about the responsibilities of the detailees as they related to information sharing, and that these responsibilities were never delineated explicitly or in writing. The Team recommends that an Accountability Board review the performance of the two Chiefs of CTC during the years before 9/11 concerning their oversight of the Center's practices in management of the detailee program.

(U) See the Team's discussions of Factual Finding 5b (The Watchlisting Failure) and Systemic Findings 9 (Information Sharing Within the IC) and 10 (Information Sharing with Non-IC Members) for elaboration on these issues.

(U) Strategic Analysis

(S) The Team, like the JI, found that the IC's understanding of al-Qa'ida was hampered by insufficient analytic focus, particularly regarding strategic analysis. The Team asked three individuals who had served as senior intelligence analysts and managers to conduct an independent review of the Agency's analytic products dealing with UBL and al-Qa'ida for the period from 1998 to 2001 and assess their quality. They found that, while CTC's tradecraft was generally good, important elements were missing. Discussion of implications was generally weak, for example. Most important, a number of important issues were covered insufficiently or not at all. The Team found:

- No comprehensive strategic assessment of al-Qa'ida by CTC or any other component.
- No comprehensive report focusing on UBL since 1993.
- No examination of the potential for terrorists to use aircraft as weapons, as distinguished from traditional hijackings.
- Limited analytic focus on the United States as a potential target.
- No comprehensive analysis that put into context the threats received in the spring and summer of 2001.

That said, CTC's analytic component, the Assessments and Information Group (AIG), addressed aspects of these issues in several more narrowly focused strategic papers and other analytic products.

(S) The personnel resources of AIG were heavily dedicated to policy-support and operational-support activities. Analysts focused primarily on current and tactical issues rather than on strategic analysis. In the two years prior to 9/11, the Directorate of Intelligence's [—just under one line deleted—] and others had raised with CTC managers the need to dedicate some proportion of the analytic work force to strategic analysis, as was the practice in many DI offices. In early 2001, the DCI specifically directed CTC to establish a strategic analysis unit within AIG. The Chief of AIG had for some time been aware of the need to strengthen the analytic work force and was working to do so. The strategic analysis unit was formed in July 2001; as of late July, it was manned by [—] analysts.

(S) The Team found that the National Intelligence Council (NIC) addressed the al-Qa'ida threat to only a limited extent. The NIC produced a National Intelligence Estimate on the terrorist threat to the United States in 1995 and an update in 1997. It did not produce a similar, comprehensive assessment from that point until after 9/11, although preparation of such a product was underway, with a CTC drafter, in the early months of 2001 and was being edited as of 9/11.

(U) See Team discussions of Factual Findings 2 (Signs of an Impending Attack), 3 (The Threat to the United States), and 4 (Aircraft as Weapons) and Systemic Finding 5 (Strategic Analysis) for further information on these topics.

(U) Operations (Unilateral and Liaison)

(S//NF) The Joint Inquiry charges that CIA did not effectively develop and use human resources to penetrate al-Qa'ida's inner circle, thus significantly limiting the IC's ability to acquire actionable intelligence before 9/11. The report argues that this lack of sources resulted from an excessive reliance on foreign liaison services and walk-ins (sources who volunteer); a focus on disruption and capture rather than collection; and adherence to the dirty asset rules (guidelines that restricted the recruitment of sources who had committed certain proscribed acts).

(S//NF) The Review Team did not find that CIA's reliance on liaison for collection was excessive but did find that [—] this reliance was not balanced with a strong focus on developing unilateral assets. The Team did not find that CIA reliance on walk-ins was misguided [—about one and a half lines deleted—] Although the CIA focused its al-Qa'ida operations on Afghanistan, possibly limiting its ability to focus elsewhere, the Team believes that this approach was reasonable and that its purpose was collection on al-Qa'ida as well as disruption of al-Qa'ida activities. While agreeing that the dirty asset rules may have created a climate that had the effect of inhibiting certain recruitment operations, the Team is unable to confirm or determine the extent of the impact. Finally, the Team found that several operational platforms [—about one and a half lines deleted—] were not effectively engaged in the battle against al-Qa'ida. In the case of [—] it reflected CTC's focus on Afghanistan and the priority of its attempts to penetrate al-Qa'ida's inner circle.

(S//NF) The Team found that the CIA's relations with foreign liaison services were critical to its ability to disrupt al-Qa'ida and thwart some terrorist attacks on the United States. While the capabilities and cooperation of liaison services were uneven, the program itself did not detract from CIA's effort to mount its own unilateral operations. The Team did not raise serious questions about whether CTC prior to 9/11 had made the most effective use of [—about two lines deleted—]

liaison services in it operations against al-Qa'ida. [—just over two lines deleted—] Nevertheless, the Team observes that the complicated dynamics of liaison relationships, including lack of common goals and counterintelligence problems, suggest that CTC managers made reasonable judgments [—about one and a half lines deleted—].

(S//NF) The Joint Inquiry particularly criticized CIA for the conduct of its operational relationship [—]. It noted that CIA had unsuccessfully pressed [—] authorities for additional information on individuals later identified as associates of some of the hijackers. It placed some of the blame for this on CIA's decisions [—just over one line deleted—]. The Team also found that CIA was unable to acquire the information cited by the JI but found that it made repeated efforts to do so and that its lack of success was the result of a difficult operating environment and limited cooperation on the part of [—]. The Team concluded that the decisions made with respect to [—] were reasonable.

(S//NF) The Joint Inquiry also argued that both the FBI and CIA had failed to identify the extent of support from Saudi nationals or groups for terrorist activities globally or within the United States and the extent to which such support, to the extent it existed, was knowing or inadvertent. While most of the JI discussion on the Saudi issue dealt with issues involving the FBI and its domestic operations, the report also [—just over one line deleted—]. The Team found that a significant gap existed in the CIA's understanding of Saudi extremists' involvement in plotting terrorist attacks. The primary reasons for this gap were the difficulty of the task, the hostile operational environment, and [—about one line deleted—].

(S//NF) The Team also found, however, that UBL Station and [—] were hostile to each other and working at cross-purposes over a period of years before 9/11. The Team cannot measure a specific impact of this counterproductive behavior. At a minimum, however, the Team found that organizational tensions clearly complicated and delayed the preparation of Agency approaches [—about a half line deleted—] thus negatively affecting the timely and effective functioning of the exchange with [—] on terrorism issues.

(U) See the Team's discussions of Systemic Findings 11 (HUMINT Operations Against Al-Qa'ida) and 15 (Reliance on Foreign Liaison), Factual Finding 5h (The Hijackers' Associates in Germany), and Related Finding 20 (Issues Relating to Saudi Arabia) for additional information.

(U) Covert Action

(C) The Joint Inquiry charged that US policymakers had wanted Usama Bin Ladin killed as early as August 1998 and believed that CIA personnel understood that. However, the government had not removed the ban on assassination and did not provide clear direction or authorization for CIA to kill Bin Ladin or make covert attacks against al-Qa'ida [—] The JI said that the CIA was reluctant to seek authority to assassinate Bin Ladin and averse to taking advantage of ambiguities in the authorities it did receive that might have allowed it more flexibility. The JI argued that these factors shaped the type of covert action the CIA undertook against Bin Ladin and that, before September 11, covert action had little impact on al-Qa'ida or Bin Ladin.

[—classification and heading deleted—] The findings and conclusions of the Review Team correspond with most but not all of the JI conclusions. The Team believes that the restrictions in the authorities given the CIA with respect to Bin Ladin, while arguably, although ambiguously, relaxed for a period of time in late 1998 and early 1999, limited the range of permissible operations. Given the law, executive order, and past problems with covert action programs, CIA managers refused to take advantage of the ambiguities that did exist. The Team believes this position was reasonable and correct. Ultimately, the Team concludes the failure of the Agency's covert action against Bin Ladin lay not in the language and interpretation of its authorities, but in the limitations of its covert action capabilities: CIA's heavy reliance on a single group of assets, who were of questionable reliability and had limited capabilities, proved insufficient to mount a credible operation against Bin Ladin. Efforts to develop other options had limited potential prior to 9/11.

[—classification and heading deleted—] The Joint Inquiry states that US military officials were reluctant to use military assets to conduct operations in Afghanistan or to support or participate in CIA operations against al-Qa'ida prior to 9/11. At least in part, this was a result of the IC's inability to provide the necessary intelligence to support military operations. The findings of the Team match those of the JI as they relate to the CIA. The Agency was unable to satisfy the demands of the US military for the precise, actionable intelligence that the military leadership required in order to deploy US troops on the ground in Afghanistan or launch cruise missile attacks against UBL-related sites beyond the August 1998 retaliatory strikes in Afghanistan and Sudan. Differences between CIA and the Department of Defense over the cost of replacing lost Predators[10] also hampered collaboration over the use of that platform in Afghanistan. The Team concludes, however, that other impediments, including the slow-moving policy process, reduced the importance of these CIA-military differences. The Team believes CIA handled its relationship with the US military responsibly and within the bounds of what was reasonable and possible.

[—classification and heading deleted—] The Joint Inquiry charges that the CIA failed to attack UBL's finances and failed to work cooperatively with the Department of the Treasury to develop leads and establish links to other terrorist funding sources. The Team, likewise, found that CIA failed to attack Bin Ladin's money successfully but finds that this was not for lack of effort. [—four lines deleted—] The Team also agrees that bureaucratic obstacles and legal restrictions inhibited CIA's partnership with the Department of the Treasury.

(U) See the Team's discussions of Systemic Findings 13 (Covert Action), 14 (Collaboration with the Military), and 16 (Strategy to Disrupt Terrorist Funding) for more information on these issues.

(U) Technology

[—classification and heading deleted—] The Joint Inquiry charged that technology had not been fully and effectively applied in support of US counterterrorism efforts. The Team found that significant differences existed between CIA and NSA over several critical issues. One of these involved a dispute over which agency had authority [—one and four-fifths lines deleted—] This dispute had not yet been resolved in September 2001. The second issue involved NSA's unwillingness to share raw SIGINT[11] transcripts with CIA; this made it more difficult for CTC to perform its mission against al-Qa'ida. In the late 1990s, however, NSA managers offered to allow a CTC officer to be detailed to NSA to cull the transcripts for useful information. CTC sent one officer to NSA for a brief period of time in 2000, but failed to send others, citing resource constraints. The Team recommends that an Accountability Board review the performance of the Chiefs of CTC for their failure to detail officers to NSA on a consistent, full-time basis to exploit this material in the years before 9/11.

(U) See the Team's discussions of Systemic Findings 4 (Application of Technology) and 7 (Computer Exploitation) for discussion of the technology issue.

Soon after the 9/11 attacks, DCI Tenet issued a memorandum to the CIA's top managers, indicating the focus and scale of the defensive and offensive tasks ahead of them. The sense of urgency comes through, but it is accompanied by an evident belief that the decades-old problems of compartmentalization, bureaucracy, and interagency coordination could be overcome by fiat and wishful thinking.

DIRECTOR OF CENTRAL INTELLIGENCE
WASHINGTON, D.C. 20505

16 September 2001

MEMORANDUM FOR:	DDCI[12]
	DDCI/CM
	ExDIR
	D/ExDIR
	ADCI/MS
	DDI
	DDO
	DDS&T
	C/NIC
	D/OCA
	C/CTC
SUBJECT:	We're at War

We must now finalize our strategy and leadership structure to wage a worldwide war against al-Qa'ida and other terrorist organizations. Our unrelenting focus must be on bringing all of our operational, analytical, and technical capabilities to bear—not only to protect the US both here and abroad from additional terrorist acts—but also, and more importantly, to neutralize and destroy al-Qa'ida and its partners.

This will require our absolute and total dedication as a leadership team. It will require your sustained focus and attention. It will require you to translate the urgency of the difficult tasks ahead to the men and women we lead by our behavior and actions.

There can be no bureaucratic impediments to success. All the rules have changed. There must be an absolute and full sharing of information, ideas, and capabilities. We do not have time to hold meetings to fix problems—fix them—quickly and smartly. Each person must assume an unprecedented degree of personal responsibility.

We must ensure that these same principles apply in dealing with our law enforcement, military, other civilian agencies, and Intelligence Community colleagues. Whatever systemic problems existed in any of these relationships must be identified and solved now.

There must be an absolute seamlessness in our approach to waging this war—and we must lead.

We must all be passionate and driven—but not breathless. We must stay cool. We must keep our heads. Never has our professionalism and discipline been at a greater premium. We must maintain these core values at all costs.

I have attached a list of priorities that we will need to coordinate and act upon immediately.

Together we will win this war and make our President and the American people proud. We will win this war on behalf of our fallen and injured brothers and sisters in New York and Washington and their families. We will win it for all that we value as a nation.

/signed/
George J. Tenet

Attachment:
As Stated [not released]

NOTES

1. George Tenet, with Bill Harlow, *At the Center of the Storm: My Years at the CIA* (New York: HarperCollins, 2007): 100.
2. Paul R. Pillar, "A Scapegoat Is Not a Solution," *New York Times* (4 June 2004). This op-ed by a CIA analyst seeks to refute the 9/11 Commission's claim that the agency paid insufficient attention to al-Qa'ida in the 1990s.
3. Quoted in Loch K. Johnson, "The Aspin-Brown Intelligence Inquiry: Behind the Closed Doors of a Blue Ribbon Commission," *Studies in Intelligence* 48:3 (2004).
4. Pillar, "A Scapegoat Is Not a Solution."
5. It appears that the "chemical plant" in Sudan was actually a pharmaceutical plant.
6. *The 9/11 Commission Report: Final Report of the National Commission on the Terrorist Attacks upon the United States* (New York: W. W. Norton, 2004).
7. The text began with the name "Steve," a reference to Deputy National Security Adviser Stephen J. Hadley, but this was crossed out and "Condi" and was written in by hand.
8. That is, the 9/11 Commission, which was led by former Governor Thomas Kean and former Representative Lee Hamilton.
9. As a result of a conflict of interest, the Inspector General recused himself from deliberations on the performance of Agency components and individuals relating to the KSM issue and to the strategic analysis issues discussed below. The two successive Deputy Inspectors General did participate in accountability discussions regarding analysis and other issues. [Note in original.]
10. Pilotless, missile-firing aircraft.
11. Signals intelligence (SIGINT) has two components. Communications intelligence (COMINT) involves the interception and processing of foreign communications, including encrypted messages. Electronic intelligence (ELINT) relates to the analysis of non-communications electromagnetic radiation, such as signals given off by radar installations or during missile tests. Here, presumably, COMINT is meant. See Jeffrey T. Richelson, *The U.S. Intelligence Community*, 5th ed. (Boulder, CO: Westview Press, 2008): 31.
12. DDCI stands for Deputy Director of Central Intelligence; DDCI/CM stands for Deputy Director of Central Intelligence for [Intelligence] Community Management; ExDIR stands for Executive Director; D/ExDIR stands for Deputy Executive Director; ADCI/MS stands for Associate Director of Central Intelligence for Military Support; DDI stands for Deputy Director for Intelligence; DDO stands for Deputy Director for Operations; DDS&T stands for Deputy Director for Science and Technology; C/NIC stands for Chairman, National Intelligence Council; D/OCA stands for Director, Office of Congressional Affairs; C/CTC stands for Chief, Counterterrorist Center.

Chapter 16

The Global War on Terrorism

After the attacks of 9/11, the war on terrorism proceeded in several directions, targeting Afghanistan, Iraq, and the international al-Qa'ida network. Within weeks of the 9/11 attacks, the United States launched a military assault against Afghanistan, where al-Qa'ida had found support from the Taliban government and where it maintained its principal operating bases.

Al-Qa'ida's ally, the Taliban, controlled about 85 percent of Afghan territory. Opposed to the Taliban were the ethnic Tajik and Uzbek militias of the Northern Alliance. The direct U.S. military effort focused on the use of air power. On the ground, starting 27 September 2001, Special Operations Forces (SOF) units and a group of CIA officers designated the Northern Alliance Liaison Team (NALT) coordinated with the Northern Alliance militias and other tribal leaders known to the CIA since the earlier war against the Soviet army. To run the operation, a new office was established in the Counterterrorist Center, CTC Special Operations (CTC/SO). The "overt" war began on 7 October. By the end of the year, the Taliban government had fallen. The U.S. ground operation consisted essentially of about 110 CIA officers and 316 SOF personnel, operating with Afghan allies.[1]

An effort by anti-Taliban Afghan troops to find Usama bin Ladin in the Tora Bora Mountains of eastern Afghanistan failed in early 2002. Many members of the Taliban and al-Qa'ida escaped across the border to the mountainous frontier region of Pakistan, which was inhabited by closely related Pathan tribes. This region officially designated the Federally Administered Tribal Areas (FATA), is "federal" only in the sense that no province runs it. In fact, no government authority is recognized by the fiercely independent tribes and the Pakistani army had not ventured there in decades. Politically, the situation was further complicated by the fact that the Pakistani government had long encouraged Islamists in the frontier region and in Afghanistan (including the Taliban at one time) because the Islamists, disdaining secular authority in general, did not claim the northwestern region of Pakistan for the state of Afghanistan.

According to reports, certain key Pakistani institutions, especially the Directorate for Inter-Services Intelligence, continued to support them. There, al-Qa'ida and the Taliban reconstituted themselves.

The next target, Iraq, was only tangentially connected to the war on terrorism as it is generally understood, and many observers have considered it a diversion of attention and resources. During 2002, with Usama bin Ladin and other key leaders still at large, CIA and military personnel who had been dedicated to the Afghan and al-Qa'ida issues were reassigned to the pending invasion of Iraq. After the initial, successful invasion phase of that war was over, the prolonged and ill-prepared occupation and counterinsurgency campaign in Iraq encouraged a new generation of militants from many corners of the Muslim world to join al-Qa'ida or to attack Western interests independently in its name. (See Chapter 17, "Iraq, Terrorism, and Weapons of Mass Destruction.")

The third aspect of the war on terrorism was not geographically focused like the Afghan and Iraqi wars. The war against the international al-Qa'ida network was more properly an intelligence operation than a military one. The various operational aspects of this clandestine war included: (a) direct action by the CIA, often in collaboration with the intelligence services of other countries, against al-Qa'ida camps, militants, and operations; (b) the detention and interrogation of captured terrorism suspects at undisclosed sites abroad, despite the fact that the U.S. government has frequently condemned other countries for engaging in secret detention and coercive interrogation; and (c) the "extraordinary rendition" of some terrorism suspects to the custody of other countries, without acknowledgment. Controversies surrounded the agency's use of secret detention and allegedly coercive interrogation techniques, as well as the practice of extraordinary rendition.

In this altogether unusual sort of conflict, the rules were invented on the fly. The normal rules of war were at times adjusted, redefined, or simply declared irrelevant. In the words of Philip Zelikow, a former State Department Counselor in the Bush administration:

> Operating under broad legal parameters set shortly after the 9/11 attacks, a series of policy choices were made, especially in 2002 and 2003, about how to conduct the armed conflict. Especially in the case of CIA, it appears from publicly available sources that, responding to some informal guidance from the White House, the Agency designed, developed, and implemented various techniques and capabilities with little substantive policy analysis or interagency consideration.[2]

Direct action against al-Qa'ida targets included attacks with antitank missiles launched from Predator unmanned aerial vehicles (UAVs). These planes could be piloted remotely from a console in a different country or even on a different continent. Such means were used to kill Abu Ali al-Harithi in Yemen in 2002, Abu Hamza Rabia and Haitham al-Yemeni in separate attacks in Pakistan in 2005, and Abu Laith al-Libi in Pakistan in 2008. An attempt was made in January 2006 to target Ayman al-Zawahiri, in Pakistan. Zawahiri, an Egyptian physician, was generally described as al-Qa'ida's second-ranking leader, although some analysts considered him even more important than Bin Ladin to the group's operations.[3] In this instance, however, Zawahiri proved not to be at the site at the time of the attack. Pakistani officials initially claimed that a number of other important al-Qa'ida leaders had been killed in the strike, but U.S. and Pakistani officials later concluded that only local villagers had died. The CIA boosted the number of its officers and agents in the border region in 2006, but still was unable to locate the al-Qa'ida leadership effectively.[4]

In January 2008 the CIA reportedly negotiated with Pakistan for less restrictive rules of engagement. The new guidelines would allegedly permit an increase in the number and scope of air strikes and allow more leeway to act without Islamabad's permission. President Pervez Musharraf, however, rejected proposals for a direct U.S. ground combat role on any scale, which he said would create a political backlash. There were also disagreements as to whether the principal target of counterterrorist efforts should be al-Qa'ida, as the United States believed, or the Taliban, as Pakistan preferred.[5]

Other types of covert operations may have been undertaken as well. One proposed "snatch-and-grab" raid into Pakistani territory became publicly known, in part, because it never happened. This was in early 2005, and again Zawahiri was a principal target. The plan, which included both the CIA and Special Operations Forces, was highly sensitive because it involved penetrating the sovereign territory of an ally. Pakistan's leader, President Musharraf, was already politically vulnerable domestically for a variety of reasons, among them his willingness to help Westerners fight Muslims. The planners thus faced conflicting pressures: Using a larger force was less risky for the participants and more likely to succeed operationally, but using a smaller force was more likely to escape the notice of Pakistan's political opposition. The plan began small, but then was expanded during the process of review at the Pentagon, eventually growing to include several hundred CIA officers, Army Rangers, and Navy Seals. At that point, Secretary of Defense Donald Rumsfeld decided that it could not be done without Musharraf's permission. Not only was this unlikely, but some analysts suspected elements of Pakistan's Inter-Service Intelligence of passing information to the Islamists and were reluctant to share this information with them. Rumsfeld canceled the operation, rejecting a last-minute appeal by CIA Director Porter Goss.[6]

The CIA and its allies did successfully capture a number of key lieutenants in the al-Qa'ida hierarchy, including Abu Zubaydah, Ramzi bin al-Shibh, and the planner of the 9/11 attacks, Khalid Shaykh Muhammad, either directly or through the cooperation of the authorities of Pakistan and other countries. A larger number of less important people were also detained. Some 770 people—many of them seized by, or turned over to, the U.S. Army in Afghanistan—were detained at a Pentagon-operated facility at the U.S. Naval Base at Guantánamo Bay, Cuba. This was, in itself, a controversial choice in that it appeared to be intended to evade the jurisdiction of U.S. courts. Many of these people were eventually processed, interrogated, and released. As of this writing, several hundred have been held indefinitely. About a dozen have been charged with crimes, but further controversies have ensued over the U.S. government's determination that the normal rules of war did not apply to people that it classified as "unlawful combatants" rather than prisoners of war.

In addition to the Pentagon's Guantánamo facilities, however, the CIA operated a number of clandestine detention centers at undisclosed sites outside the United States. It was widely reported—but could not be proved—that detainees were subject to harsh interrogation techniques tantamount to torture. This raised considerable controversy. In particular, Senator John McCain—who had been tortured as a prisoner in North Vietnam in the 1960s—led vociferous opposition, but apparently there was also controversy within the Justice Department. The administration regularly denied that it engaged in "torture," but in summer 2004 it was discovered that the Justice Department had secretly set a very narrow definition of torture. This came in a fifty-page memorandum, dated 1 August 2002, from Assistant Attorney General Jay S. Bybee, the head of the Office of Legal Counsel, to Presidential Counsel Alberto Gonzales. Referring to Sections 2340–2340A of title 18 of the U.S. Code, which make it a criminal offense to commit or attempt to commit torture, the memo finishes with the following:

Conclusion

For the foregoing reasons, we conclude that torture as defined in and proscribed by Sections 2340–2340A, covers only extreme acts. Severe pain is generally of the kind difficult for the victim to endure. Where the pain is physical, it must be of an intensity akin to that which accompanies serious physical injury such as death or organ failure. Severe mental pain requires suffering not just at the moment of infliction but it also requires lasting psychological harm, such as in mental disorders like posttraumatic stress disorder. Additionally, such severe mental pain can arise only from the predicate acts listed in Section 2340. Because the acts inflicting torture are extreme, there is significant range of acts that though they might constitute cruel, inhuman, or degrading treatment or punishment fail to rise to the level of torture.

Further, we conclude that under the circumstances of the current war against al Qaeda and its allies, application of Section 2340A to interrogations undertaken pursuant to the President's Commander-in-Chief powers may be unconstitutional. Finally, even if an interrogation method might violate 2340A, necessity or self-defense could provide justifications that would eliminate any criminal liability.

Please let us know if we can be of further assistance.

This, of course, permitted numerous possibilities short of "death or organ failure" that many people might still consider torture, quite apart from the notion that outlawing torture might be an unconstitutional restriction on presidential powers. Indeed, according to news reports, CIA Inspector General John L. Helgerson issued a secret report in the spring of 2004 warning that some of the approved interrogation techniques might violate provisions prohibiting cruel, inhuman, and degrading treatment in the international Convention Against Torture, which formed the basis for Sections 2340–2340A.[7]

In December 2004, the Justice Department quietly posted a legal opinion on its Web site that condemned torture as "abhorrent" and specifically argued against the provisions of the Bybee memo.[8] According to news reports, in February 2005, shortly after Alberto Gonzales became Attorney General, the department issued a new secret opinion endorsing all the interrogation practices then used by the CIA, whether applied singularly or in combination. This, however, did not become public knowledge until October 2007. In December 2005, Congress passed the Detainee Treatment Act, which included the provision: "No individual in the custody or under the physical control of the United States Government, regardless of nationality or physical location, shall be subject to cruel, inhuman, or degrading treatment or punishment." By that time, however, the Justice Department had already issued yet another secret memorandum, which simply declared that none of the methods used by the CIA were cruel, inhuman, or degrading.[9] By 2006, the U.S. Army was dissociating itself from techniques allegedly used by the CIA, while the Bush administration endeavored to have Congress legalize what it called "enhanced interrogation techniques" without disclosing what they actually were.

Evidently, no effort was made to determine the relative effectiveness or reliability of coercive interrogation versus other possible techniques. A study sponsored by the National Defense Intelligence College, released in December 2006, noted that effective, noncoercive interrogation techniques had been developed by the U.S. Army during World War II, but the knowledge was later lost. Interrogators in the twenty-first century were therefore required to improvise.

> With the attacks of 11 September 2001, and the initiation of the Global War on Terrorism, the Intelligence Community plunged into activities that, of necessity, involved efforts to obtain information from persons in U.S. custody who at least initially appeared uncooperative. At holding facilities in Afghanistan, Cuba, Iraq, and perhaps other sites, active duty military personnel, reservists, intelligence officers, law enforcement agents, contracted interrogators, and others worked to glean information and create intelligence that might help prevent terrorist attacks and contribute to national security. Since there had been little or no development of sustained capacity for interrogation practice, training, or research within intelligence or military communities in the post-Soviet period, many interrogators were forced to "make it up" on the fly. This shortfall in advanced, research-based interrogation methods at a time of intense pressure from operational commanders to produce actionable intelligence from high-value targets may have contributed significantly to the unfortunate cases of abuse that have recently come to light. Perhaps in the future, EI [Educing Information] professionals and researchers can develop knowledge that will inform and improve both practice and policy in these critical areas of national security.[10]

Another author in the same study highlights the simple lack of information about the relative effectiveness of coercive techniques.

> Of particular concern, we do not fully understand a complex of issues surrounding the use of coercion. Coercion is an important issue in all types of interrogation— from local police precincts and petty crimes to distant centers of detention and serious terrorist threats. The costs of coercion in human, ethical, political, and other terms vary, but can be enormous. Even when these costs are acknowledged, contemporary discussions often assume that torture, physical coercion, and psychological coercion are effective ways to obtain information, especially in emergencies (e.g., when there is little time, as with "ticking bombs"). Torture and many forms of physical and psychological coercion have been used for centuries. Whether we like it or not, coercion might be more "effective" than other methods in some circumstances. Unfortunately, much of the current debate in this area proceeds as if we actually knew what those circumstances were. In fact, we do not, beyond anecdotal evidence adduced ad hoc.[11]

The Supreme Court, in the case of *Hamdan* v. *Rumsfeld* (2006), determined that, regardless of the position of the Bush administration, Common Article 3 of the Geneva Conventions—which prohibits cruel treatment, torture, and humiliating or degrading treatment—must be applied to all detainees. Although the CIA maintained that its methods had never violated the restrictions, Common Article 3 was considered vague and open to interpretation. The interrogation program was reportedly put in limbo for nearly a year while factions within the administration argued over how far to press the legal limits as they drew up new, more specific rules.[12] The Department of Justice eventually approved a specific list of interrogation methods, which remained secret. On 20 July 2007, President Bush issued an executive order, "Interpretation of the Geneva Conventions Common Article 3 as Applied to a Program of Detention and Interrogation Operated by the Central Intelligence Agency," which prohibited certain forms of behavior and tied certain definitions to specific sections of the U.S. Code but did not specify what was allowed. Unnamed sources, however, told the media that the CIA had abandoned the practice known as "waterboarding," which induces the sensation of drowning, and exposure to extremes of heat or cold.[13] In part, the executive order reads as follows:

Sec. 3. Compliance of a Central Intelligence Agency Detention and Interrogation Program with Common Article 3. (a) Pursuant to the authority of the President under the Constitution and the laws of the United States, including the Military Commissions Act of 2006, this order interprets the meaning and application of the text of Common Article 3 with respect to certain detentions and interrogations, and shall be treated as authoritative for all purposes as a matter of United States law, including satisfaction of the international obligations of the United States. I hereby determine that Common Article 3 shall apply to a program of detention and interrogation operated by the Central Intelligence Agency as set forth in this section. The requirements set forth in this section shall be applied with respect to detainees in such program without adverse distinction as to their race, color, religion or faith, sex, birth, or wealth.

(b) I hereby determine that a program of detention and interrogation approved by the Director of the Central Intelligence Agency fully complies with the obligations of the United States under Common Article 3, provided that:

(i)   the conditions of confinement and interrogation practices of the program do not include:

(A)   torture, as defined in section 2340 of title 18, United States Code;

(B)   any of the acts prohibited by section 2441(d) of title 18, United States Code, including murder, torture, cruel or inhuman treatment, mutilation or maiming, intentionally causing serious bodily injury, rape, sexual assault or abuse, taking of hostages, or performing of biological experiments;

(C)   other acts of violence serious enough to be considered comparable to murder, torture, mutilation, and cruel or inhuman treatment, as defined in section 2441(d) of title 18, United States Code;

(D)   any other acts of cruel, inhuman, or degrading treatment or punishment prohibited by the Military Commissions Act (subsection 6(c) of Public Law 109 366) and the Detainee Treatment Act of 2005 (section 1003 of Public Law 109 148 and section 1403 of Public Law 109 163);

(E)   willful and outrageous acts of personal abuse done for the purpose of humiliating or degrading the individual in a manner so serious that any reasonable person, considering the circumstances, would deem the acts to be beyond the bounds of human decency, such as sexual or sexually indecent acts undertaken for the purpose of humiliation, forcing the individual to perform sexual acts or to pose sexually, threatening the individual with sexual mutilation, or using the individual as a human shield; or

    (F) acts intended to denigrate the religion, religious practices, or religious objects of the individual;

  (ii) the conditions of confinement and interrogation practices are to be used with an alien detainee who is determined by the Director of the Central Intelligence Agency:

    (A) to be a member or part of or supporting al Qaeda, the Taliban, or associated organizations; and

    (B) likely to be in possession of information that:

        (1) could assist in detecting, mitigating, or preventing terrorist attacks, such as attacks within the United States or against its Armed Forces or other personnel, citizens, or facilities, or against allies or other countries cooperating in the war on terror with the United States, or their armed forces or other personnel, citizens, or facilities; or

        (2) could assist in locating the senior leadership of al Qaeda, the Taliban, or associated forces;

  (iii) the interrogation practices are determined by the Director of the Central Intelligence Agency, based upon professional advice, to be safe for use with each detainee with whom they are used; and

  (iv) detainees in the program receive the basic necessities of life, including adequate food and water, shelter from the elements, necessary clothing, protection from extremes of heat and cold, and essential medical care.

(c) The Director of the Central Intelligence Agency shall issue written policies to govern the program, including guidelines for Central Intelligence Agency personnel that implement paragraphs (i)(C), (E), and (F) of subsection 3(b) of this order, and including requirements to ensure:

  (i) safe and professional operation of the program;

  (ii) the development of an approved plan of interrogation tailored for each detainee in the program to be interrogated, consistent with subsection 3(b)(iv) of this order;

  (iii) appropriate training for interrogators and all personnel operating the program;

  (iv) effective monitoring of the program, including with respect to medical matters, to ensure the safety of those in the program; and

  (v) compliance with applicable law and this order.

Apart from its own detention and interrogation program, the CIA engaged in another practice known as "extraordinary rendition," in which selected prisoners were "rendered" to other countries for detention and interrogation (although CIA personnel might still be involved in some cases). The U.S. government insisted it had assurances that detainees rendered would not be abused or tortured, but the questions of who was sent, where they were sent, why they were sent, and how they were treated all remained cloaked in secrecy, which naturally contributed to an atmosphere of rumor and suspicion.

To date, little is known of this program, but certain cases have highlighted the potential shortcomings of the practice and seriously complicated relations with U.S. allies. For example, in January 2004, U.S. agents seized Khaled el-Masri, a Lebanese-born German citizen, while he was in Macedonia. He was sent to Afghanistan, kept in secret detention, and allegedly tortured. After five months, he was sent to Albania and released. According to news reports, the CIA had mistaken him for someone else with a similar name. A German court issued thirteen arrest warrants for people said to be affiliated with the CIA, none of whom was likely to be extradited from the United States.[14]

On 17 February 2003, Hassan Mustafa Osama Nasr, also known as Abu Omar, was seized on the streets of Milan. He was dispatched to an Egyptian prison, where he says he was tortured. In this case, the Italian authorities agreed that Abu Omar was a terrorism suspect, but they also said that the abduction disrupted their own investigation of him and his associates and in any event violated Italian law. Prosecutors charged twenty-five people said to be affiliated with the CIA, as well as the head of Italian military intelligence, with kidnapping. Again, no extradition is likely. Incidentally, the CIA Chief of Station in Milan had reportedly opposed this rendition on the basis that the ongoing Italian investigation could still have gathered information.[15]

Allegations that detainees were being transported through Europe became the subject of heated debate there. One such report maintained that detainees had been flown through British territory without permission. These reports were repeatedly denied by the CIA. At the beginning of 2008, however, Director Michael V. Hayden informed the British government that the denials had been premature, although the violations had not been in Europe per se but on the Indian Ocean island of Diego Garcia. Foreign Secretary David Miliband made a public announcement of the reversal, prompting the following statement by Hayden to the CIA staff:

Statement to Employees by Director of the Central Intelligence Agency, General Mike Hayden on the Past Use of Diego Garcia

February 21, 2008

The British Government announced today that the United States recently provided information on rendition flights through Diego Garcia—a UK territory in the Indian Ocean—that contradicted earlier data from us. Our government had told the British that there had been no rendition flights involving their soil or airspace since 9/11. That information, supplied in good faith, turned out to be wrong.

In fact, on two different occasions in 2002, an American plane with a detainee aboard stopped briefly in Diego Garcia for refueling. Neither of those individuals was ever part of CIA's high-value terrorist interrogation program. One was ultimately transferred to Guantanamo, and the other was returned to his home country.[16] These were rendition operations, nothing more. There has been speculation in the press over the years that CIA had a holding facility on Diego Garcia. That is false. There have also been allegations that we transport detainees for the purpose of torture. That, too, is false. Torture is against our laws and our values. And, given our mission, CIA could have no interest in a process destined to produce bad intelligence.

In late 2007, CIA itself took a fresh look at records on rendition flights. This time, the examination revealed the two stops in Diego Garcia. The refueling, conducted more than five years ago, lasted just a short time. But it happened. That we found this mistake ourselves, and that we brought it to the attention of the British Government, in no way changes or excuses the reality that we were in the wrong. An important part of intelligence work, inherently urgent, complex, and uncertain, is to take responsibility for errors and to learn from them. In this case, the result of a flawed records search, we have done so.

Mike Hayden

In June 2007, investigators for the Council of Europe, an official body dedicated to human rights issues, charged that the CIA maintained secret detention centers in Poland and Romania from 2003 to 2005. The Polish and Romanian governments denied the existence of such facilities, although the military intelligence agencies of both countries were said to have been complicit. The local military agencies reportedly informed their presidents and defense ministers, but the prime ministers and legislators were kept in the dark. In these cases, the detention centers were said to be staffed entirely by the CIA.[17] The seventy-two page Council of Europe report notes:

> The rendition, abduction, and detention of terrorist suspects have always taken place outside the territory of the United States, where such actions would no doubt have been ruled unlawful and unconstitutional. Obviously, these actions are also unacceptable under the laws of European countries, who nonetheless tolerated them or colluded actively in carrying them out. This export of illegal activities overseas is all the more shocking in that it shows fundamental contempt for the countries on whose territories it was decided to commit the relevant acts. The fact that the measures only apply to non-American citizens is just as disturbing: it reflects a kind of "legal apartheid" and an exaggerated sense of superiority. Once again, the blame does not lie solely with the Americans but also, above all, with European political leaders who have knowingly acquiesced in this state of affairs.[18]

The government of Canada investigated the case of one particular extraordinary rendition, that of Maher Arar. A Syrian-born citizen of Canada, Arar was detained at John F. Kennedy International Airport in New York City on 26 September 2002. On 2 October, Arar was handed the following document, as transcribed by a Canadian consular official.[19]

Factual Allegation of Inadmissibility under Section 235C of the Immigration and Naturalization Act.

1) You are not a citizen of the United States.
2) You are a native of Syria and a citizen of Syria and Canada.
3) You arrived in the United States on September 26, 2002, and applied for admission as a non-immigrant in transit through the United States, destined to Canada.
4) You are a member of an organizing [sic] that has been designated by the Secretary of State as a Foreign Terrorist organization, to wit Al Qaeda aka Al Qa'ida.

Given the al-Qa'ida allegation, Canadian consular officials assumed that the FBI would investigate Arar for some time. Instead, he was rendered to Syria within days, despite the fact that Syria is listed by the U.S. government as a sponsor of terrorism. He was held there from October 2002 to October 2003. The Canadian government report notes:

> In October 2002, CSIS [Canadian Security and Intelligence Service] officials knew that the United States might have sent Mr. Arar to a country where he could be

questioned in a "firm manner." In a report to his superiors dated October 11, 2002, the CSIS security liaison officer (SLO) in Washington spoke of a trend they had noted lately that when the CIA or FBI cannot legally hold a terrorist suspect, or wish a target questioned in a firm manner, they have them rendered to countries willing to fulfill that role. He said Mr. Arar was a case in point.

On October 10, 2002, Mr. [Jack] Hooper [CSIS Assistant Director, Operations] stated in a memorandum: "I think the U.S. would like to get Arar to Jordan where they can have their way with him." Mr. Arar's whereabouts were unknown at the time.[20]

A CSIS delegation went to Syria in November 2002 and reported that "the Syrians did not appear to view this as a major case and seemed to look upon the matter as more of a nuisance than anything else."[21] According to Arar, he was kept for more than ten months in a damp, three-foot-by-six-foot cell with two blankets but no furniture. After his return to Canada, he reported in a statement:

> Interrogations are carried out in different rooms. One tactic they use is to question prisoners for two hours, and then put them in a waiting room, so they can hear the others screaming, and then bring them back to continue the interrogation.
>
> The cable is a black electrical cable, about two inches thick. They hit me with it everywhere on my body. They mostly aimed for my palms, but sometimes missed and hit my wrists. They were sore and red for three weeks. They also struck me on my hips, and lower back. Interrogators constantly threatened me with the metal chair, tire and electric shocks.
>
> The tire is used to restrain prisoners while they torture them with beating on the sole of their feet. I guess I was lucky, because they put me in the tire, but only as a threat. I was not beaten while in tire. They used the cable on the second and third day, and after that mostly beat me with their hands, hitting me in the stomach and on the back of my neck, and slapping me on the face. Where they hit me with the cables, my skin turned blue for two or three weeks, but there was no bleeding. At the end of the day they told me tomorrow would be worse. So I could not sleep.
>
> Then on the third day, the interrogation lasted about 18 hours. They beat me from time to time and made me wait in the waiting room for one to two hours before resuming the interrogation. While in the waiting room I heard a lot of people screaming. They wanted me to say I went to Afghanistan. This was a surprise to me. They had not asked about this in the United States.
>
> They kept beating me so I had to falsely confess and told them I did go to Afghanistan. I was ready to confess to anything if it would stop the torture. They wanted me to say I went to a training camp. I was so scared I urinated on myself twice. The beating was less severe each of the following days.[22]

In determining the reason for Arar's rendition, the investigating commission concluded that a report from the Royal Canadian Mounted Police had misrepresented him to U.S. authorities on the basis that he was an acquaintance of another Syrian native who had been rendered to Syria, had refused to be interviewed in Canada (in fact, he had agreed with conditions but the interview was never conducted), and had then "suddenly" fled the country (he visited his in-laws in Tunisia five months later). He was detained in New York while returning to Canada from Tunisia.

The first public acknowledgment of the CIA's secret detention centers came in a speech from President George W. Bush, on 6 September 2006, when he announced that fourteen prominent detainees were to be transferred from the secret sites to the U.S. Naval Base at Guantánamo Bay. He discussed the positive results of CIA interrogations in some detail. Of course, he said little about the interrogation methods used other than to assert their legality and did not address the question of whether the same, or more, information might have been elicited by other means.

In addition to the terrorists held at Guantánamo, a small number of suspected terrorist leaders and operatives captured during the war have been held and questioned outside the United States, in a separate program operated by the Central Intelligence Agency. This group includes individuals believed to be the key architects of the September the 11th attacks, and attacks on the USS Cole, an operative involved in the bombings of our embassies in Kenya and Tanzania, and individuals involved in other attacks that have taken the lives of innocent civilians across the world. These are dangerous men with unparalleled knowledge about terrorist networks and their plans for new attacks. The security of our nation and the lives of our citizens depend on our ability to learn what these terrorists know.

Many specifics of this program, including where these detainees have been held and the details of their confinement, cannot be divulged. Doing so would provide our enemies with information they could use to take retribution against our allies and harm our country. I can say that questioning the detainees in this program has given us information that has saved innocent lives by helping us stop new attacks—here in the United States and across the world. Today, I'm going to share with you some of the examples provided by our Intelligence Community of how this program has saved lives; why it remains vital to the security of the United States, and our friends and allies; and why it deserves the support of the United States Congress and the American people.

Within months of September the 11th, 2001, we captured a man known as Abu Zubaydah. We believe that Zubaydah was a senior terrorist leader and a trusted associate of Osama bin Laden. Our Intelligence Community believes he had run a terrorist camp in Afghanistan where some of the 9/11 hijackers trained, and that he helped smuggle al Qaeda leaders out of Afghanistan after coalition forces arrived to liberate that country. Zubaydah was severely wounded during the firefight that brought him into custody—and he survived only because of the medical care arranged by the CIA.

After he recovered, Zubaydah was defiant and evasive. He declared his hatred of America. During questioning, he at first disclosed what he thought was nominal information—and then stopped all cooperation. Well, in fact, the "nominal" information he gave us turned out to be quite important. For example, Zubaydah disclosed Khalid Sheikh Mohammed—or KSM—was the mastermind behind the 9/11 attacks, and used the alias "Muktar." This was a vital piece of the puzzle that helped our Intelligence Community pursue KSM. Abu Zubaydah also provided information that helped stop a terrorist attack being planned for inside the United States—an attack about which we had no previous information. Zubaydah told us that al Qaeda operatives were planning to launch an attack in the U.S., and provided physical descriptions of the operatives and information on their general location. Based on the information he provided, the operatives were detained—one while traveling to the United States.

We knew that Zubaydah had more information that could save innocent lives, but he stopped talking. As his questioning proceeded, it became clear that he had received training on how to resist interrogation. And so the CIA used an alternative set of procedures. These procedures were designed to be safe, to comply with our laws, our Constitution, and our treaty obligations. The Department of Justice reviewed the authorized methods extensively and determined them to be lawful.

I cannot describe the specific methods used—I think you understand why—if I did, it would help the terrorists learn how to resist questioning, and to keep information from us that we need to prevent new attacks on our country. But I can say the procedures were tough, and they were safe, and lawful, and necessary.

Zubaydah was questioned using these procedures, and soon he began to provide information on key al Qaeda operatives, including information that helped us find and capture more of those responsible for the attacks on September the 11th. For example, Zubaydah identified one of KSM's accomplices in the 9/11 attacks—a terrorist named Ramzi bin al Shibh. The information Zubaydah provided helped lead to the capture of bin al Shibh. And together these two terrorists provided information that helped in the planning and execution of the operation that captured Khalid Sheikh Mohammed.

Once in our custody, KSM was questioned by the CIA using these procedures, and he soon provided information that helped us stop another planned attack on the United States. During questioning, KSM told us about another al Qaeda operative he knew was in CIA custody—a terrorist named Majid Khan. KSM revealed that Khan had been told to deliver $50,000 to individuals working for a suspected terrorist leader named Hambali, the leader of al Qaeda's Southeast Asian affiliate known as "J-I." CIA officers confronted Khan with this information. Khan confirmed that the money had been delivered to an operative named Zubair, and provided both a physical description and contact number for this operative.

Based on that information, Zubair was captured in June of 2003, and he soon provided information that helped lead to the capture of Hambali. After Hambali's arrest, KSM was questioned again. He identified Hambali's brother as the leader of a "J-I" cell, and Hambali's conduit for communications with al Qaeda. Hambali's brother was soon captured in Pakistan, and, in turn, led us to a cell of 17 Southeast Asian "J-I" operatives. When confronted with the news that his terror cell had been broken up, Hambali admitted that the operatives were being groomed at KSM's request for attacks inside the United States—probably [sic] using airplanes.

During questioning, KSM also provided many details of other plots to kill innocent Americans. For example, he described the design of planned attacks on buildings inside the United States, and how operatives were directed to carry them out. He told us the operatives had been instructed to ensure that the explosives went off at a point that was high enough to prevent the people trapped above from escaping out the windows.

KSM also provided vital information on al Qaeda's efforts to obtain biological weapons. During questioning, KSM admitted that he had met three individuals involved in al Qaeda's efforts to produce anthrax, a deadly biological agent—and he identified one of the individuals as a terrorist named Yazid. KSM apparently believed we already had this information, because Yazid had been captured and taken into foreign custody before KSM's arrest. In fact, we did not know about Yazid's role in al Qaeda's anthrax program. Information from Yazid then helped lead to the capture of his two principal assistants in the anthrax program. Without the information provided by KSM and Yazid, we might not have uncovered this al Qaeda biological weapons program, or stopped this al Qaeda cell from developing anthrax for attacks against the United States.

These are some of the plots that have been stopped because of the information of this vital program. Terrorists held in CIA custody have also provided information that helped stop a planned strike on U.S. Marines at Camp Lemonier in Djibouti—they were going to use an explosive-laden water tanker. They helped stop a planned attack on the U.S. consulate in Karachi using car bombs and motorcycle bombs, and they helped stop a plot to hijack passenger planes and fly them into Heathrow or the Canary Wharf in London.

We're getting vital information necessary to do our jobs, and that's to protect the American people and our allies.

Information from the terrorists in this program has helped us to identify individuals that al Qaeda deemed suitable for Western operations, many of whom we had never heard about before. They include terrorists who were set to case targets inside the United States, including financial buildings in major cities on the East Coast. Information from terrorists in CIA custody has played a role in the capture or questioning of nearly every senior al Qaeda member or associate detained by the U.S. and its allies since this program began. By providing everything from initial leads to photo identifications, to precise locations of where terrorists were hiding, this program has helped us to take potential mass murderers off the streets before they were able to kill.

This program has also played a critical role in helping us understand the enemy we face in this war. Terrorists in this program have painted a picture of al Qaeda's structure and financing, and communications and logistics. They identified al Qaeda's travel routes and safe havens, and explained how al Qaeda's senior leadership communicates with its operatives in places like Iraq. They provided information that allows us—that has allowed us to make sense of documents and computer records that we have seized in terrorist raids. They've identified voices in recordings of intercepted calls, and helped us understand the meaning of potentially critical terrorist communications.

The information we get from these detainees is corroborated by intelligence, and we've received—that we've received from other sources—and together this intelligence has helped us connect the dots and stop attacks before they occur. Information from the terrorists questioned in this program helped unravel plots and terrorist cells in Europe and in other places. It's helped our allies protect their people from deadly enemies. This program has been, and remains, one of the most vital tools in our war against the terrorists. It is invaluable to America and to our allies. Were it not for this program, our Intelligence Community believes that al Qaeda and its allies would have succeeded in launching another attack against the American homeland. By giving us information about terrorist plans we could not get anywhere else, this program has saved innocent lives.

This program has been subject to multiple legal reviews by the Department of Justice and CIA lawyers; they've determined it complied with our laws. This program has received strict oversight by the CIA's Inspector General. A small number of key leaders from both political parties on Capitol Hill were briefed about this program. All those involved in the questioning of the terrorists are carefully chosen and they're screened from a pool of experienced CIA officers. Those selected to conduct the most sensitive questioning had to complete more than 250 additional hours of specialized training before they are allowed to have contact with a captured terrorist.

I want to be absolutely clear with our people, and the world: The United States does not torture. It's against our laws, and it's against our values. I have not authorized it—and I will not authorize it. Last year, my administration worked with Senator John McCain, and I signed into law the Detainee Treatment Act, which established the legal standard for treatment of detainees wherever they are held. I support this act. And as we implement this law, our government will continue to use every lawful method to obtain intelligence that can protect innocent people, and stop another attack like the one we experienced on September the 11th, 2001.

The CIA program has detained only a limited number of terrorists at any given time—and once we've determined that the terrorists held by the CIA have little or no additional intelligence value, many of them have been returned to their home countries for prosecution or detention by their governments. Others have been accused of terrible crimes against the American people, and we have a duty to bring those responsible for these crimes to justice. So we intend to prosecute these men, as appropriate, for their crimes.

In July 2007, the National Intelligence Council issued a new National Intelligence Estimate, "The Terrorist Threat to the US Homeland," assessing progress in the war on terrorism and the state of al-Qa'ida six years after 9/11. The conclusions, titled "Key Judgments," were released immediately in an unclassified version.

Key Judgments

We judge the US Homeland will face a persistent and evolving terrorist threat over the next three years. The main threat comes from Islamic terrorist groups and cells, especially al-Qa'ida, driven by their undiminished intent to attack the Homeland and a continued effort by these terrorist groups to adapt and improve their capabilities.

We assess that greatly increased worldwide counterterrorism efforts over the past five years have constrained the ability of al-Qa'ida to attack the US Homeland again and have led terrorist groups to perceive the Homeland as a harder target to strike than on 9/11. These measures have helped disrupt known plots against the United States since 9/11.

- We are concerned, however, that this level of international cooperation may wane as 9/11 becomes a more distant memory and perceptions of the threat diverge.

Al-Qa'ida is and will remain the most serious threat to the Homeland, as its central leadership continues to plan high-impact plots, while pushing others in extremist Sunni communities to mimic its efforts and to supplement its capabilities. We assess the group has protected or regenerated key elements of its Homeland attack capability, including: a safehaven in the Pakistan Federally Administered Tribal Areas (FATA), operational lieutenants, and its top leadership. Although we have discovered only a handful of individuals in the United States with ties to al-Qa'ida senior leadership since 9/11, we judge that al-Qa'ida will intensify its efforts to put operatives here.

- As a result, we judge that the United States currently is in a heightened threat environment.

We assess that al-Qa'ida will continue to enhance its capabilities to attack the Homeland through greater cooperation with regional terrorist groups. Of note, we assess that al-Qa'ida will probably seek to leverage the contacts and capabilities of al-Qa'ida in Iraq (AQI), its most visible and capable affiliate and the only one known to have expressed a desire to attack the Homeland. In addition, we assess that its association with AQI helps al-Qa'ida to energize the broader Sunni extremist community, raise resources, and to recruit and indoctrinate operatives, including for Homeland attacks.

We assess that al-Qa'ida's Homeland plotting is likely to continue to focus on prominent political, economic, and infrastructure targets with the goal of producing mass casualties, visually dramatic destruction, significant economic aftershocks, and/or fear among the US population. The group is proficient with conventional small arms and improvised explosive devices, and is innovative in creating new capabilities and overcoming security obstacles.

- We assess that al-Qa'ida will continue to try to acquire and employ chemical, biological, radiological, or nuclear material in attacks and would not hesitate to use them if it develops what it deems is sufficient capability.

We assess Lebanese Hizballah,[23] which has conducted anti-US attacks outside the United States in the past, may be more likely to consider attacking the Homeland over the next three years if it perceives the United States as posing a direct threat to the group or Iran.

We assess that the spread of radical—especially Salafi—Internet sites,[24] increasingly aggressive anti-US rhetoric and actions, and the growing number of radical, self-generating cells in Western countries indicate that the radical and violent segment of the West's Muslim population is expanding, including in the United States. The arrest and prosecution by US law enforcement of a small number of violent Islamic extremists inside the United States—who are becoming more connected ideologically, virtually, and/or in a physical sense to the global extremist movement—points to the possibility that others may become sufficiently radicalized that they will view the use of violence here as legitimate. We assess that this internal Muslim terrorist threat is not likely to be as severe as it is in Europe, however.

We assess that other, non-Muslim terrorist groups—often referred to as "single-issue" groups by the FBI—probably will conduct attacks over the next three years given their violent histories, but we assess this violence is likely to be on a small scale.

We assess that globalization trends and recent technological advances will continue to enable even small numbers of alienated people to find and connect with one another, justify and intensify their anger, and mobilize resources to attack—all without requiring a centralized terrorist organization, training camp, or leader.

- The ability to detect broader and more diverse terrorist plotting in this environment will challenge US defensive efforts and the tools we use to detect and disrupt plots. It will also require greater understanding of how suspect activities at the local level relate to strategic threat information and how best to identify indicators of terrorist activity in the midst of legitimate interactions.

A few weeks after the release of the above National Intelligence Estimate, CIA Director Michael V. Hayden addressed the Council on Foreign Relations in New York City. His talk was partly public relations but also partially an analysis of the nature of the war on terrorism. In this most unusual appearance, he publicly discussed such topics as rendition, foreign detention centers, interrogation techniques, and collaboration with foreign intelligence services, albeit without revealing details.

Remarks of Central Intelligence Agency Director
Gen. Michael V. Hayden at the Council on Foreign Relations[25]

September 7, 2007

It's a pleasure to be in New York, to spend some time with this very distinguished group, and to talk about the organization I am privileged to lead—CIA.

It's an organization with a clear objective: to protect the American people. We have a number of missions that feed into that, and one of them we share with the Council: to help our policymakers make sense of global events.

The range of issues before us is as wide as the world we study: nuclear proliferation, emerging security threats, the rise of new economic centers, the scramble for natural resources, and much more. Our nation counts on us to have the expertise and insight to flag the risks and opportunities that lie ahead. And to keep our eye on all the critical international concerns facing our nation right now.

Of the subjects we cover, none commands more attention than terrorism. It's unlikely there will ever come a time when a CIA Director visits New York and his or her thoughts aren't shaped by 9/11. We are at war, and this city, strong and vibrant, has been a battlefield in that war.

I don't make a lot of public speeches—that's probably the way it should be in my line of work. But I asked to speak here today. Like anyone who feels deeply about the safety and well being of his countrymen—and the value and integrity of his colleagues—I believe there are things that should be said. And sometimes our citizens should hear them straight from the person who's running their Central Intelligence Agency.

This afternoon, I want to talk to you about the Agency, the new kind of war that our nation has asked us to fight . . . and the question of space.

If you take nothing else from what I say, I hope it will be this: *CIA operates only within the space given to us by the American people.* That is how we want it to be, and that is how it should be.

That space is defined by the policymakers we elect and the laws our representatives pass. But once the laws are passed and the boundaries set, the American people expect CIA to use every inch we're given to protect our fellow citizens.

So first, let's talk about that space.

The intelligence services of free societies operate within strict limits. To my way of thinking, those boundaries reflect the principles of our Republic that are most worth defending. We at CIA work hard to live up to them, even as we operate in the shadows of espionage.

That sets up natural tensions, but for us they're simply part of doing business. Our Agency is absolutely convinced that it's our obligation to conform to the needs of a free society, not vice versa. That's the society we all signed up to defend. No matter the external threat, we at CIA feel just as strongly as any American that our DNA as a nation cannot be altered.

But, unlike most Americans, it's our responsibility to confront that external threat unceasingly, every minute of every hour. That too is an obligation we at CIA feel acutely.

Let me make very clear how my Agency views the fight at hand—I think it speaks to what a lot of Americans believe as well. Our nation is in a state of armed conflict with al-Qa'ida and its affiliates. It is a conflict that is global in scope, and a precondition for winning it is to take the fight to the enemy wherever he may be.

From my vantage point, as measured by the required intensity of effort and the profound nature of the threat, it's hard to see this fight as anything less than war. I've seen public references to "the *so-called* war on terrorism" or "the *Bush administration's* war on terrorism." But for us, it's simply *war*. It's a word used commonly and without ambiguity in the halls of the Pentagon and at Langley.

We who study and target the enemy see a danger more real than anything our citizens at home have confronted since our Civil War. Even when you consider the Cold War and mutually assured destruction—in which the potential danger was catastrophic—the fact is, the destruction never came.

This war is different. In a very real sense, anybody who lives or works in a major city is just as much a potential target as the victims of 9/11, or the London subway bombings, or the strikes in Madrid, or any of the other operations we've seen in Morocco, Jordan, Indonesia, Algeria, Pakistan, Kenya, and elsewhere.

That's my take on the strategic threat we face, without the precise language of an estimate. The National Intelligence Council published its findings on the threat to the homeland this summer. Analysts from CIA and throughout the Community engaged in a careful, meticulous study of the issue based on their deep expertise and on both open and classified sources. I have tremendous respect for their work, and I'd like to draw from their judgments to the extent I can in a public setting.

- First, our analysts assess with high confidence that al-Qa'ida's central leadership is planning high-impact plots against the US homeland.
- Second, they assess—also with high confidence—that al-Qa'ida has protected or regenerated key elements of its homeland attack capability. That means safe haven in the tribal areas of Pakistan, operational lieutenants, and a top leadership engaged in planning. Al-Qa'ida's success with the remaining element—planting operatives in this country—is less certain.
- Third, we assess—again, with high confidence—that al-Qa'ida is focusing on targets that would produce mass casualties, dramatic destruction, and significant economic aftershocks.

I want to be as clear as I can about the danger we face for two reasons. First, I'm a CIA Director—warning about foreign threats to our national security is part of my job.

Second, in discussing the operational space available to my Agency, I want to explain exactly why we feel so strongly about using every inch we're given. We bear responsibility for standing watch on this threat. That fact alone has the distinct effect of focusing the mind.

But we bear an additional responsibility as well. CIA is charged with prosecuting an expeditionary campaign to help capture or kill those behind that threat.

And this is a form of warfare unlike any other in our country's history. It's an intelligence war as much as a military one—maybe even more so. In the post-9/11 era, intelligence is more crucial to the security of our nation than ever before.

That's a fairly sweeping assertion, so let me spell out what I mean with a historical analogy.

The Soviet Union's most deadly forces—its ICBMs and tank armies—were relatively easy to find, but hard to kill. Intelligence was important, but overshadowed by the need for sheer firepower.

Today, the situation is reversed. We are now in an age in which our primary adversary is easy to kill, but hard to find. You can understand why so much emphasis in the last five years has been on intelligence.

Moreover, the moment of our enemy's attack may be just that—a moment, a split-second—the time it takes for an airliner to crash or a bomb to detonate. There can be little or no time to defeat him on the battlefield he's chosen.

But behind that point of attack is a trail of planning, travel, communication, training, and all the other elements that go into a large-scale terrorist operation. This is where there are secrets we can steal, operatives we can capture and interrogate, plots we can and must disrupt. This is the theater of operations for a clandestine intelligence service. This is where the American people expect us to fight.

And, in this fight, we've leveraged every inch of the space we've been given to operate. I want to briefly discuss two important aspects of our post-9/11 operations to put them in proper perspective: first, our rendition, detention, and interrogation programs, and then our close collaboration with allied intelligence services.

The first thing you need to know is that CIA's programs—which are carefully controlled and lawfully conducted—are hardly the centerpiece of our effort. Nor are they nearly as big as some think. But the intelligence they've produced is irreplaceable.

That intelligence has been used not only by this nation's national security agencies, but by our fellow members of the Atlantic Alliance and other key allies. It has been crucial in giving us a better understanding of the enemy we face, as well as leads on taking other terrorists off the battlefield.

Intelligence is sometimes described as analogous to putting the pieces of a puzzle together—except that we rarely ever get to see the picture on the box. The individuals that have been detained by CIA always provide us with new puzzle pieces, and very often they have seen the picture on the box.

For example, a substantial portion of the National Intelligence Estimate I mentioned earlier—in terms of its judgments and assumptions—is informed by the intelligence we've obtained from our detention program. More than 70 percent of the human intelligence reporting used in that estimate is based on information from detainees.

A year and a day ago, the President publicly acknowledged the existence of CIA's detention and interrogation program. Since it began with the capture of Abu Zubaidah in the spring of 2002, fewer than 100 people have been detained at CIA's facilities. And the number of renditions, apart from the fewer than 100 detainees, is itself an even smaller number.

These programs are targeted and selective. They were designed for only the most dangerous terrorists and those believed to have the most valuable information, such as knowledge of planned attacks. But they also have been the subject of wild speculation, both here and overseas.

Case in point: a European Parliament temporary committee has claimed that, and I quote, "at least 1,245 flights operated by the CIA flew into European airspace or stopped over at European airports between the end of 2001 and the end of 2005." And it said so in a context that implied that many—or even most—were rendition flights.

The actual number of rendition flights ever flown by CIA is a tiny fraction of that. And the suggestion that even a substantial number of those 1,245 flights were carrying detainees is absurd on its face.

What did some of these flights carry? It could be equipment to support our people in the field. Documents that we're sharing with our allies. Maybe even me.

Flights like the ones I take to visit our allies are good things. They are signs of our close cooperation.

As a method used against the most dangerous terrorists, there's nothing new about renditions for either America or our allies. Consider the cases of Carlos the Jackal[26] and Abdullah Öcalan,[27] whose renditions were upheld by European courts.

Renditions before and since 9/11 share some basic features. They've been conducted lawfully, responsibly, and with a clear and simple purpose: to get terrorists off the streets and gain intelligence on those still at large. Our detention and interrogation program flows from the same inescapable logic.

And a lot of what you hear about our interrogation and debriefing techniques is not only false, but it tends to obscure a point our officers understand well: when face-to-face with a detained terrorist, the most effective tool—bar none—is knowledge. That means things like familiarity with the subject's background, knowing the right questions to ask, and countering lies with facts. One detainee, for example, became quite cooperative in his debriefing when he arrived at a site and we told him not only who we were, but also who he was—and then we added where he came from and his operational history!

If CIA, with all our expertise in counterterrorism, had not stepped forward to hold and interrogate men like Abu Zubaidah and Khalid Shaykh Muhammad, people in America, Europe, and elsewhere would be right to ask why. We shouldered that responsibility for just one reason: to learn all we can about our nation's most deadly enemies so that our operations to undermine them are as effective as possible.

Serious people in free societies are still grappling with how best to address the fight against terrorists in a way that is both effective in protecting our people and consistent with our liberal democratic principles and traditions. The exchange of ideas between our societies is building a stronger consensus on the way forward.

It's not hard to see increasing signs of this cross-pollination—and of a growing realization that we all confront a distinctly new type of threat. Germany's interior minister, Wolfgang Schäuble, recently cast the situation in these terms: "The fact is that the old categories no longer apply.... The fight against international terrorism cannot be mastered by the classic methods of the police ... we have to clarify whether our constitutional state is sufficient for confronting the new threats."

While the dialogue continues on how best to conduct this fight, we and our partners stand united on its larger purpose. And this much is certain: America cannot win this war without allies.

My deputy Steve Kappes and I have gone to dozens of countries in our first year—many have been visited more than once. I cannot overstate how vital these relationships are to our overall effort.

For when I talk about winning this war, I do so in full knowledge that it is a highly complex and long-term struggle fought on two levels—what I call the close fight and the deep fight. And our foreign partners are pivotal to success on both fronts.

The close fight is very straightforward—it's about people who want to kill us. They can't be stopped unless we kill or capture them.

On this front, our foreign partners extend our reach and help us across the spectrum of our operations. The efforts of multiple services are often coordinated against a terrorist or group that has regional or global affiliations. Our collaboration has disrupted attacks that could have been on the same scale as those of 9/11.

The UK airliner plot and the takedowns of Khalid Shaykh Muhammad, Mullah Dadullah, and many, many others show what can be accomplished by close teamwork among allies. We've used that teamwork and every lawful tactic at our disposal—*every inch of the space we're given*—to protect all our citizens from terrorist brutality.

We've had strong success in the close fight. But we face an adaptive and resilient enemy who poses a heightened threat, as I mentioned earlier.

I talked recently with a reporter friend about my hard-to-find/easy-to-kill model. With his usual insight, my friend added—once again, unlike the Soviet Union—that al-Qa'ida, in addition to being hard to find, is quick to regenerate. Al-Qa'ida has compensated for losing its Afghan safehaven and key operational lieutenants by regrouping in Pakistan's tribal areas, where they've recruited from a ready pool of adherents.

And therein lies the deep fight: blunting the jihadists' appeal to disenchanted young Muslim men—and, increasingly, young Muslim women as well. The deep fight requires discrediting and eliminating the jihadist ideology that motivates the hatred and violence. It requires winning a war of ideas.

I recognize that some of the actions required by the close war can make fighting the deep war even more complicated. But it's rare in life that doing nothing is a legitimate or morally acceptable course of action. Responsibility demands action. Dealing with the immediate threat must naturally be our first priority.

Killing and capturing terrorists keeps them at bay and protects our people. But defeating the worldview responsible for producing those terrorists diminishes the threat itself. Winning the war of ideas defines the long-term victory we and our allies seek.

I want to be absolutely clear that this conflict is not about religion. The war of ideas is not about Islam. It's about fanatics whose victims most often have been Muslims. The terrorists must be exposed for the scourge they are and reviled for the horror and suffering they inflict. Only then can they be uprooted at their source.

The deep fight, which our society as a whole must wage, requires that jihadist ideas of violence, extremism, and intolerance be countered by ideas of peace, moderation, and inclusion. It requires a tireless global campaign by a broad coalition of nations and societies. But it's our friends in the Islamic world, repulsed by al-Qa'ida's savage distortion of their faith, who must take a leading role.

Any discussion of this war—and certainly this war of ideas—would be incomplete without reference to global media. It is one of the decisive battlegrounds in the post-9/11 era. It's where al-Qa'ida can attempt to spread its grand illusion of a noble struggle, or where its operatives can be revealed as murderers who try to justify their atrocities with a violent, bankrupt ideology.

The duty of a free press is to report the facts as they are found. By sticking to that principle, journalists accomplish a great deal in exposing al-Qa'ida and its adherents for what they are.

Just as they report on the terrorists, it's the job of journalists to report on the how the war against terrorism is being fought. And when their spotlight is cast on intelligence activities, sound judgment and a thorough understanding of all the equities at play are critically important. Revelations of sources and methods—and an impulse to drag anything CIA does to the darkest corner of the room—can make it very difficult for us to do our vital work.

When our operations are exposed—legal, authorized operations overseen by Congress—it reduces the space and damages the tools we use to protect Americans. After the press reported how banking records on the international SWIFT network could be monitored, I read a claim that this leak—and I quote—"bears no resemblance to security breaches, like disclosure of troop locations, that would clearly compromise the immediate safety of specific individuals."

I disagree. In a war that largely depends on our success in collecting intelligence on the enemy, publishing information on our sources and methods can be just as damaging as revelations of troop or ship movements were in the past. Now, the compromise to safety can be both immediate and lasting, extending far beyond specific individuals.

Each revelation of our methods—in tracking terrorists, WMD, or other threats—allows our enemies to cover their tracks and change their practices. And it takes us valuable time to readjust in kind.

Some say there is no evidence that leaks of classified information have harmed national security. As CIA Director, I'm telling you there is, and they have. Let me give you just two examples:

- In one case, leaks provided ammunition for a government to prosecute and imprison one of our sources, whose family was also endangered. The revelations had an immediate, chilling effect on our ability to collect against a top-priority target.
- In another, a spate of media reports cost us several promising counterterrorism and counterproliferation assets. Sources not even involved in the exposed operation lost confidence that their relationship with us could be kept secret, and they stopped reporting.

I've told you how liaison relationships with our foreign partners are critical to the war effort. Several years before the 9/11 attacks, a press leak of liaison intelligence prompted one country's service to stop cooperating with us on counterterrorism for two years.

More recently, more than one foreign service has told us that, because of public disclosures, they had to withhold intelligence that they otherwise would have shared with us. That gap in information puts Americans at risk.

Those who are entrusted with America's secrets and break that trust by divulging those secrets are guilty of a crime. But those who seek such information and then choose to publish it are not without responsibilities.

I have a very deep respect for journalists and for their profession. Many of them—especially in the years since 9/11—have given their lives in the act of keeping our citizens informed. They are smart, dedicated, and courageous men and women. I count many of them as colleagues. We each have an important role to play in the defense of the Republic.

My point is, there are times when life-and-death issues are at stake when intelligence activities are the subject of press reports. Journalists, on their own, simply don't have all the facts needed to make the call on whether the information can be released without harm. I've heard some justify a release based on their view of the sensitivity of a story's content, with no understanding of the effect the release may have on the intelligence source at the heart of the story.

As I said, both journalists and intelligence officers have important roles to play in the defense of the Republic. A free press is critical to good government. But when the media claims an oversight role on our clandestine operations, it does so in an arena where we cannot clarify, explain, or defend our actions without doing further damage to our sources and methods.

It's important to bear in mind that my Agency is subject to another oversight mechanism that has full access to our operations and takes our security requirements into account: it's the people's representatives in Congress.

CIA has asked for robust authorities so that we can better fulfill our responsibility to prevent another attack like 9/11—*but not without congressional oversight*. Close interaction with Congress is an essential part of our social contract with the American people.

I'll give you some statistics—all of them are for calendar year 2007—that underscore our vigorous support of the oversight process:

- CIA officers have testified in 57 congressional hearings and are responding to 29 congressionally legislated requests for information.
- We have answered 1,140 QFRs—that's "questions for the record"—as well as 254 other letters, questions, and requests.
- Our experts have given more than 500 briefings to congressional members and staffs.
- And we have issued some 100 congressional notifications on our sensitive programs.
- Everything is on the table. I personally have briefed the Hill nine times on renditions, detentions, and interrogations.

I mention all this because, contrary to some of the things you might read in a book, glean from a movie, or read in a newspaper, CIA acts within a strong framework of law and oversight. We are responsive to both ends of Pennsylvania Avenue. We have an Office of General Counsel that is larger than many foreign intelligence services, and our OGC officers have a defining say in how we conduct our operations.

We work very hard to earn the public trust we need to do our job. This is especially important because the counterterrorism part of our global mission isn't going to go away anytime soon. This war will define our priorities well into the future.

All of you here at the Council play a special role in informing the public debate on this and every other major issue of foreign policy and national security. I want to thank you for giving me the opportunity to talk about the work we do at CIA, and to contribute to the public's understanding of our war effort.

I came here as a member of two organizations that mean a lot to me. And this month marks the 60th anniversary of both the United States Air Force and the Central Intelligence Agency.

I've been with the Air Force for 38 of its 60 years. I'm proud to be an airman, to wear the uniform, and to be part of that great family.

I've been with CIA for about 16 months, but I've worked closely with its officers for much of my career. I have a much deeper familiarity with the Agency than those 16 months would suggest.

We at CIA are no strangers to criticism, and that's been true throughout our history. Sometimes it's justified. But often it is not.

Much of what I've seen in the press and read in some books simply doesn't square with the devotion and skill I see everyday, whether at Langley or in a war zone. The men and women of CIA are among the most gifted, talented people I've ever had the good fortune to work with. And at 130,000 applications a year, we've had the opportunity to pick some exceptionally intelligent, creative officers.

We haven't just been lucky, and it isn't as if the terrorists have been lazy. Such notions fail to explain the lack of an attack inside the United States in the last six years.

Our nation's bulwark is that group of experts—at CIA, the National Counterterrorism Center, and across the Intelligence Community—who help prosecute this war with their deep knowledge of the enemy and their tight collaboration against a shared target.

I've been out to visit our people in Iraq, Afghanistan, and other places where the risk and hardship for CIA employees are greatest. I've seen them work seamlessly with their colleagues in the armed forces, participating in joint operations that have brought the fight directly to the enemy's redoubt.

And I've seen our officers here at home take quiet satisfaction in seeing the photograph of a terrorist they've tracked for years appear on CNN after his capture. It might be a face and a name unrecognizable to most viewers, but not to those who have written countless cables, drafted finished intelligence reports, and briefed dozens of policymakers and congressmen on that one target.

Each of these victories adds up to a safer nation. Each is testimony to the tireless dedication and resolve of our men and women, for whom the memory of 9/11 is neither distant nor diminished.

At our Headquarters building, in a counterterrorism office I visit often, there's a sign that has been up for just about six years now, but it's one that never blends into the woodwork. It simply reads, "Today's date is September 12th, 2001."

That is how we at CIA approach this war. And we do so knowing we must continuously earn the trust of the American people for the operational space we need to fulfill our vital mission.

In response to questions from the audience, Hayden elaborated on the agency's view of issues surrounding the detention and rendition programs.[28]

QUESTIONER: I'm Mike Posner from Human Rights First. General Hayden, you spoke at the beginning of your remarks about the distinction between law and rules and then space. And I want to focus on the rules relating to interrogations.

Last year about this time, the president spoke, and he asked Congress for authority for the agency to be involved in what he called enhanced interrogation techniques. This is things like stress positions, use of dogs, hypothermia, mock drowning, waterboarding. The Congress said no to that, led by Senators McCain, Graham, and Warner. The military's also said no to that, and all of the senior military lawyers have been very clear that those techniques violate Common Article 3 of the Geneva Conventions, in public testimony before Congress.

And yet a month—six weeks ago, the administration passed an executive order seemingly allowing again the CIA to engage in these enhanced techniques.

From my perspective, it seems to me like this is more than asking for space; what you're really trying to do is change the rules. The question is, why do you need these enhanced techniques? Why shouldn't every U.S. agency operate by a single standard compliant with Common Article 3?

HAYDEN: First let me make comment on your listing of techniques and just frankly add that it's a pretty good example of taking something to the darkest corner of the room and not reflective of what my agency does.

Now let's talk about the history, last October. With the Hamdan decision,[29] the Supreme Court extended the protection of Common Article 3 to the unlawful combatants of al-Qa'ida. I'm not a lawyer, but I'm frankly surprised by that aspect of the decision, in that Common Article 3 refers to conflicts not of an international character. And this one does certainly seem to be conflict of an international character.

Our problem was not that we wanted the Congress to approve any techniques. Our problem was, we didn't know what Common Article 3 meant in the context of American law. When the Senate ratified a variety of other portions of the Geneva Convention, the legislative history or specific statements of the Senate clarified the meaning of the international treaty in terms of American law. For example, the Convention Against Torture is carefully hooked in the legislative history to the prohibition in domestic law against cruel and inhuman punishment articulated by the 5th, 8th, and 14th Amendments to the Constitution.

The Congress had made no clarifying language with regard to Common Article 3. And any, I think, fair reading of Common Article 3 would point out that it would be very hard for me to direct an officer of the agency to do things with the vagaries of the language in Common Article 3. So I wasn't looking for a carve out; I was looking for a definition.

One of the outs that was offered to the agency was that we in the—it turns out to be the Military Commissions Act. We in the Military Commissions Act will criminalize certain kinds of activities. And as long as your officers don't do these activities, they won't be prosecuted. And therefore you'll be safe from—well, you'll be safe from prosecution.

The agency as a whole and myself in particular rejected that solution. Because what it—what it would put me in the position of doing would be to turn to an agency officer and say, I would like you to do this with regard to this detainee, okay; I have no idea whether or not it violates the Geneva Convention, because I don't know what it means, but I'm pretty sure you'll never go to court for it, so would you go do that for me? And that's about the worst locker room speech I can imagine giving to an agency employee.

So we insisted on clarity for Common Article 3. The Congress decided that they would not offer that clarity but they then would instead reinforce the already existent presidential right to define the meaning for treaties for the United States. And so there's actual language in the Military Commissions Act that has the president doing that, and it requires him to publish his executive order in the Federal Register, which is what he did.

It's clear that what it is we do as agency is different from what is contained in the Army Field Manual. I don't know of anyone who has looked at the Army Field Manual who could make the claim that what's contained in there exhausts the universe of lawful interrogation techniques consistent with the Geneva Convention. The Army Field Manual was crafted to allow America's Army to train large numbers of young men and women to debrief and interrogate, for tactical purposes, transient prisoners on a fast-moving battlefield.

CIA handles a very small number of senior al-Qa'ida leaders. The average age of our interrogators is 43. The amount of training for this specific activity is 240 hours. So the reason we're not covered by the Army Field Manual is that we're not in the DOD [Department of Defense]. We weren't consulted about the Army Field Manual, and no one ever claimed that the Army Field Manual exhausted all the lawful tools that America could have to protect itself.

QUESTIONER: Thank you. Stephen Kass, Carter Ledyard & Milburn.

General, in view of the extensive training that you just referred to for the very highly qualified people who provide, I gather you said, 70 percent of the information that goes into the National Intelligence Estimate, in view of the critical nature of that information, what is the operating reason for sending people abroad to be interrogated by other countries with less qualified people, not under your control, when the information is so important, unless that reason is to circumvent the restrictions on U.S. operations?

HAYDEN: Thanks for the question, because it allows me to clarify the other half of detentions and renditions.... In many instances ... both justice and intelligence is better served by the movement of the individual to a country against which the individual has committed a crime or a country of which that individual is a citizen. All right? And it's a judgment case.

Now, we do not do it—we do not do it to circumvent any restrictions that we have on ourselves. There is a standard that we have to—have to apply in each and every case. We have to receive assurances—and we have to have confidence in the assurances—that this individual will be handled in a way that is consistent with international law. And we are required to maintain awareness of how this individual is handled. Now, that's not an invasive right to go to an ally with a clipboard and see how they're running day-to-day activity with a detainee, but as an intelligence agency, we have this broad responsibility that the assurances we receive at the beginning—that we continue to have confidence that we should have in those assurances.

The standard we use is that—and it's pretty straightforward—it's more or less likely—before you jump to conclusions, let me finish the explanation. We have to believe that it is less rather than more likely that the individual will be tortured. And I've had very well-informed people say, "Where did you get that standard?" And the answer is, from the Senate of the United States. That's in the legislative history for the Senate working to pass the International Convention Against Torture.

Clearly, we're not looking to shave this 49/51. All right? We want true assurances that the individual will be treated well. So we don't do it, as some have suggested, to circumvent.

QUESTIONER: I'm Carroll Bogert from Human Rights Watch. And just following on what you just said, I myself personally did research in Russia into the fate of some detainees who were rendered there on assurances from the Russian government that they would not be tortured. The State Department's own Human Rights Reports could not have been more clear that torture is very prevalent in Russia. And I wonder on what basis you think a country that conducts torture and is known to conduct torture can be trusted with—by giving a bilateral assurance to the U.S. government that somehow the spots of their leopard have changed.

HAYDEN: As I said in the prepared remarks, life rarely gives you the opportunity to just observe and do nothing. If my agency has custody of somebody, we've got to do something. And let's walk through the options: detention, Guantánamo, or renditions. And we've got to make a judgment based on the information we have available.

I should add that the statute that deals with renditions and the standards that we apply, clearly—clearly the overall history of a state has to be considered. But the statute requires us to make the judgment based upon our belief specifically about the individual on which the rendition is being conducted.

NOTES

1. George Tenet, with Bill Harlow, *At the Center of the Storm: My Years at the CIA* (New York: HarperCollins, 2007): 187, 209–213, 220. For detailed accounts, see

Gary C. Schroen, *First In: An Insider's Account of How the CIA Spearheaded the War on Terror in Afghanistan* (New York: Ballantine Books, 2005); Gary Berntsen and Ralph Pezzullo, *Jawbreaker: The Attack on Bin Laden and Al Qaeda: A Personal Account by the CIA's Key Field Commander* (New York: Crown Publishers, 2005).

2. Philip Zelikow, "Legal Policy for a Twilight War," Annual Lecture, *Houston Journal of International Law* (26 April 2007), http://www.hjil.org/lecture/2007/lecture.pdf.

3. Bruce Hoffman, "Scarier than Bin Laden," *Washington Post* (9 September 2007).

4. Craig Whitlock, "The New Al-Qaeda Central," *Washington Post* (9 September 2007).

5. Joby Warrick and Robin Wright, "Unilateral Strike Called a Model for U.S. Operations in Pakistan," *Washington Post* (19 February 2008); Eric Schmitt and David E. Sanger, "Pakistan Shift Could Curtail Drone Strikes," *New York Times* (22 February 2008); Eric Schmitt and David E. Sanger, "Pakistan Shuns C.I.A. Buildup Sought by U.S.," *New York Times* (27 January 2008).

6. Mark Mazzetti, "U.S. Aborted Raid on Qaeda Chiefs in Pakistan in '05," *New York Times* (8 July 2007); "Into Thin Air," *Newsweek* (3 September 2007).

7. Douglas Jehl, "Report Warned C.I.A. on Tactics in Interrogation," *New York Times* (9 November 2005). In a highly unusual move, the CIA Director later launched an inquiry into the activities of the Office of Inspector General apparently in connection with its investigations of the detention, interrogation, and rendition programs. Mark Mazzetti and Scott Shane, "Watchdog of C.I.A. Is Subject of C.I.A. Inquiry," *New York Times* (11 October 2007).

8. "Memoramdum for James B. Comey, Deputy Attorney General, Re: Legal Standards Applicable Under 18 U.S.C. §§ 2340–2340A" (30 December 2004), from Acting Assistant Attorney General Daniel Levin.

9. Scott Shane et al., "Secret Endorsement of Severe Interrogations," *New York Times* (4 October 2007).

10. Robert A. Fein, "Prologue: U.S. Experience and Research in Educing Information: A Brief History," in *Educing Information: Interrogation: Science and Art—Foundations for the Future* (Washington, D.C.: National Defense Intelligence College, 2006): xiii.

11. Robert Coulam, "Approaches to Interrogation in the Struggle against Terrorism: Considerations of Cost and Benefit," in ibid., 9.

12. Mark Mazzetti, "Rules Lay Out C.I.A.'s Tactics in Questioning," *New York Times* (21 July 2007); CRS Report RL33643, *Undisclosed U.S. Detention Sites Overseas: Background and Legal Issues,* by Jennifer K. Elsea and Julie Kim (Washington, D.C.: Congressional Research Service, 12 September 2006).

13. Mazzetti, "Rules Lay Out C.I.A.'s Tactics in Questioning."

14. John Goetz et al., "C.I.A. Arrest Warrants Strain U.S.-German Ties," *New York Times* (25 June 2007); Linda Greenhouse, "Supreme Court Refuses to Hear Torture Appeal," *New York Times* (10 October 2007).

15. Ian Fisher and Elisabetta Povoledo, "Italy Braces for Legal Fight over Secret C.I.A. Program," *New York Times* (8 June 2007).

16. His home country was reported to be Morocco. John F. Burns, "C.I.A. Used a British Island to Transport Terrorism Suspects," *New York Times* (22 February 2008).

17. Stephen Grey and Doreen Carvajal, "Secret Prisons in Two Countries Held Qaeda Suspects, Report Says," *New York Times* (8 June 2007); CRS Report RL33643, *Undisclosed U.S. Detention Sites Overseas.*

18. Council of Europe, Parliamentary Assembly, Committee on Legal Affairs and Human Rights, *Secret Detentions and Illegal Transfers of Detainees Involving Council of Europe Member States, Second Report* (7 June 2007): 3.

19. Commission of Inquiry into the Actions of Canadian Officials in Relation to Maher Arar, *Report of the Events Relating to Maher Arar, Factual Background: Volume 1* (Ottawa: Public Works and Government Services Canada, 2006): 190.

20. Ibid., *Addendum*, 245.

21. Ibid., 315.

22. "Maher Arar: Statement," *CBC News Online* (4 November 2003), http://www.cbc.ca/news/baclground/arar/arar_statement.html.

23. The pro-Iranian Hizballah, also spelled Hezbollah, is not affiliated with al-Qa'ida, nor does this NIE say that it is, although some readers are liable to assume a connection from the juxtaposition of the discussions. While the possibility of cooperation between the groups cannot be completely excluded, the radical Sunni Islamists of al-Qa'ida and the radical Shia Islamists of Hizballah are not natural allies.

24. Salafi, also called Wahhabi, Islam is the Sunni sect predominant in Saudi Arabia.

25. These are Hayden's remarks as prepared for delivery and as originally posted on the CIA's Web site at http://www.cia.gov.

26. An international terrorist from Venezuela with ties to the Popular Front for the Liberation of Palestine. His real name is Ilich Ramírez Sánchez.

27. Leader of the Kurdistan Workers Party (PKK), an armed secessionist movement, in Turkey.

28. The transcript of the speech as delivered, along with questions and answers, was made available by the Council on Foreign Relations (http://www.cfr.org) and then replaced the prepared version on the CIA's Web site.

29. In *Hamdan v. Rumsfeld* (2006), the Supreme Court determined the Geneva Conventions applied to the detainees at Guantánamo Bay and that the administration did not have the authority to establish the special military commissions in which it intended to try some of those detainees. Congress established the military commissions in response.

Chapter 17

Iraq, Terrorism, and Weapons of Mass Destruction

The run-up to the U.S.-led invasion of Iraq in 2003 is a study in the complex interplay of politics, intelligence, and even cognitive psychology. It is difficult to document such a contemporary case fully, as also in the case of the more general global war against terrorism, yet a limited number of original documents and a veritable treasure trove of investigative findings have emerged in recent months and years. Key issues surrounding the intelligence associated with the run-up to the Iraq War are: (1) the fact that much of the intelligence was simply wrong, (2) the fact that the intelligence (as it was thought to be) was exaggerated and used in a slipshod manner by public officials to make the case for war, and (3) the question of whether the intelligence (as it was thought to be) actually supported a case for war at all, especially after Saddam Hussein allowed international weapons inspectors to return to Iraq in November 2002.

The situation leading up to the war of 2003 was not a *tabula rasa*. The United States had fought against Iraq in 1991, in the Persian Gulf War, in order to expel its forces from Kuwait, which Iraq had invaded and annexed in August 1990. At that time, President George H. W. Bush decided not to continue the war beyond the liberation of Kuwait in order to overthrow the regime of Saddam Hussein. Not a few people thought this was a mistake at the time. This was especially the case among conservatives and, evidently, the president's son, George W. Bush. The elder Bush, however, feared the political and strategic consequences of the collapse of the Iraqi state and assumed that Saddam Hussein would, in any event, fall from power shortly after his military defeat.

The regime did survive, however, based on dictatorial rule, brutal repression, and a loyal political base recruited from among Iraq's Sunni Arab minority. As a consequence of the war, coalition forces patrolled the skies over southern and northern Iraq and bombed Iraqi antiaircraft sites whenever they were fired upon, which happened quite regularly. During the 1990s, the Republican administration of George H. W. Bush and the Democratic administration of Bill Clinton assigned the CIA to arm and support the Iraqi opposition. The opposition was for the most part small and fractious. The most effective was to be found in Kurdistan, in northern Iraq, which was essentially self-governing as a result of the Persian Gulf War.[1] Clinton's opponents considered his efforts to be half-hearted, a desire to appear to be doing something; but beyond a relatively small group of engaged conservatives, there was little public support for a more aggressive policy after the conclusion of the Persian Gulf War.

In the aftermath of a spectacular failure in the covert operation in Kurdistan in 1996 (in which the person who is now president of Kurdistan temporarily sided with Saddam Hussein against the person who is now president of Iraq) and growing tensions between the Iraqi government and UN weapons inspectors, the Republican-controlled Congress passed the Iraq Liberation Act of 1998. This act posited regime change in Iraq as the goal of the United States, but it too was at least partly for show. On the one hand, it expressed the "sense of Congress":

> It should be the policy of the United States to support efforts to remove the regime headed by Saddam Hussein from power in Iraq and to promote the emergence of a democratic government to replace that regime.

On the other hand, the bill set definite limitations:

> Nothing in this Act shall be construed to authorize or otherwise speak to the use of United States Armed Forces (except as provided in section 4(a)(2)) in carrying out this Act.

The exception, section 4(a)(2), authorized the sort of action that had already been taken, albeit on a larger scale. The Department of Defense could draw down its stocks to provide equipment, military education, and training to the opposition in Iraq, with an aggregate value not to exceed $97 million. The previous program had allowed $20 million. The opposition, however, was still small and fractious.

The invasion of 2003 was not justified on a basis of a provocation comparable to the Iraqi seizure of Kuwait, for there was no specific provocation. That fact alone made it far more difficult to gain international support for war than it had been in 1990–1991. The invasion was justified on the basis of purported intelligence that (a) Iraq had weapons of mass destruction (WMD) and was developing more and (b) Iraq was linked to international terrorism, including the al-Qa'ida movement responsible for the 9/11 attacks. Beyond that, the administration of George W. Bush posited that Iraq could or would arm those terrorists with WMD to attack the United States.

Of the two intelligence-related issues, WMD received more attention from the Intelligence Community than did links to terrorism. Regarding terrorism, Iraqi agents apparently did attempt to assassinate former president George H. W. Bush in Kuwait in April 1993 in retaliation for the Persian Gulf War. Kuwaiti authorities prevented the attempt, and President Clinton ordered a retaliatory missile strike against the headquarters of the Iraqi Intelligence Service.[2] Beyond that, Iraqi agents regularly targeted Iraqi dissidents living abroad, and Saddam Hussein provided support and refuge to groups that launched attacks against Israel and Iran.[3] The CIA had doubts about connections between Iraq and al-Qa'ida, but the Department of Defense argued strongly for this link.

As a category, WMD includes nuclear, biological, and chemical weapons. The CIA generally believed that Iraq possessed chemical and biological weapons. The agency did not think Iraq had nuclear weapons, but it believed that a program was underway that might develop nuclear weapons by the end of the decade. In the end, Iraq proved to have neither the weapons nor active programs to develop them.

Iraq had once had extensive WMD programs, but it was ordered to destroy them under UN resolutions issued during the Persian Gulf War of 1990–1991. Most of those weapons had survived that war, but an enormous number were ferreted out and destroyed by weapons inspectors from the United Nations Special Commission (UNSCOM) and the International Atomic Energy Agency (IAEA) over the course of the 1990s. The government of Saddam Hussein engaged in various subterfuges and efforts to deceive the inspectors, which made it difficult to confirm whether all the arms had been destroyed. It later emerged that Hussein believed that doubts about his capabilities would have a deterrent effect, and therefore he acted as if he had WMD even when he did not.

At the end of 1998, after a prolonged standoff, Iraq barred the inspectors in retaliation for a four-day U.S.-British bombing raid. From that time forward, there were few reliable sources of information on Iraq's weapons systems. The CIA had been relying on UN information and had apparently failed to develop independent sources. Assumptions, speculation, and extrapolations from past Iraqi behavior came to play a large role in U.S. decision making.

The gross mischaracterization of Iraq's WMD programs in the run-up to the 2003 war was a major intelligence failure and, at least potentially, a political failure. The intelligence failure was influenced by memories of the Intelligence Community's error prior to the Persian Gulf War of 1990–1991, when it underestimated Iraq's capabilities; by the lack of arms inspectors on site after 1998; by Iraq's history of dissembling and deceit; and by the Iraqi regime's efforts to exaggerate its strength, in part to deter attacks by neighboring Iran or Israel.[4] In addition, analysts had been criticized for being insufficiently imaginative in their failure to foresee the attacks of 9/11 (by failing to "connect the dots"), which may have pushed them in the opposite direction on Iraq. Yet, as intelligence and terrorism expert Richard K. Betts, a Columbia University professor and occasional consultant to the CIA, has commented, "What has been shocking is the revelation of how much of the WMD claims rested on circumstantial evidence and analytical assumptions and how little on specific reliable data."[5]

It is worth noting that the CIA was far from alone in this error. Many intelligence agencies, including those from countries opposed to the war, mistakenly believed that Iraq had some sort of WMD capability. Many Iraqi senior officials also believed it; if the CIA had succeeded in infiltrating Saddam Hussein's inner circle, it might still have come out with the wrong story.[6] On the other hand, very few governments concluded from the available evidence that there was an urgent threat necessitating immediate war. This was especially true after November 2002, when Iraq allowed the return of UN weapons inspectors.

A political failure that has been alleged involves the use, or misuse, made of that intelligence by the Bush administration. The White House succeeded in preventing an investigation of its role—part of the Senate investigation's "Phase II"—as long as the Republicans controlled Congress. (Pat Roberts, the Republican Chairman of the Senate Select Intelligence Committee, argued in 2003 that the administration's use of intelligence in making the case for war had been open and transparent and therefore did not require investigation.)[7] Some former CIA officials, however, believe that the White House decided to go to war for reasons of its own that had nothing to do with intelligence.[8]

It is known that administration officials, including President Bush and Vice President Dick Cheney, regularly and publicly questioned intelligence estimates that they considered too moderate, citing the underestimations that had preceded the Persian Gulf War.[9] Among the specific allegations made against the Bush administration are that it tended to ignore or reject intelligence that did not correspond to its preconceived notions, to seek out evidence that supported its beliefs (to the extent of creating an office—within the Defense Department's Office of Special Plans—to review evidence that the CIA had already rejected), to rely on evidence that was of questionable reliability, and even to distort evidence in the name of making the strongest possible case for war. In the end, the administration refused to allow international arms inspectors time to seek concrete evidence after Iraq permitted their return in late 2002.

The Bush administration included people who had long advocated the overthrow of the Iraqi regime. For example, in 1998, Donald Rumsfeld and Paul Wolfowitz, who respectively would become Secretary of Defense and Deputy Secretary of Defense in the Bush administration, were among eighteen people who in 1998 signed an open letter condemning Clinton's Iraq policy. They argued at that time:

> The only acceptable strategy is one that eliminates the possibility that Iraq will be able to use or threaten to use weapons of mass destruction. In the near term, this means a willingness to undertake military action as diplomacy is clearly failing. In the long term, it means removing Saddam Hussein and his regime from power. That now needs to become the aim of American foreign policy.[10]

Starting with such a predisposition, at the very least, will make one extremely receptive to evidence that Iraq is a threat and much less likely to question such evidence. Furthermore, it will often lead one to interpret objectively ambiguous information as evidence of a threat.[11] Wolfowitz in particular was a strong advocate for military action against Iraq from the first days of the Bush administration.

The first National Security Council (NSC) meeting after the inauguration of President Bush, held on 30 January 2001, was devoted largely to Iraq. It was posited that Iraq was destabilizing the Middle East but also that the country might be the key to reshaping the region. Participants agreed that they needed better intelligence, including intelligence on Iraq's WMD. At another NSC meeting two days later, Deputy Secretary Wolfowitz proposed once again arming Iraqi opposition groups to instigate an insurgency against the regime of Saddam Hussein and supporting them with U.S. troops in border areas.[12] This was consistent with public positions he had taken in the past.[13]

The attacks of 9/11 transformed the political context, changing the national mood and making a more aggressive approach politically feasible. At a meeting at Camp David on the weekend following the attacks, Wolfowitz proposed a direct war against Iraq. In his view, WMD and terrorism were key parts of an interconnected complex of reasons. This was not necessarily because he believed Iraq was responsible for that attack; rather, he argued for an all-out war against all supporters of terrorism and he considered Iraq a principal target in that regard. The combination of Iraq's past support for terrorist activities and its presumed possession of WMD—which Wolfowitz apparently assumed Saddam Hussein would share with terrorists he did not control—made it for him a higher priority than Afghanistan or even al-Qa'ida. The following is an excerpt from an interview Wolfowitz gave in early May 2003, after the invasion and the fall of the Iraqi regime but still before the realization that Iraq had no WMD:[14]

Wolfowitz: [...] And I think what September 11th to me said was this is just the beginning of what these bastards can do if they start getting access to so-called modern weapons, and that it's not something you can live with any longer. So there needs to be a campaign, a strategy, a long-term effort, to root out these networks and to get governments out of the business of supporting them. But that wasn't something that was going to happen overnight.

Q: Right. So Iraq naturally came to the top of the list because of its history and the weapons of mass terror and all the rest, is that right?

Wolfowitz: Yes, plus the fact which seems to go unremarked in most places that Saddam Hussein was the only international figure other than Osama bin Laden who praised the attacks of September 11th.

Q: [...] It's been reported in a couple of different ways, and I'd like to get it in your words if I can, the famous meetings that first weekend in Camp David where the question of Iraq came up. I believe the President heard you discussing Iraq and asked you to elaborate on it or speak more about it. Can you give us a little sense of what that was like?

Wolfowitz: Yeah. There was a long discussion during the day about what place if any Iraq should have in a counterterrorist strategy. On the surface of the debate it at least appeared to be about not whether but when. There seemed to be a kind of agreement that yes it should be, but the disagreement was whether it should be in the immediate response or whether you should concentrate simply on Afghanistan first.

There was a sort of undertow in that discussion I think that was, the real issue was whether Iraq should be part of the strategy at all and whether we should have this large strategic objective which is getting governments out of the business of supporting terrorism, or whether we should simply go after bin Laden and al Qaeda.

To the extent it was a debate about tactics and timing, the President clearly came down on the side of Afghanistan first. To the extent it was a debate about strategy and what the larger goal was, it is at least clear with 20/20 hindsight that the President came down on the side of the larger goal. [...]

The truth is that for reasons that have a lot to do with the U.S. government bureaucracy we settled on the one issue that everyone could agree on which was weapons of mass destruction as the core reason, but—hold on one second—

[The interview is interrupted.]

Wolfowitz:—there have always been three fundamental concerns. One is weapons of mass destruction, the second is support for terrorism, the third is the criminal treatment of the Iraqi people. Actually I guess you could say there's a fourth overriding one which is the connection between the first two. Sorry, hold on again.

[The interview is interrupted.]

The third one by itself, as I think I said earlier, is a reason to help the Iraqis but it's not a reason to put American kids' lives at risk, certainly not on the scale we did it. That second issue about links to terrorism is the one about which there's the most disagreement within the bureaucracy, even though I think everyone agrees that we killed 100 or so of an al Qaeda group in northern Iraq in this recent go-around, that we've arrested that al Qaeda guy in Baghdad who was connected to this guy Zarqawi whom Powell spoke about in his UN presentation.[15]

Wolfowitz speaks of WMD as the chief public justification, "the one issue everyone could agree on." Nevertheless, the crux of his argument is the combination of WMD and terrorism, which he describes as the "overriding" concern. Indeed, this nexus of WMD and terrorism would appear again and again in public arguments for war. Yet, Wolfowitz was not bothered by the fact that terrorism was the issue "about which there's the most disagreement within the bureaucracy," apparently viewing this as a shortcoming of the bureaucracy rather than as a shortcoming of the evidence. He did not seem to see a direct link to al-Qa'ida and 9/11 as necessary to justify an invasion of Iraq, but other officials, including President Bush and Secretary of State Colin Powell, would assert that Saddam Hussein had close ties to al-Qa'ida. Some officials, including Vice President Dick Cheney, would suggest that Iraq was connected to the actual 9/11 attacks.[16] Such claims were generally left to stand undisputed.

At some point, perhaps at the very beginning, the intelligence-based reasons for war with Iraq apparently became lost in a larger scheme whereby the United States would use a lightning-fast military strike to make an example of Saddam Hussein, eradicate terrorism at its roots, intimidate other potential adversaries, and initiate a transformation of the Middle East into a region of peaceful, democratic, and pro-American regimes in a chain reaction reminiscent of the collapse of communism in Eastern Europe.[17] ("Recently in Romania I was reminded of the example of [Communist leader Nicolae] Ceauşescu," Bush would lecture the Spanish prime minister. "It just took just one woman to call him a liar for the whole repressive structure to come down. That is the uncontainable power of freedom."[18]) Members of the administration were confirmed in this belief by the rapid collapse of the Taliban regime in Afghanistan in 2001. Inspired by such a vision, realistic or not, the administration may have become less interested in the specifics of intelligence reporting about the presumed Iraqi threat. Nevertheless, the public justification for the war, and the reason the Middle East was in need of transformation, was the threat implied in the nexus of terrorism and WMD.

Regarding the administration's approach to decision making on Iraq, DCI George Tenet later remarked on the lack of consideration given to alternative policy options. These comments were based on CIA participation in interagency meetings, including those at the highest level, and presumably apply as much to Tenet as to others in the administration.

There never was a serious debate that I know of within the administration about the imminence of the Iraqi threat. ... Nor was there ever a significant discussion regarding enhanced containment or the costs and benefits of such an approach versus full-out planning for overt and covert regime change. Instead, it seemed a given that the United States had not done enough to stop al-Qa'ida before 9/11 and had paid an enormous price. Therefore, so the reasoning went, we could not allow ourselves to be in a similar situation in Iraq. . . . In none of the meetings can anyone remember a discussion of the central questions. Was it wise to go to war? Was it the right thing to do? The agenda focused solely on what actions would need to be taken if a decision to attack were later made. What never happened, as far as I can tell, was a serious consideration of the implications of a U.S. invasion.[19]

The Bush administration succeeded in eliciting the support of Prime Minister Tony Blair's government in 2002. Whatever reasons Blair had for this, it does not appear that the British were persuaded by the arguments being made, at least insofar as the foreign secretary is concerned. The following memorandum was sent to Blair by Foreign Secretary Jack Straw to prepare him for a meeting with President Bush at his ranch in Crawford, Texas. The document, along with several others, was leaked to the press, and then transcribed and published in September 2004.[20]

<u>SECRET AND PERSONAL</u>

PM/02/019
<u>PRIME MINISTER</u>
<u>CRAWFORD/IRAQ</u>

1. The rewards from your visit to Crawford will be few. The risks are high, both for you and for the Government. I judge that there is at present no majority inside the PLP[21] for any military action against Iraq, (alongside a greater readiness in the PLP to surface their concerns). Colleagues know that Saddam and the Iraqi regime are bad. Making that case is easy. But we have a long way to go to convince them as to:

   (a) the scale of the threat from Iraq and why this has got worse recently;
   (b) what distinguishes the Iraqi threat from that of Iran and North Korea so as to justify military action;
   (c) the justification for any military action in terms of international law; and
   (d) whether the consequence of military action really would be a compliant, law-abiding replacement government.

2. The whole exercise is made much more difficult to handle as long as conflict between Israel and the Palestinians is so acute.

THE SCALE OF THE THREAT

3. The Iraqi regime plainly poses a most serious threat to its neighbours, and therefore to international security. However, in the documents so far presented it has been hard to glean whether the threat from Iraq is so significantly different from that of Iran and North Korea as to justify military action (see below).

WHAT IS WORSE NOW?

4. If 11 September had not happened, it is doubtful that the US would now be considering military action against Iraq. In addition, there has been no credible evidence to link Iraq with UBL [Usama bin Ladin] and Al Qaida. Objectively, the threat from Iraq has not worsened as a result of 11 September. What has however changed is the tolerance of the international community (especially that of the US), the world having witnessed on September 11 just what determined evil people can these days perpetuate.

THE DIFFERENCE BETWEEN IRAQ, IRAN AND NORTH KOREA

5. By linking these countries together in this "axis of evil" speech, President Bush implied an identity between them not only in terms of their threat, but also in terms of the action necessary to deal with the threat. A lot of work will now need to be done to delink the three, and to show why military action against Iraq is so much more justified than against Iran and North Korea. The heart of this case—that Iraq poses a unique and present danger—rests on the facts that it:

- invaded a neighbour;
- has used WMD, and would use them again;
- is in breach of nine UNSCRS.[22]

THE POSITION IN INTERNATIONAL LAW

6. That Iraq is in flagrant breach of international legal obligations imposed on it by the UNSC provides us with the core of a strategy, and one which is based on international law. Indeed, if the argument is to be won, the whole case against Iraq and in favour (if necessary) of military action needs to be narrated with reference to the international rule of law.

7. We also have better to sequence the explanation of what we are doing and why. Specifically, we need to concentrate in the early stages on:

- making operational the sanctions regime foreshadowed by UNSCR 1382;
- demanding the readmission of weapons inspectors, but this time to operate in a free and unfettered way (a similar formula to that which Cheney used at your joint press conference, as I recall).

8. I know there are those who say that an attack on Iraq would be justified whether or not weapons inspectors were readmitted. But I believe that a demand for the unfettered readmission of weapons inspectors is essential, in terms of public explanation, and in terms of legal sanction for any subsequent military action.

9. Legally there are two potential elephant traps:

(i) regime change per se is no justification for military action; it could form part of the method of any strategy, but not a goal. Of course, we may want credibly to assert that regime change is an essential part of the strategy by which we have to achieve our ends—that of the elimination of Iraq's WMD capacity; but the latter has to be the goal;

(ii) on whether any military action would require a fresh UNSC mandate (Desert Fox did not).[23] The US is likely to oppose any idea of a fresh mandate. On the other side, the weight of legal advice here is that a fresh mandate may well be required. There is no doubt that a new UNSCR would transform the climate in the PLP. Whilst that (a new mandate) is very unlikely, given the US's position, a draft resolution against military action with 13 in favour (or handsitting) and two vetoes against could play very badly here.

THE CONSEQUENCES OF MILITARY ACTION

10. A legal justification is a necessary but far from sufficient precondition for military action. We have also to answer the big question—what will this action achieve? There seems to be a larger hole in this than on anything. Most of the assessments from the US have assumed regime change as a means of eliminating Iraq's WMD threat. But none has satisfactorily

answered how that regime change is to be secured, and how there can be any certainty that the replacement regime will be better.

11. Iraq has had NO history of democracy so no-one has this habit or experience.

(JACK STRAW)
Foreign and Commonwealth Office
25 March 2002

SECRET AND PERSONAL

Blair agreed to support military action when he met with Bush in Crawford in April. He raised several conditions, however. These were: that the war be justified in terms of international law; that efforts be made to raise an international coalition; that the Israel-Palestinian situation be quiescent; and that options to eliminate WMD by means of weapons inspectors be exhausted first.[24]

British officials who met with the Bush administration in July 2002 noted a clear hardening of attitudes since the spring. The director of Britain's Secret Intelligence Service—identified only as "C" even in classified British government documents—and military officials came away from a meeting in Washington weeks earlier with the belief that the decision for war had been made.[25] Contingency plans were being drawn up. Moreover, "C" was of the opinion that the intelligence was being adjusted to suit the policy, although he did not specify whether he believed this was intentional. (Tenet says that "C" told him he was concerned that intelligence was being used in an undisciplined manner, presumably by people around the vice president.)[26] A memorandum about that meeting was leaked to the press three years later.[27]

SECRET AND STRICTLY PERSONAL—UK EYES ONLY

DAVID MANNING[28]
From: Matthew Rycroft[29]
Date: 23 July 2002
S 195 02

cc: Defence Secretary, Foreign Secretary, Attorney-General, Sir Richard Wilson, John Scarlett, Francis Richards, CDS, C, Jonathan Powell, Alastair Campbell

IRAQ: PRIME MINISTER'S MEETING, 23 JULY

Copy addressees and you met the Prime Minister on 23 July to discuss Iraq.

This record is extremely sensitive. No further copies should be made. It should be shown only to those with a genuine need to know its contents.

John Scarlett [Chairman of the Joint Intelligence Staff, or JIC] summarized the intelligence and latest JIC assessment. Saddam's regime was tough and based on extreme fear. The only way to overthrow it was likely to be by massive military action. Saddam was worried and expected an attack, probably by air and land, but he was not convinced that it would be immediate or overwhelming. His regime expected their neighbours to line up with the US. Saddam knew that regular army morale was poor. Real support for Saddam among the public was probably narrowly based.

C reported on his recent talks in Washington. There was a perceptible shift in attitude. Military action was now seen as inevitable. Bush wanted to remove Saddam, through military action, justified by the conjunction of terrorism and WMD.

But the intelligence and facts were being fixed around the policy. The NSC had no patience with the UN route, and no enthusiasm for publishing material on the Iraqi regime's record. There was little discussion in Washington of the aftermath after military action.

CDS [Chief of the Defence Staff] said that military planners would brief CENT-COM[30] on 1–2 August, Rumsfeld on 3 August and Bush on 4 August.

The two broad US options were:

(a)   Generated Start: A slow build-up of 250,000 US troops, a short (72 hour) air campaign, then a move up to Baghdad from the south. Lead time of 90 days (30 days preparation plus 60 days deployment to Kuwait).

(b)   Running Start: Use forces already in theatre (3 x 6,000), continuous air campaign, initiated by an Iraqi casus belli. Total lead time 60 days with the air campaign beginning even earlier. A hazardous option.

The US saw the UK (and Kuwait) as essential, with basing in Diego Garcia and Cyprus critical for either option. Turkey and other Gulf states were also important, but less vital. The three main options for UK involvement were:

(i)   Basing in Diego Garcia and Cyprus, plus three SF squadrons.
(ii)   As above, with maritime and air assets in addition.
(iii)   As above, plus a land contribution of up to 40,000, perhaps with a discrete role in Northern Iraq entering from Turkey, tying down two Iraqi divisions.

The Defence Secretary said that the US had already begun "spikes of activity" to put pressure on the regime. No decisions had been taken, but he thought the most likely timing in US minds for military action to begin was January, with the timeline beginning 30 days before the US Congressional elections.

The Foreign Secretary said he would discuss this with [Secretary of State] Colin Powell this week. It seemed clear that Bush had made up his mind to take military action, even if the timing was not yet decided. But the case was thin. Saddam was not threatening his neighbours, and his WMD capability was less than that of Libya, North Korea or Iran. We should work up a plan for an ultimatum to Saddam to allow back in the UN weapons inspectors. This would also help with the legal justification for the use of force.

The Attorney-General said that the desire for regime change was not a legal base for military action. There were three possible legal bases: self-defence, humanitarian intervention, or UNSC [United Nations Security Council] authorization. The first and second could not be the base in this case. Relying on UNSCR [UNSC Resolution] 1205 of three years ago would be difficult. The situation might of course change.

The Prime Minister said that it would make a big difference politically and legally if Saddam refused to allow in the UN inspectors. Regime change and WMD were linked in the sense that it was the regime that was producing the WMD. There were different strategies for dealing with Libya and Iran. If the political context were right, people would support regime change. The two key issues were whether the military plan worked and whether we had the political strategy to give the military plan the space to work.

On the first, CDS said that we did not know yet if the US battle plan was workable. The military were continuing to ask lots of questions.

For instance, what were the consequences, if Saddam used WMD on day one, or if Baghdad did not collapse and urban fighting began? You said that Saddam could also use his WMD on Kuwait. Or on Israel, added the Defence Secretary.

The Foreign Secretary thought the US would not go ahead with a military plan unless convinced that it was a winning strategy. On this, US and UK interests converged. But on the political strategy, there could be US/UK differences. Despite US resistance, we should explore discreetly the ultimatum. Saddam would continue to play hardball with the UN.

John Scarlett assessed that Saddam would allow the inspectors back in only when he thought the threat of military action was real.

The Defence Secretary said that if the Prime Minister wanted UK military involvement, he would need to decide this early. He cautioned that many in the US did not think it worth going down the ultimatum route. It would be important for the Prime Minister to set out the political context to Bush.

Conclusions:

(a) We should work on the assumption that the UK would take part in any military action. But we needed a fuller picture of US planning before we could take any firm decisions. CDS should tell the US military that we were considering a range of options.

(b) The Prime Minister would revert on the question of whether funds could be spent in preparation for this operation.

(c) CDS would send the Prime Minister full details of the proposed military campaign and possible UK contributions by the end of the week.

(d) The Foreign Secretary would send the Prime Minister the background on the UN inspectors, and discreetly work up the ultimatum to Saddam.

He would also send the Prime Minister advice on the positions of countries in the region, especially Turkey, and of the key EU member states.

(e) John Scarlett would send the Prime Minister a full intelligence update.

(f) We must not ignore the legal issues: the Attorney-General would consider advice with FCO/MOD [Foreign and Commonwealth Office/Ministry of Defence] legal advisers.

(I have written separately to commission this follow-up work.)
MATTHEW RYCROFT

Vice President Dick Cheney, in a speech before the Veterans of Foreign Wars on 26 August 2002, was the first to suggest in public that Iraq posed such an immediate threat that preemptive war would be necessary and that time was already running out.

There is a full agenda for the fall, and beyond. Yet the President and I never for a moment forget our number one responsibility: to protect the American people against further attack, and to win the war that began last September 11th. [...]

At the same time, we realize that wars are never won on the defensive. We must take the battle to the enemy. We will take every step necessary to make sure our country is secure, and we will prevail. [...]

The case of Saddam Hussein, a sworn enemy of our country, requires a candid appraisal of the facts. After his defeat in the Gulf War in 1991, Saddam agreed under to U.N. Security Council Resolution 687 to cease all development of weapons of mass destruction. He agreed to end his nuclear weapons program. He agreed to destroy his chemical and his biological weapons. He further agreed to admit U.N. inspection teams into his country to ensure that he was in fact complying with these terms.

In the past decade, Saddam has systematically broken each of these agreements. The Iraqi regime has in fact been very busy enhancing its capabilities in the field of chemical and biological agents. And they continue to pursue the nuclear program they began so many years ago. These are not weapons for the purpose of defending Iraq; these are offensive weapons for the purpose of inflicting death on a massive scale, developed so that Saddam can hold the threat over the head of any-one he chooses, in his own region or beyond. [...]

Saddam has perfected the game of cheat and retreat, and is very skilled in the art of denial and deception. A return of inspectors would provide no assurance whatsoever of his compliance with U.N. resolutions. On the contrary, there is a great danger that it would provide false comfort that Saddam was somehow "back in his box." [...]

Simply stated, there is no doubt that Saddam Hussein now has weapons of mass destruction. There is no doubt he is amassing them to use against our friends, against our allies, and against us. And there is no doubt that his aggressive re-gional ambitions will lead him into future confrontations with his neighbors—confrontations that will involve both the weapons he has today, and the ones he will continue to develop with his oil wealth. [...]

America in the year 2002 must ask careful questions, not merely about our past, but also about our future. The elected leaders of this country have a responsibility to consider all of the available options. And we are doing so. What we must not do in the face of a mortal threat is give in to wishful thinking or willful blindness. We will not simply look away, hope for the best, and leave the matter for some future administration to resolve. As President Bush has said, time is not on our side. Deliverable weapons of mass destruction in the hands of a terror network, or a murderous dictator, or the two working together, constitutes as grave a threat as can be imagined. The risks of inaction are far greater than the risk of action.

DCI Tenet later said he was startled by Cheney's speech. It had not under-gone CIA review as was customary when speeches touched upon intelligence-related matters. The speech went well beyond the available evidence on WMD. The CIA did not expect Iraq to be able to complete a nuclear weapon before late in the decade. Nevertheless, Tenet seems to have done nothing about this.[31]

In September 2002, the Bush administration began a concerted move to pre-pare the grounds for war. Officials made public remarks suggesting a lack of interest in further intelligence, if not denigrating the importance of evidence altogether. In particular, National Security Adviser Condoleezza Rice made a comment in September, later repeated by others, that was clearly designed to cut off debate. In this it proved quite effective.

> No one can give you an exact timeline as to when he [Saddam Hussein] is going to have this or that weapon, but given what we have experienced in history and given what we have experienced on September 11, I don't think anyone wants to wait for the 100 percent surety that he has a weapon of mass destruction that can reach the United States, because the only time we may be 100 percent sure is when something lands on our territory. We can't afford to wait that way. [...]
>
> The problem here is that there will always be some uncertainty about how quickly he can acquire nuclear weapons. But we don't want the smoking gun to be a mushroom cloud.[32]

About the same time, the administration issued a new national security strat-egy. For the first time, the United States made "preemption" a central part of its policy.

> It has taken almost a decade for us to comprehend the true nature of this new threat. Given the goals of rogue states and terrorists, the United States can no lon-ger solely rely on a reactive posture as we have in the past. The inability to deter a

potential attacker, the immediacy of today's threats, and the magnitude of potential harm that could be caused by our adversaries' choice of weapons, do not permit that option. We cannot let our enemies strike first. . . .

The United States has long maintained the option of preemptive actions to counter a sufficient threat to our national security. The greater the threat, the greater is the risk of inaction—and the more compelling the case for taking anticipatory action to defend ourselves, even if uncertainty remains as to the time and place of the enemy's attack. To forestall or prevent such hostile acts by our adversaries, the United States will, if necessary, act preemptively.[33]

Preemption, of course, puts an extra high premium on intelligence because as a justification for war it requires *knowing* that you are threatened. While the administration spoke of "preemption," however, and cited numerous legal justifications for preemption, what it actually had in mind went beyond preemption to "preventive war," which is a much harder case to make legally, politically, or morally. National security expert Ivo Daalder explained the difference in memorandum for the Council on Foreign Relations and the American Society of International Law:

The legal justification for this doctrine [preemption] resides in the concept of anticipatory self-defense—that is, the notion, long recognized in international law, that states can take defensive action even before an attack has occurred if the threat is truly imminent (traditionally when an opposing force mobilizes in anticipation of an attack). . . . Preventive war refers to a premeditated attack of one state against another, which is not provoked by any aggressive action of the state being attacked against the state initiating the conflict. In contrast, a preemptive attack is launched only after the state being attacked has either initiated or has given a clear indication that it will initiate an attack. A war against Iraq that is justified by the belief that Baghdad will soon acquire nuclear weapons which it then may use to threaten the interests of others would be a preventive war; an attack against an Al Qaeda cell believed to be plotting a terrorist strike would be a preemptive strike. While the latter can readily be justified on the basis of self-defense, preventive war, especially if launched by a single state on its own accord, cannot. And every time when our nation's leaders confronted the question of launching a war to [prevent] an adversary from acquiring nuclear weapons—whether against the Soviet Union in the late 1940s, against Cuba in 1962, or against China in 1964—they decided against it.[34]

Also in September, President Bush pressed Congress to approve a joint resolution authorizing war. The president insisted that it was urgent to pass the measure quickly, before recessing for elections in November. This timing put pressure on Congress to comply and highlighted the political implications of appearing "weak on terrorism" just prior to an election.[35] On 7 October, Bush gave a major speech in Cincinnati outlining his arguments for war and for urgency in highly emotional terms.

Some citizens wonder, after 11 years of living with this problem, why do we need to confront it now? And there's a reason. We've experienced the horror of September the 11th. We have seen that those who hate America are willing to crash airplanes into buildings full of innocent people. Our enemies would be no less willing, in fact, they would be eager, to use biological or chemical, or a nuclear weapon.

Knowing these realities, America must not ignore the threat gathering against us. Facing clear evidence of peril, we cannot wait for the final proof—the smoking gun—that could come in the form of a mushroom cloud. As President Kennedy said in October of 1962, "Neither the United States of America, nor the world community of nations can tolerate deliberate deception and offensive threats on the part of any nation, large or small. We no longer live in a world," he said, "where only the actual firing of weapons represents a sufficient challenge to a nation's security to constitute maximum peril."

Bush evidently forgot that, in the end, President Kennedy opted for restraint and was glad that he did. In addition to emotional appeals and the use of evidence that later proved to be untrue, Bush made sloppy use of evidence. For example, he remarked:

In 1995, after several years of deceit by the Iraqi regime, the head of Iraq's military industries defected. It was then that the regime was forced to admit that it had produced more than 30,000 liters of anthrax and other deadly biological agents. The inspectors, however, concluded that Iraq had likely produced two to four times that amount. This is a massive stockpile of biological weapons that has never been accounted for, and capable of killing millions.

The president glibly slid from an amount that was "likely produced" to a "massive stockpile ... that has never been accounted for." Beyond that, however, according to a study by the Carnegie Endowment, what the inspectors actually said was that the Iraqis failed to account for a quantity of bacteria growth media that—if they in fact had it—could have been used to produce about three times as much anthrax as they admitted to. This is a few steps away from "a massive stockpile of biological weapons that has never been accounted for." Moreover, it required sophisticated delivery systems to be capable of killing millions.[36]

Members of the Senate Select Committee on Intelligence pressed DCI Tenet to produce a National Intelligence Estimate (NIE) on Iraq's WMD program in time for the vote in October.[37] This meant compressing the normal NIE process of several months into a few weeks. The NIE that was produced, *Iraq's Continuing Programs for Weapons of Mass Destruction*, was 96 pages long. A hastily produced, unclassified white paper with fewer qualifications on its assertions accompanied the NIE and was intended to support the administration's public case for war.

Reproduced below is a redacted version of pages 5–9 of the original, secret NIE, titled "Key Judgments," which was declassified in April 2004. A close reading indicates that the NIE pairs a series of bold assertions with supporting discussions that are much more tentative. Note also that the State Department's Bureau of Intelligence and Research (INR) refused to endorse the interagency consensus regarding nuclear (although not necessarily chemical or biological) weapons, appending a dissenting view at the end.

Key Judgments

[—] Iraq's Continuing Programs for Weapons of Mass Destruction

[—] We judge that Iraq has continued its weapons of mass destruction (WMD) programs in defiance of UN resolutions and restrictions. Baghdad has chemical and biological weapons as well as missiles with ranges in excess of UN restrictions; if left unchecked, it probably will have a nuclear weapon during this decade. (See INR alternative view at the end of these Key Judgments.)

[—] **We judge that we are seeing only a portion of Iraq's WMD efforts, owing to Baghdad's vigorous denial and deception efforts.** Revelations after the Gulf war starkly demonstrate the extensive efforts undertaken by Iraq to deny information. We lack specific information on many key aspects of Iraq's WMD programs.

[—] **Since inspections ended in 1998, Iraq has maintained its chemical weapons effort, energized its missile program, and invested more heavily in biological weapons; in the view of most agencies, Baghdad is reconstituting its nuclear weapons program.**

- Iraq's growing ability to sell oil illicitly increases Baghdad's capabilities to finance WMD programs: annual earnings in cash and goods have more than quadrupled, from $580 million in 1998 to about $3 billion this year.
- Iraq has largely rebuilt missile and biological weapons facilities damaged during Operation Desert Fox and has expanded its chemical and biological infrastructure under the cover of civilian production.
- Baghdad has exceeded UN range limits of 150 km with its ballistic missiles and is working with unmanned aerial vehicles (UAVs), which allow for a more lethal means to deliver biological and, less likely, chemical warfare agents.
- Although we assess that Saddam does not yet have nuclear weapons or sufficient material to make any, he remains intent on acquiring them. Most agencies assess that Baghdad started reconstituting its nuclear program about the time that UNSCOM inspectors departed—December 1998.

[—] **How quickly Iraq will obtain its first nuclear weapon depends on when it acquires sufficient weapons-grade fissile material.**

- If Baghdad acquires sufficient fissile material from abroad it could make a nuclear weapon within several months to a year.
- Without such material from abroad, Iraq would not be able to make a weapon until 2007 to 2009, owing to inexperience in building and operating centrifuge facilities to produce highly enriched uranium and challenges in procuring equipment and expertise.
  - Most agencies believe that Saddam's personal interest in and Iraq's aggressive attempts to obtain high-strength aluminum tubes for centrifuge rotors—as well as Iraq's attempts to acquire magnets, high-speed balancing machines, and machine tools—provide compelling evidence that Saddam is reconstituting a uranium enrichment effort for Baghdad's nuclear weapons program. (DOE agrees that reconstitution of the nuclear program is underway but assesses that the tubes probably are not part of the program.)
  - Iraq's efforts to re-establish its cadre of weapons personnel as well as activities at several suspect nuclear sites further indicate that reconstitution is underway.
  - All agencies agree that about 25,000 centrifuges based on tubes of the size Iraq is trying to acquire would be capable of producing approximately two weapons' worth of highly enriched uranium per year.
- In a much less likely scenario, Baghdad could make enough fissile material for a nuclear weapon by 2005 to 2007 if it obtains suitable centrifuge tubes this year and has all the other materials and technological expertise necessary to build production-scale uranium enrichment facilities.

[—] **We assess that Baghdad has begun renewed production of mustard, sarin, GF (cyclosarin), and VX;**[38] its capability probably is more limited now than it was at the time of the Gulf war, although VX production and agent storage life probably have been improved.

- An array of clandestine reporting reveals that Baghdad has procured covertly the types and quantities of chemicals and equipment sufficient to allow limited CW agent production hidden within Iraq's legitimate chemical industry.[39]
- Although we have little specific information on Iraq's CW stockpile, Saddam probably has stocked at least 100 metric tons (MT) and possibly as much as 500 MT of CW agents—much of it added in the last year.
- The Iraqis have experience in manufacturing CW bombs, artillery rockets, and projectiles. We assess that they possess CW bulk fills for SRBM [short-range ballistic missile] warheads, including for a limited number of covertly stored Scuds, possibly a few with extended ranges.[40]

[—] **We judge that all key aspects—R&D, production, and weaponization—of Iraq's offensive BW are active and that most elements are larger and more advanced than they were before the Gulf war.**[41]

- We judge Iraq has some lethal and incapacitating BW agents and is capable of quickly producing and weaponizing a variety of such agents, including anthrax, for delivery by bombs, missiles, aerial sprayers, and covert operations.

  - Chances are even that smallpox is part of Iraq's offensive BW program.
  - Baghdad probably has developed genetically engineered BW agents.

- Baghdad has established a large-scale, redundant, and concealed BW agent production capability.

  - [—paragraph deleted; replaced by text in errata sheet below—]

[—] **Iraq maintains a small missile force and several development programs, including for a UAV probably intended to deliver biological warfare agents.**

- Gaps in Iraqi accounting to UNSCOM suggests that Saddam retains a covert force of up to a few dozen Scud-variant SRBMs with ranges of 650 to 900 km.
- Iraq is deploying its new al-Samoud and Ababil-100 SRBMs, which are capable of flying beyond the UN-authorized 150-km range limit; Iraq has tested an al-Samoud variant beyond 150 km—perhaps as far as 300 km.
- Baghdad's UAVs could threaten Iraq's neighbors, US forces in the Persian Gulf, *and if brought close to, or into, the United States, the US Homeland.*

  - An Iraqi UAV procurement network attempted to procure commercially available route planning software and an associated topographical database that would be able to support targeting of the United States, according to analysis of special intelligence.
  - The Director, Intelligence, Surveillance, and Reconnaissance, US Air Force, does not agree that Iraq is developing UAVs *primarily* intended to be delivery platforms for chemical and biological warfare (CBW) agents. The small size of Iraq's new UAV strongly suggests a primary role of reconnaissance, although CBW delivery is an inherent capability.

- Iraq is developing medium-range ballistic missile capabilities, largely through foreign assistance in building specialized facilities, including a test stand for engines more powerful than those in its current missile force.

[—] **We have low confidence in our ability to assess when Saddam would use WMD.**

- Saddam could decide to use chemical and biological warfare (CBW) preemptively against US forces, friends, and allies in the region in an attempt to disrupt US war preparations and undermine the political will of the Coalition.
- Saddam might use CBW after an initial advance into Iraqi territory, but early use of WMD could foreclose diplomatic options for stalling the US advance.
- He probably would use CBW when he perceived he irretrievably had lost control of the military and security situation, but we are unlikely to know when Saddam reaches that point.
- We judge that Saddam would be more likely to use chemical weapons than biological weapons on the battlefield.
- Saddam historically has maintained tight control over the use of WMD; however, he probably has provided contingency instructions to his commanders to use CBW in specific circumstances.

[—] **Baghdad for now appears to be drawing a line short of conducting terrorist attacks with conventional or CBW against the United States, fearing that exposure of Iraqi involvement would provide Washington a stronger case for making war.**

[—] **Iraq probably would attempt clandestine attacks against the US Homeland if Baghdad feared an attack that threatened the survival of the regime were imminent or unavoidable, or possibly for revenge. Such attacks—more likely with biological than chemical agents—probably would be carried out by special forces or intelligence operatives.**

- The Iraqi Intelligence Service (IIS) probably has been directed to conduct clandestine attacks against US and Allied interests in the Middle East in the event the United States takes action against Iraq. The IIS probably would be the primary means by which Iraq would attempt to conduct any CBW attacks on the US Homeland, although we have no specific intelligence information that Saddam's regime has directed attacks against US territory.

[—] **Saddam, if sufficiently desperate, might decide that only an organization such as al-Qa'ida—with worldwide reach and extensive terrorist infrastructure, and already engaged in a life-or-death struggle against the United States—could perpetrate the type of terrorist attack that he would hope to conduct.**

- In such circumstances, he might decide that the extreme step of assisting the Islamist terrorists in conducting a CBW attack against the United States would be his last chance to exact vengeance by taking a large number of victims with him.

[—] **State/INR Alternative View of Iraq's Nuclear Program**

[—] The Assistant Secretary of State for Intelligence and Research (INR) believes that Saddam continues to want nuclear weapons and that available evidence indicates that Baghdad is pursuing at least a limited effort to maintain and acquire nuclear weapon-related capabilities. The activities we have detected do not, however, add up to a compelling case that Iraq is currently pursuing what INR would consider to be an integrated and comprehensive approach to acquire nuclear weapons. Iraq may be doing so, but INR considers the available evidence inadequate to support such a judgment. Lacking persuasive evidence that Baghdad has launched a coherent effort to reconstitute it nuclear weapons program, INR is unwilling to speculate that such an effort began soon after the departure of UN inspectors or to project a timeline for the completion of activities it does not now see happening.

As a result, INR is unable to predict when Iraq could acquire a nuclear device or weapon.

[—] In INR's view Iraq's efforts to acquire aluminum tubes is central to the argument that Baghdad is reconstituting its nuclear weapons program, but INR is not persuaded that the tubes in question are intended for use as centrifuge rotors. INR accepts the judgment of technical experts at the U.S. Department of Energy (DOE) who have concluded that the tubes Iraq seeks to acquire are poorly suited for use in gas centrifuges to be used for uranium enrichment and finds unpersuasive the arguments advanced by others to make the case that they are intended for that purpose. INR considers it more likely that the tubes are intended for another purpose, most likely the production of artillery rockets. The very large quantities being sought, the way the tubes were tested by the Iraqis, and the atypical lack of attention to operational security in the procurement efforts are among the factors, in addition to the DOE assessment, that lead INR to conclude that the tubes are not intended for use in Iraq's nuclear weapon program.

(U) Confidence Levels for Selected Key Judgments in This Estimate

[—] **High Confidence:**

- Iraq is continuing, and in some areas expanding, its chemical, biological, and nuclear and missile programs contrary to UN resolutions.
- We are not detecting portions of these weapons programs.
- Iraq possesses proscribed chemical and biological weapons and missiles.
- Iraq could make a nuclear weapon in months to a year once it acquires sufficient weapons-grade fissile material.

[—] **Moderate Confidence:**

- Iraq does not yet have a nuclear weapon or sufficient material to make one but is likely to have a weapon by 2007 to 2009. (See INR alternative view, page 84).

[—] **Low Confidence:**

- When Saddam would use weapons of mass destruction.
- Whether Saddam would engage in clandestine attacks against the US Homeland.
- Whether in desperation Saddam would share chemical or biological weapons with al-Qa'ida.

[—] **Errata sheet for NIE 2002-16HC, October 2002:** *Iraq's Continuing Programs for Weapons of Mass Destruction*

Change 1

[—] Page 7, first sub-bullet under first full bullet, Replace

[—paragraph deleted—]

With this language:

- Baghdad has mobile facilities for producing bacterial and toxin BW agents; these facilities can evade detection and are highly survivable. Within three to six months these units probably could produce an amount of agent equal to the total that Iraq produced in the years prior to the Gulf War.

After the issuance of the NIE and the release of the associated white paper, some members of the Senate Select Committee on Intelligence objected to the failure to include several points in the public version, including the assessments that Iraq was more likely to use WMD if it was attacked than otherwise and the information on the extent of CIA knowledge about Iraqi–al-Qa'ida relations. Deputy Director of Central Intelligence John McLaughlin responded on Tenet's behalf with a letter to Senator Bob Graham, the committee chairman, on 7 October 2002, authorizing the declassification of further excerpts from the "Key Judgments" and of selected quotes from McLaughlin's own closed testimony before the committee a few days earlier.[42]

October 7, 2002

Hon. Bob Graham
Chairman, Select Committee on Intelligence
U.S. Senate
Washington, D.C.

Dear Mr. Chairman:

In response to your letter of 4 October 2002, we have made unclassified material available to further the Senate's forthcoming open debate on a Joint Resolution concerning Iraq.

As always, our declassification efforts seek a balance between your need for unfettered debate and our need to protect sources and methods. We have also been mindful of a shared interest in not providing to Saddam a blueprint of our intelligence capabilities and shortcomings, or with insight into our expectation of how he will and will not act. The salience of such concerns is only heightened by the possibility of hostilities between the U.S. and Iraq.

These are some of the reasons why we did not include our classified judgments on Saddam's decision-making regarding the use of weapons of mass destruction (W.M.D.) in our recent unclassified paper on Iraq's Weapons of Mass Destruction. Viewing your request with those concerns in mind, however, we can declassify the following from the paragraphs you requested:

Baghdad for now appears to be drawing a line short of conducting terrorist attacks with conventional or C.B.W. [chemical and biological weapons] against the United States.

Should Saddam conclude that a U.S.-led attack could no longer be deterred, he probably would become much less constrained in adopting terrorist actions. Such terrorism might involve conventional means, as with Iraq's unsuccessful attempt at a terrorist offensive in 1991, or C.B.W.

Saddam might decide that the extreme step of assisting Islamist terrorists in conducting a W.M.D. attack against the United States would be his last chance to exact vengeance by taking a large number of victims with him.

Regarding the 2 October closed hearing, we can declassify the following dialogue:

Senator Levin [Carl Levin, Democrat of Michigan]: ... If (Saddam) didn't feel threatened, did not feel threatened, is it likely that he would initiate an attack using a weapon of mass destruction?

Senior Intelligence Witness [John McLaughlin]: ... My judgment would be that the—probability of him initiating an attack—let me put a time frame on it—in the foreseeable future, given the conditions we understand now, the likelihood I think would be low.

Senator Levin: Now if he did initiate an attack you've ... indicated he would probably attempt clandestine attacks against us ... But what about his use of weapons of mass destruction? If we initiate an attack and he thought he was *in extremis* or otherwise, what's the likelihood in response to our attack that he would use chemical or biological weapons?

Senior Intelligence Witness: Pretty high, in my view.

In the above dialogue, the witness's qualifications—"in the foreseeable future, given the conditions we understand now"—were intended to underscore that the likelihood of Saddam using W.M.D. for blackmail, deterrence, or otherwise grows as his arsenal builds. Moreover, if Saddam used W.M.D., it would disprove his repeated denials that he has such weapons.

Regarding Senator Bayh's [Evan Bayh, Democrat of Indiana] question of Iraqi links to al-Qa'ida. Senators could draw from the following points for unclassified discussions:

Our understanding of the relationship between Iraq and al-Qa'ida is evolving and is based on sources of varying reliability. Some of the information we have received comes from detainees, including some of high rank.

We have solid reporting of senior level contacts between Iraq and al-Qa'ida going back a decade.

Credible information indicates that Iraq and al-Qa'ida have discussed safe haven and reciprocal nonaggression.

Since Operation Enduring Freedom [the war in Afghanistan in 2001], we have solid evidence of the presence in Iraq of al-Qa'ida members, including some that have been in Baghdad.

We have credible reporting that al-Qa'ida leaders sought contacts in Iraq who could help them acquire W.M.D. capabilities. The reporting also stated that Iraq has provided training to al-Qa'ida members in the areas of poisons and gases and making conventional bombs.

Iraq's increasing support to extremist Palestinians coupled with growing indications of a relationship with al-Qa'ida, suggest that Baghdad's links to terrorists will increase, even absent U.S. military action.

Sincerely,
John McLaughlin
(For George J. Tenet, Director)

The suggestion in the letter that a U.S. attack would make Iraq *more* likely to use WMD elicited a furious phone call from National Security Adviser Condoleezza Rice. At Rice's insistence, Tenet issued a "clarification" to the media.[43]

Statement by DCI George Tenet, October 8, 2002

There is no inconsistency between our view of Saddam's growing threat and the view as expressed by the President in his speech. Although we think the chances of Saddam initiating a WMD attack at this moment are low—in part because it would constitute an admission that he possesses WMD—there is no question that the likelihood of Saddam using WMD against the United States or our allies in the region for blackmail, deterrence, or otherwise grows as his arsenal continues to build. His past use of WMD against civilian and military targets shows that he produces those weapons to use not just to deter.

Despite lingering doubts on the part of some members, Congress approved the joint resolution with the general understanding that the nation would go to war only as a last resort. It was left to the president to determine when other means had been exhausted. Disputes over the quality of intelligence continued but seemed to have little impact on policy decisions. The administration next turned to the United Nations Security Council and succeeded in eliciting unanimous approval of Resolution 1441 on 8 November 2002. The resolution declared Iraq to be in material violation of its 1991 obligations to disarm and called upon it to disarm immediately and fully and to allow unfettered access to the inspectors of the United Nations Monitoring, Verification, and Inspection Commission (UNMOVIC, which had replaced UNSCOM). In order to achieve unanimous support, the administration agreed to drop language that implied immediate authorization of war.

The final push to justify attacking Iraq and build public support behind it came in the first months of 2003. This consisted above all of President Bush's State of the Union address on 28 January 2003 and Secretary of State Colin L. Powell's remarks to the UN Security Council on 5 February 2003. The administration had been reluctant to involve the UN at all, but in the end it attempted to do so to placate certain allies, especially the British.

Spain agreed to join the United States and Britain in submitting a draft "second resolution" to the UN Security Council stating that Iraq had failed to comply with Resolution 1441. President Bush and National Security Adviser Rice met with Prime Minister José María Aznar in Texas on 22 February 2003. While certain of his own convictions and ostensibly assured that the intelligence would convince the other permanent and rotating members of the Security Council, Bush was impatient with the process and evidently prepared to apply pressure. Iraq, however, had permitted the UN weapons inspectors to return on 27 November 2002. While the Bush administration tended to be dismissive of them, the other Security Council members would put much more weight on their anticipated report.

Prime Minister Aznar: How will the resolution and the inspectors' report be combined?

Condoleezza Rice: Actually there won't be a report on February 28, the inspectors will present a written report on March 1, and their appearance before the Security Council won't happen until March 6 or 7 of 2003. We don't expect much from that report. As with the previous ones, it will be six of one and half a dozen of the other.

I have the impression that [the chief inspector Hans] Blix will now be more negative than before about the Iraqis' intentions. After the inspectors have appeared before the Council we should anticipate the vote on the resolution taking place one week later. Meanwhile, the Iraqis will try to explain that they're meeting their obligations. It's neither true nor sufficient, even if they announce the destruction of some missiles.

President Bush: This is like Chinese water torture. We have to put an end to it.

Prime Minister Aznar: I agree, but it would be good to be able to count on as many people as possible. Have a little patience.

President Bush: My patience has run out. I won't go beyond mid-March.

Prime Minister Aznar: I'm not asking for indefinite patience. Simply that you do everything possible so that everything comes together.

President Bush [listing Security Council members]: Countries like Mexico, Chile, Angola, and Cameroon have to know that what's at stake is the United States' security and act with a sense of friendship toward us.

[Chilean President Ricardo] Lagos has to know that the Free Trade Agreement with Chile is pending Senate confirmation, and that a negative attitude on this issue could jeopardize ratification. Angola is receiving funds from the Millennium Account that could also be compromised if they don't show a positive attitude. And Putin must know that his attitude is jeopardizing the relations of Russia and the United States.

Both the State of the Union address and Powell's UN speech relied heavily on information derived from intelligence and on inferences culled from that information. Here is the portion of Bush's State of the Union address that deals with Iraq:

Our nation and the world must learn the lessons of the Korean Peninsula and not allow an even greater threat to rise up in Iraq. A brutal dictator, with a history of reckless aggression, with ties to terrorism, with great potential wealth, will not be permitted to dominate a vital region and threaten the United States. (Applause.)

Twelve years ago, Saddam Hussein faced the prospect of being the last casualty in a war he had started and lost. To spare himself, he agreed to disarm of all weapons of mass destruction. For the next 12 years, he systematically violated that agreement. He pursued chemical, biological, and nuclear weapons, even while inspectors were in his country. Nothing to date has restrained him from his pursuit of these weapons—not economic sanctions, not isolation from the civilized world, not even cruise missile strikes on his military facilities.

Almost three months ago, the United Nations Security Council gave Saddam Hussein his final chance to disarm. He has shown instead utter contempt for the United Nations, and for the opinion of the world. The 108 UN inspectors were sent to conduct—were not sent to conduct a scavenger hunt for hidden materials across a country the size of California. The job of the inspectors is to verify that Iraq's regime is disarming. It is up to Iraq to show exactly where it is hiding its banned weapons, lay those weapons out for the world to see, and destroy them as directed. Nothing like this has happened.

The United Nations concluded in 1999 that Saddam Hussein had biological weapons sufficient to produce over 25,000 liters of anthrax—enough doses to kill several million people. He hasn't accounted for that material. He's given no evidence that he has destroyed it.

The United Nations concluded that Saddam Hussein had materials sufficient to produce more than 38,000 liters of botulinum toxin—enough to subject millions of people to death by respiratory failure. He hadn't accounted for that material. He's given no evidence that he has destroyed it.

Our intelligence officials estimate that Saddam Hussein had the materials to produce as much as 500 tons of sarin, mustard, and VX nerve agent. In such quantities, these chemical agents could also kill untold thousands. He's not accounted for these materials. He has given no evidence that he has destroyed them.

U.S. intelligence indicates that Saddam Hussein had upwards of 30,000 munitions capable of delivering chemical agents. Inspectors recently turned up 16 of them—despite Iraq's recent declaration denying their existence. Saddam Hussein has not accounted for the remaining 29,984 of these prohibited munitions. He's given no evidence that he has destroyed them.

From three Iraqi defectors we know that Iraq, in the late 1990s, had several mobile biological weapons labs. These are designed to produce germ warfare agents, and can be moved from place to a place to evade inspectors. Saddam Hussein has not disclosed these facilities. He's given no evidence that he has destroyed them.

The International Atomic Energy Agency confirmed in the 1990s that Saddam Hussein had an advanced nuclear weapons development program, had a design for a nuclear weapon and was working on five different methods of enriching uranium for a bomb. The British government has learned that Saddam Hussein recently sought significant quantities of uranium from Africa. Our intelligence sources tell us that he has attempted to purchase high-strength aluminum tubes suitable for nuclear weapons production. Saddam Hussein has not credibly explained these activities. He clearly has much to hide.

The dictator of Iraq is not disarming. To the contrary; he is deceiving. From intelligence sources we know, for instance, that thousands of Iraqi security personnel are at work hiding documents and materials from the UN inspectors, sanitizing inspection sites, and monitoring the inspectors themselves. Iraqi officials accompany the inspectors in order to intimidate witnesses.

Iraq is blocking U-2 surveillance flights requested by the United Nations. Iraqi intelligence officers are posing as the scientists inspectors are supposed to interview. Real scientists have been coached by Iraqi officials on what to say. Intelligence sources indicate that Saddam Hussein has ordered that scientists who cooperate with UN inspectors in disarming Iraq will be killed, along with their families.

Year after year, Saddam Hussein has gone to elaborate lengths, spent enormous sums, taken great risks to build and keep weapons of mass destruction. But why? The only possible explanation, the only possible use he could have for those weapons, is to dominate, intimidate, or attack.

With nuclear arms or a full arsenal of chemical and biological weapons, Saddam Hussein could resume his ambitions of conquest in the Middle East and create deadly havoc in that region. And this Congress and the America people must recognize another threat. Evidence from intelligence sources, secret communications, and statements by people now in custody reveal that Saddam Hussein aids and protects terrorists, including members of al Qaeda. Secretly, and without fingerprints, he could provide one of his hidden weapons to terrorists, or help them develop their own.

Before September the 11th, many in the world believed that Saddam Hussein could be contained. But chemical agents, lethal viruses, and shadowy terrorist networks are not easily contained. Imagine those 19 hijackers with other weapons and other plans—this time armed by Saddam Hussein. It would take one vial, one canister, one crate slipped into this country to bring a day of horror like none we have ever known. We will do everything in our power to make sure that that day never comes. (Applause.)

Some have said we must not act until the threat is imminent. Since when have terrorists and tyrants announced their intentions, politely putting us on notice before they strike? If this threat is permitted to fully and suddenly emerge, all actions, all words, and all recriminations would come too late. Trusting in the sanity and restraint of Saddam Hussein is not a strategy, and it is not an option. (Applause.)

The dictator who is assembling the world's most dangerous weapons has already used them on whole villages—leaving thousands of his own citizens dead, blind, or disfigured. Iraqi refugees tell us how forced confessions are obtained—by torturing children while their parents are made to watch. International human rights groups have catalogued other methods used in the torture chambers of Iraq: electric shock, burning with hot irons, dripping acid on the skin, mutilation with electric drills, cutting out tongues, and rape. If this is not evil, then evil has no meaning. (Applause.)

And tonight I have a message for the brave and oppressed people of Iraq: Your enemy is not surrounding your country—your enemy is ruling your country.

(Applause.) And the day he and his regime are removed from power will be the day of your liberation. (Applause.)

The world has waited 12 years for Iraq to disarm. America will not accept a serious and mounting threat to our country, and our friends and our allies. The United States will ask the UN Security Council to convene on February the 5th to consider the facts of Iraq's ongoing defiance of the world. Secretary of State Powell will present information and intelligence about Iraqi's legal—Iraq's illegal weapons programs, its attempt to hide those weapons from inspectors, and its links to terrorist groups.

We will consult. But let there be no misunderstanding: If Saddam Hussein does not fully disarm, for the safety of our people and for the peace of the world, we will lead a coalition to disarm him. (Applause.)

Tonight I have a message for the men and women who will keep the peace, members of the American Armed Forces: Many of you are assembling in or near the Middle East, and some crucial hours may lay ahead. In those hours, the success of our cause will depend on you. Your training has prepared you. Your honor will guide you. You believe in America, and America believes in you. (Applause.)

Sending Americans into battle is the most profound decision a president can make. The technologies of war have changed; the risks and suffering of war have not. For the brave Americans who bear the risk, no victory is free from sorrow. This nation fights reluctantly, because we know the cost and we dread the days of mourning that always come.

We seek peace. We strive for peace. And sometimes peace must be defended. A future lived at the mercy of terrible threats is no peace at all. If war is forced upon us, we will fight in a just cause and by just means—sparing, in every way we can, the innocent. And if war is forced upon us, we will fight with the full force and might of the United States military—and we will prevail. (Applause.)

And as we and our coalition partners are doing in Afghanistan, we will bring to the Iraqi people food and medicines and supplies—and freedom. (Applause.)

Many challenges, abroad and at home, have arrived in a single season. In two years, America has gone from a sense of invulnerability to an awareness of peril; from bitter division in small matters to calm unity in great causes. And we go forward with confidence, because this call of history has come to the right country.

Americans are a resolute people who have risen to every test of our time. Adversity has revealed the character of our country, to the world and to ourselves. America is a strong nation, and honorable in the use of our strength. We exercise power without conquest, and we sacrifice for the liberty of strangers.

Americans are a free people, who know that freedom is the right of every person and the future of every nation. The liberty we prize is not America's gift to the world, it is God's gift to humanity.

The speech was extremely powerful and it made a strong impression on the public. Of course, much of the information that underlay it was simply incorrect. In addition, one can point out conclusions and inferences that existed apart from the intelligence or went beyond the information that officials believed they had. For example, Iraq's inability to account for weapons could have had numerous explanations, such as bad record keeping or the distorted flow of information in tyrannical regimes. (In fact, according to the Duelfer Report, "The members of the [biological warfare] program were too scared to tell the [Iraqi] Regime that they had dumped deactivated anthrax within sight of one of the principal presidential palaces." This dumping had occurred back in 1991.)[44] Moreover, Iraq could have had many uses for WMD (if it had the weapons) other than "to dominate, intimidate, or attack." It might have wanted them to protect itself from rebellion, an attack by Iran, or an invasion by the United States. It was, after all, an unpopular regime with no end of enemies at home and abroad. Finally, what exactly is the connection between gassing the Kurdish people (which occurred in response to a Kurdish rebellion at the time when most of the Iraqi army was tied down in Iran) and attacking the United States? Have other countries that savagely repressed rebellions attacked the United States? We knew that Saddam Hussein's regime was heinous, we had known it for years, but it was not the world's only heinous regime and that was not the justification given for war. Even Deputy Secretary Wolfowitz—probably the war's most enthusiastic advocate—said in the interview cited above that "the criminal treatment of the Iraqi people" was "not a reason to put American kids' lives at risk, certainly not on the scale we did it."

Once again, the crux of the argument was the nexus of WMD and terrorism, but it was accompanied by no intelligence-based evidence and, indeed, by no real argument other than the notion that connecting the two would be a bad thing. Saying that "he *could* provide one of his hidden weapons to terrorists, or help them develop their own" is not the same as saying that he would. In principle, the same thing could be said of anyone with "hidden weapons." No reason is given as to why a tyrant who strives to keep such strict control over so many aspects of life at home would choose to give deadly weapons to terrorists (we assume the president means Islamist terrorists like al-Qa'ida) who, frankly, do not like him any more than they like the Americans. If Hussein had weapons of mass destruction and wanted to attack the United States, why did he not do it years ago and why would he need Islamist terrorists instead of using his own people? The forensic evidence connecting Iraq to the deed would probably come from the bomb itself as much as from the people carrying it.

The most famous line in the State of the Union speech, of course, was this: "The British government has learned that Saddam Hussein recently sought significant quantities of uranium from Africa." Its fame was due to the controversy over its origins after former diplomat Joseph Wilson announced that he had investigated the matter in March 2002 on behalf of the CIA and believed it to be unfounded.[45] The claim had been based on forged papers purportedly showing Iraq to be purchasing 500 tons of uranium oxide (also known as "yellowcake") from Niger. The White House had already tried to insert this claim into a speech made by the president in Cincinnati in October 2002, but CIA intervention prevented it on that occasion.[46]

A year before the invasion of Iraq, a cable from the Office of Analysis for Africa (AA) in the State Department's Bureau of Intelligence and Research (INR)—under the subject heading "INR/AA ANALYSIS FOR FEBRUARY 25–MARCH 3, 2002"—had dismissed the claim as unlikely. The relevant passages were partially declassified in November 2005. Each paragraph was originally classified as "Secret" (S) or "Secret/No Foreign Distribution" (S/NF).

(S/NF) NIGER: SALE OF URANIUM TO IRAQ IS UNLIKELY

32. (S/NF) NIGER PROBABLY IS NOT PLANNING TO SELL URANIUM TO IRAQ, IN PART BECAUSE FRANCE CONTROLS THE URANIUM INDUSTRY AND WOULD TAKE ACTION TO BLOCK A SALE [—about six lines deleted—]

BUT NEITHER PRESIDENT TANDJA NOR KEY OFFICIALS OF HIS GOVERN-MENT, WHO UNDERSTAND THE VALUE OF GOOD RELATIONS WITH THE U.S. AND OTHER AID DONORS, WOULD RISK JEOPARDIZING THEM BY SELLING URANIUM TO IRAQ. IN ADDITION, THE SALE WOULD VIOLATE UN SECURITY COUNCIL RESOLUTION 687.

33. (S) FRANCE, WHICH USES NUCLEAR POWER TO PRODUCE ABOUT 80 PERCENT OF ITS ELECTRICITY, OBTAINS AROUND 40 PERCENT OF ITS URA-NIUM FROM TWO MINES AT ARLIT, DEEP IN THE SAHARA IN NORTHERN NIGER—THE ONLY OPERATING URANIUM MINES IN THE COUNTRY. FRANCE AND NIGER JOINTLY OWN THE MINES; JAPAN AND SPAIN HAVE A MINORITY INTEREST IN ONE OF THEM. FRANCE UNEQUIVOCALLY CON-TROLS THE OVERALL OPERATION; THERE ARE FRENCH MANAGERS AND ENGINEERS AT EVERY POINT IN THE MINING, MILLING, AND TRANSPOR-TATION PROCESS.

34. (S/NF) A CORRUPT FORMER PRESIDENT MAY HAVE NEGOTIATED WITH IRAQ. [—just over one line deleted—] AT THAT TIME NIGER WAS RULED BY PRESIDENT BARE MINASSARA, AN UNSOPHISTICATED AND VENAL INDI-VIDUAL WHO WOULD NOT HAVE BEEN ABOVE TRYING TO SELL URA-NIUM TO A ROGUE STATE. BUT BARE'S PRESIDENTIAL GUARD KILLED HIM IN APRIL 1999. THE JUNTA THAT GOVERNED NIGER FOR THE NEXT NINE MONTHS RELINQUISHED POWER TO TANDJA'S FREELY ELECTED GOVERNMENT IN DECEMBER 1999.

35. (S/NF) TANDJA NOT LIKELY TO RISK AID FOR SHORT-TERM GAIN. THE REPORT FURTHER STATES THAT NIGER AND IRAQ SIGNED THE SALES AGREEMENT IN JULY 2000, WITH FULL SUPPORT FROM TANDJA (AND FOL-LOWING A FULL LEGAL REVIEW). IN VIEW OF TANDJA'S [—two-thirds of a line deleted—] RELUCTANCE TO DO ANYTHING THAT MIGHT ENDANGER HIS RELATIONS WITH WESTERN AID DONORS, IT IS IMPROBABLE ANY SUCH AGREEMENT WAS SIGNED WITH HIS KNOWLEDGE. NIGER IS DE-PENDENT ON FOREIGN ASSISTANCE—NOT ONLY FOR DEVELOPMENT AID, BUT ALSO FOR FINANCING MUCH OF THE SAY-TO-DAY OPERATIONS OF THE GOVERNMENT. A PAYOFF FROM IRAQ OF $50 MILLION OR EVEN $100 MILLION WOULD NOT MAKE UP FOR WHAT WOULD BE LOST IF THE DONOR COMMUNITY TURNED OFF THE TAPS TO NIGER. [—about three and a half lines deleted—]

36. (S/NF) THE DIFFICULTY OF MOVING SECRETLY 500 TONS OF URANIUM. THOUGH THE ALLEGED AGREEMENT WITH IRAQ IS NOT SPECIFIC, IT APPARENTLY CALLS FOR THE 500 TONS TO BE DELIVERED [—] IN ONE YEAR. THIS WOULD MEAN THAT [—] 25 HARD-TO-CONCEAL 10-TON TRACTOR-TRAILERS WOULD BE USED TO TRANSPORT THE OFF-THE-BOOKS URANIUM. BECAUSE NIGER IS LANDLOCKED THE CONVOY WOULD HAVE TO CROSS AT LEAST ONE INTERNATIONAL BORDER AND TRAVEL AT LEAST 1,000 MILES TO REACH THE SEA. MOVING SUCH A QUANTITY SECRETLY OVER SUCH A DISTANCE WOULD BE VERY DIFFICULT, PARTICU-LARLY BECAUSE THE FRENCH WOULD BE INDISPOSED TO APPROVE OR CLOAK THIS ARRANGEMENT.

POWELL

To these points Tenet added that Iraq already had a substantial supply of uranium oxide and would not have needed to buy it from Niger. Moreover, the CIA had already expressed its doubts on this issue in a briefing to Congress.[47]

The White House opted to use the claim anyway. After the war started, the president conceded that using it was a mistake.

On 5 February 2003, Secretary of State Powell presented the administration's case for war before the United Nations Security Council. The speech was based on the general argument that had been developed to that point, but Powell, with CIA assistance, downplayed elements for which the evidence was weakest, for instance leaving aside the suggestion of Iraqi involvement in the 9/11 attacks (Bush had not used this in the State of the Union, either) and the uranium oxide issue, although he did mention aluminum tubes as evidence of a nuclear program. The speech was filled with circumstantial evidence, inferences, and references to questions still unanswered. Powell accompanied his speech with images from satellite photos suggesting that the Iraqis were cleaning weapons sites before the arrival of international weapons inspectors. Intercepts from telephone calls indicated that Iraqi officials were nervous about the return of the inspectors, were monitoring the inspectors, and were being uncooperative. They had hidden some classified documents. Dual-use equipment had been acquired. Rockets had been built that marginally exceeded permitted range limits. This was behavior consistent with the intent to hide weapons and other prohibited activities, but other explanations could have been equally valid. In each case, ambiguous evidence was interpreted in the most sinister way.

A key portion of Powell's presentation dealt with the mobile laboratories that produced biological weapons, which Bush had also mentioned in the State of the Union address. Regarding this, Powell noted:

> The source was an eyewitness, an Iraqi chemical engineer who supervised one of these facilities. He actually was present during biological agent production runs. He was also at the site when an accident occurred in 1998. Twelve technicians died from exposure to biological agents.

In fact, this information was based on a story that an Iraqi refugee—codenamed Curveball by the CIA—had invented some four years earlier in order to get political asylum in Germany. The story apparently became increasingly exaggerated with repeated retellings. Germany's Federal Intelligence Service (Bundesnachrichtendienst, BND) had forwarded the information to the U.S. Defense Intelligence Agency, which in turn sent it to the CIA. The CIA did not directly interview Curveball, who had entered the German equivalent of the federal witness protection program, until March 2004. At that time they declared him a fabricator. The Germans, themselves, pointed out in late 2002 that they were not able to verify anything that Curveball had said. (Of course, verification probably would have required investigating sites in Iraq that had not been available.)[48]

After addressing weapons of mass destruction in the main portion of his speech, Powell concluded with a discussion of Iraq's purported links to al-Qa'ida. Here is that portion of the speech in full:

> My friends, the information I have presented to you about these terrible weapons and about Iraq's continued flaunting of its obligations under Security Council Resolution 1441 links to a subject I now want to spend a little bit of time on, and that has to do with terrorism.
>
> Our concern is not just about these illicit weapons; it's the way that these illicit weapons can be connected to terrorists and terrorist organizations that have

no compunction about using such devices against innocent people around the world.

Iraq and terrorism go back decades. Baghdad trains Palestine Liberation Front members in small arms and explosives. Saddam uses the Arab Liberation Front to funnel money to the families of Palestinian suicide bombers in order to prolong the Intifadah. And it's no secret that Saddam's own intelligence service was involved in dozens of attacks or attempted assassinations in the 1990s.

But what I want to bring to your attention today is the potentially much more sinister nexus between Iraq and the al-Qaida terrorist network, a nexus that combines classic terrorist organizations and modern methods of murder. Iraq today harbors a deadly terrorist network headed by Abu Musab al-Zarqawi an associate and collaborator of Usama bin Ladin and his Al-Qaida lieutenants.

Zarqawi, Palestinian born in Jordan, fought in the Afghan war more than a decade ago. Returning to Afghanistan in 2000, he oversaw a terrorist training camp. One of his specialties, and one of the specialties of this camp, is poisons.

When our coalition ousted the Taliban, the Zarqawi network helped establish another poison and explosive training center camp, and this camp is located in northeastern Iraq. You see a picture of this camp.

The network is teaching its operatives how to produce ricin and other poisons. Let me remind you how ricin works. Less than a pinch—imagine a pinch of salt—less than a pinch of ricin, eating just this amount in your food, would cause shock, followed by circulatory failure. Death comes within 72 hours and there is no antidote. There is no cure. It is fatal.

Those helping to run this camp are Zarqawi lieutenants operating in northern Kurdish areas outside Saddam Hussein's controlled Iraq. But Baghdad has an agent in the most senior levels of the radical organization Ansar al-Islam that controls this corner of Iraq. In 2000, this agent offered al-Qaida safehaven in the region.

After we swept al-Qaida from Afghanistan, some of those members accepted this safehaven. They remain there today.

Zarqawi's activities are not confined to this small corner of northeast Iraq. He traveled to Baghdad in May of 2002 for medical treatment, staying in the capital of Iraq for two months while he recuperated to fight another day.

During his stay, nearly two-dozen extremists converged on Baghdad and established a base of operations there. These al-Qaida affiliates based in Baghdad now coordinate the movement of people, money and supplies into and throughout Iraq for his network, and they have now been operating freely in the capital for more than eight months.

Iraqi officials deny accusations of ties with al-Qaida. These denials are simply not credible. Last year, an al-Qaida associate bragged that the situation in Iraq was "good," that Baghdad could be transited quickly.

We know these affiliates are connected to Zarqawi because they remain, even today, in regular contact with his direct subordinates, include the poison-cell plotters. And they are involved in moving more than money and materiel. Last year, two suspected al-Qaida operatives were arrested crossing from Iraq into Saudi Arabia. They were linked to associates of the Baghdad cell and one of them received training in Afghanistan on how to use cyanide.

From his terrorist network in Iraq, Zarqawi can direct his network in the Middle East and beyond. We in the United States, all of us, the State Department and the Agency for International Development, we all lost a dear friend with the cold-blooded murder of Mr. Laurence Foley in Amman, Jordan, last October. A despicable act was committed that day, the assassination of an individual whose sole mission was to assist the people of Jordan. The captured assassin says his cell received money and weapons from Zarqawi for that murder. After the attack, an associate of the assassin left Jordan to go to Iraq to obtain weapons and explosives for further operations. Iraqi officials protest that they are not aware of the whereabouts of Zarqawi or of any of his associates. Again, these protests are not credible. We know of Zarqawi's activities in Baghdad. I described them earlier.

Now let me add one other fact. We asked a friendly security service to approach Baghdad about extraditing Zarqawi and providing information about him and his close associates. This service contacted Iraqi officials twice and we passed details that should have made it easy to find Zarqawi. The network remains in Baghdad. Zakawi still remains at large, to come and go.

As my colleagues around this table and as the citizens they represent in Europe know, Zarqawi's terrorism is not confined to the Middle East. Zarqawi and his network have plotted terrorist actions against countries including France, Britain, Spain, Italy, Germany, and Russia. According to detainees, Abu Atiya, who graduated from Zarqawi's terrorist camp in Afghanistan, tasked at least nine North African extremists in 2001 to travel to Europe to conduct poison and explosive attacks.

Since last year, members of this network have been apprehended in France, Britain, Spain, and Italy. By our last count, 116 operatives connected to this global web have been arrested.

We know about this European network and we know about its links to Zarqawi because the detainees who provided the information about the targets also provided the names of members of the network. Three of those he identified by name were arrested in France last December. In the apartments of the terrorists, authorities found circuits for explosive devices and a list of ingredients to make toxins.

The detainee who helped piece this together says the plot also targeted Britain. Later evidence again proved him right. When the British unearthed the cell there just last month, one British police officer was murdered during the destruction of the cell.

We also know that Zarqawi's colleagues have been active in the Pankisi Gorge, Georgia, and in Chechnya, Russia. The plotting to which they are linked is not mere chatter. Members of Zarqawi's network say their goal was to kill Russians with toxins.

We are not surprised that Iraq is harboring Zarqawi and his subordinates. This understanding builds on decades-long experience with respect to ties between Iraq and al-Qaida. Going back to the early and mid-1990s when Bin Ladin was based in Sudan, an al-Qaida source tells us that Saddam and Bin Ladin reached an understanding that al-Qaida would no longer support activities against Baghdad. Early al-Qaida ties were forged by secret high-level intelligence service contacts with al-Qaida, secret Iraqi intelligence high-level contacts with al-Qaida.

We know members of both organizations met repeatedly and have met at least eight times at very senior levels since the early 1990s. In 1996, a foreign security service tells us that Bin Ladin met with a senior Iraqi intelligence official in Khartoum and later met the director of the Iraqi Intelligence Service.

Saddam became more interested as he saw al-Qaida's appalling attacks. A detained al-Qaida member tells us that Saddam was more willing to assist al-Qaida after the 1998 bombings of our embassies in Kenya and Tanzania. Saddam was also impressed by al-Qaida's attacks on the USS Cole in Yemen in October 2000.

Iraqis continue to visit Bin Ladin in his new home in Afghanistan. A senior defector, one of Saddam's former intelligence chiefs in Europe, says Saddam sent his agents to Afghanistan sometime in the mid-1990s to provide training to al-Qaida members on document forgery.

From the late 1990s until 2001, the Iraqi Embassy in Pakistan played the role of liaison to the al-Qaida organization.

Some believe, some claim, these contacts do not amount to much. They say Saddam Hussein's secular tyranny and al-Qaida's religious tyranny do not mix. I am not comforted by this thought. Ambition and hatred are enough to bring Iraq and al-Qaida together, enough so al-Qaida could learn how to build more sophisticated bombs and learn how to forge documents, and enough so that al-Qaida could turn to Iraq for help in acquiring expertise on weapons of mass destruction.

And the record of Saddam Hussein's cooperation with other Islamist terrorist organizations is clear. HAMAS, for example, opened an office in Baghdad in 1999, and Iraq has hosted conferences attended by Palestine Islamic Jihad. These groups are at the forefront of sponsoring suicide attacks against Israel.

Al-Qaida continues to have a deep interest in acquiring weapons of mass destruction. As with the story of Zarqawi and his network, I can trace the story of a senior terrorist operative telling how Iraq provided training in these weapons to al-Qaida. Fortunately, this operative is now detained and he has told his story. I will relate it to you now as he, himself, described it.

This senior al-Qaida terrorist was responsible for one of al-Qaida's training camps in Afghanistan. His information comes firsthand from his personal involvement at senior levels of al-Qaida. He says Bin Ladin and his top deputy in Afghanistan, deceased al-Qaida leader Mohammed Atef, did not believe that al-Qaida labs in Afghanistan were capable enough to manufacture these chemical or biological agents. They needed to go somewhere else. They had to look outside of Afghanistan for help.

Where did they go? Where did they look? They went to Iraq. The support that the operative describes included Iraq offering chemical or biological weapons training for two al-Qaida associates beginning in December 2000. He says that a militant known as Abdullah al-Araqi had been sent to Iraq several times between 1997 and 2000 for help in acquiring poisons and gasses. Abdullah al-Araqi characterized the relationship he forged with Iraqi officials as successful.

As I said at the outset, none of this should come as a surprise to any of us. Terrorism has been a tool used by Saddam for decades. Saddam was a supporter of terrorism long before these terrorist networks had a name, and this support continues. The nexus of poisons and terror is new. The nexus of Iraq and terror is old. The combination is lethal.

With this track record, Iraqi denials of supporting terrorism take their place alongside the other Iraqi denials of weapons of mass destruction. It is all a web of lies.

When we confront a regime that harbors ambitions for regional domination, hides weapons of mass destruction, and provides haven and active support for terrorists, we are not confronting the past; we are confronting the present. And unless we act, we are confronting an even more frightening future.

DCI Tenet would later state that the CIA was skeptical of allegations linking Iraq to al-Qa'ida. He noted that Deputy Secretary of Defense Wolfowitz and Vice President Cheney's chief of staff, I. Lewis "Scooter" Libby, "never seemed satisfied with our answers regarding allegations of Iraqi complicity with al-Qa'ida."[49] Wolfowitz authorized Under Secretary of Defense for Policy Douglas J. Feith to establish the Policy Counter Terrorism Evaluation Group (PCTEG; often misidentified as the Office of Special Plans). Although not part of the Intelligence Community, the group combed through evidence already rejected by the CIA looking specifically for links between Iraq and al-Qa'ida and purported to find them. They then briefed ranking decision makers on their findings in the summer of 2002. The briefing was well received by the Office of the Secretary of Defense, the Office of the Deputy Secretary of Defense, the Office of the Vice President, and the Deputy National Security Adviser, but it appears that it did not impress the Intelligence Community.[50]

As evidence of cooperation between Saddam Hussein and Usama bin Ladin, Feith's people pointed to the presence of Ansar al-Islam and Abu Musab al-Zarqawi in Iraq and to a meeting between Muhammad Atta, the leader of the 9/11 terrorists, and an Iraqi intelligence officer in Prague in 2001. Ansar al-Islam was the "al-Qa'ida group in northern Iraq" mentioned by Wolfowitz in his interview. It was a radical Islamist group that was operating in a secluded corner of the northern zone—the region that was otherwise under the control of the anti-Hussein Kurdish regime since the Persian Gulf War. Ansar al-Islam objectively served the Iraqi government's purposes in that it attacked Kurdish forces, the enemy of both, but that hardly constitutes evidence of Hussein's ties to al-Qa'ida. If Hussein really had an agent operating within it, as Powell stated, it does not necessarily follow that the agent made authoritative decisions on the organization's behalf. Ansar al-Islam later split into rival groups, Ansar al-Sunna and the Tawid and Jihad Group.[51]

Abu Musab al-Zarqawi was affiliated for a time with Ansar al-Islam and then became the leader of Tawhid and Jihad. He had earlier run a training camp in Afghanistan, but it was separate from al-Qa'ida's facilities. Regional experts now believe that Zarqawi and Bin Ladin were rivals. While Bin Ladin focused on the "far enemy"—the United States—for its support of Israel and secular Middle East regimes, Zarqawi insisted on targeting the "near enemy"—"apostates" within the Muslim world, that is, people like Saddam Hussein. The U.S. invasion of Iraq brought the "far" enemy "near" and thus created the basis for a tactical alliance between the two rival terrorist groups.[52] In 2004, after the invasion had ended and the Iraqi insurgency had begun, Zarqawi changed the name of his organization from "Tawhid and Jihad" to "al-Qa'ida in Iraq."[53]

Documents and detainee testimony after the invasion of Iraq substantially filled in the gaps in the Intelligence Community's understanding of the relationships among Iraq, Ansar al-Islam, and al-Qa'ida. These reassessments were brought together by the Senate Select Committee on Intelligence in 2006.

In contrast to prewar foreign intelligence service reports that al-Zarqawi had allied with bin Ladin, in April 2003 the CIA learned from a senior al-Qa'ida detainee that al-Zarqawi had rebuffed several efforts by bin Ladin to recruit him. The detainee claimed that al-Zarqawi had religious differences with bin Ladin and disagreed with bin Ladin's singular focus against the United States. The CIA assessed in April 2003 that al-Zarqawi planned and directed independent terrorist operations without al-Qa'ida direction, but assessed that he "most likely contracted out his network's services to al-Qa'ida in return for material and financial assistance from key al-Qa'ida facilitators."

A postwar CIA assessment on al-Zarqawi notes that both captured former regime documents and former regime officials show that the IIS [Iraqi Intelligence Service] did respond to a foreign request for assistance in finding and extraditing al-Zarqawi for his role in the murder of U.S. diplomat Lawrence Foley. In the spring of 2002, the IIS formed a "special committee" to track down al-Zarqawi, but was unable to locate and capture him. The CIA, the DIA [Defense Intelligence

Agency], and FBI all reported that no evidence suggests that al-Zarqawi had been warned by a former Iraq regime element that he had been located in Baghdad by the IIS. The CIA assessed that Zarqawi left Baghdad in late November 2002. [...]

In 2005, the CIA assessed that prior to the war, "the regime did not have a relationship, harbor, or turn a blind eye toward Zarqawi and his associates." [...]

[...] In addition, "detainees that originally reported on AI-IIS [Ansar al-Islam–Iraqi Intelligence Service] links have recanted, and another detainee, in September 2003, was deemed to have insufficient access and level of detail to substantiate his claims.

According to DIA, detainee information and captured document exploitation indicate that the regime was aware of Ansar al-Islam and al-Qa'ida presence in northeastern Iraq, but the groups' presence was considered a threat to the regime and the Iraqi government attempted intelligence collection operations against them. The DIA stated that information from senior Ansar al-Islam detainees revealed that the group viewed Saddam's regime as apostate, and denied any relationship with it. The DIA said that one detainee speculated that al-Zarqawi may have had contacts with the former regime prior to Operation Iraqi Freedom, but all other detainees' information, from both the former regime and members of al-Zarqawi's network, denied such contacts occurred.[54]

In addition to such inferences about the location of people and groups believed to be associated with al-Qa'ida, the CIA had one principal human source that linked Iraq to al-Qa'ida, the one cited repeatedly by Powell as a former ranking al-Qa'ida official now in custody. That was Ibn al-Shaykh al-Libi, who had been captured in Pakistan in December 2001 and rendered the following month to Egypt for interrogation. (The network of clandestine CIA interrogation sites had not yet been established.) There, in response to coercive interrogation techniques, al-Libi reported that al-Qa'ida had received weapons training from Iraq. However, in a report issued on 14 February 2004, the CIA informed senior administration officials that al-Libi had recanted his story after being confronted with contradictory testimony from other al-Qa'ida detainees. In fact, he now denied ever having been a member of al-Qa'ida. At best, intelligence officials were left wondering which version was true.[55] There had already been doubts about al-Libi within the Defense Intelligence Agency from early on, as shown in the following excerpt from a DIA memorandum dated February 2002.[56] It indicates that al-Libi presented his original story connecting al-Qa'ida to Iraq only after his transfer to Egyptian authorities. Although the word *torture* is not mentioned, it is clearly the implication.

This is the first report from Ibn al-Shaykh in which he claims Iraq assisted al-Qaida's CBRN [chemical, biological, radiological, or nuclear] efforts. However, he lacks specific details on the Iraqi's involved, the CBRN materials associated with the assistance, and the location where training occurred. It is possible he does not know any further details; it is more likely this individual is intentionally misleading the debriefers. Ibn al-Shaykh has been undergoing debriefs for several weeks and may [be] describing scenarios to the debriefers that he knows will retain their interest.

Saddam's regime is intensely secular and is wary of Islamic revolutionary movements. Moreover, Baghdad is unlikely to provide assistance to a group it cannot control.

Feith's reporting regarding Iraq's links to al-Qa'ida was later criticized in a report by the Senate Armed Services Committee Minority (Democratic) Staff,

Report of an Inquiry into the Alternative Analysis of the Issue of an Iraq-Al Qaeda Relationship (21 October 2004), which was released by Senator Carl Levin. The Senate Select Committee on Intelligence had put off an evaluation of the PCTEG's assessments until its Phase II report because the group was not officially part of the Intelligence Community. Feith also received a mild rebuke from the Department of Defense Office of Inspector General.[57]

> The Office of the Under Secretary of Defense for Policy developed, produced, and then disseminated alternative assessments on the Iraq and al-Qaida relationship, which included some conclusions that were inconsistent with the consensus of the Intelligence Community, to senior decision makers. While such actions were not illegal or unauthorized, the actions were, in our opinion, inappropriate given that the intelligence assessments were intelligence products and did not clearly show the variance with the consensus of the Intelligence Community. This condition occurred because of an expanded role and mission of the Office of the Under Secretary of Defense for Policy from policy formulation to alternative intelligence analysis and dissemination. As a result, the Office of the Under Secretary of Defense for Policy did not provide "the most accurate analysis of intelligence" to senor decision makers.

In 2004, Senator Levin directed a number of questions to DCI Tenet. One of them specifically addressed the purported meeting in Prague between an Iraqi intelligence official and 9/11 leader Muhammad Atta. Tenet's response came nearly three months later.

July 1, 2004 Response of Director of Central Intelligence George Tenet to Senator Levin Question for the Record, March 9, 2004 Armed Services Committee Hearing

Question 8: Director Tenet, do you believe it is likely that September 11 hijacker Muhammad Atta and Iraqi Intelligence Service officer Ahmed al-Ani met in Prague in April 2001, or do you believe it is unlikely that the meeting took place?

Answer: Although we cannot rule it out, we are increasingly skeptical that such a meeting occurred. The veracity of the single-threaded reporting on which the original account of the meeting was based has been questioned, and the Iraqi official with whom Atta was alleged to have met has denied ever having met Atta.

We have been able to corroborate only two visits by Atta to the Czech Republic: one in late 1994, when he passed through en route to Syria; the other in June 2000, when, according to detainee reporting, he departed for the United States from Prague because he thought a non-EU member country would be less likely to keep meticulous travel data.

In the absence of any credible information that the April 2001 meeting occurred, we assess that Atta would have been unlikely to undertake the substantial risk of contacting any Iraqi official as late as April 2001, with the plot already well along toward execution.

It is likewise hard to conceive of any single ingredient crucial to the plot's success that could only be obtained from Iraq.

In our judgment, the 11 September plot was complex in its orchestration but simple in its basic conception. We believe that the factors vital to success of the plot were all easily within al-Qa'ida's means without resort to Iraqi expertise: shrewd selection of operatives, training in hijacking aircraft, a mastermind and pilots well-versed in the procedures and behavior needed to blend in with US society, long experience in moving money to support operations, and the openness and tolerance of US society as well as the ready availability of important information about targets, flight schools, and airport and airline security practices.

Administration officials had frequently spoken of a relationship between Iraq and al-Qa'ida that went back at least a decade. Some meetings had, in fact, occurred. Post-invasion intelligence reassessments of the relationship, based on captured documents and detainee testimony, indicated that the meetings generally involved al-Qa'ida making requests for equipment and training and Iraq turning down those requests.[58] For example:

> During the meeting in Khartoum [in 1995], bin Ladin reportedly asked that Iraq allow him to open an office in the country, provide him with Chinese sea mines, provide military training, and broadcast the speeches of a radical anti-Saudi cleric Shaykh Salman al-Awdah. [IIS officer Faruq] Hijazi told debriefers that once he returned to Iraq, he "wrote a negative report on the meeting with bin Ladin." Hijazi "criticized bin Ladin for his hostile speech and his insistence on the Islamization of Iraq." Hijazi said that he assessed that "working with bin Ladin would damage relations with Arab countries through the region."
>
> According to Hijazi, Saddam immediately refused bin Ladin's requests for the office, mines, and military training, but expressed some willingness to broadcast the requested speeches from the anti-Saudi cleric. Hijazi did not know if Iraq ever actually broadcast the speeches because he stated that Saddam delegated the decision to a lower level of the Iraqi government. Soon after Hijazi filed the report, he "received word from his IIS chain-of-command that he should not see bin Ladin again." Hijazi told debriefers that, "this was his sole meeting with bin Ladin or a member of al-Qa'ida and he was not aware of any other individual following up on the initial contact."[59]

Regarding weapons of mass destruction, as noted above, the Iraqi government had allowed UN weapons inspectors back into the country starting 27 November 2002. On 7 December 2002, Iraq submitted a 12,200-page declaration, claiming that it did not in fact have any WMD whatsoever. The inspectors, although complaining of inadequate cooperation from the Iraqis, failed to find any evidence of WMD, even when U.S. intelligence directed them to likely sites. Rather than being "more negative," as Condoleezza Rice had predicted, the inspectors simply concluded that they would require several more months to complete their assignment thoroughly. The United States, Britain, and Spain introduced a draft resolution on 24 February 2003 declaring that Iraq had failed to comply with Resolution 1441 of November 2002, its last chance to avoid war. The same day, France and Germany issued a joint memorandum calling for a delay of at least four months to give weapons inspectors time to complete their mission. Russia and China immediately endorsed the proposed delay, while only Bulgaria supported the U.S. draft. Having failed to find sufficient support, the United States, Britain, and Spain finally gave up and formally withdrew their draft resolution on 17 March 2003. No vote was ever held.

Having dismissed the inspections as irrelevant, the Bush administration now warned weapons inspectors to leave the country before the war started. Indeed, by this time, war preparations had advanced so far that—for political, psychological, and organizational reasons—only intelligence that was both over-whelming and unambiguously contradictory, the kind one rarely sees, could have stopped it. The Intelligence Community appears to have come to a similar conclusion independently. Apparently, no effort was made to reassess intelligence estimates of Iraqi WMD based on new information coming from the UN inspectors.[60] (Even though UN inspectors investigated a site identified by Curve-ball as a biological weapons factory and found that his claim was not true.[61])

This disinterest must have been based, at least in part, on the Intelligence Community's reading of the administration. For instance, a Department of Defense analyst detailed to the CIA—a specialist on biological warfare and the only U.S. intelligence official to have met Curveball—repeatedly raised questions about the source's reliability. On 4 February 2003, he specifically questioned the use of Curveball's information in Secretary Powell's UN speech. The Deputy Chief of the CIA's Iraqi Task Force responded to the analyst's concerns with this e-mail message:

> Greetings. Come on over (or I'll come over there) and we can hash this out. As I said last night, let's keep in mind the fact that this war's going to happen regard-less of what Curve Ball said or didn't say, and that the Powers That Be probably aren't terribly interested in whether Curve Ball knows what he's talking about. However, in the interest of Truth, we owe somebody a sentence or two of warning, if you honestly have reservations.[62]

The Deputy Chief later told Senate staffers that this opinion had not been the result of political pressure or any other interactions with CIA officials or government policymakers. It resulted from his reading of the *Washington Post.*

Air strikes against Baghdad began on 19 March 2003. The land invasion, relying primarily on U.S. and British troops and a few Australian commandos, began the next day. Baghdad fell on 9 April. On 1 May, President Bush declared major combat operations to be at an end, although a major insurgency, or rather several insurgencies, against occupation forces would soon emerge. The Iraq Survey Group, led first by David Kay and then by Charles Duelfer, fanned out across the country to uncover Iraq's weapons of mass destruction. Not one was found.[63] Nor was evidence found of links to al-Qa'ida.

The WMD issue was subjected to more scrutiny than the issue of links to terrorist groups in the aftermath of the invasion. This was the subject of the Iraq Survey Group, which reported directly to the Director of Central Intelligence, and a presidential commission led by former Senator Charles S. Robb and former Deputy Attorney General Laurence H. Silberman. An internal investigation, led by former Deputy Director of Central Intelligence Richard Kerr, examined the Iraq case for what it said about U.S. intelligence practices.

The Iraq Survey Group produced a multifaceted report, commonly known as the Duelfer Report, that was more than 1,000 pages in length. While Duelfer placed emphasis on Saddam Hussein's continuing desire to produce WMD, the ultimate conclusions were that he had not done so and that his capacity to do so in the future had been steadily deteriorating. The Iraqis had been working on new delivery systems, which were permitted if they remained within strict range limits. They were in the process of destroying some of them under UN instructions when the invasion started. Some of the key findings of the Duelfer Report follow:

Comprehensive Report of the Special Advisor to the DCI on Iraq's WMD
23 September 2004

Regime Strategic Intent

Key Findings

Saddam Husayn so dominated the Iraqi Regime that its strategic intent was his alone. He wanted to end sanctions while preserving the capability to reconstitute his weapons of mass destruction (WMD) when sanctions were lifted.

- *Saddam totally dominated the Regime's strategic decision making.* He initiated most of the strategic thinking upon which decisions were made, whether in matters of war and peace (such as invading Kuwait), maintaining WMD as a national strategic goal, or on how Iraq was to position itself in the international community. Loyal dissent was discouraged and constructive variations to the implementation of his wishes on strategic issues were rare. Saddam was the Regime in a strategic sense and his intent became Iraq's strategic policy.

- *Saddam's primary goal from 1991 to 2003 was to have UN sanctions lifted, while maintaining the security of the Regime.* He sought to balance the need to cooperate with UN inspections—to gain support for lifting sanctions—with his intention to preserve Iraq's intellectual capital for WMD with a minimum of foreign intrusiveness and loss of face. Indeed, this remained the goal to the end of the Regime, as the starting of any WMD program, conspicuous or otherwise, risked undoing the progress achieved in eroding sanctions and jeopardizing a political end to the embargo and international monitoring.

- *The introduction of the Oil-For-Food program (OFF) in late 1996 was a key turning point for the Regime.* OFF rescued Baghdad's economy from a terminal decline created by sanctions. The Regime quickly came to see that OFF could be corrupted to acquire foreign exchange both to further undermine sanctions and to provide the means to enhance dual-use infrastructure and potential WMD-related development.

- *By 2000–2001, Saddam had managed to mitigate many of the effects of sanctions and undermine their international support.* Iraq was within striking distance of a *de facto* end to the sanctions regime, both in terms of oil exports and the trade embargo, by the end of 1999.

Saddam wanted to recreate Iraq's WMD capability—which was essentially destroyed in 1991—after sanctions were removed and Iraq's economy stabilized, but probably with a different mix of capabilities to that which previously existed. Saddam aspired to develop a nuclear capability—in an incremental fashion, irrespective of international pressure and the resulting economic risks—but he intended to focus on ballistic missile and tactical chemical warfare (CW) capabilities.

- *Iran was the pre-eminent motivator of this policy.* All senior level Iraqi officials considered Iran to be Iraq's principal enemy in the region. The wish to balance Israel and acquire status and influence in the Arab world were also considerations, but secondary.

- *Iraq Survey Group (ISG) judges that events in the 1980s and early 1990s shaped Saddam's belief in the value of WMD.* In Saddam's view, WMD helped to save the Regime multiple times. He believed that during the Iran-Iraq war, chemical weapons had halted Iranian ground offensives and that ballistic missile attacks on Tehran had broken its political will. Similarly, during Desert Storm, Saddam believed WMD had deterred Coalition Forces from pressing their attack beyond the goal of freeing Kuwait. WMD had even played a role in crushing the Shi'a revolt in the south following the 1991 cease-fire.

- *The former Regime had no formal written strategy or plan for the revival of WMD after sanctions.* Neither was there an identifiable group of WMD policymakers or planners separate from Saddam. Instead, his lieutenants understood WMD revival was his goal from their long association with Saddam and his infrequent, but firm, verbal comments and directions to them.

Delivery Systems

Key Findings

Since the early 1970s, Iraq has consistently sought to acquire an effective long-range weapons delivery capability, and by 1991 Baghdad had purchased the missiles and infrastructure that would form the basis for nearly all of its future missile system developments. The Soviet Union was a key supplier of missile hardware and provided 819 Scud-B missiles and ground support equipment.

Iraq's experiences with long-range delivery systems in the Iran/Iraq war were a vital lesson to Iraqi President Saddam Husayn. The successful Iraqi response to the Iranian long-range bombardment of Baghdad, leading to the War of the Cities, probably saved Saddam.

By 1991, Iraq had successfully demonstrated its ability to modify some of its delivery systems to increase their range and to develop WMD dissemination options, with the Al Husayn being a first step in this direction. The next few years of learning and experiments confirmed that the Regime's goal was for an effective long-range WMD delivery capability and demonstrated the resourcefulness of Iraq's scientists and technicians.

Iraq failed in its efforts to acquire longer-range delivery systems to replace inventory exhausted in the Iran/Iraq war. This was a forcing function that drove Iraq to develop indigenous delivery system production capabilities.

Desert Storm and subsequent UN resolutions and inspections brought many of Iraq's delivery system programs to a halt. While much of Iraq's long-range missile inventory and production infrastructure was eliminated, Iraq until late 1991 kept some items hidden to assist future reconstitution of the force. This decision and Iraq's intransigence during years of inspection left many UN questions unresolved.

- Coalition airstrikes effectively targeted much of Iraq's delivery systems infrastructure, and UN inspections dramatically impeded further developments of long-range ballistic missiles.
- *It appears to have taken time, but Iraq eventually realized that sanctions were not going to end quickly.* This forced Iraq to sacrifice its long-range delivery force in an attempt to bring about a quick end to the sanctions.
- After the flight of Husayn Kamil in 1995, Iraq admitted that it had hidden Scud-variant missiles and components to aid future reconstitution but asserted that these items had been unilaterally destroyed by late 1991. The UN could not verify these claims and thereafter became more wary of Iraq's admissions and instituted a Regime of more intrusive inspections.
- *The Iraq Survey Group (ISG) has uncovered no evidence Iraq retained Scud-variant missiles, and debriefings of Iraqi officials in addition to some documentation suggest that Iraq did not retain such missiles after 1991.*

While other WMD programs were strictly prohibited, the UN permitted Iraq to develop and possess delivery systems provided their range did not exceed 150 km.

This freedom allowed Iraq to keep its scientists and technicians employed and to keep its infrastructure and manufacturing base largely intact by pursuing programs nominally in compliance with the UN limitations. ***This positioned Iraq for a potential breakout capability.***

- Between 1991 and 1998, Iraq had declared development programs underway for liquid- and solid-propellant ballistic missiles and unmanned aerial vehicles (UAVs).

Iraq's decisions in 1996 to accept the Oil-For-Food program (OFF) and later in 1998 to cease cooperation with UNSCOM and IAEA spurred a period of increased activity in delivery systems development. The pace of ongoing missile programs accelerated, and the Regime authorized its scientists to design missiles with ranges in excess of 150 km that, if developed, would have been clear violations of UNSCR 687.

- By 2002, Iraq had provided the liquid-propellant Al Samud II—a program started in 2001—and the solid-propellant Al Fat'h to the military and was pursuing a series of new small UAV systems.
- *ISG uncovered Iraqi plans or designs for three long-range ballistic missiles with ranges from 400 to 1,000 km and for a 1,000-km-range cruise missile, although none of these systems progressed to production and only one reportedly passed the design phase. ISG assesses that these plans demonstrate Saddam's continuing desire—up to the beginning of Operation Iraqi Freedom (OIF)—for a long-range delivery capability.*

Procurements supporting delivery system programs expanded after the 1998 departure of the UN inspectors. Iraq also hired outside expertise to assist its development programs.

- ISG uncovered evidence that technicians and engineers from Russia reviewed the designs and assisted development of the Al Samud II during its rapid evolution. ISG also found that Iraq had entered into negotiations with North Korean and Russian entities for more capable missile systems.
- According to contract information exploited by ISG, Iraq imported at least 380 SA-2/Volga liquid-propellant engines from Poland and possibly Russia or Belarus. While Iraq claims these engines were for the Al Samud II program, the numbers involved appear in excess of immediate requirements, suggesting they could have supported the longer-range missiles using clusters of SA-2 engines. Iraq also imported missile guidance and control systems from entities in countries like Belarus, Russia, and Federal Republic of Yugoslavia (FRY). (Note: FRY is currently known as Serbia and Montenegro but is referred to as FRY in this section.)

In late 2002 Iraq was under increasing pressure from the international community to allow UN inspectors to return. Iraq in November accepted UNSCR 1441 and invited inspectors back into the country. In December Iraq presented to the UN its Currently Accurate, Full, and Complete Declaration (CAFCD) in response to UNSCR 1441.

- While the CAFCD was judged to be incomplete and a rehash of old information, it did provide details on the Al Samud II, Al Fat'h, new missile-related facilities, and new small UAV designs.
- In February 2003 the UN convened an expert panel to discuss the Al Samud II and Al Fat'h programs, which resulted in the UN's decision to prohibit the Al Samud II and order its destruction. Missile destruction began in early

March but was incomplete when the inspectors were withdrawn later that month.

The CAFCD and United Nations Monitoring, Verification, and Inspection Commission (UNMOVIC) inspections provided a brief glimpse into what Iraq had accomplished in four years without an international presence on the ground.

Given Iraq's investments in technology and infrastructure improvements, an effective procurement network, skilled scientists, and designs already on the books for longer range missiles, ISG assesses that Saddam clearly intended to reconstitute long-range delivery systems and that the systems potentially were for WMD.

- Iraq built a new and larger liquid-rocket engine test stand capable, with some modification, of supporting engines or engine clusters larger than the single SA-2 engine used in the Al Samud II.
- Iraq built or refurbished solid-propellant facilities and equipment, including a large propellant mixer, an aging oven, and a casting pit that could support large diameter motors.
- Iraq's investing in studies into new propellants and manufacturing technologies demonstrated its desire for more capable or effective delivery systems.

Nuclear

Key Findings

Iraq Survey Group (ISG) discovered further evidence of the maturity and significance of the pre-1991 Iraqi Nuclear Program but found that Iraq's ability to reconstitute a nuclear weapons program progressively decayed after that date.

- Saddam Husayn ended the nuclear program in 1991 following the Gulf war. ISG found no evidence to suggest concerted efforts to restart the program.
- Although Saddam clearly assigned a high value to the nuclear progress and talent that had been developed up to the 1991 war, the program ended and the intellectual capital decayed in the succeeding years.

Nevertheless, after 1991, Saddam did express his intent to retain the intellectual capital developed during the Iraqi Nuclear Program. Senior Iraqis—several of them from the Regime's inner circle—told ISG they assumed Saddam would restart a nuclear program once UN sanctions ended.

- Saddam indicated that he would develop the weapons necessary to counter any Iranian threat.

Initially, Saddam chose to conceal his nuclear program in its entirety, as he did with Iraq's BW program. Aggressive UN inspections after Desert Storm forced Saddam to admit the existence of the program and destroy or surrender components of the program.

In the wake of Desert Storm, Iraq took steps to conceal key elements of its program and to preserve what it could of the professional capabilities of its nuclear scientific community.

- Baghdad undertook a variety of measures to conceal key elements of its nuclear program from successive UN inspectors, including specific direction by Saddam Husayn to hide and preserve documentation associated with Iraq's nuclear program.
- ISG, for example, uncovered two specific instances in which scientists involved in uranium enrichment kept documents and technology. Although

apparently acting on their own, they did so with the belief and anticipation of resuming uranium enrichment efforts in the future.

- Starting around 1992, in a bid to retain the intellectual core of the former weapons program, Baghdad transferred many nuclear scientists to related jobs in the Military Industrial Commission (MIC). The work undertaken by these scientists at the MIC helped them maintain their weapons knowledge base.

As with other WMD areas, Saddam's ambitions in the nuclear area were secondary to his prime objective of ending UN sanctions.

- Iraq, especially after the defection of Husayn Kamil in 1995, sought to persuade the IAEA that Iraq had met the UN's disarmament requirements so sanctions would be lifted.

ISG found a limited number of post-1995 activities that would have aided the reconstitution of the nuclear weapons program once sanctions were lifted.

- The activities of the Iraqi Atomic Energy Commission sustained some talent and limited research with potential relevance to a reconstituted nuclear program.
- Specific projects, with significant development, such as the efforts to build a rail gun and a copper vapor laser could have been useful in a future effort to restart a nuclear weapons program, but ISG found no indications of such purpose. As funding for the MIC and the IAEC increased after the introduction of the Oil-for-Food program, there was some growth in programs that involved former nuclear weapons scientists and engineers.
- The Regime prevented scientists from the former nuclear weapons program from leaving either their jobs or Iraq. Moreover, in the late 1990s, personnel from both MIC and the IAEC received significant pay raises in a bid to retain them, and the Regime undertook new investments in university research in a bid to ensure that Iraq retained technical knowledge.

Iraq's Chemical Warfare Program

Key Findings

Saddam never abandoned his intentions to resume a CW effort when sanctions were lifted and conditions were judged favorable:

- Saddam and many Iraqis regarded CW as a proven weapon against an enemy's superior numerical strength, a weapon that had saved the nation at least once already—during the Iran-Iraq war—and contributed to deterring the Coalition in 1991 from advancing to Baghdad.

While a small number of old, abandoned chemical munitions have been discovered, ISG judges that Iraq unilaterally destroyed its undeclared chemical weapons stockpile in 1991. There are no credible indications that Baghdad resumed production of chemical munitions thereafter, a policy ISG attributes to Baghdad's desire to see sanctions lifted, or rendered ineffectual, or its fear of force against it should WMD be discovered.

- The scale of the Iraqi conventional munitions stockpile, among other factors, precluded an examination of the entire stockpile; however, ISG inspected sites judged most likely associated with possible storage or deployment of chemical weapons.

Iraq's CW program was crippled by the Gulf war and the legitimate chemical industry, which suffered under sanctions, only began to recover in the mid-1990s.

Subsequent changes in the management of key military and civilian organizations, followed by an influx of funding and resources, provided Iraq with the ability to reinvigorate its industrial base.

- Poor policies and management in the early 1990s left the Military Industrial Commission (MIC) financially unsound and in a state of almost complete disarray.
- Saddam implemented a number of changes to the Regime's organizational and programmatic structures after the departure of Husayn Kamil.
- Iraq's acceptance of the Oil-for-Food (OFF) program was the foundation of Iraq's economic recovery and sparked a flow of illicitly diverted funds that could be applied to projects for Iraq's chemical industry.

The way Iraq organized its chemical industry after the mid-1990s allowed it to conserve the knowledge-base needed to restart a CW program, conduct a modest amount of dual-use research, and partially recover from the decline of its production capability caused by the effects of the Gulf war and UN-sponsored destruction and sanctions. Iraq implemented a rigorous and formalized system of nationwide research and production of chemicals, but ISG will not be able to resolve whether Iraq intended the system to underpin any CW-related efforts.

- The Regime employed a cadre of trained and experienced researchers, production managers, and weaponization experts from the former CW program.
- Iraq began implementing a range of indigenous chemical production projects in 1995 and 1996. Many of these projects, while not weapons-related, were designed to improve Iraq's infrastructure, which would have enhanced Iraq's ability to produce CW agents if the scaled-up production processes were implemented.
- Iraq had an effective system for the procurement of items that Iraq was not allowed to acquire due to sanctions. ISG found no evidence that this system was used to acquire precursor chemicals in bulk; however documents indicate that dual-use laboratory equipment and chemicals were acquired through this system.

Iraq constructed a number of new plants starting in the mid-1990s that enhanced its chemical infrastructure, although its overall industry had not fully recovered from the effects of sanctions, and had not regained pre-1991 technical sophistication or production capabilities prior to Operation Iraqi Freedom (OIF).

- ISG did not discover chemical process or production units configured to produce key precursors or CW agents. However, site visits and debriefs revealed that Iraq maintained its ability for reconfiguring and "making do" with available equipment as substitutes for sanctioned items.
- ISG judges, based on available chemicals, infrastructure, and scientist debriefings, that Iraq at OIF probably had a capability to produce large quantities of sulfur mustard within three to six months.
- A former nerve agent expert indicated that Iraq retained the capability to produce nerve agent in significant quantities within two years, given the import of required phosphorous precursors. However, we have no credible indications that Iraq acquired or attempted to acquire large quantities of these chemicals through its existing procurement networks for sanctioned items.

In addition to new investment in its industry, Iraq was able to monitor the location and use of all existing dual-use process equipment. This provided Iraq the ability to rapidly reallocate key equipment for proscribed activities, if required by the Regime.

- One effect of UN monitoring was to implement a national level control system for important dual-use process plants.

Iraq's historical ability to implement simple solutions to weaponization challenges allowed Iraq to retain the capability to weaponize CW agent when the need arose. Because of the risk of discovery and consequences for ending UN sanctions, Iraq would have significantly jeopardized its chances of having sanctions lifted or no longer enforced if the UN or foreign entity had discovered that Iraq had undertaken any weaponization activities.

- ISG has uncovered hardware at a few military depots, which suggests that Iraq may have prototyped experimental CW rounds. The available evidence is insufficient to determine the nature of the effort or the timeframe of activities.
- Iraq could indigenously produce a range of conventional munitions, throughout the 1990s, many of which had previously been adapted for filling with CW agent. However, ISG has found ambiguous evidence of weaponization activities.

Saddam's Leadership Defense Plan consisted of a tactical doctrine taught to all Iraqi officers and included the concept of a "red-line" or last line of defense. However, ISG has no information that the plan ever included a trigger for CW use.

- Despite reported high-level discussions about the use of chemical weapons in the defense of Iraq, information acquired after OIF does not confirm the inclusion of CW in Iraq's tactical planning for OIF. We believe these were mostly theoretical discussions and do not imply the existence of undiscovered CW munitions.

Discussions concerning WMD, particularly leading up to OIF, would have been highly compartmentalized within the Regime. ISG found no credible evidence that any field elements knew about plans for CW use during Operation Iraqi Freedom.

- Uday—head of the Fedayeen Saddam—attempted to obtain chemical weapons for use during OIF, according to reporting, but ISG found no evidence that Iraq ever came into possession of any CW weapons.

ISG uncovered information that the Iraqi Intelligence Service (IIS) maintained throughout 1991 to 2003 a set of undeclared covert laboratories to research and test various chemicals and poisons, primarily for intelligence operations. The network of laboratories could have provided an ideal, compartmented platform from which to continue CW agent R&D or small-scale production efforts, but we have no indications this was planned. (See Annex A.)

- ISG has no evidence that IIS Directorate of Criminology (M16) scientists were producing CW or BW agents in these laboratories. However, sources indicate that M16 was planning to produce several CW agents including sulfur mustard, nitrogen mustard, and Sarin.
- Exploitations of IIS laboratories, safe houses, and disposal sites revealed no evidence of CW-related research or production, however many of these sites were either sanitized by the Regime or looted prior to OIF. Interviews with key IIS officials within and outside of M16 yielded very little information about the IIS' activities in this area.
- The existence, function, and purpose of the laboratories were never declared to the UN.
- The IIS program included the use of human subjects for testing purposes.

ISG investigated a series of key pre-OIF indicators involving the possible movement and storage of chemical weapons, focusing on 11 major depots assessed to have possible links to CW. A review of documents, interviews, available reporting, and site exploitations revealed alternate, plausible explanations for activities noted prior to OIF which, at the time, were believed to be CW-related.

- ISG investigated pre-OIF activities at Musayyib Ammunition Storage Depot— the storage site that was judged to have the strongest link to CW. An extensive investigation of the facility revealed that there was no CW activity, unlike previously assessed.

Biological Warfare

Key Findings

The Biological Warfare (BW) program was born of the Iraqi Intelligence Service (IIS) and this service retained its connections with the program either directly or indirectly throughout its existence.

- The IIS provided the BW program with security and participated in biological research, probably for its own purposes, from the beginning of Iraq's BW effort in the early 1970s until the final days of Saddam Husayn's Regime.

In 1991, Saddam Husayn regarded BW as an integral element of his arsenal of WMD weapons, and would have used it if the need arose.

- At a meeting of the Iraqi leadership immediately prior to the Gulf war in 1991, Saddam Husayn personally authorized the use of BW weapons against Israel, Saudi Arabia and US forces. Although the exact nature of the circumstances that would trigger use was not spelled out, they would appear to be a threat to the leadership itself or the US resorting to *"unconventional harmful types of weapons."*
- Saddam envisaged all-out use. For example, all Israeli cities were to be struck and all the BW weapons at his disposal were to be used. Saddam specified that the *"many years"* agents, presumably anthrax spores, were to be employed against his foes.

ISG judges that Iraq's actions between 1991 and 1996 demonstrate that the state intended to preserve its BW capability and return to a steady, methodical progress toward a mature BW program when and if the opportunity arose.

- ISG assesses that, in 1991, Iraq clung to the objective of gaining war-winning weapons with the strategic intention of achieving the ability to project its power over much of the Middle East and beyond. Biological weapons were part of that plan. With an eye to the future and aiming to preserve some measure of its BW capability, Baghdad in the years immediately after Desert Storm sought to save what it could of its BW infrastructure and covertly continue BW research, hide evidence of that and earlier efforts, and dispose of its existing weapons stocks.
- From 1992 to 1994, Iraq greatly expanded the capability of its Al Hakam facility. Indigenously produced 5 cubic meter fermentors were installed, electrical and water utilities were expanded, and massive new construction to house its desired 50 cubic meter fermentors were completed.
- With the economy at rock bottom in late 1995, ISG judges that Baghdad abandoned its existing BW program in the belief that it constituted a potential embarrassment, whose discovery would undercut Baghdad's ability to reach its overarching goal of obtaining relief from UN sanctions.

In practical terms, with the destruction of the Al Hakam facility, Iraq abandoned its ambition to obtain advanced BW weapons quickly. ISG found no direct evidence that Iraq, after 1996, had plans for a new BW program or was conducting BW-specific work for military purposes. Indeed, from the mid-1990s, despite evidence of continuing interest in nuclear and chemical weapons, there appears to be a complete absence of discussion or even interest in BW at the Presidential level.

Iraq would have faced great difficulty in re-establishing an effective BW agent production capability. Nevertheless, after 1996 Iraq still had a significant dual-use capability—some declared—readily useful for BW if the Regime chose to use it to pursue a BW program. Moreover, Iraq still possessed its most important BW asset, the scientific know-how of its BW cadre.

- Any attempt to create a new BW program after 1996 would have encountered a range of major hurdles. The years following Desert Storm wrought a steady degradation of Iraq's industrial base: new equipment and spare parts for existing machinery became difficult and expensive to obtain, standards of maintenance declined, staff could not receive training abroad, and foreign technical assistance was almost impossible to get. Additionally, Iraq's infrastructure and public utilities were crumbling. New large projects, particularly if they required special foreign equipment and expertise, would attract international attention. UN monitoring of dual-use facilities up to the end of 1998 made their use for clandestine purposes complicated and risk-laden.

Depending on its scale, Iraq could have re-established an elementary BW program within a few weeks to a few months of a decision to do so, but ISG discovered no indications that the Regime was pursuing such a course.

- In spite of the difficulties noted above, a BW capability is technically the easiest WMD to attain. Although equipment and facilities were destroyed under UN supervision in 1996, Iraq retained technical BW know-how through the scientists that were involved in the former program. ISG has also identified civilian facilities and equipment in Iraq that have dual-use application that could be used for the production of agent.

ISG judges that in 1991 and 1992, Iraq appears to have destroyed its undeclared stocks of BW weapons and probably destroyed remaining holdings of bulk BW agent. However ISG lacks evidence to document complete destruction. Iraq retained some BW-related seed stocks until their discovery after Operation Iraqi Freedom (OIF).

- After the passage of UN Security Council Resolution (UNSCR) 687 in April 1991, Iraqi leaders decided not to declare the offensive BW program and in consequence ordered all evidence of the program erased. Iraq declared that BW program personnel sanitized the facilities and destroyed the weapons and their contents.
- Iraq declared the possession of 157 aerial bombs and 25 missile warheads containing BW agent. ISG assesses that the evidence for the original number of bombs is uncertain. ISG judges that Iraq clandestinely destroyed at least 132 bombs and 25 missiles. ISG continued the efforts of the UN at the destruction site but found no remnants of further weapons. This leaves the possibility that the fragments of up to 25 bombs may remain undiscovered. Of these, any that escaped destruction would probably now only contain degraded agent.
- ISG does not have a clear account of bulk agent destruction. Official Iraqi sources and BW personnel state that Al Hakam staff destroyed stocks of bulk agent in mid-1991. However, the same personnel admit concealing details of the movement and destruction of bulk BW agent in the first half of 1991. Iraq continued to present information known to be untrue to the UN up to OIF. Those involved did not reveal this until several months after the conflict.

- Dr. Rihab Rashid Taha Al 'Azzawi, head of the bacterial program, claims she retained BW seed stocks until early 1992, when she destroyed them. ISG has not found a means of verifying this. Some seed stocks were retained by another Iraqi official until 2003, when they were recovered by ISG.

ISG is aware of BW-applicable research since 1996, but ISG judges it was not conducted in connection with a BW program.

- ISG has uncovered no evidence of illicit research conducted into BW agents by universities or research organizations.
- The work conducted on a biopesticide (*Bacillus thuringiensis*) at Al Hakam until 1995 would serve to maintain the basic skills required by scientists to produce and dry anthrax spores (*Bacillus anthracis*) but ISG has not discovered evidence suggesting this was the Regime's intention. However in 1991, research and production on biopesticide and single cell protein (SCP) was selected by Iraq to provide cover for Al Hakam's role in Iraq's BW program. Similar work conducted at the Tuwaitha Agricultural and Biological Research Center (TABRC) up to OIF also maintained skills that were applicable to BW, but again, ISG found no evidence to suggest that this was the intention.
- Similarly, ISG found no information to indicate that the work carried out by TABRC into single cell protein (SCP) was a cover story for continuing research into the production of BW agents, such as *C. botulinum* and *B. anthracis*, after the destruction of Al Hakam through to OIF.
- TABRC conducted research and development (R&D) programs to enable indigenous manufacture of bacterial growth media. Although these media are suitable for the bulk production of BW agents, ISG has found no evidence to indicate that their development and testing were specifically for this purpose.
- Although Iraq had the basic capability to work with *variola major* (smallpox), ISG found no evidence that it retained any stocks of smallpox or actively conducted research into this agent for BW intentions.

The IIS had a series of laboratories that conducted biological work including research into BW agents for assassination purposes until the mid-1990s. ISG has not been able to establish the scope and nature of the work at these laboratories or determine whether any of the work was related to military development of BW agent.

- The security services operated a series of laboratories in the Baghdad area. Iraq should have declared these facilities and their equipment to the UN, but they did not. Neither the UN Special Commission (UNSCOM) nor the UN Monitoring, Verification, and Inspection Commission (UNMOVIC) were aware of their existence or inspected them.
- Some of the laboratories possessed equipment capable of supporting research into BW agents for military purposes, but ISG does not know whether this occurred although there is no evidence of it. The laboratories were probably the successors of the Al Salman facility, located three kilometers south of Salman Pak, which was destroyed in 1991, and they carried on many of the same activities, including forensic work.
- Under the aegis of the intelligence service, a secretive team developed assassination instruments using poisons or toxins for the Iraqi state. A small group of scientists, doctors, and technicians conducted secret experiments on human beings, resulting in their deaths. The aim was probably the development of poisons, including ricin and aflatoxin to eliminate or debilitate the Regime's opponents. It appears that testing on humans continued until the mid-1990s. There is no evidence to link these tests with the development of BW agents for military use.

In spite of exhaustive investigation, ISG found no evidence that Iraq possessed or was developing BW agent production systems mounted on road vehicles or railway wagons.

- Prior to OIF there was information indicating Iraq had planned and built a breakout BW capability, in the form of a set of mobile production units, capable of producing BW agent at short notice in sufficient quantities to weaponize. Although ISG has conducted a thorough investigation of every aspect of this information, it has not found any equipment suitable for such a program, nor has ISG positively identified any sites. No documents have been uncovered. Interviews with individuals suspected of involvement have all proved negative.
- ISG harbors severe doubts about the source's credibility in regards to the breakout program.
- ISG thoroughly examined two trailers captured in 2003, suspected of being mobile BW agent production units, and investigated the associated evidence. ISG judges that its Iraqi makers almost certainly designed and built the equipment exclusively for the generation of hydrogen. It is impractical to use the equipment for the production and weaponization of BW agent. ISG judges that it cannot therefore be part of any BW program.

The Robb-Silberman Commission was assigned to examine several cases involving CIA assessments of various countries' WMD programs in light of the Iraqi episode in order to evaluate its capacity to make such judgments. The following is a summary of their findings regarding Iraq.

Commission on the Intelligence Capabilities of the United States Regarding Weapons of Mass Destruction

31 March 2005

Iraq: An Overview

In October 2002, at the request of members of Congress, the National Intelligence Council produced a National Intelligence Estimate (NIE)—the most authoritative intelligence assessment produced by the Intelligence Community—which concluded that Iraq was reconstituting its nuclear weapons program and was actively pursuing a nuclear device. According to the exhaustive study of the Iraq Survey Group, this assessment was almost completely wrong. The NIE said that Iraq's biological weapons capability was larger and more advanced than before the Gulf War and that Iraq possessed mobile biological weapons production facilities. This was wrong. The NIE further stated that Iraq had renewed production of chemical weapons, including mustard, sarin, GF, and VX, and that it had accumulated chemical stockpiles of between 100 and 500 metric tons. All of this was also wrong. Finally, the NIE concluded that Iraq had unmanned aerial vehicles that were probably intended for the delivery of biological weapons, and ballistic missiles that had ranges greater than the United Nations' permitted 150-kilometer range. In truth, the aerial vehicles were not for biological weapons; some of Iraq's missiles were, however, capable of traveling more than 150 kilometers. The Intelligence Community's Iraq assessments were, in short, riddled with errors.

Contrary to what some defenders of the Intelligence Community have since asserted, these errors were not the result of a few harried months in 2002. Most of the fundamental errors were made and communicated to policymakers well before the now-infamous NIE of October 2002, and were not corrected in the months between the NIE and the start of the war. They were not isolated or random failings. Iraq had been an intelligence challenge at the forefront of U.S. attention for over a decade. It was a known adversary that had already fought one war with the United States and seemed increasingly likely to fight another. But, after ten years of effort, the Intelligence Community still had no good intelligence on the status of Iraq's weapons programs. Our full report examines these issues in detail. Here we limit our discussion to the central lessons to be learned from this episode.

The first lesson is that the Intelligence Community cannot analyze and disseminate information that it does not have. The Community's Iraq assessment was crippled by its inability to collect meaningful intelligence on Iraq's nuclear, biological, and chemical weapons programs. The second lesson follows from the first: lacking good intelligence, analysts and collectors fell back on old assumptions and inferences drawn from Iraq's past behavior and intentions.

The Intelligence Community had learned a hard lesson after the 1991 Gulf War, which revealed that the Intelligence Community's pre-war assessments had underestimated Iraq's nuclear program and had failed to identify all of its chemical weapons storage sites. Shaken by the magnitude of their errors, intelligence analysts were determined not to fall victim again to the same mistake. This tendency was only reinforced by later events. Saddam acted to the very end like a man with much to hide. And the dangers of underestimating our enemies were deeply underscored by the attacks of September 11, 2001.

Throughout the 1990s, therefore, the Intelligence Community assumed that Saddam's Iraq was up to no good—that Baghdad had maintained its nuclear, biological, and chemical technical expertise, had kept its biological and chemical weapons production capabilities, and possessed significant stockpiles of chemical agents and weapons precursors. Since Iraq's leadership had not changed since 1991, the Intelligence Community also believed that these capabilities would be further revved up as soon as inspectors left Iraq. Saddam's continuing cat-and-mouse parrying with international inspectors only hardened these assumptions.

These experiences contributed decisively to the Intelligence Community's erroneous National Intelligence Estimate of October 2002. That is not to say that its fears and assumptions were foolish or even unreasonable. At some point, however, these premises stopped being working hypotheses and became more or less unrebuttable conclusions; worse, the intelligence system became too willing to find confirmations of them in evidence that should have been recognized at the time to be of dubious reliability. Collectors and analysts too readily accepted any evidence that supported their theory that Iraq had stockpiles and was developing weapons programs, and they explained away or simply disregarded evidence that pointed in the other direction.

Even in hindsight, those assumptions have a powerful air of common sense. If the Intelligence Community's estimate and other pre-war intelligence had relied principally and explicitly on inferences the Community drew from Iraq's past conduct, the estimate would still have been wrong, but it would have been far more defensible. For good reason, it was hard to conclude that Saddam Hussein had indeed abandoned his weapons programs. But a central flaw of the NIE is that it took these defensible assumptions and swathed them in the mystique of intelligence, providing secret information that seemed to support them but was in fact nearly worthless, if not misleading. The NIE simply didn't communicate how weak the underlying intelligence was.

This was, moreover, a problem that was not limited to the NIE. Our review found that after the publication of the October 2002 NIE but before Secretary of State Colin Powell's February 2003 address to the United Nations, intelligence officials within the CIA failed to convey to policymakers new information casting serious doubt on the reliability of a human intelligence source known as "Curveball."

This occurred despite the pivotal role Curveball's information played in the Intelligence Community's assessment of Iraq's biological weapons programs, and in spite of Secretary Powell's efforts to strip every dubious piece of information out of his proposed speech. In this instance, once again, the Intelligence Community failed to give policymakers a full understanding of the frailties of the intelligence on which they were relying.

Finally, we closely examined the possibility that intelligence analysts were pressured by policymakers to change their judgments about Iraq's nuclear, biological, and chemical weapons programs. The analysts who worked Iraqi weapons issues universally agreed that in no instance did political pressure cause them to skew or alter any of their analytical judgments. That said, it is hard to deny the conclusion that intelligence analysts worked in an environment that did not encourage skepticism about the conventional wisdom.

The Kerr Group, led by former Deputy Director of Central Intelligence Richard Kerr, examined the Iraq-related intelligence failures and what they said about the state of intelligence in the United States in the post–Cold War era. The group issued three reports. Only the third report has been released to the public, although it briefly summarizes the first two.

Intelligence and Analysis on Iraq: Issues for the Intelligence Community

29 July 2004

Introduction

This is the third in a series of reports by the Kerr Group (Richard Kerr, Thomas Wolfe, Rebecca Donegan, and Aris Pappas) supporting the Director of Central Intelligence's evaluation and critique of intelligence and analysis associated with the war in Iraq that began in 2003. The analysis and judgments in this report were informed by the Group's two previous reports.

- The Group's first report was a documentation of the Intelligence Community's judgments before the war. It characterized the intelligence process, product content, and analytic shortcomings but was not a commentary on the accuracy of those judgments. The report (without annexes) is attached. [The first report has not been declassified.]
- The second report reviewed the intelligence used to support judgments regarding weapons of mass destruction in Iraq. Specifically, it reviewed the reporting used to develop the National Intelligence Estimate Iraq's Continuing Programs for Weapons of Mass Destruction published in October 2002. The report is attached. [The second report has not been declassified.]

The Intelligence Community's uneven performance on Iraq over the past two years has raised significant questions concerning the condition of intelligence collection, analysis, and policy support. This third report assesses the performance of the Intelligence Community from a broad perspective, focusing on systemic issues that channeled analysts' evaluations and analyses. The discussion of shortcomings and failures in this report is not meant to imply that all surprises can be prevented by even good intelligence. There are too many targets and too many ways of attacking them for even the best intelligence agencies to discover all threats in time to prevent them from happening. Nonetheless, improving performance requires an acknowledgement of past mistakes and a willingness to change.

The Group recognizes that the Community itself has made some useful changes and recommended others. Several fixes also have been proposed from outside the Community, for example a Director of National Intelligence, which might be helpful but do not address some of the core problems identified by the Group. This report addresses the question: Does the Community's flawed performance on Iraq represent one-time problems, not to be repeated, or is it symptomatic of deeper problems?

The First Two Reports: A Summary of Principal Findings and Issues

The central focus of national intelligence reporting and analysis prior to the war was the extent of the Iraqi programs for developing weapons of mass destruction (WMD). The analysis on this issue by the Intelligence Community clearly was wide of the mark. That analysis relied heavily on old information acquired largely before late 1998 and was strongly influenced by untested, long-held assumptions. Moreover, the analytic judgments rested almost solely on technical analysis, which has a natural tendency to put bits and pieces together as evidence of coherent programs and to equate programs with capabilities. As a result the analysis, although understandable and explainable, arrived at conclusions that were seriously flawed, misleading, and even wrong.

Intelligence produced prior to the war on a wide range of other issues accurately addressed such topics as how the war would develop and how Iraqi forces would or would not fight. It also provided perceptive analysis on Iraq's links to al-Qa'ida; calculated the impact of the war on oil markets; and accurately forecast the reactions of the ethnic and tribal factions in Iraq. Indeed, intelligence assessments on post-Saddam issues were particularly insightful. These and many other topics were thoroughly examined in a variety of intelligence products that have proven to be largely accurate.

The national intelligence produced on the technical and cultural/political areas, however, remained largely distinct and separate. Little or no attempt was made to examine or explain the impact of each area on the other. Thus, perspective and a comprehensive sense of understanding of the Iraqi target *per se* were lacking. This independent preparation of intelligence products in these distinct but interrelated areas raises significant questions about how intelligence supports policy. In an ironic twist, the policy community was receptive to technical intelligence (the weapons program), where the analysis was wrong, but apparently paid little attention to intelligence on cultural and political issues (post-Saddam Iraq), where the analysis was right.

With respect to the weapons programs, some critics have argued that the off-the-mark judgments resulted largely from reinforcement of the Community's assumptions by an audience that was predisposed to believe them. This, however, seems to have been less a case of policy reinforcing "helpful" intelligence judgments than a case of policy deliberations deferring to the Community in an area where classified information and technical analysis were seen as giving it unique expertise.

On the other hand, the Intelligence Community's analysis of post-Saddam Iraq rested on little hard information, was informed largely by strong regional and country expertise developed over time, and yet was on the mark. Intelligence projections in this area, although largely accurate, however, had little or no impact on policy deliberations.

The bifurcation of analysis between the technical and the cultural/political in the analytic product and the resulting implications for policy indicates systemic problems in collection and analysis. Equally important, it raises questions about how best to construct intelligence products to effectively and accurately inform policy deliberations.

The Context

Any examination of the Intelligence Community must acknowledge the impact of more than ten years of turmoil that adversely affected all collection and analytic efforts, including those on Iraq. The Intelligence Community was designed to focus on the Soviet Union. It had developed a single-minded rigor and attention to detail that enriched its analysis, particularly with respect to Soviet military issues. The end of the Cold War, however, brought to a close that "stable" bi-polar world and left the United States without a principal enemy. Although never perfect, the Intelligence Community's analytic efforts against the Soviet threat were generally insightful and its collection largely effective, reflecting the accumulation of deeper understanding over many years.

Absent this singular focus, in the post–Cold War environment the Intelligence Community struggled to reestablish its identity and purpose in what had become a world of multiple crises and transient threats. The effort to define its priorities was further complicated as policymakers and others raised questions not only about the role of but even the need for intelligence. Accordingly, intelligence came to be seen as an area where the Government could reap resource savings. The resulting cutbacks in collection (technical and HUMINT) and analytic resources had a significant adverse impact on Intelligence Community capabilities.

Nonetheless, during the 1990s the Intelligence Community confronted numerous crises in which to demonstrate the relevance of intelligence analysis to policy deliberations. Regional conflicts, such as the first Gulf war and follow-on sanctions on Iraq, the breakup of Yugoslavia, and emerging threats from North Korea and Iran provided tests for intelligence. The Community's collection and analysis performance over this period, however, was seen as inconsistent and sometimes faulty, leaving important customers still wondering about the relevance of the intelligence input to policy deliberations.

A significant contributor to this uneven performance was, and still is, the Community's tendency to establish single-issue centers and crisis-response task forces. By stripping expertise from regional offices they diminish the overall ability to provide perspective and context for those issues. The resources seldom get returned to the line offices, which historically have been better equipped to provide complete perspectives on country and regional issues.

Although resources increased marginally over the decade, they were not as robust or focused as the capabilities devoted to the Soviet Union and were seen by the Intelligence Community as inadequate to deal conclusively with the multiplicity of threats. Accordingly, the Community in critical situations has faltered in its analyses and failed to collect pertinent information. This has occurred over a length of time and across crises sufficient in number, quite apart from Iraq, to indicate systemic issues rather than just occasional missteps.

Collection Impeded and Misdirected

Intelligence collection against Iraq fell far short of the mark. The intelligence base for collection and analysis was thin and sketchy. The Intelligence Community had nothing like the richness, density, and detail that it worked hard to develop and became accustomed to having on Soviet issues during the Cold War. To a significant extent this resulted from the reduction over the past decade of the professional collection management cadre capable of integrating HUMINT, imagery, and signals intelligence capabilities into coherent strategies. This development was compounded by the increased separation of collection professionals from the analytic cadre who had been intimately involved in identifying collection gaps, needs, and priorities and developing collection strategies.

Placing these developments in a broader context, however, is important. Iraq was not the only significant intelligence problem facing the Community in the years immediately preceding the war. Counterterrorism and counterproliferation were given higher priority and absorbed much of the clandestine service capability and leadership attention. Weapons programs in both North Korea and Iran received higher priority than those in Iraq until late 2002. In Iraq, technical collection priorities emphasized coverage of the Iraqi air defense system in southern Iraq in support of US military operations and prevented collection on other important targets in Iraq.

A number of other factors added to the difficulty of clandestine collection on the Iraq target. The Iraqis took pains to carefully hide their WMD programs. People and operations were protected from US intelligence by a variety of methods, including isolating scientists and technicians involved in the programs and employing effective camouflage, concealment, and deception efforts. The Iraqis had learned well about US intelligence during more than ten years of confrontation and war.

Nevertheless, collection of information on difficult targets is the core mission of intelligence and in the Iraq case it did not measure up. Many of the more sophisticated clandestine technical collection techniques did not produce results. The Iraq WMD target was given a high priority over more than a decade, even if not the highest. Still, the Intelligence Community did not have conclusive evidence on what the Iraqis were working on, what they had achieved, which programs were ongoing, who was working them, or what the doctrines for use might be. Conversely, the Community saw no evidence that WMD programs were slowed, put on hold, or even nonexistent. Nor did it understand why Saddam's devious and obstructionist behavior continued if, as he claimed, he had no stockpiles of banned weapons.

US intelligence collection strategies contributed to the problem. Looking for information on a particular subject with a preconception of what is needed is almost certain to result in data that reinforces existing assumptions. The Community directed its collection capabilities to filling in what it thought were gaps in information about WMD programs, monitoring progress, looking for new developments in weapons and delivery systems, and identifying efforts to acquire materiel and technology abroad. Based on the hard information collected by US military forces and UN inspectors during and following the first Gulf war, reinforced by subsequent bits of information, the Intelligence Community and the US defense establishment had little doubt that Iraq was continuing development of weapons of mass destruction.

Collection was not focused or conceptually driven to answer questions about the validity of the premise that the WMD programs were continuing apace. This problem is well illustrated by a comprehensive collection support brief describing intelligence needs published by the DCI Center for Weapons Intelligence, Nonproliferation, and Arms Control. It was published contemporaneously with the 2002 National Intelligence Estimate on WMD. The support brief describes in great detail the information required to support analysis of Iraq's weapons programs. The intent of the brief was to expose gaps in knowledge about what was believed to be aggressive, ongoing Iraqi weapons programs. The revealed gaps in knowledge were not, however, raised as requirements to address what was not known nor did such gaps raise doubts about prevailing intelligence judgments.

Discussing largely space-based collection systems at an unclassified level is difficult, but a few observations are possible. Despite a wide variety of technical capabilities available to the US, these systems were able to provide accurate information on relatively few critical issues. Monitoring Iraqi reactions to inspectors was informative as was reporting on Iraqi acquisition efforts. Technical collection lends itself to monitoring large-scale, widespread targets, a condition not met in the Iraqi case. Analysis of Iraq's WMD programs, therefore, provides an excellent case study for an assessment of the limitations of relying too heavily on technical collection systems with little acknowledgement of the political/cultural context in which such programs exist.

Accordingly, surprisingly little collection was directed against several key issues. Neglected topics for collection included the social, cultural, and economic impacts on Iraq of nearly twenty years of war and ten years of sanctions and isolation. Little attention appears to have been paid, for example, to collecting information on the oil-for-food program. Considerable speculation was voiced that several countries and individuals were profiting from this program. Despite the fact that many of the targets for this subject were outside Iraq, it received only sporadic attention.

Although collection itself was a problem, analysts were led to rely on reporting whose sourcing was misleading and even unreliable. In the case of US clandestine reporting, it too often used different descriptions for the same source, leading analysts to believe they had more confirmatory information from more sources than was actually the case. In addition, some critical judgments were made on the basis of intelligence provided by foreign intelligence services. Some of those sources were not available to the US, and some key information obtained from liaison proved to be false.

The Intelligence Community knows how to collect secret information, even though in the Iraq situation it did not perform this function well. On the other hand, the acquisition of "softer" intelligence on societal issues, personalities, and elites presents an even greater challenge. This latter information can be found in databases, but they are too often only accessible indirectly and with considerable effort. It may also reside in the minds of groups of people who are accessible but not easily approachable and who do not fall into the category of controlled agents. Although there is a strong argument that the clandestine service should not divert its attention away from collecting "secrets," information on the stresses and strains of society may be equally, if not more, important. This type of information, however, does not fit with the reward system in the collection world and can be difficult to fully assess and to integrate with other information.

In the case of Iraq, collection strategies were too weak and unimaginative to get the richness and density of information required. A careful examination might have addressed the long-neglected question of the value added by the different types of intelligence, e.g., SIGINT [signals intelligence] and IMINT [imagery intelligence], relative to the resources devoted to them. Collection on Iraq was the victim of inadequate funding and too intense competition between top priority targets. Finally, Iraq demonstrates that collection strategies must take into account that the absence of dangerous activity in a targeted country cannot be convincingly demonstrated in the presence of a secretive and devious regime. Or, put differently, collection strategies should recognize the extreme difficulty of requiring such a regime to prove the negative in the face of assumptions that it is dissembling. Overall, the Intelligence Community did not acquit itself well in developing collection strategies on Iraq.

Analysis Adversely Affected

No single act of omission or commission accounts for the inconsistent analytic performance of the Intelligence Community with regard to Iraq. It appears to be the result of decisions made, and not made, since the fall of the Soviet Union, which had an impact on the analytical environment analogous to the effect of the meteor strikes on the dinosaurs. Nothing was the same afterwards.

In response to changed priorities, and decreased resources, the Intelligence Community's analytic cadre underwent changes in both its organization and its methodological orientation. Perhaps the most significant change was the shift away from long-term, in-depth analysis in favor of more short-term products intended to provide direct support to policy. Done with the best of intentions, this shift seems to have had the result of weakening elements of the analytic discipline and rigor that characterized Intelligence Community products through the Cold War.

The kind of "intellectual capital intensive" analysis that traditionally and effectively preceded policy deliberations was unavailable because of the shift away from research-oriented analytic investments. In reviewing the national intelligence products associated with Iraq, we found that they too often dealt, *seriatim*, with a broad range of subjects, but without extensive cross-reference, and with no attempt to synthesize a macro understanding of Iraq out of the many detailed pieces that were prepared. The absence of such a contextual effort contributed to assessments that failed to recognize the significance of gaps in collection that may have been more evident when viewed from a larger perspective. The absence of a unifying analysis was also disguised by the rapidity and volume of interactions between intelligence and policy deliberations. Eagerly responsive to quickly developed policy requirements, the quick and assured response gave the appearance of both knowledge and confidence that, in retrospect, was too high.

Of all the methodological elements that contributed, positively and negatively, to the Intelligence Community's performance, the most important seems to be an uncritical acceptance of established positions and assumptions. Gaps in knowledge were left undiscovered or unattended, which to some degree is explainable by the absence of persuasive, intrusive, and effective collection in Iraq. Although many products were appropriately caveated, the growing need to caveat judgments to explain the absence of direct intelligence did not seem to provoke internal review within the Intelligence Community. Indeed, although certain gaps were acknowledged, no product or thread within the intelligence provided called into question the quality of basic assumptions, hastening the conversion of heavily qualified judgments into accepted fact.

As noted earlier, the growing use of centers also contributed to what was at best a problematic result. The Intelligence Community has generally considered centers a useful organizational concept to concentrate analytic and collection capabilities against a carefully defined target set or issue. They also have the effect, however, of drawing resources away from more broadly based organizations. The post–Cold War reductions throughout the Intelligence Community made this a critical but insidious factor. Analysis of Iraq's weapons of mass destruction thus became the purview of technically competent analysts, but as has been described elsewhere, their efforts were not leavened through review by more broadly based colleagues.

Finally, quality control was weakened. The extensive layers of critical management review that traditionally served to insure both the validity and standing of finished intelligence products seem to have been ineffective in identifying key issues affecting collection and analysis. Allowing for a satisfying sense of voluminous production, and reflecting the approval of receptive consumers, the policy-heavy process provided positive feedback, while the narrowly focused internal architecture lacked the self-awareness that could otherwise have raised serious and timely warnings.

Interaction with the Policy Community

Few issues have engaged greater policymaker interest in intelligence than those concerning Iraq—particularly the questions of weapons of mass destruction and

Saddam's links to al-Qa'ida. The demands for intelligence in the months leading up to the war were numerous and intense. The Intelligence Community responded to the overwhelming consumer demand with an ever-increasing stream of analysis—both written and oral. Neither means of communication, however, served the policy community as well as they might have.

In periods of crisis, when demands are high and response time is short, most written intelligence production is in the form of policy-driven memos and briefs and pieces written for daily publications. The result of this narrowly focused and piecemeal intelligence flow is that it does not foster continuity of analysis nor does it provide a context within which to place seemingly unrelated information. In the case of Iraq, national intelligence did not provide a comprehensive picture of how the country functioned as a whole. The Intelligence Community has made substantial, although sporadic, efforts over the past decade and a half to explore better and more technologically advanced methods of communicating with consumers. The results, however, have been modest at best. The requirement to have background and contextual information available at the policymaker's fingertips in a timely fashion remains unfulfilled.

The policy community was also ill served by the National Intelligence Estimate (NIE) process. NIEs rarely represent new analysis or bring to bear more expertise than already exists in analytic offices; indeed, drafters of NIEs are usually the same analysts from whose work the NIE is drawn. Little independent knowledge or informed outside opinion is incorporated in estimative products. The preparation of an NIE therefore consists primarily of compiling judgments from previous products and debating points of disagreement. The Iraqi WMD estimate of October 2002 was characterized by all of these weaknesses and more. It was done under an unusually tight time constraint—three weeks—to meet a deadline for Congressional debate. And it was the product of three separate drafters, each responsible for independent sections, drawing from a mixed bag of analytic product. Consistent application of analytic or evidentiary standards became next to impossible.

The fundamental question is whether National Intelligence Estimates add value to the existing body of analytic work. Historically, with few exceptions, NIEs have not carried great weight in policy deliberations, although customers have often used them to promote their own agendas. The time may have come to reassess the value of NIEs and the process used to produce them.

Oral communications have their own set of problems. While direct engagement with the policy community is essential for intelligence to have an impact, too close association with policy deliberations can be troublesome. In the case of Iraq, daily briefings and other contacts at the highest levels undoubtedly influenced policy in ways that went beyond the coordinated analysis contained in the written product. Close and continuing personal contact, unfettered by the formal caveats that usually accompany written production, probably imparted a greater sense of certainty to analytic conclusions than the facts would bear.

Some in the Intelligence Community and elsewhere hold the view that intense policymaker demands in the run-up to the war constituted inappropriate pressure on intelligence analysts. Although viewed in that context as a problem, serious pressure from policymakers almost always accompanies serious issues. The more relevant issue is how the Intelligence Community responded to the climate of policy-level pressure and expectations. Whether or not this climate contributed to the problem of inconsistent analytic performance, however, remains an open question.

The cases of WMD and Iraq's links to al-Qa'ida illustrate two different responses to policy pressure. In the case of al-Qa'ida, the constant stream of questions aimed at finding links between Saddam and the terrorist network caused analysts to take what they termed a "purposely aggressive approach" in conducting exhaustive and repetitive searches for such links. Despite the pressure, however, the Intelligence Community remained firm in its assessment that no operational or collaborative relationship existed. In the case of Iraq's possession of WMD, on the other hand, analytic judgments and policy views were in accord, so that the impact of pressure, if any, was more nuanced and may have been considered reinforcing. Although it is possible that in the absence of strong policy interest, analysts would have been more inclined to examine their underlying assumptions, it is unlikely that such examination would have changed judgments that were longstanding and firmly held.

Final Thoughts

The intelligence world is one of ambiguity, nuance, and complexity. Dealing with these elements is difficult in the world intelligence serves, where success or failure is the uncomplicated measure by which the Intelligence Community is judged. The controversies over Iraq intelligence can be expressed in the contrast between these two worlds: carefully crafted national intelligence that ultimately failed in its singular mission to accurately inform policy deliberations. This report, the result of over two years of review and consideration, reflects the same contrast. On the one hand, it recognizes the enormous efforts undertaken, the long hours, and the intense debate. On the other hand, it describes failures and weaknesses that cannot be ignored or mitigated.

Failures of collection, uncritical analytical assumptions, and inadequate management reviews were the result of years of well-intentioned attempts to do the best job with the resources provided. Decisions were made and their potential risks weighed, but the outcome on important issues proved unacceptably bad. Recognition of these problems must bring a rapid response.

US Intelligence is a robust, highly capable, and thoroughly motivated community that represents an invaluable asset to the nation and its citizens. It must reveal itself as sufficiently mature to both adapt to changing circumstances and counteract the evolutionary processes that have conspired to threaten its reputation and its ability to successfully perform its assigned mission. The alternative is unacceptable and unthinkable.

In closing, it should be noted that the Intelligence Community, while certainly not perfect, actually fared much better at predicting potential negative political trends that could be expected in Iraq and the region after a war. The two major National Intelligence Estimates, *Regional Consequences of Regime Change in Iraq* and *Principal Challenges in Post-Saddam Iraq*, were both completed in January 2003. That being the case, they were almost certainly produced too late to influence the decision of whether to go to war. Unfortunately, they appear to have had little influence on early decisions regarding occupation policies. Ironically, the Bush administration adhered closely to incorrect assessments, such as those on weapons of mass destruction, and ignored those that later proved closer to the truth. In 2007, the Senate Select Committee published the following conclusions on the Intelligence Community's predictions about a postwar Iraq[64]:

CONCLUSIONS

Democracy
The Intelligence Community assessed prior to the war that establishing a stable democratic government in postwar Iraq would be a long, difficult and probably turbulent challenge. In January 2003, the Intelligence Community assessed

that building "an Iraqi democracy would be a long, difficult and probably turbulent process, with potential for backsliding into Iraq's tradition of authoritarianism." The greatest medium-to-long term challenge in Iraq would be the "introduction of a stable and representative political system." The Intelligence Community noted that Iraqi political culture did "not foster liberalism or democracy" and was "largely bereft of the social underpinnings that directly support development of broad-based participatory democracy." Although the idea of free and democratic elections probably would be a popular concept with the vast majority of the Iraqi population, "the practical implementation of democratic rule would be difficult in a country with no concept of loyal opposition and no history of alternation of power."

The Intelligence Community noted factors that favored the development of democracy: "the relatively low politicization of Iraqi Shiism" and "discredited" secular authoritarian nationalism. This did "not mean, however, that the trend [political Islam] could not take root in postwar Iraq, particularly if economic recovery were slow and foreign troops remained in the country for a long period." In addition, the Intelligence Community cited "the contributions that could be made by four million exiles—many of whom are Westernized and well educated—and by the now impoverished and underemployed Iraqi middle class," but noted that opposition parties did "not have popular, political or military capabilities to play a leading role after Saddam's departure without significant and prolonged external economic, political and military support."

Terrorism

The Intelligence Community assessed prior to the war that al-Qa'ida probably would see an opportunity to accelerate its operational tempo and increase terrorist attacks during and after a US-Iraq war. In January 2003, the Intelligence Community stated that al-Qa'ida "probably would try to exploit any postwar transition in Iraq by replicating the tactics it has used in Afghanistan during the past year to mount hit-and-run operations against US personnel." According to the Intelligence Community, "some militant Islamists in Iraq might benefit from increases in funding and popular support and could choose to conduct terrorist attacks against US forces in Iraq." The Intelligence Community assessed that, "If Baghdad were unable to exert control over the Iraqi countryside, al-Qa'ida or other terrorist groups could operate from remote areas." The Intelligence Community assessed that, "To the extent that a new Iraqi government effectively controlled its territory, especially in northern Iraq, and was friendlier to US interests and backed by US military power, al-Qa'ida's freedom of movement inside Iraq almost certainly would be hampered. If al-Qa'ida mobilized significant resources to combat a US presence in Iraq, it could, at least in the near term, reduce its overall capability to strike elsewhere." The Intelligence Community noted that "Use of violence by competing factions in Iraq against each other or the United States—Sunni against Shia; Kurd against Kurd; Kurd against Arab; any against the United States—probably also would encourage terrorist groups to take advantage of a volatile security environment to launch attacks within Iraq." Additionally, rogue ex-regime elements "could forge an alliance with existing terrorist organizations or act independently to wage guerrilla warfare against the new government or Coalition forces."

The Intelligence Community assessed prior to the war that a heightened terrorist threat resulting from a war with Iraq, after an initial spike, probably would decline slowly over the subsequent three to five years. The Intelligence Community assessed that al-Qa'ida probably would see an opportunity to "accelerate its operational tempo and increase terrorist attacks during and after a US-Iraq war." The lines between al-Qa'ida and other terrorist groups around the world "could become blurred" in the wake of a US attack and counterattacks by al-Qa'ida and jihadists. "The targeting by less capable groups and planners operating on short notice would mean that such softer targets as US citizens overseas would become more inviting for terrorists." The Intelligence Community also noted that al-Qa'ida "would try to take advantage of US attention on postwar Iraq to reestablish its presence in Afghanistan." The Intelligence Community assessed that "if al-Qa'ida mobilized significant resources to combat a US presence in Iraq, it could—at least in the near term—reduce al-Qa'ida's overall capability to strike elsewhere."

Domestic Conflict

The Intelligence Community assessed prior to the war that Iraq was a deeply divided society that likely would engage in violent conflict unless an occupying power prevented it. In January 2003, the Intelligence Community assessed that "a post-Saddam authority would face a deeply divided society with a significant chance that domestic groups would engage in violent conflict with each other unless an occupying force prevented them from doing so." The threat of Shia reprisals for their oppression under Saddam was a "major concern to the Sunni elite and could erupt if not prevented by an occupying force." Sunni Arabs would face possible loss of their longstanding privileged position while Shia would seek increased power. Although some Sunni who had extensive contact with Shia in urban life might be open to a representative political system, some reporting indicated that elements of Sunni society would oppose a regime that did not allow the Sunnis to continue to prevail in the military security services and government. Kurds could try to take advantage of Saddam's departure by seizing some of the large northern oilfields, a move that would elicit a forceful response from Sunni Arabs. According to the Intelligence Community, "score settling would occur throughout Iraq between those associated with Saddam's regime and those who have suffered the most under it." The Intelligence Community assessed that "underlying causes for violence involve political reprisals more than ethnic or sectarian division."

Political Islam

The Intelligence Community assessed prior to the war that the United States' defeat and occupation of Iraq probably would result in a surge of political Islam and increased funding for terrorist groups. In January 2003, the Intelligence Community assessed that a "US-led defeat and occupation of Arab Iraq probably would boost proponents of political Islam" and would result in "calls from Islamists for the people of the region to unite and build up defenses against the West." Assessments concluded that "funds for terrorist groups probably would increase as a result of Muslim outrage over US action." The Intelligence Community also underscored that "in some countries an increase in Islamist sentiment also probably would take the form of greater support for Islamic political parties that seek to come to power through legitimate means."

Influence of Iraq's Neighbors

The Intelligence Community assessed prior to the war that Iraq's neighbors would jockey for influence in Iraq, with activities ranging from humanitarian reconstruction assistance to fomenting strife among Iraq's ethnic and sectarian groups. In January 2003, the Intelligence Community assessed that the objective of most Middle Eastern states regarding a post-Saddam Iraq would be for the territorial integrity of Iraq to remain intact and for a new regime to become neither a source of regional instability nor dominant in the region. The Intelligence Community assessed that Iraq's immediate neighbors would have the greatest stakes in protecting their interests and would be most likely to pose challenges for US goals in post-Saddam Iraq.

The Intelligence Community assessed prior to the war that Iranian leaders would try to influence the shape of post-Saddam Iraq to preserve Iranian

security and demonstrate that Iran is an important regional actor. In January 2003, the Intelligence Community assessed that "the degree to which Iran would pursue policies that either support or undermine U.S. goals in Iraq would depend on how Tehran viewed specific threats to its interests and the potential US reaction." The Intelligence Community assessed that the "more that Iranian leaders perceived that Washington's aims did not challenge Tehran's interests or threaten Iran directly, the better the chance that they would cooperate in the postwar period, or at least not actively undermine US goals." The Intelligence Community assessed that "some elements in the Iranian government could decide to try to counter aggressively the U.S. presence in Iraq or challenge U.S. goals following the fall of Saddam by attempting to use their contacts in Kurdish and Shia communities to sow dissent against the US presence and complicate the formation of a new, pro-US Iraqi government." The Intelligence Community noted that elements in the regime also could "employ their won operatives against US personnel, although this approach would be hard to conceal."

The Intelligence Community assessed that "guaranteeing Iran a role in the negotiations on the fate of post-Saddam Iraq might persuade some Iranian officials to pursue an overt and constructive means to influence reconstruction in Iraq." [— just under two lines deleted—] When possible, the establishment of "a mechanism for US and Iranian officials to communicate on the ground in Iraq could facilitate dialogue, [—about one line deleted—]

WMD

The Intelligence Community assessed prior to the war that military action to eliminate Iraqi WMD would not cause other regional states to abandon their WMD programs, or their desire to develop such programs. The Intelligence Community assessed that for many countries in the Middle East and South Asia, WMD programs "would continue to be viewed as necessary and integral components of an overall national security posture." The Intelligence Community cited several reasons that other regional states would not give up WMD, including the need "to survive in a dangerous neighborhood, enhance regional prestige, compensate for conventional military deficiencies, and deter threats from superior adversaries." The Intelligence Community said "states also would be driven to acquire WMD capabilities or accelerate programs already in train with the hope of developing deterrent capabilities before the programs could be destroyed preemptively."

Security

The Intelligence Community assessed prior to the war that the Iraqi government would have to walk a fine line between dismantling the worst aspects of Saddam's police, security, and intelligence forces and retaining the capability to enforce nationwide peace. In January 2003, the Intelligence Community assessed that "if responsibility for internal security had been passed from an occupying force to an Iraqi government, such a government would have to walk a fine line between dismantling the worst aspects of Saddam's police, security, and intelligence forces and retaining the capability to enforce nationwide peace." The Iraqi Regular Army "has been relatively unpoliticized below the command level and, once purged of security and intelligence officers embedded within it, could be used for security and law enforcement until police or a local gendarme force is established." Over the longer term, the police and security forces "would need to be rebuilt and restructured if they were to gain the trust of the Iraqi people and avoid the excesses similar to those under Saddam's rule."

Oil

The Intelligence Community assessed prior to the war that Iraq's large petroleum resources would make economic reconstruction a less difficult challenge

than political transformation, but that postwar Iraq would nonetheless face significant economic challenges. Intelligence assessments prior to the war differed on the likelihood that the Iraqi oil system would contribute to reconstruction efforts in the short-term. The Intelligence Community, for example, noted that "if Iraq's oil facilities were relatively undamaged by a war, Baghdad could increase crude oil production from 2.4 million barrels a day (b/d) to about 3.1 million b/d within several months of the end of hostilities." Assessments noted that while Iraq could draw on its own oil resources for economic reconstruction, political transformation lacked an equivalent domestic resource. The Intelligence Community also assessed that aside from oil, Iraq's economic options would remain "few and narrow without forgiveness of debt, a reduction in reparations from the previous Gulf War, or something akin to a Marshall Plan."

Humanitarian Issues

The Intelligence Community assessed prior to the war that major outside assistance would be required to meet humanitarian needs. In January 2003, the Intelligence Community assessed that a prolonged struggle to depose Saddam and install a new regime would be likely to cause more flight of refugees and internally displaced persons and to disrupt severely the distribution of food and health services. The Intelligence Community assessed that the "internal security situation would affect the humanitarian challenge" and that the impact on humanitarian needs of a war "would depend on its length and severity." On the topic of refugees, the Intelligence Community reported that a Baghdad-centered military occupation would displace 900,000 persons internally and create 1.45 million refugees. Assessments emphasized that the Iraqi population depended heavily on the rations distributed by the government, and that securing the government's food warehouses after the war and implementing a food distribution system "would be critical to avoiding widespread hunger." The civilian healthcare situation probably "would be severely damaged by the war and widespread civil strife."

Infrastructure

The Intelligence Community assessed prior to the war that the new Iraqi government would require significant outside assistance to rebuild Iraq's water and sanitation infrastructure. The Intelligence Community reported that such basic services as electricity and clean water reached less than half the population prior to the war. The Intelligence Community assessed that the "difficulty of restoring such services as water and electricity after a war would depend chiefly on how much destruction was caused by urban combat." Assessments noted that, "civil strife would cause disruptions in electricity and water purification or distribution if generators, pumps, or plants became damaged, seized, or looted." The Intelligence Community noted that, "cuts in electricity or looting of distribution networks could have a cascading disastrous impact on hospitals at a time when casualty rates are likely to be high." Although Iraq's infrastructure already had suffered extensive degradation, the Intelligence Community reported that Iraqis had restored their physical infrastructure quickly after previous wars.

NOTES

1. Tim Weiner, "Iraqi Offensive into Kurdish Zone Disrupts U.S. Plot to Oust Hussein," *New York Times* (7 September 1996); Tim Weiner, "For 3d Time in 21 Years, Saddam Hussein's Foes Pay Price for Foiled U.S. Plot," *New York Times* (11 September 1996).

2. Office of the Inspector General, "Section D: The Bush Assassination Attempt," in *The FBI Laboratory: An Investigation into Laboratory Practices and Alleged Misconduct in Explosives-Related and Other Cases* (Washington, D.C.: U.S. Department of Justice, April 1997).

3. "Overview of State-Sponsored Terrorism: Iraq," in *Patterns of Global Terrorism, 2002* (Washington, D.C.: U.S. Department of States, 2003): 79.

4. Regarding Saddam Hussein's calculations, see Kevin Woods, James Lacey, and Williamson Murray, "Saddam's Delusions: The View from the Inside," *Foreign Affairs* 85:3 (May/June 2006).

5. Richard K. Betts, "The New Politics of Intelligence," *Foreign Affairs* 83:3 (May/June 2004): 4.

6. Robert Jervis, "Reports, Politics, and Intelligence Failures: The Case of Iraq," *The Journal of Strategic Studies* 29: 1 (February 2006): 19.

7. Pat Roberts, "A Panel above Politics," *Washington Post* (13 November 2003). The Democrats won control of both houses of Congress in the elections of 2006. The Senate Select Committee on Intelligence released a portion of its "Phase II" report in September 2006 and completed it in May 2007. The final portion was then sent to the Director of National Intelligence for declassification review.

8. See, for example, Paul R. Pillar, "Intelligence, Policy, and the War in Iraq," *Foreign Affairs* 85:2 (March/April 2006); idem, "Great Expectations," *Harvard International Review* 27:4 (Winter 2006); Tyler Drumheller, with Elaine Monaghan, *On the Brink: An Insider's Account of How the White House Compromised American Intelligence* (New York: Carroll & Graf, 2006); George Tenet, with Bill Harlow, *At the Center of the Storm: My Years at the CIA* (New York: HarperCollins, 2007).

9. CRS Report RS21696, *U.S. Intelligence and Policymaking: The Iraq Experience* (Washington, D.C.: Congressional Research Service, Updated 2 December 2005): 4–5.

10. The text can be found at http://www.newamericancentury.org/iraqclintonletter.htm.

11. Robert Jervis, *Perception and Misperception in International Politics* (Princeton, NJ: Princeton University Press, 1976).

12. Ron Suskind, *The Price of Loyalty* (New York: Simon & Schuster, 2004): 70–76, 96–97. Suskind's book draws from extensive interviews with former Treasury Secretary Paul O'Neill.

13. Paul Wolfowitz, "Rising Up," *The New Republic* (7 December 1998): 12–13.

14. The interview was done with Sam Tannenhaus for *Vanity Fair*. The excerpts presented here are taken from a transcript provided by the Department of Defense after it said Tannenhaus had distorted Wolfowitz's words in the magazine. The full transcript can be found at http://www.defenselink.mil/transcripts/transcript.aspx?transcriptid=2594. An added benefit noted by Wolfowitz: The invasion of Iraq allowed the United States to withdraw its forces from Saudi Arabia, where they had been stationed since the Persian Gulf War to deter further Iraqi aggression. The U.S. presence in the country of the Muslim holy sites, however, was considered politically destabilizing and aided Usama bin Ladin's recruiting efforts. Wolfowitz also said that removing Hussein would eliminate a source of instability in the Middle East and that a democratic regime would foster stability in the long run.

15. Abu Musab al-Zarqawi is now believed by at least some regional experts to have been a rival of Usama bin Ladin. Bin Ladin focused on the "Far Enemy," the United States. Zarqawi targeted the "Near Enemy," Israel and secular Arab states like Iraq. The U.S. invasion of Iraq brought the far enemy near and created the basis for an alliance between the two terrorist groups. Zarqawi later renamed his organization "al-Qa'ida in Iraq." At the time, U.S. officials pointed to Zarqawi's presence in Iraq as evidence of cooperation between Iraq and al-Qa'ida.

16. CRS Report RL32217, *Iraq and Al Qaeda,* by Kenneth Katzman (Washington, D.C.: Congressional Research Service, Updated 27 July 2007). For the evolution of the administration's justification for war, see Louis Fisher, "Deciding on War against Iraq: Institutional Failures," *Political Science Quarterly* 118:3 (Fall 2003): 389–410.

17. See the various "insider" journalist reports of prewar decision making, Bob Woodward, *State of Denial: Bush at War, Part III* (New York: Simon & Schuster, 2006) and Ron Suskind, *The One Percent Doctrine* (New York: Simon & Schuster, 2006).

18. Texto de Referencia: Acta de la Conversación entre George W. Bush y José María Aznar—Crawford, Tejas, 22 de Febrero de 2003," *El País* (26 September 2007); reprinted in translation in *The New York Review of Books* (8 November 2007).

19. Tenet, *At the Center of the Storm*, 305, 312.

20. *Telegraph* (18 September 2004).

21. PLP stands for Parliamentary Labour Party, that is, the Labour caucus within Parliament.

22. UNSCRS stands for United Nations Security Council Resolutions.

23. Operation Desert Fox was the four-day U.S.–U.K. bombing campaign against Iraq in December 1998.

24. "Cabinet Office Paper: Conditions for Military Action," *Sunday Times* [London] (12 June 2005).

25. The Secret Intelligence Service (SIS) is still popularly known by an outdated designation, MI6. "C" was the initial of the service's first director, Sir Mansfield Cumming. In 2002, "C" was Sir Richard Dearlove.

26. Tenet, *At the Center of the Storm*, 310.

27. "The Secret Downing Street Memo," *Sunday Times* [London] (1 May 2005).

28. A foreign policy adviser to Prime Minster Tony Blair.

29. An aide to David Manning.

30. CENTCOM stands for Central Command, the U.S. military command with operational responsibilities for the Persian Gulf region.

31. Tenet, *At the Center of the Storm*, 315–316.

32. *CNN Late Edition with Wolf Blitzer* (8 September 2002), http://transcripts.cnn.com/TRANSCRIPTS/0209/08/le.00.html.

33. *The National Security Strategy of the United States of America, September 2002*, p. 15, http://www.whitehouse.gov/nsc/nss.pdf.

34. Ivo Daalder, "Policy Implications of a Bush Doctrine of Preemption" (16 November 2002), http://www.cfr.org/publication.html?id=5251.

35. Fisher, "Deciding on War against Iraq."

36. Joseph Cirincione et al., *WMD in Iraq: Evidence and Implications* (Washington, D.C.: Carnegie Endowment for International Peace, January 2004): 53.

37. Tenet, *At the Center of the Storm*, 321–323.

38. Poisonous gases.

39. CW stands for chemical warfare.

40. SRBM stands for short-range ballistic missile; SCUD stands for a particular missile used by Iraq in the Persian Gulf War.

41. R&D stands for research and development; BW stands for biological warfare.

42. Tenet, *At the Center of the Storm*, 335. Text is from *Congressional Record—Senate* (9 October 2002): S10154.

43. Tenet, *At the Center of the Storm*, 336. Text is from *Congressional Record—Senate* (9 October 2002): S10154.

44. *Comprehensive Report of the Special Advisor to the DCI on Iraq's WMD*, rev. ed. (Washington, D.C.: Central Intelligence Agency, 2005): 56. For further examples of fear distorting information flows, see Woods, et al. "Saddam's Delusions."

45. Joseph C. Wilson 4th, "What I Didn't Find in Africa," *New York Times* (6 July 2003).

46. See Joseph Wilson, *The Politics of Truth* (New York: Carroll & Graf, 2004). The White House apparently orchestrated a campaign to tell journalists that Wilson had been sent by Valerie Plame, his wife and a CIA officer, illegally revealing her identity as a clandestine officer in the process. Wilson holds that they did this to ruin her career as revenge for his op-ed, which undermined the justification for the war. It seems more likely that the intent was to separate Wilson's mission from Vice President Cheney. Wilson claimed that Cheney's queries prompted the mission, which implies that Cheney would have received the report that the uranium claim was unlikely to be true.

47. Tenet, *At the Center of the Storm*, 449–450.

48. On Curveball, see Bob Drogin, *Curveball* (New York: Random House, 2007); Drumheller, *On the Brink*; John Prados, "Electronic Briefing Book: The Curveball Affair" (5 November 2007), available from the National Security Archive, http://www.gwu.edu/~nsarchiv. Curveball's real name, Rafid Ahmed Alwan, was revealed publicly for the first time by CBS News' *60 Minutes* on 4 November 2007. See "Faulty Intel Source 'Curve Ball' Revealed," http://www.cbsnews.com/stories/2007/11/01/60minutes/printable3440577.shtml.

49. Tenet, *At the Center of the Storm*, 302.

50. U.S. Senate, Select Committee on Intelligence, *Report on the U.S. Intelligence Community's Prewar Intelligence Assessments on Iraq together with Additional Views* (9 July 2004): 307–312. Extensive excerpts from one of their memos can be found in Stephen F. Hayes, "Case Closed," *The Weekly Standard* (24 November 2003): 20–25.

51. "Tawhid," translated sometimes as "monotheism" and sometimes as "unity," refers to the unity of God. The term is not mentioned in the Qur'an, yet Islamist activists since the mid-twentieth century have latched onto it as the defining characteristic of Islam. "Jihad" can refer to many kinds of struggle, but here it means armed struggle against nonbelievers. See "Jihad" and "Tawhid" in *Oxford Encyclopedia of the Modern Islamic World*, ed. John L. Esposito et al. (New York: Oxford University Press, 1995).

52. See, for example, Brian Fishman, "After Zarqawi: The Dilemmas and Future of Al Qaeda in Iraq," *Washington Quarterly* 29: 4 (Autumn 2006): 19–32. Fishman is an associate of the Combating Terrorism Center at the U.S. Military Academy, West Point, NY.

53. The group's new name is actually the Qa'ida Jihad Organization in Bilad al-Rafidayn. It uses an ancient Arabic name for the region, meaning "land of two rivers," rather than the modern name Iraq. It is generally translated as al-Qa'ida in Iraq or as al-Qa'ida in Mesopotamia, using the ancient Greek name for the region, which has a similar meaning.

54. U.S. Congress, Senate, Select Committee on Intelligence, *Report on Postwar Findings about Iraq's WMD Programs and Links to Terrorism and How They Compare with Prewar Assessments together with Additional Views* (8 September 2006): 90–93.

55. U.S. Senate, Select Committee on Intelligence, *Report on Postwar Findings*, 79–82.

56. The excerpt, reprinted in a letter, http://levin.senate.gov/newsroom/supporting/2005/DIAletter.102605.pdf.

57. Department of Defense Office of Inspector General, Report No. 07-INTEL-04, *Review of Pre-Iraqi War Activities of the Office of the Under Secretary of Defense for Policy: Executive Summary* (9 February 2007). Feith dismissed the criticism. See, for example, "Douglas Feith, Former Undersecretary of Defense, Responds to Pentagon Inspector General's Report on NPR News' *Day to Day* (9 February 2007), http://www.npr.org/about/press/2007/020907.feith.html.

58. U.S. Senate, Select Committee on Intelligence, *Report on Postwar Findings*, 69–75.

59. U.S. Senate, Select Committee on Intelligence, *Report on Postwar Findings*, 72–73.

60. Jervis, "Reports, Politics, and Intelligence Failures," 37.

61. CBS News, "Faulty Intel Source 'Curve Ball' Revealed."

62. U.S. Congress, Senate, Select Committee on Intelligence, *Report on the U.S. Intelligence Community's Prewar Intelligence Assessments on Iraq together with Additional Views* (9 July 2004): 249.

63. *Comprehensive Report of the Special Advisor to the DCI on Iraq's WMD*, rev. ed. (Washington, D.C.: Central Intelligence Agency, 2005).

64. U.S. Congress, Senate, Select Committee on Intelligence, *Report on Prewar Intelligence Assessments about Postwar Iraq together with Additional Views* (2007): 6–12. The full report is 226 pages and includes redacted versions of the National Intelligence Estimates. Footnotes have been deleted, but all footnotes cite one or the other of the two NIEs. Also deleted is the blacked-out classification code at the beginning of every paragraph and subhead.

_____ *Chapter 18* _____

The Iran National Intelligence Estimate

As the Iraq War unfolded after 2003, tensions rose anew between the United States and the Islamic Republic of Iran. The two countries had still not had publicly acknowledged negotiations since 1979, yet each U.S. administration had had contacts of some sort—the administration of George W. Bush, prior to the Iraq War, more than most.

The main controversy between the two nations centered on the discovery that Iran had been developing a clandestine nuclear program since the mid-1980s. Yet in late 2007, the National Intelligence Council—based on intelligence newly discovered by the CIA and citing the lessons of Iraq—would dramatically reverse its assessment of Iran's nuclear weapons program and then publicize that reversal (two weeks after the Director of National Intelligence had said he would no longer release intelligence findings). Presumably, the reasons for publicizing the turnaround included the desire to avoid having intelligence misused as it had been in the run-up to the Iraq War. Arguably, it may also have disrupted a behind-the-scenes effort to launch a preventive attack on Iran, although that cannot be proved at this time.

Apart from the nuclear question, the United States accused Iran, which is dominated by Shia Muslim clerics, of supporting Islamist militant groups abroad, especially Hizballah (also spelled Hezbollah)[1] in Lebanon and Hamas[2] and Palestinian Islamic Jihad in the Palestinian territories (even though the latter two represent Sunni, not Shia, Muslims). These armed militant groups also are supported by the secular government of Syria, Iran's only Arab ally. Both Iran and Syria backed them as a way to retain influence in Lebanon and to pressure the common enemy, Israel.

Complicating the picture was the fact that, to a greater or lesser degree, Iran had ties to all the major parties representing the Shia majority in Iraq after 2003. That included the Supreme Council of the Islamic Revolution in Iraq (later, the Supreme Islamic Iraqi Council), the largest party in the Iraqi parliament, which had been formed by exiles in Iran and had fought on Iran's side in the Iran-Iraq War (1980–1988); the Islamic Call (al-Dawa al-Islamiya), the party of Prime Ministers al-Ja'afari and al-Maliki; and also the party of Muqtada al-Sadr, who has fought against U.S. troops and other Shia militias as well as the Sunnis who constitute the core of the Iraqi insurgency, even while serving in the government. Of the three, Sadr had the most ambiguous ties to Iran, in part because he was viewed as an upstart, has fought other Shia, and has based his political appeal on class issues more than religion. These ties have put post–Saddam Hussein Iraq in the unique position of being closely allied to both the United States and Iran, and they have made the U.S. government suspicious of Iranian intentions in Iraq.

Also complicating the picture is Iran's complex political system, which includes elements of both democracy and authoritarianism. The highest authority is not the elected president, but the *faqih*, an expert in religious law who is chosen by an elected council of senior Muslim clerics called the Assembly of Experts. The faqih serves a fixed term, but there is no limit on the number of terms. To date there have been only two faqihs, the Ayatollah Ruhollah Khomeini, from 1979 until his death in 1989, and then the Ayatollah Ali Khamenei. The faqih is the commander in chief of the armed forces and is responsible for setting general policy guidelines. The faqih also chooses six members of the Council of Guardians. Another six are chosen by the parliament from among candidates selected by the judiciary, who are in turn selected by the faqih.

Elections are held for parliament and the president; elections have been meaningful, yet the powers of elected officials are circumscribed. Although there was just one political party until 1998, multiple parties have been legal since then. All parties, however, must accept the "guardianship of the faqih."[3] All candidates, regardless of party, must be approved in advance by the Ministry of the Interior and the Council of Guardians. The Council of Guardians, in particular, disqualified many reformist candidates prior to the legislative elections of 2004. The Council of Guardians also decides on the constitutionality of all bills enacted.

The faqih rarely involves himself in the day-to-day decisions of government. The precise relationship between faqih and president has varied with personalities over the years. For his part, Ayatollah Khamenei strives to balance the various political factions in the government, including the pragmatic and hard-line conservatives.[4] Beyond that, there are many ill-defined power centers, including the military, government agencies, and the religious foundations that control large parts of the nonpetroleum economy. Lines of authority are often vague, and rival factions are highly competitive.

Iran is a signatory of the Nuclear Nonproliferation Treaty (NPT). Under that agreement, it has the right to develop nuclear energy for peaceful purposes as long as it keeps its facilities open to the inspectors of the International Atomic Energy Agency (IAEA). Iran's hard-line conservatives have taken that right very seriously, maintaining that anyone who disagreed was necessarily motivated by a desire to oppress the country.[5]

Iran's first nuclear research reactor was purchased from the United States in 1959. A far more ambitious program to develop a civilian nuclear energy industry was initiated in the 1970s with assistance from West Germany, France, and South Africa. Reportedly, the Shah's intention at that time was to develop the nuclear technology and infrastructure that would be necessary to build nuclear weapons later.[6] The public argument, then as now, was that Iran needed nuclear energy for domestic consumption so that it could sell more of its oil and gas abroad to raise revenues. The nuclear program was disrupted by the revolution of 1979 and the start of the Iran-Iraq War. The program was then resumed during that war and proceeded with fits and starts into the 1990s. Dr. A. Q. Khan, who ran a clandestine nuclear assistance program out of Pakistan, provided technical information and equipment. In 1995, Russia began assisting with the construction of a nuclear reactor at Bushehr, which had been started with the assistance of West Germany in the 1970s.[7]

At the time of the Afghan invasion of 2001, Iran had a relatively liberal president, Muhammad Khatami. The United States and Iran were already conducting quiet negotiations at the time of the 9/11 terrorist attacks. Those negotiations continued, and the Iranian regime actually cooperated with the United States in overthrowing Afghanistan's Taliban regime and in negotiating its replacement by the government of Hamid Karzai. (Although Iran and Afghanistan both had Islamic regimes, one Shia and the other Sunni, relations between the two had been tense.) There was a brief interruption in that cooperation after President George W. Bush branded Iran, Iraq, and North Korea the "Axis of Evil" in his State of the Union address in early 2002. Negotiations then resumed and continued until after the U.S. invasion of Iraq.[8]

Over the course of 2002, according to his memoirs, Director of Central Intelligence George Tenet discovered that two figures from the Iran-Contra affair, Michael Ledeen and Manucher Ghorbanifar, were endeavoring to convince the Pentagon and the National Security Council to back Iranian officials who were "in violent opposition to the regime" without informing the CIA. The agency had a low opinion of both men; it had issued a "burn notice" on Ghorbanifar, warning other intelligence agencies not to trust him, even before the Iran-Contra affair. The CIA was also suspicious of any further unauthorized, "off-the-books" covert operations. In any event, preparations were already under way for the Iraq War. It is unclear how receptive the Pentagon and the NSC had been, although Tenet received reports from Italy that two members of the staff of Under Secretary of Defense for Policy Douglas Feith were apparently in Europe discussing a possible $25 million program to support Iranian oppositionists. Ledeen also claimed to have briefed the vice president's office but refused to cooperate with the CIA. The incident was apparently ended after a CIA lawyer threatened to file a "crimes report" against Ledeen with the Department of Justice.[9]

Later in 2002, an exile group, the National Council of Resistance of Iran, declared that in addition to Iran's publicly acknowledged nuclear energy program, the country had undeclared nuclear sites at Natanz (for enriching uranium) and Arak (for heavy water production).[10] In February 2003, the IAEA confirmed that Iran had been secretly working on a uranium-enrichment program. Enriched uranium can be used either for fuel to generate electricity or for a nuclear weapon—depending on the degree to which it is enriched—but the fact that Iran had been running a clandestine nuclear development program put it in violation of the NPT. The CIA had evidently been unaware of these activities.

In May 2003, in the aftermath of these discoveries and the U.S. invasion of Iraq, President Khatami, via the Swiss ambassador, proposed negotiations with the United States to discuss the countries' differences. Iran was willing to discuss its support for Hizballah, its nuclear program, and its role in Iraq; in return, it expected the United States to discuss the normalization of relations and an end to sanctions. Shortly after the proposal, however, intelligence connected a terrorist incident in Saudi Arabia to a telephone call from Iran, and a debate ensued in the Intelligence Community over its significance. President Bush then rebuffed the Iranian offer, shut down the U.S.-Iranian negotiating channel, and lodged a formal complaint against Switzerland for interfering.[11] It is impossible to say what further negotiations might have produced, if anything. Khatami might have been unable to sustain the initiative in the face of likely opposition from rival factions in the Iranian government. The Saudi terrorist incident may even have been intended to torpedo the offer. On the other hand, there have been cases in which Iran has ceased terrorist attacks against countries that improved relations with it.[12]

In any event, Britain, France, and Germany—representing the European Union and called the EU-3—began negotiations with Iran, not on a "grand bargain" to normalize relations but on Iran's nuclear program. From that time on, Iran engaged in a two-track negotiating process on the nuclear issue, dealing separately with the IAEA and the EU-3. By October 2003, Iran had been persuaded to suspend its uranium-enrichment program. The Bush administration, however, considered suspension to be inadequate and insisted that it would not negotiate with Iran until the latter had completely abandoned enrichment activities. In November 2003, the IAEA formally declared that Iran had been violating the Nuclear Nonproliferation Treaty by concealing key parts of its nuclear program for eighteen years.

On 24 February 2004, DCI Tenet delivered the following assessment as part of a prepared statement to the Select Committee on Intelligence (SSCI), during the committee's annual review of current and projected security threats to the United States.

> **IRAN** is taking yet a different path [from Libya and North Korea], acknowledging work on a covert nuclear fuel cycle while trying to preserve its WMD options. I'll start with the good news: Tehran acknowledged more than a decade of covert nuclear activity and agreed to open itself to an enhanced inspection regime. Iran for the first time acknowledged many of its nuclear fuel cycle development activities—including a large-scale gas centrifuge uranium enrichment effort. Iran claims its centrifuge program is designed to produce low-enriched uranium to support Iran's civil nuclear power program. This is permitted under the Nonproliferation Treaty, but—and here's the downside—the same technology can be used to build a military program as well.
>
> • The difference between producing low-enriched uranium and weapons-capable high-enriched uranium is only a matter of time and intent, not technology. It would be a significant challenge for intelligence to confidently assess whether that red line had been crossed.
>
> Finally, Iran's missile program is both a regional threat and a proliferation concern. Iran's ballistic missile inventory is among the largest in the Middle East and includes the 1300-km range Shahab-3 MRBM as well as a few hundred SRBMs.[13] Iran has announced production of the Shahab-3 and publicly acknowledged development of follow-on versions. During 2003, Iran continued R&D on its longer-range ballistic missile programs, and publicly reiterated its intention to develop space launch vehicles (SLVs)—and SLVs contain most of the key building

blocks for an ICBM. Iran could begin flight-testing these systems in the mid- to latter-part of the decade.

- Iran also appears willing to supply missile-related technology to countries of concern and publicly advertises its artillery rockets and related technologies, including guidance instruments and missile propellants.

At some point in mid-2004, the CIA obtained from an unidentified Iranian source a laptop computer that had evidently belonged to an engineer in the Iranian nuclear program. According to news reports published later, the contents were so voluminous that they appeared to represent the work of a team of engineers. Included were studies and computer simulations for a number of nuclear warhead designs. The documents were taken as evidence that the goals of the nuclear program were not confined to the production of electricity.[14] It was assumed that the work was current and active.

On 2 February 2005, at a time when the prospects of the Iraq War appeared to be improving, President Bush again used his State of the Union address to denounce Iran.

Today, Iran remains the world's primary state sponsor of terror—pursuing nuclear weapons while depriving its people of the freedom they seek and deserve. We are working with European allies to make clear to the Iranian regime that it must give up its uranium enrichment program and any plutonium reprocessing, and end its support for terror. And to the Iranian people, I say tonight: As you stand for your own liberty, America stands with you. (Applause.)

At the next review of current and potential security threats by the SSCI, on 16 February 2005, DCI Porter J. Goss's statement appeared to indicate a hardening of positions compared to Tenet's statement of the year before. Goss made no reference to the laptop, the existence of which remained a secret at that time.

IRAN

In early February, the spokesman of Iran's Supreme Council for National Security publicly announced that Iran would never scrap its nuclear program. This came in the midst of negotiations with EU-3 members (Britain, Germany, and France) seeking objective guarantees from Tehran that it will not use nuclear technology for nuclear weapons.

- Previous comments by Iranian officials, including Iran's Supreme Leader and its Foreign Minister, indicated that Iran would not give up its ability to enrich uranium. Certainly they can use it to produce fuel for power reactors. We are more concerned about the dual-use nature of the technology that could also be sued to achieve a nuclear weapon.

In parallel, Iran continues its pursuit of long-range ballistic missiles, such as an improved version of its 1,300 km range Shahab-3 MRBM, to add to the hundreds of short-range SCUD missiles it already has.[15]

Even since 9/11, Tehran continues to support terrorist groups in the region, such as Hizballah, and could encourage increased attacks in Israel and the Palestinian Territories to derail progress toward peace.

- Iran reportedly is supporting some anti-Coalition activities in Iraq and seeking to influence the future character of the Iraqi state.

     o Conservatives are likely to consolidate their power in Iran's June 2005 presidential elections, further marginalizing the reform movement last year.

     o Iran continues to retain in secret important members of Al-Qai'ida—the Management Council—causing further uncertainty about Iran's commitment to bring them to justice.

On the same occasion, on 16 February 2005, Vice Admiral Lowell E. Jacoby, Director of the Defense Intelligence Agency, stated the following with regard to Iran:

> Iran is likely continuing nuclear weapon-related endeavors in an effort to become the dominant regional power and to deter what it perceives as the potential for US or Israeli attacks. We judge Iran is devoting significant resources to its weapons of mass destruction and ballistic missile programs. Unless constrained by a nuclear non-proliferation agreement, Tehran probably will have the ability to produce nuclear weapons early in the next decade. [. . .]
>
> We judge Iran will have the technical capability to develop an ICBM by 2015. It is not clear whether Iran has decided to field such a missile. Iran continues to field 1300-km range Shahab III MRBMs capable of reaching Tel Aviv. Iranian officials have publicly claimed they are developing a new 2000-km-range variant of the Shahab III. Iranian engineers are also likely working to improve the accuracy of the country's SRBMs.

In May 2005, the National Intelligence Council issued a new National Intelligence Estimate on Iran. No portion of the NIE was released to the public, but within months news of it was leaked to the press. The estimate was, no doubt, influenced by the information from the Iranian laptop but also by the growing backlash from the failure of the intelligence preceding the Iraq War, which by this time had become the subject of numerous investigations. (Unlike the Iraqi case, the Bush administration had not referred specifically to intelligence in its accusations against Iran.) The estimate held that the Iranian government was determined to develop a nuclear weapon, although a good deal of the news reporting focused on an extension of the time frame for developing a weapon to ten years. A longer time frame implied less urgency and a greater opportunity for negotiation. The NIE also noted that technologies developed in Iran's open nuclear energy program could easily be transferred to a military program at a later time. Regarding Iran's contention that it kept its program secret for eighteen years for fear of being attacked by the United States or Israel, the NIE commented that this was plausible but unverifiable.[16] Vice President Dick Cheney and John R. Bolton, who had recently transferred from Under Secretary of State for Arms Control to Permanent Representative to the United Nations, had already spoken publicly about the possibility of air strikes against Iranian nuclear facilities.

    In the summer of 2005, the liberal Khatami's second term came to an end. A "pragmatic conservative" candidate was expected to win the presidential election, but victory went to the hard-line conservative Mahmud Ahmadi-Nejad (also spelled Ahmadinejad). Ahmadi-Nejad proceeded to make a number of inflammatory remarks, especially regarding Israel and the Jews. (Although Ahmadi-Nejad is clearly hostile toward Israel, there are conflicting translations for several of these remarks and the Western press has generally reported the most inflammatory versions.[17]) The civilian uranium-enrichment program was reactivated, and, in April 2006, Ahmadi-Nejad announced that Iran had successfully enriched a small quantity of uranium to a level of 3.5 percent, sufficient to fuel a nuclear reactor but not nearly the 90 percent required for a bomb. (It should be remembered that, as president, Ahmadi-Nejad did not necessarily control military programs, which would remain in the hands of the faqih, Ayatollah Khamenei.)

Director of National Intelligence John D. Negroponte had delivered the Annual Threat Assessment to the SSCI on 2 February 2006. The portion pertaining to Iran was becoming longer.

Iran and North Korea: States of Highest Concern

Our concerns about Iran are shared by many nations, by the IAEA, and of course, Iran's neighbors.

Iran conducted a clandestine uranium enrichment program for nearly two decades in violation of its IAEA safeguards agreement, and despite its claims to the contrary, we assess that Iran seeks nuclear weapons. We judge that Tehran probably does not yet have a nuclear weapon and probably has not yet produced or acquired the necessary fissile material. Nevertheless, the danger that it will acquire a nuclear weapon and the ability to integrate it with the ballistic missiles Iran already possesses is a reason for immediate concern. Iran already has the largest inventory of ballistic missiles in the Middle East, and Tehran views its ballistic missiles as an integral part of its strategy to deter—and if necessary retaliate against—forces in the region, including US forces.

As you are aware, Iran is located at the center of a vital—and volatile—region, has strained relations with its neighbors, and is hostile to the United States, our friends, and our values. President Ahmadi-Nejad has made numerous unacceptable statements since his election, hard-liners have control of all the major branches and institutions of government, and the government has become more effective and efficient at repressing the nascent roots of personal freedom that had emerged in the late 1990s and earlier in the decade.

Indeed, the regime today is more confident and assertive than it has been since the early days of the Islamic Republic. Several factors work in favor of the clerical regime's continued hold on power. Record oil and other revenue is permitting generous public spending, fueling strong economic growth, and swelling financial reserves. At the same time, Iran is diversifying its foreign trading partners. Asia's share of Iran's trade has jumped to nearly match Europe's 40 percent share. Tehran sees diversification as a buffer against external efforts to isolate it.

Although regime-threatening instability is unlikely, ingredients for political volatility remain, and Iran is wary of the political progress occurring in neighboring Iraq and Afghanistan. Ahmadi-Nejad's rhetorical recklessness and his inexperience on the national and international stage also increase the risk of a misstep that could spur popular opposition, especially if more experienced conservatives cannot rein in his excesses. Over time, Ahmadi-Nejad's populist economic policies could—if enacted—deplete the government's financial resources and weaken a structurally flawed economy. For now, however, Supreme Leader Khamenei is keeping conservative fissures in check by balancing the various factions in government.

Iranian policy toward Iraq and its activities there represent a particular concern. Iran seeks a Shia-dominated and unified Iraq but also wants the US to experience continued setbacks in our efforts to promote democracy and stability. Accordingly, Iran provides guidance and training to Shia militant groups to enable anti-Coalition attacks. Tehran has been responsible for at least some of the increasing lethality of anti-Coalition attacks by providing Shia militants with the capability to build IEDs [improvised explosive devices] with explosively formed projectiles similar to those developed by Iran and Lebanese Hizballah.

Tehran's intentions to inflict pain on the United States in Iraq has been constrained by its caution to avoid giving Washington an excuse to attack it, the clerical leadership's general satisfaction with trends in Iraq, and Iran's desire to avoid chaos on its borders.

Iranian conventional military power constitutes the greatest potential threat to Persian Gulf states and a challenge to US interests. Iran is enhancing its ability to project its military power in order to threaten to disrupt the operations and reinforcement of US forces based in the region—potentially intimidating regional allies into withholding support for US policy toward Iran—and raising the costs of our regional presence for us and our allies.

Tehran also continues to support a number of terrorist groups, viewing this capability as a critical regime safeguard by deterring US and Israeli attacks, distracting and weakening Israel, and enhancing Iran's regional influence through intimidation. Lebanese Hizballah is Iran's main terrorist ally, which—although focused on its agenda in Lebanon and supporting anti-Israeli Palestinian terrorists—has a worldwide support network and is capable of attacks against US interests if it feels its Iranian patron is threatened. Tehran also supports Palestinian Islamic Jihad and other groups in the Persian Gulf, Central and South Asia, and elsewhere.

In April 2006, the month Ahmadi-Nejad announced Iran's achievement in enriching uranium, the IAEA referred the Iran issue to the United Nations Security Council. The EU-3 was replaced by the P5 + 1, consisting of the five permanent members of the UN Security Council plus Germany. Negotiations with Iran, however, were conducted by Javier Solana, the European Union's High Representative for the Common Foreign and Security Policy. In July, the Security Council demanded that Iran cease its enrichment activities or face international sanctions.

The Bush administration launched a series of initiatives in the first half of 2006. In February, Secretary of State Condoleezza Rice, acknowledging that Congress had already authorized $10 million "to develop support networks for Iranian reformers, political dissidents, and human rights activists" in fiscal year 2006, requested a further "$75 million in supplemental funding for the year 2006 to support democracy in Iran" through broadcasts, public diplomacy, and scholarships.[18]

In April 2006, journalist Seymour Hersh reported in the *New Yorker* magazine that the Bush administration was developing plans for air strikes against Iranian nuclear facilities, despite the continuing quagmire in Iraq.[19] It seemed evident that the Bush administration—or someone within the administration—had planted or encouraged the story. Several current or recently retired officials (including "a government consultant with close ties to the civilian leadership in the Pentagon" and "one former defense official who still deals with sensitive issues for the Bush administration") were available to discuss the secret matter with Hersh, who was not known as a friend of the administration.[20] More difficult to determine was whether this reflected a real intention to launch an attack, an effort to intimidate Iran into being more forthcoming in negotiations, or more likely, an attempt by a faction within the administration to structure the internal policy debate. Hersh—among others—speculated that the administration's ultimate goal in Iran was "regime change."

The United States' concern about Iran only grew. In January 2006, Israel had permitted elections in the occupied Palestinian territories after U.S. prodding. The result was a victory by Iran's ally Hamas, which led to factional fighting between Hamas and the secular Palestinian organization Fatah[21] as well as efforts by the United States to isolate the government born of the elections it had championed. In the summer of 2006, Iran's Lebanese ally Hizballah became increasingly prominent after surviving an attempt by Israel to destroy it through military intervention in southern Lebanon.

In late 2006 and early 2007, the Bush administration made a number of accusations concerning Iranian interference in Iraq. Several Iranians who claimed to be diplomats were detained by U.S. military forces. The accusations concerned the training and equipping of Iraqi Shia militias and sometimes even of Sunni insurgents. (In some instances, the Iraqi authorities demanded and obtained the release of detained Iranians.) The United States also succeeded in organizing the approval of the UN Security Council for two rounds of relatively mild sanctions against Iran in December 2006 and March 2007.

Negroponte again delivered the Annual Threat Assessment to Congress on 11 January 2007.

The Middle East—An Emboldened Iran

In the Middle East, Iran and its neighbors see a strategic shift: Iran's influence is rising in ways that go beyond the menace of its nuclear program. The fall of the Taliban and Saddam, increased oil revenues, HAMAS's electoral victory, and Hizballah's perceived recent success in fighting against Israel all extend Iran's shadow in the region. Our Arab allies fear Iran's increasing influence, are concerned about worsening tensions between Shia and Sunni Islam, and face heightened domestic criticism for maintaining their decades-old strategic partnerships with Washington.

Iran's growing influence has coincided with a generational change in Tehran's leadership. Iranian President Ahmadi-Nejad's administration—staffed in large part by second-generation hardliners imbued with revolutionary ideology and deeply distrustful of the US—has stepped up the use of more assertive and offensive tactics to achieve Iran's longstanding goals.

However, Ahmadi-Nejad's supporters suffered setbacks in the recent Assembly of Experts and local council elections. Moreover, ethnic tensions in Iran's Baloch, Kurdish, and, to a lesser extent, Arab and Azeri areas continue to fester, creating concern in Tehran about the potential for broader ethnic unrest to generate large-scale anti-regime activity. While record oil revenues and manageable debt suggest that Iran is capable, for now, of weathering shocks to the economy, inflationary pressures, exacerbated by Ahmadi-Nejad's expansionary fiscal and monetary policies, are harming Iran's consumer and investment climates and causing employment opportunities to decline.

Regarding Tehran's regional policies, Iran continues to be active in Iraq, seeking to influence political, economic, religious, and cultural developments to ensure a non-threatening, cooperative, and Shia-dominated regime to its west.

- o Iran uses radio, television, and print media to influence Iraqi public opinion and help promote pro-Iranian individuals in the Iraqi government at all levels. It has offered financial and other support to its political allies in the United Iraqi Alliance, but its electoral impact appears to have been marginal, given the likelihood that Shia voters would have voted for the unified Shia ticket anyway.

Iranian conventional military power threatens Persian Gulf states and challenges US interests. Iran is enhancing its ability to project its military power—primarily with ballistic missiles and naval power—with the goal of dominating the Gulf region and deterring potential adversaries. It seeks a capacity to disrupt the operations and reinforcement of US forces based in the region—potentially intimidating regional allies into withholding support for US policy—and raising the political, financial, and human costs to the US and our allies of our presence in Iraq. Tehran views its growing inventory of ballistic missiles (it already has the largest inventory of these missiles in the Middle East) as an integral part of its strategy to deter—and if necessary retaliate against—forces in the region, including US forces.

We assess that Iran regards its ability to conduct terrorist operations abroad as a key element of its national security strategy; it considers this capability as helping to safeguard the regime by deterring US or Israeli attacks, distracting and weakening Israel, enhancing Iran's regional influence through intimidation, and helping to drive the US from the region.

At the center of Iran's terrorism strategy is Lebanese Hizballah, which relies on Tehran for a substantial portion of its annual budget, military equipment, and specialized training. Hizballah is focused on its agenda in Lebanon and supporting anti-Israeli Palestinian terrorists, but, as I indicated earlier, it has in the past made contingency plans to conduct attacks against US interests in the event it feels its survival—or that of Iran—is threatened.

Syria has strengthened ties with Iran and grown more confident about its regional policies, largely due to what it sees as vindication of its support to Hizballah and HAMAS and its perceptions of its success in overcoming international attempts to isolate the regime. Damascus has failed to crack down consistently on militant infiltration into Iraq and continues to meddle in Lebanon. Lebanon remains in a politically dangerous situation as Damascus, Hizballah, and other pro-Syrian groups attempt to topple the government of Prime Minister Siniora.

In the Palestinian territories, inter-factional violence, which has intensified in the Gaza Strip and the West Bank since the establishment of the HAMAS-led Palestinian Authority (PA) government in March, threatens to escalate further absent success in forming a national unity government. Talks have stalled over disputes about the political platform and control of key cabinet positions. HAMAS has continued to reject Quartet[22] and Israeli demands for explicit recognition of Israel, renunciation of armed resistance to Israeli occupation, and acceptance of previous PLO and international agreements.

In late 2006, an independent commission called the Iraq Study Group had proposed, among other things, direct negotiations with Iraq's neighbors, including Iran and Syria, in order to foster greater stability in Iraq and the wider region.[23] The Bush administration initially dismissed the prospect but then engaged in such meetings in spring 2007 with the understanding that only Iraq-related issues could be discussed.

Congress requested an updated National Intelligence Estimate on Iran, the previous one dating from May 2005. The new NIE was expected to be released in the spring of 2007, but was delayed several times. As work on it continued during the summer, the CIA came into the possession of new information. According to later news reports, the information consisted of the notes taken during conversations and deliberations among Iranian military officials in which one complains bitterly about a government decision in late 2003 to shut down the engineering effort to design nuclear weapons, including a warhead that would fit Iranian missiles, and also a journal or diary documenting the decisions to shut it down.[24]

The new information, combined with the recent experience of faulty assessments on Iraqi nuclear programs, led to an overall review of the Iran assessment. The Counterintelligence Staff was put to the task of determining whether the information was legitimate or a deception and concluded that it was reliable. Past information was reviewed anew. Alternative-analysis teams were assigned to examine the issue from various perspectives. The outcome was a complete reversal on the key issue of Iran's intentions regarding nuclear weapons.

President Bush was informed in August that a reassessment was under way, although it is unclear how explicit the information was. Nevertheless, the president and the vice president continued to speak as though nothing had changed. On 17 October 2007, President Bush startled many observers by alluding during a press conference to the possibility of world war erupting over the issue of Iran's nuclear program.

> **Q:** But you definitively believe Iran wants to build a nuclear weapon?
> **THE PRESIDENT:** I think so long—until they suspend and/or make it clear that they—that their statements aren't real, yeah, I believe they want to have the capacity, the knowledge, in order to make a nuclear weapon. And I know it's in the world's interest to prevent them from doing so. I believe that the Iranian—if Iran had a nuclear weapon, it would be a dangerous threat to world peace.
>
> But this—we got a leader in Iran who has announced that he wants to destroy Israel. So I've told people that if you're interested in avoiding World War III, it seems like you ought to be interested in preventing them from have the knowledge necessary to make a nuclear weapon. I take the threat of Iran with a nuclear weapon very seriously. And we'll continue to work with all nations about the seriousness of this threat. Plus we'll continue working the financial measures that we're in the process of doing. In other words, I think—the whole strategy is, is that at some point in time, leaders or responsible folks inside of Iran may get tired of isolation and say, this isn't worth it. And to me, it's worth the effort to keep the pressure on this government.
>
> And secondly, it's important for the Iranian people to know we harbor no resentment to them. We're disappointed in the Iranian government's actions, as should they be. Inflation is way too high; isolation is causing economic pain. This is a country that has got a much better future, people have got a much better—should have better hope inside Iran than this current government is providing them.
>
> So it's—look, it's a complex issue, no question about it. But my intent is to continue to rally the world to send a focused signal to the Iranian government that we will continue to work to isolate you, in the hopes that at some point in time, somebody else shows up and says it's not worth the isolation.

Later, when it became public that Bush had been advised in August that the Intelligence Community was revising its assessment of Iran's nuclear weapons program, people would ask how he could have taken such a position in October. In fact, the statement may actually reflect that information. Previously, Bush had always warned that Iran could not be allowed to have a nuclear weapon. Now, he was saying that it could not be allowed to have "the *knowledge* necessary to make a nuclear weapon."[25] A purely civilian nuclear energy program would provide knowledge necessary to make a nuclear weapon. The nature of the objection had been adjusted to match the changing facts.

Four days later, on 21 October 2007, Vice President Dick Cheney spoke before the Washington Institute for Near East Policy. His address was a general broadside against Iran reminiscent of his speeches advocating war against Iraq five years earlier.

Across the Middle East, further progress will depend on responsible conduct by regional governments; respect for the sovereignty of neighbors; compliance with international agreements; peaceful words, and peaceful actions. And if you apply all these measures, it becomes immediately clear that the government of Iran falls far short, and is a growing obstacle to peace in the Middle East.

Given the recent appearance by the Iranian President in New York City, no one can fail to understand the nature of the regime this man represents. He has called repeatedly for the destruction of Israel; has spoken of his yearning for a world without the United States. Under their current rulers, the people of Iran live in a climate of fear and intimidation, with secret police, arbitrary detentions, and a hint of violence in the air. In the space of a generation, the regime has solidified its grip on the country and grown ever more arrogant and brutal toward the Iranian people. Journalists are intimidated. Religious minorities are persecuted. A good many dissidents and freedom advocates have been murdered, or have simply disappeared. Visiting scholars who've done nothing wrong have been seized and jailed.

This same regime that approved of hostage-taking in 1979, that attacked Saudi and Kuwaiti shipping in the 1980s, that incited suicide bombings and jihadism in the 1990s and beyond, is now the world's most active state sponsor of terror. As to its next-door neighbor, Iraq, the Iranian government claims to be a friend that supports regional stability. In fact, it is a force for the opposite. As General Petraeus has noted, Iran's Quds Force is trying to set up a "Hezbollah-like force to serve its interests and to fight a proxy war against the Iraqi state and coalition forces in Iraq." At the same time, Iran is "responsible for providing the weapons, the training, the funding and, in some cases, the direction for operations that have indeed killed U.S. soldiers."

Operating largely in the shadows, Iran attempts to hide its hands through the use of militants who target and kill coalition and Iraqi security forces. Iran's real agenda appears to include promoting violence against the coalition. Fearful of a strong, independent, Arab Shia community emerging in Iraq, one that seeks religious guidance not in Qom, Iran, but from traditional sources of Shia authority in Najaf and Karbala [in Iraq], the Iranian regime also aims to keep Iraq in a state of weakness that prevents Baghdad from presenting a threat to Tehran.

Perhaps the greatest strategic threat that Iraq's Shiites face today in consolidating their rightful role in Iraq's new democracy is the subversive activities of the Iranian regime. The Quds Force, a branch of Iran's Islamic Revolutionary Guard Corps, is the defender of the theocracy. The regime has used the Quds Force to provide weapons, money, and training to terrorists and Islamic militant groups abroad, including Hamas; Palestinian Islamic Jihad; militants in the Balkans; the Taliban and other anti-Afghanistan militants; and Hezbollah terrorists trying to destabilize Lebanon's democratic government.

The Iranian regime's efforts to destabilize the Middle East and to gain hegemonic power is a matter of record. And now, of course, we have the inescapable reality of Iran's nuclear program; a program they claim is strictly for energy purposes, but which they have worked hard to conceal; a program carried out in complete defiance of the international community and resolutions of the U.N. Security Council. Iran is pursuing technology that could be used to develop nuclear weapons. The world knows this. The Security Council has twice imposed sanctions on Iran and called on the regime to cease enriching uranium. Yet the regime continues to do so, and continues to practice delay and deception in an obvious attempt to buy time.

Given the nature of Iran's rulers, the declarations of the Iranian President, and the trouble the regime is causing throughout the region—including direct involvement in the killing of Americans—our country and the entire international community cannot stand by as a terror-supporting state fulfills its most aggressive ambitions. (Applause.)

The Iranian regime needs to know that if it stays on its present course, the international community is prepared to impose serious consequences. The United States joins other nations in sending a clear message: We will not allow Iran to have a nuclear weapon. (Applause.)

The irresponsible conduct of the ruling elite in Tehran is a tragedy for all Iranians. The regime has passed up numerous opportunities to be a positive force in the Middle East. For more than a generation, it had only isolated a great nation, suppressed a great people, and subjected them to economic hardship that gets worse every year. The citizens of Iran deserve none of this. They are the proud heirs of a culture of learning, humanity and beauty that reaches back many centuries. Iranian civilization has produced shining achievements, from the Persian Book of Kings, to the poetry of Rumi and Khayyam, to celebrated achievements in astronomy and mathematics, to art and music admired on every continent. The Iran of today—a nation of 70 million, a majority of them under the age of 30—is a place of unlimited potential. And the Iranian people have every right to be free from oppression, from economic deprivation, and tyranny in their own country.

The spirit of freedom is stirring in Iran. The voices of change and peaceful dissent will not be silent. We can expect to hear more from the courageous reformers, the bloggers, and the advocates of rights for women and ethnic and religious minorities, because these men and women are more loyal to their country than to the regime. Despite the regime's anti-American propaganda, the Iranian people can know that America respects them, cares about their troubles, and stands firmly on the side of liberty, human dignity and individual rights. America looks forward to the day when Iranians reclaim their destiny; the day that our two countries, as free and democratic nations, can be the closest of friends.

The new National Intelligence Estimate on Iran was finally issued in November. Then, on 3 December 2007, the NIE's "Key Judgments" were released to the public.

National Intelligence Estimate
Iran: Nuclear Intentions and Capabilities
Scope Note

This National Intelligence Estimate (NIE) assesses the status of Iran's nuclear program, and the program's outlook over the next 10 years. This time frame is more appropriate for estimating capabilities than intentions and foreign reactions, which are more difficult to estimate over a decade. In presenting the Intelligence Community's assessment of Iranian nuclear intentions and capabilities, the NIE thoroughly reviews all available information on these questions, examines the range of reasonable scenarios consistent with this information, and describes the key factors we judge would drive or impede nuclear progress in Iran. This NIE is an extensive reexamination of the issues in the May 2005 assessment.

This Estimate focuses on the following key questions:

- o   What are Iran's intentions toward developing nuclear weapons?
- o   What domestic factors affect Iran's decision-making on whether to develop nuclear weapons?

- ○ What external factors affect Iran's decision-making on whether to develop nuclear weapons?
- ○ What is the range of potential Iranian actions concerning the development of nuclear weapons, and the decisive factors that would lead Iran to choose one course of action over another?
- ○ What is Iran's current and projected capability to develop nuclear weapons? What are our key assumptions, and Iran's key chokepoints/vulnerabilities?

This NIE does *not* assume that Iran intends to acquire nuclear weapons. Rather, it examines the intelligence to assess Iran's capability and intent (or lack thereof) to acquire nuclear weapons, taking full account of Iran's dual-use uranium fuel cycle and those nuclear activities that are at least partly civil in nature.

This Estimate does assume that the strategic goals and basic structure of Iran's senior leadership and government will remain similar to those that have endured since the death of Ayatollah Khomeini in 1989. We acknowledge the potential for these to change during the time frame of the Estimate, but are unable to confidently predict such changes or their implications. This Estimate does not assess how Iran may conduct future negotiations with the West on the nuclear issue.

This Estimate incorporates intelligence reporting available as of 31 October 2007.

Key Judgments

A. A. We judge with high confidence that in fall 2003, Tehran halted its nuclear weapons program*; we also assess with moderate-to-high confidence that Tehran at a minimum is keeping open the option to develop nuclear weapons. We judge with high confidence that the halt, and Tehran's announcement of its decision to suspend its declared uranium enrichment program and sign an Additional Protocol to its Nuclear Nonproliferation Treaty Safeguards Agreement, was directed primarily in response to increasing international scrutiny and pressure resulting from exposure of Iran's previously undeclared nuclear work.

- ○ We assess with high confidence that until fall 2003, Iranian military entities were working under government direction to develop nuclear weapons.
- ○ We judge with high confidence that the halt lasted at least several years. (Because of intelligence gaps discussed elsewhere in this Estimate, however, DOE and the NIC assess with only moderate confidence that the halt to those activities represents a halt to Iran's entire nuclear weapons program.)[26]
- ○ We assess with moderate confidence Tehran had not restarted its nuclear weapons program as of mid-2007, but we do not know whether it currently intends to develop nuclear weapons.
- ○ We continue to assess with moderate-to-high confidence that Iran does not currently have a nuclear weapon.
- ○ Tehran's decision to halt its nuclear weapons program suggests it is less determined to develop nuclear weapons than we have been judging since 2005. Our assessment that the program probably was halted primarily in response to international pressure suggests Iran may be more vulnerable to influence on the issue than we judged previously.

---

*For the purposes of this Estimate, by "nuclear weapons program" we mean Iran's nuclear weapon design and weaponization work and covert uranium conversion-related and uranium enrichment-related work; we do not mean Iran's declared civil work related to uranium conversion and enrichment. [Note in original.]

B. We continue to assess with low confidence that Iran probably has imported at least some weapons-usable fissile material, but still judge with moderate-to-high confidence it has not obtained enough for a nuclear weapon. We cannot rule out that Iran has acquired from abroad—or will acquire in the future—a nuclear weapon or enough fissile material for a weapon. Barring such acquisitions, if Iran wants to have nuclear weapons it would need to produce sufficient amounts of fissile material indigenously—which we judge with high confidence it has not yet done.

C. We assess centrifuge enrichment is how Iran probably could first produce enough fissile material for a weapon, if it decides to do so. Iran resumed its declared centrifuge enrichment activities in January 2006, despite the continued halt in the nuclear weapons program. Iran made significant progress in 2007 installing centrifuges in Natanz, but we judge with moderate confidence it still faces significant technical problems operating them.

   o We judge with moderate confidence that the earliest possible date Iran would be technically capable of producing enough HEU [highly enriched uranium] for a weapon is late 2009, but that this is very unlikely.

   o We judge with moderate confidence Iran probably would be technically capable of producing enough HEU for a weapon sometime during the 2010–2015 time frame. (INR[27] judges Iran is unlikely to achieve this capability before 2013 because of foreseeable technical and programmatic problems.) All agencies recognize the possibility that this capability may not be attained until *after* 2015.

D. Iranian entities are continuing to develop a range of technical capabilities that could be applied to producing nuclear weapons, if a decision is made to do so. For example, Iran's civilian uranium enrichment program is continuing. We also assess with high confidence that since fall 2003, Iran has been conducting research and development projects with commercial and conventional military applications—some of which would also be of limited use for nuclear weapons.

E. We do not have sufficient intelligence to judge confidently whether Tehran is willing to maintain the halt of its nuclear weapons program indefinitely while it weighs its options, or whether it will or already has set specific deadlines that will prompt it to restart the program.

   o Our assessment that Iran halted the program in 2003 primarily in response to international pressure indicates Tehran's decisions are guided by a cost-benefit approach rather than a rush to a weapon irrespective of the political, economic, and military costs. This, in turn, suggests that some combination of threats of intensified international scrutiny and pressures, along with opportunities for Iran to achieve its security, prestige, and goals for regional influence in other ways, might—if perceived by Iran's leaders as credible—prompt Tehran to extend the current halt to its nuclear weapons program. It is difficult to specify what such a combination might be.

   o We assess with moderate confidence that convincing the Iranian leadership to forgo the eventual development of nuclear weapons will be difficult given the linkage many within the leadership probably see between nuclear weapons development and Iran's key national security and foreign policy objectives, and given Iran's considerable effort from at least the late 1980s to 2003 to develop such weapons. In our judgment, only an Iranian political decision to abandon a nuclear weapons objective would plausibly keep Iran from eventually producing nuclear weapons—and such a decision is inherently reversible.

F. We assess with moderate confidence that Iran probably would use covert facilities—rather than its declared nuclear sites—for the production of highly enriched uranium for a weapon. A growing amount of intelligence indicates Iran was engaged in covert uranium conversion and uranium enrichment activity, but we judge that these efforts probably were halted in response to the fall 2003 halt, and that these efforts probably had not been restarted through at least mid-2007.

G. We judge with high confidence that Iran will not be technically capable of producing and reprocessing enough plutonium for a weapon before about 2015.

H. We assess with high confidence that Iran has the scientific, technical, and industrial capacity eventually to produce nuclear weapons if it decides to do so.

Key Differences between the Key Judgments of This Estimate on Iran's Nuclear Program and the May 2005 Assessment

2005 IC Estimate	2007 National Intelligence Estimate
Assess with high confidence that Iran currently is determined to develop nuclear weapons despite its international obligations and international pressure, but we do not assess that Iran is immovable.	Judge with high confidence that in fall 2003, Tehran halted its nuclear weapons program. Judge with high confidence that the halt lasted at least several years. (DOE and the NIC have moderate confidence that the halt to those activities represents a halt to Iran's entire nuclear weapons program.) Assess with moderate confidence Tehran has not restarted its nuclear weapons program as of mid-2007, but we do not know whether it currently intends to develop nuclear weapons. Judge with high confidence that the halt was directed primarily in response to increasing international scrutiny and pressure resulting from exposure of Iran's previously undeclared nuclear work. Assess with moderate-to-high confidence that Tehran at a minimum is keeping open the option to develop nuclear weapons.
We have moderate confidence in projecting when Iran is likely to make a nuclear weapon; we assess that it is unlikely before early-to-mid next decade.	We judge with moderate confidence that the earliest possible date Iran would be technically capable of producing enough highly enriched uranium (HEU) for a weapon is late 2009, but that this is very unlikely. We judge with moderate confidence Iran probably would be technically capable of producing enough HEU for a weapon sometime during the 2010–2015 time frame. (INR judges that Iran is unlikely to achieve this capability before 2013 because of foreseeable technical and programmatic problems.)
Iran could produce enough fissile material for a weapon by the end of the decade if it were to make more rapid and successful progress than we have seen to date.	We judge with moderate confidence that the earliest possible date Iran would be technically capable of producing enough highly enriched uranium (HEU) for a weapon is late 2009, but that this is very unlikely.

One question that rose immediately was why the Intelligence Community released the "Key Judgments" at all. As recently as 13 November 2007, Director of National Intelligence Mike McConnell had told reporters that he would not release an unclassified version of the NIE on Iran requested by Congress.[28] In any event, public release was an extremely rare occurrence. Many commentators quickly assumed that the CIA feared the intelligence would be distorted for partisan purposes if not made immediately clear. On the day of the NIE's release, McConnell's principal deputy issued a statement on the decision.

December 3, 2007

Statement by the Principal Deputy Director of National Intelligence Dr. Donald M. Kerr

The Office of the Director of National Intelligence, National Intelligence Council prepared a National Intelligence Estimate (NIE) on Iran's nuclear program titled, *Iran: Nuclear Intentions and Capabilities.* NIEs are generated to help U.S. civilian and military decision-makers develop policies to protect national security interests.

The decision to release unclassified conclusions from any NIE is based upon weighing the importance of the information to open discussions about our national security against the necessity to protect classified information and the sources and methods used to collect intelligence. It is also important to ensure that the unclassified judgments accurately reflect the broad strategic framework the NIE is assessing.

The decision to release an unclassified version of the Key Judgments of this NIE was made when it was determined that doing so was in the interest of our nation's security. The Intelligence Community is on the record publicly with numerous statements based on our 2005 assessment on Iran. Since our understanding of Iran's capabilities has changed, we felt it was important to release this information to ensure that an accurate presentation is available. While the decision to release the declassified Key Judgments was coordinated with senior policy makers, the IC took responsibility for what portions of the NIE Key Judgments were to be declassified.

These unclassified Key Judgments are consistent with the findings of this National Intelligence Estimate.

The reference to senior policy makers was noteworthy. The document could not have been released without the concurrence of the president, yet the sudden reversal of the assessment of the Iranian nuclear threat appeared to undermine the president's policy. Moreover, the administration went out of its way to downplay the relevance of the change and to assert that the policy would continue as before. On the same day as the release, National Security Adviser Stephen Hadley issued the following statement:

Today's National Intelligence Estimate offers some positive news. It confirms that we were right to be worried about Iran seeking to develop nuclear weapons. It tells us that we have made progress in trying to ensure that this does not happen. But the intelligence also tells us that the risk of Iran acquiring a nuclear weapon remains a very serious problem. The estimate offers grounds for hope that the problem can be solved diplomatically—without the use of force—as the Administration has been trying to do. And it suggests that the President has the right strategy: intensified international pressure along with a willingness to negotiate a solution that serves Iranian interests while ensuring that the world will never have to face a nuclear armed Iran. The bottom line is this: for that strategy to succeed, the international community has to turn up the pressure on Iran—with diplomatic isolation, United Nations sanctions, and with other financial pressure—and Iran has to decide it wants to negotiate a solution.

At a press conference on 4 December 2007, President Bush also depicted the new assessment as a victory for current policy.

> **Q:** Mr. President, a new intelligence report says that Iran halted its nuclear weapons program four years ago, and that it remains frozen. Are you still convinced that Iran is trying to build a nuclear bomb? And do the new findings take the military option that you've talked about off the table?
>
> **THE PRESIDENT:** Here's what we know. We know that they're still trying to learn how to enrich uranium. We know that enriching uranium is an important step in a country that wants to develop a weapon. We know they had a program. We know the program is halted.
>
> I think it is very important for the international community to recognize the fact that if Iran were to develop the knowledge that they could transfer to a clandestine program it would create a danger for the world. And so I view this report as a warning signal that they had the program, they halted the program. And the reason why it's a warning signal is that they could restart it. And the thing that would make a restarted program effective and dangerous is the ability to enrich uranium, the knowledge of which could be passed on to a hidden program.
>
> And so it's a—to me, the NIE provides an opportunity for us to rally the international community—continue to rally the community to pressure the Iranian regime to suspend its program.
>
> You know, the NIE also said that such pressure was effective, and that's what our government has been explaining to other partners in keeping the international pressure on Iran. The best diplomacy, effective diplomacy, is one of which all options are on the table.

The Intelligence Community presented the new assessment as an example of how it had successfully learned the lessons of Iraq. They had carefully assessed the credibility of the new evidence, comprehensively reexamined past evidence, and applied alternative analysis to ferret out any weaknesses in the argument. The situation, however, was still not unambiguous, as the Intelligence Community would admit. A number of commentators—not all of them from the same end of the political spectrum—noted that Iran could still use its civilian nuclear program to develop the technology and infrastructure necessary to build nuclear weapons at a later date, much as the Shah had intended to do; that some of the technology already being developed had little purpose in a purely civilian program; and that there are legitimate concerns about Iran apart from nuclear weapons.[29] For their part, Senate Republicans demanded an investigation of the new assessment and the intelligence that went into it.[30]

In terms of visible policy changes, what some have termed the most dramatic intelligence turnaround on record appeared to have remarkably little impact. The Bush administration soon succeeded in eliciting statements of support for further UN sanctions against Iran from the new conservative leaders of France and Germany.[31] Israel, while agreeing that Iran ceased its nuclear weapons program in 2003, asserted that it resumed development in 2005.[32] Russia remained opposed to further sanctions, arguing as before that there was no evidence of an active arms program in Iran. Two weeks later, Russia began delivering eighty tons of enriched uranium to fuel the nuclear power plant at Bushehr (under the supervision of the IAEA), which was finally nearing completion.[33] Indeed, the only country whose overt policy was immediately affected by the NIE was China, which had appeared on the verge of supporting new sanctions but now backed away.[34]

Many commentators have argued that Hadley overstated the degree to which the United States had engaged in diplomacy. They note that the Europeans engaged in diplomacy, while the United States at best offered grudging support but generally opposed any proposal that could be interpreted as a concession to Iran. That argument probably misses the point insofar as the Bush administration has never followed the conventional concept of diplomacy.

According to the traditional realist school, one can negotiate with adversaries and even regard them as potential future allies. That practice declined, but did not disappear, in the ideologically driven conflicts of the twentieth century. For the Bush administration, however, certain adversaries are designated as contemptible and beyond redemption. (U.S. policy toward Cuba is a precedent in this regard.) One may negotiate with them on occasion as long as those negotiations constitute a demand for concessions without reciprocation, for to reciprocate would be to "reward bad behavior" even if the adversary is being cooperative at the moment. True peace can only be assured through "regime change" that makes the adversary more like America. In such situations, diplomacy does not mean negotiating with the adversary but negotiating with allies and others to isolate, sanction, and pressure the adversary.

This concept is not traditional diplomacy, but on the other hand, neither is it bombing. Note that, in Hadley's words, the NIE showed that the Iran problem could be solved "without the use of force." Note, too, that indirect evidence such as the Hersh article of April 2006 and the Cheney speech of October 2007 suggested that a faction within the administration may have been pressing for a preventive strike against Iran. It is possible—but not provable at this early date (December 2007)—that the release of the Iran estimate had its greatest impact behind the scenes. If a faction was pressing for an attack, the public knowledge that Iran was not actively pursuing a nuclear weapon at the moment seriously undermined the argument that the urgency of the situation outweighed any need for caution.[35]

A pro-war faction would already have been weakened by the departure in 2005 and 2006 of several key players who had been instrumental in promoting the Iraq War. These included Secretary Donald Rumsfeld, Deputy Secretary Paul Wolfowitz, and Under Secretary Douglas Feith, all of the Defense Department, and Chief of Staff I. Lewis "Scooter" Libby of the Office of the Vice President. To suggest an opposing faction that might have favored the release would be the purest speculation—but possibilities include the CIA, which was blamed by some for the rush to war in Iraq; the Joint Chiefs of Staff, who were sure to be concerned about the already overstretched condition of the armed forces; and the new Secretary of Defense, Robert M. Gates, who happened to be a former Director of Central Intelligence and was on the record as advocating a new approach to Iran.[36]

NOTES

1. *Hizballah* is Arabic for "Party of God."
2. *Hamas* is the Arabic word for "zeal," but in this case it serves as an acronym for Harakat al-Muqawama al-Islamiya (Islamic Resistance Movement).

3. On the Iranian government, see "Country Profile: Iran" (March 2006), by the Federal Research Service of the Library of Congress, http://lcweb2.loc.gov/frd/cs/profiles/ Iran.pdf, and "Background Note: Iran" at the State Department Web site, http://www. state.gov/r/pa/ei/bgn/5314.htm.

4. On Khamenei's balancing, see Ray Takeyh, "Time for Détente with Iran," *Foreign Affairs* 86:2 (March/April 2007).

5. Vali Nasr and Ray Takeyh, "The Costs of Containing Iran," *Foreign Affairs* 87:1 (January/February 2008); Kenneth M. Pollack, "Bringing Iran to the Bargaining Table," *Current History* 105:694 (November 2006).

6. Colin Dueck and Ray Takeyh, "Iran's Nuclear Challenge," *Political Science Quarterly* 122:2 (Summer 2007): 189–192.

7. CRS Report RS21592, *Iran's Nuclear Program: Recent Developments,* by Sharon Squassoni (Washington, D.C.: Congressional Research Service, Updated 6 September 2006); Joseph Cirincione, "The Clock's Ticking: Stopping Iran before It's Too Late," *Arms Control Today* 36:9 (November 2006):17–21.

8. Hillary Mann, "U.S. Diplomacy with Iran: The Limits of Tactical Engagement," and James Dobbins, "Negotiating with Iran," both delivered on 7 November 2007 as testimony before the Subcommittee on National Security and Foreign Affairs of the House Committee on Oversight and Government Reform. They are available at http://nationalsecurity.oversight.house.gov.

9. George Tenet, with Bill Harlow, *At the Center of the Storm: My Years at the CIA* (New York: HarperCollins, 2007): 311–314.

10. Alireza Jafarzadeh, *The Iran Threat: President Ahmadinejad and the Coming Nuclear Crisis* (New York: Palgrave Macmillan, 2007). Jafarzadeh is a former spokesman for the National Council of Resistance of Iran.

11. Mann, "U.S. Diplomacy with Iran;" John H. Richardson, "The Secret History of the Impending War with Iran that the White House Doesn't Want You to Know," *Esquire* 168:5 (November 2007).

12. Takeyh, "Time for Détente with Iran."

13. MRBM stands for medium-range ballistic missile; SRBM stands for short-range ballistic missile.

14. William J. Broad and David E. Sanger, "Relying on Computer, U.S. Seeks to Prove Iran's Nuclear Aims," *New York Times* (13 November 2005); William J. Broad and David E. Sanger, "How Did a 2005 Estimate Go Awry?" *New York Times* (4 December 2007).

15. SCUD is the code name for a missile based on a Soviet design.

16. Dafna Linzer, "Iran Is Judged 10 Years From Nuclear Bomb," *Washington Post* (2 August 2005); Steven R. Weisman and Douglas Jehl, "Estimate Revised on When Iran Could Make Nuclear Bomb," *New York Times* (3 August 2005).

17. Ethan Bronner, "Just How Far Did They Go, Those Words against Israel?" *New York Times* (11 June 2006).

18. "President's FY 2007 International Affairs Budget Request," http://state.gov/ secretary/rm/2006/61262.htm.

19. Seymour M. Hersh, "The Iran Plans," *New Yorker* (16 April 2006).

20. This was the same Seymour Hersh who had vexed William Colby regarding the "Family Jewels" file thirty years earlier.

21. Fatah is the most prominent member of the Palestine Liberation Organization (PLO), a coalition formed in the 1960s to unite several secular, leftist parties dedicated to the creation of a Palestinian state. Fatah had only recently reconciled itself to the continued existence of Israel and in the 1990s negotiated the establishment of the Palestinian Authority in the Israeli occupied territories (the West Bank and the Gaza Strip) as an interim stage toward independence. It resented the relatively recent rise of anti-Israeli Islamist movements, which continued to call for the elimination of Israel.

22. The "Quartet" refers to representatives of the United States, the Russian Federation, the European Union, and the United Nations assigned to foster a Middle Eastern peace settlement.

23. *The Iraq Group Report*, James A. Baker III and Lee H. Hamilton, co-chairs (New York: Vintage Press, 2006).

24. Mark Mazzetti, "With New Data, U.S. Revises Its View of Iran," *New York Times* (5 December 2007); Greg Millier, "Anatomy of an About-Face on Iran," *Los Angeles Times* (5 December 2007); Joby Warrick and Walter Pincus, "Lessons of Iraq Aided Intelligence on Iran," *Washington Post* (5 December 2007); David E. Sanger and Steven Lee Myers, "Details in Military Notes Led to Shift on Iran, U.S. Says," *New York Times* (6 December 2007).

25. See the interview with former CIA analyst Flynt Leverett in Mark Follman, "An Iran Bombshell for Bush," *Salon* (5 December 2007), http://www.salon.com/news/feature/2007/12/05/iran_nie/.

26. DOE stands for Department of Energy; NIC stands for National Intelligence Council.

27. INR stands for State Department Bureau of Intelligence and Research.

28. "Remarks and Q&A by the Director of National Intelligence, Mr. Mike McConnell," 6–7, http://www.odni.gov/speeches/20071113_speech.pdf.

29. John R. Bolton, "The Flaws in the Iran Report," *Washington Post* (6 December 2007); Valerie Lincy and Gary Milhollin, "In Iran We Trust?" *New York Times* (6 December 2007).

30. Robin Wright and Glenn Kessler, "Review of Iran Intelligence to Be Sought," *Washington Post* (7 December 2007).

31. Katrin Bennhold, "Despite Report, France and Germany Keep Pressure on Iran," *New York Times* (7 December 2007).

32. Steven Erlanger, "Israelis Brief Top U.S. Official on Iran," *New York Times* (11 December 2007).

33. Helene Cooper, "Iran Receives Nuclear Fuel in Blow to U.S.," *New York Times* (18 December 2007). Russia had been stalling the delivery for several months.

34. Steven Lee Myers and Helene Cooper, "Bush Insists Iran Remains a Threat Despite Arms Data," *New York Times* (5 December 2007).

35. See Robert Baer, "Commentary: Was Bush Behind the Iran Report?" *Time* (4 December 2007), http://www.time.com/time/world/article/0,8599,1690696,00.html.

36. Gates had been a member of the Iraq Study Group, although he left the group to become Secretary of Defense shortly before its final report was published. Two years earlier, he had been cochair of a Council on Foreign Relations task force that called for selective engagement with Iran. See Council on Foreign Relations Independent Task Force, *Iran: Time for a New Approach*, Zbigniew Brzezinski and Robert M. Gates, co-chairs (New York: Council on Foreign Relations, July 2004).

---- *Chapter 19* ----

Concluding Remarks

In conclusion, let us consider some points regarding the range of CIA activities. These will touch upon intelligence, covert operations, and the general role of secrecy.

INTELLIGENCE

The 9/11 Commission proposed a series of intelligence reforms that led to the Intelligence Reform and Terrorism Prevention Act of 2004. The key organizational change was the creation of the post of Director of National Intelligence, an official who would coordinate and take responsibility for the entire intelligence community but would not run any portion of it directly. The desired outcomes, based on the commission's analysis of the sources of surprise on 9/11, were greater coherence of effort and improved information sharing within the intelligence community.

Critics have complained that the real shortcomings of the intelligence community had little to do with coordination and information sharing and would not be rectified with an additional layer of bureaucracy.[1] They contended that the real needs were simpler but harder to bring about by decree. The CIA and the rest of the Intelligence Community, after 9/11 as before, required more human intelligence sources, better-quality analysis, and a more adaptive institutional culture.[2] The existing situation had been worsened by a 22 percent reduction in intelligence staffing in the years following the end of the Cold War.[3]

Both positions have their strengths but tend to overlook the nature of the task itself. There is a fundamental problem at the heart of intelligence activities. What we want most of all from intelligence is effective warning of an attack to prevent another Pearl Harbor or 9/11. Yet that is arguably where the performance of intelligence agencies is weakest and probably always will be. This is not the fault of any particular agency, organizational structure, or director. It is inherent in the nature of the task. While certain specific practices or organizational structures may be more effective than others, no amount of reforms or investigative committee recommendations will make the job easy or success likely. Nevertheless, trying to understand the outside world will always produce better results than not trying, even if the outcome cannot be perfect.

Predicting an attack requires putting the clues together in one place. This is obvious, and it forms the basic rationale for information-sharing reforms. The problem is that clues are not necessarily recognizable as clues until after the fact.[4] Prior to that, clues are drops dispersed in a sea of irrelevant information. Distinguishing "signals" from "noise" is an impossible task until one knows that one is looking for something and what that something is. Clues will grow increasingly identifiable in the course of a mounting crisis or over the long run in a hostile, long-term, bilateral relationship. If an attack is truly unexpected, however, one can hardly expect analysts to know what to look for.

Predicting an attack also requires assessing the intentions of others. That, in turn, may require access to the mental activities of a relatively few individuals. Intentions are difficult to decipher and easy to conceal, at times even from one's own side, especially in dictatorial regimes. Intentions are also notoriously subject to change.

Moreover, the attacker always has advantages over the intended target. The plotter, for instance, knows that there is a plan and what that operation consists of. The plotter can devise plans specifically to take advantage of weaknesses in an adversary's defenses or choose a target toward which the adversary has devoted the least attention. The defender, on the other hand, must operate in an environment in which it does not know the intended target, the method, the timing, the perpetrator ... or even whether a threat actually exists, even though all of these things seem obvious after the fact.

The difficulty of knowing that one is under a threat is often overlooked. Sometimes attacks come as a surprise; at other times attacks are predicted but never occur. It is always easy to assert that a country has avoided attack because of its deterrent measures—as the United States did throughout the Cold War and again after 9/11—but it is much more difficult to prove whether an adversary was actually deterred, failed to find an opportunity, or never actually intended to attack. As much as officials like to say that they "know" an attack is being planned—and they may be right—they usually have no way of knowing any such thing.

In the case of 9/11, the CIA was aware that al-Qa'ida existed and posed some level of threat, and was actively watching the group. The agency also had a good idea that an attack was coming. Nonetheless, the most that analysts knew in advance of the event—based on the active monitoring of terrorist communications—was that there might be an attack against U.S. interests coming at some time in the not-too-distant future by someone from some direction by some means against some target possibly in the United States or perhaps elsewhere. Consequently, these analysts had a great deal of difficulty getting busy officials to take them seriously. Such a vague situation makes it extremely hard to prepare effectively, but that is more likely to be the case than otherwise. Moreover, when warnings are not followed by an immediate attack, or at least an immediate proof of a threat, the result can be "receptivity fatigue" (or the "Crying Wolf" syndrome) on the part of policy makers.[5]

Compared with the deciphering of intentions, it is far easier to keep track of military capabilities, such as missiles or large-scale troop concentrations, especially with modern satellite surveillance technology. In some instances, this will make the prediction of an imminent conventional military attack much easier. Nevertheless, assessing military capabilities presents problems of another sort. For one thing, it may still be hard to assess quality even when you know quantity. More important, however, is the fact that the purpose cannot always be derived from the capability. To take an example from the Iraq War, some analysts argued that Iraq's aluminum tubes (incorrectly believed to be intended for centrifuges to enrich uranium) could not have been intended for use as simple rocket bodies (which were permitted to the Iraqi military) because the specifications were much more precise than required for that purpose. The explanation turned out to be simple, if unexpected: The Iraqis had ordered rocket bodies with much more precise specifications than they needed. Thus, the intended purpose of a given set of capabilities may not be what analysts assume it to be. With capabilities, the facts on the ground may seem clear, but the conclusions are still subject to interpretation.

The capabilities necessary for a terrorist attack are, of course, far smaller and more difficult to detect than those required for an invasion. Yet look at the problems presented by a large-scale invasion. In 1950, even without satellites, the United States had a fairly good idea of the size of the Chinese army and knew more or less where it was deployed in relation to North Korea. Nonetheless, a misinterpretation of Chinese intentions—based on a U.S. assumption of what the global consequences of a Chinese intervention would be—meant that U.S. intelligence not only failed to predict the Chinese entry into the Korean War but also failed for some time to recognize that it had already happened.

As many observers point out, gathering information about intentions requires human intelligence, or HUMINT. Human intelligence, however, carries its own special set of problems. The Iraq war offers several examples of the potential shortcomings of human intelligence. One human source falsely told Egyptian interrogators that Iraq had trained al-Qa'ida operatives in weapons use, but evidently at that point he was prepared to say anything to stop the torture. Another source told the Germans that Iraq had mobile germ-warfare factories, but he was lying in an effort to gain asylum in Germany. Unnamed sources linked the terrorist group Ansar al-Islam to Saddam Hussein. All of these sources recanted after the invasion, but by then it was too late.

Another potential problem is the distortion of information that is common in dictatorial regimes. Even if the CIA had been able to find a well-placed source within the Iraqi regime, it turned out that many high-ranking Iraqi officials did not know what Iraqi military capabilities—or Saddam Hussein's intentions—really were. Some officials assumed that Iraq did have weapons of mass destruction, in part because the Americans seemed so sure of it, but thought that Hussein had simply not deemed them worthy of informing them.[6]

The lesson, however, is not to avoid human intelligence sources but to multiply them. Human intelligence requires multiple sourcing and cross-verification. This is especially the case when the informant or informants are not well known, even though, historically, some of the most dramatic intelligence breakthroughs have involved strangers walking into embassies and offering secrets.[7] It may also require eliminating prohibitions against dealing with "unsavory" characters.[8] When multiple sourcing (including "walk-ins") is not possible, as was the case regarding several aspects of Iraq, caution should prevail.

The intelligence failure in the case of Iraq's weapons of mass destruction is more difficult to explain. The task in this case should have been easier than that of predicting an attack. The CIA and other intelligence agencies knew what the target country was, knew that it was weapons they were looking for, knew what kind of weapons they were looking for, and thought they had a pretty good idea of where the weapons were. That is quite a bit. However, they were confounded by their lack of access on the ground (and, unfortunately, the places you want to know about most of all are likely to be the ones to which you cannot get ready access) and by the fact that they thought they knew more than they did. Analysts, for example, thought they could reliably extrapolate from past Iraqi behavior to explain present behavior and predict future behavior. Often, in fact, this can be done usefully, but as a basis for war it is rather thin. Ironically, the same logic led many CIA critics to assume the agency was responsible for the 1973 coup d'état in Chile because the CIA knew about its role in the failed attempt of 1970.

As in the case of the missile gap of the 1950s, U.S. intelligence also assumed that the Iraqi adversaries would produce as many arms as it was capable of making once inspectors were gone and that they would do so efficiently (despite the fact that neither the Soviet Union nor Iraq was particularly known for efficiency). In both cases the adversary had simply decided not to do it. Saddam Hussein compounded the difficulty by trying to convince the Iranians, the Israelis, and his own population that he was not defenseless at the same that he was trying to convince the United States that he had disarmed as promised. The general history of the case and the ongoing atmosphere encouraged analysts and policy makers alike to interpret ambiguous evidence as confirming worst-case scenarios.

It is worth noting in this regard that the various investigative reports that followed the Iraq War generally concluded that politicians did not overtly pressure analysts to produce a particular interpretation in favor of war. In fact, the CIA did not endorse all of the Bush administration's positions. The CIA incorrectly believed that Iraq had chemical and biological weapons programs, but it was very reluctant to draw links between Iraq and al-Qa'ida (as President Bush publicly did), much less to tie Iraq directly to the 9/11 attacks (as Vice President Cheney did, although Bush did not). Regarding the imminence of a nuclear threat, CIA analysts incorrectly believed that Iraq had a nuclear development program but did not expect it to produce results for several years. Rather than press for different results (or, for all we know, after pressing unsuccessfully), Cheney, in his speech of August 2002, suggested that the threat was imminent, openly questioned the value of intelligence on this one issue, and highlighted the underestimates made prior to the war of 1991. Bush did something quite similar in Cincinnati two months later. In addition, Bush and Condoleezza Rice both alluded to the desirability of avoiding "mushroom clouds" without any reference to intelligence whatsoever. As general advice, this hardly requires an intelligence estimate, but again it is not much of a basis for war.

On the other hand, it has been noted that the 2002 National Intelligence Estimate on Iraq's weapons of mass destruction was quite different from the more modest and more accurate analyses produced by the CIA, presumably using the same methods, in the years immediately preceding the Iraq invasion. Some observers have seen this as indirect evidence that the administration began pressing for particular results at that point.[9]

One can also argue that the analysis put out by the CIA—minus the public embellishments added by policy makers—did not necessarily justify war. President Bush has frequently argued that many foreign intelligence services basically agreed with the analysis. He fails to mention that relatively few of those countries concluded that war was a necessary response. Paul Pillar, the National Intelligence Officer for the Middle East from 2000 to 2005, has admitted that there were problems with the intelligence, but he argues that the administration did not use intelligence in its decision making but rather misused it in public justifications for decisions already made.[10]

Pillar's position is supported by the fact that certain key members of the administration were making essentially the same arguments in the 1990s, when they were out of office and presumably had no access to intelligence. In addition, civilian leaders in the Pentagon established an amateur intelligence office to find evidence to support their views when the CIA failed to do so. Clearly, at least some minds were already made up. Nevertheless, much of the intelligence was wrong, and that must have assisted the initial pro-war faction in convincing others within the administration. Moreover, the CIA's concern for the truth apparently did not lead it to reexamine its conclusions in view of new evidence being gathered by international weapons inspectors after November 2002.[11] This may have been because analysts (or managers) assumed that new evidence would not change their conclusions, because they assumed that new conclusions would not change the president's decision to go to war, or because of some combination of the two. Still, if it is true, a failure to pursue the fact that inspectors were not finding weapons seems difficult to justify.

It is worth noting that the CIA did a better job when it came to predicting the possibility of a chaotic postwar situation in Iraq. This is ironic because this was by its nature an essentially speculative task. It was based not on "hard facts" but on a general understanding of Iraqi history, society, and politics and the application of a few social science concepts and realpolitik assumptions. Perhaps that is the reason that it had so little impact on decision makers. It is also worth noting, however, that the administration had not requested the assessment. According to Pillar, administration officials asked constantly for proof of Iraqi links to al-Qa'ida but never requested an overall assessment of Iraq until a year into the war. Congress had requested the 2002 NIE on weapons of mass destruction, and the CIA had produced the assessment on postwar Iraq on its own initiative.[12]

Policy makers often have great demands and great expectations of intelligence. When those expectations are not fulfilled, this can lead to equally great disillusionment, fault-finding, and endless demands for organizational reforms that will fix the problem. Yet organizational restructuring and admonitions to "connect the dots" will never make the unknowable known. If the surprise attacks of 9/11 resulted from a failure to connect the "dots," then the faulty intelligence regarding Iraq was the consequence of connecting dots that were never meant to be connected. In essence, this problem cannot be fixed. Conclusions and predictions will always be more modest, more hedged, and more conditioned than people wish. As Carl von Clausewitz observed 200 years ago, "Many intelligence reports in war are contradictory; even more are false, and most are uncertain."[13] Two centuries of technological change have not fundamentally changed the balance; it has merely increased the flow.

Policy makers are never obliged to follow the recommendations of intelligence agencies. Such agencies are not even supposed to make recommendations. Intelligence is supposed to be unsullied by policy advocacy. It is merely one of the inputs available for policy makers to consider. That is why the CIA was established as a separate entity, set apart from the policy-making institutions of the government. Nevertheless, it would be naive to think that intelligence agency officials never have an impact on policy. Issues can be framed and options can be structured to favor one choice over another. The publication of part of the Iran estimate of 2007 may have eliminated preventive military action as a viable option in regard to that country—a major policy impact, indeed—although we shall have to wait for the details of the internal debates to emerge before we really know.

Even in normal situations, the intelligence function can be an important one. Without it, policy could well depend on the assumptions, "rules of thumb," and "gut feelings" of politicians even more than it does already. If done properly, intelligence can highlight possibilities, draw attention to alternatives, and discredit unlikely or harmful contingencies. However, intelligence will never eliminate all surprises, and it will rarely if ever form a sound foundation for preventive war. Policy makers should learn to accept both the usefulness and the shortcomings of intelligence.

COVERT OPERATIONS

Covert action is a separate function from intelligence gathering and analysis. It has, nevertheless, been an official function of the CIA since the secret National Security Council directive NSC 10/2 of 1948. It accounted for many of the controversies that surrounded the agency in the 1970s because of the moral implications of activities such as overthrowing governments, clandestine warfare, or assassination.* Moreover, they do not seem to succeed very often. Note the CIA's efforts at political assassination (which would seem to be an easy task, at least in a technical sense), the attempted coup in Chile in 1970, the paramilitary operations in Cuba in the early 1960s, or the effort to induce Iran to secure the release of hostages in Lebanon.

According to advocates, covert operations are the necessary "middle option." They are the alternative between "doing nothing" and "sending in the marines," as if no issue had ever been resolved any other way. Advocates also claim that the success record is far better than people realize because, unlike the failures, the successes remain secret. The successes that we know about, however, seem questionable. The assassination cases—regardless of whether they were actually committed by the CIA—highlight the complications of defining success. Some commentators have advocated assassination as a quick, clean, and easy solution to complicated problems, arguing that the efficacy overcomes any moral implications. Yet, are they so efficacious? The deaths of Lumumba, Trujillo, and Diem were all followed by periods of instability rather than

---

*At one time, the category of covert operations included discreet payments to aid the survival of pro-democracy parties or other aspects of civil society in foreign lands, but the Reagan administration moved that sort of activity (as far as we know) to public entities, such as the National Endowment for Democracy. This was intended to remove support for democracy from the political taint associated with the CIA in many countries.

resolution. In the Congo and South Vietnam, this included years of warfare. The Dominican Republic was the calmest of the three cases, and there the ultimate resolution involved U.S. military intervention.

War is always a blunt instrument. War by proxy is even less likely to be swift, precise, or anesthetic. The Contra war in Nicaragua has been deemed a success in retrospect because it eventually led to the fall of the Sandinista government in elections. Yet as the Contra war was coming to a close, its principal backers in the CIA and elsewhere in the Reagan administration considered it a failure, for which they blamed Congress. The success came about only later and owing to fortuitous timing. Congress had cut off resources to the Contras at the same time that the Sandinistas were running low on alternatives, and both sides felt compelled to negotiate. While the backers of the war said their purpose, in addition to arms interdiction, was to force the Sandinistas to make political concessions, they clearly did not believe the Sandinistas would do so without constant military pressure.

The intervention and overthrow of the Taliban regime in Afghanistan in 2001, in large measure a CIA operation, was a startling success, especially when one considers the Soviet Union's unsuccessful ten-year war in the same country. Nevertheless, as of this writing—six years after the startling success—the war in Afghanistan is still going on, and the U.S. military commitment to it has only grown.[14]

Some famous success cases not covered in this volume, such as the projects to overthrow the Mossadeq government in Iran (1953) and the Arbenz government in Guatemala (1954), did not actually go according to plan, either. For example, the Guatemalan army stopped the CIA-backed force in its tracks and then overthrew the Arbenz government itself.[15] Neither Mossadeq nor Arbenz looks so threatening in retrospect. The United States learned to live with worse. Moreover, the coups left negative political legacies that complicated U.S. diplomacy for years. Iran eventually turned from ally to adversary, while Guatemala suffered from guerrilla warfare for decades. We shall never know how the subsequent course of events in these countries might have differed if the coup plots had never been carried out. At the very best, planning for covert operations should include consideration of who is going to cleanup the mess.

SECRECY

Another fundamental problem of intelligence work might be called the corrupting influence of secrecy. This is an inherent problem because secrecy remains fundamental to the task of intelligence. Yet this does not negate its corrosive effects.

Daniel Patrick Moynihan—the late Harvard professor, bureaucrat, diplomat, and senator—likened secrecy to government regulation. Most regulations in domestic politics prescribe what a citizen may do; regulations in foreign policy prescribe what a citizen may know. Regulations on business, in his view, distort the natural patterns of economic activity; secrecy distorts the marketplace of ideas.[16] It appears from this study that there are at least three levels at which secrecy disrupts political relationships with regard to the CIA: It distorts the relationship between the government and the electorate, between agencies within the government, and within the CIA itself.

The key dilemma of maintaining a secret government agency in an open society is the most obvious. The government is supposed to be accountable to the people, but the people cannot hold it to account if they do not know what it is doing; however, the government cannot perform some of its basic functions that most people would insist on it fulfilling without maintaining secrecy. Congress tries to mitigate the situation through oversight, but even that is constrained as the executive limits the number of members entitled to know its secrets and forbids them to tell the others. Furthermore, centralizing intelligence functions in the name of efficiency—as was the intent of the 2004 reform—will probably exacerbate the negative impact of secrecy to the extent that it is successful. At least in a decentralized intelligence community, rival agencies must compete with each other in the marketplace of secret ideas.

One well-known drawback of secrecy is the temptation of impunity. The Congressional hearings of the 1970s created an image of the CIA as a rogue agency, an image that Senator Frank Church helped disseminate even if his committee report did not fully bear it out. A look into the documents suggests that it is not the agency itself so much as the president who succumbs to the temptation. Illegal operations initiated by the CIA, to the extent we know about them, tended to be limited to the surveillance of its own staff or recent retirees (or the long-term incarceration of Yuriy Nosenko). It was the president who initiated the bigger operations—be it domestic spying, assassinations,[17] coups, or covert wars. Various presidents took advantage of the agency's impunity to achieve goals for which there were no legal means or public support. Sometimes the CIA was an eager accomplice; at other times it carried out its tasks with some reluctance and foreboding, realizing that it would also take the blame if the operation came to light.

The second distortion of secrecy involves relations between entities within the government. The requirement for secrecy prevents the CIA from objecting when it is blamed for failures or illegal activities initiated by others. Also, secrecy prevents it from objecting when public officials make false claims about the content of intelligence. For example, the minutes of the DCI Richard Helms's morning staff meeting of 10 December 1970, included in the "Family Jewels" file, contain the following comment from the Deputy Director for Intelligence:

<u>10 December 1970</u>

DDI noted press accounts of FBI Director J. Edgar Hoover's 19 November statement that the Black Panthers are supported by terrorist organizations. He said that we have examined the FBI's related files and our own data and find no indication of any relationship between the fedayeen and the Black Panthers. He provided the Director with a memorandum on this topic.

What does one do when one cannot speak publicly? Evidently, one provides the director with a memorandum. There is no indication that Hoover retracted the statement (or even whether it was Hoover or, more likely, Helms who received the memo). DCI George Tenet was in a similar situation when Vice President Dick Cheney went beyond (what was then believed to be) the evidence in public statements regarding Iraq's nuclear program in August 2002. In this case, it does not appear that Tenet even provided a memorandum.

Likewise, President Bush claimed that Iraq was seeking uranium in Africa in his 2003 State of the Union address even after the CIA successfully excised the same claim from his October 2002 Cincinnati speech. What does one do when top leaders just do not care what the truth is (or what the CIA believes the truth to be)? In this regard, secrecy makes the CIA a very weak bureaucratic player.

Secrecy, however, also disrupts power relations in other ways. The image comes to mind of the top officials of the Reagan administration sitting around the table in the White House Situation Room on 25 June 1984 discussing whether it would be legal and desirable to induce foreign governments to fund the Contras in the event that Congress defunded them. Most of these decision makers had not been informed that the CIA was already doing precisely that without waiting for Congress to cut off funds. In this case, secrecy made the CIA a powerful player, but it also raises fundamental questions of accountability, even within the executive branch, let alone the Constitutional power of Congress to control the purse.

In the instances cited here, the variable that determines whether secrecy strengths or weakens the CIA lies outside the agency's control. In the one case, higher-level officials used the CIA's secrecy against the agency itself, and in the other, they used it against others. While the CIA was no a passive bystander, the key decisions were made elsewhere.

Finally, secrecy must distort both the functioning and the administration of the CIA itself. Not only is the agency wrapped in secrecy vis-à-vis the outside world, its own subdivisions are cut off from one another by the control of information on a need-to-know basis. Often that need to know is defined quite narrowly. Thus, the Directorate of Intelligence was expected to analyze the political situation in Nicaragua without being informed about what the Directorate of Operations was planning or actively doing there. Citing secrecy, Maxwell Taylor did not want to give the operational plans for Operation Mongoose to the people expected to carry it out.

The reluctance of the Directorate of Operations to name its secret sources, even in internal documents, compels it to describe them (for example, "a ranking al-Qa'ida official" or "a well-placed Iraqi scientist") in memoranda addressed to the Directorate of Intelligence. When Joseph Wilson reported the unlikelihood that Niger had sold uranium to Iraq, he was described in DO memos not as Joseph Wilson or even as a U.S. diplomat, but as "a contact with excellent access who does not have an established reporting record."[18] In the run-up to the Iraq War, the use of different descriptors to refer to the same source gave the Directorate of Intelligence the impression that there were several sources for information when there was, in reality, only one. This gave the DI a higher degree of confidence in the validity of the information than it would have had if it had realized the true situation. In addition, it turns out that the DO and the DI use different definitions for the term "credible source." For the DO, a credible source is one that has been fully vetted, but for the DI, it is one whose information fits in with what is already believed to be true.

William Colby, who rose to the position of Director of Central Intelligence in a career spent entirely within the CIA Directorate of Operations (called the Directorate of Plans until he took over), was startled by some of the things he learned about his own agency—indeed, even about the past activities of the Directorate of Operations—once he arrived at the top. It was that much more of a shock for James Schlesinger, who came to the job from outside the agency. He learned about CIA issues from newspapers that no one had ever briefed him on. Presumably, if the subject had not come up in the press, he never would have known. Neither Colby nor Schlesinger knew that James McCord had written letters to both Helms and the CIA Office of Security accusing the White House of pressing him to blame the CIA for Watergate, a matter that should have been of considerable concern to both of them.

Schlesinger, of course, issued a memorandum to find out what illicit activities the agency might have undertaken. From all appearances, most of the responses—the bulk of the contents of the "Family Jewels" file—were written on the spot from memory. Probably as a consequence of this, the file covers very little that occurred more than a few years earlier. It may be that Schlesinger wanted the responses so quickly that CIA officials did not have time to go through their records. On the other hand, this at least raises the question of how complete the record-keeping was on questions that might prove embarrassing. The internal memoranda that are available frequently refer to certain facts by allusion, apparently either requiring the reader to know in advance what the reference is or tacitly saying that it is none of the addressee's business.

Secrecy also feeds an atmosphere of rumor and suspicion. Memoranda from the "Family Jewels" file about MHCHAOS and the complaints of the Management Advisory Group show the extent to which rumors and suspicion fill the gaps left by a deficit of credible information. After the MAG incident, the CIA Office of Security had to conduct an internal investigation of the Ballou affair just to find out what the MAG members were talking about. In the end, the incident proved to be based on a misinterpretation of something overheard during a seminar.

Secrecy also inhibits learning. The CIA was very effective in covering up for decades the failure of its secret, behind-the-lines operations in the Korean War. Even if some officials within the agency knew about them at the time, future CIA leaders and presidents would not know that this was something that had been tried and that it had failed miserably, much less why it failed.

Finally, and related to the previous statement, one must consider the effect of secrecy on future generations. The release of the thirty-four-year-old "Family Jewels" file was accompanied by a chorus of voices in newspapers and on blogs describing what a disappointment it was compared to the things people expected to find inside. If the past activities of the CIA have in fact been exaggerated, which is a likely consequence of secrecy, then the present generation of CIA officials and other government leaders grew up believing exaggerated notions of what the CIA does. What past CIA leaders found embarrassing, or actively opposed as immoral, a new generation will accept on the assumption that it has been happening all along. Such a pattern, *ceteris paribus*, predicts an escalating spiral of ill-conceived operations and weakening standards of judgment over the long run. That is a heavy price to pay just to be able to keep a secret.

NOTES

1. Richard A. Posner, "The 9/11 Report: A Dissent," *New York Times Book Review* (29 August 2004) argues that the Director of National Intelligence will not in any event

coordinate the Intelligence Community because his time will be taken up in endless turf battles with the Secretary of Defense and other bureaucratic rivals with overlapping jurisdictions.

2. See, for example, Richard L. Russell, *Sharpening Strategic Intelligence: Why the CIA Gets It Wrong and What Needs to Be Done to Get It Right* (New York: Cambridge University Press, 2007).

3. Mike McConnell, "Overhauling Intelligence," *Foreign Affairs* 86:4 (July/August 2007).

4. The classic treatment of the "signal-to-noise ratio" problem is Roberta Wohlstetter, *Pearl Harbor: Warning and Decision* (Stanford, CA: Stanford University Press, 1962). See also Richard K. Betts, *Enemies of Intelligence: Knowledge and Power in American National Security* (New York: Columbia University Press, 2007).

5. Charles F. Parker and Eric K. Stern, "Blindsided? September 11 and the Origins of Strategic Surprise," *Political Psychology* 23:3 (2002): 614–615.

6. Kevin Woods, James Lacey, and Williamson Murray, "Saddam's Delusions: The View from the Inside," *Foreign Affairs* 85:3 (May/June 2006): Footnote #1: 6.

7. Richard L. Russell, "A Weak Pillar for American National Security: The CIA's Dismal Performance against WMD Threats," *Intelligence and National Security* 20:3 (September 2005): 479–483.

8. Joshua Rovner, "Why Intelligence Isn't to Blame for 9/11," MIT Center for International Studies, *Audits of the Conventional Wisdom*, 05–13 (November 2005).

9. Joseph Cirincione, Jessica T. Mathews, George Perkovich, with Alexis Orion, *WMD in Iraq: Evidence and Implications* (Washington, DC: Carnegie Endowment for International Peace, January 2004): 50–51.

10. Paul R. Pillar, "Intelligence, Policy, and the War in Iraq," *Foreign Affairs* 85:2 (March/April 2006): 15–27. Pillar describes "subtle" forms of pressure to make intelligence conform to expectations but maintains that the substance of the intelligence was not changed.

11. Robert Jervis, "Reports, Politics, and Intelligence Failures: The Case of Iraq," *The Journal of Strategic Studies* 29:1 (February 2006): 37.

12. Pillar, "Intelligence, Policy, and the War in Iraq," 18.

13. Cited in Robert Jervis, "The Politics and Psychology of Intelligence and Intelligence Reform," *The Forum* 4:1 (2006): 1–9.

14. On recent trends in Afghanistan, see Caroline P. Wadhams and Laurence J. Korb, *The Forgotten Front* (Washington, DC: Center for American Progress, November, 2007); Gen. James L. Jones and Amb. Thomas R. Pickering, *Afghanistan Study Group Report: Revitalizing Our Efforts, Rethinking Our Strategies* (Washington, DC: Center for the Study of the Presidency, January 2008); *Saving Afghanistan: An Appeal and Plan for Urgent Action* (Washington, DC: The Atlantic Council of the United States, January 2008); *Afghanistan, The Need for International Resolve*, Asia Report No. 145 (Brussels: International Crisis Group, February 2008).

15. Nick Cullather, *Secret History: The CIA's Classified Account of Its Operations in Guatemala, 1952–1954*, 2nd ed. (Stanford, CA: Stanford University Press, 2006); Richard H. Immerman, *The CIA in Guatemala: The Foreign Policy of Intervention* (Austin, TX: University of Texas Press, 1982).

16. Daniel Patrick Moynihan, *Secrecy: The American Experience* (New Haven, CT: Yale University Press, 1998).

17. The Trujillo case is ambiguous in this regard. Apparently, the Dominicans initiated it. The CIA aided and then tried to restrain it, or at least dissociate itself from it. Kennedy apparently learned of it late, but Eisenhower may have known earlier.

18. Senate Select Committee on Intelligence, *Report on the U.S. Intelligence Community's Prewar Intelligence Assessments on Iraq together with Additional Views* (Washington, DC: U.S. Government Printing Office, 2004): 43.

Appendix A: Leaders of the United States Intelligence Community

DIRECTORS OF CENTRAL INTELLIGENCE[*]

Director	Years in Office	President
Sidney W. Souers	1946	Truman
Hoyt S. Vandenberg	1946–1947	Truman
Roscoe H. Hillenkoetter	1947–1950	Truman
Walter Bedell Smith	1950–1953	Truman
Allen W. Dulles	1953–1961	Eisenhower, Kennedy
John A. McCone	1961–1965	Kennedy, Johnson
William F. Raborn, Jr.	1965–1966	Johnson
Richard Helms	1966–1973	Johnson, Nixon
James R. Schlesinger	1973	Nixon
William E. Colby	1973–1976	Nixon, Ford
George H. W. Bush	1976–1977	Ford
Stansfield Turner	1977–1981	Carter
William J. Casey	1981–1987	Reagan
William H. Webster	1987–1991	Reagan, G. H. W. Bush
Robert M. Gates	1991–1993	G. H. W. Bush
R. James Woolsey	1993–1995	Clinton
John M. Deutch	1995–1996	Clinton
George J. Tenet	1997–2004	Clinton, G. W. Bush
Porter J. Goss	2004–2005	G. W. Bush

[*]The terms of the first two Directors of Central Intelligence and part of the term of the third preceded the establishment of the Central Intelligence Agency. These officials functioned solely as coordinators of the intelligence community.

DIRECTORS OF THE CENTRAL INTELLIGENCE AGENCY[**]

Director	Years in Office	President
Porter J. Goss	2005–2006	G. W. Bush
Michael V. Hayden	2006–	G. W. Bush

DIRECTORS OF NATIONAL INTELLIGENCE[**]

Director	Years in Office	President
John D. Negroponte	2005–2007	G. W. Bush
Mike McConnell	2007–	G. W. Bush

[**]In 2005 the position of Director of Central Intelligence was replaced by two positions, the Director of the Central Intelligence Agency and the Director of National Intelligence.

Appendix B: Agencies of the United States Intelligence Community*

Office of the Director of National Intelligence
Central Intelligence Agency
Defense Intelligence Agency
Department of Energy: Office of Intelligence and Counterintelligence
Department of Homeland Security: Office of Intelligence and Analysis
Department of State: Bureau of Intelligence and Research
Department of the Treasury: Office of Intelligence and Analysis
Drug Enforcement Administration: Office of National Security Intelligence
Federal Bureau of Investigation: National Security Branch
National Geospatial-Intelligence Agency
National Reconnaissance Office
National Security Agency
United States Air Force Intelligence
United States Army Intelligence
United States Coast Guard Intelligence
United States Marine Corps Intelligence
United States Navy Intelligence

Source: *An Overview of the United States Intelligence Community* (Washington, DC: Office of the Director of National Intelligence, 2007).

---

*After 2006.

Appendix C: Some Common Acronyms

ADDI: Assistant Deputy Director for Intelligence
A/DDS: Associate Deputy Director for Support
BNDD: Bureau of Narcotics and Dangerous Drugs
C/CI: Chief, Counterintelligence
COS: Chief of Station
CTC: Counterterrorist Center
DCI: Director of Central Intelligence
DCIA: Director of the Central Intelligence Agency
DDCI: Deputy Director of Central Intelligence
DDI: Deputy Director for Intelligence
DDO: Deputy Director for Operations
DDP: Deputy Director for Plans
DDS&T: Deputy Director for Science and Technology
DI: Directorate of Intelligence (sometimes DDI)
DIA: Defense Intelligence Agency
DNI: Director of National Intelligence
DO: Directorate of Operations (sometimes DDO)
D/OCI: Director of the Office of Current Intelligence
ELINT: Office of Electronic Intelligence
FBIS: Federal Broadcast Information Service
FI: Foreign Intelligence
HUMINT: Human Intelligence
IAEA: International Atomic Energy Agency
IC: Intelligence Community
IEC: Intelligence Evaluation Committee
IES: Intelligence Evaluation (Committee) Staff
LEAA: Law Enforcement Assistance Agency
MAG: Management Advisory Group
NARCOG: Narcotics Coordination Group
NCS: National Clandestine Service

NCTC:	National Counterterrorism Center
NIC:	National Intelligence Council
NIE:	National Intelligence Estimate
NPT:	Nuclear Nonproliferation Treaty
NRO:	National Reconnaissance Office
NSA:	National Security Agency
NSC:	National Security Council
ODNI:	Office of the Director of National Intelligence
OEL:	Office of Electronic Intelligence
OIG:	Office of Inspector General
OTS:	Office of Technical Services
SDB:	Special Development Branch
SIGINT:	Signals Intelligence
TSD:	Technical Services Division
UAV:	Unmanned Aerial Vehicle

Selected Bibliography

Alleged Assassination Plots Involving Foreign Leaders: An Interim Report of the Select Committee to Study Governmental Operations with Respect to Intelligence Activities, United States Senate: Together with Additional, Supplemental, and Separate Views. New York: W. W. Norton, 1976.

Andrew, Christopher. *For the President's Eyes Only: Secret Intelligence and the American Presidency from Washington to Bush.* New York: HarperCollins, 1995.

Barratt, David M. *The CIA and Congress: The Untold Story from Truman to Kennedy.* Lawrence, KS: University Press of Kansas, 2005.

Betts, Richard K., *Enemies of Intelligence: Knowledge and Power in American National Security.* New York: Columbia University Press, 2007.

Bissel, Richard M., Jr. *Reflections of a Cold Warrior.* New Haven, CT: Yale University Press, 1996.

Born, Hans, Loch K. Johnson, and Ian Leigh, eds. *Who's Watching the Spies? Establishing Intelligence Service Accountability.* Washington, D.C.: Potomac Books, 2005.

Clarke, Richard A. *Against All Enemies: Inside America's War on Terror.* New York: Free Press, 2004.

Colby, William, and Peter Forbath. *Honorable Men: My Life in the CIA.* New York: Simon & Schuster, 1978.

Conboy, Kenneth J., and James Morrison. *The CIA's Secret War in Tibet.* Lawrence, KS: University Press of Kansas, 2002.

Final Report of the Select Committee to Study Governmental Operations with Respect to Intelligence Activities, United States Senate: Together with Additional, Supplemental, and Separate Views. Report No. 94-755, 6 vols. Washington, D.C.: United States Government Printing Office, 1976.

Fischer, Benjamin B., ed. *At Cold War's End: U.S. Intelligence on the Soviet Union and Eastern Europe, 1989–1991.* Washington, D.C.: Central Intelligence Agency, 1999.

Gates, Robert M. *From the Shadows: The Ultimate Insider's Story of Five Presidents and How They Won the Cold War.* New York: Simon & Schuster, 1996.

Helms, Richard, with William Hood. *A Look over My Shoulder: A Life in the CIA.* New York: Random House, 2003.

Jeffreys-Jones, Rhodri. *The CIA and American Democracy*, 3rd ed. New Haven, CT: Yale University Press, 2003.

Johnson, Loch K. *America's Secret Power: The CIA in a Democratic Society.* New York: Oxford University Press, 1989.

Johnson, Loch K. *A Season of Inquiry: The Senate Intelligence Investigation.* Lexington: University Press of Kentucky, 1985.

Johnson, Loch K., ed. *Handbook of Intelligence Studies.* New York: Routledge, 2007.

Johnson, Loch K., ed. *Strategic Intelligence*, 3 vols. Westport, CT: Praeger Security International, 2007.

Laqueur, Walter. *The Uses and Limits of Intelligence.* New Brunswick, NJ: Transaction Publishers, 1993.

Lowenthal, Mark M. *Intelligence: From Secrets to Policy*, 3rd ed. Washington, D.C.: CQ Press, 2006.

Matthias, Willard C. *America's Strategic Blunders: Intelligence Analysis and National Security Policy, 1936–1991.* University Park, PA: Pennsylvania State University Press, 2001.

Olmsted, Kathryn. *Challenging the Secret Government: The Post-Watergate Investigations of the CIA and FBI.* Chapel Hill, NC: University of North Carolina Press, 1996.

Prados, John. *Lost Crusader: The Secret Wars of CIA Director William Colby.* New York: Oxford University Press, 2003.

Prados, John. *Safe for Democracy: The Secret Wars of the CIA.* Chicago: Ivan R. Dee, 2006.

Richelson, Jeffrey T. *The U.S. Intelligence Community*, 5th ed. Boulder, CO: Westview Press, 2008.

Richelson, Jeffrey T. *The Wizards of Langley: Inside the CIA's Directorate of Science and Technology.* Boulder, CO: Westview Press, 2001.

Risen, James. *State of War: The Secret History of the CIA and the Bush Administration.* New York: Free Press, 2006.

Tenet, George, with Bill Harlow. *At the Center of the Storm: My Years at the CIA.* New York: HarperCollins, 2007.

Troy, Thomas F. *Donovan and the CIA: A History of the Establishment of the CIA.* Frederick, MD: Aletheia Books, 1981.

Turner, Stansfield. *Burn before Reading: Presidents, CIA Directors, and Secret Intelligence.* New York: Hyperion, 2005.

Weiner, Tim. *Legacy of Ashes: The History of the CIA.* New York: Doubleday, 2007.

Westerfield, H. Bradford, ed. *Inside CIA's Private World: Declassified Articles from the Agency's Internal Journal, 1955–1992.* New Haven, CT: Yale University Press, 1995.

Zegart, Amy B. *Flawed by Design: The Evolution of the CIA, JCS, and NSC.* Stanford, CA: Stanford University Press, 1999.

Zegart, Amy B. *Spying Blind: The CIA, the FBI, and the Origins of 9/11.* Princeton, NJ: Princeton University Press, 2007.

Further information about the Central Intelligence Agency and related subjects may be found online at the following Web sites.

The Central Intelligence Agency
http://www.cia.gov.

The Department of Defense
http://www.defenselink.mil.

The Department of State
http://www.state.gov.

The Federation of American Scientists
http://www.fas.org.

The National Security Archive
http://www.gwu.edu/~nsarchiv/.

The Office of the Director of National Intelligence
http://www.odni.gov.

The United States Intelligence Community
http://www.intelligence.gov/index.shtml.

The White House
http://www.whitehouse.gov.

Index

About the Author

SCOTT C. MONJE is a professional editor and an independent scholar. He holds a Ph.D. in political science from Columbia University and has taught at Rutgers University, New York University, and Purchase College of the State University of New York.